HISTORY OF THE POPES.

VOL. IV.

PASTOR'S HISTORY OF THE POPES.

THE HISTORY OF THE POPES. Translated from the German of Dr. LUDWIG PASTOR. Edited, as to Vols. I.-VI., by the late FREDERICK IGNATIUS ANTROBUS, and, as to Vols. VII.-XIV., by FRANCIS RALPH KERR of the London Oratory. In 14 Volumes.

THE
HISTORY OF THE POPES,

FROM THE CLOSE OF THE MIDDLE AGES.

DRAWN FROM THE SECRET ARCHIVES OF THE VATICAN AND OTHER
ORIGINAL SOURCES.

FROM THE GERMAN OF

Dr. LUDWIG PASTOR,

PROFESSOR OF HISTORY IN THE UNIVERSITY OF INNSBRUCK.

EDITED BY

FREDERICK IGNATIUS ANTROBUS

OF THE ORATORY.

FOURTH EDITION.

VOLUME IV.

LONDON
KEGAN PAUL, TRENCH, TRUBNER & CO., LTD.
BROADWAY HOUSE, 68-74 CARTER LANE, E.C.4.
1923

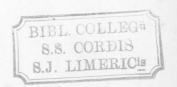

Printed in Great Britain by Butler & Tanner, *Frome and London*

CONTENTS OF VOL. IV.

TABLE OF CONTENTS OF VOLUME IV.

BOOK I.

CHAPTER I.

ELECTION OF PAUL II.

CHAPTER II.

PAUL II. AND THE RENAISSANCE.

CHAPTER III.

THE WAR AGAINST THE TURKS.

CHAPTER IV.

EUROPEAN POLICY OF PAUL II. REFORMS.

CHAPTER V.

THE NEW CARDINALS.   CHURCH QUESTIONS IN BOHEMIA.

CHAPTER VI.

PAUL II.'S CARE FOR THE STATES OF THE CHURCH.

CHAPTER VII.

DEATH OF PAUL II.

BOOK II.

CHAPTER I.

ELECTION OF SIXTUS IV.

CHAPTER II.

RISE OF THE ROVERE AND RIARIO FAMILIES.

CHAPTER III.

THE KING OF DENMARK IN ROME.

CHAPTER IV.

THE JUBILEE YEAR.

CHAPTER V.

BEGINNING OF THE RUPTURE WITH LORENZO DE' MEDICI.

CHAPTER VI.

THE CONSPIRACY OF THE PAZZI.

CHAPTER VII.

THE TUSCAN WAR.

CHAPTER VIII.

THE TURKISH WAR.

CHAPTER IX.

ALLIANCE BETWEEN THE POPE AND VENICE. ITALIAN WAR.

CHAPTER X.

THE POPE'S STRUGGLE WITH VENICE AND THE COLONNA. DEATH OF SIXTUS IV.

CHAPTER XII.

SIXTUS IV. AS THE PATRON OF ART AND LITERATURE.

LIST OF UNPUBLISHED DOCUMENTS
IN APPENDIX.

BOOK I.

PAUL II. 1464-1471.

CHAPTER I.

THE CONCLAVE AND THE ELECTION.—CAPITULATION OF 1464.
—PAUL II.'S CHARACTER AND MANNER OF LIFE.—HIS CARE
FOR THE CITY OF ROME AND FOR THE STATES OF THE
CHURCH.

THE Cardinals in attendance on Pius II. had hastened to
Rome as soon as it was decided that the election should be
held in that city. The period of the vacancy of the Holy
See was one of great disquiet, as it had often been before.
The Sienese in Rome suffered much, and were assailed
by a hostile crowd wherever they appeared.*

Cardinal Roverella returned from his Mission to Naples
on the 23rd August, and Cardinal Gonzaga reached Rome
on the 24th. The Sacred College assembled in the morning
of the 25th in the house of Cardinal Scarampo. In this
preliminary meeting, doubts were expressed as to the
prudence of holding a Conclave in the Vatican while
Antonio Piccolomini, Duke of Amalfi, still kept possession
of the Castle of St. Angelo, and many Cardinals advised

* **Letter from Cardinal Gonzaga to his father, dated Rome, 1464,
Aug. 25. See *Despatch of G. P. Arrivabene, dated Rome, 1464,
Aug. 27 : " Quelli de Fermo hanno brusato quello castello de S.
Petro de Laio, vituperato le donne, menato via li fanciulli et usato
mille crudelitate etiam contra li luochi sacri, che è uno stupore ad
udire. Li Senesi dove se trovano sono a furia perseguitati." Jacobus
de Aretio writes on the 27th Aug., 1464, to Marquess Lodovico Gonzaga : *" Molti latrocinii et correrie se fanno vacante questa benedetta
sedia et maxime per la strada de Ancona a Roma." All these letters
are in the Gonzaga Archives, Mantua.

that the Election should take place in the Minerva or at the Capitol.*

The Duke of Amalfi, who was at this time absent from Rome, seems to have been an object of suspicion, principally because of the close relations which existed between him, the Orsini, and King Ferrante of Naples. Some of the Cardinals feared that, in the event of a Pope being chosen who was not agreeable to the King, he might make difficulties about giving up St. Angelo. On the other side, it was maintained that Antonio Piccolomini had given the most positive assurances, and that regard for his brothers, one of whom was a member of the Sacred College, would deter him from doing anything that could interfere with the liberty of the Conclave. This consideration prevailed, and it was determined that the Election should be held in the Vatican.†

On the evening of the 28th August,‡ the Cardinals went

* **Letter from Cardinal Gonzaga on the 25th Aug., 1464, *loc. cit.* For Roverella's arrival, see *Acta Consist., f. 33b, Secret Archives of the Vatican.

† See AMMANATI, Comment. 347 ; **Letter of the 25th Aug., from Cardinal Gonzaga ; and a **Despatch of J. P. Arrivabene of the 27th Aug., 1464 (Gonzaga Archives, Mantua) ; also the *Report of Jo. An. Ferrofinus to Cecco Simoneta, dated Rome, ex palatio S. Petri die xxix. Augusti, 1464. State Archives, Milan, Cart. Gen.

‡ AMMANATI, *loc. cit.*, says the 27th August. This date, which is repeated by CANCELLIERI, Stagioni, 15 ; GREGOROVIUS, VII., 206, 3rd ed. ; REUMONT, III., 1, 152 ; and ROHRBACHER-KNÖPFLER, 232, is wrong, as is also that given by PETRUCELLI, 285, the 26th August. The Cron. Rom., 30, name the 22nd ; the Diario Nepesino, 141, has the 18th ; Infessura, 1139, the 24th August ; CREIGHTON, III., 3, follows this last. The 28th is established as the day of entrance into Conclave by the following authorities :—(*a*) *Despatches of J. P. Arrivabene of the 27th Aug. and 1st Sept., 1464 ; (*b*) *Despatch of Jacopo de Aretio of the 1st Sept., 1464 (Gonzaga Archives) ; (*c*) the *Report of J. A. Ferrofinus of the 29th August : "Heri sera da

into Conclave. We have a graphic account of the proceedings from the Duke of Mantua's Envoy. The little Chapel of the Palace was chosen for the actual Election. The doors and windows were walled up. The chambers to be occupied during the election were like monks' cells; they were twenty-five feet square, and were so dark that artificial light was almost constantly necessary. The cells were marked with a letter of the alphabet, and assigned to the different Cardinals by lot. Each Cardinal had his meals brought to him at regular hours by his servants, in a coffer called a cornuta, adorned with his coat of arms. These coffers had to pass three sets of guards who surrounded the Conclave. The first was composed of Roman citizens, the second of Ambassadors, and the third of Prelates; they carefully examined the contents of the coffers, so that no letters should be introduced with the provisions.*

Bessarion was invested with the dignity of Dean, and for a long time it seemed likely that the tiara would fall to his share.† After him the most notable among the Cardinals were, d'Estouteville, the head of the French party; Carvajal, with his untiring zeal; Torquemada, who was looked upon as the first theologian of his time; and the two antipodes, Scarampo and Barbo. Of the more youthful members of the Sacred College, Roderigo Borgia was distinguished by his position of Vice-Chancellor.

le xxiii. a le xxiv. hore li rev^mi S^ri cardinali intrarono in conclave numero xix. che'l rev. card. de Theano nondum venit et S. Sisto propter infirmitatem nondum e venuto o rectius stato portato fin a questo matina si che adesso sonno xx^ti" (State Archives, Milan); (d) Cronica di Bologna, 758 ; (e) *Acta Consist., f. 33b, Secret Archives of the Vatican.

* **Report of Arrivabene of the 1st Sept., 1464. Gonzaga Archives.

† VESPASIANO DA BISTICCI, 192 ; CORTESIUS, De cardinalatu, CXXI b.

His private life, like that of Francesco Gonzaga, was anything but edifying. Cardinals Filippo Calandrini, Francesco
Todeschini Piccolomini, Juan de Mella, Angelo Capranica,
Lodovico Libretto, and Bartolomeo Roverella,* by their
irreproachable conduct formed a great contrast to Borgia
and Gonzaga. In Ancona, Roverella had, like Capranica,
Carvajal, and Calandrini, been named as a candidate for
the papacy.† On the other hand, even in June, 1464,
when the condition of Pius II. had become worse, Cardinal
Barbo's prospects had been highly thought of. The
Milanese Ambassador advised his master at that time to
make a friend of this Cardinal.‡

On the 27th August, one of the Ambassadors then in
Rome wrote as follows: "The negotiations regarding the
Papal Election are being carried on in every direction in
secret, and with great zeal. God grant that the Holy
Spirit, and not human passions, may preside! Some few
persons conclude, from certain predictions, that Cardinal
Torquemada will be Pope, but he is very suffering, and
this morning was said to be dead, which, however, I do not
believe. Others are of opinion that the choice will fall on
one who is not a member of the Sacred College, and, in
virtue of some prophecies, Battista Pallavicini, Bishop of
Reggio, is named."§

* AMMANATI, Comment. 348b *seq.*; GASPAR. VERONEN., 1028–
1038; GREGOROVIUS, VII., 205–206, 3rd ed.; CIAMPI, Forteguerri,
17–18.

† So Raphael Caymus informs us in a *Letter of the 15th August,
1464. State Archives, Milan.

‡ *O. de Carretto to Fr. Sforza, dated Rome, 1464, June 14th.
Ambrosian Library.

§ **Despatch of J. P. Arrivabene, dated Rome, 1464, Aug. 27th.
See the **Letter of Jacopo de Aretio, dated Rome, 1464, Sept. 1.
(Gonzaga Archives, Mantua.) At Ancona it was believed that
d'Estouteville's Election was very probable; see *Despatch of

The statements regarding Cardinal Torquemada's prospects of election are confirmed by one of the Duke of Milan's Envoys. On the 29th August he informed his master of the general impression that Cardinal Torquemada, who had that morning been carried into the Conclave, would never return to his own dwelling, but would either become Pope or die, as he was so old and feeble.* After Torquemada, Scarampo was thought by many likely to be the favoured candidate.†

The discourse pronounced by Domenico de' Domenichi, the eloquent Bishop of Torcello, in St. Peter's, before the Conclave began, gives a picture of the general state of affairs, and describes the disposition of the Electors.‡ The

S. Nardini to Fr. Sforza, dated Ancona, 1464, Aug. 16th. (State Archives, Milan.) For an account of the pious and learned B. Pallavicini, who was a disciple of Vittorino of Feltre, see AFFO, Scritt. Parmiz., II., 242 *seq.* ; MARINI, II., 181, 199.

* "*Communis est opinio che'l rev. Monsig. S. Sisto, quale questa matina fu portato al conclave, piu non debia tornare ad casa essendo aut creato pontifice aut posto in sepultura, adeo est senex et infirmis." Despatch of J. A. Ferrofinus of the 29th Aug , 1464. State Archives, Milan.

† *Letter from Jacopo de Aretio to Marchioness Barbara of Mantua, dated Rome, 1464, Sept. 1. Gonzaga Archives, Mantua.

‡ **Rev. patris Dominici episcopi Torcellani ad rev^{mos} dominos S. R. E. cardinales oratio pro electione summi pontificis habita Romae in basilica S. Petri. I am acquainted with four MS. copies of this Discourse, three of which are in the Vatican Library : (1) Cod. Vat., 3675 ; (2) Cod. Vat., 4589, f. 25-48 ; (3) Ottob., 1035, pp. 10-18b ; (4) Cod. CXXXIV., f. 105 *seq.*, of the Library at Turin. The last MS. states that the Discourse was pronounced on the iv. Cal. Sept. MSS. N. 2 and 3, give viii. Cal. Sept.=25th Aug., N. 1, v. Cal. Sept.=28th Aug. As the customary Discourse de eligendo s. pontifice was pronounced before the Cardinals went into Conclave, and Cod. Vat., 4589, expressly speaks of the Discourse as "habita in basilica S. Petri," the last named date must be the correct one. On the 28th, the Cardinals heard the Mass of the Holy Ghost in St. Peter's ; see

preacher took for his text the words of Jeremias, " To what shall I equal thee, O virgin, daughter of Sion ? For great as a sea is thy destruction : who shall heal thee ? " and applied them to the state of Christendom. He recalled the fall of Constantinople, and the Christian losses, in the East, which followed on that deplorable event. Things had now, he said, reached such a point that tidings of defeat were frequently, indeed almost daily, received ; and yet the Princes took no heed, and were, as had been evident during the life-time of Pius II., deaf to the exhortations of the Supreme Head of Christendom. After an affecting picture of the dangers from without, Domenichi turned to the contemplation of the ills which the Church had to suffer from her own sons. The clergy, he said, are slandered, the goods of the Church plundered, ecclesiastical jurisdiction impeded, and the power of the keys despised. He frankly blamed the Popes for their compliance with the unjust demands of Princes, and attributed the sad condition of the times to the fact that those in authority had sought their own interests, and not those of Jesus Christ. Help, he maintained, could be looked for only from a Chief Pastor who would give back to the Church her former liberty, and would not fear the power of Princes.* He pointed out that the relations between the Pope and the Bishops had also been impaired. " Burdened by you," exclaimed the Orator, addressing the Cardinals, "the Bishops favour your enemies ; oppressed by the Princes, they turn, not to the Mother who appears to them in the guise of a step-mother, but seek the favour of those into whose power they have been allowed to fall." Finally, Domenichi declared that the position of the Sacred College

*Report of J. A. Ferrofinus of the 29th August, 1464. State Archives, Milan.

* *Cod. Vatic., 4589, f. 38b, 39.

itself was not what it had been. "Where," he asked, "is
the former splendour of your authority? where is the
Majesty of your College? Once, whatever was to be done,
was first laid before your Senate, hardly anything was
determined without your counsel." Domenichi concluded
by lamenting the complete change that had taken place,
and pronouncing the existing state of things to be insupportable, inasmuch as the authority, dignity, and splendour
of the Sacred College had well-nigh disappeared.*

These last words were hailed with delight by those
Cardinals who sought as much as possible to limit the
Papal authority. On the first day of the Conclave this
party framed an Election Capitulation, which all the
Cardinals, except Scarampo, signed, and swore to observe.†

The provisions of this document would necessarily have
involved a transformation of the monarchical character
of the Church's Constitution, and have reduced the Pope
to the position of the mere President of the College of
Cardinals.

The Capitulation began by binding the future Pope to
prosecute the Turkish war, and to devote to this purpose

* *Cod. Vatic., cit. f. 40b, 42.   There is a passage on this subject in
GREGOROVIUS, VII., 206–207, 3rd ed.

† Despatch of Arrivabene of Sept. 1, 1464. (Gonzaga Archives,
Mantua.)   The Election Capitulation is in AMMANATI, Comment.
350–51, and has often been published from his version, as in
RAYNALDUS, ad an. 1464, N. 55; CIACONIUS, II., 1071; QUIRINI,
Vind., XXII.–XXIX.; DÖLLINGER, Beiträge, III., 344.   HÖFLER,
Zur Kritik und Quellenkunde Karls V., 2nd Abth. (Wien, 1878),
prints it, pp. 62–3, from a very incorrect MS. in the Court Library at
Munich (Cod. Lat., 151), as if it had not previously been published.
Otto de Carretto promises soon to send the Duke of Milan a copy of
the Election Capitulation, which, when he wrote, he had not himself
seen.   *Despatch, dated Rome, 1464, Sept. 11.   Ambrosian Library,
Milan, Cod. Z.—219, Supp.

all the revenue derived from the Alum quarries. He was, moreover, to reform the Roman Court, was not to remove it to any other Italian city without the consent of the majority of the Cardinals, nor to any place out of Italy without the consent of the whole body. A General Council was to be summoned within three years' time. This Council was to reform Ecclesiastical affairs, and to summon the temporal Princes to defend Christendom against the Turks. It was further decided that the number of the Cardinals should never exceed four and twenty, and that one only should be of the Pope's kindred ; no one was to be admitted into the Sacred College under the age of thirty, and also no one who did not possess the requisite amount of learning. Creations of new Cardinals, and nominations to the greater benefices, were only to be made with the express consent of the Sacred College. The Pope was further to bind himself not to alienate any of the posses-sions of the Church, not to declare war, or enter into any alliance without the consent of the Cardinals ; to confer the more important fortresses in the Patrimony of St. Peter exclusively on Clerics, who, however, were not to be his kinsmen ; no relation of his was to occupy the position of Commander-in-Chief of his troops. In State documents, the formula, "after consultation with our Brethren," was only to be used when the Cardinals had actually been summoned together in Council. Every month these re-solutions were to be read to the Pope in Consistory, and twice in the year the Cardinals were to examine whether he had faithfully observed them ; should this not be the case they were, "with the charity due from sons towards their parents," to remind him three times of his promise. What was to take place, in the event of these warnings being unheeded, is not stated. Schism was the only course open.

The arrangement of the Election Capitulation was followed by the Election, which, on this occasion, was very rapidly concluded. The first scrutiny took place on the 30th August.* Scarampo had seven votes, d'Estouteville nine, and Pietro Barbo eleven. The last-named Cardinal, who, six years before, had almost obtained the tiara,† now at once received three more votes by way of *accessit*. His election was accordingly secured. The other Cardinals also agreed, invested him with the Papal robes, and did him homage. Thus the high-born but needy Sienese Pope was succeeded by a rich Venetian noble. The populace assembled in front of the Vatican received the news with joy. The Pope was then carried to St. Peter's, where the throng was so great that it was most difficult to find a passage through it.‡

* The principal authority for the completely new information given above is **Despatch of Arrivabene of the 1st Sept., 1464. (Gonzaga Archives, Mantua.) See, in the same Archives, the *Despatch of Jacopo de Aretio to Lodovico Gonzaga of the 1st Sept., and Cardinal Gonzaga's Letter of the 13th Sept., 1464.

† See our account, Vol. II., p. 322.

‡ Various dates are given, not only for the beginning of the Conclave but also for the actual Election of Paul II., and this even by contemporaries who ought to have been well informed. In a *Letter from Albertino de Cigognara to Marchioness Barbara, dated Rome, 1464, Sept. 1, the Pope is said to have been elected on the 28th August. (Gonzaga Archives.) PLATINA, 762, and the Istoria di Chiusi, 994, name the 31st August, and are followed by CHEVALIER, 1740, and KRAUS, 802, while L'ÉPINOIS, 435, mentions the 29th. The 30th August, however, is established by the testimony of many chroniclers; see Cronica di Bologna, 758; Diario Nepesino, 141; NOTAR GIACOMO, 107; Chron. Eugub., 1008; PH. DE LIGNAMINE, 1310; *GHIRARDACCI, Cron. di Bologna (see our Vol. III., p. 354), and a number of other well-informed contemporaries, such as Gaspar. Veron. in MARINI, II., 178; F. HANKO, Polit. Corresp. Breslau's, IX., 94; *Arrivabene, *Jacopo de Aretio (see preceding note*); and Cardinal Gonzaga, in a Letter of the 30th August to his father; also by the College of Cardinals itself in a *Letter

The unusual rapidity of Cardinal Barbo's Election was looked upon by many as a miracle, for an Election preceded by less than three scrutinies had not occurred within the memory of man; but a little consideration enables us to understand the motives for the haste of the Cardinals.* The first of these was the anxious state of public affairs, together with fear of the King of Naples and of the Duke of Amalfi, the latter of whom had his troops encamped on the frontiers of the States of the Church;† moreover, Torquemada, Scarampo, and Barbo were very ailing, and Rodrigo Borgia had not yet recovered from his illness; he appeared in the Conclave with his head bound up.‡ The confinement and privations of the Conclave must necessarily have been doubly irksome to these invalids, and made them desirous to get through the Election without delay.

Cardinal Ammanati says that Barbo at first wished to take the name of Formosus; the Cardinals, however, objected, on the ground that it might seem to be an allusion to his good looks. Barbo, who had been Cardinal Priest of St. Mark's, then thought of selecting Mark, but this was the war-cry of the Venetians, and was therefore deemed unsuitable. Finally, he decided to be known as Paul II.§

---

to Lodovico Gonzaga, d. d. Romae die sexta Sept. A°, 1464, assumptionis dom. nostri pape prefati die octava. (Gonzaga Archives.) To these may be added the statement in the *Acta Consist., *loc. cit.*, of the Secret Archives of the Vatican.

* Besides CANENSIUS, 32, see the *Despatch of Jacopo de Aretio of Sept. 1, 1464: "Facta questa electione al mio parer miraculosa-mente, perho che tutti dicono non esser mai fatto meno che tre scruptinii." Gonzaga Archives.

† **Despatch of J. P. Arrivabene to Marchioness Barbara, dated Rome, 1464, Aug. 27. Gonzaga Archives.

‡ **Despatch of the same, 1st Sept., 1464.

§ AMMANATI, Comment. 348. This historian, who certainly was

The new Pope was, as Ammanati in a confidential autograph letter informed the Duke of Milan, indebted for his elevation to the elder Cardinals, that is to say, to those who had been members of the Sacred College before the time of Pius II. ; they were of opinion that the late Pope had shewn so little regard to the Cardinals, because his own experience as a member of the Sacred College had been very short. Some of the younger Cardinals, and amongst them Ammanati, joined the party of the elders.*

The Prelate so quickly elevated to the Supreme dignity of Christendom was at this time in the 48th year of his age.† His pious mother was sister to Eugenius IV.,

not prejudiced in favour of Paul II., writes : " Indiderat autem sibi Formosi pontificis nomen secutus credo religionem animi quandam qua historiam eius legens innocentiam adamarat." It is, however, not true that Paul II. wished to be called Formosus on account of his personal beauty, as PALACKY, IV., 2, 237, and others have stated. This writer charges Paul II., who would never allow a capital sentence to be carried out (see Platina in VAIRANI, I., 34) with cruelty (p. 326), and also affirms that the Election Capitulation required the immediate summoning of a Council. Two names are spoken of in the *Despatch of Jacopo de Aretio to Marchioness Barbara, dated Rome, 1464, Sept. 1 (Gonzaga Archives), which is unfortunately mutilated. Otto de Carretto and the Archbishop of Milan, in their *Letter to Fr. Sforza, dated Rome, 1464, Aug. 30, only mention the name of Mark. State Archives, Milan.

* *Letter of Card. Ammanati to Fr. Sforza, written on the 1st Sept., 1464 (Ambrosian Library): see Appendix, N. 1. GREGOROVIUS' assertion, VII., 208, 3rd ed., that "he owed the tiara to the alliance of the Roman Court with Venice against the Turkish war," lacks proof.

† AMMANATI, 348, expressly says : "Annos 48 natus." REUMONT, III., 1, 153 ; GREGOROVIUS, VII., 207, 3rd ed. ; CHEVALIER, 1740 ; ZÖPFFEL in Herzog, Real-Encykl., XI., 318, 2nd ed. ; MÜNTZ, II., 129 ; Rohrbacher-Knöpfler and others must therefore be mistaken in giving 1418 as the year of his birth. CANENSIUS' statement (p. 9) that Barbo was born on the 23rd February, 1417, agrees with that of Ammanati.

and the youth, originally destined for a mercantile career, had been very carefully brought up, and owed his education, as well as his ecclesiastical advancement, to that Pope.* The teachers selected by Eugenius IV. for his nephew were men of ability,† yet the progress of the latter was but slow; he took no interest in Humanistic studies, History and Canon Law had more attraction for him. Barbo's favourite pursuit at that time was the collection of coins, gems, and other antiquities.‡

As early as 1440, Barbo was, together with his rival Scarampo, raised to the purple; he also became Cardinal Deacon of Sᵗᵃ Maria Nuova (now Sᵗᵃ Francesca Romana), which Church he afterwards exchanged for S. Marco.§ Under Nicholas V. and Calixtus III., he continued to occupy the same influential position as he had enjoyed

Regarding his family, which, of course, was in no way connected with the Domitii Aenobarbi, see LITTA, 146, where are given engravings of the coat of arms, of a ring, and of a Bust of Paul II., now in a Palace in Venice.

* CANENSIUS, 9.

† Barbo, when Pope, shewed his gratitude to them. See PLATINA, 763; CANENSIUS, 11; and a *Despatch from Otto de Carretto, dated Rome, Oct. 9, 1464. State Archives, Milan, Cart. Gen.

‡ MÜNTZ, II., 2, 3, 129. It may here be remarked that the Venetian nobles as a class were indifferent towards Humanism; see VOIGT, I., 416, 2nd ed.

§ See our Vol. I., 302. The nomination took place in Florence, and, on the 8th Sept., 1466, Paul II. gratefully alluded to it in writing to the Florentines: "Insuper cum in minoribus agebamus, multum familiariter in ea urbe versati sumus et consuetudinem multorum habuimus ibique dignitatem cardinalatus accepimus, ut profecto eam patriam quasi nostram omni dilectione et paterna caritate complectamur." Cl. X. Dist. II., N. 23, f. 148b–149b. In a *Brief d. d. Rom., 1468, Maii 16, Paul II. again declares his affection for Florence: "ubi adolescentiam summa consolatione et benivolentia omnium bonorum civium egimus ac demum cardinalatus honorem suscepimus;" ibid., f. 172. State Archives, Florence.

during the pontificate of his uncle.* His relations with
Pius II. were not of so agreeable a character. The
Cardinal of S. Marco† derived a princely income from
his numerous benefices, and made a most generous use
of it, sometimes for the benefit of less wealthy colleagues,
such as Cusa and Æneas Sylvius. A lover of splendour, like
all Venetians, he began in 1455 to build a great palace,
and in 1458 undertook the restoration of his titular Church.
He was also a diligent collector of antiques and artistic
treasures, and in this respect, rivalled even the Medici.‡

The Cardinal of Venice, as Barbo was also styled, was
one of the most popular personages in the Court and City
of Rome. His generosity, liberality, affability, and gentleness, soon won all hearts. His devotion to his friends was
manifested on the occasion of the fall of the Borgia.§
Any one who enjoyed his patronage was deemed fortunate.
He used to visit the sick in his neighbourhood with kindly

---

* See PLATINA, 764; and B. JUSTINIANUS in LÜNIG, Orat. I., 8.
Barbo's appointment as generalis gubernator in prov. Campanie et
Maritime, dat. 1456, prid. Non. Julii A° 2°, is in Regest. 458, f. 4b.
Secret Archives of the Vatican.

† His contemporaries generally called him by this title. The
Cardinal in his *Letters used to sign himself:

> P. tit. s. Marci presb. ⎱
> Car^lis Venetiar. ⎰ episc. Vicentin.

I found *Letters with this heading, but unimportant in their contents,
in the Gonzaga Archives, Mantua (to Lodovico Gonzaga, dat. Rome,
1456, May 15 and Dec. 20), and in the State Archives, Milan (to Fr.
Sforza, d. d. ex urbe, 1454, March 11, 1455, Febr. 3. Autogr. pontif. I.).

‡ REUMONT, III., 1, 153 *seq.*; Lorenzo de' Medici, II., 131, 2nd ed.
Regarding the glorious choir-books, restored by Barbo, and now in
the Archives of the Papal Chapel, see HABERL, Bausteine zur Musik-
gesch., Fasciculus II.

§ See our Vol. II., p. 477. The great "humanita" of Barbo is particularly praised by Jacopo de Aretio in a letter of the 1st Sept., 1464,
to Marchioness Barbara. Gonzaga Archives, Mantua.

solicitude, and had a little pharmacy from which he dispensed medicines gratis. The poor were loud in their praises of the open-handed and tender-hearted Prince of the Church, and strangers were delighted with the kindness of his welcome and his readiness to serve them. Any one who had matters of business at the Roman Court, might reckon on success if Barbo took an interest in him. Genial wit and good humour reigned at his table, and he used to say in jest that when he became Pope each Cardinal should have a beautiful villa, to which he might retire during the heat of summer.*

Cardinal Barbo added to his amiable qualities the charm of an imposing appearance ; he was tall, well-made, and his bearing was dignified, advantages which have always been greatly valued by the Italians. For half a century, says a chronicler, a handsomer man had not been seen in the Senate of the Church.† The weak points in his character were his jealousy, his vanity, and an overweening love of pomp, which betrayed his Venetian and mercantile origin.

According to the rude custom of the age the Romans used to plunder the abode of a new-made Pontiff; even Cardinals who had not been elected, frequently suffering on these occasions, Barbo and Scarampo had taken the precaution of placing military guards in their Palaces. An attack made on Scarampo's Palace, when a report of his election had been circulated, was repulsed.‡ After Barbo's

---

* VOIGT, Enea Silvio, III., 507 ; CHRISTOPHE, 110–119 ; BARBO'S "humanita, amore et benivolentia" towards his friends and servants are praised by Jacopo de Aretio in a second *Letter of the 1st Sept., 1464, addressed to the Marquess of Mantua. Gonzaga Archives.

† N. DELLA TUCCIA, 89, see 100, N. 1 ; ÆN. SILVIUS, De viris illustr., 2 (Stuttgart, 1842); Gaspar. Veron., in MARINI, II., 187 ; and SCHIVENOGLIA, 136.

‡ *Jacopo de Aretio to Marchioness Barbara, dated Rome, 1464, Sept. 1. Gonzaga Archives.

elevation became known, his Palace, which was full of treasures and works of art, was besieged by the rabble. Nothing but a haystack, however, fell into their hands. Some of the marauders then rushed to the Convent of Sta Maria Nuova, under the erroneous impression that property belonging to the newly-elected Pope was hidden there. Defensive preparations had, however, been made, and the mob returned to the Palace. They seemed about to storm it, but were pacified by a present of 1300 ducats.*

Extensive preparations for the Pope's Coronation were undertaken by three Cardinals chosen for the purpose.† Even before this solemnity took place, he was delivered from the anxiety which had beset the first days of his reign in regard to the Duke of Amalfi. After the Election, the Castle of St. Angelo and the fortresses of Tivoli, Spoleto, and Ostia, were still held by Sienese captains in the Duke's name; the garrisons declared that they would not give up these strongholds until the sum of 30,000 ducats, which he said he had advanced to the Roman Church, had been repaid.‡ In order to guard against the recurrence of such a danger, the Pope entrusted St. Angelo, which was finally given up to him on the 14th September, to the learned Spaniard, Roderigo Sancio de Arevalo. In compliance with the stipulations of the Election Capitulation, the Pope also arranged that for the future the governors of all the fortresses in the States of the Church should be Prelates.§

* See the *Letter cited in the previous note. Paul II. was, however, unable to hinder the plunder of his chamber in the Conclave; see *Arrivabene's Letter of the 1st Sept., 1464. Gonzaga Archives.

† See the two *Letters already cited, written by Jacopo de Aretio, 1st Sept., 1464; and a *Despatch of this Ambassador, dated Rome, 1464, Sept. 14.

‡ *Despatch of W. Molitoris of 9th Sept., 1464. Gonzaga Archives.

§ *Report of J. P. Arrivabene of the 16th Sept., 1464, *loc. cit.*

The Pope's Coronation took place on the 16th September.* Cardinal Borgia, as the senior of the Cardinal Deacons, was entitled to perform the ceremony, but, as he was indisposed, Cardinal Forteguerri acted in his stead.† The ceremony took place on a tribune erected in front of St. Peter's. It was observed that Paul II. did not, like other Popes, get a new tiara made for himself, but used the old one, which is said to have belonged to Pope St. Sylvester.

After his Coronation the Pope took possession of the Lateran. It was long since the Romans had witnessed more splendid festivities. More than 23,000 florins were spent on this occasion, according to the accounts of the Apostolic Treasury.‡ The Pope rode from St. Peter's to Sta Maria Nuova on a palfrey adorned with crimson and silver, which had been presented to him by Cardinal Gonzaga. Ancient custom gave the Roman populace a claim to the horse ridden by the Pope to the Lateran; and, after the Coronation of Pius II., as well as on many other occasions, a riot had been the result. To avoid this,

According to the Diario Nepesino, 142, the Castle was not given over until the 16th Sept.

* Hitherto nothing has been known of Paul II.'s Coronation and the *Possesso*, save the date; see CANCELLIERI, Possessi, 44-5. The description we give is founded on Arrivabene's Report, cited in preceding note, together with the *Despatches of Jacopo de Aretio and W. Molitoris, dated, respectively, the 17th and 21st Sept., both of which are in the Gonzaga Archives, Mantua. See also *Acta Consist., f. 33b. Secret Archives of the Vatican.

† The statement of REUMONT (III., 1, 154) and HÖFLER (Rod. de Borgia, 24) that Card. Borgia crowned the Pope is mistaken. Jacopo de Aretio, writing on the 17th Sept., expressly says: *"Et perche lo rev^{mo} Monsig. Vicecancelliere, a cui spectava porre la cor[ona] in testa a N. S^{re} come a piu antiquo diacono cardinale, non se sentiva bene perche an[cora non] è ben guarito, Monsig. de Thyano suppli e fece la incoronatione." Gonzaga Archives.

‡ MÜNTZ, II., 124-6.

Paul II. dismounted at the Convent ot Sta Maria Nuova, leaving the palfrey there, and having himselt carried in a litter the rest of the way. The function in the Lateran was followed by a banquet. The Pope spent the night in the Palace of Sta Maria Maggiore, and on the following morning, after he had heard Mass, returned to the Vatican.*

Many Embassies soon arrived to pay homage to the new Pontiff. The first was from the King of Naples, which was admitted to an audience two days after the Coronation, when Paul II. reminded the Envoys of the benefits received by King Ferrante from the Apostolic See.† The Neapolitan Embassy was followed by others from Lucca, Siena, Mantua, Milan, and Florence, this latter being remarkable for its magnificence. All these were received in public, but the Embassies from the States ot the Church in Secret Consistories; which furnished an opportunity for making complaints and asking for favours. Paul II., who, especially at the beginning of his reign, appeared to think a good deal of his own importance,‡ was not very ready to comply with these requests, and disputes with the Bolognese arose in consequence.§ Some ot the speeches made by the

---

* *Acta Consist., *loc. cit.*   Secret Archives of the Vatican.

† *Despatch of W. Molitoris of 21st Sept., 1464. See Jacopo de Aretio's **Letter of the 29th Oct., 1464. Gonzaga Archives.

‡ See NOTAR GIACOMO, 107.

§ Besides Jacopo de Aretio's *Letter, cited in note †, see *Letter written by him on the 9th Oct., 1464 ; Polit. Corresp. Breslau's, IX., 97 ; and a *Letter of W. Molitoris, dated Rome, 1464, Oct. 28. (Gonzaga Archives.) Regarding the complaints brought forward by the Ambassadors from Ascoli, see the *Letter of the Archbishop of Milan to Fr. Sforza, dated Rome, 1464, Dec. 14. (Ambrosian Library, *loc. cit.*). The *Oratio of Giulia della Mirandola's Ambassador ad pontif. summ. Paulum, II., 1464, is to be found in the Campori Library, Modena,

Ambassadors were masterpieces of Humanistic eloquence,
filled with quotations from the ancient authors.   That
of the Jurist, Francesco Accolti, who was attached to the
Milanese Embassy, was specially admired.*   On the 2nd
December the Ambassadors of the Emperor Frederick III.
arrived ; they were commissioned to treat also of the
affairs of Bohemia.†

Some of the Articles of the Election Capitulation were
so obnoxious that even a Pope less imbued with a sense

App. Cod. 169 (saec., 15).   The *Instruction for the Florentine
Embassy, dated 1464, Oct. 6, is in the State Archives, Florence,
X.-I.-53, f. 125.   GUIDICINI, Miscell., 16, speaks of the relations
between Paul II. and Bologna.   See LA MANTIA, I., 316 ; CIPOLLA,
541.

* A MS. copy of Accolti's discourse is in the Chapter Library
at Lucca ; it is printed in BALUZE-MANSI, Miscell., III., 166 *seq.*
See VAHLEN, 415-16 ; and MAZZUCHELLI, I., 1, 68 *seq.*   Vahlen
makes Accolti arrive in Rome at the end of 1464.   This is incorrect.
He delivered his discourse in the October of that year : *" Il nostro
Misser Francesco d'Arezo ha facto il dovere cum grande comen-
datione dogni persona che l'ha udito."   Otto de Carretto to Fr.
Sforza, dated Rome, 1464, Oct. 22.   (Ambrosian Library, *loc. cit.*)
The *Speeches of the Ambassadors of Naples, Lucca, Siena, Ferrara,
Venice, and Florence are in Cod. 537 of the University Library,
Padua.

† PALACKY, IV., 2, 328 *seq.*   "To-day the Emperor's Ambassadors
arrived," says Jacopo de Aretio in a *Despatch of the 2nd Dec., 1464.
(Gonzaga Archives.)   The Archbishop of Milan, in a *Letter of the
14th Dec., 1464, Ambrosian Library, *loc. cit.*, mentions a night attack
upon the Imperial Embassy, which greatly displeased the Pope.
(The war-cry of the rioters was "Austria.")   In November, the Knights
of St. John, at Rhodes, sent an Embassy to offer their homage ; see
BOSIO, 228.   Regarding a French Embassy which, perhaps, was connected with this occasion, see JEAN DE REILHAC, I., 183.   He is
mistaken in asserting that the Acts of the French Nunciature in
the Secret Archives only begin some years after the commencement
of Paul II.'s Pontificate.

of his own importance than Paul II. would have been driven to resist this fresh attempt to introduce an oligarchical character into the government of the States of the Church, and, as a necessary consequence, into that of the Church itself. As a Venetian, the Pope was only too well-acquainted with the defects of this system, and was firmly resolved not to allow himself to be reduced "to the helpless position of a Doge, controlled by Committees of the Nobles."* He was encouraged in this resolve, if we may believe Ammanati, by two Bishops who were aspiring to the purple.†

The Pope, himself, prepared the Ambassadors for an alteration in the Election Capitulation. To one of them he bitterly complained that its stipulations tied his hands so that he could hardly do anything without the consent of the Cardinals. "I perceive," wrote the Duke of Milan's Ambassador on the 21st September, "that His Holiness will endeavour, if he possibly can, to mitigate the Election Capitulation."‡

One of the reasons which, from Paul II.'s point of view, compelled him to take this course was, that, under existing circumstances, any limitation of the Monarchical power of the Pope in the States of the Church would necessarily interfere with the free exercise of that power in matters purely ecclesiastical.

* GREGOROVIUS, VII., 3rd ed. ; CREIGHTON, III., 6.

† Stefano Nardini, Archbishop of Milan, and Teodoro de Lelli, Bishop of Treviso. AMMANATI, Comment. 351 ; see Epist., 114. Nardini's efforts to become a Cardinal are mentioned in a *Letter to Fr. Sforza of the 6th Dec., 1464, which we shall cite, and in a *Despatch from Otto de Carretto, dated Rome, 1464, Sept. 21. Ambrosian Library, *loc. cit.*

‡ **Letter of Otto de Carretto to Fr. Sforza, dated Rome, 1464, Sept. 21. (Ambrosian Library, *loc. cit.*) See *Arrivabene's Letter of 1st Sept., 1464. Gonzaga Archives.

According to the Catholic Doctrine, the Constitution of the Church is, by Divine appointment, monarchical; any attempt, therefore, to alter it was unlawful, and the oath to observe the Election Capitulation invalid. It is, moreover, an article of Faith that each Pope receives the plenitude of power as directly from God as when it was first conferred by the Divine Founder of the Church. Prescriptions of limitation, therefore, whether contained in an Election Capitulation or in the enactments of a predecessor, can only affect the new Pope as counsels or directions, not as binding obligations.*

According to trustworthy contemporaneous testimony, the intentions of many of the Cardinals in framing the Election Capitulation were far from disinterested. In reality, their aim was, not the removal of prevailing abuses, but an unlawful elevation and extension of the authority of the Sacred College. At the head of this party was the worldly-minded Cardinal d'Estouteville, who would have had much to apprehend from a genuine reform.† A very

---

* See our Vol. I., 179 *seq.*, 282. Papa subsequens non potest ligari constitutione praedecessoris sui. See Declaratio Innoc. III., c. 20, de electione. Bonif. VIII., c. fin. de rescriptis in VI.—juncta glossa ad "nostris successoribus indicamus." Eugen. IV., Constit., "Quum ad nos" an. 1433, ap. RAYNALDUS. The Pope ought not without reason to neglect such indications, accordingly, some Canonists hold that he is bound *honestatis* not *necessitatis causa* to be guided by them : *honestatis causa*, that is to say, non sine rationabili causa ab illis constitutionibus recedere potest ; ita tamen ut penes ipsum pontificem (et non penes alios) sit judicare de existentia et rationabilitate causae recedendi a statutis praedecessorum. If this holds good in the case of enactments of a predecessor, far less has the College of Cardinals power to establish limitations. See BENEDICTUS XIV., De synod. dioec., XIII., c. 13, N. 20. PHILLIPS, V., 900.

† **Report of Otto de Carretto of the 26th Sept., 1464. (Ambrosian Library.) VAST (283) attributes the origin of the Election Capitulation to Bessarion, but gives no decisive evidence to support this statement.

well-informed Ambassador, writing on the 11th September, 1464, says that the stipulation regarding the Council was not made in good faith by the Cardinals, but adopted by them as a means of keeping the Pope in fear, and inducing him to comply with their demands.* Paul II., who thoroughly understood these designs, soon made it clear how much this resolution displeased him.

The Pope was required to publish a Bull, confirming the Election Capitulation, on the third day after his Coronation; but the Bull did not appear and, instead of framing it, Paul II. was occupying himself in devising means of recovering the free exercise of the Monarchical power.† He caused several legal authorities to draw up opinions on the question, whether the articles to which he had sworn in the Conclave were binding on him. These authorities answered in the negative,‡ and the Pope then

* **Report of Otto de Carretto of the 11th Sept., 1464. (Ambrosian Library.) FRANTZ, Sixtus IV., 23, is therefore mistaken in considering the Election Capitulation as an expression of serious purposes of reform.

† **Report of Otto de Carretto of the 26th Sept., 1464. Ambrosian Library.

‡ See ANDREAS DE BARBATIA, Consilia, I., c. 1 (see SCHULTE, II., 306–311 ; and Jahrb. d. preuss. Kunsts., II , 37), and the treatise dedicated to Paul II. in the MS. Theol. Lat. quart., 184, of the Royal Library, Berlin : *"Ad beatiss. Paulum P. M. contra supercilium eorum, qui plenitudinem potestatis Christi vicario divinitus attributam ita cardinalibus communicatam censent, ut Romanum pontificem nec quae sunt fidei terminare nec cardinales creare nec ardua quaeque sine eorum consilio et consensu asserant posse disponere libellus." Lib., II., cap. XIII., defends the principle : "quod nulla pactio facta sede vacante etiam si voto vel jurejurando ante vel post electionem firmata fuerit Romani pontificis auctoritatem vel circa creationem cardinalium vel regimen universalis ecclesiae possit astringere." The copy in the Berlin Library, bound in red velvet and adorned with Miniatures, and with the arms of Paul II., is the one presented to the

laid a document, differing very essentially from the Election
Capitulation, before the Cardinals, and persuaded, or constrained, them to sign it. All yielded, with the exception of the aged Carvajal, who was immovable in his
opposition.*

The excitement in the Sacred College reached such a
height that Cardinal Alain, brother of the Admiral of
France, told the Pope to his face that his whole life for
twenty-four years had been nothing but a plot to deceive
them.† Cardinal Gonzaga, whose relations with Paul II.
were in general friendly, and who had received many
favours from him, wrote word to his father, on the 4th
September, that the Pope was very much taken up with

Pope. The treatise of an unknown author in DÖLLINGER, Beiträge,
III., 343–6, is directed against Barbatia. Döllinger is certainly mistaken in ascribing this to the time of Paul II. ; SOUCHON (Die
Papstwahlen, Braunschweig, 1888, p. 16), believes Paris de Grassis,
Master of the Ceremonies to Julius II., to have been its author. The
*Disceptatio an capitula jurata a cardinalibus sede vacante obligent
futurum pontificem D. Clementis Tosii monachi et abbatis Silvestrini
et s. congreg. indicis consultoris ad Alexand. VII., P. O. M., appeals
to Barbatia, Cod. J.–II.–36 (not 31, as it is printed, Vol. I., p. 283),
f. 425–443, Chigi Library, Rome. The treatise of Domenico de'
Domenichi : An papa ligetur vinculis sui juramenti, &c., also belongs
to this matter, Turin Library, Cod. 134, f. 111 seq. See PASINIUS,
II., 30.

   * AMMANATI, Comment., 351 ; see Epist., 113b seq. Ammanati's
representation is not sine ira et studio, and it is much to be regretted
that the version of the other party is not before us. The following
passage from an Ambassador's Report is, however, interesting, and
gives us the date of the abolition of the Capitulation (which Ammanati
does not mention) : * " Come per l'altra mia (unfortunately not to be
found), ho dicto ad V. Ill. S. dopoy se sonno tolti in parte et in parte
modificati questi capituli del conclave, che e stato una saluberrima
cosa." Letter from Archbishop S. Nardini of Milan to Fr. Sforza,
dated Rome, 1464, Dec. 6. Ambrosian Library, loc. cit.

   † AMMANATI, Epist., 115.

his dignity, and was proceeding in a most dictatorial manner. "Possibly," he added, "the council which is to take place in three years may humble him."* Even in October, it was reported at the French Court that a schism had begun.†

Happily this danger was averted, but the relations between the Pope and the Cardinals continued for a long time far from friendly. No improvement took place, even though he granted pensions to the poorer members of the Sacred College, and to all Cardinals in general the privilege of wearing the red biretta, and a large mitre of silk damask, embroidered with pearls, such as had hitherto been worn only by the Popes.‡

Cardinal Ammanati, who now fell into complete disgrace, was the most bitter in his complaints of Paul II. "All," he wrote, "is suddenly changed, affability has given place to harshness, friendliness to a distant and repellent behaviour, a happy commencement to an evil progress."§

---

* Cardinal Gonzaga to his father, dated Rome, 4th Sept., 1464 ; see Appendix, N. 3. Regarding the kindness shewn by Paul II. to Gonzaga, see Arrivabene's Despatch of the 1st Sept., cited *supra*, p. 15, note §.

† **Despatch of the Milanese Ambassador in France to Fr. Sforza, of the 5th Oct., 1644. National Library, Paris.

‡ The following Reports from Ambassadors which I have found, have served to supplement the former account of this matter (in PHILLIPS, VI., 279 *seq.*), and to settle its date : (*a*) *J. P. Arrivabene to Marchioness Barbara, d. d. Roma, 1464, Sett. 13 : "Vole el papa che da qui inanti li cardinali habbiano le lor mitre bianche raccamate de perle." (*b*) *Jacopo de Aretio, d. d. Roma, 1464, Sett. 14 : "Vole N. S^re che differentia sia fra le mitre de questi S. cardinali et altri prelati et per tanto ha ordinato quelle de li cardinali sieno de domaschino et cum alcune perle." (*c*) *Cardinal Gonzaga to his mother, 1464, Dec. 28 ; see Appendix, N. 7 ; (*d*) B. Suardo to Marchioness Barbara, dated Rome, 1465, Jan. 7, regarding the Cardinals' red biretta. All these are in the Gonzaga Archives, Mantua.

§ AMMANATI, Epist., 113b, f. 93.

The estrangement was aggravated by the Pope's inaccessibility, induced by his peculiar manner of life. Changes, which he considered necessary for the sake of his health, were made in the arrangements of the Court ; day was turned into night, and night into day.* Audiences were only granted at night. A German Ambassador writes : " His Holiness gives no more audiences by day, and, as mine was the first, I sat all night in the Pope's chamber until 3 o'clock in the morning." † Other accounts say that even good friends of the Pope had to wait from fifteen to twenty days before they could see him.‡ To obtain an audience, the Envoy from Breslau writes, has now become quite an art. He had recently spent as much as five hours in the Palace, and had then been put off till the following evening. " It has now become three times as difficult to have an audience as it was under Papa Pio," says this same Ambassador, adding that he had often seen even Cardinals obliged to go away, after waiting two hours, without having obtained their object.§ It is not astonishing to find that business was greatly delayed and continued to accumulate.

* Besides CANENSIUS, 48 and 69 ; PLATINA, 767–93 ; AMMANATI, Comm., 350 ; Cronica di Bologna, 788 ; and N. DELLA TUCCIA, 100, n. 1, 269 ; see, in regard to the nocturnal habits of Paul II., *Otto de Carretto's Letter of the 9th Oct., 1464, and a *Despatch of Augustinus de Rubeis, dated Rome, 1465, June 18. Ambrosian Library, *loc. cit.*

† VOIGT, Stimmen, 158. See BARROCIUS, in Anecdot. Veneta, ed. Contarini, 266.

‡ See the *Despatch of the Milanese Ambassador of the 9th Oct., 1464. (Ambrosian Library.) *J. P. Arrivabene, writing on the 3rd Oct., 1464, says that the old Secretaries of the Pope are much displeased, most of them not yet having had an audience. Gonzaga Archives.

§ Polit. Corresp. Breslau's, IX., 110 ; see 100–101. See *Jacopo de Aretio's Despatch of the 31st Jan., 1465. (Gonzaga Archives.) See Appendix, N. 10. Augustinus de Rubeis in a *Despatch, dated Rome, 1466, Dec. 6, complains of the difficulty of obtaining an audience. State Archives, Milan.

The progress ot affairs was further hindered by the slowness, indecision, and distrustfulness which were natural to Pope Paul II.* In many cases he went so far as to instruct the Chancery not to accept authentic copies of documents, but to require the originals.†

The Ambassadors also lamented the difficulties which the Pope made in granting dispensations and important favours.‡ All these causes tended seriously to diminish the incomes of the officials, and discontent soon prevailed amongst them.§ This dissatisfaction led to the expression

* All the Ambassadors repeatedly complain of these hindrances. See, amongst others, the Reports of Otto de Carretto of the 9th Oct., 1464 ; of Augustinus de Rubeis, dated Rome, 1465, May 12 (Ambrosian Library, *loc. cit.*) ; of Jacobus Trottus, dated Rome, 1467, Dec. 1 (State Archives, Modena) ; of W. Molitoris, dated 1464, Dec. 20 (Gonzaga Archives, Mantua). *Augustinus de Rubeis on the 18th June, 1465, tells Fr. Sforza that the Pope is "longo, tardo et suspectuoso." (Ambrosian Library.) In a *Letter of the 22nd Oct., 1464, Otto de Carretto complains of the inconstancy of Paul II. The same reproach is made by Augustinus de Rubeis in a *Despatch, dated Rome, 1466, Nov. 29. State Archives, Milan.

† VOIGT, Stimmen, 158. In a *Letter to Fr. Sforza, dated Rome, 1465, Oct. 24, Otto de Carretto speaks of the "suspicione mirabile che ha (Paul II.) quasi dogniuno." (Ambrosian Library, *loc. cit.*) Jacobus Trottus in a *Despatch, dated Rome, 1467, July 13, says the Pope is slow, wishes to do everything himself, and trusts no one. State Archives, Modena.

‡ See *Despatch of Jacopo de Aretio of the 31st Jan., 1465 (Gonzaga Archives), and the Milanese Ambassador's Reports, especially the *Letter of Augustinus de Rubeis, dated Rome, 1465, May 12 (Ambrosian Library). Jacobus Trottus writes on the 2nd Sept., 1467, to Ferrara : *"Voglio che V. Ex. sapia che *il papa* (the words are in cipher) non serve ni fa conto de servire ni de far piacere a potentia alcuna de Italia indifferenter." He gives an example. State Archives, Modena.

§ Polit. Corresp. Breslau's, IX., 103 ; Cronica di Bologna, 788 ; *Letter of Augustinus de Rubeis, dated Rome, 1465, June 18. Ambrosian Library.

of unfavourable opinions regarding the Pope, which have not always been received with due caution.

There is certainly no foundation for the charge of parsimony so often made and repeated against Paul II. Cardinal Ammanati, who originated it, must have had many opportunities of witnessing the Pope's generosity. He granted 100 florins a month to Cardinals whose income was under 4000 golden florins; he was most liberal in assisting Bishops who were poor or exiled from their Sees. Impoverished nobles, destitute widows and orphans, the weak and the sick, and especially the members of the dethroned families from the East, who had taken refuge in Rome, were all partakers of his princely beneficence.*

Almost every page of the account books of his reign furnishes documentary proof of his magnificent benevolence. Entry after entry records alms bestowed on needy widows and maidens, on nobles, on invalids or fugitives from the countries which had fallen under Turkish domination, from Hungary, and from the East.† He made admirable arrangements for the care of the poor of Rome, and by his orders the Apostolic Treasury, every month, "for the love of God" (amore Dei), distributed 100 florins to those in want.‡

---

* AMMANATI, Comment., 350; CANENSIUS, 66 *seq.*; Gasp. Veron. in MURATORI III., 2, 1019, 1047. See CHRISTOPHE, II., 177 *seq.*; MÜNTZ, II., 12. See *infra*, Chap. III.

† State Archives, Rome. *Div. Pauli II., Vol. I., 1464-1466. Payments, f. 104: pro duobus pauperibus Ungaris fugitivis a captivit. Turcor., 18th Sept. 1465; f. 113: pro honest mulieri Felicie pauperrime et egrote, Oct., 1465; f. 139: pro duobus pauperibus Indis, 5th Dec., 1465; f. 163: pro pauperibus Indis, Mart. 1466; pro pauperibus personis, Mart. 1466; f. 208: pro pauperibus Indis qui hodie proiecerunt se ad pedes, S. D. N. pape eundo ad S. Petrum, 29 Junii, 1466, *Lib. II., Bulletar. Pauli II.; f. 80: 100 duc. pro pauperibus puellis, 12th Dec., 1466, &c.

‡ These 100 florins are entered every month; see *loc. cit.*, *Vol. I, f. 175, 199; *Bullet., II., f. 1, 17b, 41, 75, &c.; *Bullet., III.

Fixed sums were also received at regular intervals by a number of poor Convents and Churches in Rome ; as, for example, S. Agostino, S. Marcello, Sta Maria sopra Minerva, Sta Maria Ara Celi, Sta Maria del Popolo, Sta Sabina, S. Martino ai Monti, S. Giuliano, S. Clemente, S. Onofrio, SS. Giovanni e Paolo, Sta Susanna, S. Alessio, S. Francesco in Trastevere, S. Cosimato and S. Pietro in Vincoli ; but his bounty was not confined within the limits of the Eternal City ; the Hospital of S. Matteo at Florence looks upon Paul II. as, after Leo XI., one of its chief benefactors.*

From the beginning of his Pontificate, Paul II. devoted much care to the concerns of the City of Rome,† a care rendered all the more necessary on account of the series of calamities, floods, tempests, and earthquakes by which it had then been visited.‡ These were followed by pestilential epidemics, which raged in the autumn of 1464 to such a degree that one of the Ambassadors says that all the Cardinals' houses had become hospitals.§ This Plague

(March 1468 to March 1469) ; *Lib. quart. Bullet. (April 1469 to July 1470) ; *Lib. V. Bullet. (Aug. 1470 to July 1471), regularly on the first of each month. See also in the Secret Archives of the Vatican. *Introit. et Ex. 466 ; and CANENSIUS, 67.

* RICHA, VII., 92. Evidence regarding the support given to the Roman Convents in the State Archives, Rome. *Div. Pauli II., Vol. I., f. 175, 188 ; Bullet., II., 1467, Jan. 11, April 2, &c.

† Arch. d. Soc. Rom., IV., 268 *seq.* ; MÜNTZ, II., 8.

‡ INFESSURA, 1141 ; AMMANATI, Epist., 49. See also a *Letter from Jacopo de Aretio to Marchioness Barbara, dated Rome, 1465, Jan. 20, in which he speaks of a violent storm which had visited Rome during the previous night, and goes on to say : " Caschò secondo intendo la saetta in casa de Mons. Vicecancelliere (R. Borgia), ma non ha fatto danno." (Gonzaga Archives, Mantua.) An account of an earthquake in the neighbourhood of Rome on the 15th Jan., 1466, is to be found in Cod. Δ., a. XV., at Grottaferrata. See ROCCHI, Cod. 316.

§ *J. P. Arrivabene to Marchioness Barbara, dated Rome, 1464,

lasted on into the colder months, and returned in the
following years.*   Paul II. rightly judged that the sanitary
condition of the city could only be improved by a greater
attention to cleanliness ; he accordingly caused the streets
to be purified, and sewers and aqueducts to be repaired.†

A great benefit was conferred on Rome by Paul II., in
the revision of its Statutes, which was completed in 1490,
and had for its object the better and more rapid administration of justice.   The revised Statutes were printed in
the time of this Pope, probably in the year 1471.   They
are divided into three books: Civil Law, Criminal Law,

Oct. 3 : many died of the Plague ; " Quasi in ugni casa de cardinali e
uno hospitale." See the *Despatches of Jacopo de Aretio of the
9th Oct. (Plague and fever prevail, many courtiers are dying) and
16th Oct., 1464. Gonzaga Archives.

* See the *Despatch of Jacopo de Aretio, dated Rome, 1464, Nov.
13, and Arrivabene's of the 16th Nov. (Scarampo fled from the Plague
to Albano). A *Letter from Cardinal Gonzaga to his parents, dated
Rome, 1465, Feb. 12, speaks of the continuance of the Plague, which,
during May (see the *Despatch of Jacopo de Aretio of the 21st May,
Gonzaga Archives) and June (see AMMANATI, Epist., 69b, 70, 71, 72b),
continually claimed fresh victims. It again visited Rome in 1468 and
1469 ; see AMMANATI, *loc. cit.*, 145–6, 175. The question whether
it was right to flee from an infectious malady was then discussed.
It is dealt with in the *Epistola Dominici episcopi Torcellani quod
liceat pestem fugere ad rev., &c., Jacobum S. R. E. card. S. Crisogoni Papien. nunc in Cod. B.–51 of the Chapter Library, Padua.
A little work against the Plague was also written in the time of
Paul II. : it begins with the following words : "*Jesus.* Questo è un
consiglio optimo contra lo morbo pestilentiale, Cioè anguinaglie ;
Carbunculi antrace : apostemie : et altri mali cativi et apostemosi.
Composto per Mastro Francesco da Siena doctore nell arte medicinale.
In fine : Laus omnipotenti Deo Finis. *s. l. et a.*" A copy of this very
rare little volume, which I do not find mentioned by bibliographers,
was sold in 1888 in Florence by the Bookseller, Franchi (Cat. 66,
N. 1006).

† CANENSIUS, 99 ; MÜNTZ, II., 96 *seq.*

and Administrative Law. This reform did not materially alter the principles of the Statutes of 1363, and the external and internal rights of the city remained unaltered.* Paul II. took great pains to win the affection of the Roman people. In 1466 he gave them the Golden Rose, and the precious gift was borne in triumph through the streets.† But they appreciated still more the variety and splendour with which the popular festivals, and especially the Carnival, were now celebrated.

Hitherto the Carnival had been confined to the Piazza Navona, the Capitol, and Monte Testaccio. In 1466, Paul II. allowed the races to be held in the principal street of Rome, which from that time came to be called the Corso. The triumphal Arch of Marcus Aurelius, near S. Lorenzo in Lucina, was the starting point, and the Palace of S. Marco was the goal.‡ Games and prizes were multiplied.

* LA MANTIA, I., 173–8 ; GREGOROVIUS, VII., 213 seq., 3rd ed. The ed. princeps of the Statutes reformed by Paul II., is, however, not so rare as CORVISIERI, Arch. Rom., I., 484, supposes ; LA MANTIA, I., 176, enumerates eight copies. See also Riv. Europ., XII., 456 (1879). Regarding the form of the oath taken by the Roman Senate under Paul II., see Arch. d. Soc. Rom., IV., 268 seq.

† "*La rosa heri foe data al populo de Roma e cussi tuto hoggi cum gran triumpho l'hanno per la citade accompagnata ; queste cose molto gratificano questo populo, el quale se ne piglia piacere assai." J. P. Arrivabene to Marchioness Barbara, d. d. Rom., 1466, Mart. 17. (Gonzaga Archives.) To complete the account of the Golden Rose, given in Vol. I., 320 and 321, note 1, we may here observe that the "Meisterwerke Schwäbischer Kunst aus der kunsthistorischen Abtheilung der Schwäbisch. Kreisausstellung" (München, 1886), Plate XXI., N. 5, gives a very good Phototype (a quarter the size of the original) of the Rose presented by Nicholas V., in 1454, to Duke Albrecht of Bavaria, and now in the possession of the Benedictine Priory of Andechs.

‡ ADEMOLLO, Il Carnevale di Roma, 1 (Roma, 1883), is wrong

" In order," writes Canensius, in his Life of Paul II., "that
none of the elements, out of which Roman society was
formed, might be left out, he instituted races for Jews, for
boys, for grown men, and, finally, for old people, each with
its suitable prize. The palls which it was customary to
bestow as prizes on the successful race-horses were, by
his directions, made of more costly materials." The great
banquets, in the Square of S. Marco, to which the Pope
invited the magistrates and the people, formed a new
feature in the festivities. From a window of his Palace,
Paul II. looked down upon these entertainments, and at
their conclusion money was distributed amongst the people.
To give greater variety to the scene, donkey and buffalo
races were added.* Amusement of a higher grade was
provided in the magnificent processions " which represented
the triumphs of the ancient Roman Emperors, a favourite
theme of the imagination of the period." No doubt these
" pictures of old Roman days were, in all archæological
simplicity, clad in the brightest colours of the style of the
early Renaissance, but that only gave more life and variety
to the scene."† These worldly proceedings were even at
the time condemned by some, but Paul II. paid no heed.
He counted much on these popular amusements for
counteracting the evil influences of the revolutionary

in giving the year 1467 as the date of Paul II.'s regulation ; see
the testimony of the contemporary, Cron. Rom., 31 ; see NATALI,
Il Ghetto di Roma, 98 seq. (Roma, 1887). Besides the materials
collected by *CANCELLIERI, Il Carnevale di Roma (the MS. is in
the Archives of the Capitol), I found other unpublished Documents
relating to the history of the Roman Carnival ; these I intend to
publish in a separate work, as to treat this subject adequately would
lead me too far from the purpose of the present volume.

  * CANENSIUS, 50 seq. ; BAYER, Aus Italien, 158.

  † BURCKHARDT, I., 230, II., 160, 163, 3rd ed.; BAYER, Aus
Italien, 191.

demagogues.* How much the festivities were generally
appreciated may be gathered from the detailed and
enthusiastic descriptions given by different chroniclers.†
The care with which Paul II. promoted the better supply
of provisions for the City, and his measures against the
robbers who infested its neighbourhood, gave him a
further title to the gratitude of the Romans.‡ The Pope
likewise endeavoured to check the vendettas and blood-
feuds, to which so many lives were sacrificed in Rome
and in all the Italian cities.§

Paul II. hated violence, and made it his special object to
ensure the preservation of peace in the City. His government displayed a happy combination of firmness and
gentleness. No malefactor escaped punishment, but the
sentence of death was hardly ever carried out. The Pope
met remonstrances against this great leniency by asking
whether it were indeed a small thing to take the life of so
wonderful a work of God as is man,—and a being upon
whom Society has for many years expended so much
pains. Criminals who had deserved death were generally
sent to the galleys, but he gave express orders that they
should not be treated with cruelty. The Pope was so
tender-hearted and compassionate that he could not bear
to see beasts led to the slaughter, and often bought them
back from the butchers. It is said that he had great difficulty in refusing any request, and was obliged to shun

* ROHRBACHER-KNÖPFLER, 235.

† Cron. Rom., 31–4 ; see N. DELLA TUCCIA, 90.

‡ N. DELLA TUCCIA, 89, N. 2 ; CANENSIUS, 35 ; Gasp. Veronen. in
MURATORI, III., 2, 1006 seq. In a poem of the year 1468, published
by P. L. GALLETTI, Verona, 1787, D. Galletti celebrates the restoration
of peace, both in Rome and outside it.

§ L'ÉPINOIS, 436 ; BURCKHARDT, II., 207, 3rd ed. From CHMEL,
Materialien, II., 306, we learn that Paul II. insisted also on the
Jews being justly treated.

doubtful petitioners lest he should, against his own better judgment, grant what they asked.*

Paul II. was a true friend and benefactor, not only to the Romans, but to all his other subjects. He was zealous in the promotion of all useful public works. In poor places such as Cesena† and Serra San Quirico,‡ he contributed towards the repair of the harbours and the city walls. He repeatedly took measures to protect the Bolognese territory from being flooded by the Reno.§ In the second year of his reign, he issued very salutary regulations for the better organisation of the Mint in the States of the Church. For a long time the rule prevailed that money should be coined nowhere but in Rome; afterwards, however, the privilege was extended to the cities of Fermo, Ancona, Ascoli, and Recanati, with the stipulation that the conditions previously laid down should be exactly observed.‖ In 1471 the Senate of the City of Rome was strictly enjoined to be diligent in proceeding against all who coined false money, or clipped the silver from the Papal mint.¶

* CANENSIUS, 39-40 ; CORTESIUS, LIIII.

† *Brief to Cesena of the 29th April, 1471, Lib. brev. 12, f. 139-139b. Secret Archives of the Vatican.

‡ *Document in the Archives of the place. The people of Ancona also received a grant "in reparationem murorum vestrorum"; see **Brief of Paul II., dated Rome, 1464, Sept. 25. Archivi Comm. at Ancona.

§ See the *Briefs of the 29th April, 1466, and 6th March, 1469 (Bologna Archives) ; see Appendix, N. 13 and N. 27.

‖ For the subject in general, see PERUZZI, Ancona, 371 seq. The *Permission for Fermo and the other cities is dated Febr. 4 and July 4, and is to be found in the State Archives of Venice. Regarding the erection of a Mint in Rome, see AMMANATI, Ep., 61 ; and, in relation to the great number of coins of the reign of Paul II., see CINAGLI, 42 seq. ; and MÜNTZ, II., 6.

¶ Secret Archives of the Vatican, Lib. brev. 12, f. 90. *Senatori urbis, dat. Romae, 1471, Febr. 1 ; see ibid., fol. 180 : *Brief for

A very wholesome Decree of this Pontiff forbade all Legates, Governors, and Judges to receive presents, and their conduct in this matter was closely watched.* In grateful recognition of his excellent government the inhabitants of Perugia determined, in the year 1466, to erect a bronze statue of the Pope in their city.†

Joh. Bapt. de Sabellis prov. Marchie gubernatori, dat. Romae, 1471, Febr. 7. Similar *Orders concerning the exact observance of the ordinances for the coinage were sent on the 25th July, 1471, to all Rectors and Legates in the States of the Church.

* See Appendix, N. 34. Bull to the Governor of Spoleto of the 5th April, 1471. Secret Archives of the Vatican.

† PELLINI, 690; and BONAZZI, 682. A *Brief from Paul II., dated 15th Dec., 1466, thanking the people of Perugia for their proposal to erect the statue, is preserved in the Municipal Archives of the city.

CHAPTER II.

PAUL II. AND THE RENAISSANCE.—THE CONSPIRACY OF 1468,
AND THE ABOLITION OF THE ROMAN ACADEMY.—PLATINA
AND POMPONIUS LAETUS.—THE ART OF PRINTING IN ROME.—
THE POPE'S COLLECTION OF WORKS OF ART IN THE PALACE
OF S. MARCO, AND HIS CARE FOR ANCIENT MONUMENTS.

THE great intellectual movement of the Renaissance was
at the time of Paul II., still expanding and developing.
Through each one of its phases the two currents of heathen
and Christian tendency are always clearly discernible, but
the attentive observer cannot fail to recognise a considerable difference between its condition under Nicholas V. and
under Paul II.

In the time of Nicholas V. the genuine and noble Renaissance, which had grown up on Christian principles, and,
while embracing classical studies with enthusiasm, had
made them subordinate and subservient to Christian aims
and ideas, still thoroughly held its own against the other
tendency. Subsequently, a change took place, and the
school which inclined to substitute the heathen ideal of
beauty for the central sun of Christianity, became predominant. In the second generation of Humanists that
one-sided devotion to classical antiquity, which led to a
completely heathen view of life, gained considerably in
extent and importance.

Opposition on the part of the highest ecclesiastical
authority was inevitable. Even before the accession of
Paul II. the Church and the heathen Renaissance would

already have come into collision, had it not been so
extremely difficult to lay hold of this tendency by any
external measures. A formal heresy might be condemned,
but it was much harder to discern the many byways into
which this new, and, in itself, lawful and salutary form of
culture had strayed, and any interference with its course
would almost necessarily have destroyed not only that
which was evil, but also much that was excellent. Moreover, the partisans of the heathen Renaissance carefully
avoided any appearance of conflict between their learning
and theology, and altogether contrived to assume such an
innocent air of dilettanteism that it would have seemed
ridiculous to attempt to deal seriously with them.

If, however, a case arose which did not admit of being
excused as mere harmless classicism, the Humanists at
once made the strongest professions of submission to the
dogmas of the Church, and either altered or abandoned the
theories which had been called in question. Thus, by their
very frivolity and utter want of principle, the Literati were
able to avoid any serious conflict with authority.*

But however complaisant the Literati might be in
matters of this kind, it was quite another affair wherever
their material interests were concerned. Any one who
failed to treat them in this respect with the greatest indulgence and consideration must be prepared for the most
violent attacks. Neither age nor rank were any protection
against the envenomed tongues and pens of the disciples
of Cicero. Lies and slanders pursued Calixtus III. and
Pius II., even to their graves. And the same fate in a
yet greater degree befell Paul II.

A measure passed in the very beginning of his Pontificate gave occasion to a calumny which has not even
yet completely died out, and which represents him as a

* See our Vol. I., pp. 21 and 38.

barbarous enemy of classical studies and of all intellectual
activity, in fact a "hater of learning."*

The measure in question affected the College of the
Abbreviators of the Chancery.   In November, 1463, Pius II.
had made a Decree that this body should be composed
of seventy members, of whom only twelve were to be
appointed by the Vice-Chancellor.   The work and the
pay were to be distributed only amongst these seventy,
and not directly by the Vice-Chancellor.   In May, 1464,
Pius II. reorganised the College ; the former officials
were suppressed, and a number of Sienese, chosen from
the Humanist party, were appointed, some by favour and
others by purchase.†   Paul II., who had always kept up
friendly relations with the Cardinal Vice-Chancellor, re-
instated him in his former powers, and reversed the
arrangements made by his predecessor.‡   Thus the

---

* GEIGER, 149.   Similar unjust judgments on the part of other
modern historians have been collected by L'ÉPINOIS, Paul II., 278
seq.

† CIAMPINI, 25 seq. ;   VOIGT, Enea Silvio, III., 553 ;   VAHLEN, 411.
See in Appendix, N. 5, the *Despatch of Jacopo de Aretio of the
9th Oct., 1464.   (Gonzaga Archives.)   Regarding the Abbreviators,
see PHILLIPS, IV., 394 seq. ;   OTTENTHAL, Bullenregister, 49 seq. (Innsbruck, 1885) ;   BRESSLAU, Urkundenlehre, I., 235 (1889).

‡ The Decree of Paul II., dated 1464, Dec. 3, is in CIAMPINI, 31.
It may be questioned whether the date of " Dec. 3 " is correct, for
the **Letters of J. P. Arrivabene and Jacopo de Aretio of the 15th
and 16th October, 1464 (Gonzaga Archives), speak of the change
as having already taken place.   The time mentioned by PLATINA,
766, (statim ubi magistratum iniit), accords with October rather
than December.   To this may be added the testimony of the
*Despatch of Jacopo de Aretio of the 9th Oct., 1464 (Gonzaga
Archives), which we print in Appendix, N. 5.   It is much to be
regretted that we have not the key to the *Cipher Letters of Otto
de Carretto of the 15th and 21st, 1464, in the State Archives at
Milan, Cart. Gen.   GREGOROVIUS, VII., 210, 3rd ed. ;   REUMONT,

Abbreviators, who had enjoyed the favour of Pius II., lost both their places and their means of living. This was undoubtedly a hardship to those who had bought their positions, although an order was given that the purchase money should be refunded.*

The indignation of those affected by this change was extreme. The secretaries, poets, and Humanists at the Roman Court really considered themselves the most important persons in the world ; they seriously believed that they " conferred on the Papal Court as much honour as they received from it," and were firmly persuaded that " men of their stamp were absolutely necessary to the Pope, and that he must seek them out from all parts of the world, and attach them to himself by the promise of rich rewards."†

The distress of these self-important men was equal to their astonishment. They resolved, in the first instance, to have recourse to friendly representations ; and even the lowest members of the Papal Court were importuned for assistance to obtain them an audience. For twenty consecutive nights they besieged the entrance to the Palace without gaining access to the presence of Paul II.

One of their number, Bartolomeo Sacchi da Piadena (a small place between Cremona and Mantua), known as an author by the name of Platina, the Latin form of Piadena, then resolved on a desperate measure.‡ He

III., 1, 155 ; ZÖPFFEL, in HERZOG, Real-Enc., XI., 318, 2nd ed. ; ROHRBACHER-KNÖPFLER, 234 ; L'ÉPINOIS, 435, &c., are undoubtedly wrong in placing this event in the year 1466. This error may have arisen from the fact that Raynaldus relates the matter under that year (N. 21).

* See in Appendix, N. 5, the record of this order.

† PLATINA, 766 ; BURCKHARDT, I., 273, 3rd ed.

‡ See in CHEVALIER, 1850, a notice of the literature regarding Platina ; the important work of Vairani is here omitted. See also

wrote a pamphlet in the form of a letter, and, by his own confession, addressed the Pope in the following terms :— " If it is permissible for you to despoil us, without a hearing, of that which we had justly and fairly purchased, it must be allowable for us to complain of so undeserved an injury. Since we find ourselves contemptuously repulsed by you, we will address ourselves to the Kings and Princes, and urge them to assemble a Council, before which you will be constrained to justify yourself for having robbed us of our lawful possession." The letter concluded with the subscription :—" Servants of Your Holiness, if the new regulations are cancelled."*

Platina gave this letter sealed to the Bishop of Treviso, the Pope's most confidential Counsellor, remarking that it was written by the Humanist, Ognibene da Lonigo.†

Hitherto Paul II. had kept silence ; now he acted. Platina was summoned to the Papal Palace, where he appeared with a defiant air, and, when the Bishop of Treviso called him to account for his conduct, answered very insolently. He was committed to St. Angelo, where, notwithstanding the intercession of Cardinal Gonzaga, he had that same evening to undergo an examination by torture, " I am very anxious on his account," wrote one of the Ambassadors, then in Rome, on the 15th of October, " for the Pope has spoken very violently about him to many, and no one ventures to take the part of a man guilty of so

SCHMARSOW, 25 *seq.*, 338 *seq.*   The account given by BISSOLATI, 15 *seq.*, is very unsatisfactory.

* PLATINA, 767, and **Arrivabene's Despatch of the 16th Oct., 1464. (Gonzaga Archives.)   According to Platina, it was on this occasion that Paul II. said : " Omnia iura in scrinio pectoris nostri collocata esse."   The character of the reporter makes it very uncertain whether these words were ever really uttered.

† **J. P. Arrivabene's Letter of the 15th Oct., 1464. Gonzaga Archives, Mantua.

great a crime."* On the following day another writer mentions that Paul II. had talked of having him beheaded. "As Platina is an excellent author," he adds, "every one laments this mischance, more particularly Cardinal Gonzaga, in whose service he was at one time; but he is unable to help him in this matter. It is true, however, that when the Pope spoke to the Cardinal, he excused Platina as a madman. This deed of folly, indeed, proves him to be such."†

In the cold solitude of St. Angelo, Platina had full time for reflection. When, after four months of confinement, Cardinal Gonzaga's persevering intercession procured his release, he could hardly stand. He was obliged to promise that he would not leave Rome.‡ The Papal enactment was never repealed, and the ejected Literati, and more especially, their ill-starred leader continued to meditate vengeance.

The meeting of these malcontents, and of the heathen-minded Humanists, took place in the house of a scholar well known throughout Rome for his intellectual gifts and for his eccentricity. Julius Pomponius Laetus § was an ille-

---

* See the **Letter cited in preceding note.

† **Letter of Jacopo de Aretio, of the 16th Oct., 1464. Gonzaga Archives.

‡ PLATINA, 768 ; GREGOROVIUS, VII., 211, 3rd ed., wrongly refers to Card. Gonzaga the words "admonet ne ab urbe, &c."

§ Regarding P. Laetus and his studies, see AP. ZENO, Diss. Voss., II., 232 *seq.*; TIRABOSCHI, VI., 1, 92 *seq.*, 185 *seq.*; A. ZAVARRONI, Bibl. Calabra, 59 *seq.* (Neapoli, 1753); TAFURI, Scritt. Nap., II., 2, 364 *seq.*; TOPPI, Bibl. Nap., 213 *seq.*; NAEKE, De Julio Pomponio Sabino, Virgilii interprete (Bonn., 1824); VILLARI, I., 128 ; NOLHAC, in Mél. d'Arch. et d'Hist., VI., 139 *seq.* (1886); DE ROSSI, Inscript., II., 401 *seq.*; and in Studi e Doc., III., 49 *seq.*, VII., 129 *seq.*; also Arch. d. Soc. Rom., X., 635 *seq.*, 696 *seq.* A critical Biography of P. Laetus, drawn from original sources, would be a great boon. I have been dis-

gitimate scion of the princely house of Sanseverino, had
come to Rome at an early age from his home in Calabria,
and had become Valla's disciple, and afterwards succeeded
him as Professor in the University. "Of all the worshippers
of antiquity, whose exclusive ideal was ancient Rome
and the oldest words of the Latin tongue," he was the most
extreme.* No scholar, perhaps, ever lived so completely in
the heathenism of the past ; "the present was to him a mere
phantom ; the world of antiquity was the reality in which
he lived and moved and had his being."†

Pomponius Laetus lived in antique style, in haughty
poverty, like a second Cato. In the cultivation of his vine-
yard he followed the rules of Varro and Columella. He
would often come down, with buskined feet, before day-
break to the University, where the hall could hardly contain
the crowd of his eager scholars. The vivacious little man
might frequently be seen wandering alone through the
ruins of ancient Rome, suddenly arrested, as if in a rapture,
before some heap of stones, or even bursting into tears.
He despised the Christian religion, and passionately
inveighed against its adherents. As a deist, Pomponius
believed in a Creator, but, as one of his most devoted
disciples tells us, as an antiquarian he revered the "Genius
of the City of Rome," or what would, in modern language,
be called "the Spirit of Antiquity."‡

appointed with the Memorie di P. Leto in the Cod. G., 285, Inf., of the
Ambrosian Library, cited by DE ROSSI, Roma Sott., I., 7 ; they contain
nothing new.

    * VOIGT, II., 239, 2nd ed.

    † HÖRSCHELMANN, 150–51 ; see SCHMARSOW, 26.

    ‡ "Fuit ab initio contemptor religionis, sed ingravescente aetate
coepit res ipsa, ut mihi dicitur, curae esse," says Sabellicus. See ‾
P. CORTESIUS, De Cardinalatu, LXXXVII. ; CREIGHTON, III., 42 ;
GREGOROVIUS, VII., 566 seq., 3rd ed. ; GEIGER, 158. "Even from a
by no means rigorous point of view, P. Laetus can hardly be any

His house on the Quirinal was filled with fragments of ancient Architecture and sculpture, inscriptions and coins.* Here, in an atmosphere charged with the spirit of heathen Rome, he assembled his disciples and friends. Disputations were held on ancient authors, and philosophical questions, discourses and poems were read, Comedies of Plautus and Terence were sometimes performed, and an infatuated admiration for the old Republic was cherished.

Such was the origin of a " literary sodality," called the Roman Academy, whose object was the cultivation of pure Latinity, and of the ancient national life of Rome. " Pomponius, the founder of the Society, went so far as to refuse to learn Greek, lest he should injure the perfection of his Latin pronunciation."†

Around Pomponius, the representative of pagan Humanism, soon gathered a number of young freethinkers, semi-heathen in their views and morals, who sought to make up for their lost faith by a hollow worship of antiquity.

The members of the Academy looked upon themselves as a Confraternity ; they laid aside their ordinary names, and adopted ancient ones instead. The original name of Pomponius, who was venerated by all as their leader and teacher, is not even known. Bartolomeo Platina and Filippo Buonaccorsi, who was called Callimachus, are the most noted of the other members. We also hear of Marcantonio Coccio of the Sabine country, called Sabellicus ; Marcus Romanus, or Asclepiades ; Marinus Venetus,

longer considered a Christian," according to GEBHARDT, Adrian of Corneto, 79 ; JANITSCHEK, 19, is of the same opinion.

* "Leto's chief merit, in the judgment of posterity, is the initiation of a practical interest in antiquity," says REUMONT, III., 1, 341 ; VILLARI, I., 129, expresses a similar opinion.

† HÖRSCHELMANN, 151.

or Glaucus ; a certain Petrus or Petrejus ; Marsus Demetrius, Augustinus Campanus, &c.*

It may be admitted that this use of heathen names was a mere fancy, for which a parallel may be found in the increasing preference for such names, and even those which were of evil repute, in baptism. But other practices of the Academicians cannot be thus explained. The fantastic "enthusiasm of the adherents of the old Calabrian heathen" found vent in religious practices which seemed like a parody of Christian worship. The initiated constituted their learned Society into "a formal Antiquarian College of Priests of the ancient rite, presided over by a pontifex maximus, in the person of Pomponius Laetus." The sentiments and the conduct of these "pantheistic votaries of Antiquity" were certainly more heathen than Christian.† Raphael Volaterranus, in his Roman Commentaries, dedicated to Julius II., plainly declared that the meetings of these men, their antique festivities in honour of the birthday of the City of Rome and of Romulus, were " the first step towards doing away with the Faith." ‡

There was certainly some ground for the charges brought against the Academicians of contempt for the Christian religion, its servants and its precepts, of the worship of

* PAPENCORDT, 513 ; CORSIGNANI, II., 494 ; and NOLHAC in Mél. d'Arch., VI., 140 seq.

† See SCHMARSOW, 26 ; REUMONT, III., 1, 342 ; CANTÙ, I., 187. GREGOROVIUS, VII., 568, 3rd ed., writes : "Among the Academicians there was scarcely a trace of Christianity . . . They despised the dogmas and the hierarchical constitution of the Church, for they were of the School of Valla and Poggio." In another passage he speaks of the Academy "as a classical Freemasons' lodge." Regarding Platina's immorality, see infra. Sabellicus died in 1506, leaving an illegitimate son ; see CORSIGNANI, II., 494-5.

‡ Commentarii, XXI., f. 246 ; see GEBHARDT, Adrian of Corneto, 79.

heathen divinities and the practice of the most repulsive vices of ancient times. Pomponius Laetus was the disciple of Valla, and was certainly an adherent and disseminator of the destructive doctrines of his master. A heathen idea of the State, hostility to the clergy, and the dream of substituting for the existing government of Rome a Republic of the ancient type, prevailed in this circle, together with Epicurean and materialistic views of life. "Experience had already sufficiently shewn that the enthusiastic veneration of the old Roman commonwealth was not unlikely to have practical consequences."[*]

This heathen and republican secret society seemed all the more dangerous in the increasingly excited state of the Roman populace. Many of the youths of the city were ready for any sort of mischief, and numerous exiles lurked on the Neapolitan frontiers. In the June of 1465, when Paul II. went to war with Count Everso of Anguillara, there was a decided movement in favour of the tyrant.[†] A year later, many adherents of the Fraticelli were discovered; their trial revealed the opposition of their rites and doctrines to those of the Church. Further inquiry shewed that the partisans of this sect were at work not only in the March of Ancona, but also in the Roman Campagna and in Rome itself. There is no proof of any connection between these heretics and the Roman Academy.[‡] It is, however, certain that various fanatical demagogues, and some of the angry Abbreviators, held

---

[*] ROHRBACHER-KNÖPFLER, 321 ; VOIGT, II., 239, 2nd ed., also thinks it very probable that P. Laetus and his disciples may have had their heads full of heathen and republican aspirations. Regarding Valla's doctrine, see our Vol. I., p. 12 *seq.*

[†] CANENSIUS, 56–9 ; see also AMMANATI, Epist., 54b.

[‡] It is even improbable that such existed. Platina only condemns the excessive pomp of the Church "ecclesiae pompam." Regarding the Fraticelli, see *infra.*

intimate relations with the Academicians, and that in their
assemblies strong language against the Pope was freely
indulged in.   Thus " all the hostile elements of Heathenism,
Republicanism and Heresy seemed to have their centre in
the Academy."*

In the last days of February, 1468,† the inhabitants
of Rome suddenly learned that the police had discovered
a conspiracy against the Pope, and had made numerous
arrests, chiefly among the Literati and members of the
Roman Academy.‡

Disquieting reports of various kinds had, for some time,
been prevalent in the city, and predictions of the Pope's
speedy death had been circulated.§   Paul II. had attached

---

* GREGOROVIUS, VII., 570, 3rd ed. ; CREIGHTON, III., 44 ;
SCHMARSOW, 27.   It need not surprise us, REUMONT observes (III.,
1, 345 and 509), that the Academy was looked upon with suspicion,
when we see how, subsequently, in the 16th century, the Academy
sided with the party of opposition in politics.   In that of Florence, for
example, a jargon, known only to the initiated, was framed for party
purposes.   See also REUMONT, Gesch. Toskana's, I., 258 seq. (Gotha,
1876).

† Not 1467, as CIAMPI, I., 27, and ZÖPFFEL in Herzog, Real-Enc.,
XI., 318, 2nd ed., state ; nor in 1469, as REUMONT, III., 1, 344 ; MAR-
CELLINO, III., 78 ; L'ÉPINOIS, Paul II., 27 ; CHRISTOPHE, 192 ;
ROHRBACHER-KNÖPFLER, 320 ; SCHMARSOW, 27, and others have it.

‡ The chief authorities for the following details are the Despatches
of the Milanese Ambassadors.   Hitherto none was known but that of
J. Blanchus of 28th Febr., 1468, which MOTTA published in the Arch.
della Soc. Rom., VII., 555-9.   I succeeded in finding two other *Reports of J. Blanchus of 28th and 29th Febr., as well as Aug. de Rubeis'
Despatches of the 28th Febr. and 4th March, in the State Archives,
Milan.   See Appendix, N. 19-22.

§ A *Prognostic of Gistoldus de Melodia, for the year 1469, speaks of
"mundi evacuacio, cleri decisio, christianitatis deposicio, &c." Cod.
4764, f. 193b, of the Court Library, Vienna.   A long *Prognostic for
1470, by a Servite, Paulus Venetus, is preserved in the State Archives,
Milan, Astrologia.

no importance to these rumours, but, after receiving a
warning letter from a temporal Prince, he looked on the
matter in a more serious light. His anxiety increased,
and his determination to act was confirmed, when some of
the Cardinals also made communications of an alarming
character. On the same night an order was issued for
the arrest of the ringleaders of the Conspiracy. Four
members of the Roman Academy, viz., Callimachus,
Glaucus, Petrejus, and Platina, had been named to the
Pope as the chiefs. The first three, having received intimation of the danger which threatened them, succeeded
in making their escape. Callimachus, himself, in a letter
subsequently written for his own justification, declares that
he had at first remained hidden in Rome, and then fled
secretly to Apulia.*

Others who had been connected with the Academicians
were, together with Platina, incarcerated in St. Angelo,
and afterwards examined by torture. "Every night some
one is arrested," wrote the Milanese Ambassador, Johannes
Blanchus, on the 28th February, "and every day the
matter is better understood; it is not, as Cardinal
Ammanati supposed, a dream, but a reality. The plan
would have succeeded if God had not protected the
Pope."†

It is most interesting to observe the manner in which
Paul II. himself took the whole affair. Hitherto, we have
had little save the somewhat scanty account of his
biographer, Canensius, to guide us. He informs us that
the Pope had taken measures to make an example
of an infamous band of young Romans of corrupt

* ZEISSBERG, 352. Pomponius Laetus was in Venice at the time
when the conspiracy was discovered.

† Arch. della Soc. Rom., VII. 557. PLATINA, 781, says that about
twenty persons in all were imprisoned.

morals and insolent behaviour. They had maintained that the Christian religion was a fraud, trumped up by a few Saints, without any foundation in facts. Hence, it was allowable to copy the Cynics, and give themselves up to the gratification of their passions. "These persons," Canensius goes on to say, "despise our religion so much that they consider it disgraceful to be called by the name of a Saint, and take pains to substitute heathen names for those conferred on them in baptism. The leader of this Sect, whom I will not here name, was a well-known teacher of Grammar in Rome, who, in the first instance, changed his own name, and then those of his friends and disciples in this manner. Some abandoned men associated themselves with him : as, for example, the Roman, Marcus, who is called Asclepiades ; the Venetian, Marinus, who is called Glaucus ; a certain Petrus, who has styled himself Petrejus ; and Damian, a Tuscan, who is known as Callimachus. These had bound themselves to murder the Pope."*

This account enables us to look at the affair from the point of view of the Pope's position as " Guardian of Faith and Morals," and recently discovered Reports of the Milanese Ambassadors serve yet more clearly to elucidate its significance in this respect. Their independent character, and the direct nature of their testimony, entitle them to be considered as documents of the greatest importance.†

It was not easy for the Ambassadors of the League,

---

* CANENSIUS, 78–9. VOIGT, II., 240 *seq.*, 2nd ed., observes that this account is all the more unprejudiced, inasmuch as it is written without a suspicion of the deeper significance of these events.

† The Milanese Ambassadors were by no means prejudiced against Platina, and PLATINA, himself, says (789) that the Venetian and Milanese Ambassadors afterwards made interest on his behalf with Paul II.

then in Rome, to obtain really authentic information regarding the events which had just taken place there, for the most varied and fantastic accounts were circulated.*

Many different statements were made as to the day fixed upon for carrying the plot into effect. Some said that Paul II. was to have been murdered on Ash-Wednesday, at the Papal Mass, others that the crime was to have been perpetrated on Carnival Sunday, when all the people, and even the Papal Guards, would have gone to Monte Testaccio for the accustomed festivities. Others again declared Palm Sunday to be the day selected. It was further reported that the conspirators had, with a view to the accomplishment of their purpose, associated with themselves Luca de Tocio, a banished Roman, belonging to the party of the Orsini, who was a member of the Council at the Court of Ferrante I. at Naples. This man was believed to be in league with other banished persons. Four or five hundred of them were to enter the city secretly, and to hide themselves in the ruins of the houses which had been pulled down in order to enlarge the Papal Palace. On the other side, forty or fifty partisans were to join the conspirators, and begin an attack on the attendants of the Cardinals and Prelates, who would be waiting in the Square in front of the Palace. By this means the Pope's small Guard would be occupied, and the conflict was to serve as a signal to the hidden outlaws, who would then make their way into the Church and murder the Pope and those about him. General pillage was to ensue, and Luca de Tocio was to establish a new Constitution.†

* The following description is from the *Reports of A. de Rubeis and Joh. Blanchus of the 28th and 29th Febr., 1468, given in Appendix, *loc. cit.* State Archives, Milan.

† The resemblance between this plot and that of Porcaro is obvious ; see our Vol. II., p. 224 *seq.*

Even more alarming than the plot itself was the reported extent of its ramifications. The King of Naples was accused of taking part in it, and some were of opinion that the King of France was also engaged, while others declared Sigismondo Malatesta to be one of the conspirators.*

These varied accounts led the Ambassadors of the League to seek from the Pope himself more accurate information, and, at the same time, to express their sympathy and offer assistance on behalf of their several masters. An account of the Audience was drawn up by the Milanese Ambassadors personally, and in duplicate.† This document makes it perfectly evident that, from the very first, the Pope clearly distinguished between the Anti-Christian and immoral life of many Academicians, or their "heresy," as the Ambassadors shortly style it, and the Conspiracy against his person.‡

On the first of these points Paul II. made some very important statements, representing the Academicians as complete heathens and Materialists. They deny, he said, the existence of God, they declare that there is no other world than this, that the soul dies with the body, and that, accordingly, man may give himself up to the indulgence of his passions without any regard to the law of God; all that is

* J. BLANCHUS in the Arch. della Soc. Rom., VII., 559.

† See Appendix, N. 20 and 21 (State Archives, Milan). The Perugians, according to PELLINI, 695, also sent an Ambassador to Rome to offer Paul II. assistance against the conspirators, and to invite him to come to Perugia. This Ambassador must, no doubt, have written home, but I have not been able to find the Letters in the Perugian Archives ; another may, perhaps, be more fortunate.

‡ Paul II. did not alter the accusation in the tenth month after the imprisonment of the conspirators, as PLATINA, 785, would have us believe.

needed is to avoid coming into collision with the temporal power.*

Paul II. had much more to tell of the evil deeds of these Epicureans, who seem, indeed, to have adopted the doctrines promulgated by Valla in his book "on pleasure." They despised the commands of the Church, he said, ate meat on fast-days, and reviled the Pope and the Clergy. They said that the priests were the enemies of the laity, that they had invented fasting and forbidden men to have more than one wife.† Moses, they taught, deceived the Jews, his law was a forgery, Christ was a deceiver, Mahomet a great intellect, but also an impostor.‡ They were ashamed of their Christian names and preferred those which were heathen, and they practised the most shameful vices of antiquity. Some of these free-thinkers are said to have contemplated an alliance with the Turks. Predictions of the speedy death of the Pope were circulated by them ; then there would be a new Election and a complete change in the state of affairs.

Paul II. named Callimachus, Petrejus, Glaucus, and Platina as the ringleaders of the Conspiracy. He deeply regretted that the first three had escaped beyond the reach of justice. He evidently considered the matter to be most important, and expressed to the Ambassadors his determination to root out this "heresy," and his regret that he had not sooner become aware of its existence.

In regard to the Conspiracy against his person, the Pope said he had heard the prevalent reports, but added that he

* It will be observed that this account agrees with that of Canensius, mentioned p. 48.

† It is known that, in the above-mentioned work, Valla advocated the community of women desired by Plato ; see our Vol. I., p. 16.

‡ This teaching is concealed beneath the leading idea of the work : De tribus impostoribus. See WELLER'S edition, Heilbronn, 1876.

could form no decided opinion as to whether they were well-founded or not, because those believed to be the leaders in the plot had escaped. According to the report of one of the Ambassadors, Paul II. had, at first, a suspicion that Podiebrad, the Hussite King of Bohemia, might be implicated; it appeared to him not improbable that one heretic might help another.*

The Pope was particularly disquieted by the rumour about Luca de Tocio, who had taken part in the troubles in the time of Pius II. He at once sent a courier to Naples to ascertain whether he had really left that city. As it was also affirmed that Tocio had given 1000 ducats to the guards of St. Angelo, as a bribe to induce them to deliver up the fortress, the Pope caused searching enquiries to be made, but very little information was obtained. Even at the time, it was suspected that these reports had been set afloat by persons whose interest it was to raise a cloud of dust as a stratagem to escape punishment.†

A reward of 300 ducats was offered for the discovery of the whereabouts of Callimachus, Glaucus, and Petrejus, and 500 for that of Luca de Tocio. The Pope hoped to get hold of some, if not all, of the conspirators.‡ On the 29th February, it was believed that a clue to Callimachus' abode had been found; he was considered next in importance to Luca de Tocio.§

The houses of the fugitives were, of course, searched, and

* *Despatch of Joh. Blanchus of the 29th Febr., 1468. (State Archives, Milan.) See Appendix, N. 21.

† *Loc. cit.*

‡ *Report of Augustinus de Rubeis of the 28th Febr., 1468. (State Archives, Milan.) See Appendix, N. 20.

§ *Report of Joh. Blanchus of the 29th Febr., 1468. (State Archives, Milan.) See Appendix, N. 21.

the licentious poems which were found furnished fresh proof of the immorality of the Academicians.*

"We cannot wonder that the Pope did not consider the existence of such a Conspiracy as in itself incredible. He had incurred the bitter hatred of the aggrieved Abbreviators. Stefano Porcaro, the head of the conspiracy against Nicholas V., had also been a Humanist, and had dreamed of the restoration of the ancient Republic. The Ghibelline bands in Rome were still in existence, and their alliance with the party-chiefs of the city, and with the fugitives and exiles beyond its limits, constituted an abiding danger. Again, in the days of Pius II., young Tiburzio, at the head of a similar Catiline band, had stirred the people up to cast off the priestly yoke, and revive the ancient liberty of Rome. By his decided action, Paul II., at any rate, repressed disorder, and provided himself with material for investigation."†

Until the official documents are brought to light, it will be impossible to give an exact account of these proceedings, which were conducted by Cardinal Barbo, and watched with the greatest interest by Paul II. They would furnish us with the means of checking the detailed relation of Platina, whose participation in the events renders it necessary to receive his statements with the greatest caution.‡ In many cases they are, moreover, at variance with facts otherwise established.§

He certainly is guilty of gross misrepresentation in his

* See the *Report cited in preceding note.

† VOIGT, II., 240, 2nd ed.

‡ For critical observations on Platina, see ZEISSBERG, 351 *seq.*; VOIGT, II., 237 *seq.*, 2nd ed. ; BURCKHARDT, II., 277 *seq.*, 5th ed. ; GREGORO-VIUS, VII., 571, 3rd ed. ; L'ÉPINOIS, Paul II., 278 *seq.*; CREIGHTON III., 274 *seq.* ; TRIPEPI, Religione e Storia, Roma, 1872.

§ See especially ZEISSBERG, 351.

Life of Paul II., when he affirms that, in his examination, he had shewn the indolent Callimachus to be incapable of independently originating a Conspiracy. In Platina's letters, written during his imprisonment, we find him, on the contrary, laying the whole blame on the blustering folly of Callimachus. "Who," he asks, in one of these letters, "would believe that the drunken dreams of this man, whom we mocked at and despised, could have brought us into such trouble? Alas! for us, poor wretches, who must pay for the silly temerity of another! That crazy bestower of treasures and kingdoms roams about freely, drunk with wine and glutted with food, while we, for being imprudent enough not to reveal his mad dreams, are tortured and shut up in dungeons." In almost all the other letters of this period Platina reiterates these accusations.*

The constancy with which Platina claims to have undergone examination and endured torture must also be relegated to the domain of fiction.

The letters written during his imprisonment also testify against him. Anything more abject than his petitions addressed to the Pope can hardly be imagined. His error, in not shewing up the drunken Callimachus, had been one of negligence, not of malice. For the future, however, he promised, whenever he hears anything against the name or the welfare of the Pope, even from a bird of the air, at once to report it to His Holiness. He approves of the measures taken for the repression of Humanistic license, inasmuch as it is the duty of a good shepherd to preserve his flock from contagion. He confesses that, when turned out of his office, he accused God and man; he repents of this, and will not again so far forget himself. Finally, he promises, if restored to liberty and secured from want, to

* VAIRANI, I., 30, 32, 33, 37.

become the Pope's most ardent panegyrist, to celebrate in prose and verse "the golden age of his most happy Pontificate"; he is even ready to abandon classical studies and devote himself entirely to Holy Scripture and Theology. The Humanist, however, again comes out when he reminds the Pope that poets and orators confer immortality on Princes: Christ was made known by the Evangelists, and Achilles by Homer. The prevailing tone of the letter is expressed in its concluding words: "Only give hope to us who, with clasped hands and bended knees humbly await your mercy."*

Utterly broken and crushed, Platina in his distress built much on the assistance of Rodrigo Sanchez de Arevalo, Bishop of Calahorra and Prefect of St. Angelo, and besieged him with elegant letters. Rodrigo had the courtesy to grant Platina's request that he would refresh him with a letter. This led to a brisk correspondence between the two Humanists, one of whom was a representative of the Christian and the other of the heathen Renaissance. Rodrigo sought to calm and elevate Platina's mind by presenting to him religious motives of consolation. It is curious to see how difficult the latter found it to respond to the Bishop's thoughts. In spite of some convulsive snatches after Christian reminiscences, the antique element is the one that predominates in his letters, and certain fatalistic observations which escaped from his pen, induced Rodrigo to enlighten him as to the manner in which a Catholic ought to speak of Fortune and of Fate.†

The letters in which Platina invoked the intercession

* See the original text of this Letter in VAIRANI, I., 30–32.

† See VAIRANI, I., 45–66. Concerning Rodrigo Sanchez de Arevalo, see, besides the works cited in our Vol. II., p. 44, SAXIUS, Onom., II., 460; CHEVALIER, 2036, and *supra*, p. 17.

of a number of the Cardinals and Prelates are as deplorable as the "abject and fulsome flatteries" with which he overwhelmed his gaoler. All these letters are full of the praises of those to whom they are addressed, and of Paul II. and Sanchez de Arevalo. In one of them Platina confesses that he contemplated suicide. In answer to the accusation of irreligion, he maintains that, as far as human frailty permitted, he had always fulfilled his religious duties, and denies that he had ever impugned any article of Faith. He is conscious of no crime save his silence regarding the babble of Callimachus.*

Pomponius Laetus, who was delivered up to the Pope by Venice, during his detention at St. Angelo's shewed little of the ancient Roman stoicism which he had so ostentatiously professed. At first he seems to have given some sharp answers to his examiners;† but he soon followed the example of his friend Platina, and sought by obsequious flattery to win the favour of his gaoler and of the Pope.‡ He protested in the strongest terms that he was innocent, and, at the same time, begged for some books to read in his solitude. Instead of Lactantius and Macrobius, for which Pomponius asked, Rodrigo de Arevalo sent him his treatise on the errors of the Council of Basle. Pomponius was little gratified by the substitution, but thanked him in an offensively fulsome letter. This was meant to pave the way for another petition, and, on the same day, he expressed a wish for a cheerful companion, with whom he

* See especially the Letter to Cardinal Ammanati in VAIRANI, I., 36-7.

† This appears from a Letter of Platina's to P. Laetus, in VAIRANI, I., 38.

‡ CREIGHTON, III., 44-5, 276-284; here the original text of the letters is given from Cod. 161, of the Library of Corpus Christi College, Cambridge.

might interchange ideas. In support of his request, he quoted the words of Scripture : " Bear ye one another's burthens, and so you shall fulfil the law of Christ." This application was granted.

The Apology drawn up by Pomponius Laetus, while in prison, is also a pitiful production.* He meets an accusa-tion, in regard to his relations with a young Venetian, by an appeal to the example of Socrates. He had withdrawn from all intimate intercourse with Callimachus from the time he had become aware of his wickedness. Every-where, and especially in Venice, he had extolled Paul II. He confesses with regret that he had spoken strongly against the clergy; he had said these things in anger because he had been deprived of his maintenance; he begs to be forgiven for the sake of the sufferings of Christ. He brings forward witnesses to prove that he had fulfilled his Easter duties, explains his disregard of the law of fasting by the state of his health, and declares that he had received the necessary dispensation. Finally, in evidence of his Christian sentiments, he refers to the verses which he had composed on the Stations of the Cross, to his discourse in honour of the Blessed Virgin, and his treatise on the Immortality of the Soul. He concludes by a penitent admission that he has done wrong, and prays that, for the sake of the Risen Saviour, mercy may prevail over justice.

This pitiful document seems to have decided the fate of Pomponius. Paul II. came to the conclusion that the

---

* **Defensio Pomponii Laeti in carceribus et confessio. Cod. Vatic., 2934, P. I, p. 305-308b. (Vatican Library.) This Document was not, as GEIGER, 150, supposes, discovered by Gregorovius ; DE ROSSI first drew attention to it (Roma Sott., I., 7). GREGOROVIUS' extracts, VII., 571-2, 3rd ed., are more perfectly accurate ; the correct reading must be " *effusissimo* ore laudavi," and " ignoscate " should be "ignoscite."

writer of such a letter was incapable of originating a Conspiracy, and, with regard to the other charges against him, he probably considered that the severe lesson which he had received was sufficient to reform him. The reason of Platina's far longer detention in prison was evidently that the suspicions against him were stronger, owing to his former conduct.*

Paul II. still hoped that the ringleaders of the Conspiracy would fall into his hands, and, if we may believe Platina, Petrejus was actually apprehended, but confessed nothing.†

That the affair had a political side is evidenced by the fact that, immediately on the discovery of the plot, the Pope transferred his residence from St. Peter's to S. Marco, "in order to remove from the neighbourhood of the Orsini and place himself near the Colonna." " But," as the Ambassador, from whom we learn of this change, remarks, "danger is everywhere."‡

Things, however, did not now seem so alarming. The report of the departure from Naples of Luca de Tocio, the partisan of the Orsini, and of his participation in the Conspiracy, proved to be mistaken. Paul II., nevertheless, considered it well to surround himself with a strong guard. The Carnival amusements, as Augustinus de Rubeis, on the 4th March, informed the Duke of Milan, took place just as usual. "Regarding the Conspiracy against the Pope's person," writes the same Ambassador, "enquiries have been most carefully made, but as yet nothing has been discovered but some blustering talk of murdering the Pope, which may easily have arisen in the way I have already

---

* CREIGHTON, III., 46 ; VOIGT, II., 240, 2nd ed.

† PLATINA, 784.

‡ *Report of Joh. Blanchus of the 28th Febr., 1468 ; see Appendix, N. 19. State Archives, Milan.

described.   As the populace and the whole Court are discontented, it was only necessary for some one to make a beginning in order to carry all with him." *

The obscurity in which this Conspiracy is involved will never be completely cleared away.   Platina and Pomponius Laetus, " with touching unanimity concur in laying all the blame on the cunning of the fugitive who was not there to defend himself."   Even in distant Poland, where he hoped to find sure refuge with Paul II.'s enemy, King Casimir, Callimachus had good cause to guard his lips, for the Pope made great, though ineffectual, efforts to get him into his power.   Again, in the year 1470, the Papal Legate, Alexander, Bishop of Forli, urged the General Diet at Petrikau to deliver up the conspirator, who only escaped through a combination of favourable circumstances.†

Although enquiries regarding this Conspiracy were finally abandoned in Rome for want of evidence, yet the prosecution of what was designated as the "heresy" of the Academicians, was carried on, and this with all the more reason, inasmuch as Platina himself had not ventured to deny the charge of heathen practices.   Unfortunately, trustworthy information on this subject is but scanty. From many sources, however, we learn that Paul II. meditated measures of extreme severity against the heathen and philosophical extravagances of the Professors and Literati.

"If God preserves my life," said the Pope to one of the Ambassadors very soon after the discovery of the plot, " I will do two things ; in the first place, I will forbid the study of these senseless histories and poems, which are full of heresies and blasphemies, and, secondly, I will prohibit the

* See Appendix, N. 21.

† See ZEISSBERG, 354 and *seq.*; Acta Tomic., I., Appendix ; and CARO, V., I, 322 *seq.*

teaching and practice of Astrology, since so many errors
arise thence." "Children," continued the Pope, "when
hardly ten years old, even without going to school, know a
thousand villanies. What, then, must they become when,
later on, they read Juvenal, Terence, Plautus, and Ovid?
Juvenal certainly makes a shew of blaming vice, but he
leads his readers to the knowledge of it."* There are
many other books, he added, through which a sufficient
amount of learning may be attained; it is better to call
things by their true names and to avoid poetical circum-
locution. These Academicians are worse than the heathen,
for they believed in God, while these deny Him. The
Ambassadors expressed their agreement with the Pope,
especially Lorenzo of Pesaro, who delighted him by
demonstrating the faith of the ancients with a great display of learning. The Ambassadors also considered it
very advisable to forbid Ecclesiastics to study Poetry and
Astrology. The Pope concluded by declaring that he also
meant to take measures against the Roman habit of
spreading false reports.†

* This admirable discourse furnishes a fresh proof that Paul II.
was not so unlearned as Platina represents him.

† For the above, see the interesting *Report of Joh. Blanchus of 29th
Febr., 1468. (State Archives, Milan.) See Appendix, N. 21. Amongst
other reproaches brought by Ammanati (see FRIEDRICH, Astrologie
u. Ref., 20 seq., München, 1864) against Paul II., is that of having,
in 1465, firmly believed in Astrological predictions. I have not yet
found any confirmation of the statement of this witness, who is certainly
open to suspicion : the assertion, however, cannot be an absolute invention, and the general prevalence of Astrology in the Renaissance
age must be borne in mind. See BURCKHARDT, II., 279 and 346, 3rd
ed., concerning Sixtus IV.; see also GOTHEIN, 446, and PASTOR in
the Freib. Kirchenlexikon, I., 1525 seq., 2nd ed. In 1441, Domenico de
Domenichi even pronounced a *Discourse in laudem astrologiae et
confutationem opinionum ei adversantium. (Manuscript in the Mantua
Library ; see ZACHARIAS, Iter, 135.)

In the consultations, which were held during this time, to devise the best means of attacking the false Renaissance, the Pope may have had in his mind a treatise which Ermolao Barbaro, the excellent Bishop of Verona, had dedicated to him in 1455. This author, looking at the matter exclusively from a moral point of view, vehemently protests against the undue estimation in which the ancient poets were commonly held, and in some places altogether condemns the whole of the old heathen poetry. He goes through the whole series, first of the Greek, and then of the Latin poets, and cites a number of extracts from the writings of the Fathers, in which immoral poets are condemned. In his opposition to the fanatical admirers of ancient poetry, Barbaro sometimes flies to the other extreme, and completely condemns the art in itself. The conclusion which he deduces is, that if the study of these heathen writers, even by the laity, requires much circumspection, this must be still more necessary in the case of religious and priests.*

One of the Ambassadors expressly states that, in the middle of March, 1468, all the teachers in Rome were, on account of the danger of heresy, forbidden to make use of the old poets ; further details are wanting.†   It is,

* Ad rev. in Christo patrem et dominum dom. Petrum tit. S. Marci presbiterum card. dignissimum Hermolai dei paciencia episcopi Veronensis oratio contra poetas. The preface is dated : ex Verona, Cal. April. 1455. I found this remarkable treatise in Cod. Reg., 313, f. 167–192, of the Vatican Library. Barbaro looks only at one side of the question, and his adversaries at the other, the former blaming, and the latter praising, the poets. He dwells almost exclusively on the bad poets, and the evil contained in the writings of the good ones, while his opponents only mention the good. Barbaro died in 1471 ; see OROLOGIO, Canonici, 23.

† The *Despatch of "Laurentius de Pensauro" to Fr. Sforza, unfortunately a very short one, which, in accordance with the Pope's

however, probable that the Papal prohibition was confined
to the schools. At any rate, it did not apply to all poets,
but only, as the Pope clearly explained to the Ambassadors
of the League, to those who were objectionable on the score
of morals. Every one must admit that the moral aspect
was the one which a Pope was bound to consider in forming a judgment on the Classics. The vindication of the
Christian moral law in this domain was, therefore, a most
salutary act. Poison is poison still, even if contained in
crystal vials.

As regards the issue of the trial, we have only Platina's
report, and it cannot be looked upon as trustworthy.
According to him, the Academicians were acquitted from
the charge of actual heresy, nothing more than flippancy
and undue licence in language being proved against them.
Accordingly, the prisoners were now no longer shut up,
but merely detained in the Papal Palace, then within the
precincts of the Vatican, and finally, at the intercession
of some of the Cardinals, especially Bessarion, only in the
City of Rome;* but the Academy was dissolved, and
certain limitations were imposed upon classical studies.

The severe lesson given by Paul II. to the wanton
insolence of the Humanists, was no doubt a salutary
one. No one can deny that the Pope was acting within
his rights when he took measures against the practical
heathenism of the Academicians. Platina, himself, in a
letter to Pomponius Laetus, confessed that the heathenish
practices of the Academy must, necessarily, give offence.

explanation, must refer to the immoral poets only, runs as follows:
"Il papa ha prohibito a tutti li maestri de scole che non vole S. Sᵗᵃ che
legano poeti per la heresia era intrata in certi che se delectavano de
questi poeti. Dat. Romae, xvi. Martii, 1468." State Archives, Milan,
Cart. Gen.

  * PLATINA, 788.

"And so," he adds, "we must not complain if the Pope defends himself and the Christian religion."*

The action of Paul II. towards the Roman Academy has received a remarkable justification from recent investigations in the Catacombs.

Until the 15th century the subterranean necropolis of the early Christians had, with the exception of the Catacomb of St. Sebastian, been completely forgotten. Traces of visitors begin to reappear from the year 1433. First, we have names of Monks and Pilgrims, led there by devotion. "I came here," writes Brother Laurentius of Sicily, "to visit this holy place, with twenty companions of the Order of the Friars Minor, on the 17th January, 1451." Then, suddenly, we come upon the autograph scratches (Graffiti) of Humanists and Roman Academicians : of Pomponius, Platina, Volscus, Campanus, Pantagathus, Ruffus, Histrius, Partenopaeus, Perillus, Calpurnius, &c. They call themselves "a company of venerators and students of Roman antiquity, under the leadership of the pontifex maximus, Pomponius." Pantagathus describes himself as "Priest of the Roman Academy."† These men were in search, not of Christian, but of heathen, antiquity. In his large collection of inscriptions Pomponius inserted but

* "Justus fuit pontificis dolor; honesta tanta suspicione questio. Proinde et nos ferre aequo animo debemus, si saluti suae, si christianae religioni cavit." VAIRANI, I., 38. See GEBHARDT, A. of Corneto, 79 ; FRIEDRICH, J. Wessel, 63 seq., and JANITSCHEK, 19. The last-named author says : "I do not believe the charge to be false, that the Academicians were enemies of the Christian religion and intended to bring back the heathen worship."

† DE ROSSI, Roma Sott., I., 3 seq. ; REUMONT, III., 1, 342 seq. "The date 1475," observes Reumont, "points to the time of Sixtus IV., when, the meaning of these things being known, the danger was at an end. But, undoubtedly, this was a repetition, in a more public manner, of what had formerly been connected with a sort of secret society."

one which is Christian, and this one because it was metrical, and its polished form had a flavour of heathenism.* Even more characteristic is the fact that these "modern heathens" ventured, in the venerable vaults of the Catacombs, where the very stones preach the Gospel, to scrawl flippant inscriptions on the walls! † With this evidence before us, therefore, we cannot wonder that, even after their liberation from prison, the contemporaries of the Academicians should persist in maintaining that they were heathens rather than Christians.‡

Of all the Academicians no one had been treated with more severity than Platina. After his release he cherished the hope that his cringing flattery would, at least, have secured him some appointment from the Pope.§ Paul II. however, did not see any necessity for employing the pen of this violent and immoral man.‖ This disappointment

---

* DE ROSSI, Inscript., II., 402.

† DE ROSSI, Roma Sott., I., 6. The inscriptions have no individual character, and are written in the ordinary capitals.

‡ KRAUS, Roma Sott., 3 (Freiburg, 1879).

§ BALAN, V., 196, concludes from a letter of Platina's that he had been set at liberty some time before the September of 1469. A *Letter of the Cardinal of Ravenna's of the 7th July, 1469, in the Gonzaga Archives, proves this unfortunate man to have been at liberty at that date.

‖ At this time Platina intended to dedicate to Paul II. his work, " De falso ac vero bono." In the printed version, however, it is dedicated to Sixtus IV. (see ARISIUS, I., 317 ; and SCHMARSOW, 338 seq.), but Cod. 805 of the Trivulzio Library, Milan, shews that Platina originally offered or intended to offer it "divo Paulo II., P. M." Testimony as to Platina's immorality is furnished by the *Letter of the Bishop of Ventimiglia, from which DE ROSSI, I., 3-4, has only given the passage cited above. The Bishop here complains that Platina had recently loaded him with abuse in his own house. The cause of the quarrel was Platina's jealousy of a member of the Bishop's household, who was, he feared, likely to turn away his mistress from him : " vereris ne

intensified the hatred of the Humanist. He swore that he would have his revenge, and took it, after the death of Paul II., in his wide-spread " Lives of the Popes."

In this work he describes his enemy as a monster of cruelty, and a barbarian who detested all learning. This " biographical caricature" * has for centuries imposed itself on history. Even scholars, well aware of Platina's bias, have not succeeded in avoiding the influence of the portrait, drawn with undeniable skill and in a bright and elegant style. Some few over-partial attempts to vindicate his character have only served to increase the confusion, until, at length, recent critical investigation of the Archives has brought the truth to light.†

It must always be remembered that Paul II. was not an

illa tua adolescentula a tuis amoribus abducatur." The young person in question is then characterised as "puellam turpissimam monstroque similem," and Platina is reminded that he is no longer young. Cod. Vatic., 9020, f. 11. Vatican Library.

* BURCKHARDT, II., 50, 3rd ed.; BAYER, Aus Italien, 160, calls Platina's Biography of Paul II. 'a pamphlet.'

† The merit of this investigation is due to E. MÜNTZ, II., 1 seq., where the new literature on the subject is quoted. See also GEOFFROY, 383 seq. "Platina," observes CREIGHTON, III., 274, "without saying anything that is obviously untrue, has contrived to suggest a conception of Paul II. which is entirely contrary to known facts, yet which is so vivid, so definite, so intelligible, that it bears the stamp of reality." The influence of this work on Gregorovius is, therefore, quite comprehensible, especially as its sentiments accord with the prejudice against the Popes which even the Sybels'chen Zeitschr., N. F., XXI., 358, admits to exist in his mind. The great authority of Platina and Pomponius Laetus with their contemporaries has also had its effect, and so has the unfavourable opinion of Ammanati and of the author of the Cronica di Bologna, in regard to Paul II. The party feeling, which colours the writings of the Cardinal and the chronicler, has not been duly taken into account. See CREIGHTON, 273 seq. The disputes between Paul II. and Bologna warped the mind of the chronicler.

opponent of the Renaissance in itself, yet he is not to be looked upon as a Humanist, like Nicholas V. The boastfulness and conceit of its adherents repelled him : he preferred men of practical knowledge and practical tendencies. Poetasters had little to expect from him, and, in view of the pseudo-classical rhymes of a Porcello or a Montagna, this was not much to be regretted.*

The favours which Paul II. granted to the Roman and other High Schools,† as well as his generosity to a number of learned men, prove him to have been no enemy of culture and learning. While still a Cardinal he repeatedly visited Flavio Biondo in his last sickness, gave him assistance, and promised to provide for his children. As Pope, he fulfilled this promise by giving the charge of the Registers to Gasparo Biondo, in recognition of his father's deserts.‡ When the pious and enthusiastic scholar, Timoteo Maffei, fell ill, Paul II. sent him a present of money and a skilful physician, and, on his recovery, he conferred on him the Bishopric of Ragusa. Bishoprics were also bestowed on the three former preceptors of the Pope, and one of them, Amicus Agnifilus, was even raised to the purple. Learned men,

---

* MÜNTZ, II., 3, where there is proof from the *Epigrams of L. Montagna. Cod. 103 of the Bibl. de l'Institut, Paris.

† RENAZZI, I., 175, 185, 193 ; PAPENCORDT, 515. In regard to the other Universities, see DENIFLE, I., 514 ; PRANTL, I., 15–18 ; FROMMANN, Zur Gesch. d. Buchh., II., 23 ; BULAEUS, V., 674 seq. ; Ungar. Revue, 1881, p. 503. "Hatred of learning" is not indicated by the fact that Paul II. excommunicated those who removed the books from the Library of S. Spirito in Florence (RICHA, IX., 58), or, by his command, that the Bishop of Modena should take care that the MSS. to be transferred from Monte Cassino to Rome suffered no injury on the way from rain or from any other cause. *Brief of the 20th March, 1471, in the State Archives, Venice.

‡ Gött. Gel. Anz., 1879, p. 1501 seq. Regarding Atti camerali rogati dal notaro G. Biondo, see Studi e Doc., 1886, VII., 59 seq.

like Perotti, were promoted to positions of some importance in the States of the Church. Niccolo Gallo, Professor of Jurisprudence, when seriously ill, asked for a Confessor furnished with faculties to absolve from every sin ; the Pope granted his request, and added a present of 20 ducats.* He summoned to Rome many scholars whose acquaintance he had made while a Cardinal ; for example, Domizio da Caldiero and Gasparo da Verona, who was subsequently his biographer.† The Florentine, Lionardo Dati, was made Bishop of Massa, and Sigismondo de' Conti and Vespasiano da Bisticci bear witness to the Pope's affection for him ; the latter declares that, if the life of Paul II. had been prolonged, Dati would have been a Cardinal.‡ In the year 1470, Paul II. shewed the interest he took in historical studies by causing some Chronicles to be copied for him.§

Among the scholars advanced by Paul II. to the Episcopal dignity, was Cardinal Cusa's intimate friend, Giovan Andrea Bussi of Vigevano, a man who deserves the highest praise for his labours in the diffusion of printing throughout Italy. The numerous books dedicated by this Prelate to the Pope prove the interest taken by Paul II. in the

---

* CANENSIUS, 66-7 ; QUIRINI, XIII. See also MUTIUS PHOE-BONIUS, Hist. Marsorum cum catal. episcop., p. 35 (Neapol. 1678); and CORSIGNANI, II., 559. Regarding Maffei, see, besides the account in our Vol. I., 8, note 1, and Vol. II., 205 *seq.*, GIULIARI, 39, 163, 167 *seq.* ; MONTFAUCON, Bibl. bibl., I., 98 ; and ENGEL, Gesch. von Ragusa, 184 *seq.*

† RENAZZI, I., 234 ; see 211, and GIULIARI, 40-44.

‡ MAI, Spic., I., 275. Sigismondo de' Conti, in his *Treatise pro secretariis addressed to Sixtus IV., wrote : *"Gratus jocundusque fuit Paulo II., pontifici sapientissimo Leonardus Dathus Massanus praesul vir summa innocentia, summa prudentia, summa in rebus omnibus temperantia, stilo praeterea erudito et gravi praeditus." Vatic., 2934, P. II., f. 600, Vatican Library.

§ MÜNTZ, Bibl., 133, 134 ; see CANENSIUS, 97-8.

introduction of the newly discovered " divine art." " Your
pontificate, most glorious already, will never be forgotten,"
says Bussi, " because this art has been taken up to your
Throne."*

It is impossible to say, with certainty, who it was that
summoned the first German printers—Conrad Schweinheim
from Schwanheim, opposite Höchst on the Maine, Arnold
Pannartz from Prague, and Ulrich Hahn from Ingolstadt—
to Italy. Cusa was deeply interested in the important
discovery, but he died before these Germans arrived in
Italy. There can be no doubt that to Subiaco, " the Mother

---

* QUIRINI, 135 ; see MÜNTZ, Bibl., *loc. cit.*, who, like PAPENCORDT,
515, and FALKENSTEIN, 209, maintains that the Pope patronised the
new discovery. It is evident that Bussi's dedications were acceptable
to the Pope, as the Bishopric of Aleria was conferred upon him in
1469 (regarding which, compare MAZZUCHELLI, I., 2, 701 *seq.* ; MOTTA,
P. Castaldi . . . ed. il vesc. d'Aleria, Torino, 1884 ; and Riv. St. Ital.,
I.) ; and, moreover, a dedication to the Pope always implies his consent ;
it is, therefore, somewhat surprising to find H. V. D. LINDE, I., 165,
assert that " Paul II. was by no means a friend to the innovation ;"
and that Bussi had provided his editions with letters of dedication
to the Pope in order to convince him of the utility of typography.
Tiraboschi's account of the Pope's proceedings against the heathen
Academicians is quoted by H. v. d. Linde in support of his theory.
Those proceedings cannot be understood to imply any aversion on
the part of Paul II. to the art of printing, for Bussi, in one of his
dedicatory epistles (QUIRINI, 134), speaks of the humbling of these
restless men as favouring his efforts. A great many other passages
in these epistles (QUIRINI, 115, 152, 194, 196, 233) not only exclude
the idea of Paul's aversion to printing, but shew it to be absolutely at
variance with facts. FALK, Die Druckkunst, &c., draws a vivid picture
of the manifold encouragements afforded by the Church, in all European
countries, to Gutenberg's invention during its first decades. His work
is founded on materials gathered from a very wide field, many of which
have as yet been hardly, if at all, turned to account. This view has
since prevailed, even on the Protestant side, over the prejudices of
former days ; see, *e.g.*, B. HASE, Die Koberger, Leipzig, 1885, 2nd ed.

House of the Benedictine Order, which has done so much for the cause of learning, is due the honour of having given a home to the first German printers."* Constant relations between this great seat of Western culture and Germany had been maintained ever since the days of the excellent Abbot Bartholomaus III. (1362, &c.), who, in his zeal for the improvement of the monastic spirit, had invited from beyond the Alps many German monks, remarkable alike for their learning and their austerity of life.† Again, also, in the middle of the 15th century there were many German Benedictines at St. Scholastica.

In the retirement of Subiaco, Schweinheim and Pannartz printed, first the Latin Grammar of Donatus, which was extensively used in the Middle Ages, then Cicero's work on Orators, and the Instructions of Lactantius against the Heathen. The last of these books was completed on the 29th October, 1465. Two years later, an edition of St. Augustine's "City of God" issued from the Convent printing press at Subiaco.‡ The States of the Church may therefore claim, after Germany, the honour of first producing printed books.

---

* GREGOROVIUS, VII., 515, 3rd ed.

† Cronaca Subl., 394, 396–7. The holy life of the monks in their solitude is described by PIUS II. Comment. 168. Cod. 211, Juvenal, written in 1455 by Peter Paul Dominici de Subiaco, bears witness to the cultivation of classical studies in the monastery of Subiaco.

‡ See C. FUMAGALLI, Dei primi libri a stampa e specialmente di un Codice Sublacense impresso avanti il Lattanzio e finora creduto posteriore, Lugano, 1875; see FALKENSTEIN, 209; LAIRE, Specimen Hist. Typogr. Rom., Romae, 1778; AUDIFFREDI, Cat. Rom. edit. saec., XV., Romae, 1783; and OTTINO in the review, L'Arte della Stampa, 1870–71. Of the first edition of Lactantius but one copy now exists at Subiaco (before the French Revolution there was, according to BLUME, II., 241, a second); see the description in GORI, II., 325. The copy in the Casanatense Library, valued at 15,000 francs, dis-

Of Ulrich Hahn's labours at Subiaco no trace now remains. The learned Cardinal Torquemada induced him to come to Rome, and here, in 1467, Hahn, who is generally known by the name of Gallus, finished printing the " Contemplations " on the picture in the Court of Sᵗᵃ Maria sopra Minerva, which his patron had composed.* In the September of the same year, 1467, Schweinheim and Pannartz had also migrated to the Eternal City.† Here

appeared in 1885. The theft was, according to the " Frankf. Ztg." supposed to have been perpetrated by one of the officials of the library, and they were all severely punished ; the last of the Dominicans had a short time previously been removed. BERLAN'S opinion (La invenzione della stampa a tipo mobile revendicata all' Italia, Firenze, 1882), that Italy was the first country to make use of moveable type, is briefly refuted in the Jahresberichten der Geschichtswissenschaft, VI., 2, 268.

* Thirty-four folio pages with thirty-three woodcuts. LINDE, III., 715. See FALKENSTEIN, 211 ; and SCHMARSOW, 57. FROMMANN, Zur Gesch. d. Buchh., II., 5, says : " With the aid of the German monks, Torquemada caused the German printers, Schweinheim and Pannartz, to come to Subiaco and set up a printing press in the monastery." This is a conjecture for which evidence is wanting. Moveover, Falkenstein ought not to have confounded Cardinal Torquemada with the Spanish Inquisitor.

† The time when the German printers arrived at Subiaco cannot exactly be determined (FROMMANN, II., 5, thinks it was about the beginning of 1464, and so does VILLARI, I., 130, but Ph. de Lignamine does not agree with them) ; I can, however, confidently give 1467 as the date when they settled in Rome. GASP. VERONEN, Paulus II., 1046, adds to his account of Carvajal's return from his mission to Venice, the remark : " Hac tempestate ad sanct. Romam quidam juvenes accesserunt et ii quidem Teutonici qui Lactantium Firmianum de hominis opificio, de Dei ira necnon contra gentiles mense uno formaverunt et ducentos hujusmodi libros quoque mense efficiebant." Carvajal's return took place on the 17th Sept., 1467, as we learn from the *Acta Consist., f. 35b. (Secret Archives of the Vatican.) PH. DE LIGNAMINE, loc. cit., relates the arrival of Schweinheim and

in the Massimi Palace, near the German National Hospice, they established their printing press. Its first production was the " Letters of Cicero to his Friends." In the course of a few years this was followed by two editions of Lactantius, a second edition of Cicero's Letters, St. Augustine's City of God, the works of St. Jerome, the Holy Scriptures, St. Cyprian's Letters, the Catena of St. Thomas, and, amongst other classical works, those of Cæsar, Livy, Virgil, Ovid, Pliny, Quintilian, Suetonius, Gellius and Apulius.*

The corrector, or, as we should now say, the editor, of these works was the indefatigable classical scholar, Bussi. Almost all the books we have mentioned had fervid dedications to the Pope from his pen, and contained verses written by him. On one occasion he thus alludes to the names of his typographers, which had to the ears of his countrymen a barbarous sound :—

> The harsh-sounding German names awaken a smile :
> Let the admirable art soften the unmelodious tones.†

The friendly attitude of the Pope towards the new art, and the extraordinary liberality with which he allowed Bussi to make use of the precious Manuscripts in the Vatican Library, greatly contributed to promote the success of the Bishop's efforts. ‡

The important post of Corrector—with whom scientific textual criticism had its beginning—was also filled at Hahn's printing-house by a Bishop, Giantonio Campano, a

---

Pannartz in Rome, in June, 1465, but this must allude to their first visit, after which they went to Subiaco.

* QUIRINI, 107 *seq.* The Roman types were not so fine as the older ones employed at Subiaco.

† REUMONT, III., 1, 347, 510. Most of Bussi's prefaces are in QUIRINI, *loc. cit.* See BOTFIELD, Prefaces to the first editions of the Greek and Roman Classics, London, 1861.

‡ QUIRINI, 188.

fact which shews the esteem in which typography was held at this period.*

After the death of Torquemada, Caraffa became a warm patron of the art of printing ; nor did he stand alone among his colleagues in this respect.   In 1469 Bussi writes, "We have as yet found no one in the Sacred College of Cardinals who has not been favourable to our efforts, so that the higher the dignity the greater has been their zeal in learning.   Would that we could say as much for other orders."†   As time went on, the Roman clergy maintained an unflagging interest in the "sacred art" which, in the dedication to Paul II. prefixed to the letters of St. Jerome, is said to be "one of the most auspicious of all the Divine gifts bestowed during his pontificate on the Christian world, enabling even quite poor men at small cost to procure books." ‡

The account-books of Paul II.'s pontificate, which have lately been brought to light, shew how little he can be charged with systematic hostility towards classical antiquity.   They lead us to the conclusion that this so-called barbarian watched over the preservation of ancient remains even more carefully than the scholarly Pius II.   The triumphal arches of Titus and Septimius Severus, the Colossus of Monte Cavallo, and the equestrian statue of Marcus Aurelius were restored by his desire, and many forgotten and neglected relics of antiquity were brought to the Palace of S. Marco. §

The magnificent collection of antiquities and works of art, which Paul II. had brought together in this Palace while yet a Cardinal, contained the most important treasures

* FALKENSTEIN, 211 ; FALK, 18 ; GREGOROVIUS, VII., 517, 3rd ed.
† QUIRINI, 202.
‡ QUIRINI, 135 ; FALK, 19–20 ; LINDE, III., 705.
§ MÜNTZ, II., 4, 92–5.

of this kind from the time of the destruction of the Roman Empire. It contained numerous rare and most precious examples of antique Cameos and engraved gems, medals, and bronzes. From Byzantium there were pictures with golden backgrounds, little domestic altars with mosaics, reliquaries, ivory carvings, and gorgeously embroidered vestments. To these objects, whose value was enhanced by their age or their origin, was added a splendid selection of more recent works of art, such as Flemish tapestries, Florentine work in gold, vases and jewels. An inventory of this collection, taken in 1457, while Barbo was still a Cardinal, is one of the most interesting documents in the Roman State Archives,* and is of great value in connection with the history of art and civilisation in the Renaissance period. A comparison of the objects here mentioned with those in the Museums of the present day, enables us to realise the wealth of the Collection at S. Marco's. The Museum of Vienna contains about 200 ancient Cameos, and the Paris Library about 260 ; the inventory of Barbo's collection mentions 227. The Cardinal collected about a hundred ancient gold, and a thousand ancient silver, coins. He had twenty-five domestic altars with mosaics, a number greater than that now possessed by all the Museums of Europe together.†

But all these ancient, modern, and Eastern treasures were not sufficient to satisfy the soul of a collector like Paul II. On the contrary, now that the means at his disposal were greater, his schemes assumed yet larger propor-

---

* Published with some later additions by MÜNTZ, II., 181–287. Regarding Paul II. as a collector, see *ibid.*, 128 *seq.* ; and MÜNTZ, Précurseurs, 159, 170, 184, 193. His long sojourn in Florence, of which Paul II. speaks with so much enthusiasm in his *Letter of Sept. 8, 1466, cited on p. 14, must have had an important influence on his taste for collecting.

† MÜNTZ., II , 140, 143.

tions. He seems to have seriously entertained the idea of transferring the whole of the library of Monte Cassino to his palace, and he is said to have offered to construct a new bridge for the inhabitants of Toulouse in exchange for a Cameo.*

The Pope, however, was not merely an enthusiastic collector, but also an expert in matters of art. His memory was so extraordinary that he never forgot the name of a person or a thing, and he was able at a glance to tell where an ancient coin came from, and give the name of the Prince whose image it bore.†

The Churches of the Eternal City shared the care which he bestowed on the ancient monuments ; works of restoration, of a more or less extensive character, were carried on at the Lateran, S. Lorenzo in Piscibus, Sta Lucia in Septemviis, Sta Maria in Araceli, Sta Maria Maggiore, Sta Maria sopra Minerva and the Pantheon. The bridges, gates, walls, and many of the public buildings in Rome were repaired by his command. Similar benefits were conferred upon Tivoli, Ostia, Civitavecchia, Terracina, Viterbo and Monte Cassino.‡

The progress of Architecture, under Paul II., was most

---

* Proof of this statement is to be found in MÜNTZ, II., 133.

† Gasp. Veronen. in MARINI, II., 179 ; CANENSIUS, 31-2.

‡ MÜNTZ, II., 85-90, 94, 96, 98-107. See MÜNTZ, Les Anciennes Basiliques, 8, 17, 18, 19, 20-21, and Rev. Archéol., VII., 339, IX., 171. FORCELLA, XIII., 6. Regarding the Artists employed by Paul II., see also the Doc. e Stud., published by the Deput. di St. Patria, I. (Bologna, 1886), Studi, p. 4 *seq.* On one of the doors of the Palazzo Pubblico, at Viterbo, I saw the arms of Paul II., with the inscription : PA PP II. 1465. Paul II. also contributed to the rebuilding of the Cathedral of Loreto ; see TURSELLINUS, 133 *seq.* (SCHMARSOW, 122), and the *Brief of this Pope to the "episcop. Parentinus, eccl. Rachanaten. vicarius," dated Romae, 1 Martii, 1471. Lib. brev. 12, f. 12. Secret Archives of the Vatican.

remarkable,* and in this branch ot creative art the Pope appears as the champion of the Renaissance. In the erection of the magnificent Palace of S. Marco he was the first to apply the theories of Vitruvius and definitely to break with the Gothic style. The splendid and extensive buildings at the Vatican secured the triumph of the new style in Rome.† The fact that Paul II. reverted to Nicholas V.'s grand scheme for the reconstruction of St. Peter's, and proceeded with the erection of the Tribune, is of the higest interest. A medal and a couple ot lines in Canensius' Biography ot the Pope were, until lately, our only sources of information on this subject, and, accordingly, it came to be supposed that only works of restoration were alluded to. The accounts preserved in the Roman State Archives, however, furnish absolute proof of the magnificent projects entertained by the Pope. A passage, unfortunately very laconic, in a letter from Gentile Becchi to Lorenzo de' Medici, confirms this statement.‡

The transportation of the Obelisk on St. Peter's square—another scheme of his great predecessor's—was also taken in hand by Paul II. The distinguished architect, Ridolfo Fioravante degli Alberti, one of the first men of his day,

---

* Painting was not at this time very flourishing. See MÜNTZ, II., 30 *seq.*, 32, 107-108, and JANITSCHEK'S Repert., VI., 215 *seq.*

† MÜNTZ, II., 8, 32-43.

‡ "*Sam Marco si sta. La tribuna di Sam Piero diseguita." Gentile Becchi to Lorenzo de' Medici, 1470 (stil. flor.), da Roma a di III. di Gennaio (Ricevuta a di V. detto). The Original is in the State Archives at Florence. Av. il princ. filza 61, fol. 119. This recently discovered information perfectly agrees with the extracts from accounts given by MÜNTZ, II., 45 *seq.*, and with his conjecture regarding the date of the medals given by Litta (note 11). The juxtaposition in these of the works at S. Marco and S. Peter's, leads us to conclude that a great new building had also been in contemplation on the site of the latter.

had prepared the plans, and the work had already been commenced when the Pope died.*

The Palazzo di S. Marco, now Palazzo di Venezia, is the most magnificent creation of Paul II. Recent investigations of the Archives have thrown some light on the history of this gigantic work, but many questions regarding it are still unanswered.† Medals struck on this occasion, and frequently found during restorations in earthenware caskets, together with an inscription on the façade, bear witness that these extensive works were begun in the year 1455.‡ This magnificent building was designed in truly Roman proportions. A whole quarter had to be pulled down in order to make room for it, and, although the works went on during the whole of Paul II.'s pontificate, the Palace "within which the newly decorated Basilica of St. Mark was contained like a chapel" was not completed at the time of his death. But even in its unfinished state it is one of the grandest of Roman Monuments,§ and, in a remarkable manner, exhibits the transition from the mediæval

---

* Müntz, II., 4, 24–5. See our Vol. II., p. 184. To the works concerning Fioravante, cited by Müntz, I., 83, may be added the Arch. St. Lomb., 1882, and the Giornale dell' Ingegnere Architetto of 1872.

† Here again the investigations of Müntz, II., 49 seq., are our principal authority; they are supplemented by his articles in L'Art (1884), and in Gli Studi in Italia, A°, VII., 1, fasc. 2 (which also appeared separately at Rome in 1884). See also Schmarsow, 62 seq., and Studi e Doc., VII., 67 seq. (1886).

‡ Bonanni, I., 71. The inscription is as follows : " Petrus Barbus Venetus cardinalis S. Marci has aedes condidit A° Chr., 1455."

§ All contemporary writers mention this building with admiration. Fr. Ariostus, in his *Description of Borso's elevation to the dukedom of Ferrara, which we shall hereafter quote, says, in regard to the passage of this Prince through Rome, that he came "per quella regione dove si fabrica quello alto e superbo pallazzo pontificale a S. Marco cum tanta incomparabile spesa, cum tanto maraveglioso

fortress to the modern Palace, and from the Gothic to the Renaissance style. In the Palace proper, the character of a fortress predominates. " It is," to quote the words of a gifted historian of art, "a speaking monument of an age of violence, presenting to the mob a stern and imposing aspect, devoid of all grace or charm, jealously concealing all the beauty of its spacious and decorated halls, destined to be the home of a luxurious life, and the scene of many a gorgeous spectacle." * The grand unfinished court, with its portico ornamented with pilasters in the Doric-Tuscan style below and Corinthian above, the Palazzetto, begun in 1466, joining it at the right-hand corner, and the vestibule of S. Marco, connected with the Palace, are all in the Renaissance style.

From 1466, Paul II. had, during a great part of the year, taken up his abode in this stupendous Palace, which was

artificio, cum piu ingegno, cum piu magnificentia che per adriedo si sia usitado edificare in Roma." Cod. J., VII., 261. Chigi Library, Rome.

* SCHMARSOW, 63, who conjectures that the purpose of this edifice was to put an end to the banishment of the Popes to the Leonine City. That political motives actually induced Paul II. frequently to dwell in the new Palace, is evident from the *Despatch in the Archives at Milan, cited *supra*, p. 58. See PAPENCORDT, 516 *seq.*; GSELL-FELS, 188 ; BURCKHARDT-BODE, 98 ; REDTENBACHER, 155; BURCKHARDT, Gesch. der Renaiss., 55, 160. Regarding S. Marco, see ARMELLINI, 327. Calixtus III., in 1458, tertio Non. Maii A° 4°, granted an Indulgence to promote the restoration of S. Marco, and, on this occasion, mentioned the care and expense bestowed by Card. Barbo on this Church. Regest., 452, f. 40. (Secret Archives of the Vatican.) Compare also Stevenson's remarkable treatise, "Sur les tuiles de plomb de la basilique de S. Marc, ornées des armoiries de Paul II. et des médaillons de la Renaissance," in the Mél. d'Arch., p. 439 *seq.* (1888). The area of the Palace, together with the Church and the Palazzetto, is (as the Architect, F. Pokorny, kindly informs me) 12,174 square metres. The Ecclesialogist, XXIX., 160,

situated in the middle of the City, at the foot of the Capitol and in the domain of the friendly Colonna family. The Apostolic Treasury was also transferred there.* Subsequent Popes frequently, as their Bulls bear evidence, lived there. Just a century after the Election of Paul II., this grand building was given by Pius IV. to the Republic of Venice.† Afterwards, when Venice fell into the hands of Austria, it became the property of that Empire, whose Ambassadors now occupy it.

* See GOTTLOB, Cam. Apost. Especially in summer, when the neighbourhood of the Vatican is infested with fever, the Pope lived at S. Marco, which is accordingly called by Fr. Ariostus in the MS. cited *supra*, p. 76, the 'stantia estiva de la Sta de N. S.' His sojourn there was often prolonged into the winter months ; in 1464, Paul II. was still at S. Marco on the 16th November, as appears from the *Acta Consist., f. 34a. (Secret Archives of the Vatican.) The investigations of MÜNTZ (Arts, II., 13, 15, 16, 53 ; Palais, 9) shew that Giacomo da Pietrasanta, who first came into notice in the time of Nicholas V., may justly claim to be considered the architect of this Palace. See REDTENBACHER, 146. Giuliano da San Gallo, then a youth, Meo del Caprino, and Giovannino de' Dolci, were all fellow-workers with him. Blocks of Travertine freestone, taken from the Colosseum, were employed in the building. See MÜNTZ, II., 7. Over and over again, valuable ancient stones were also sent out of Rome. On the 16th Sept., 1464, *Cardinal Gonzaga writes from Rome to his mother, Barbara : "Mando etiam per questo mestiere alcuni pezzi de alabastri et altre antiquitate tuolte qui." (Gonzaga Archives, Mantua.) A metrical inscription on the Church and Palace of S. Marco, which has not previously been published, will be found in Appendix, N. 9.

† See CECCHETTI, l., 333, note. The transfer was symbolised by the shutting and opening of the gates ; see the *Act regarding the Traditio of the Palace by Card. Guido Ascanius Sforza, Procurator of Pius IV., to the Orator Jacobus Superantius, dated 1564, 2, VII., in the State Archives, Venice. (Kindly communicated by Prof. F. Kaltenbrunner.)

CHAPTER III.

THE WAR AGAINST THE TURKS.—SKANDERBEG IN ROME.

THE death of Pius II. inflicted a heavy blow upon the Church, more especially because its effect was to arrest the movement for the defence of Christendom against Islam, which had then just commenced. Cardinal Bessarion, one of Greece's noblest sons, gave expression to his sorrow in touching words.* The Crusade was, for the time, at a standstill, but the idea lived on in the minds of the Popes. Paul II. had, even while a Cardinal, taken a deep interest in the Turkish question, and his friends hoped great things from him.†

The first steps taken by the new Pope in no way disappointed these expectations. In the letters by which he informed the Italian Princes of his election, he gave expression to his zeal for " the defence of the Christian Faith against the fury of the Turks." ‡ One of the principal

* Report of the Milanese Ambassador of the 23rd Oct., 1464. Ambrosian Library.

† JÄGER, II., 428. The letter of Paul Morizeno, of the 4th Sept., 1464, here cited, is no longer to be found in the Government Archives of Innsbruck.

‡ CONTELORIUS, 57-9 (see RAYNALDUS, ad an. 1464, N. 59). The Letters to Florence (of which a copy exists in the Archives of that city) and to the Marquis of Mantua (Original in the Gonzaga Archives) are similar to that here published. In a *Brief to Bologna, dated Rome, 1464, Sept. 20, Paul II. also asserts his intention of carrying on the war against the Turks which Pius II. had begun. (State Archives, Bologna, Q. 3.) See also THEINER, Mon. Hung., II., 398.

hindrances in the way of Pius II.'s magnificent schemes
had been his constant financial difficulties.   Paul II., the
practical Venetian, sought to remedy this state of things,
by removing the charge of the revenue derived from the
Alum monopoly, and, in virtue of the Election Capitulation, destined for the Holy War, from the Apostolic
Treasury to a Commission composed of Cardinals Bessarion,
d'Estouteville and Carvajal.*   These Cardinals, who were
styled " Commissaries General of the Holy Crusade," were
to deliberate on all measures necessary for the prosecution
of the war, and to report accordingly.   " Also the income
from Indulgences and from the tithes paid by the clergy
for this purpose, as far as it had hitherto been at the disposal of the ' Camera Apostolica,' was now, for the most
part, directly handed over to the Commission, or expended
according to its decision." †   The magnificent support
afforded by the Commission to the brave Hungarians has
won for it an abiding and honourable remembrance.‡

In the autumn of 1464, when the Envoys of the Italian
States came to Rome to do homage, the Pope took the
opportunity of bringing forward the Turkish question.§

* Letter of Cardinal Gonzaga to his Mother, dated Rome, 1464, Nov.
23. (Gonzaga Archives, Mantua.)   See *ibid.*, *Letter of Jacopo de
Aretio of the 1st Sept., 1464; AMMANATI, Epist., f. 26, 60 ; and
CANENSIUS, 47.

† GOTTLOB, Cam. Ap.

‡ Further particulars will be found, *infra*, p. 83.   A Papal Bull, " Ad
sacram," dated Romae, 1465, III. Id. April (=11 April), renews the
prohibition of trade with the Infidels and of any interference with
the alum trade.   (Regest., 519, f. 153, Secret Archives of the Vatican.
Copy in the State Archives, Milan.)   GOTTLOB, Cam. Ap., shews that
Paul II. called upon the other powers to protect the Papal monopoly
of Alum.

§ See Paul II.'s Brief to Louis XI. in D'ACHERY, III., 824, and
the *Letter of the Milanese Ambassadors of the 14th Oct., 1461.
Ambrosian Library.

Special negotiations were set on foot with the splendid Embassy of the Venetian Republic.* They proceeded to treat with the Commission of Cardinals, and a fresh scheme was proposed for the Italian States, according to which the Pope and Venice were each to contribute 100,000 ducats, Naples 80,000, Milan 70,000, Florence 50,000, Modena 20,000, Siena 15,000, Mantua 10,000, Lucca 8,000 and Montferrat, 5,000.†

The plan was by no means well received by the Italian powers. The Pope, who declared himself ready to pay the 100,000 ducats, even if he should have to take it out of his household expenditure,‡ had great difficulty in obtaining a promise to let the matter be again brought under discussion in Rome. The deliberations lasted for six months. No one was prepared to pay the appointed contributions, which the Pope intended to devote to the assistance of the Hungarians. Each sought to diminish his own share, and the more powerful States attached onerous conditions to their compliance. Venice, Florence and Milan demanded the remission of the Papal tax of the tenth, twentieth and thirtieth, and the King of Naples the complete remission of the tribute which he owed to the Holy See. In order to enforce his request, Ferrante informed the Pope that the Sultan had made offers of alliance to him, with a sum of 80,000 ducats, if he would stir up a war in Italy. Subsequently, when the relations between Rome and Naples had become still more un-

---

* Regarding this Embassy, see ROMANIN, IV., 321.

† AMMANATI, Epist., 41. See Mon. Hung., II., 234, where the document on the subject is wrongly assigned to the year 1471, instead of the autumn of 1464. The proposal is also interesting as giving an idea of the wealth of the Italian States. See the Table of 1455 in MÜNTZ, Renaiss., 50.

‡ Mon. Hung., II., 234.

friendly, he openly threatened to ally himself with the Turks.*

The Ambassadors assembled in Rome displayed a true Italian talent for evasion and procrastination. It was evident that not one amongst them would do anything.† This "hopeless state of things" induced Paul II. to lift the veil, and let all the world know whose fault it was that, after six months of deliberation, not a single step in advance had been made. The just displeasure of Paul II. found vent in bitter complaints. "The outcry against the burdens imposed is only raised in order to avoid giving support to the Venetians. May it not prove that, in thus forsaking the Venetians, people are forsaking themselves and all the faithful." They desire to discharge their obligations with the money of the Church, and thus to render it impossible for her to assist the Hungarians. The consequence will be that Hungary will be compelled to make peace with the Turks. What is left for the Venetians but to take the same course, especially as Mahomet has offered them tolerably favourable conditions? When both these champions are removed, the way to Italy by land and sea lies open to the enemies of Christendom.‡

These complaints were as powerless to rouse the Italian powers from their lethargy as the tidings of the immense

---

* Besides the authorities cited by CHRISTOPHE, II., 120 *seq.*, 152 *seq.*, see the *Letter of Augustinus de Rubeis to Fr. Sforza, dated Rome, 1465, Febr. 20. (Ambrosian Library.) Particulars regarding the conflict between Rome and Naples will be found in Chapter VI.

† Jacopo de Aretio, one of the Ambassadors, writes (dat. Roma, 1465, Marzo 18), regarding the negotiations with the Commission of Cardinals : *"Secondo a mi parse comprendere in quelle volte che me so ritrovato in simil congregatione non compresi alcuno che vollese offerire alcuna cosa." Gonzaga Archives, Mantua.

‡ AMMANATI, Epist., f. 60b ; ZINKEISEN, II., 309 *seq.*

naval preparations of the Turks, which reached Rome in May, 1465, denoted immediate danger to Italy.* Yet at this very time Florence refused the payment of a yearly contribution for Hungary demanded by the Pope.†

Even in the States of the Church the Pope encountered obstinate opposition to the payment of the Turkish tithes. Not only the smaller towns, like Viterbo, Toscanella and Soriano, but even the wealthy city of Bologna had to be seriously admonished to fulfil the obligation.‡ Tivoli and Foligno begged for a remission of the tax ; Ferentino lay for a long time under an Interdict for resisting the claims of the Apostolic Treasury; the Counts of Conti in the Campagna were utterly recalcitrant. Ecclesiastical penalties proved useless, and in the end it was necessary to resort to force.§

Meanwhile, Paul II. maintained the war against the enemies of the Faith as well as his own resources permitted, making great sacrifices, especially on behalf of Hungary. A modern historian,|| after mentioning 42,500 (or 40,000) ducats given to Matthias Corvinus at Ancona, speaks of "some smaller" sums of money sent by Paul to Hungary. This statement is directly contradicted by the testimony of the Pope's contemporary, Vespasiano da Bisticci, who says that Paul II. sent about 80,000 ducats to Hungary in 1465, and also promised an annual contribution.¶ The

* *Letter of J. P. Arrivabene of the 21st May, 1465. Gonzaga Archives, Mantua.

† MÜLLER., Docum., 202-3.

‡ *Brief to Bologna, dated Rome, 1464, Sept. 20. (State Archives, Bologna, Q. 3.) Regarding the other cities, see *Cruciata Pauli II., f. 10b. State Archives, Rome.

§ GOTTLOB, Cam. Ap.

|| HUBER, Gesch. Oesterr., III., 212.

¶ MAI, Spic., I., 297.

account-books preserved in the Roman State Archives shew that on the 23rd May, 1465, the Commissaries General of the Crusade paid 57,500 golden florins to the Ambassadors of King Matthias of Hungary from the proceeds of the Alum monopoly alone, and, on the 28th April, 1466, a further sum of 10,000 Hungarian ducats.* The expense of the mercenaries meanwhile was so heavy that the Hungarian Monarch felt obliged to give up all offensive warfare against the Turks. Venice, also, at this time thought of making peace with the enemy. The deplorable policy of the Italian States, which Paul II. had vainly endeavoured to gain to the common cause, explains this universal discouragement. " Naples and Milan kept on good terms with the Porte, Genoa and Florence hankered after the reversion of the commerce of Venice in the Levant." Under these circumstances, it was well that the heroic Skanderbeg and the war in Asia Minor, " by which the feudatory kingdom of Caramania was annexed in 1466," fully occupied the Turkish forces.†

To prevent the conclusion of a peace with the Turks, Paul II. made large offers of money, and resolved to send Cardinal Carvajal, the most distinguished member of the

---

* *Cruciata Pauli II. See GOTTLOB, Cam. Ap., and GORI, Arch., III., 39. I will not blame Huber for having overlooked the last mentioned treatise, but I ask why he has completely ignored the statements of Vespasiano da Bisticci in a work which is generally accessible. It is absolutely incomprehensible that HUBER, *loc. cit.*, should speak of "some few smaller sums of money also sent" by Paul II., while he himself cites the Brief of that Pope of May 26th, 1465, published by TELEKI, XI., 124 *seq.*, in which the transmission of 57,500 florins is expressly mentioned. The zeal of Paul II. in resisting the Turks has been generally acknowledged, even by the Venetians, who were not favourably disposed towards him. See Mon. Hung., I., 321 ; *ibid.*, 324, 332, 339, 343, 375.

† HERTZBERG, Griechenland, II., 591. See ROMANIN, IV., 324 *seq.*

Sacred College, to Venice. This prelate, who had through life ardently espoused the cause of the Holy War, was of all others the best fitted to accomplish so difficult a mission. His appointment as Legate for Venice took place on the 30th July, 1466 ; he left Rome on the 20th August, and did not return till the autumn of the following year.*

In November, 1466, a Diet, energetically promoted by Paul II., was held at Nuremberg† to consider the Turkish question. The despatch of an army to the assistance of Hungary was discussed at great length, but neither this Assembly nor those which followed had any definite result.‡

* GASP. VERONEN., 1046, expresses himself in a very mysterious manner regarding Carvajal's Mission, but declares that the Cardinal accomplished the object in view. MALIPIERO, 38, says even more. The above dates, which have hitherto been unknown, are from the *Acta Consist. of the Secret Archives of the Vatican, f. 34b–35 ; the purpose of the journey is here mentioned in the following terms : "sollicitaturus aliqua contra nephandissimum Turcum et alia etc." Concerning his return, see *infra*, p. 140, note †. From a *Letter of Card. Gonzaga's, dated Rome, 1466, July 31, in which the 30th July is mentioned as the day of his appointment, we learn that Carvajal was to enter into negotiations not only about the Turkish War, but also concerning the other matters then in dispute between Rome and Venice. (Gonzaga Archives, Mantua.) See *infra*, Chap. IV.· Carvajal had also to treat of the entry of Venice into the Italian League ; see *Report of A. de Rubeis, dated Rome, 1466, December 6. State Archives, Milan.

† The Cardinal of Augsburg sent out the Papal Briefs, in which the "great peril of the Christian Faith" was laid before the States, and they were called upon to send delegates to Nuremberg. The Original of a *Letter to Frankfort-on-Maine (dated Dillingen, 1466, Oct. 15) is in the Archives of that City, Reichssachen, 5537. Paul II. himself also exhorted the powers to attend the Diet appointed, also to meet at Nuremberg on the 15th June, 1467. See JANSSEN, Reichscorr., I., 251, and Cod. Dipl. Sax., 170–171. A list of those who at this time received these Papal Briefs is in the City Archives of Strasburg, AA. 205.

‡ See REISSERMAYER, I., 20 *seq.*, where the dignity of Cardinal is

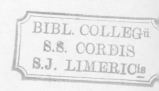

In July, 1466, the Pope invoked the assistance of the European Princes on behalf of Skanderbeg. For two years had this hero resisted all the attacks of the Turks, who had been repeatedly defeated by him.* To avenge this disgrace, the Sultan determined on an expedition against Albania. In the spring of 1466 a Turkish force, 200,000, or, as some few writers say, 300,000 strong,† began its march against Croja, the capital city. At the end of May a messenger reached Ragusa with the news that Skanderbeg had been defeated by treachery, and that a number of Christians had been slain ; a second Turkish army was also said to threaten Hungary.‡ The Italians were panic-stricken. Piero de' Medici shed tears over the fate of Albania and promised help.§ The Pope, who had already aided Skanderbeg, again sent money,‖ and lost no time in calling on the Christian powers to bestir themselves. He spoke in moving terms of the affliction of Christendom, of the terror of the nations on the Adriatic coast, and of the fugitives who were constantly arriving from the East. "One cannot without tears behold those ships that flee from the Albanian shore

wrongly ascribed to Fantinus. Besides the Acts of the Electoral Chancery in the State Archives of Vienna, the *Händelung auf dem päpstlichen und kaiserlichen Tage zu Nürnberg, A° 66, in the City Archives at Oberehenheim, may be consulted in regard to this Diet.

* PAGANEL, 327 seq., 349 seq.

† **Letter from the Ambassador of Mantua to Rome, 31st May, 1466. Gonzaga Archives.

‡ **Letter of Bartol. de Maraschis to the Marchioness of Mantua, dated Rome, 1466, May 31. Gonzaga Archives.

§ *Letter of T. Maffei of the 15th May, 1466, according to the Florentine State Archives, in Appendix, N. 14. See the complaints of the Venetians in MAKUSCEV, Slaven in Albanien, 108.

‖ Documentary evidence of this fact, taken from the Roman State Archives (*Cruciata Pauli II.), is given by Bertolotti in GORI, Archivio, III., 39, and also by GOTTLOB, who was unacquainted with Bertolotti's work, in Hist. Jahrb., VI., 443.

to take refuge in Italian harbours ; those naked, wretched families, driven from their dwellings, who sit by the sea, stretching out their hands to heaven and filling the air with lamentations uttered in an unknown tongue." The account-books of his pontificate bear witness to the magnificent liberality with which Paul II. succoured these unhappy creatures. The Pope might indeed say that he had done what lay in his power ; the Hungarians alone had in the preceding year received 100,000 golden florins, but he could not do everything ; effectual support from the Christian powers was more than ever a necessity.[*]

Happily the apprehensions regarding the fate of Albania were not realised. The heroic valour of its champion rendered Croja invincible. "Skanderbeg pursued his ancient, well-tried tactics, and from the woodlands of Tumenistos he ceaselessly harassed the besiegers, inflicting so much loss and disgrace on the Turkish army, that the Sultan, finding corruption and force alike useless, left Balaban with 80,000 men to continue the siege of Croja and starve it into submission, and himself retired with the bulk of his troops into winter quarters at Constantinople."[†]

The fate of Albania depended on the deliverance of Croja, which Balaban had encircled with a girdle of fortresses, and the task was beyond the unassisted powers of the Albanians and Venetians. Skanderbeg, therefore, resolved to go in

---

[*] Papal Letter to the Duke of Burgundy in AMMANATI, Epist., 102b–104, and in RAYNALDUS, ad an. 1466, N. 2–6. The date, July 1466, wanting in CIPOLLA, 535, may be gathered from the contents, and from a comparison with the Brief cited by LICHNOWSKY, Urkunden, p. CCCLXVIII., addressed to Duke Sigismund of the Tyrol. I have, however, vainly sought for this Document in the Ferdinandeum at Innsbruck.

[†] FALLMERAYER, 87. See HOPF, 156, and MAKUSCEV, Slaven, 109.

person to Italy to beg for money and arms from Rome and Naples.*

In the middle of December, 1466, the Albanian champion reached Rome, where he was received with honours. " He is," to quote the words of an eye-witness, " an old man in his sixtieth year ; he came with but few horses, in poverty ; I hear that he will ask for help."†

It has been again and again falsely asserted that, in consequence of his " too Venetian sympathies," Skanderbeg obtained nothing from the Pope beyond the Indulgence and the Proclamations addressed to the deaf ears of Western Christendom, together with some pious exhortations and the renewal of the never fulfilled promise of the crown of Epirus and Macedonia.‡

His biographer, on the contrary, not only relates the honourable and friendly reception of the hero in Rome, but expressly observes that the Pope, like the Cardinals, had generously responded to his requests. " With many

---

* MALIPIERO, 38 ; BARLETIUS, I., XII., p. 355.

† PAGANEL, 356, gives 1465 as the date of Skanderbeg's journey to Rome ; ZINKEISEN, II., 393, places it in the beginning of 1466 ; FALLMERAYER, 87, and HOPF, 156, in the summer of that year. They are all mistaken. The Cron. Rom., 32, expressly mention his arrival in the December of 1466, and the *Account-books of Paul II. in the Roman State Archives, as well as a *Letter of Card. Gonzaga's of the 15th Dec., 1466 (Gonzaga Archives), concur in the statement. In the Gonzaga Archives a *Letter from J. P. Arrivabene, dated Rome, xiv. Decemb., 1466, contains the following words :—*" El S. Scanderbeo gionse qui veneri [=12 Dec.] et incontra li forono mandate le famiglie de' cardinali. È homo molto de tempo passa li 60 anni ; cum puochi cavalli è venuto e da povero homo. Sento vorrà subsidio." Beneath the Quirinal, Vicolo di Scanderbeg No. 116–117, is to be seen on the house where he is said to have dwelt, his image with the inscription : "Geor. Castriota a Scanderbeg princeps Epiri‖ad fidem iconis rest. an. dom. MDCCCXLIII." See BELLI, Case, 58.

‡ FALLMERAYER, 88, where the Pope is twice called Paul III. !

presents, and with a considerable sum of money," says
Barletius, " Skanderbeg returned cheered and encouraged
to his people."* Other authentic documents give fuller
particulars as to the results of the journey to Rome. In
the account-books of Paul II. we find that first of all
Skanderbeg received for his maintenance on one occasion
250, and on another, 200 ducats, and that furthermore on
the 19th April, 1467, 2700, and on the 1st September
1100 ducats were paid to him.† Regarding the Secret
Consistory of January 7th, 1467, in which the assistance to
be given to the Albanian hero was considered, we have
the testimony of Cardinal Gonzaga, who took part in it.‡
He says that the Pope at once declared his readiness to
pay 5000 ducats ; the necessity of protecting his own
country was his reason for not contributing yet more
largely ; Cardinal Orsini, who was hostile to Paul II.,
ventured to observe that the Pope had nothing to apprehend from any quarter. This remark greatly angered the
Pope, and provoked some interesting disclosures as to his
relations with Naples. He said that he knew with certainty that Ferrante was eager to attack the States of the
Church. One of the King's five confidants on this matter
had given information to Rome. It is evident that, under
these circumstances, the Holy See could not do more for
the champion of Albania. A Secret Consistory of the 12th
January, 1467, determined that in any case Skanderbeg
should have 5000 ducats.§ Not only Venice, but also

* BARLETIUS, I., XII., p. 358. The speech of Skanderbeg here
related is no more genuine than that which the hero is said to have
made on his death-bed.

† Authorities are given in the articles by BERTOLOTTI and GOTT-
LOB, cited p. 86, *supra.* See also CANENSIUS, 74.

‡ See in Appendix, N. 18, the text of this *Document, which I found
'n the Gonzaga Archives.

§ *" Questa matina de novo foe havuto ragionamento in consistorio

Ferrante, whose relations with Skanderbeg had long been of an intimate character, received him and sent money, provisions and munitions.* On his return to his beloved country he soon won fresh laurels ; in April, 1467, the Turks were defeated and Balaban's brother taken prisoner. A second victory quickly followed, in which Balaban fell and his troops took to flight.† Croja was saved. The danger, however, was not at an end ; a second Turkish army appeared, and Skanderbeg had to keep the field throughout the whole year. In the midst of these conflicts, death overtook the Albanian champion ; on the 17th January, 1468, Skanderbeg succumbed at Alessio to the effects of a fever.‡

No greater loss had befallen Christendom since the death of Hunyadi and St. John Capistran. This was but too plain to the enemies of the Faith. It is said that when the Sultan heard the news, he exclaimed, "At last Europe and Asia are mine. Woe to Christendom ! she has lost her sword and her shield !"

---

secr [eto circa] li fatti de Scandarbeo al qual se daranno pur li cinquemilia ducati." Letter from Card. Gonzaga to his father, dated Rome, 12 Januarii, 1467. Gonzaga Archives, Mantua.

* TRINCHERA, I., 90.

† This is related by Zacharius Barbarus, writing on the 10th May, 1467, from Letters from Alessio. See MAKUSCEV, Slaven, 110.

‡ HAMMER, II., 91, 94, makes Skanderbeg die in 1466 ; PAGANEL, 377 ; ROHRBACHER-KNÖPFLER, 227, and CIPOLLA, 539, fix 1467 as the date ; and REUMONT, III., 1, 189, February, 1468. The date we have given above, to which FALLMERAYER, 95, also adheres, is confirmed by the Letter of Condolence in TRINCHERA, I., 439, and the Milanese Report in the Mon. Hung., II., 93. See also HOPF, Griechenland, 157. Skanderbeg's helmet, with a goat's head erect embossed, and his sword, with the inscription in Arabic, "God's hero, Iskender Beg," are preserved in the Ambras Collection at Vienna ; see VON SACKEN, Ambras Sammlung, 211–212 (Wien, 1855).

The effect of the blow was felt at once by the hard-pressed Albanians. The Turks overran their country—" in the whole of Albania we saw nothing but Turks," says a contemporary account—8000 unhappy creatures were sent away as slaves within a few weeks.* But Albania was not yet completely vanquished : Scutari and Croja, whose garrisons were strengthened by Venetian troops, continued to hold out. The enthusiastic honour paid by the afflicted people to the memory of their departed chief was most touching. " Choirs of Albanian maidens," Sabellicus informs us, " though surrounded with the din of battle and the clang of barbarian arms, assembled regularly every eighth day in the public squares of the cities of the principality to sing hymns in praise of their departed hero." † The valour with which the little nation resisted the overwhelming power of Mahomet for more than a decade is a proof that the spirit of Skanderbeg still survived amongst them, though he himself had passed away.

* HOPF, Griechenland, LXXXVI., 157.
† SABELLICUS, Decad., III., 568 ; FALLMERAYER, 100.

CHAPTER IV.

Struggle against the Domineering Policy of the Venetians and Louis XI. of France.—Efforts to give Greater External Splendour to the Holy See.—Reforms.—Punishment of the Fraticelli.—Regulations Regarding the Jubilee. — Attempt to Unite Russia with the Church.

THE independent attitude which the island city of Venice maintained towards the other Italian States is equally marked in the domain of ecclesiastical politics. In no portion of the Appenine Peninsula do we meet with such early and persistent efforts for the extension of the authority of the State at the expense of the liberty of the Church. The Popes were the natural opponents of these efforts, and more than once found themselves under the sad necessity of inflicting the sharpest ecclesiastical penalties on the proud Republic.*

The great piety of the Venetians, to which their numerous churches still bear silent witness, seems to contrast strangely with these efforts to subjugate the Church to the State. A deeply religious spirit no doubt existed among the people, and of this the rulers of the Republic, who loved to call it by the name of St. Mark, were obliged to take some account. Yet this St. Mark was almost constantly

* See *Collect. Scripturar. spectantium ad interdictum reipubl. Venetae inflictum a variis summis pontificibus. Cod. L. 27 of the Vallicell. Library, Rome.

in conflict with the Holy See, because it strove in every way to degrade the freeborn Church into the position of handmaid to the State. Further contests with Rome were also occasioned by the efforts of the Republic to obtain possession of the Romagna. In 1441 the Venetians had gained a footing in Ravenna, and ever since that period they had been constantly bent on the extension of their dominion to the detriment of the States of the Church. These more external disputes, however, were driven into the background, by the contests which arose from the pretensions of the Venetian oligarchy to absolute dominion over the whole life of its subjects, even in regard to ecclesiastical matters.*

Even while a Cardinal, Paul II. had come into collision with the government of his native city. In 1459, on the death of Fantin Dandolo, Bishop of Padua, Pius II. had conferred the See on Cardinal Barbo.† By this appointment he intended to please both the Cardinal and the Republic,‡ which had always been glad to see her Bishoprics occupied by the sons of her noble families. The Venetian government had, however, on this occasion selected another candidate, Gregorio Correr, and now made every effort to give effect to their choice. It was resolved that, unless the Cardinal should within twenty days renounce his Bishopric, all his revenues derived from Venetian territory should be sequestrated. Moreover, Paul Barbo was to put pressure

---

* FRIEDBERG, II., 688 *seq.*, follows almost exclusively the unsatisfactory article of SAGREDO, in Arch. St. Ital., 3 Serie, II., 92 *seq.* See also LEBRET, II., 2, 668 *seq.* Many fresh details are given by CECCHETTI, V., e la C. di Roma, 2 vols., but ill-arranged and very defective.

† May, 1459 ; see DONDI OROLOGIO, Canonici, 24.

‡ PII II. Comment. 44. See DONDI OROLOGIO, Dissert. nona s. l'Istoria Eccl. Padovana, 50 *seq.* (Padova, 1817.)

on his brother in the same direction, and if he failed to induce him to resign, was to be banished from the Venetian territory and deprived of his possessions!* Soon afterwards, the Signoria wrote many urgent letters on the matter to the Pope and to various Cardinals.† As Cardinal Barbo did not yield, the Venetian Ambassador was strictly charged not to visit him.‡ So firmly did the Signoria adhere to their purpose§ that the Cardinal was at last obliged to give way. Jacopo Zeno, however, not Gregorio Correr, became Bishop of Padua. He was required to pay 2000 ducats yearly to Cardinal Barbo, and the resolutions against Paul Barbo were rescinded.‖

Great was the embarrassment of the Venetian statesmen when, a few years later, the Cardinal who had been treated in this manner was elevated to the Papal throne. No elec-

---

* *Decision of the 5th March, 1459. Sen. Secr. XX., f. 177b–178. State Archives, Venice.

† *Letters to Pius II., dated 1459, March 8 and 27, and to Card. Scarampo, dated 1459, March 27. Sen. Secr. XX., f. 178–9, *loc. cit.*

‡ *"Bene autem commemoramus et mandamus vobis, quod desistere debeatis a visitatione rmi card. S. Marci ex causis et respectibus vobis notis." *Instruction for the Envoys for Mantua, 17th Sept., 1459. Sen. Secr. XX., f. 190. DARU, and after him VOIGT, III., 70, are mistaken in speaking of a prohibition to speak to the Pope or to salute him.

§ See especially the discourteous *Letter to the Envoys to the Pope of the 4th January, 1459 (st. fl.), in Sen. Secr. XX., f. 203.

‖ See SANUDO, 1167; CANENSIUS, 97. The resolution against P. Barbo was repealed on the 5th March, 1460; see *Sen. Secr. XX., f. 177b. Memmo's Memoir of 1709, printed in Arch. St. Ital., 3 Serie, II., 120 *seq.*, incorrectly gives 1443 as the date, and speaks of a Cardinal of Mantua instead of S. Marco. FRIEDBERG, II., 692, has simply adopted the chronological error, although any list of Bishops, *e.g.*, UGHELLI, V., 456, might have served to correct it. CAVACIUS' opinion (Hist. coenobii D. Justinae Patav., p. 228, Venetiis, 1606) that Barbo was Bishop of Padua for a year is a mistake.

tion could have been less agreeable to them. They were, however, prudent enough carefully to conceal their vexation. Arrangements for public rejoicings were made immediately, and an Embassy of surpassing splendour was sent to Rome to proffer obedience to Paul II. The usual number of Envoys on such occasions was four. In the case of Eugenius IV., who was a Venetian, this number was doubled; but now ten were sent.* The Pope perfectly understood the value of these outward tokens of honour. Even before the arrival of the Mission he spoke in bitter terms to the Milanese Ambassador about the arrogance and the personal hostility of certain Venetian statesmen, and expressed his opinion that before the Envoys had been a fortnight in Rome, disputes would break out.† In fact, unpleasant explanations began almost immediately,‡ and the tension kept on growing from day to day, for no European power was viewed in Venice with such jealousy as the Roman See.§ At the end of 1465, Paul II. poured forth a whole list to the Milanese Ambassador of charges against his fellow-countrymen. In the Turkish matter, he said, they had, by a simple act of arbitrary power, imposed a tithe on the clergy. They claimed tribute from Cardinals visiting Venice, a thing which no Christian Prince had ever done. They were perpetually incurring reprimands for contemptuous conduct towards their Bishops. They had forbidden

* MALIPIERO, 32; SANUDO, 1181; Ist. Bresc., 900. The Pope knew that the festivities in Venice were intended to obliterate the memory of former injuries; see Carretto's *Letter to Fr. Sforza, dated Rome, 1464, Oct. 24. (Ambrosian Library.) Regarding the Embassy to do homage, see also *GHIRARDACCI, ad an. Cod. 768 of the Library at Bologna.

† See Appendix, N. 6. Ambrosian Library.

‡ *Letter of S. Nardini to Fr. Sforza, dated Rome, 1464, Dec. 6. Ambrosian Library.

§ LEBRET, II., 2, 670; Gesch. d. Republik Venedig.

the Archbishop of Spalatro to enter his See. They were seeking to take possession of the Morea, which belonged to Thomas Palæologus. The Venetian Merchants, by buying alum from the Turks, put Christian money in the pockets of their enemies. The penalty of Excommunication would have to be pronounced against them. Assuming the position of mistress of the Adriatic, Venice oppresses Ancona ; she holds wrongful possession of Cervia and Ravenna. The Knights of St. John at Rhodes, and the Emperor, complain of the Republic, and indeed every one has some grievance against her. The law which prohibits any one who has a relation among the clergy from being a member of the Council is absolutely intolerable ; the infidels themselves could not do worse ; this measure must be repealed.*

Nothing of the kind was contemplated in Venice ; the remonstrances of the Pope were utterly unheeded.† In the following spring the appointment to the Patriarchal Throne gave occasion for further conflicts with Rome, which were aggravated in the summer, when the Signoria took advantage of the scare about the Turks again arbitrarily to impose taxes on ecclesiastical property. Many in Rome were of opinion that this was done with the object of concealing a secret understanding with the Sultan.‡ It is quite certain that a powerful party in Venice favoured a peace with the Porte ; some few Venetians, according to

---

* **Report of S. Nardini, Archbishop of Milan, to Fr. Sforza, dated Rome, 1465, Dec. 11. (Ambrosian Library.) Concerning the dispute about the tithes, see NAVAGIERO, 1125 ; the notice in CECCHETTI, I., 154 ; and also ROSMINI, Milano, IV., 67.

† See in Appendix, N. 8, the undated *Brief to the Doge. Cod. Ottob. of the Vatican Library.

‡ Cardinal Gonzaga mentions this on the 5th July, 1466. (Gonzaga Archives, Mantua.) See Appendix, N. 15. For further particulars relating to the question of the Patriarchate, see Arch. St. Ital., *loc. cit.*, 121 *seq.*

the report of the Milanese Ambassador, even went so far as to say that it would be well, not merely to make peace with the Turk, but also to open the way to Rome for him, that he may punish these priests ! * In the summer of 1466 the Republic raised the question of the Council. This so incensed Paul II. that he spoke of excommunicating them, and laying them under Interdict.† Several Consistories took place, in which these extreme measures were seriously considered. Two grave motives weighed against a breach with Venice : in the first place, the necessity of previously securing the support of an Italian Power,‡ and secondly, the fear that the Signoria might actually conclude peace with the Infidels. Even in July the Milanese Ambassador was persuaded that, notwithstanding the threats which had been pronounced, the Pope would in the end endeavour to come to an amicable understanding.§ This difficult undertaking was entrusted to Cardinal Carvajal, who, however, was empowered, in case of necessity, to pronounce the Interdict. What has transpired of the instructions given to him, makes it evident that the Pope sincerely endeavoured to bring about a satisfactory understanding. Cardinal Gonzaga believed Paul II. to have contemplated an alliance with Venice, as

* Mon. Hung., II., 14.

† *Report of the Milanese Ambassador, dated Rome, 1466, Aug. 4. Paul II., he says, fears the Council "piu che l'inferno." Fonds Ital., 1591, f. 362-3, of the National Library, Paris.

‡ See in Appendix, N. 16, Card. Gonzaga's *Letter of July 19, 1466.

§ "*Questi signori preti faranno ogni cosa per abonizare dicta signoria." *Letter of A. de Rubeis to the Duke and Duchess of Milan, dated Rome, 1466, July 20. (Fonds Ital., 1591, f. 358 of the National Library, Paris.) The presence of the Duke of Urbino, who is spoken of in the *Report of 4th August, cited above, was no doubt connected with the Venetian dispute.

a protection against the animosity of the King of Naples.* Details regarding the protracted negotiations carried on by the distinguished Cardinal are unfortunately wanting. He is, however, said to have admirably discharged his arduous mission. If he was not successful in bringing all questions between Rome and Venice to a solution, he at any rate prevented the conclusion of a peace with the Porte, and prepared the way for better relations between Paul II. and the Republic.† The question of the tithes having been settled in 1468, in a manner which contented the Venetians, in the May of the following year the Pope and the Signoria entered into an alliance directed chiefly against the treacherous Roberto Malatesta. The double game which the Venetians subsequently played,‡ and fresh disputes regarding the Turkish tithes, again caused discord between the allies. When Paul II. died, things had reached such a pass that there was no Venetian Ambassador at the Roman Court.§

Paul II. had repeated differences with Florence on matters connected with the liberty of the Church, and in

* *Letter of Card. Gonzaga to his father, dated Rome, 1466, July 31. (Gonzaga Archives, Mantua.) The Milanese Ambassador, in the *Report of August 4th, 1466, which we have already cited, expresses his belief that Carvajal was charged to bring about a reconciliation between the Republic and the Holy See.

† See *supra*, Chap. III., and also the two very short notices in CECCHETTI, I., 154, regarding the solution of the tithe question. See also Mon. Hung., II., 33, 35, 63.

‡ See *infra*, Chap. VI.

§ MALIPIERO, 239. Regarding the joy of the Venetians at the death of Paul II., see Arch. d. Soc. Rom., XI., 254. In the year 1472, Paul's sister, Isabella Zeno, mother of the Cardinal, was imprisoned and banished because she was said to have revealed State secrets to the Roman Court. Isabella subsequently came to Rome. Her last resting-place was in St. Peter's ; see REUMONT, III., 1, 494, and CECCHETTI, I., 419 *seq.*

1466* and 1469 about the arbitrary taxation of ecclesiastical property.   The obstinacy of the opposition encountered by the Pope may be estimated by the frequency of
his remonstrances.†   One was published but a few days
before his death.‡   Beyond the Italian frontier the appointment to the See of Brixen also gave rise to a conflict.§

The omnipotence claimed by the State was also the
occasion of considerable tension in the relations between
the Pope and the French King.   Louis XI. wished to reign
alone, alike in State and Church ; his will was to be in all
things supreme.∥   Even in the beginning of November, 1464,
fresh anti-Roman measures of the King were reported in
Rome.   It was said that Louis XI. had announced that the

---

* *Paul II.'s Brief to Florence, dated 1466, March 25.   State
Archives, Florence, X., II., 23 f., 141 *seq.*

† *Paul II.'s Brief to Florence, dated 1469, Aug. 25, *loc. cit.*, X., II.,
25, f. 14b–15.

‡ Paulus II., Florentinis, dat. 1471, Julii 23.   Lib. brev. 12, f. 180.
(Secret Archives of the Vatican.) *Ibid.*, f. 45b, is a *Brief which must
here be mentioned, inasmuch as it treats of the protection of ecclesiastical rights : * " Regi Aragonum.   Non absque magna admiratione
intelleximus quod adhuc possessionem monasterii S. Victoriani ac
prioratus de Roda Ilerd. dioc. dil. fil. noster L.[udovicus] tit. s. 4
coronator. S. R. E. presb. card[lis] assequi non potuit."   Threats follow.
Dat. 1470, Dec. 5.

§ The account given of this matter by EGGER, I., 595, is very imperfect ; the author's attack on his own fellow-countrymen speaks for
itself.   Regarding Paul II.'s measures for the protection of ecclesiastical
liberty in Hungary, see TELEKI, XI., 133 *seq.*, 139 *seq.*, 141 *seq.*   I am
indebted to the kindness of Dr. Fraknói, Vice-President of the
Hungarian Academy, for having made known to me a *Brief of Paul
II. to the Abbot of the Convent of S. Maximiani extra muros Trev.,
in which the latter is blamed for having invoked the assistance of a
layman in a dispute : " Hoc enim non videtur ius suum velle defendere,
sed monasterium et ecclesiam laicis ipsis quodammodo subicere."

∥ See FIERVILLE, 137.

publication of Apostolic Bulls throughout the whole of his kingdom must depend on his permission, and had also prohibited *expectances*. " These things," wrote the Milanese Ambassador, " are poor tokens of obedience ; these measures are worse than the Pragmatic Sanction, which formerly prevailed in France." No wonder that Paul II. distrusted the French Monarch, whose tyrannical and ambitious disposition was well known to him.*

A treatise, written by Thomas Basin about the end of the year 1464, shews the state of feeling which then prevailed at the court of Louis XI.   He twisted the words in which homage was paid to Louis XI. so as to deduce from them that this document only bound the King to Pius II. personally.   By the death of that Pope, Louis XI. was freed from all further obligation.   Basin also insisted on the necessity of speedily convening a French National Synod.†

Evil counsels of other kinds came to the French King from Milan.   In March, 1466, an Envoy from that State was charged to advise Louis XI. to defer his profession of obedience as long as possible, on the ground that, while this matter was in suspense, the Pope would be obliged to shew himself pliable.‡   The French Monarch, however, did not take this view ; his honour, he thought, allowed of no further delay, and that which had already taken place had been injurious to him.§   When, however, the representative of Milan again brought forward his request, the

* **Letter from O. de Carretto to Fr. Sforza, dated Rome, 1464, Nov. 6. (Ambrosian Library.)   See also BULAEUS, V., 671 *seq.* ; Ordonnac., XVI., 244 ; GUETTÉE, VIII., 24.

† BASIN-QUICHERAT, IV., 69, 73–90.

‡ See in Appendix, N. 12, the *Instruction of the 3rd March, 1466, to the Milanese Envoys.   National Library, Paris.

§ Paul II. had not granted the concessions asked by the French Ambassador, Pierre Gruel, in the name of Louis XI. ; see FIERVILLE, 136.

King consented to procrastinate as long as possible. "As the French fear the heat and the Plague," adds the Milanese Envoy, "the Embassy which is to do homage in the usual form will not start before September. The Archbishop of Lyons, Charles of Bourbon, will be its leader; Cardinal Jouffroy, who is to accompany and support the Envoys, will not, his people say, begin his journey before September." * This last piece of news was untrue, for Jouffroy reached Rome on the 4th October, 1466.† The great Embassy, however, did not leave Lyons until the end of the month.‡ In a letter to the Pope the King excused his tardiness on the plea of the troubles in his kingdom. The instructions given to the Envoys seemed to promise a favourable change in the ecclesiastical policy of France. They were desired, in the first place, to express the sincere devotion of the King to the Holy See, of which the decree abrogating the Pragmatic Sanction, in spite of the opposition of almost all the kingdom, was a token. Besides making the profession of obedience in the form which, since the days of Martin V., had been

* *Letter of Joh. Petrus Panicharolla to the Duke and Duchess of Milan, dated Montargis, 1466, June 25. Fonds Ital., 1611, of the National Library, Paris.

† *Acta Consist. of the Secret Archives of the Vatican. Jouffroy's Biographer, Fierville, fails to give us any information regarding these dates.

‡ "*Li revmi arcivescovo di Lione, fratello del duca di Borbon et monsig. da Mans, fratello del conte San Pollo et li altri ambassatori che vanno a Roma di presente sono per partire da Lione." Emanuel de Jacopo and J. P. Panicharolla to the Duke and Duchess of Milan, dated Orleans, 1466, Oct. 26. (Cod. 1611 of the Fonds Ital. of the National Library, Paris.) FIERVILLE, 137, is mistaken in his statement that the Embassy started as early as "towards the end of 1465. or beginning of 1466." See also Lettres de Louis XI., III., 99, 107 *seq.*. 112 *seq.*

in use, the Ambassadors were charged to apologise in Louis's name for the anti-Roman ordinances of 1464 ; and to explain that they were not the act of the King, but due to the Bishop of Bayeux and the Patriarch of Jerusalem. The King would be an obedient son of the Holy See; in return he asked for the right of appointing to twenty-five Bishoprics.*

Paul II. was not deluded by these fair words, for he was well aware that the Bishop of Bayeux had acted by the directions of the King. The Ambassadors obtained nothing. At this time, Jean de La Balue, Bishop of Evreux, and afterwards of Angers, another favourite of Louis, took part with Cardinal Jouffroy in the negotiations concerning the ecclesiastical policy of France.† This designing man, who was exactly of the same stamp as Jouffroy and his apt pupil, sought, like him, to win the purple by means of the question of the Pragmatic Sanction.‡ For a while Paul II. resisted the admission of such a man into the Senate of the Church, but the hope that Louis XI. would now really suppress the Pragmatic Sanction induced him at last to yield. "I know the faults of this priest," he is reported to have said, " but I was constrained to cover them with this hat."

In return for the red hat conferred upon his favourite,§

---

* RAYNALDUS, ad an. 1466, N. 15–16, and FIERVILLE, *loc. cit.*

† For the literature regarding La Balue, see CHEVALIER, 214 and 2439. Also Lettres de Louis XI., III., 225–6.

‡ GUETTÉE, VIII., 27.

§ 18th Sept., 1467, according to the *Acta Consist. of the Secret Archives of the Vatican. FRIZON, 517, is mistaken in making Balue Cardinal as early as 1464. For satires concerning this nomination, see Bibl. de l'École d. Chartes, Series IV., I., 565. The Harenga facta per rev. card. Albiensem in eccl. Paris , A° 1468, qua die cardinalatus dignitatem recepit dom. card. Andegavens. in D'ACHERY, nov. edit., III., 825 to 830. See FIERVILLE, 141–6. Cardinal Alain took part in

Louis XI. issued a declaration against the Pragmatic Sanction of a more stringent nature than those which had preceded it. When La Balue, on the 1st October, 1467, appeared in Parliament with this document, the Procurator-General refused to register it. In order to work upon the mind of the King, much stress was laid upon the abuse of *commendams*,* and the large sums of money sent to Rome from France.†

The University of Paris, like the Parliament, declared against the abrogation of the Pragmatic Sanction. An appeal to a future Council was even issued. Now, however, the Procurator-General resigned his post, and the Royal Declaration remained in full force, although not registered.‡ The ecclesiastical policy of France, nevertheless, remained as unsatisfactory and disquieting as ever, for the King never relaxed his efforts to bind the Church fast within the toils of the State. His favourites, Jouffroy and La Balue, turned the position of affairs to their own advantage. His acceptance of the anti-Roman project of a Council, put forward by the Hussite King of Bohemia, enables us to estimate the value of the "filial obedience" to the Holy See so often spoken of by his Envoys in Rome. In 1468, when the French demand for a general Council was again mentioned to Paul II., he said that he would hold one that very year, but that it should be in Rome.§

the ceremony of giving the red hat. His Recessus versus Galliam is noted in the *Acta Consist., Secret Archives of the Vatican, as taking place on the 12th June, 1468.

* Paul II. looked into this abuse, and gave advice regarding its abolition. It was not, however, thoroughly remedied. See AMMANATI, Epist., f. 59 ; FIERVILLE, 18.

† PICOT, I., 426, note 2, considers the statements respecting the money made by the excited Parliament of 1467 to be exaggerated.

‡ GUETTÉE, VIII., 29-32.

§ This is stated by the Milanese Ambassador, Joh. Blanchus, in the

Meanwhile, in the person of the new Duke of Burgundy, Charles the Bold, the King encountered so dangerous a political adversary, that ecclesiastical affairs were again for a time completely in abeyance. Ever since the subjugation of Liège, Charles had reigned more absolutely than any of his predecessors, and his immense financial resources gave him a great advantage over the French King. Louis fought his enemy with the weapons of treachery and corruption. He had an interview with him at Peronne, during which tidings arrived of a fresh rising of the Liégeois, excited by the agents of Louis. The Duke of Burgundy was furious, and, it is said, contemplated the murder of the King, who was in his power. The demands which the Duke now made would have appeared to a high-minded man worse than death: Louis was to proceed in person against Liège, which he had himself incited to revolt. Utterly destitute of every feeling of honour, he made no difficulty, and at once consented to join the Duke in his expedition against the Netherlands, and thus witness with his own eyes the barbarous sack of Liège.*

The immediate consequence of these events was the downfall of La Balue, by whose advice the meeting at Peronne had taken place. His good fortune was short-

---

Postscript to a *Despatch, dated Rome, 1468, March (the date effaced), State Archives, Milan, Cart. Gen. Regarding the Bohemian project of a Council, see the next Chapter.

* See SCHMIDT, Gesch. Frankr., II., 432 seq.; HENRARD, Les Campagnes de Charles-le-Téméraire contre les Liégeois (Bruxelles, 1867). Paul II. had, in 1468, sent Onofrius de S. Cruce, Bishop of Tricarico, as Legate to Liège to appease the discord between Bishop Louis of Bourbon and his subjects, and to prevent Charles the Bold from turning his victory to the prejudice of the liberty of the Church; this mission failed. The Legate wrote a Memorandum in his own justification. It is published in BORMANS, Mém. du Légat Onofrius sur les affaires de Liège en 1468 (Bruxelles, 1886).

lived, and the King thought that he had before him
evidence of a treacherous understanding between the
Cardinal and the Duke of Burgundy.   He resolved to
take signal vengeance on the man whom he had raised
from nothing to be the first of his subjects.   La Balue was
despoiled of his possessions and imprisoned.   A like fate
befell the Bishop of Verdun, who was believed to be in
league with him.   Even a tyrant like Louis XI. saw that
a Cardinal could not be tried without the Pope, and two
Envoys were charged to enter into negotiations on this
subject with Rome.   The conditions which the Pope laid
down for the trial were perfectly in accordance with the
prescriptions of the Canon law, but they were not to the
King's taste.   Under these circumstances, it was deferred,
and La Balue remained in prison.*

The hostility of Louis XI. to the Holy See was further
evinced by the efforts which he made, in the year 1470,
to induce the Pyrenean Princes, as well as those in the
Appenine Peninsula, to support his Conciliar projects,
which were aimed directly against Paul II.†   All these anti-
Roman machinations, however, led to no definite result.

---

* Details are given in AMMANATI, Comment., I., VII.; GUETTÉE,
VIII., 33 ; LEGEAY, II., 8-9.   Regarding the canonical prescriptions,
see PHILLIPS, VI., 283 seq.

† See Mariana in FIERVILLE, 198 ; and MOUFFLET, Étude sur une
négociat. dipl. de Louis XI. (Marseilles, 1884).   Here is given the text
of the Speech addressed to the Duke of Milan and other Italian
Princes by Guillaume Fichat on the question of the Council.   Corrections and additions to Moufflet's work were furnished by GHINZONI
(G. Maria Sforza e Luigi XI., in Arch. St. Lomb., Series II., part 1,
1885).   It is evident, from a *Report of the Milanese Envoys, dated
Rome, 1468, April 27, that even at that period Louis XI. was seeking,
by threats of a Council, to extort concessions from Paul II.   The
same Report informs us that similar threats were used by Charles the
Bold.   State Archives, Milan.

Paul II. was a steadfast defender of the privileges of the Holy See, not only against the temporal power, but also against ecclesiastical encroachments. On the 1st June, 1466, he strictly prohibited the use of the Tiara* by the Archbishop of Benevento, and reserved the right of consecrating the Agnus Dei to the Holy See.† In 1469 a stop was put to the loss inflicted on the Apostolic Treasury by the frequent practice of uniting benefices to each other which were subject to Annates. It was decided that henceforth all ecclesiastical Corporations were, every fifteenth year, to contribute what were called "Quindennium," instead of Annates, for the benefices united by them.‡

This last measure, and the great delight which the Pope took in pomp and splendour, have been made the subject of severe strictures. It cannot be said that these reproaches are altogether unfounded ; but, on the other hand, the surrounding circumstances must be taken into account. In a time of such general magnificence as the period of the Renaissance, the Papacy could not, without a loss of dignity, be clothed in Apostolical simplicity. Paul II. was firmly persuaded that the Pope ought to appear in a style befitting the highest position on earth. His private life§ was as simple as his appearance in public

* MARINI, II., 161.

† Bull. V., 199-200. The Agnus Dei, which hold the first place amongst all Sacramentals, are little tablets of wax with the image of the Lamb of God imprinted. Their use is extremely ancient. See Breve notizia dell' origine, uso e virtù degli Agnus Dei (Roma, 1829); Freib. Kirchenlexikon, I., 344 seq., 2nd ed.; MORONI, I., 127 seq.

‡ PHILLIPS, V., 2, 581 seq.

§ Paul II., as a rule, ate only plain dishes ; he always mixed water with the wine he drank. See CANENSIUS, 98-9 ; CHRISTOPHE, II., 179 ; GEBHART, 183.

was sumptuous. He always went in state from the Vatican to his Palace at S. Marco, scattering money amongst the crowd.* All Church Festivals in which he took part were celebrated with exceptional magnificence. His coronation and the ceremony of taking possession of the Lateran had given the Romans a foretaste of future glories.† The following Christmas the Pope appeared in gorgeous vestments and wore the Tiara.‡ It was then reported that a new Tiara, more costly and splendid than any that had yet been seen, was to be made. At the Easter of 1465 the Pope wore this work of art, which was the wonder of his contemporaries.§ Holy Week and Easter were always celebrated with great pomp and solemnity. Thousands of foreigners crowded on these occasions to the tombs of the Apostles.‖ The Pope had a new litter made for the Christmas of 1466, and it must have been a marvel of workmanship. It is said to have cost more than a palace.¶

* See the *Description given by Augustinus de Rubeis in a *Letter, dated Rome, 1465, Oct. 28. Ambrosian Library.

† See *Letter of Jacobus de Aretio, dated Rome, 1464, Nov. 13. Gonzaga Archives, Mantua.

‡ *Letter of J. P. Arrivabene to Marchioness Barbara, dated Rome, 1464, Dec. 26. Gonzaga Archives.

§ See Appendix, N. 11 : Letter of A. de Rubeis of the 21st April, 1465. Ambrosian Library.

‖ Bart. Marasca, writing from Rome, 1467, May 30, mentions this to Marchioness Barbara, and adds : *"lo officio d'heri fu molto solenne cum quello regno in modo che a hora 20 fu finito." (Gonzaga Archives, Mantua.) The importance attached to great functions by Paul II. and also by Sixtus IV. (BURCKHARDT, I., 149, 3rd ed.) cannot be deemed surprising by a Catholic. If the magnificent Liturgy of the Church is the mantle of the mysteries of religion, its worthy celebration is an efficacious means of promoting the honour that is due to her.

¶ "*Ha similiter facto fare una cadrega da farse portare a questo natale che es dice costa piu che non faria uno bono palazo. Et

At these great festivals all beholders were deeply impressed by the noble figure and countenance of the Pope,
the magnificence of his vestments, and his majestic bearing.
Even on the lesser festivals the ceremonial was very carefully carried out.* The love of splendour which belonged
to his artistic temperament led him to surround the person
of the Vicar of Christ with corresponding magnificence.
We have already mentioned the measures taken at the
beginning of his reign to give greater external dignity to
the Cardinals.† Another change was made at the same
time. Any one who has seen the Papal leaden seals will
be able to recall the ancient type : the heads of SS. Peter
and Paul are on one side, and on the reverse the name of
the Pope of the day. In the time of Paul II., we find on
the face of the seal the Pope himself enthroned and
dispensing graces, with two Cardinals by his side, and
in the foreground a number of other persons ; on the
reverse are the full-length figures of the Princes of
the Apostles, seated.‡ This alteration, however was

demum Sua Sta è tutta piena de magnanimita et magnificentia quemad
modum se po intendere per le cose grande chel fa." Augustinus de
Rubeis from Rome, 1466, December 6. State Archives, Milan.

* See the *Letter of Giacomo d'Arezzo to Marchioness Barbara,
describing the distribution of candles by the Pope, of whom he
observes : "molto è ceremonioso." This letter is dated Rome, 1465,
Febr. 13. (Gonzaga Archives.) See Gasp. Veronen. in MARINI, II.,
178, and in MURATORI, III., 2, 1009.

† See *supra*, p. 25.

‡ COMTE DE MAS-LATRIE, Les éléments de la dipl. pontificale, in the
Rev. d. Quest. Hist., XLI., 434 (April, 1887), considers these leaden seals
of Paul II.'s to be "sceaux spéciaux soit pour confirmer les décisions
des conciles soit pour d'autres usages moins définis," and cites the
Bull of 13th June, 1468, confirming the privileges of the University of
Paris as an example "de ce *rare* type." (Archives Nat. Paris, Bull. L.,
234, N. 3.) All the seals of Paul II. are, however, of this design, as, for
instance, that affixed to a Bull of 17th Sept., 1464, in the Innsbruck

not maintained, and the ancient type reappears under Sixtus IV.*

The necessity of reforms, especially in Rome, had been insisted on by Paul II., immediately after his election,† and soon the question as to the manner in which they were to be accomplished arose. In the very first Consistory the matter was seriously considered, and a number of wholesome regulations were framed. It was on this occasion that several Cardinals declared themselves in favour of the abolition of *reservations;* no less a personage, however, than the excellent Carvajal adduced such weighty reasons against this measure that it was abandoned.‡ It is certain that Paul II. was anxious to introduce a thorough reform amongst the officials of the Court, and also that, at the very outset of his reign, he opposed the simoniacal and corrupt practices which prevailed there.§

Archives (L. 3, 16 A). That the measure was a general one, adopted by the Pope immediately after his Election, is evident from J. P. Arrivabene's *Report of the 3rd Oct., 1464, in Appendix, N. 4. Gonzaga Archives, Mantua.

* See, *e.g.*, the *Bull of Sixtus IV. regarding the appointment of Georgius Golser, decretor. doctor. et canonicus Brix., to the Episcop. ecclesiae Brix., dated Romae, 1471, 17 Cal. Jan. A° 3°, from the Brixen Archives in the Government Archives, Innsbruck, L. 3, 21d.

† *Letter of J. P. Arrivabene, dated Rome, 1464, Sept. 1. Gonzaga Archives, Mantua.

‡ AMMANATI, Epist., 58b–59 ; PHILLIPS, V., 530.

§ In the Corp. jur. can. (C. 2, de simonia) [l. 5 tit. 1] Paul II.'s Constitution of the year 1464 against simoniacal persons was adopted. See also ROD. SANCIUS, Hist. Hispaniae, IV., c. 40 ; see FRANTZ, Sixtus IV., 18, and GREGOROVIUS, VII., 211 *seq.*, 3rd ed. Regarding the corruption which prevailed among the Roman officials, see SS. rer. Siles., IX., 97, 101, 103, 104, 111, 114, 115. ÆGIDIUS of Viterbo, in his *Hist., XX. secul., greatly praises Paul II. for the strict morality which he tried to enforce amongst those immediately around him. Cod. C. 8, 19, f. 308b. Angelica Library, Rome.

If, in the sequel, the Venetian Pope did not prove such a zealous reformer as the sad state of affairs perhaps required, he cannot be charged with absolute inaction. " The abuse of the *commendams* and *expectances* was, if not removed, yet practically much restrained ; simoniacal practices were combated, the receiving of gifts by Legates, Governors and Judges was forbidden, and also the aliena- tion of Church property, or leasing it for more than three years ; and the interests of benevolent foundations were protected."* In the matter of refusing presents, the Pope himself set a good example. When the Ambassadors who came to congratulate him on his elevation offered the customary gifts, he steadfastly declined them all, whatever their value might be. He desired nothing, he said, but perfect fidelity to the Holy See.† During the whole of his reign he adhered to this practice. In the spring of 1471, the Archbishop of Trèves sent him an ornament composed of diamonds and rubies, and the Pope, who did not think it possible to refuse the present, at once sent in return a cross adorned with similar stones, adding that it was not his habit to receive gifts.‡

The high and fixed principles on which Paul II. acted in making appointments to ecclesiastical offices was greatly calculated to improve the condition of the Church. In other matters, he is reported to have said, the Pope may be a man, but in the choice of Bishops he must be an Angel, and in that of members of the Sacred College, God.§ Canensius expressly informs us that he conferred ecclesi-

* REUMONT, III., 1, 155. See Bull. V., 183–6, 194–5, and Bull. Ord. Praed., III., 458.

† CANENSIUS, 31.

‡ See the *Brief of the 19th April, 1471, in Appendix, N. 36. Venice Archives.

§ Ægidius of Viterbo in RAYNALDUS, ad an. 1471, N. 63.

astical dignities only after mature and impartial deliberation, having strict regard to the merits of the recipients,
and he adds that many excellent men were appointed
Bishops without their previous cognisance and in their
absence.*

Paul II. did much to promote monastic reform, particularly in Lombardy, Modena, Ferrara and Venice ;† as also
in Western and Southern Germany, especially in Cologne,
Bavaria and Würtemberg.‡ In 1469 he issued a Bull for
the better regulation of the Augustinian Congregation in
Lombardy.§ A few months before his death the Pope
exhorted the Patriarch of Venice to proceed against all
clergy and monks who led irregular lives, without respect
of persons,‖ and also took measures for raising the stand-
ard of education amongst the clergy in the Diocese of
Valencia.¶ The evil star which presided over the Briefs
of Paul II. has consigned much interesting information on
this subject to unmerited oblivion.

The fact that Paul II. was always surrounded by men of
worth is one that speaks well for his own character. In the
autumn of 1466 the Milanese Ambassador mentions the
Archbishop of Spalatro, Lorenzo Zane, who became Treas-
urer; Stefano Nardini, Archbishop of Milan; and Teodoro de'
Lelli, Bishop of Feltre and, after the 17th September, 1466,

* CANENSIUS, 48, 99.

† RICHA, IX., 187 ; Bull. Ord. Praedic., III., 469 ; *Lib. brev. 12,
f. 111b ; see below, note ‖.

‡ Bull. Ord. Praed., III., 449 ; Anal. Francisc., 413, 417 seq., where is
also information regarding the reform of the Convents of St. Francis
and St. Clare at Eger. See also Deutsche Chroniken aus Böhmen,
III., 12, 277 seq.

§ KOLDE, Augustiner Congregation, 106 seq.

‖ *Patriarchae Venetiarum, VI. Martii, 1471. Lib. brev. 12, f. 111b.
Secret Archives of the Vatican.

¶ *Brief dated Romae, 1471, 28 Martii, loc. cit., 251.

of Treviso, as possessing much influence with the new Pope.
The Bishop of Aquila, who had been his preceptor, is also
named amongst those who occupied positions immediately
about him.　Lelli, as it was at once surmised, took the first
place.*　No letter, or decree of importance, was issued until
it had been examined by this excellent man.†　On his
death in 1466, the Pope took his nephew Marco Barbo, and
Bessarion into his confidence.　Agapito Cenci de' Rustici,
Bishop of Camerino, who had been greatly valued by both
Pius II. and Paul II., had passed away in October, 1464.‡
Giovanni Barozzi, Patriarch of Venice from the year 1465;
the learned Angelus Faseolus, Lelli's successor in the See
of Feltre; Valerius Calderina, Bishop of Savona; Pietro
Ferrici, Bishop of Tarasona, afterwards a Cardinal;
and Corrado Capece, subsequently Archbishop of Bene-

---

* *Letter of O. de Carretto to Fr. Sforza, dated Rome, 1464, October
9. (State Archives, Milan, Cart. Gen.)　Nardini was at once given a
lodging in the Papal Palace ; see the *Despatch of J. P. Arrivabene,
dated Rome, 1464, Sept. 1.　In this Ambassador's *Reports of the 11th
Sept. and 3rd Oct., 1464, we have evidence that the Pope's relations with
Lelli were of a very intimate character.　These three documents are
in the Gonzaga Archives, Mantua.　Fr. Sforza, writing from Rome
on the 11th Sept., 1464, informs Jo. Jacobus de Plumbo Parmen. that
Lelli is one of the 'principali homini' about the new Pope.　(State
Archives, Milan.)　Regarding Lelli's appointment as Bishop of
Treviso, see *Reg. Bull. Pauli II., A. 2, tom. II., f. 203.　(Secret
Archives of the Vatican.)　See Appendix, N. 4.

† AMMANATI, Epist., 109b.　See also, regarding Lelli, A. M.
QUIRINI, Ad. S. D. N. Benedictum XIV. Monum. lit. episc. Venetor.
ditionis, 1742.

‡ "*A questi di mori lo rev. mons. vescovo de Camerino notabilis-
simo prelato pianto da tutta la corte per la integrita et virtu sue . . . fu
in somma gratia di papa Pio" [see Vol. III., p. 41], who entrusted to him
the Signatura delle supplicationi.　Paul II. also loved him and visited
him during his illness. *Jacopo de Aretio, dated Rome, 1464, Oct. 9.
(Gonzaga Archives.)　See also MARINI, II., 157.

vento,* were also in the Pope's confidence. Most of the
Sienese had left Rome ; many of them were called to account
by the Pope for extortion or embezzlement.† Even Platina
bears witness to the strict order and discipline which he
maintained in his Court and among his dependents.‡ Moreover, at the very beginning of his pontificate it was observed
that Paul II. engaged no Venetians among his guards.§

The disorders of the Fraticelli (fraticelli de opinione)
were, like the abuses at the Court, energetically repressed
by Paul II. In the summer of 1466 it became evident
that the partisans of this sect had gained a footing, not
only in the March of Ancona and the adjacent district of
Romagna, but also in the Campagna, and even in Rome
itself.‖ The headquarters of these dangerous heretics were
Assisi and the little town of Poli near Palestrina, where
Stefano de' Conti was accused of being in league with
them.¶ The Pope caused this Baron and all the rest

---

* Gasp. Veronen. in MARINI, II., 192 *seq.* See CHRISTOPHE, II.,
205 *seq.*

† See VOIGT, III., 556.   ‡ PLATINA, 794.

§ In Carretto's Letter of the 9th Oct., 1464, cited *supra*, p. 112, he
observes : *" Scuderi ce sono Milanesi, Alexandrini, Monferrini, Man-
tuani e daltre natione. Fina qui non ce nullo Venetiano bence ne sono
de Friuoli e Vicentini." State Archives, Milan.

‖ DRESSEL, Documente, IV. ; INFESSURA (1140–1141) wrongly
assigns the prosecution of the Fraticelli to the year 1467. So does
LEA, III., 178, who is unacquainted with Dressel's Documents and
with Canensius ! Besides the pieces published by Dressel, may be
cited for the year 1466 the *Letter of B. de Maraschis of Sept. 1, 1466,
in Appendix, N, 17. (Gonzaga Archives, Mantua.) It is, however, true
that some of these heretics were punished in 1467 ; this appears from
*Lib. II., Bullet. Pauli II., where, on the 6th July, 1467, are entered
payments for " xii. vestibus, ferram. lignis et aliis oportunis rebus . . .
emendis in faciendo cert. act. nonnullor. hereticor." State Archives,
Rome.

¶ CANENSIUS, 78, and DRESSEL, Documente, 9.

of the accused to be confined in St. Angelo, where they were tried. Five Bishops were appointed to conduct the enquiry.* Many statements made by the accused are extant, but as most of them were extorted by the rack their value may be questioned. One of their principal doctrines seems to have been, that of all the successors of St. Peter, no one had really been the Vicar of Christ who had not imitated the poverty of his Chief; from the time of John XXII., who spoke against the poverty of Christ, in particular, all Popes had been heretics and excommunicate, as also had all Cardinals, Bishops and Priests consecrated by them. Paul II. was no true Pope. These heretics were, moreover, charged with immoral practices in their assemblies, and other crimes. In the record of the trial, mention is made of a small codex found in the possession of a priest of this sect, which confirmed the truth of these allegations. A Fraticelli bishop is named in this, thus a formal Church must have been contemplated. The Hussite principle, that unworthy priests lose their powers,† was also a part of their teaching. It is certain, at any rate, that the movement was one which threatened great danger to the Papacy, and which had for a long time been making progress in the locality we have named. One of the women accused said that St. Jacopo della Marca had converted her, and that she

---

* "*Cum apud Asisium plures deprensi fuerint fraticelli della oppinione vulgariter nuncupati, ii autem ad urbem vincti ducti sunt et in castro s. Angeli duris carceribus mancipati per summum pontificem Paulum II., causa Mediolanen. archiepiscopo, Zamorensi, Farensi, Tarraconensi et mihi Ortano episcopi commissa, &c." NIC. PALMERIUS, De paupertate Christi. (Cod. Vatic., 4158, f. 1., Vatican Library.) See DRESSEL, Doc. 24.

† Processus contra haereticos de opinione dampnata A° 1466, from Cod. Vatic., 4012, in DRESSEL, Documente, 7, 12, 17, 20–22, 25, 31 ; see NIEDNER'S Zeitschr., 1859, III., 436 seq.

had again relapsed into error.* All these heretics, Platina says, were punished: those who continued obstinate, with the greatest severity. Such as acknowledged their errors, and sought for pardon, were treated more leniently.†

The extent to which these doctrines had spread, and the serious manner in which they were viewed in Rome, may be estimated from the numerous refutations which at once appeared, although the Franciscan, St. Jacopo della Marca, had already published a work dealing thoroughly with the subject.‡ Nicholas Palmerius, Bishop of Orte, one of the prelates who took part in the enquiry, composed a treatise on the poverty of Christ, and dedicated it to Cardinal Jouffroy.§ Rodericus Sancius of Arevalo offered his work on the same subject to the Pope himself; in this treatise he shews that there is no contradiction between the statements of Nicholas III. and John XXII. in regard to the poverty of Christ.‖ There are also treatises on this sub-

* *Loc. cit.*, p. 46.

† PLATINA, 776 ; CANENSIUS, 78. In 1471 the Fraticelli reappeared on the coast of Tuscany.

‡ Dialogus contra fraticellos in MANSI, Miscell., IV., 595–610. See JEILER in the Freiburg Kirchenlexikon, IV., 1930 *seq.*, 2nd ed., who, however, is mistaken in saying that after 1449 the name of the Fraticelli vanishes from history.

§ R^do J[oan.] tit. s. [Stephani in monte Coelio] presb. card. Albiensi nuncupato de paupertate Christi. (Cod. Vatic., 4158.—70 pages). This beautifully adorned copy is evidently the one presented to the Cardinal.

‖ In the Vatican Library, *Cod. Vatic., 969, I found the copy presented to Paul II., adorned with his arms and with miniatures : Ad sanct. et clem. patrem et dom. d. Paulum papam II. pont. max. libellus incipit de paupertate Christi creatoris et dominatoris omnium nec non apostolor. eius . . . editus a Roderico episc. Zamoren. eiusdem Sanct^tis in castro suo s. Angeli de urbe fidelissimo castellano et referendario.

ject from the pens of Torquemada* and of Fernando of Cordova.†

At this time tidings reached Rome of the discovery in Germany of a sect similar to that of the Fraticelli.‡   The copy of a letter, addressed to Bishop Henry of Ratisbon by Rudolf of Rüdesheim, Bishop of Lavant and the Papal Legate, on the 11th June, 1466, contains details regarding these dreamy fanatics, whose chiefs were Brothers John and Livin of Wirsberg.   A member of this sect called himself John of the East; he was to be the forerunner of the anointed Redeemer, the One Shepherd of whom Christ had spoken.   These heretics declared the Pope to be Antichrist, and all Catholics who did not believe in the "anointed Redeemer" to be members of Antichrist.   "John of Wirsberg promulgated his doctrines in Eger as well as in the country, and even in the Bishopric of Eichstätt; his most zealous adherent, however, was his brother Livin," who died in prison in 1467, after having abjured his errors.§

It is very probable that Paul II. also took measures

---

* *Libellus velociter compositus et editus contra certos haereticos noviter impugnantes paupertatem Christi et suorum apostolorum. (Cod. Vatic., 974, f. 55 *seq*.)   MONTFAUCON, Bibl., II., 1382, saw this work also in the Library at Metz, where it is no longer to be found.

† Fernandi Cordubensis (see regarding him, HAVET in the Mém. de la Soc. d'Hist. de Paris, IX., 193 *seq*.), adversus haereticos qui fraterculi dela opinione vulgo appellantur ad rev. in Christo patrem et ill. dom. G. episcop. Hostiensem S. R. E. card. Rotomagens. vulgo appell. tractatus.   I found this work, which FABRICIUS, I., 570, does not cite, in the Cod. Vatic., 1127 ; it occupies 166 pages.

‡ See in Appendix, N. 17, the *Letter of B. de Maraschis of the 1st September, 1466.   Gonzaga Archives, Mantua.

§ JANNER III., 564–71, and GRADL, Die Irrlehre der Wirsperger, in the Mittheilungen des Vereins für Gesch. der Deutschen in Böhmen (1881), XIX., 270 *seq*.

against these sectaries.   Direct evidence, however, is wanting, for the Secret Archives of the Vatican only contain
Briefs belonging to the second half of the seventh year
of his pontificate.   These Briefs shew that he proceeded
against heretics in the Diocese of Amiens, and afterwards
in Bologna.*

The solicitude of Paul II. for the spiritual welfare of the
faithful committed to his charge is manifested by his
decision that the Jubilee should, for the future, be celebrated
once in every twenty-five years.   The Bull on this subject
was published on the 19th April, 1470.   " The thought of
all that the Church had suffered from schism at two
periods, and all that it had cost her to end it ; the terror of
Western Christendom when, by the fall of Constantinople,
the Turks gained a footing in Europe ; the alarming outbreaks of devastating maladies ; finally, the ruin which
ceaseless wars had wrought in the very life of the Western
kingdoms, led men to turn their eyes to Heaven, and
shewed that, in order to avert the strokes of the chasten-
ing hand of God, it was needful that all should tread the
paths of penance."   Moved by considerations such as
these, and by the fact that, under the former regulations,
but few could partake of the Jubilee Indulgence, the Pope
made the Decree we have mentioned, which was at once
solemnly announced throughout Christendom.†   But Paul

---

* Lib. brev. 12, f. 26 : *heret. pravit. inquisitori in prov. Remen. et in
dioc. Ambianen., dat. Romae, xviii. Oct., 1470, A° VII°., f. 121 : *Simoni
de Novaria Ord. Praed. prof. heret. pravit. inquisitori, dat. xiii. Martii,
1471.   Here is also mentioned a letter to the Bishop of Bologna,
which has not been preserved.   (Secret Archives of the Vatican.)   See
also Annal. Bonon., 897.

† Bull. V., 200–203 (in RAYNALDUS, ad an. 1470, N. 55, the beginning
is wanting, and there is an error in the date).   See NÖTHEN, 65 seq.,
and FESSLER, Schriften, 23.   Regarding the publication, see N.
DELLA TUCCIA, 98, and Istoria di Chiusi, 995–6.   The Bull is to be

II. was not destined to see the beginning of the new Jubilee year.

Towards the end of this pontificate a remarkable effort was made to prepare the way for the union of the Russian with the Roman Church, and also to gain the Grand Duke Iwan III. as a champion against the Turks. The idea originated with Bessarion, and found great favour with Paul II., who had just at that time expressed to the Maronites his wish that they should conform more closely to the Roman ritual.* An Ambassador was sent to Moscow to propose a marriage between the Grand Duke and Zoe (Sophia), the daughter of the unfortunate Thomas Palæologus. Iwan entered into the project, and the Ambassadors were at once sent back to Rome to bring a portrait of the bride. After a time things were so far settled that a Russian Embassy was sent to Rome to conduct Zoe to her new home. When this Embassy, bearing letters to Bessarion and to the Pope, reached Italy, Paul II. had ceased to live. His successor, however, took up the matter with equal zeal.†

---

found in many Manuscripts, as, *e.g.*, in Cod. 12,262 of the State Library, Munich (see Catal., IV., 2, 63); Cod. 3496, f. 6a–8b, Court Library, Vienna; and in Cod. LXXVI., f. 159a–160b, of the Cathedral Library, Zeitz.

* RAYNALDUS, ad an. 1469, N. 28 *seq.*

† See FR. PIERLING'S remarkable article, " Le Mariage d'un Tsar," 353 *seq.*, which is much better than the account of FIEDLER. (Sitzungsberichte der Wiener Akademie, XL., 29 *seq.*), or PICHLER, II., 54, and PELESZ, I., 261.

CHAPTER V.

The New and the Old Cardinals.—Church Questions in Bohemia.

THE appointment of new Cardinals was spoken of in the earliest months of Paul II.'s pontificate. At the Christmas of 1464, or, at the latest, in the following Lent, he seems to have contemplated an increase of the members of the Sacred College. Marco Barbo, Bishop of Vicenza, and Stefano Nardini, Archbishop of Milan,* were named as candidates. No nomination, however, according to Canensius, actually took place until the second year of his reign, and Teodoro de' Lelli, Bishop of Treviso, and Giovanni Barozzi, Patriarch of Venice, the only Prelates then elevated to the purple, both died before their publication.† A creation of Cardinals was positively announced for December, 1466;‡ but it did not take place. The consent

---

* *Letter of Stefano Nardini to Fr. Sforza, dated Rome, 1464, Dec. 6, in which he asks for his good offices with Paul II. Ambrosian Library.

† CANENSIUS, 100. Although the *Acta Consist. are silent regarding this nomination, we cannot, like CONTELORIUS, 63, completely reject it. Canensius was in all matters very well-informed. PANVINIUS, 315, is mistaken in assigning the first nomination to the year 1464. Regarding the death of the two who were created, see GAMS, 792 and 804.

‡ *Despatch of J. P. Arrivabene, dated Rome, 1466, Dec. 19, who says it was believed that L. Zane, Archbishop of Spalatro, would be made Cardinal. Gonzaga Archives, Mantua.

of the Sacred College probably could not be obtained.
At last, in the beginning of the fourth year of his reign,
on the 18th September, 1467, Paul II. was able to create
a large number of Cardinals.* Three of the eight then
admitted to the Sacred College were foreigners : Thomas
Bourchier, Archbishop of Canterbury ; Stephan de Varda,
Archbishop of Colocsa,† and Jean de La Balue, Bishop of
Angers. The last-named prelate, who, "by his cleverness
and cunning," had risen from a very obscure position, was
at this time Louis XI.'s Ambassador to Rome, and was
engaged in negotiations regarding the repeal of the Pragmatic Sanction ; this explains his appointment.

Of the five Italians promoted, one of the most distinguished was Olivieri Carafa, Archbishop of Naples.
"He was a jurist, a theologian, an antiquarian, and a
statesman ; he had even taken part in warfare as Admiral
against the Turks. Highly esteemed and influential in his
own country, he was remarkably popular in Rome. His
popularity was due to the use which he made of his ample
income and to his affability. He was generous in supporting learning and learned men ; many youths were won by
him for the Church and for serious studies." ‡ Paulus

---

* *Acta Consist., f. 35b, Secret Archives of the Vatican. See
*Despatch of J. Trottus of the 18th Sept., 1467 : " N. S. ha facto hoggi
li cardinali descripti ne la presente cedula" (State Archives, Modena),
and *Letter of Card. Gonzaga of the 18th Sept., 1467 : " Questa matina
sono pronuntiati octo cardinali cioè, etc." (Gonzaga Archives, Mantua.)
N. DELLA TUCCIA, 271, is mistaken in naming the 19th December.

† The King of Hungary had, from the year 1464, exerted himself on
his behalf ; see Mon. Hung., I., 305 ; also Arch. St. Ital. (Series 3),
XX., 311.

‡ REUMONT, III., 1, 259-60. See CHIOCARELLUS, 286 seq. ;
CIACONIUS, II., 1097 seq. ; CARDELLA, 159 seq. ; TOPPI, Addiz. alla
Bibl. Neapolit., 189 seq. (Neap. 1683) ; MÜNTZ, II., 87. MIGNE,
622, and CHEVALIER, 392, are mistaken in stating that 1464 was the

Cortesius praises his great discretion, his uprightness, and his blamelessness.*

The character of Paul II.'s nephew, Marco Barbo, Bishop, first of Treviso (1455–64) and afterwards of Vicenza, was still more admirable.† A singular sweetness of disposition and deep piety were in his case united with a rare capacity for business and great learning. He was absolutely disinterested. During his lifetime he gave almost all his income to the poor, to whom he afterwards bequeathed what remained, " for," he said, " the goods of the Church are, according to the teaching of the Fathers, the inheritance of Christ's poor." His fine library was the only gratification he allowed himself.‡ Of all the Pope's relations, he was the one most closely united with him ; his " inexhaustible power of work and his consummate prudence" were of great use to Paul II.§

year of Carafa's appointment.   Regarding Ferrante's exertions for Carafa, see TRINCHERA, I., 33 *seq.*

* CORTESIUS, De cardinalatu, f. LXIb. and CCXXXVIb.

† In the Library at Würzburg, I found in Cod. Q., 1 : *Leonelli Chieregati oratio in laudem Marci Barbi episc. Vicentini pro ingressu suo in civitatem, dat. Vicentiae, Kal. Octob., 1464.

‡ LITTA, Famiglie : Barbo ; MÜNTZ, II., 153 ; MAZZUCHELLI, II., 1, 318–19 ; Tiara et purp. Venet., 31 *seq.*, 66 *seq.*, 368.   In the Lib. confrat. b. Mariae de anima, p. 23, is the entry : "Marcus episc. Prenest. card. hospitalis nostri protector et singularis promotor, 1479." Barbo's sweetness is particularly praised by P. CORTESIUS, De Card., CCXXXVII. ; see CXXb.   A work dedicated to him by Amelius Trebanus, De felicitate, is in Cod. Vat., 2924. See ABEL, I., CXXX. On the 15th March, 1471, *Paul II. informs the Doge that he has conferred the Bishopric of Vicenza on Cardinal M. Barbo. Lib. brev. 12, f. 113.   Secret Archives of the Vatican.

§ See SCHMARSOW, 25. The confidential relations of Barbo to the Pope are mentioned by the Ambassador of Este, J. Trottus, in a *Despatch of the 19th Sept., 1467, in which he advises his master to congratulate the Cardinal of Vicenza : " il quale è lo ochio destro del

Amicus Agnifilus, the third of the Cardinals nominated on the 18th of September, 1467, had been a member of the household and a friend of Domenico Capranica, and subsequently tutor to Paul II. When raised from low estate to be Bishop of Aquila, he had chosen, for his armorial bearings, a lamb and a book. His epitaph praises his generosity to the poor, his discretion, and his thorough knowledge of Canon Law.* Little has been handed down concerning the fourth Cardinal, the Protonotary, Marquess Theodore of Montferrat,† and even less concerning Francesco della Rovere, the General of the Franciscans, on the occasion of whose elevation to the purple Paul II. is said to have observed that he had chosen his successor.‡

On the 19th September, the Red Hat was conferred on those among the newly-created Cardinals who were at the time in Rome. On the 2nd October, the mouth of Cardinal Barbo was opened, and S. Marco assigned to him as his titular Church. On the 22nd of the month, Agnifilus reached Rome; the Cardinal's Hat was at once given to him in a Public Consistory, and, on the 13th November, he received the Church of Sta Balbina, which, on the 13th October, 1469, he exchanged for that of Sta Maria in Trastevere. S. Pietro in Vincoli was the titular Church of Francesco della Rovere, and SS. Pietro e Marcellino that of Carafa, who arrived in Rome on the 3rd December, 1467.

---

papa e ragiona in concistorio de darli il suo titulo de S. Marco," in order that his palace may be left to him. See also a *Despatch of this Ambassador, dated Rome, 1469, Sept. 30. State Archives, Modena.

* CIACONIUS, II., 1111 ; CARDELLA, 172 *seq.* ; CHEVALIER, 39, is mistaken in regard to the appointment as well as the title of Agnifilus.

† CARDELLA, 174–5. The Hist. Monteferrat. (MURATORI, XXIII., 136) is wrong in giving 1466 as the date of his nomination. The Cardinal had a benefice in Mayence ; see JOANNIS, II., 288.

‡ FULGOSUS, I. c. 2.

Cardinal Theodore of Montferrat did not make his entry into Rome until the 21st April, 1468, when S. Teodoro was assigned to him.*

On the 21st November, 1468, Paul II. created two more Cardinals, who, like Marco Barbo, were of his own kindred : these were Battista Zeno and Giovanni Michiel, the sons of two of his sisters.   They received the Red Hat, and the Churches of Sta Maria in Porticu and Sta Lucia, on the 22nd Nov., and the ceremony of the opening of their mouths took place on the 9th December.†   The Popes nephews were both men of unblemished character.   None of the Cardinals were excessively wealthy or influential.‡

Towards the end of his reign, Paul II. created four other Cardinals.   This was done in a secret Consistory, and with the proviso that, in the event of his death, they were to be considered as published.§   They were Johann Vitéz, Archbishop of Gran, Pietro Foscari, Giovan Battista Savelli, and Francesco Ferrici.‖

---

* All these statements are from the *Acta Consist. of the Secret Archives of the Vatican.   From the same authority it appears that, on the 13th May, 1468, Bourchier, S. de Varda, and La Balue received respectively the Churches of S. Ciriaco, SS. Nereo ed Achilleo, and Sta Susanna.   The Cardinal's hat was not transmitted to S. de Varda until 1471 ; see Appendix, N. 28.

† *Acta Consist., f. 39.   Secret Archives of the Vatican.

‡ CREIGHTON, III., 50, who, at p. 51, observes : "In the creations of cardinals, Paul II. shewed his general impartiality and his good intentions."   For a further account of Zeno and Michiel, see Tiara et purp. Venet., 34 *seq.*, 369 ; CIACONIUS, II., 1112 *seq.* ; and CARDELLA, 175 *seq.*

§ CONTELORIUS, 62-3 ; CIACONIUS, II., 1114.   The publication was deferred out of consideration for the French King ; see *Letter of J. P. Arrivabene, dated Rome, 1471, June 8.   Gonzaga Archives.

‖ Regarding Vitéz, who died in 1472, see REUMONT, in Arch. St. Ital., 1874, and the Monograph of FRAKNÓI (Budapest, 1879) ; regarding the others, see *infra*; for Foscari, see Tiara et purp. Venet., 39 and 371.

Between the Cardinals created by Paul II., who were
called the " Pauleschi," and the " Piischi,"* who owed their
elevation to his predecessor, a certain opposition existed.
Of the latter number, Ammanati fell into complete dis-
favour, while Forteguerri, Roverella, and Eroli enjoyed the
good graces of Pope Paul II., and the first of these three
Cardinals enjoyed great influence with him.† At the
beginning of the pontificate, Richard Longueil,‡ who,
on the 1st October, 1464, was sent as Legate to Perugia,
was also at the French Court believed to have considerable
influence.§ Cardinals Borgia and Gonzaga also received
marked favours ; the latter, however, was not a friend of
the Pope.|| On the 18th February, 1471, he was appointed
Legate at Bologna, possibly with the object of removing
him from the Court.¶

The relations which existed between the Pope and

Frederick III. sought in vain to obtain the elevation of Domenico
de Domenichi (DOMINICUS, De dignit. episc., 32), and King René
that of the Archbishop of Arles, his Ambassador to Rome ; see LECOY
DE LA MARCHE, I., 542.

* These appellations are, as far as I know, found for the first time in a
*Despatch, which I shall speak of later, written by Joh. Blanchus on
the 29th July, 1471.   State Archives, Milan.

† N. DELLA TUCCIA, 98.   Concerning Ammanati, see *supra*, p. 25.

‡ *Letter of A. Malletta to Fr. Sforza, dated Abbeville, 1464, Oct. 8.
Fonds Ital., 1611, National Library, Paris.

§ *Acta Consist.   Secret Archives of the Vatican.

|| See *supra*, p. 24, and Appendix, N. 2.   Gonzaga Archives.

¶ Card. Gonzaga to his father, dated Rome, 1471, Febr. 18 :
*" Questa mattina è piaciuto a la Sta de N. S. deputarmi legato ad
Bologna." (Gonzaga Archives.)   See *Acta Consist. of the Secret
Archives of the Vatican.   According to this authority, Card. Gonzaga
did not set off until the 5th July.   *Ghirardacci speaks of his entry on
the 21st July.   A *Bull granting numerous faculties for his new sphere
of work, dated Rome, 1471, tertio Non. Julii A° 7°, is in the State
Archives, Bologna, Q. 22.

Cardinal Scarampo were of a peculiar character. The latter, whose contemporaries deemed him remarkable for his cunning, had, shortly after his rival's elevation, made peace with him. The reconciliation seems to have been tolerably complete, for, in September, 1464, the Pope had no hesitation in granting to Scarampo the full exercise of his post of Cardinal-Camerlengo. " Neither Calixtus III., nor Pius II., nor even Nicholas V., would have done this," observed a secretary in Cardinal Gonzaga's service.* The fact that, after the death of Cardinal Pierre de Foix, Paul II. conferred the Bishopric of Albano upon Scarampo shews that some degree of friendly feeling existed.† That there was, however, a certain amount of friction in the relations between the former rivals, is far from improbable. For instance, in answer to a pointed remark of the Cardinal's regarding the cost of the Palace of S. Marco, the Pope is said to have declared that it was far better to spend his money in buildings than to play it away.‡

At the beginning of March, 1465, Scarampo fell ill, and, on the 22nd, he died.§ He was a thoroughly worldly man,

---

* "*Item dom. papa voluit quod rev. dom. camerarius debeat officium suum exercere libere in curia Romana quod tempore pape Calisti et pape Pii (see VOIGT, III., 544) et eciam pape Nicolai facere non potuit." W. Molitor, in a *Letter, dated Rome, 1464, Sept. 21. Gonzaga Archives, Mantua.

† *Report of Giacomo d'Arezzo to Marchioness Barbara, dated Rome, 1465, January 9. Gonzaga Archives.

‡ CORTESIUS, De cardinalatu, CXXXIIII.

§ VOIGT, III., 508, attributes Scarampo's death to vexation at the election of Paul II. *J. P. Arrivabene, writing on March 1, 1465, reports Scarampo to be suffering from gout. Cardinal Gonzaga seems to have been on good terms with Scarampo, for in a *Letter to his parents, dated Rome, 1465, March 21, he expresses his sorrow that Scarampo "laborat in extremis ne se gli ha speranza alcuna." Gonzaga Archives, Mantua.

and was known at the Roman Court by the name of Cardinal Lucullus. As a Prince of the Church, his example was bad. As a statesman and politician, however, by restoring regular government in Rome, by promoting employment, and looking after the welfare of the people, by his consummate skill in the conduct of the negotiations with the Italian Princes, as well as by his care for the army and fleet, he did good service to the restored Papacy at a critical period.*

The close of Scarampo's career was followed by a somewhat painful episode. He had availed himself of the right conceded to him of making testamentary dispositions to bequeath his whole property, amounting to 200,000, or, according to some accounts, to 400,000 golden florins, to his nephews. Scarcely anything was left to the Church in whose service he had amassed these riches. To the general satisfaction, Paul II. set aside this will and devoted the whole of the property to charitable purposes, such as churches, the poor, and refugees from the countries which had been conquered by the Turks. The nephews of the deceased were also remembered ; even Platina here admits the kindness of the Pope.†

---

* Such is the opinion of GOTTLOB, Cam. Ap. See our Vol. I., p. 301 *seq.*

† CANENSIUS, 40 *seq.* ; FULGOSUS, VII., c. 7, see VI., c. 10 ; GREGOROVIUS, VII., 210, 3rd ed. According to *GHIRARDACCI, Cronica di Bologna, 759, the Cardinal left 600,000 ducats. Here there is a mistake as to the day of his death : the date we give is established by the *Acta Consist., Secret Archives of the Vatican. See Annal. Bonon., 895, and Cronica Borselli (GUIDICINI, Miscel., 44), which add, "Oh! Che buon elemosiniere !" *Carlo de Franzoni, writing to the Marchioness of Mantua, speaks of the "infinita di denari e goije" left by the Cardinal. (Gonzaga Archives.) For an account of Scarampo's tomb in S. Lorenzo in Damaso, see MÜNTZ, II., 81 *seq.* ; GATTULA, II., 568 ; and FORCELLA, V., 171.

His friendship for Cardinal Bessarion speaks well for Paul II. The dispute about the Election Capitulation had temporarily estranged them, but, in the year 1468, the Duke of Este's Ambassador spoke of Bessarion as enjoying more consideration than all the other Cardinals, and, in the following year, he wrote word that Barbo and the Greek Cardinal were much in the Pope's confidence, and were the only men trusted with the most secret affairs.* In fact, "in the history of this period Bessarion stands forth almost like a father of the Church ; his majestic presence, his noble Greek profile with his long flowing beard, also contributed to enhance the esteem and deference which were everywhere accorded to him."†

Bessarion, who was an ardent patriot, not only took the deepest interest in the proposed Crusade, but also endeavoured in every way to awaken the compassion of Western Christendom on behalf of his exiled countrymen. The unselfishness with which he assisted the scattered fugitives, and his "noble efforts to preserve and render profitable whatever it had been possible to rescue from a vanishing civilisation, call upon us to deal leniently with his weaknesses."‡

* Report o Jacobus Trottus, dated Rome, 1468, Nov. 2 (*Niceno, Rohano e S. Angelo son contra il Re a morsi et a calci et piu Niceno che è tuto Venetiano et che ha piu auctoritate chal resto de cardinali), and 1469, Sept. 30. (State Archives, Modena.) See Vespasiano da Bisticci in MAI, I., 193, and CANENSIUS, 101.

† SCHMARSOW, 4. See also our Vol. I., p. 319 *seq.*, Vol. II., 69 *seq.* I have since had an opportunity of seeing the Russian Monograph of Alex. Sadov (St. Petersburg, 1883) there mentioned, and it has disappointed my expectations. The author brings forward no new documents or authorities, but rests exclusively on foreign literature. As Vast's work is also unsatisfactory, a new life of the Greek Cardinal, based on original sources, is still greatly to be desired.

‡ GOTHEIN, 400–401.

The Greek Cardinal's state of health became so much worse during Paul's reign that, in 1466, he caused the simple tomb, which is still well-preserved in the Church of the SS. Apostoli, to be prepared.* In the following year he stayed for a considerable time at Viterbo, where he had on former occasions taken the baths.† In spite of his bodily sufferings he devoted himself as zealously as ever to study ; his celebrated work in defence of Plato appeared at this time. He was also in constant intercourse with the Humanist Scholars in Rome. His house at SS. Apostoli was common ground for the most noted Greeks and Italian Hellenists, where all were welcomed by their learned host with the most winning kindness.‡ "Here Andronikos Callistos, Constantine Laskaris, and Theodore Gaza held brilliant and genial converse with the Cardinal in friendly rivalry with his pupil and favourite, Niccolo Perotto, who translated Polybius, and composed a metrical poem." Francesco della Rovere, afterwards Sixtus IV., Domizio da Caldiero, Johannes Müller Regiomontanus, the great astronomer and geographer, and many others, also frequented his house,§ and Bessarion

* VAST, 293 *seq*.

† N. DELLA TUCCIA, Pref. XX. and 91. That Bessarion was also at Viterbo, in 1468, is shewn by his Letter to the Doge, dated from that city, giving his valuable library to the Republic of Venice ; see Serapeum, II., 94 *seq*. Regarding this gift, see also Arch. St. Ital., 3 Series, IX., 2, 193 *seq*. (here, p. 198, is also an account of a College, founded by Bessarion in Candia, for the education of clergy of the Greek Rite), and OTTINO-FUMAGALLI, Bibl. bibliograph. Italica, 350 *seq*. (Roma, 1889).

‡ CORTESIUS, De cardinalatu, LXXIII., says that Bessarion, like Torquemada and Cusa, was always most courteous to the learned men who visited him.

§ SCHMARSOW, 26. See VOIGT, II., 130 *seq*., 2nd ed. ; GASPARY, 110 ; VAST, 308 *seq*. ; Arch. St. Ital., 1887, XIX., 314 *seq*. Among the learned men whom Bessarion assisted we must also mention Michael

took part in their learned disputations with unfailing interest.*

As Protector of the Basilian Order, the Greek Cardinal's labours were both extensive and important. The reforms which the Order at this time required, and which Martin V. had already attempted, were energetically taken in hand. "Persuaded that the extent of the malady demanded a comprehensive remedy, Bessarion began by drawing up a Rule in Italian and in Greek, which he strictly imposed upon the Monasteries in Italy and Sicily. He increased their revenues by recovering lands which had been alienated, and by regulating their household expenses, and endeavoured to give new splendour to the Order by beautifying its ancient buildings and by constructing on the old lines skilfully arranged additions." Bessarion everywhere insisted on serious study; he encouraged the monks to apply themselves to the Greek classics, to transcribe and collect Manuscripts and to establish good schools. Among these, the Gymnasium of Messina acquired a great reputation. Laskaris, whom Bessarion appointed Professor at this Institution in 1467, soon attracted scholars from all parts of Italy.†

In recognition of these important services Pius II., in August 1462, nominated Bessarion Commendatory Abbot of Grottaferrata. This celebrated Abbey, which had long been considered as a link uniting East and West, had, at the period of which we are speaking, fallen into a state of dilapidation. Bessarion at once devoted himself most ardently to the work of restoration, and quickly succeeded in effecting a thorough renovation, both material and

---

Apostolios, concerning whom see LEGRAND, Bibl. Hell., I., LVIII. *seq.*, and NOIRET'S work, Lettres inéd. de M. A. (Paris, 1889).

* CORTESIUS, De Cardinalatu, XXXIX.

† VOGEL, C. Laskaris in the Serapeum, VI., 45 *seq.*; VAST, 224 *seq.*; LEGRAND, I., LXXIX.

spiritual, in this interesting spot, so rich in classical associa-
tions and Christian memories.* His chalice, his famous
Inventory (Regestum Bessarionis †), and some valuable
Manuscripts, presented by him to his Abbey, are still preserved at Grottaferrata.‡

The Vatican Basilica, the Camaldolese Abbey at Avel-
lana, and the Church of the Holy Apostles in Rome, were
also generously enriched by Bessarion.§ The last-named
Church, which Eugenius IV. had assigned as his title, was
the special object of his paternal solicitude. In the beginning of Paul II.'s pontificate the Cardinal caused the
Chapels of the Archangel Michael, of St. John the Baptist,
and of Saint Eugenia, at the left of the High Altar, to be
completely restored and decorated by the painter Anto-
nazzo Romano. "In the centre of the vaulting appeared
the figure of Our Lord, enthroned and surrounded with nine
choirs of Angels, in a blue firmament strewn with stars and
encircled by a frieze. In the corners were the four Evangelists, with a Latin and a Greek Father of the Church writing
in his cell beside each. On the upper part of the wall behind
the Altar was the apparition of the Archangel Michael on
Monte Gargano, and beneath this the birth of St. John the
Baptist. On the side walls, between two real and two painted
windows, stood two Archangels above, and the third with St.
John the Baptist below. From half-way up the wall down
to the ground, curtains ornamented with patterns in flowers

* ROCCHI, Grottaferrata, 38 *seq.*, 65, 80, 138, 162. The Catalogue of
the Manuscripts of Grottaferrata, commenced by order of Bessarion in
1462, has been published by BATIFFOL in DE WAAL'S Quartalschrift,
III., 39 *seq.*

† Description in ROCCHI, Cod. Crypt., 513.

‡ A liturgical Manuscript, Γ. β. I., which Cesarini gave to his friend
Bessarion, and the magnificent Codex Z. δ. I., are particularly worthy
of notice. See ROCCHI, Cod. Crypt., 220 and 500.

§ MÜNTZ, II., 298 *seq.*; MALVASIA, 80 *seq.*, 83 *seq.*

and gold were painted. On each of the six pilasters was the figure of a Saint under a canopy. The framing-arch was adorned with a frieze, and three shields with the arms of the founder."*

Amongst the nearest and dearest of Bessarion's friends was Juan de Carvajal, the most devoted of all the sons of the Church. His motto was " To suffer all things for Christ and His Church ! " In consequence of his extreme modesty, and utter disregard of fame, the memory of this distinguished man has not been honoured as it deserves. The student of history can discover but scanty records of the life of this saintly Cardinal, who proved his fidelity and self-sacrificing devotion to the cause of the Church in twenty-two Legations and " from all his journeys brought back nothing but the reputation of an unspotted priesthood."†

Since the autumn of 1461 Carvajal had again been living in Rome. " The vigorous man, whom Pope Calixtus had sent to Hungary at the time when Belgrade was threatened by the Turks, had grown old and feeble in that severe climate, amid the turmoils of the Court and camp, and the fatigues of travel. His teeth were so loose in his mouth that he could only use them with the aid of artificial appliances. Yet it was political reasons rather than considerations of health, which at last induced him to abandon this bleak country of moorlands and marshes.

* SCHMARSOW, 57. See MALVASIA, 36 *seq.*; MÜNTZ, II., 82 *seq.* The first of these writers draws attention to the similarity of these frescos, which were whitewashed over in the 17th Century, and Fra Angelico's paintings in the Vatican.

† See our Vol. II., p. 7 and p. 390 *seq.* The scarcity of materials for a life of Carvajal is evident from the Monograph of LOPEZ, Rome, 1754. A College, which he founded at Salamanca, is mentioned by DENIFLE, I., 813. FRAKNÓI, in an article which has just appeared, and which I have not yet seen, gives the history of the Cardinal's Legations in Hungary.

He left behind him the memory of a pure and beneficent
life, and his merits, which have never been questioned by
any historian, met with an honourable appreciation in
Rome. No other Cardinal, it was justly observed, did so
much and endured such sufferings as Carvajal in the six
years during which he was Legate for Hungary, while
championing the Church's highest interest, the purity of
her faith."*   Extreme simplicity and exemplary order
prevailed in his modest dwelling near S. Marcello.† His
ascetic manner of life enabled him to be very liberal to
the poor, and to provide for needy churches. He was
never absent from any great ecclesiastical function or
from a Consistory. In Consistory he expressed his
opinion freely, but in a conciliatory manner. In their
"brevity, simplicity, and clearness, their strict logic and
their utter absence of rhetoric," his discourses form a
striking contrast to the bombastic and artificial productions of the literary men of his day; his Reports while
a Legate have the same "restrained and impersonal
character."‡

Though always genial in his intercourse with others,
there was a something about Carvajal which inspired a
certain awe in all who saw much of him. Cardinal

---

* VOIGT, III., 511–12, who remarks that Carvajal would have been
a Pope suited to the period, after the Tridentine Reforms. In regard
to the date of his return, which is given wrongly by all writers, see our
Vol. III., p. 225, note §, the extract from the *Acta Consist., Secret
Archives of the Vatican.

† Carvajal's mortal remains found their last resting-place in this
church. The inscription on the monument, erected by Bessarion, has
the following lines :—

>   "Pontificum splendor iacet hic sacrique senatus ;
>   Namque animo Petrus, pectore Caesar erat."
>   —CIACONIUS, II., 926.

‡ VOIGT, I., 260.

Ammanati observed of him : " our age may rightly place him by the side of the ancient Fathers of the Church," and these words expressed the general opinion of the members of the Sacred College.   It might be said that Rome did not contain a single man who had not done homage to " the height and depth of his character."   Pomponius Laetus, " who admired nothing in ruined Rome but the heroic grandeur of its earliest founders ; who hardly deigned to bestow a glance on the Barons and Prelates of the Papal City,—the proud Platonist, the cynic scorner of all flattery and of every kind of dignity, who never uncovered his head, or bowed to any one, made but one exception, and that was the aged Cardinal of S. Angelo."*

Subsequent historians have unanimously endorsed the esteem and admiration of his contemporaries for Carvajal. The latest biographer of Pius II., who is generally disposed to believe the worst of men,† speaks of Carvajal with the greatest reverence.   Even the Hussite historian of Bohemia says of him : " Not only in zeal for the Faith, in moral purity and strength of character, was he unsurpassed, but he was also unequalled in knowledge of the world, in experience of ecclesiastical affairs, and in the services which he rendered to the Papal authority.   It was chiefly due to his labours, prolonged during a period of twenty years, that Rome at last got the better of Constance and Basle, that the nations returned to their allegiance, and that her power and glory again shone before the world with a splendour that had not been seen since the time of Boniface VIII. Carvajal's colleagues knew and acknowledged this, and in

* M. Fernus, J. Pomp. Leti Elogium Hist., in FABRICIUS-MANSI, VI., 630 ; VOIGT, III., 514. We have shewn, *supra*, p. 57, that P. Laetus had his hours of weakness.

† This is the opinion of VAHLEN, Valla, LXI., 371.

all important matters were guided by his counsels. Paul
II. himself feared him, and yielded to all his wishes. Thus,
his personal influence, and his opinion regarding King
George and the doctrine of the Hussites, had great weight
in Rome."*

As a member of the Commission appointed by Paul II.
to consider the state of ecclesiastical affairs in Bohemia,
Carvajal was associated with Bessarion and d'Estouteville.†
From the beginning he advocated stern measures. The
ill-advised conduct of the King of Bohemia, who omitted
to send any one from his Court to offer the congratulations
usual from Princes to a new Pope, had confirmed the
Cardinal in the conviction "that it would be absolutely
necessary to employ the knife in the case of wounds which
admitted of no other remedy, and to guard against fatal
corruption by severing the decayed members from the body
of Holy Church."‡

The Pope at first hoped that gentleness might be
successful with George Podiebrad. The proceedings which
Pius II. had commenced were at once suspended. Paul II.
declared that, if the Bohemian King fulfilled his promises,
he would be to him not a Pope, but a loving brother.§ It
soon became evident that the double-tongued monarch had
no thought of keeping his oath. When all Christian
Princes sent Ambassadors to Rome, none appeared from
Bohemia. Fresh complaints were constantly made by the

* PALACKY, IV., 2, 372. Regarding Carvajal's influence with Paul
II., see CANENSIUS, 101.

† BACHMANN, I., 548, and other historians mention Cardinal
"William of Ostia," without giving his real name. This is not a
scientific way of speaking.

‡ PALACKY, IV., 2, 325. See Fontes Rer. Austr., XLIV., 589.

§ This is related by Johann Rohrbacher to Procopius von Rabenstein in PALACKY, Urkundl. Beitr., 338, Gesch., IV., 2, 329.

Catholics. The "pacific inclinations" of Paul II. gradually vanished. The letter which the King of Bohemia sent to Rome on the 7th March, 1465, only apologises in a passing way for the delay of the Embassy; its main purpose is to explain the reasons why George did not think it well to comply with the Pope's desire, and raise the siege of the fortress of Zornstein, which belonged to the Catholic Heinrich von Lichtenburg. Paul II.'s reply to this letter was not addressed to the King himself, but to the Bohemian Prelates and Barons (13th May, 1465),* a fact which shews the change in his feeling. By the middle of the summer of this year the stern views of Carvajal had completely prevailed, and from henceforth guided the Pope in all his decisions. On the 2nd August, Podiebrad was summoned by Cardinals Bessarion, Carvajal and Eroli, who were entrusted with the management of the Bohemian affair, to appear at Rome within 180 days to answer charges of heresy, of relapse into heresy, of perjury (in regard to the breach of his coronation oath), of spoliation of churches, and of blasphemy. "In order, however, to guard against a further outbreak of heresy during the trial, and to protect the oppressed Catholics," the Pope, on the 6th August, empowered the Legate Rudolf, Bishop of Lavant, to inflict ecclesiastical censures on all George's adherents, and to declare all engagements entered into with him null and void.†

Meanwhile George's position had become much worse, the chief lords of Bohemia, dissatisfied with his arbitrary government, having become more and more hostile to him. He therefore made new proposals of accommodation with Rome; but Rome was weary of these endless negotiations.

* BACHMANN, I., 549 *seq.*, 553.

† SS. Rer. Siles., IX, 135–9; PALACKY, Urk. Beitr., 362–6; FRIND, IV., 65.

" Long years of prevarication had destroyed all confidence
in George, so that even those who had once depended upon
his word now turned from him with feelings embittered by
disappointment, and firmly resolved never again to be
deceived by him."* As early as the 8th December, 1465,
Paul II. had released George's subjects from their oath of
allegiance ; on the 6th February, 1466, the proposals made
through Duke Louis of Bavaria in favour of the King of
Bohemia were absolutely rejected.

In order to understand the severe language of this
document, we must remember the shameful manner in
which George had trifled with Calixtus III. and Pius II.
regarding the Turkish question. It is strange to find the
King now bringing forward this question, and demanding
to be rewarded beforehand for his return to the Church,
and his participation in the Crusade, by the title of Emperor
of Constantinople for himself, and the Archbishopric of
Prague for one of his sons. Is a relapsed heretic, a per-
jured man, Paul II. remarks, to ask, instead of penance
and punishment, for a reward such as could hardly be
granted to the most Christian Princes, who had rendered
the greatest services to religion ? He desires to traffic
with his conversion to the Faith, and sell his conscience for
gain. His feigned obedience would indeed be a precious
boon to the Church, while the old leaven would still
ferment throughout the kingdom. Is the Apostolic See
to beg for this, while he reserves to himself the right
to accept or reject what is offered ? The proposed Archbishop is a youth, scarce twenty years of age, who has
grown up in the midst of his father's crimes and deceits, in

* BACHMANN, I., 574. Regarding the League among the Lords, see
Markgraf's article in SYBEL'S Hist. Zeitschr., XXXVIII., 49 *seq.*,
where, however, at pp. 54 and 65, the date of Paul's accession and Pius
II.'s death are wrongly given.

ignorance of all law, either human or Divine; he has but just ceased to be a heretic, and is now to be made a Bishop! Equally obnoxious is the request that the Archbishop should have as assistant an Inquisitor who will prosecute all "heresies outside the Compact." That is very cunningly devised : is it not equivalent to a covert demand that the Compacts should be re-established? Again, what is the meaning of the petition for the Imperial Crown of Constantinople? Evidently its object is only to secure an easier passage from one Confession of Faith to another (the Greek). But the dominion of the Infidels, who have never known the truth, is a lesser evil than the rule of a heretic and schismatic, who has apostatised from that which he professed. The Church has not yet fallen so low as to be compelled to seek the protection of heretics and robbers of churches.*

The fact that Podiebrad, in the summer of 1466, took the excommunicated Gregor Heimburg into his service is a proof that the Pope had not judged him too severely. His connection with this unscrupulous man, who, "for twenty years, had been at the head of every opposition offered outside the limits of Bohemia to the restoration of the Papal power," was equivalent to a renunciation of all idea of reconciliation with the Church.† Even on the 28th July, Heimburg, who had formerly made a parade of his German sympathies, published a manifesto in defence of the "honour and innocence" of the Czech monarch, who

* Paul II. to Duke Louis of Bavaria, 1466, Febr. 6. SS. Rer. Siles., IX., 156–63. See PALACKY, IV., 2, 375 *seq.*; BACHMANN, I., 575 *seq.*; KLUCKHOHN, Ludwig, 261 *seq.*; JORDAN, 195 *seq.*; Markgraf in SYBEL'S Hist. Zeitschr., XXXVIII., 72 *seq.* Paul II.'s Brief to the people of Breslau (Fontes, XLIV., 593), which Bachmann erroneously assigns to the year 1465, refers to this occasion.

† BACHMANN, I., 583 ; PALACKY, IV., 2, 391.

had been treated by Rome worse "than the fratricide Cain and the Sodomites!" George, he said, was no private individual whom the Pope might summon to Rome at his pleasure, but a King, and a King of great merit. This advocate found excuses for everything, even for the imprisonment of Fantinus, which was a breach of the law of nations. The Pope was accused of credulity, and his conduct characterised as hasty, as an offence against Divine and natural law, and opposed to reason and Scripture. He further insisted that a Diet should be summoned, at which the Envoys of the temporal Princes should, in the presence of a Legate, deliberate on the ecclesiastical affairs of Bohemia.* As this manifesto was at once sent, not only to all the German Courts, but also to the King of France and the other Princes of Christendom, it was impossible for the Papal party to be silent. The autumn had not passed before letters in answer appeared from Rudolf von Rüdesheim, Bishop of Lavant, and from Cardinal Carvajal. The former sought to surpass his opponent in violence of language, and lost himself in prolix explanations, while Carvajal, in his brief, simple and logical style, exposed the treacherous arts of the Czech monarch and of his advocate. In particular, he brought forward the sacrilegious manner in which George had violated the right of nations by his conduct towards Fantinus and the double-faced policy by which he had trifled with the Holy See. What Rome now commanded was the result of mature deliberation, and was in accordance with justice. George's intrigues are unmasked, the axe is laid to the roots ; he must prove his innocence or else experience the rigour of justice.†

* SS. Rer. Siles., IX., 181–90; MÜLLER, Reichstagstheater, II., 250–58; BROCKHAUS, 286 seq. ; JORDAN, 227 seq.

† Instead of "ut penas juris paciatur oportet" (SS. Rer. Siles., IX., 209) we must surely read "aut penas," as the copy in Cod. 4, f. 74b–76b,

Heimburg soon wrote a second apology for King George, in which he gave vent to his violent hatred of the two heads of Christendom and for the Cardinals. All manner of false charges were here made against both Pope and Emperor, and amongst others that of immorality. The " very violence and indecency of these accusations destroyed their effect."* The only result of this letter was entirely to put an end to the friendly relations which had existed between George Podiebrad and Frederick III. The action of George's counsellor was certainly not that of a states-man.

of the Library at Kremsmünster has it. This Manuscript also gives f. 45a–68b, the above-mentioned *Letter of Rudolf von Rüdesheim contra venenosum hereticum Georgium. I also found in a collection formerly belonging to the Convent of Ebrach : *Scripta in causa G. Podiebradii Bohemiae regis, f. 53–79, now Cod. Q. 15, of the University Library, Würzburg.

* MARKGRAF in SS. Rer. Siles., IX., 190, where it is observed that PALACKY, who (Urkundl. Beitr., 647 *seq.*) publishes the Apology, is mistaken in giving 1467 as its date. The charges of immorality made by Heimburg against Paul II. are also to be found in B. CORIO, 264. SCHMARSOW, 14, had not been able to receive this man's evidence because of its very general character (uomo molto dedito alla libidine), and because of the close relations which existed between him and Galeazzo Maria Sforza, who was hostile to Paul II.; in the earlier parts of his history he is very untrustworthy (see ANNONI, Un plagio dello storico B. Corio, a reprint from the Rivist. Ital., and Arch. St. Lomb., II., 155), and also in the later period tells his readers many incredible stories and reports (see the example from the time of Alexander VI. in DÖLLINGER, Papstfabeln, p. 32, note, 2nd ed.). Nor is Janus Pannonius a more credible authority ; according to VOIGT, II., 325, 2nd ed., he brought "all the moral filth of Italian Humanism into Hungary," and derided the precepts of the moral law and found pleasure in turning ecclesiastical things and persons into ridicule. The passage on the subject (in WOLF, II., 112) is, for all purposes of historical criticism, properly characterised as a biting epigram. JANUS, 372, rightly perceives that in such a case the testimony of partisans

The decided measures advocated by Carvajal did not meet with universal approval at the Roman Court. Looking at the matter from a merely human point of view, some urged that there was no one who could carry into effect the sentence of the Holy See. Nothing was to be expected from the irresolute Emperor, and Poland also displayed little inclination to be of use. King Matthias of Hungary had, indeed, given the best assurances of good-will, but it was generally desired that he should reserve his forces for the Turkish war. It was doubtful whether the power of the Bohemian nobles was equal to the occasion. In the face of these grave difficulties, Carvajal remained unmoved in his opinion that justice ought to take its course, and that there was a duty to be accomplished. God would, he believed, provide for all.*

After Carvajal had left Rome as Legate to Venice, on the 20th August, 1466, Cardinals Ammanati and Piccolomini were the chief advocates of strong measures. After long deliberations their opinion finally prevailed.† On the

like Heimburg (see BROCKHAUS, 369) and Corio, or the obscene Pannonius, is inadmissible ; that adduced from Attilio Alessio (in BALUZE-MANSI, IV., 519) must also be rejected, inasmuch as he wrote after 1530. In the numerous Ambassadorial Reports in the Archives of Milan, Mantua, and Modena, which I have gone through, there is no trace of a charge against the moral character of Paul II., although his other faults are by no means concealed. The silence of his bitterest enemy,—Platina,—who, if grounds of accusation had really existed, would certainly not have passed them over, ought to be deemed conclusive.

* See Fabian Hanko's Report of the 17th July, 1466, in SS. Rer. Siles., IX., 181. Further particulars regarding the attitude of Poland will be found in CARO, V., 1, 269 seq., 273 seq.

† AMMANATI, Comment., 401–402 (Frankfort ed., p. 437), speaks as if the energetic words of Carvajal had at once, and of themselves, brought about the Consistory of Dec. 23, 1466. PALACKY, IV., 2, 419, and BACHMANN, I., 592, who follow this later account, might have

23rd December a Consistory was held, in which George Podiebrad was deposed from his dignities of King, Marquis and Prince, his posterity declared disqualified for any honour or inheritance, and his subjects absolved from their oath of allegiance.*

The Papal Bull announcing this decision made a deep impression on loyal Catholics, and in order to lessen its effect, Podiebrad, on the 14th April, 1467, published a solemn appeal to a General Council, which ought properly, he said, to have been assembled before this time, and

learnt from the final sentence of 23rd Dec., 1466 (SS. Rer. Siles., IX., 211), that Carvajal was not at the time in Rome. The *Acta Consist. in the Secret Archives of the Vatican also expressly declare that Carvajal was absent from Rome from the 20th August, 1466, until the 17th Sept., 1467. See also HÖFLER, Geschichtsschr. der Husitischen Bewegung, III., 224 ; and Cardinal Gonzaga, who wrote from Rome on the 18th Sept., 1467 : *" Heri sera tornoe el rev. mons. de S. Agnolo." (Gonzaga Archives.) Probably the Cardinal was exerting himself in opposition to Podiebrad in Venice, while Heimburg was endeavouring to gain the Republic over to the Bohemian side. (BACHMANN, I., 584, note 3.) The above-mentioned controversial letter must also have originated there.

* Besides Balthasar of Piscia's Report in SS. Rer. Siles., IX., 214–215, see *J. P. Arrivabene's letters from Rome. (1) Dat. 1466, Dec. 19 : " P. S. Fornito el consistorio de hoggi niente si è saputo de cardinali. Sono stati sopra questa materia del Re de Bohemia." Probably a Public Consistory was to be held on the Monday. (2) Dat. 1466, Dec. 23 : " P. S. Nel consistorio publico che foe differito ad hoggi è sta dechiarato quello Georgio che se pretende Re de Bohemia heretico e privato d'ugni dignitate regale ducale e marchionale e d'ugni bene spirituale e temporale e inhabilitato li figlioli e l'acto foe sollemne secundo el stilo de ragione. Ad' esso che è xxiv. hore e giunto Alexio." (Gonzaga Archives, Mantua.) A *Commentary on the Bull of Deposition was written by Rodericus Sancius de Arevalo, and dedicated to Paul II. Bessarion's Copy of the Document is preserved at the Marciana in Venice (see ANDRES, Cartas, III., 73 [Madrid, 1790]) ; present number, Z. L. CXCIV.

had been put off only by the Pope's negligence. This document, which attacked the Pope personally, was drawn up by Heimburg. It was immediately sent to all the German Princes.* At the same time an Ambassador was despatched from Prague to the Court of the French King. He was to propose the conclusion of an offensive and defensive alliance between Louis XI. and Podiebrad, into which the Poles and a number of the German Princes were to be drawn, especially the rulers of Saxony and Brandenburg, whose sympathies were with Bohemia. The immediate object of the allies was to be the humiliation of Burgundy. When this was accomplished, Louis XI. was to summon a Council, "which should be held by the nation," and which should put down all strife and all arrogance, especially the pretensions of the Pope and the Emperor, who were to be brought low and punished! At the French Court the Ambassador maintained that the Pope was endeavouring " to get both swords into his hands, and thus subject all rulers to himself, so that the clergy might have their way in everything." Words like these found a ready access to the ear of a tyrant like Louis XI. He promised to exert himself in Podiebrad's favour in Rome, and also to use his influence " to maintain the Compacts of the Holy Council of Basle in force " ; he further advised that the German Princes should be persuaded to advocate the assembling of the Council. George's efforts in this matter were unsuccessful, and complications in his own dominions, and with England, so fully occupied the French King, that he was unable to pursue his anti-Roman project of the Council.† The close relations which

* Fontes Rer. Austr. Dipl., XX., 454–8, XLII., 410 ; SS. Rer. Siles., IX., 226.

† J. Pažout, G. v. Böhmen und die Concilsfrage im Jahre 1467, in the Archiv. für Œsterr. Gesch., XL., 333 *seq.* See *supra*, p. 104.

continued to exist between Louis XI. and the Bohemian monarch is evidenced by the fact that when, in the following year, Paul II. wished to have the Bull of Maundy Thursday, in which Podiebrad was mentioned by name, published in France, the French King at once raised objections, and the Duke of Milan did the same.*

While Podiebrad was somewhat unsuccessfully labouring to elevate his personal contest with Rome into a matter of general importance to all the temporal powers, the opposing party within his kingdom did not remain idle. Nothing decisive, however, was done, even after the formation of a great Catholic League in the December of 1467. It became more and more evident that the League could only hope to prevail against George if assisted by some powerful Prince. All efforts to obtain such aid proved fruitless, and accordingly in the end no alternative remained to the Pope and the League, save to listen to the overtures made to them by the King of Hungary.†

The adversaries of George greatly rejoiced when Matthias Corvinus (1468, March 31) declared war against Bohemia. Cardinal Ammanati's letters to Paul II. and Carvajal bear witness to their satisfaction.‡ The necessary interruption

---

* DAUNON, 265 *seq.* See FRIEDBERG, Grenzen, 479. From a command on the subject to the Archbishop of Lyons on the 25th Febr., 1469, we find that Paul continued his efforts to have Podiebrad's Excommunication published in France. D'ACHERY, III., 834 (nov. edit.). The Maundy Thursday Bull, expressly naming Podiebrad, was also disseminated in the vernacular in Italy. I found a contemporary Italian translation of the Bull *Cœna Domini*, of 1469, in the State Archives at Modena ; Bolle. In reference to the opposition made by the Duke of Milan, see a contemporary *Notice on the copy of the Maundy Thursday Bull in the State Archives, Milan.

† This is the opinion of HUBER, III., 208, see 215 ; and CARO, V., 1, 293.

‡ AMMANATI, Epist., f. 151b, 152b, pp. 655–6 (Frankfort ed.).

of the war with the Turks was looked upon as a lesser
evil. The Apostolic Faith was deemed to be in imminent danger unless the Bohemian King should voluntarily
abandon his schismatic position, or be forcibly deprived
of the power of doing harm.*   On the 20th April, 1468,
the Pope had again pronounced the severest ecclesiastical
penalties on all the adherents and abettors of George, and
had moreover promised a number of Indulgences to those
who should either personally, or by pecuniary contributions,
take part in the war against him.†   Lorenzo Roverella,
the Bishop of Ferrara, who had but lately returned to
Rome, was again sent to Germany to publish these Indulgences, and furnished with fuller powers.‡

During the year 1468 the fortunes of war favoured the
King of Hungary. In the following February, Matthias
advanced into Bohemia, but was completely shut in by
Podiebrad in the defiles near Wilimow, and his case seemed
hopeless. He then began to negotiate for a truce, and
promised to obtain from the Pope the toleration of the
Compacts for the Bohemians. On the 24th March, the
two Kings purposed to meet at Olmütz, and conclude a
permanent peace. The Papal Legate, Roverella, hastened
to the spot to prevent this, and succeeded in doing so.§

* See the passage from Joh. von. Rabenstein's Dialog. in the Archiv
für Œsterr. Gesch., LIV., 382.

† SS. Rer. Siles., IX., 265–9.

‡ RAYNALDUS, ad an. 1468, N. 2–3. A *Letter of Credentials,
given by Paul II. to L. Roverella for the City of Ratisbon, dated
1468, April 20, is in Regensb. R–T–A. in the Records Office in
Munich. Even on the 8th April, 1468, there appears in *Cruciata
Pauli II., f. 84, an entry of 1000 ducats, "pro dom. episc. Ferrariensi,
nuncio et oratori S. D. N. papae in partibus Alamanniae pro negotiis
Bohemiae rem fidei concernentibus ituro."   State Archives, Rome.

§ PALACKY, IV., 2, 573 seq. See Urkundl. Beiträge, 569 seq.; and
Fontes, XLIV., 661 seq.

In July, 1469, the war broke out afresh, Matthias having been two months previously solemnly elected King of Bohemia. No decisive advantage was gained by either party during that year or the next. The war was one of mutual devastation, and seemed likely to be endless. Notwithstanding all the efforts of his opponents, George held his ground, paying his partisans out of the spoils of the Church. He failed, however, to accomplish his plan of founding a Czech dynasty by securing the succession to one of his sons.*

Meanwhile, the "greatest, and, in regard to his moral character, the most estimable, of the enemies of Bohemia in the Sacred College," Juan Carvajal, had died in Rome (6th December, 1469).† At the same time it was reported that one of the Cardinals had advocated a pacific arrangement with Podiebrad; this induced the latter to express to the Cardinal in question, whose name is unfortunately unknown, his desire for reconciliation with Rome. He declared that he had never intended to injure the Holy Father, and yet had undeservedly to endure his severe displeasure. He had never believed himself to be outside the Holy Church, in which alone is salvation. If in any way he had departed from the unity of the Faith, he had done it in ignorance. Although he had already entrusted his reconciliation with Rome to King Casimir of Poland, he

---

* FRIND, IV., 73; GRÜNHAGEN, I., 321, 324.

† RAYNALDUS, ad an. 1470, N. 48; and PALACKY, IV., 2, 657, both give 1470 as the year of Carvajal's death. They are contradicted by AMMANATI, Comment., lib. VII., and the precise statement of the *Acta Consist., that on the 6th Dec., 1469, at the first hour of the night, the Card. Joannes tit. S. Angeli episc. Portuens., Camerlengo of the Sacred College, died "cuius anima per dei misericordiam propter sua infinita benemerita requiescat in pace." (Secret Archives of the Vatican.) A complete and really critical biography of Carvajal would be a very valuable work.

now sent another Ambassador, whom he hereby accredited to the Pope.*

If these endeavours at reconciliation were really sincere, the increasing danger from the Turkish power gave them a prospect of success. But when matters had gone so far a higher Hand intervened. On the 22nd February, 1471, Rokyzana, "the soul of all the anti-Catholic efforts of the Utraquists," died in Prague, and on the 22nd March George Podiebrad followed him. The opinion that the King was, before his death, reconciled to the Church is erroneous.† It is, however, certain that Gregor Heimburg, the man who had exercised so potent an influence on his anti-Roman policy, did, before his death (1472), make his peace with the Church.‡

The struggle about the Compacts, which were not really observed in any of the Utraquist Churches, was not terminated by the deaths of the spiritual and temporal chiefs of the party ; the Polish Prince Wladislaw, when elected by the Bohemians in May, 1471, as their King, was obliged expressly to bind himself to uphold them. The hopes cherished by the father of the newly-elected sovereign, that

---

* PALACKY, IV., 2, 657 seq.; see Urk. Beiträge, 639 seq.

† FRIND, IV., 75, speaks decidedly of George's conversion, and considers his interment in the Cathedral to be evidence of his reconciliation with the Church ; see, on the other hand, PALACKY, IV., 2, 665, N. 458. The testimony of COCHLAEUS, l. XII. (followed by PESSINA, Phosphorus septicornis, 292 [Prag., 1673], and VOIGT, III., 501, who does not reject the statement), cannot be considered of weight in this question ; every doubt, however, is removed by the Letter of Paul II. to Roverella (in THEINER, II., 425), where he expressly mentions "Georgius de Podiebrad damnate memorie."

‡ Heimburg applied by letter to Sixtus IV., who, inasmuch as the Holy See is not wont to refuse forgiveness to penitent sinners, gave the Bishop of Meissen full power to absolve him. BROCKHAUS, 383-4 ; and Cod. Dipl. Sax., 211 seq.

the Bohemian position would be recognised by Rome were accordingly without foundation ; for this was no mere question of externals, but a deep-seated and essential separation which might be for a time concealed by a formula of union, but could not be conclusively settled by any such means.*

* See HÖFLER, Gesch. der Husitischen Bewegung, I., xxxvi. ; III., 205. The fanaticism which possessed many of the Bohemians appears in the "Manifesto of Satan," written in the time of Sixtus IV., and published by JORDAN, 520 *seq*. This letter begins as follows : "We, Lucifer, by the power of fraud, King of the Kings of earth, holding the sceptre of the most illustrious Roman Emperor by virtue of our presence and residence near the tombs of the Holy Apostles Peter and Paul, where we have achieved the complete abandonment of the doctrine of Jesus and trodden His faith under our feet."

CHAPTER VI.

PAUL II.'S CARE FOR THE STATES OF THE CHURCH.—DESTRUC-
TION OF THE BANDIT FAMILY OF ANGUILLARA.—THE PEACE
OF 1468.—THE POPE'S DIFFERENCES WITH FERRANTE OF
NAPLES.—SECOND JOURNEY OF FREDERICK III. TO ROME.—
THE STRUGGLE REGARDING RIMINI.

PAUL II., who was by nature anything but warlike, was in
the early part of his reign more successful in his conflicts
with tyrants in the States of the Church than in his
expeditions against the Turks and Hussites.* The robber
Knights of Anguillara were the first to claim his attention.

The cruel Count Everso of Anguillara had already given
great trouble to his immediate predecessors. "During the
Pontificate of Pius II. he had taken possession of all the
territory formerly held by the Prefects, and there in his
mountain fortresses securely guarded the spoils gathered
from the plunder of towns, pilgrims, and merchants. Like
Malatesta, he had been the ally of all the enemies of the
Pope." Cardinal Ammanati says that he despised God and
the Saints and yet made pious foundations.† Much has

---

* Jacobus Trottus, Ambassador of Este, in a Postscript to a
*Despatch, dated Rome, 1469, Sept. 6, remarks of Paul II., "non e de
natura bellicosa." (State Archives, Modena.) See also CANENSIUS,
83.

† GREGOROVIUS, VII., 218, 3rd ed. See AMMANATI, Comment.,
351b; MASSIMO, Torre Ang., 12 *seq.*; ADINOLFI, Laterano e Via
Maggiore (Rome, 1857), Doc. 4; ROHAULT, Pl. 63; ARMELLINI,
272.

lately been heard of the portion of his Palace which still exists, a gloomy tower in Trastevere, which was in danger of falling a sacrifice to a destructive work of restoration. Happily this interesting building, which commands a splendid view of the City, has for the present escaped ; who can say, however, how long it may be spared ?

Count Everso, who had to the last defied Pius II., died on the 4th September, 1464.* His two sons, Francesco and Deifobo, began by making the fairest promises to the Pope, but soon betrayed a disposition to follow in the footsteps of their father, and ruin the peace of the whole neighbourhood. Paul II. then determined to make war upon this race of tyrants, who had braved the authority of four successive Popes, and were a scourge to that portion of the States of the Church. His prudence and caution enabled him to take the Counts completely by surprise.

At the end of June, 1465, the sentence of Excommunication was pronounced against them, and Cardinal Niccolo Forteguerri, Federigo of Urbino, and Napoleone Orsini,† at once advanced with an armed force. They were joined by troops from the King of Naples, who had a personal quarrel with Deifobo. Thirteen castles, some of which had been deemed impregnable from their position and fortifications, were taken almost without a blow. In these robbers' nests were found implements for coining Papal money, correspondence of a compromising character, and numbers of unhappy captives, doomed by the tyrants to perpetual

---

* Not on the 3rd September, as GREGOROVIUS, VII., 218, 3rd ed., says, following INFESSURA (1140), who is most unreliable, especially as to dates ; see in MASSIMO, 15, Everso's epitaph, which was formerly to be found in Sta Maria Maggiore ; this agrees with the statement in the Diario Nepesino, 141.

† See Paul II.'s Brief to Cesare de Varano, 10th June, 1465.   State Archives, Florence (Urbino).

imprisonment. Deifobo escaped to Venice; Francesco was imprisoned, together with his children, but was soon liberated at the instance of Stefano Colonna.* Twelve days sufficed to break the power of the Anguillara; the conquered towns and fortresses came under the immediate rule of the Holy See.†

The year 1465 also witnessed an extension of Papal authority in the Romagna. By virtue of the treaty concluded in 1463 with Pius II., the towns possessed by the Malatesta were, on the extinction of their line, to revert to the Holy See. Malatesta Novello, Lord of Cesena, dying childless on the 20th November, 1465, his nephew, Roberto, sought to occupy Cesena and Bertinoro. His efforts were, however, frustrated by the loyalty with which these cities adhered to the promise given to the Holy See. The inhabitants had good reasons for preferring immediate

* "*Francescho fiolo che fu del conte de Aversa è cavato de presone mediante la intercessione de Stefano Colona, quale ha fatto securtate de cento milia ducati," writes Bartholomaus de Maraschis to Marchioness Barbara, under date Rome, 1465, July 24. (Gonzaga Archives, Mantua.) Francesco seems to have been again imprisoned subsequently, for, on the 13th Aug., 1471, Sixtus IV. set him at liberty. This we learn from *Petrus de Modegnano in his Report of August 14. (State Archives, Milan.) REUMONT, III., 1, 175, gives 1475 as the year of Francesco's death. The epitaph in SCHRADER, Mon. Ital., 129, and GALLETTI, III., 156, however, have 1473, and FORCELLA, IV., 385, agrees with them. I found in Cod. Vat. 939, Vatican Library, an *Epistola ad nob. vir. Franc. de Anguilaria exhortatoria ad pacientiam (belonging to the time when he was in confinement at S. Angelos).

† For an account of the war against the Anguillara, see AMMANATI, Comment., 355 *seq.*, Epist., 71b, 77; Gasp. Veronen. in MURATORI, III., 2, 1014 *seq.*; N. DELLA TUCCIA, 270; CANENSIUS, 51–64; Diario Nepesino, 149–52; PLATINA, 772–3; Cronica di Bologna, 760–61; Chron. Eugub., 1009; BALDI, Fed. di Montef., III., 71 *seq.*; CIAMPI, Forteguerri, 14; ROSMINI, Milano, IV., 65; Arch. d. Soc. Rom., VII., 117–18, 179–82; X., 425–6.

dependence on the government of the Church, which allowed them far greater liberty, and did not harry them with oppressive taxation. In order to conciliate and win over the warlike Robert, Paul II. invested him with the fiefs of Meldola, Sarsina, and some other small places, and took him into his service as a captain of mercenaries.*

Not long after the downfall of the Anguillara, the Pope came into conflict with the King of Naples, " the terrible and faithless Ferrante."†

The unreasonable demands of the King, and his prevarications about the payment of his tribute, had, even at the beginning of the Pontificate, caused some estrangement between Naples and the Pope.‡ Although, according to the Bull of Investiture granted by Pius II., the severest penalties—such as Excommunication, Interdict, deposition from the throne, and forfeiture of his fief—were to be incurred by non-payment of the tribute, Ferrante steadily neglected it. " When called upon to pay, he never failed to find some excuse ; at one time he pleaded the great difficulties occa-

* SUGENHEIM, 341 ; REUMONT, Lorenzo, I., 179, 2nd ed. ; BALDI, III., 86 *seq.* ; TONINI, V., 308 *seq.* ; L'ÉPINOIS, 437. Rob. Malatesta's pay is entered on the 10th Oct., 1466, in *Div. Pauli II., Vol. II., f. 43. State Archives, Rome.

† Thus designated by GREGOROVIUS in the Augsburg Allg. Zeitung, 1870, N. 146. See GOTHEIN, 32. Bartholomaus de Maraschis, in the *Despatch of the 24th July, 1465, cited on p. 150, note*, tells how the Neapolitan troops, immediately after the downfall of the Anguillara, oppressed the Romans.

‡ See the *Letter of Otto de Carretto to Fr. Sforza, dated Rome, 1464, Oct. 14 and 24 (Ambrosian Library, Milan), and a *Letter of the 21st Oct., 1464, from the same Carretto in the State Archives at Milan. See the passage from a *Despatch of Nicodemus of the 31st Oct., 1469 (State Archives, Milan), given *infra*, p. 172, note *. When Federigo, the son of the King of Naples, came to Rome in April, 1465, he was treated with great honour. *Div. Pauli II., 1464–66, fol. 82b, contains records of money expended on this occasion. State Archives, Rome.

sioned by internal troubles, at another the expenses in which
he had been involved by his share in the war against the
Anguillara." The tension constantly increased. When
Ferrante, who already owed the Pope 60,000 golden ducats,
sent the customary palfrey, but not a farthing with it, the
Pope returned it. The King went so far as to threaten
that, if the claim were still insisted upon, he would entei
into alliance with the Turks, whereupon the Pope answered
that he would provide for having Ferrante driven from
his kingdom, and the Turks expelled from the Christian
dominions.*

The complicated relations which existed between Naples
and the Apostolic See made it possible for the King to
keep the Pope in perpetual alarm, by constantly making
fresh demands. The real ground of Ferrante's hostility
was the jealousy with which he viewed the consolidation
of the Papal power in the States of the Church, and
accordingly he harassed the Pope in every way that he
could.

The energetic measures of Paul II. against the lawless
Barons in the Roman territory " had not perfectly restored
peace ; feuds were constantly breaking out amongst them,
as well as amongst the lesser nobles, while bloody and
barbarous revenges were of frequent occurrence. Yet
much had been gained. The Pope laboured unremittingly,
by means of his Cardinals and Prelates, to bring about
reconciliations."† At the same time he did what he could

* CANENSIUS, 74-5 ; GASP. VERONEN., 1041 ; REUMONT, Lorenzo,
I., 220, 2nd ed. ; BORGIA, Dom. temp. nelle Sicil., 196-7, Rome, 1789,
2nd ed. According to GOTTLOB, Cam. Ap., Part 3, the *Introitus-
register of Paul II.'s pontificate records no payment of tribute by
Ferrante.

† REUMONT, III., 1, 157. See L'ÉPINOIS, 436. Regarding the
Pope's efforts to promote peace in Orvieto, see the documents in

to maintain among the Italian powers that peace which the danger of Turkish invasion rendered so necessary. His prompt action at the critical moment of the death of Francesco Sforza, which occurred on the 8th March, 1466, after an illness of but two days, was specially judicious and effective. This unexpected event caused the greatest consternation at the French Court,* as well as in Florence and in Rome, where the news arrived on the 16th March.† A Consistory was at once held, in which, at the Pope's suggestion, it was determined that the Holy See should use every possible means for the maintenance of peace. Paul II. forgot all previous differences with Milan, and sent a special Ambassador to express his sympathy, and declare his intention of standing by the Duchess and her children.‡ He also addressed Briefs to all the Italian Governments, informing them of his determination to maintain peace in the Peninsula, and earnestly exhorting them to avoid all disturbances.§ The warning was needed,

FUMI, 724–8. Paul II.'s *Briefs of the 17th Nov., 1470, to Card. S. Clementis (Ravenna), and the Episc. Firmanus, deal with troubles in the dominions of Todi and Spoleto. Lib. brev., 12, f. 36, Secret Archives of the Vatican.

* See the *Despatches of Panigarola and Em. de Jacopo to the Duchess of Milan, dated Orleans, 1466, March 23. Fonds Ital., 1611, National Library, Paris.

† *Letter of J. P. Arrivabene, dated Rome, 1466, March 17. (Gonzaga Archives.) See BUSER, Beziehungen, 134 seq.

‡ See A. de Rubeis' Report of the 18th March. Fonds Ital., 1613, National Library, Paris.

§ See PLATINA, 775 ; *PARENTI, Hist. Fiorent. (Original Manuscript in the National Library, Florence) ; MAGLIAB., XXV.–2–519, f. 2 ; and CANENSIUS, 70 seq. ; see also DESJARDINS, I., 137. A *Brief of Paul II. to Florence, dated Rome, 1466, xiii. Cal. April., and relating to this subject, is in the State Archives, Florence (X.–II.–23, f. 142–3) : the Republic is here urged to maintain peace in Italy. In the State Archives, Milan, I found a copy of a *Brief of similar import addressed

especially in regard to the Republic of St. Mark, whose policy had given the Pope just cause for dissatisfaction.* Many exiles from Florence had at this time betaken themselves to Venice to hatch in safety conspiracies against the rule of the Medici. The Signoria, ever ready to fish in troubled waters, while avoiding any open breach of the peace, by no means discouraged these plots. "The old grudge against Florence, on account of the defeat of their schemes against Milan by Cosmo, revived. The resentment of the banished Florentines was to be turned to account to establish a government there, which should be dependent on the support of Venice, and to overthrow the Sforzas in Milan."† Bartolommeo Colleone, an ambitious and avaricious Condottiere, was to be the instrument employed for the accomplishment of these designs. In order to enable the exiled Florentines to avail themselves of his services, the Signoria dismissed him with promises of money.‡

In face of the threatening attitude of Colleone, the Ambassadors of Florence, Naples and Milan, on the 4th January, 1467, entered into a defensive alliance at Rome, under the protection of Paul II., with a view of securing the

by Paul II. to the Doge of Venice, dated 1466, April 17, with an observation appended to the effect that letters of the same character had been sent to Naples, Ferrara, Mantua, and Siena.

* See Appendix, N. 14. *Letter of T. Maffei of the 15th June, 1466, and *supra*, p. 96 *seq*.

† REUMONT, Lorenzo, I., 173-4, 182, 2nd ed.   See BUSER, Beziehungen, 135 *seq*. Regarding the conspiracy in Florence, see PERRENS, 313 *seq*. Paul II. wrote a *Letter of condolence, dated Rome, 1466, Sept. 8, to the Florentine Government in reference to these troubles, which he characterises as dangerous to the city, and injurious to the peace of Italy and the war against the Turks. State Archives, Florence, X.-II.-23, f. 148b-149b.

‡ See PERRENS, 328.

peace of Italy.* This was a time of great anxiety for the
Pope; he placed no confidence in Ferrante, who shewed
symptoms of meditating an attack on the temporal possessions of the Holy See.† In the month of March the
Ambassador of Modena was of opinion that Ferrante would
declare war on the Pope.‡

Besides Colleone, the Florentine exiles took Ercole of
Este, Alessandro Sforza of Pesaro, Pino degli Ordelassi,
Lord of Forli, the Lords of Carpi and Galeotto de' Pici
della Mirandola into their pay. An army, 14,000 strong,
was assembled. The Republic of Florence engaged the
services of the Count of Urbino, while Ferrante sent
auxiliary troops, and Galeazzo Maria himself hurried to the
front, at the head of 6000 men. The two most famous
Italian Generals of the day, Colleone and Federigo of
Urbino, thus stood opposed to one another, each at the
head of a considerable force. On the 23rd July, 1467,
they met at La Molinella, in the territory of Imola; but
the battle led to no decisive result.§

After this action, more than half a year was spent "in
useless marches and entrenchments, and in wrangling,

---

* See MALIPIERO, 212 ; TRINCHERA, I., 1 *seq*., 6 *seq*. ; BUSER, Beziehungen, 139 ; DESJARDINS, I., 144 *seq*.; REUMONT, Lorenzo, I., 173,
183, 2nd ed. GREGOROVIUS, VII., 221, 3rd ed., is wrong in giving the
2nd January as the date of the conclusion of the League. A *Letter of
Augustinus de Rubeis, dated Rome, 1466, Dec. 6, throws important
light on the negotiations which preceded the treaty. State Archives,
Milan.

† *Letter of Card. Gonzaga of the 7th Jan., 1467. Gonzaga Archives ;
see Appendix, N. 18.

‡ "*Il me pare vedere che Re Ferrando [ha] voglia di guerra col
papa." Report of Jacobus Trottus, dated Rome, 1467, March 15.
State Archives, Modena.

§ LEO, III., 410 *seq*. ; REUMONT, Lorenzo, I., 183 *seq*., 2nd ed. ;
PERRENS, 331.

recriminations and negotiations."* At last Paul II. determined, on the Feast of the Purification, 1468, after Mass at Araceli on the Capitol, to proclaim peace by his own authority.† The Bull published on this occasion first insists on the necessity of peace in face of the danger from Turkey, then relates the efforts made by the Pope for the restoration of tranquillity, and requires Venice, Naples, Milan, and Florence, within the space of thirty days, to come to terms. Colleone was named General of the Christians, with a salary of a hundred thousand florins, to which all the Italian States were to contribute, and he was to carry on the war with the Turks in Albania ; the territory which he had won from the Florentines, and from Taddeo Manfredi of Imola, was to be restored within fifty days.‡

* REUMONT, Lorenzo, I., 188, 2nd ed. See SYBEL'S Hist. Zeitschr., XXIX., 329 seq. ; and CIPOLLA, 541 seq. Further lights are needed to explain the attitude of Paul II. during these negotiations. AMMANATI, Comment., lib. IV., is by no means an absolutely trustworthy authority ; nor can we, like SISMONDI, X., 324 seq., place complete confidence in G. B. PIGNA, l. VIII., who wrote in the time of Alfonso II.

† Until this time war had been threatening ; not till the 28th Jan., 1468, could Card. Gonzaga declare : *" Heri matina in concistoro secreto la Sta de N. S. concluse che omnino voleva pronunciare questa pace el di de la purificatione." Gonzaga Archives, Mantua.

‡ RAYNALDUS, ad an. 1468, N. 14–21 ; Bull. V., 189–94, where the Bull is wrongly assigned to the year 1467. See AMMANATI, Comment., l. IV. ; N. DELLA TUCCIA, 272 ; MALIPIERO, 231 seq. ; PALMERIUS, 250–51 ; SANUDO, 1185 ; Chron. Eugub., 1015 ; also SUMMONTE, IV., 564 ; and Arch. St. Napol., IX., 217. The Brief to Colleone, which accompanied the Bull, is in the Istor. Bresc., 911–12. On the 2nd February the Florentines were also informed by a *Brief of the conclusion of peace ; a Copy is in the State Archives, Florence, X.-II.-23, f. 170. A detailed account of the proclamation in Araceli is given in a *Report of Aug. de Rubeis and Joh. Blanchus, dated Rome, 1468, Febr. 3. (State Archives, Milan, Cart. Gen.) Expenses pro luminaribus pro pace publicanda are entered on the 1st Febr., 1468, in *Div.

Milan and Naples, however, would not do anything towards paying Colleone. A chronicler sums up their reply in the following words : " We desire peace, but as to Colleone, we will not give him even a biscuit." * Other difficulties were also raised ; and for some time it seemed as if the war must break out again. Paul II. was obliged to give up the stipulation regarding Colleone. On the 25th April peace was proclaimed in Rome, and soon afterwards in Florence, and celebrated everywhere with brilliant festivities. Some fresh obstacles were now created by Venice,† but finally these, too, were happily overcome, and on the Feast of the Ascension peace was proclaimed in the territories of the Republic.‡ By the 8th May the conditions

Pauli II., Vol. II. (State Archives, Rome.) Gold medals were struck to commemorate the conclusion of peace (MALIPIERO, 233). Domenico Galletti, on this occasion, addressed several poems to Paul II.; these are preserved in Cod. Vat., 3694 and 3695 ; Piero Luigi Galletti published them in a very rare pamphlet (Nozze-Publ.), Verona, 1787.

* Chron. Eugub., 1015.

† RAYNALDUS, ad an. 1468, N. 22 ; LANDUCCI, 10 ; Cr. di Bologna, 773 ; TRINCHERA, I., p. LVIII. seq.; *Letter of August. Patritius to Campanus, dated Rome, 1468, April 27 ; Cod. S. I. I., f. 117, of the Angelica Library, Rome ; *Letter of Card. Gonzaga, dated Rome, 1468, April 25 (Gonzaga Archives, Mantua) ; and *Despatch of Lorenzo da Pesaro to the Duke of Milan of the same date. This last Document begins with the words : *" Ad laude et gloria del omnipotente dio, de la sua madre madona S. Maria semper vergine et de S. Ambroscio, de S. Agnese, de S. Petro matiro et de tucta la corte celestiale, ad exaltation et grandeza del stato de V. J. S., &c., hoggi havemo firmata la pace in lo infrascr. modo." The Original and Copy are in the State Archives, Milan. Regarding the festivities in the States of the Church on occasion of the peace, see also PERUZZI, Ancona, 376 ; BONAZZI, Perugia, 683. As to the Republic of Florence, see P. BIGAZZI, Miscell. Stor., N. 3, p. 25 seq. (Florence, 1849).

‡ Ist. Bresc., 912. See CIPOLLA, 584 seq.; and ROMANIN, IV., 332, for the ratification.

had been officially drawn up in Rome in the Pope's presence.*

On Ascension Day there was a magnificent procession, in which Paul II. himself took part on foot. Hymns were composed for the occasion by Lionardo Dati and an eloquent discourse was pronounced by Domenico de' Domenichi.†

Paul II.'s satisfaction at the advent of peace was enhanced by the hope which it encouraged that Italy would now offer a serious resistance to the Turks. For this object he had already expended no less than the sum of two hundred thousand florins,‡ and his disappointment, when clouds again overspread the political horizon, must have been in proportion to his interest in the cause.

Ferrante of Naples was the disquieting element. In the summer of 1468, when Paul II. had attempted to occupy the important fortress of Tolfa, which commanded the alum mines, he had been prevented by the Neapolitan troops, who not only supported the Orsini, who were the lords of the soil, in their resistance, but even threatened Rome itself. The Pope was so much alarmed that he meditated flight. His most valuable property had already been hidden in St. Angelo, when the Neapolitan army turned against Sora.§

---

* Secret Archives of the Vatican. *Lib. rubeus (see our Vol. III., p. 245), f. 81 seq., and *Cod. B–19, f. 49, of the Vallicellana Library, Rome. RAYNALDUS, ad an. 1468, N. 25, makes use of the latter manuscript. See also MITTARELLI, Access. Faventinae, 337 (Venet., 1771).

† CANENSIUS, 82 ; AMMANATI, Epist., f. 143 seq., 165, 166b, 167. Domenichi's *Discourse, which QUIRINI, 287, intended to publish, is preserved in Cod. A 44, N. 9, of the Chapter Library, Padua, and in Cod. Ottob., 1035, f. 46–53, Vatican Library. Disbursements for the peace rejoicings on Ascension Day appear in the *Lib. III., Bullet. Pauli II., on the 22nd May, 1468. State Archives, Rome.

‡ See the *Brief of the 16th May, 1468, addressed to Florence. State Archives, Florence ; also Appendix, N. 23.

§ CANENSIUS, 84. See REUMONT, Diplomazia, 371.

During the contest for the throne of Naples, Pius II. had become Sovereign of this important Duchy, and he had maintained his rights over it against all the efforts of Ferrante. On the accession of Paul II., the King had again endeavoured to recover Sora. He now deemed the moment to have arrived for the forcible accomplishment of his object, and certainly the opportunity seemed favourable. Paul II., who always shrank from outlay for military purposes, was almost defenceless; in vain did he reproach the faithless Monarch with ingratitude towards the Holy See, to whose favour he owed his crown. Fortunately for him, Cardinal Roverella was successful in persuading Ferrante not to advance any further. In October, 1468, the Pope gave orders that fresh troops should be levied, to occupy the frontier between the States of the Church and Naples, which shews how little confidence he had in his neighbour.* Paul II. was unsuccessful in his attempts to obtain possession of Tolfa; subsequently, an amicable arrangement was arrived at, and in June, 1469, the Apostolic Treasury purchased the place for 17,300 golden ducats.†

Ferrante was also the Pope's chief opponent in regard to the territory of Malatesta.

In the October of 1468, Sigismondo Malatesta, who had

---

* Jacobus Trottus in a *Letter, dated Rome, 1468, October 28, says : *"Il papa ha molto ben forniti de fanti quelli suoi luoghi de confine dove el dubitava del Re." (State Archives, Modena.) See CONTA-TORE, 239–40. Blanchus, in a Report of the 28th March, 1468, in LAMANSKY, 765, speaks of the labours of Bessarion in favour of the Venetians. Regarding the claims of Ferrante, see Chron. Eugub., 1016.

† PLATINA, 774, 791; AMMANATI, Comment., 368 *seq*.; CANENSIUS, 83–8 ; THEINER, Cod. 456–8. *Lib. III., Bullet. Pauli II., contains entries of payments for war material for the conquest of the castrum Tolphe as late as August, 1468. State Archives of Rome.

not long returned from the Turkish war, died without leaving any legitimate heir, and accordingly, in virtue of the treaty which had been made, Paul II. justly claimed Rimini. Sigismondo's wife, Isotta, however, assumed the government of the city. Roberto Malatesta, who was at the time in Rome, promised the Pope, by oath and in writing, that he would deliver up Rimini to him.* Upon this he was at once commissioned to take possession of the city on behalf of the Holy See. But no sooner had he succeeded, with the assistance of the inhabitants, and by means of the subsidies granted by Paul II., in getting rid of the Venetian garrison and making himself master of the citadel, than he informed the Pope that he did not consider himself bound by the promise he had given. A secret alliance with the King of Naples encouraged him to venture on this step. "The Pope, finding himself thus betrayed, collected an army, and in a short time nearly all the Italian States were involved in the war about Rimini."†

Such was the political situation of the Italian Peninsula when Frederick III. determined to undertake a pilgrimage to Rome, in fulfilment of a vow which he had made in 1462, while a prisoner in the Castle of Vienna, and of which he had repeatedly postponed the accomplishment.‡ The

---

* On the 16th June, 1469, the Pope communicated copies of this promise to the King of Naples, the Duke of Milan, and the Florentines. *Transcripts of the letters, which are all of similar import, are in the State Archives at Venice and Florence.

† GREGOROVIUS, VII., 220 *seq.*, 3rd ed. ; SUGENHEIM, 342 ; LILIUS, Hist. di Camerino, II., 215 ; UGOLINI, I., 485 *seq.* ; TONINI, V., 325 *seq.* ; YRIARTE, 341 *seq.*

‡ Regarding the postponement of the journey, see LICHNOWSKY, VII., 113, and also TRINCHERA, I., 106, where is given a letter of the 8th April, 1467, from the King of Naples ; but even on the 16th February, 1467, J. P. Arrivabene wrote : *"La venuta del imperatore da octo di in qua se fa piu dubia che prima." Gonzaga Archives.

Emperor's suite was not a large one; it consisted of four-teen Princes and Counts, and a number of knights, and amounted altogether to 700 horsemen. All were in mourn-ing garb on account of the death of the Empress.*

Frederick travelled by the same route as that which he had followed sixteen years before; it led through Treviso to Padua, where the Venetian Ambassadors met him and paid their respects, then by Rovigo to Ferrara.† At Fran-colino on the Po, Borso d'Este welcomed his noble visitor.‡ From Ferrara the pilgrims continued their journey by Ravenna along the coast to the Sanctuary of Loreto.§ The gates of Rimini were closed by Robert Malatesta, who distrusted the Emperor. This obliged him to alter his route, but the swampy character of the ground compelled him again to approach the city. The inhabitants at once armed themselves and hastened to the walls, where they remained until the travellers were out of sight.‖ He met with even greater rudeness from the Ambassadors of Duke Galeazzo Maria Sforza, who, when informed by Frederick that he looked upon Milan as belonging to the Empire, had, we are told, the audacity to reply, that Galeazzo's father had won the Duchy by the sword,

* Gesch. W. von Schaumburg, 7; and GRAZIANI, 641. *LANDO FERRETTI, Storia d'Ancona (original Manuscript in Cod. H., III., 70, of the Chigi Library, Rome), f. 304, mentions "sei cento cavalli ben guarniti et molto all' ordine." The Diario Ferrar., 215, and CANENSIUS, 88, speak of only 500 as accompanying the Emperor.

† See in Appendix, N. 25, Tommaso Soderini's *Letter of the 29th Nov., 1468. State Archives, Florence.

‡ For an account of the honour paid to the Emperor in Ferrara, see Diario Ferrar., *loc. cit.*; Cronica di Bologna, 776; Annal. Bonon. 897.

§ On the 18th December, Frederick III. was at Ancona. See CIAVARINI, I., 186 (see PERUZZI, 373), and *L. FERRETTI, *loc. cit.*

‖ TONINI, V., 329, where for 1464 *read* 1468.

and that his son would not lose it save by the sword.*

Paul II. looked forward with some apprehension to the Emperor's arrival. He took precautions against possible disturbances in Rome by bringing large bodies of troops into the city.† Special Briefs were sent to all the officials of the States of the Church, desiring them to receive Frederick III. with honour, and to entertain him at the expense of the Holy See.‡ The Governor of the March of Ancona, by order of the Pope, accompanied the Emperor to Rome,§ and a number of members of the Papal Court were appointed to meet him.‖ On Christmas Eve Frederick approached the walls of Rome. He had proceeded by water from Otricoli to Castell Valcha, where Cardinals d'Estouteville and Piccolomini met him with a numerous escort.¶

He was met at Ponte Molle by the Vice-Camerlengo, the City Prefect, the Conservators, and the rest of the municipal authorities, with the Roman nobles, by command of the Pope. The Sacred College had a long time to wait at the Porta del Popolo. The late hour at which Frederick arrived made it difficult to carry out the order of the procession, every detail of which had been arranged by Paul II.**

* Chronic. Eugub., 1017.

† Chronic. Eugub., 1016 ; PLATINI, 785, and *Report of J. P. Arrivabene of Dec. 26, 1468, Gonzaga Archives, Mantua ; see Appendix, N. 26.

‡ *Brief to "Joh. Bapt. de Sabellis notario nostro civit. nostre Bononien. gubernatori," dated Romae, ap. S. Petrum, 1468, Dec. 6. (State Archives, Bologna.) Bolle e brevi, Q. 22. See also CANENSIUS, 89.

§ *L. FERRETTI, loc. cit., f. 305. Chigi Library, Rome.

‖ See Paul II.'s Brief to the Emperor, in MÜLLER, II., 320.

¶ *Report of J. P. Arrivabene ; see Appendix, N. 26.

** PATRITIUS, 207.

At this gate of the city, Bessarion made a speech, and he and Cardinal d'Estouteville then took their places, one on each side of the Emperor.   They then proceeded first to S. Marco, all the streets through which they passed being richly decorated.   The Emperor, clad in black, rode with the Cardinals under a baldacchino of white silk damask, embroidered with gold, and bearing the Papal and Imperial arms.   One of Frederick's suite estimated the number of torches in the procession at 3000.*

The Imperial pilgrim was met in front of St. Peter's by the clergy of the city bearing a cross and relics.   At the fifth hour of the night he entered the venerable Basilica, and, going at once to the tomb of the Prince of the Apostles, knelt " for a long time in prayer."   The Pope, who was very exact in matters of the kind, had most minutely arranged the ceremonial to be observed at the meeting of the two chief powers of Christendom.   This appeared to their contemporaries so significant as a token of the relations then existing between them, that Augustinus Patritius, the Papal Master of Ceremonies, carefully tran-scribed the whole in a special note-book.†

" As soon," Patritius says, " as the Emperor beheld the

---

* Gesch. W. von Schaumburg, 8. See AMMANATI, Comment., Lib. 7; Storia Napolit., 235; INFESSURA, 1141; and the *Report of J. P. Arriva-bene in Appendix, N. 26. (Gonzaga Archives.) Payments ad explan-andum et mundandum stratam de Ponte Mollo ad portam populi et . . . palatium s. Marci are noted in *Lib. III., Bullet. Pauli II.   State Archives, Rome.

† First made use of by RAYNALDUS, ad an. 1469, N. 1, from Cod. F., N. 73, of the Vallic. Library, and afterwards published from the same MS. by MABILLON, II., 256–72; PEZ, II., 609–622; and MURATORI, XXIII., 205 seq. I cite from this last. Patritius' account is also in Cod. Vat., 8090. There is nothing of interest to us in the Notula hist. de Frid. III. Imp. Romam, 1469, visitante in Cod. 4455, f. 366, of the Court Library, Vienna.

Pope upon his throne, he bent the knee before him, and repeated this act several times during his approach. When he had got up to the Pope, he did homage to the Vicar of Christ by kissing his feet. Paul II. bent his eyes upon Frederick with an expression of great benevolence, put his arms round him, and permitted him to kiss both his knees ; then he rose a little and embraced him warmly. He pointed out to him the place he was to take on his right hand above the Cardinals. The Emperor's seat, which had a back, was covered with green cloth, embroidered with gold ; the Papal throne was so placed that the Emperor's seat was at the same height as the feet of the Pope." After the conclusion of the ceremonies in St. Peter's, which were accompanied with chanted psalms, "the Emperor departed to a noble palace, hung with cloth of gold and precious tapestry, wherein he was to have his abode, and every one of his people, according to his rank and dignity, was conducted to a well-appointed chamber therein."*

The Christmas festival was celebrated with great splendour. "When it came to the holy Gospel," says Wilwolt von Schaumburg, "the Emperor put on a dalmatic. The Pope gave him, as was fitting, a costly hat ; they say that it must have been worth 8000 ducats. And when the Emperor was to begin singing the Gospel, one of the highest of his servants, who was appointed for the purpose, took the hat from his head, and put the naked sword, which was commonly carried before him, into his hand. The Emperor held it solemnly aloft, and ever and anon, while he sang the Gospel, he brandished the sword lustily."

After the Offertory, the Emperor was incensed next

---

* Gesch. W. von Schaumburg, 8. The Emperor lived in the part of the Palace which he had occupied in 1452. PATRITIUS, 209.

after the Pope; Paul II., having given him Holy Communion with his own hand, bestowed on him the kiss of peace. The Pope administered the Blessed Sacrament to the Emperor, Deacon and Sub-Deacon, under the species of Bread only, although it was usual to give the Chalice in such cases to all who communicated with him. On this occasion the practice was discontinued on account of the erroneous teaching of the Hussites.[*]

After the conclusion of Mass, the Pope and the Emperor venerated the veil of St. Veronica. Then Paul II. solemnly imparted his Blessing, and an Indulgence was proclaimed. After the customary form, the words, " and for our Emperor Frederick, that the Lord God may grant him victory over the heretical Bohemians, the Turks, and the other enemies of the Christian name," were added.

Throughout these solemnities, and during the days which followed them, Frederick III. behaved towards the Pope with the utmost respect and deference. When Paul II. returned his visit, he accompanied him back to his chamber, and, on New Year's Eve, when they quitted the Lateran together, Frederick sprung forward to hold the Pope's stirrup. The Pope, however, declared that he would not allow this, and refused to mount until the Emperor had dispensed him from receiving, and himself from rendering, this service. " The Pope's affability," Patritius observes, " was thought all the more of, because the credit of the Papacy is no less than in former times, and its power is far more considerable ; for God has so disposed things, that the Roman Church, through the sagacity of her Pontiffs, and especially of the present Pope, has so increased in power and wealth, that she can hold her own by the side

[*] PATRITIUS, 212. See AMMANATI, *loc. cit.* Heimburg's Apology in PALACKY, Urkundl. Beiträge, 657, shews that the Pope's precaution was not uncalled for.

of kingdoms of the first rank. The Roman Empire, on the other hand, has fallen into such deep decay, that nothing but the name is left to its chief. Under these altered circumstances, the smallest mark of honour comes to be very highly regarded." In the sequel he lays much stress on the Pope's courtesy towards the Emperor, and says that he treated him in all points as an equal.*

The ceremony at which, in presence of the Pope, the Emperor conferred knighthood on 125 Germans in the middle of the bridge over the Tiber, provided an imposing pageant for the Romans. On this occasion Frederick III. also declared Galeazzo Maria to have forfeited the Duchy of Milan, and granted investiture of this fief to his grandson.†

The first point to be discussed between Frederick III. and the Pope was the war against the Turks and the Hussites. A Public Consistory for this purpose was held but four days after Christmas. The Emperor began by declaring, through his spokesman, that it was not merely his vow which had brought him to Rome, but also his concern for the general good, and that he desired to learn the views of the Holy Father in regard to the measures to be adopted against the Turks. Paul II. caused all the efforts of the Holy See for this great object to be related, saying that his resources were now exhausted, and it had become the duty of the Emperor to counsel and to act. When Frederick explained that he had come to receive, and not to give, counsel, the Pope repeated what he had

---

* PATRITIUS, 215-6. See CANENSIUS, 89, and the *Report of J. P. Arrivabene of the 26th Dec., 1468, Gonzaga Archives ; see Appendix, N. 26. Regarding the visit to the Lateran, see ROHAULT, 251 *seq.*, 500, 502.

† CANENSIUS, 90 ; Chron. Eugub., 1017 ; PLATINA, 785 ; Gesch. W. von Schaumburg, 9 ; GREGOROVIUS, VII., 223, 3rd ed. See ADINOLFI, I., 16-17.

already said. The Emperor then, with his Counsellors and all the Ambassadors who were present, withdrew into an adjoining hall to deliberate on the subject, and remained there for an hour. As the result of their consultation, he proposed that a general assembly should be held at Constance, in the presence of the Emperor and the Pope. Afterwards, Ammanati informs us, most of those who were accustomed to weigh matters at that period doubted whether the proposal had originated from the Emperor, who might have been anxious to shew his zeal for the Faith, or from the politic Venetians. The Pope and the Cardinals, however, were agreed that the existing state of affairs did not demand such a measure, which past experience had shewn to be dangerous. It was at last settled that the Ambassadors of all the Christian Princes should be invited, in the name of the two heads of Christendom, to a Congress, to be held in Rome in September, and that the Venetians should be allowed to levy a tenth part from the clergy, the twentieth part from the Jews, and the thirtieth from the laity, in their dominions.*

It is equally hard to ascertain the exact nature of the claims which Frederick at this time made on the Pope, and the special purpose of the Imperial pilgrimage. According to Dlugoss,† he sought, but did not obtain, from the Holy See the confirmation of the succession in Hungary and Bohemia to himself and his son Maximilian. He would " seem also to have tried unsuccessfully to procure the transfer of the electoral vote belonging to the Crown of Bohemia to the house of Austria. The

* AMMANATI, Comment., I., 7, and Frederick III.'s letter in BONELLI, III., 271. See GEBHARDT, 46. As to the negotiations now carried on regarding the Brixen affair, see SINNACHER, VI., 558.

† DLUGOSSI Hist. Pol., II., 439.

Court of Rome looked upon King Matthias as its principal
champion in Christendom, and would consent to nothing
that would be distasteful to him. In reference to the
Crown of Bohemia, moreover, its views differed wholly
from those of the Emperor, as it desired the suppression
of this dignity."* The Emperor, on the other hand,
obtained the confirmation of the Order of St. George, as
also the commencement of the process of canonisation
of Margrave Leopold of the house of Babenberg, and the
erection of two Bishoprics, one at Vienna and one at
Wiener-Neustadt.† This last measure fulfilled a desire
which had been ardently cherished by Rudolf of Hapsburg.

On the 9th January, 1469, the Emperor left Rome,
enriched with many Indulgences, relics, precious stones,
and pearls.‡ The Pope had borne all the expenses of
his suite.§ Cardinals Capranica and Borgia escorted him

---

* PALACKY, IV., 2, 554 ; RAUCH, 34.

† GAMS, 321–2 ; POTTHAST, Bibl. Suppl., 440 ; and WIEDEMANN,
Beitr. z. Gesch. d. Bisthums Wiener-Neustadt, in the Œsterr. Viertel-
jahrschrift für Kath. Theol., 1864, III., 514 *seq.*, all give the year 1468
as that of the foundation of the Bishopric. The Bull in Cod. 9309
of the Court Library, Vienna, which the last-named author cites,
is certainly dated Romae, anno 1468, Jan. 18, but the note " pontif
nostri anno quinto " shews the document to belong to the year 1469.
The Bull for the erection of the Bishopric of Vienna, whose original
is in the Consistorial Archives of the Archbishop at Vienna, has
also " pont. nostri a° quinto" (this Bull is printed in Bull. V., 195 *seq.*,
but wrongly placed in the year 1468). On account of the opposition
of the Bishop of Passau it was not solemnly published until 1480 ;
see details in the exhaustive Study of Prof. KOPALLIK, in Wiener
Diöcesanbl., 1887, N. 2, and KEIBLINGER, I., 659.

‡ PATRITIUS, 216 ; INFESSURA, 1141 ; GRAZIANI, 641. The Cron. Rom.,
34, gives a wrong date, 19th, which is repeated by LICHNOWSKY, 115.

§ According to GOTTLOB, Cam. Ap., the festivities, the lodging,
and entertainment of Frederick's suite cost 6000 flor. auri ; the Pope
contributed 3690 florins from his private purse.

as far as Viterbo.   Here, as well as in Rome and throughout his return journey, Frederick III. conferred many
honours.*

Soon after the Emperor's return, the war, which Roberto
Malatesta's treacherous usurpation of Rimini had rendered
inevitable, broke forth.   The Pope and the Republic of
Venice, formerly rival claimants for the possession of the
city, now united against Roberto, who had deceived them
both.   On the 28th May, 1469, an alliance was concluded,
by which Venice undertook to assist the Pope energetically,
both by land and sea.†   Paul II. made haste to collect
troops, and took Napoleone Orsini and Alessandro Sforza
into his service.‡   Lorenzo Zane, Archbishop of Spalatro,
was appointed Legate for the Papal army.   The war began
in the month of June, and it seemed as if the crafty
Malatesta was doomed to destruction.§

Things, however, took a different turn.   Roberto's escape
was principally due to " Federigo of Montefeltre, an ancient

* N. DELLA TUCCIA, 94.   For an account of Frederick's homeward
journey, see SANSI, Storia, 64-5 ; PELLINI, 69 seq. ; BONAZZI, 684 ;
CRISTOFANI, 327 ; CINELLI, L'Imperiale castello presso Pesaro,
1881 ; Jahrb. der Preuss. Kunstf., IX., 166 ; BURCKHARDT, I.,
18 seq., 3rd ed. ; MURATORI, Ann. ad an. Regarding his sojourn
in Venice, see SANUDO, 1188 ; MALIPIERO, 237 ; Gesch. W. von
Schaumburg, 10 seq. ; MITTARELLI, 1015 ; and TODERINI, 13 seq.

† DUMONT, III., 1, 405 ; RAYNALDUS, ad an. 1469, N. 24 ;
ROMANIN, IV., 333, N. 2.

‡ A *Letter of Napoleone Orsini (S. R. E. armorum generalis
capitaneus) to Piero de' Medici, d. d. ex felicibus castris S. D. N.
apud flumen Toppini prope Fulgin. die II. Aug., 1469, is in the
State Archives, Florence, Av. il princ., f. 17, f. 736.

§ J. P. Arrivabene wrote from Rome to Mantua on the 20th June,
1469 : *" La impresa de Arimino per quanto se comprende dara
occasion de rumpere in tuto la guerra, perche se sente pur chel Re
fa adunare le gente suoe al Tronto."   Gonzaga Archives, Mantua.

enemy of his house, who unexpectedly became his friend and helper." Federigo, "the most powerful feudal lord in the States of the Church," looked upon "the Pope's zealous and successful efforts to diminish the number of feudal potentates in his territory" as a danger to himself.* For the same reason, not only the King of Naples, who was almost always more or less at variance with the Pope,† but also Milan and Florence, declared against him.‡ All these powers were agreed that "any increase of the authority of the Popes in their temporal principality," at the expense of its feudal nobility, was to be strenuously resisted. "The element of weakness, caused by the partition of the States of the Church among a number of feudal nobles," must be retained.§

The support of these allies emboldened Roberto Malatesta to command his General, Federigo of Montefeltre, to assume the offensive. On the 30th August, just when Rome was celebrating the sixth anniversary of Paul II.'s elevation to

---

* SUGENHEIM, 345.

† Jacobus Trottus, writing on the 15th April, 1469, says that the Pope was disposed for war, and only contemplated the ruin of the King. Another Ambassador from Este, Agostino de Bon, wrote on the 14th April, 1469 : *"Questo papa me pare ogni di ingrossa le sue gente. Lo cardinale de Napoli, che fu mio compagno in studio, me ha ditto, che lo Re de Napoli ha mandato a dire al papa che el volle intendere che homo el debba esser o de dio o del diavolo ; queste sono le parole formale e par voria fare certi capituli cum el papa, non sa ancora se se poterano acordare, ma pure me pare che lo Re ogni otto di ge da una spelazata." State Archives, Modena.

‡ On the 16th June, 1469, Paul II. wrote to Florence : *"Hortamur in domino et summopere rogamus devotionem vestram ut tametsi Robertus ipse ad vestra stipendia conductus existit, nihilominus in hac re nihil ipsum iuvetis aut presidis prosequamini contra nos et S. R. E." State Archives, Florence, 11, X., dist. II., 25, f. 10–11.

§ SUGENHEIM, 344 ; UGOLINI, I., 487, 496 ; REUMONT, Diplomazia, 372 seq.

the Chair of St. Peter,* he attacked the Papal army, and completely routed it. Three thousand prisoners, a number of guns and other booty from the enemy's camp, were seized by the victors. Amongst the spoils was all the Legate's silver plate.†

The consequences of this victory might have been serious, but Federigo of Montefeltre shrank from attacking the actual territory of the Holy See. He contented himself with subjugating thirty castles and the territories of Rimini and Fano to the authority of Roberto Malatesta, and then, in November, 1469, disbanded his troops.‡

The co-operation of Florence and Naples, which had made this successful resistance on the part of his rebellious vassal possible, deeply incensed the Pope. Before the assembled Consistory he broke forth into bitter complaints of the Medici and of Ferrante. "The King," he said to the Milanese Ambassador, " immediately after my elevation, demanded the surrender of Ascoli and other things so preposterous that I can never be his friend. He is so

---

* J. Trottus' account in a **Letter of the 30th August, 1469. State Archives, Modena.

† See AMMANATI, Comment., I., 5, f. 375 *seq.* ; Epist., 174 *seq.*, 176 *seq.* Vespas. da Bisticci in MAI, I., 107–108 ; TONINI, V., 336 *seq.* ; SUGENHEIM, 344 ; REUMONT, III., 1, 157 ; and ROHRBACHER-KNÖPFLER, 236, follow Muratori in naming the 23rd August as the day of the battle. The date given above is that in the Annal. Forliv., 228, and in the document in REUMONT, Diplomazia, 373. The Cronica di Bologna, 777, has the 29th ; CANENSIUS, 92, and NOTAR GIACOMO, 116–17, mention the 31st August. On the 5th Sept., 1469, *J. Trottus declares that the Pope had received a letter concerning the defeat. (State Archives, Modena.) *Angelus Azarolus informs Pietro Dietisalvi, ex Ferrara, 2nd Sept., 1469, that the army of the Church had been defeated, " e forsi piu grossamente che non si dice qui." State Archives, Florence, Strozz., 365, f. 88.

‡ Cronica di Bologna, 777.

crafty and malignant that no one can trust him.   Moreover, he is no son of King Alfonso's; Pope Calixtus told me the names of his real parents."*

The confederates were in no way intimidated either by Paul II.'s complaints or by the warlike preparations which he carried on with much energy.†   On the contrary, in July, 1470, Naples, Milan, and Florence renewed their alliance, and determined, with their united forces, to protect Malatesta against the Pope, not only in the possession of Rimini, but also "in that of all the conquests which he had since made in the States of the Church or might yet make, unless within two months the Pope should agree, on his restoration of these spoils, to be reconciled to him and to invest him with the remainder of his family dominions."‡

Hard as it was for Paul II., he was compelled to yield, for he knew that his Venetian countrymen and allies were

---

* I find this statement, which has not hitherto been made public, in a *Letter from Nicodemus de Pontremoli, dated Rome, 1469, Oct. 31. Speaking of Paul II., he says : *"Poi disse de le stranie cose havia volute da lui fui ad havergli facto domandare Ascoli quamprimum fo assumpto al pontificato et altre domande adeo enorme che mai gli poria esser amico, ne persona se posseva fidare de lui, tanto è ficto e de mala natura, fin a dirmi non è figliolo del Re Alphonso et como papa Calisto gli havia dicto el patre et la matre, quali ha dicti ad me." State Archives, Milan, Pot. Est.

† In a *Despatch, dated Rome, 1469, Sept. 14, J. P. Arrivabene says : *"Qui non se attende ad altro se non a le provision de remetter queste gente eccles." (Gonzaga Archives, Mantua.) The preparations were considered very onerous. "All the Cardinals," wrote *Angelo Acciaioli from Rome on the 12th Dec., 1469, "wish for peace, but with honour to the Pope and the maintenance of the States of the Church." On the 20th Dec., 1469, he wrote : *"La S. de N. S. non può lasciare Arimino sanza gran vergogna e carico suo e damno della chiesa." Both these *Despatches are in the State Archives, Modena.

‡ DUMONT, III., 1, 354 seq., 408 ; MORBIO, VI., 377, 393 seq. ; SUGENHEIM, 345.

playing a very double game, "more intent on the extension of their own power in the Romagna than on the support of the Papal government."* A yet more decisive influence was exercised by an event which now filled Christendom in general and Italy in particular with fear : Negropont was taken by the Turks.†

* REUMONT, III., 1, 157–8 ; BALAN, V., 198. Regarding the delay of the Venetian subsidies, see the *Letter of J. Trottus of the 30th Aug., 1469. State Archives, Modena.

† Malatesta was not actually put in possession of the fief of Rimini and its territory until after the death of Paul II. ; see TONINI, V., 347 seq. ; BALDI, III., 208.

CHAPTER VII.

THE FALL OF NEGROPONT, AND THE NEGOTIATIONS IN ITALY AND
GERMANY REGARDING THE TURKISH QUESTION.—THE DIGNITY
OF DUKE OF FERRARA CONFERRED UPON BORSO D'ESTE.—
SUDDEN DEATH OF THE POPE.

EVER since the naval fortunes of Venice had, under the
command of Niccolò Canale (1468), taken a more favourable
turn, Sultan Mahomet, with the energy which was his
characteristic, had laboured to increase and improve his
fleet. Many new ships of war were built, and numerous
Jews and Greeks, then deemed the best seamen, were
engaged to man them. In the spring of 1470, he thought
that the favourable moment had arrived for avenging his
former defeat and dealing a crushing blow to the Venetian
power. Mahomet himself set out for Greece at the head of
an army more than 100,000 strong, while Mahmoud Pasha,
with a fleet of about 400 vessels, 100 of which were men-of-war,
put to sea. In the latter half of June the tidings that this
great expedition was on the way reached Venice, and from
thence passed on to Rome.* It was not yet known for
certain that Euboea, " the pearl of the Italian dominions in

* **Letter of Cardinal Gonzaga to his father, dated Rome, 1470,
June 30 (Gonzaga Archives, Mantua); here, as well as in MALIPIERO,
51, the number of Turkish vessels is given at 400 ; other authorities
mention 300 ; see Cronica di Bologna, 779 ; *Letter of A. Hyvanus of
the 19th Aug., 1470, Cod. 3477, f. 3b, of the Court Library, Vienna.
See also MAGISTRETTI, 341.

Greece," was its goal, but the greatness of the peril was manifest. A Consistory was at once summoned in an unusual manner by the Pope ; Cardinal Gonzaga informs us that he was prepared, for the sake of restoring peace in Italy, to renounce his claim to Rimini and the other places taken from him in the war, and that a Congregation of Cardinals was appointed to take counsel regarding further measures.* In view of the confusion prevailing in the whole of Europe, and more particularly in Italy, and the failure of all former attempts † at combination against the ancestral enemy of Christian civilisation, the task was somewhat hopeless. Yet Paul II. at once issued an urgent general appeal for help. King Ferrante of Naples, who, next to Venice, seemed the most immediately threatened, declared his readiness not only to join a general alliance of all the Christian powers, but also to enter into a special agreement with Venice and Rome. As the bitter enmity which existed between Venice and Milan left little prospect of a general alliance among the Princes of Christendom, Paul II., forgetting the injuries which he had received from

---

* This Consistory, which has hitherto remained unknown, is mentioned by Cardinal Gonzaga in the **Letter cited in note on previous p.

† The accounts of the Congress held in Rome, in the autumn of 1469, to deliberate on the measures to be taken against the Turks and Hussites, are very scanty. Frederick III. sent Hinderbach on this occasion as his representative (BONELLI, III., 270-71). The passage of many Envoys is mentioned by N. DELLA TUCCIA, 97. It appears from a *Letter of the City of Cologne to Dr "Wolter van Bilssen," dated 1469, June 22 (Cologne City Archives, Letter-book 29, f. 33b), that even the German cities were called upon by Frederick III. to send Envoys. Nicodemus de Pontremoli, the representative of Milan, who was himself devoid of zeal for the Turkish war (see BUSER, Beziehungen, 153), in a *Letter dated Rome, 1469, Nov. 20, admits that the Pope had the cause much at heart (ha molto al core). State Archives, Milan.

the Neapolitan monarch, accepted his second proposal. He gave orders that eight of the Cardinals, postponing all other business, should assemble once in every four days to take counsel regarding the measures to be adopted. Their first meeting was held on the 8th August, at which time no answer had yet been received from either Milan or Florence to the Papal Briefs despatched to them at the same date as that to Naples. From the outset it was evident to all experienced persons that the negotiations were likely to be extremely protracted.* On the 3rd of August a fresh Brief had been addressed to Florence, and also to Milan, insisting on the imminent danger with which the siege of Negropont threatened Italy, and exhorting these powers to despatch Envoys.†

Meanwhile, the growing power of Islam had again given proofs of its strength ; on the 12th July, after a desperate resistance on the part of the besieged, Negropont, which had been accounted impregnable, had fallen into the hands of the Turks.‡ The terrible tidings caused the greatest consternation throughout Italy, and nowhere was the feeling more intense than in Venice. The Milanese Ambassador to that city, in a despatch of the 7th August, said that he had seen the proud nobles weep as if their own wives and children had been slain. "All Venice,"

---

* **Report of Jacobus Trottus to Borso of Este, dated Rome, 1470, Aug. 8. State Archives, Modena.

† MÜLLER, Doc., 211–12 ; where is also to be found the answer of the 8th of August expressed in terms of general goodwill.

‡ ZINKEISEN, II., 322 *seq.* ; VAST, 379 *seq.* ; ROMANIN, IV., 337 *seq.* ; Rivista Maritt., 1886, Luglio-Agosto, and Arch. Veneto, XXXII., P. II., p. 267. The Brief concerning Niccolo de Canale, given in part and without date by RAYNALDUS, ad an. 1470, N. 17, is in *Lib. brev. of the Secret Archives of the Vatican, 12, f. 61, dated 24th Dec., 1470. See Bibliofilo, VII., 40.

he added, some days later, "is struck with dismay ; the inhabitants, half-dead with fear, say that the loss of all their possessions on the mainland would have been a less disaster."* " The glory and credit of Venice are destroyed," wrote the chronicler Malipiero, " our pride is humbled."†

The conquest of Euboea by the Turks was in fact an event of such importance that the latest historian of Greece considers it as the close of an epoch. All the Greeks, with the exception of a small fraction, were now in the clutch of the Sultan. Venice "was driven back into Crete and a few small islands and fortresses on the outer rim of Greece."‡

The alarm of the Venetians was increased by the strained relations which existed between them and the Pope, the Emperor and the King of Hungary, as well as by the openly hostile attitude of Duke Galeazzo Maria Sforza, who was the centre of a party which sought to take advantage of the misfortunes of the Republic, and recover the territory surrendered in 1454. In Bergamo, Crema, and Brescia an immediate invasion of Milanese troops was apprehended ; guards were doubled, and the work of strengthening the defences was carried on day and night.§ Happily, the King of Naples declared to the representative of Milan that, in presence of the actual danger from Turkey, he would take no part in any attack upon Venice.‖ The attitude of the King of

* See the Despatch from the Milanese State Archives in MAGIS-TRETTI, 347, see 101.

† MALIPIERO, 59. The terror was great in Naples and Sicily, where all the harbours were placed in a state of defence ; see BLASI, Storia di Sicilia, II., 648.

‡ HERTZBERG, II., 603 ; see III., 3 *seq.*

§ MAGISTRETTI. 81, 89, 92-4, 101, 106.

‖ *Ibid.*, 114, 116.

Hungary, on the other hand, was by no means reassuring. Paul II., however, with a true sense of his high position, laid aside all resentment against Venice, and laboured earnestly for the restoration of peace and the conclusion of an alliance against the Turks.* On the 25th August he informed all the Christian powers of the fall of Negropont, drew a vivid picture of the danger which lowered from the East, and urgently implored assistance: prompt action on their part, he said, would give him the greatest consolation.† The Pope earnestly entreated the Duke of Milan, who had attacked the Lords of Correggio, to lay down his arms, and urgently admonished the Venetians to desist from the works they had begun on the Mincio, which were a menace to the Marquess of Mantua, and were calculated to excite fresh troubles.‡ Paul II. himself set a good example, by determining to waive his rights regarding Rimini, and to refrain from punishing the Neapolitan King. On the 18th of September an invitation was addressed to all the Italian powers, calling upon them to send Ambassadors as soon as possible to Rome, in order to consult on measures for the general defence and the preservation of their own liberties.§

* See Paul II.'s *Brief to Florence of the 23rd Aug., 1470. State Archives, Florence, X.–II.–25, f. 25–6.

† **Brief to Frankfort-on-Maine, dat. Romae, 1470, Octavo Cal. Sept., in the Archives of that City. A similar Letter to Joh. de Sabaudia comes Gebennensis is in the State Archives, Turin, and the one to Cologne in the City Archives, Or. Pgm., arrived with the appended Bull, according to the entry in the Chancery, Nov. 23, 1470. I found in the R. T. A., I. (Sect. V.), f. 135, of the Kreisarchiv, Bamberg, a German translation of the Brief, also addressed to Margrave Albrecht of Brandenburg on the 25th August, 1470.

‡ RAYNALDUS, ad an. 1470, N. 39–40.

§ Ibid., ad an. 1470, N. 41. The reports prevalent at this time

The Pope had no more zealous supporter in his labours than Cardinal Bessarion, who addressed several long circular letters to the Italian Princes and people, vividly representing the magnitude of the common peril and the necessity for unanimous action against their cruel foe.* With the impression of his soul-stirring words fresh on their minds, the Italian Envoys commenced their deliberations in Rome. There were apprehensions to be removed and disputes to be settled, but at length the efforts of Paul II. were crowned with success.† On the 22nd December, 1470, a general defensive alliance of the Italian States against the Turks was concluded, on the basis of the League of Lodi, Roberto Malatesta being included among its members.‡ Public thanksgivings were offered and bonfires kindled throughout the States of the Church by desire of Paul II.§

concerning a defeat of the Turkish fleet were not confirmed; see the *Letter of Jacobus Azzarolus to Pietro Dietisalvi, dated Rome, 1470, Sept. 20: "Le novelle vostre della ropta della armata del Turcho non graniscono." C. STROZZ., 365, f. 106. State Archives, Florence.

* VAST, 385 *seq.* On the 13th Dec., 1470, Bessarion sent them to Guillaume Fichat, Prof. in Paris. See the *Cardinal's Letter of that date in Cod. Vat., 3586, Vatican Library.

† See RAYNALDUS, ad an. 1470, N. 38; and WÜRDTWEIN, Nov. Subs., XIII., pp. 68–70. Paul II. also speaks of his labours to promote a league of Italians in the *Brief of the 20th Dec., 1470, to the Duke of Modena, and explains that the representative of Modena, Jacobus Trottus, had been unjustly calumniated. Lib. brev., 12, f. 58, Secret Archives of the Vatican.

‡ LEIBNIZ, Cod. 429–30; DU MONT, III., 2, 29–30; RAYNALDUS, ad an. 1470, N. 42. See TRINCHERA, I., LX.

§ RAYNALDUS, ad an. 1470, N. 43. In the State Archives at Bologna I saw the original of the Brief published by Raynaldus from Lib. brev., and also by LÜNIG, Cod. Dipl. Ital., IV., 184–5. It bears the address: Joh. Bapt. de Sabellis, gub. Bononiae. (The Cr. di Bologna, 783, speaks of the joy which it awakened.) Similar

" But this time again the hopes of the Pope were far from
being realised.   Sforza did not ratify the treaty, ostensibly
because his wishes were disregarded in some unimportant
points in the draft of the document, but in reality because
he disliked committing himself to a war against the Turks.
Although the Florentine Signoria sent their ratification,
Guicciardini put it aside, because Lorenzo, who desired to
hold with Milan, and, like his grandfather, not to break
with the Sultan, had secretly instructed him not to sign."*

In France and Germany the prospect was not any
brighter.   The Pope sent special envoys to both countries.†
Cardinal Francesco Piccolomini, the Legate for Germany,
left Rome on the 18th March, 1471,‡ to proceed in the first
instance to Ratisbon, where a Diet was to open at the end
of April.

Piccolomini was chosen for this mission, first, on account
of his " distinguished personal qualities," and secondly,
because he could speak German,§ and was " a nephew of
Pius II., whose memory was still warmly cherished at the
Imperial Court."‖

---

*Documents were sent to gubernat. Marchie, rect. Campanie, gub.
Fani, Cesenae, Sore, &c.   (Information kindly furnished by Dr.
Fraknói, Vice-President of the Hungarian Academy.)

* REUMONT, Lorenzo, I., 222, 2nd ed.

† CANENSIUS, 95.

‡ *Acta Consist., f. 42, Secret Archives of the Vatican. Piccolomini's nomination as Legate in Alemaniam had taken place on the
18th February, *loc. cit.*

§ See A. Patritius in FREHER, II., 145. In a letter of 1485, the
Cardinal again alludes to his knowledge of the German language ; see
JANNER, III., 543.   It was, at this time, the custom of the Roman Court,
when possible, to send representatives acquainted with the language
of the countries to which they were accredited ; the contemporary
French Nuncio understood French ; see AMMANATI, Comment., l. VII.

‖ REISSERMAYER, I., 28-9 ; see II., 15.

He entered Ratisbon on the 1st May, where all his energies had first to be applied to the allaying of the ill-feeling occasioned by the prolonged delay of the Emperor. His position was by no means an easy one : " he desired and was even bound to defend the Emperor, and yet he could not altogether deny the justice of the complaints made by the impatient Assembly." * At last, on the 16th June, Frederick III. arrived, and "the great Christian Diet" began on the 24th. During the deliberations which ensued, the zeal displayed by Cardinal Piccolomini fully justified the repeated commendations of the Pope.† But neither his acknowledged eloquence, nor the urgent entreaties of the unhappy victims of the Turkish invasion from Croatia, Carniola, and Styria, sufficed to remove the manifold obstacles in the way of unanimous and energetic action. "The question of aid against the Turks proceeds so slowly," wrote an Italian Ambassador on the 7th July, "that the Cardinal Legate is wearied to death, and looks for little result from this Diet, on which he had built such great hopes." ‡ After fully four weeks of negotiations, no decisive resolution binding all the states of the Empire had been arrived at. "All went well till it came to the determination of the amount to be contributed by each power, because, up to that point, general promises and offers sufficed ; but when definite engagements were to be set down in black and white, difficulties of all kinds were raised, absurd pretexts invented, conditions imposed, and fresh proposals made to escape the obnoxious task." For a little while, to the delight of the Cardinal, things seemed again to take a more favourable turn ; but the issue of this

---

* REISSERMAYER, I., 54-5.

† See in Appendix, N. 37 and 39, the two *Briefs from the Secret Archives of the Vatican.

‡ Report of A. Bonattus in REISSERMAYER, II., 126.

Diet, the largest within the memory of man, was no better than that of those which had preceded it. "Private interests on all sides outweighed the general interests of the Empire."* Only two among the Princes—Ernest, Elector of Saxony, and Albrecht of Brandenburg, who had made his peace with the Pope at Ratisbon†—sent troops to the threatened frontiers; none of the others stirred.

"O the blindness of men!" exclaims Rodericus de Arevalo. "The Catholic Princes see the blazing torch of the infidel at their very doors, ready to set fire to all the kingdoms of Christendom, while they are squabbling each one for his portion. With their own eyes they behold the destruction of the Faithful, while every heathen jeers at their struggles to conquer each other, without thinking of saving themselves."‡

Besides the threatened danger from Turkey, the year 1471 had brought many other troubles to Paul II. At its very outset, disturbances had broken out in the Bolognese territory;§ in Florence, as well as in Venice, there had

* REISSERMAYER, II., 73 seq., 113 seq. See SCHWEIZER, Vorgesch. des schwäb. Bundes, 55 seq. (Zurich, 1876); and GOTHEIN, Volksbewegungen, 3 seq. and 42.

† See in Appendix, N. 41, the *Brief of 20th June, 1471. Secret Archives of the Vatican.

‡ "O mortalium ingenia sinistris passionibus tenebrata : vident catholici principes commune omnium regnorum incendium ab infidelibus parari, dum ipsi inter se super regnis concertant. Cernunt omnium fidelium naufragium, ipsi vero non de salute, sed ut ethnicus ille dicebat aut potius irridebat super gubernatione contendunt. Rodericus episc. Calagurritan. ad rev. patr. et dom. d. Rodericum Borja S. R. E. diacon. card. et vicecanc. liber de origine et differentia principatus imperialis et regalis et de antiquitate et iusticia utriusque." Cod. Vat., 4881, f. 1, Vatican Library. This MS. is richly adorned with miniatures, and is no doubt the copy presented to the Cardinal.

§ See Paul II.'s *Brief to Alex. de Perusio episcopatus nostri Bonon. vicarius, dat. Romae, 1471, Jan. 11. State Archives, Bologna, Q. 22.

been "troublesome discussions" about the contributions
for the Turkish war, and scarcely anywhere, either in
Italy or elsewhere, was any genuine zeal for the defence
of Christendom to be found.* Tidings of a very anxious
nature had come from the Knights of St. John at Rhodes.
It would appear that, for some time past, the Christians in
that island had completely lost heart. Paul II. hastened
to encourage the Knights to stand firm, promised assistance,
and exhorted them to put the fortifications of the island
into a state of thorough repair.† A serious attack
of the Turks might, under the actual circumstances of
the island, have been successful. Happily, no such
attempt was made, the attention of Mahomet being
at that time much engaged by the Turcoman Prince
Usunhassan.

Of all the Italian Princes, no one was on more friendly
terms with Paul II. than Duke Borso of Modena ; there
was much intellectual sympathy between them, both were
warm patrons of Art, and had a taste for external splendour,
which the Duke, as well as the Pope, believed to have a
great effect on the popular mind.‡ Borso's most ardent
desire was to add the ducal title of Ferrara to that of
Modena ; during the pontificate of Pius II. he had vainly

* In the *Brief of the 20th Dec., 1470, to the Duke of Modena,
mentioned in *supra*, p. 179, note †, Paul II. dwells on the confidence with
which he had hoped for aid from the Italians. Secret Archives of the
Vatican.

† See in Appendix, 30, 31, and 33, the *Briefs of 20th Jan. and 12th
March, 1471. With regard to the General Chapter of the Knights
of St. John, held in Rome, and the appointment by Paul II. of
Giambattista Orsini as Grand-Master (1467); see BOSIO, 234 *seq.*,
243 *seq.*

‡ See MÜNTZ, Renaissance, 328. Regarding Borso's promotion of
Art, see Atti d. Romagna, III., 388 *seq.*, 3rd Series ; and VENTURI in
the Rivist. St. Ital., II., 689-749.

laboured for the realisation of this wish.*   Under Paul II.
further negotiations were carried on, and, in the spring of
1471, they were brought to a successful conclusion.†

Borso came to Rome to receive his new dignity.   On
the 13th March he left Ferrara with an almost royal train.
The Lords of Carpi, Correggio, Mirandola, and Scandiano
formed part of the company, and a host of nobles and
knights ; there were more than 700 horses and 250 mules, all
adorned with costly trappings, and some of them bearing the
arms of Este.   Paul II. sent his friend, the Archbishop of
Spalatro, to welcome the Duke,‡ who, on his arrival in
Rome, was received by Cardinals Barbo and Gonzaga, all
the great Barons, the Ambassadors, the Senate, and all
the other city dignitaries.   A contemporary informs us
that, in the opinion of the Romans, no such honours had
ever been accorded to any King or Emperor as were now
paid to Borso.§   Festal music resounded through the
richly-decorated streets which he traversed on his way
to the Vatican.   Shouts of " Paulo, Paulo ! Borso, Borso !"

* See a *Letter from Card. Gonzaga to his father, dated Rome, 1463,
Feb. 15.   Gonzaga Archives, Mantua.

† Considering the good relations which existed between Paul II.
and Borso, it is somewhat strange to find a *Brief addressed to him
on the 31st Dec., 1470, admonishing him to pay his tribute, inasmuch
as the Apostolic Treasury has to meet great expenses in the defence
of the Catholic Faith.   Lib. brev., 12, f. 63b.   Secret Archives of the
Vatican.

‡ See in Appendix, N. 32, the *Brief of 3rd March, 1471, from the
State Archives, Modena.

§ Atti d. deput. p. le prov. Moden., II., 307 (1864).   Besides the
description here given from the Archives of Modena, see the continua-
tion of the Chron. Estense in MURATORI, XV., 542 ; INFESSURA,
1142, and especially a very detailed *Report from the Jurist Franciscus
Ariostus to Ercole d'Este, dated Rome, 1471, April 3 (not 1, as
GREGOROVIUS, VII., 224, 3rd ed., has it).   Cod. J., VII., 261, Chigi
Library, Rome.

from the crowd mingled with the clang of the trumpets. The Pope received his visitor seated on a throne adorned with gold and ivory, and the Palace of Cardinal Castiglione, which adjoined the Vatican, was assigned to him as his residence.* The rest of his followers were provided for, at the expense of the Apostolic Treasury, in the numerous inns which then existed in Rome.†

On Palm Sunday, after Mass, Paul II. assembled the Cardinals and informed them of his intention regarding Borso. They all approved of the Pope's decision, and the Duke was then called in. Paul II. told him what had passed, and Borso warmly expressed his gratitude.‡

* "*Questo e uno magno regale et eminente pallazo non molto distante dal pontificale quale gia la recolenda memoria de monsignor Constanciense haveassi fabricado cum spesa non vulgare e cum admirabile inzegno." F. Ariostus in the *Report cited in note § on preceding page. I intend elsewhere to publish his description of the street decorations, which is of value as bearing on the history of Renaissance Art and culture.

† *Lib. quintus Bullet. Pauli II., p. 205 *seq.*, gives the payments pro infrascriptis personis hospitibus in alma urbe et pro expens. fact. d. march. Ferrarie—in all flor. aur. de cam. septem millia noningentos triginta octo, b. XLIIII., d. XII. This sum represents only a part of the outlay, which, according to CANENSIUS, 96, amounted to 14,000 golden florins ; in the same *Lib. quintus other payments are entered, *e.g.*, "pro luminaribus in dicto castro [S. Angeli] pro adventu ill. ducis Mutine." 1st April, 1471. These records have a special interest from the fact that they give the names of the Roman inns of the period. We have *Hospes ad solem, ad spatam, ad turrim, ad navim, ad stellam, ad navim in campo florae, ad camellum, ad coronam, ad lunam, ad scutum, ad angelum, ad S. Catherinam, ad galeam* and *Hospitissa ad dalphinum* and *ad S. Triffonem*. (State Archives, Rome.) Some of these names are still kept up. See the unhappily incomplete Notizie storiche intorno alla origine dei nomi di alcune osterie, etc., di Roma, by A. Rufini, Roma, 1855.

‡ *Letter of Cardinal Fr. Gonzaga of 1st April, 1471. Gonzaga Archives, Mantua.

Easter Sunday (14th April) was the day fixed for Borso's
solemn investiture with the title of Duke of Ferrara.*
All the Cardinals, Bishops, and Prelates then in Rome,
together with all the members of the Court, were assembled
in the Basilica of the Prince of the Apostles, where Borso
was in the first place made a Knight of St. Peter.   The
Pope himself handed him a naked sword, saying : " Take
this in the name of the Father, the Son, and the Holy
Ghost, and use it for your own defence and that of God's
Holy Church, and for the destruction of the enemies of
the holy Cross and of the Faith."   The High Mass then
began, the music being rendered by the Papal Choir.†
When the Epistle had been sung, Borso took the oath
of allegiance to the Pope.   After the Communion, he
and his followers received the Sacred Host from the
hands of Paul II., who then bestowed on Borso the

---

* For the following account, see, besides Borso's short letter of
the 16th April, 1471, which was known to PIGNA, Hist. d. princ.
d'Este, 617 (Ferrara, 1570), and is published in the Atti d. st. patr.
d. prov. Mod., II., 307–308 ; (*a*) Lettera inedita di Borso d'Este
scritta in Roma il di 15 Aprile 1471, al suo segretario Giovanni
di Compagno, printed in honour of a wedding, Ferrara, 1869 ;
(*b*) a *Description (Latin and Italian) of all the festivities by
the Ferrarese, Franciscus Ariostus, dated ex urbe Roma Cal. Maii,
1471, and dedicated to Duke Ercole (regarding F. Ariostus, see
MAZZUCHELLI, I., 2, 1058), in Cod. J., VII., 261 (not T. VII., as
CORVISIERI, in his otherwise correct description of the MS. in Arch.
Rom., I., 467, has it), Chigi Library, Rome.   My copy of this MS.
occupies 160 quarto pages, which may give an idea of the detailed
character of the Report.   It is of special interest in connection with
the history of civilisation, and I shall again revert to it.

† " *Non altramente haresti sentido, magnanime signore divo
Hercule, ussire di quel choro de piu excellentissimi cantori un
concerto de tante melodie nello intonar quello sancto introito
ricevendo cum maravigliosi signi de letitia la S. Sanctita."   F.
Ariostus, *loc. cit.*

Ducal robes and the other insignia of his new dignity. The veneration of the Veil of St. Veronica, the Papal Benediction, and the proclamation of a Plenary Indulgence closed this imposing function, which was witnessed by an immense multitude gathered from far and near.* When Borso sought to accompany the Pope back to his apartments, his Holiness desired the Cardinals to pay that token of respect to the Duke, who was enchanted with the distinctions heaped upon him. He wrote to his Secretary: "We have been treated as if we were a King or an Emperor."

On the following day Borso accompanied the Pope to St. Peter's, and there received the Golden Rose. From there he rode, carrying the Rose, to the Palace of S. Marco, where a great banquet was prepared. During the ensuing days the same pomp and ceremony were displayed in various other entertainments provided for the new Duke, especially at a grand hunting-party, in which many of the Cardinals took part.†

After all these festivities were over, the Duke still lingered in Rome. The extraordinary honours of which he was the object, and his frequent interviews with the Pope, had, from the time of his arrival, attracted general attention. Even the Cardinals were kept in the dark as to the subjects of these conversations. With a view of obtaining some information, Cardinal Gonzaga told Borso of the pleasure which it had given him to hear it said at the Court that the Pope meant to accompany the Duke back to Ferrara ; and further expressed his opinion, that, considering the dispositions of Germany and the perpetual demands of

---

* The Diario Ferrar., 228, and F. Ariostus give 200,000 as the number of those present, but this is certainly an exaggerated estimate.

† CANENSIUS, 96.

France for a Council, such an Assembly might with advantage be held in that City. Borso replied that the Cardinal's view was most reasonable, adding: "Would to God that every one thought the same." "These words," wrote the Cardinal to his father, "make me think that something of the sort may be in the wind." In a second conversation the Duke expressed his confident hope of bringing the Pope to Ferrara. Cardinal Battista Zeno, the Pope's nephew, at this time said that it would be wise to hold a Congress at some suitable place in Italy, for that by doing so in time, and of his own accord, the Pope would avoid the danger of having it forced upon him, when also some undesirable place would probably be selected.*

The learned Bishop of Calahorra, Rodericus Sancius de Arevalo, had some years previously, in a treatise dedicated to Cardinal Bessarion, declared against the holding of a Council, the demand for which had always been the war-cry of the opposition. Nothing of the sort was required to deal with either the Turkish question or that of Reform. Hard fighting, not a Congress, was the means by which the Infidels must be repelled. From the outset of his pontificate, Paul II. had done everything in his power to protect Christendom against them. The example of the Synod of Basle was not one to encourage another attempt of the kind. And as to the Congress of Mantua, it had

* These particulars, previously unknown, are taken from a *Letter of Cardinal Gonzaga, written on the 10th April, 1471, which I found in the Gonzaga Archives, Mantua, and have printed in Appendix, N. 35. The first half of the *Considerationes de concilium generale congregandi utilitate et necessitate, belonging to the year 1471, in Cod. 4 of the Kremsmünster Library, deals with the demand for a Council. See thereon H. SCHMID, Cat. Cod. manuscript, Bibl. Cremf., I., 66. From ROMANIN, IV., 353, where, unfortunately, the exact quotation is wanting, it appears that Venice also at this time asked for a Congress or Council.

been utterly fruitless, and even prejudicial, for it had made the disunion of Christendom patent to the Turks.*

Another project to which Paul II. had turned his mind seemed far more likely to prove beneficial than the meeting of a Congress. This was an alliance with the enemies of the Sultan in the East, and especially with the Turcoman Prince, Usunhassan, who was now at the summit of his power.† Following the example of the Venetians and of his predecessors, Calixtus III. and Pius II., Paul II. leagued himself with this Prince, the only one among the Oriental rulers who could venture to measure swords with Mahomet. Usunhassan indeed made such solemn promises of co-operation against the common foe,‡ that powerful aid from the East seemed a certainty. At this crisis Paul II. suddenly died.

The Pope, whose constitution was naturally strong, had appeared to be in excellent health. At the beginning of his reign he had suffered from the dangerous Roman fever ; § in 1466, and again in 1468, he had been ill, but had quite recovered ;‖ at this moment there seemed no cause for apprehension.

---

* *Roderici Calaguritani, De remediis afflictae ecclesiae, Cod. Z.-L.-XC., f. 11 and 27b, St. Mark's Library, Venice. Regarding other manuscript copies of this work, see our Vol. II., p. 55, note *. In the year 1466 Rodericus Sancius dedicated to Pope Paul II. his *Defensorium ecclesie et status ecclesiastici contra querulos, detractores et emulos sublimitatis, auctoritatis et honoris Romani pontificis nec non praelatorum et ceterorum ministrorum ecclesie. Cod. Vat., 4106. Vatican Library.

† MÜLLER, Islam, 325 *seq.*, 340 ; HEYD, II., 326.

‡ RAYNALDUS, ad an. 1471, N. 48.

§ *Despatch of Laurentius de Pensauro to Fr. Sforza of 27th Oct., 1464. (State Archives, Milan.) See also *Card. Gonzaga's Letter of 8th Oct., 1464. Gonzaga Archives.

‖ See CANENSIUS, 101, and the *Letter of Barth. de Maraschis of 1st Sept., 1466, in the Gonzaga Archives, Mantua, see Appendix, N. 17.

On the morning of the 26th July the Pope was perfectly well, and had held a Consistory lasting for six hours ; he then dined bare-headed in the garden* and freely indulged his taste for melons and other indigestible food. At the first hour of the night he felt ill, and his chamberlain advised him to postpone the audiences usually granted at that time, and to rest for a while. Paul II. was suffering from a sense of oppression and lay down on a bed, while the chamberlain left the room to dismiss those who were waiting without. After an hour had passed, he heard a knocking on the door of the bed-chamber, hurried in, and found the Pope half-insensible and foaming at the mouth. With difficulty he lifted the sick man on to a bench and rushed out to summon assistance. By the time he returned the Pope had expired, having died of a stroke. Cardinal Barbo was at once called, and the corpse, accompanied by a few torches, was borne to St. Peter's.† Here the obsequies

---

In reference to the illness of 1468, Giacomo Trotti, in a *Despatch, dated Rome, 1468, May 21, says : *" N. S. hora non da audientia ni a cardinali ni a persona del mondo. Il se ha sentito malo e se medecina." According to a *Despatch of 15th June, the indisposition of the Pope continued up to that time : no audiences were granted. The Plague was then raging in Rome ; see in Appendix, N. 24, the *Letter of G. Trotti of 8th July, 1468. All these letters are in the State Archives, Modena.

* CANENSIUS, 103.

† See in the Appendix, N. 42, Nicodemus of Pontremoli's Report, which I found in the State Archives at Milan. One of the last cares of Paul II. regarded the health of the Duke of Ferrara ; see in Appendix, N. 38 and 40, the *Briefs of the 10th and 20th July, 1471. (Secret Archives of the Vatican.) On the 27th July the Archbishop of Milan, writing to Galeazzo Maria Sforza, to inform him of the Pope's death, said, " che è stato uno stupore maraviglioso ateso che era sanissimo piu fosse stato gran tempo fa." The Cardinals at once assembled, made some preliminary arrangements, and summoned their absent colleagues. Nardini reluctantly undertook the " governo di Roma."

for the departed took place ; * the mortal remains of Paul
II. were deposited in an imposing monument erected by
Cardinal Barbo in the Chapel of St. Andrew.   It was the
work of Mino da Fiesole, " an artist who exercised a very
important influence on sepulchral decoration, and with
whom began a new and brilliant epoch in monumental
art."   Fragments of the tomb are still to be seen scattered
about in the Grotto of St. Peter's.†

   " Pope Paul," says the chronicler of Viterbo, " was a
just, holy, and   peaceable   man ;   he   established   good
government in all parts of his dominions." ‡   His labours,
as a practical ruler, to strengthen and consolidate the
authority of the Holy See throughout the States of the
Church, may   indeed   be   considered   one   of the   chief
characteristics of his reign.   A modern historian sums
up his judgment of the Pope in the following words :
" Paul II. was certainly a born ruler, and one animated
by the most noble intentions.   It may be regretted that
the mitre was compelled to give way too much to the
tiara, and that his pontificate displayed an   excess of
worldly splendour, but it cannot be said that ecclesiastical
interests suffered in any direct way from this.   In many

(State Archives, Milan.)   On the 27th July the Cardinals announced
the death of the head of the Church.   Letters to this effect are to be
seen in the Archives of Florence (X.–II.–25, f. 35a, b), and in those of
Milan ; the latter is marked, *cito, cito.*

   * According to information kindly furnished by Dr. Gottlob, 13,610
pounds of wax, costing about 1852 florins, were consumed on this
occasion ; 6062 flor. 10 bolog. were also paid " pro broccato auri ac
pro pannis lane ac aliis rebus eiusmodi . . . ratione exequiarum fe. re.
dom. Pauli pape II."   State Archives, Rome.

   † REUMONT, III., 1, 399 *seq.* See GREGOROVIUS, Grabmäler, 98.
BURCKHARDT, Cicerone, II., 372 *seq.*, 4th ed., speaks in less favourable
terms of this monument.   See also MÜNTZ, II., 48-9.

   ‡ N. DELLA TUCCIA, 98.

matters he was a zealous reformer.   Witnesses who are
above suspicion attest his determination in opposing all
simoniacal practices.   If, weighed down beneath the burden
of affairs, he was not always successful in accomplishing
the good he desired, we must not be harsh in our judgment
of one whose uprightness is admitted even by his enemies.
The nepotism from which he was not free, never took
the offensive and mischievous form which we have to
lament in his immediate successor.   Even his enemies
do not venture to say that it was ever hurtful to the
Church." *   In opposition to Platina's calumnies, it must
be remembered that Paul II. opposed only that heathen
abuse of learning which seemed dangerous to religion ;
apart from that he encouraged it.   It was not the learning
of the Humanists that he hated, but that tendency which
Dante characterised as the stench of heathenism.†   All
Platina's other charges against the Pope are merely in-
sinuations, not facts.   " How virtuous," concludes a non-
Catholic scholar, " must he have been when so diligent
and malicious an enemy as this Humanist could bring
forward so little against him." ‡

The statement that Paul II. did not realise the Turkish
danger is also unjust.   It is true that this war was not
the one all-engrossing object of his life, as it had been
with Pius II., but the silence of those who hated him
most is in itself a proof that no cause of complaint can be
found against him on this head.   Recent investigations,
moreover, have brought to light many facts which are
much to his credit.§   It is impossible that a conclusive
judgment can be formed until our information is completed

* ROHRBACHER-KNÖPFLER, 238 ; REUMONT, III., 1, 160.

† Parad., XX., 125.

‡ CREIGHTON, III., 275.

§ See GOTTLOB in the Hist. Jahrb., IV., 443, and Cam. Apost.

by further examination of the Archives. We have, as yet, before us but scanty particulars as to the negotiations which took place in 1471 for the purpose of organising defensive measures against the Osmanli. A newly-discovered letter of Cardinal Gonzaga, written on the 17th of January in that year, shews that Paul II. was prepared to devote 50,000 ducats, the quarter of his annual income, to the expenses of the Turkish war.* This sum does not include the revenue derived from the Alum monopoly, which, from the beginning of his reign, he had assigned to the objects of the Crusade. Subsidies and pensions were provided out of these funds for all the unfortunate exiles who had been driven by Turkish conquests to take refuge in the States of the Church. The account-books of his pontificate are full of entries of this description, sometimes reaching the annual amount of 20,000 to 30,000 ducats. The name of Thomas, the dethroned Despot of the Morea, appears as the recipient of a monthly pension of 300 florins. After the death of Thomas, the Pope continued this allowance to his children, who were brought up under the care of Cardinal Bessarion.† Catherine, Queen-Mother of Bosnia, who migrated to Rome in 1466, from that time received 100 florins a month, and in the following year a further annual allowance of 240 florins was made to her for the rent of her house.‡ To the Despot Leonard of Arta, were

* The Venetians were dissatisfied with these offers of the Pope. See Appendix, N. 29.

† FALLMERAYER, Morea, II., 404. See our Vol. III., p. 251, and also, for an account of the death of Thomas, **J. de Aretio's Despatch of the 21st May, 1465. (Gonzaga Archives.) In the *Div. Pauli II., 1464–1466, f. 100 (also f. 112, 126, 135, &c.), payments are entered "pro filiis bon. mem. olim dom. Thome Paleologi Amoree despoti" from Sept. 5, 1465. State Archives, Rome.

‡ She lodged with the "prudens vir Jacobus Mentebone." For

granted, " as assistance in the war against the Turks,"
1000 golden florins on the 12th March, 1465, 1200 on the
18th July, 1466, and another 1000 on the 2nd April, 1467.
Monthly pensions were likewise bestowed on Queen
Charlotte of Cyprus, Prince John Zacharias of Samos,
Nicolaus Jacobus, a citizen of Constantinople, Thomas
Zalonich, and many others. From the year 1467 the
Archbishop of Mitylene and the Despot of Servia also
received regular allowances, which were supplemented by
occasional presents.*

These facts prove the princely liberality of Paul II. It
is also worth noting that now, as on many subsequent
occasions, possession of the States of the Church enabled
the Holy See to offer an asylum to the persecuted and
exiled, and to succour the oppressed and unfortunate.
" The dominions of the Church have a characteristic which
distinguishes them from all other kingdoms ; in contra-
distinction to the exclusiveness of other States, they partake
of the Catholicity of the Church. They form a separate
realm ; but as their Monarch is the Supreme Head of
Christendom, this realm is the common patrimony of all
Christians. No nationality is excluded from its offices and
dignities, and its educational institutions and Convents are
open to all races." †

these particulars I am indebted to the kindness of my friend, Dr.
Gottlob, who intends to publish a complete list of those assisted by
the funds of the Cruciata, founded on accurate study of the *Account-
books preserved in the Roman State Archives. Hist. Jahrb., VI., 443.
See *supra*, p. 28.

* As on 17th Dec., 1467, 200 gulden. State Archives, Rome.

† PHILLIPS, V., 708. In regard to the international character of the
Roman Court in the 15th Century, see our Vol. I., p. 242 *seq*. Amongst
Pius II.'s officials we find numerous Germans, several Englishmen, a
Burgundian, Bohemians, and Spaniards. At the Court of Paul II.
there were three Henrys, all of them Germans ; see MARINI, 152, 202.

BOOK II.

SIXTUS IV. 1471–1484.

CHAPTER I.

The Papal Election of 1471.—Ecclesiastical Career of Sixtus IV. and First Acts of his Government.—His Zeal for the War against the Turks.—Successes of the Papal Fleet.

THE death of Paul II. had occurred at a most critical moment. Steadily, like an advancing flood, the Turks streamed on to overwhelm the distracted West. It was not Italy alone which now found all barriers swept away between her coasts and the enemy. The defenceless frontiers of the Holy Roman Empire were overrun by these barbarian hordes, carrying rapine, murder, and devastation in their train as they pressed through Croatia into Styria. The terrible tidings of the destruction which threatened Italy and Germany alike, were well calculated to startle the most slothful from their slumber. Nevertheless, at the Diet which met at Ratisbon, under the "influence of the Turkish panic," next to nothing was accomplished ; the Papal Legate, Piccolomini, preached to deaf ears.[*] Italy, like Germany, was rent by internal dissensions : no one seemed to realise the serious character of the times. "As wave follows wave upon a storm-swept sea, so one political combination was perpetually giving way to another

[*] See *supra*, p. 181. Regarding the inroads of the Turks, see ZINKEISEN, II., 362 *seq.*; HASELBACH, 42; ILWOLF in the Mittheil. des Historischen Vereins für Steiermark, X., 222 *seq.*; and HUBER, III., 224.

in a restless, aimless succession. This everlasting change of relations, this possibility of being at once mutually friendly and hostile; the impossibility of having any clear certainty of the position, at any given moment, of any State towards its neighbour, became more and more the characteristic of Italian political life."*

During the vacancy of the Holy See in 1471, the Province of Romagna, always more or less unquiet, gave special cause for anxiety.† Considerable excitement also prevailed in Rome. Immediately after the death of Paul II., the Secular Canons of the Lateran had, with the assistance of their Roman friends, driven out the Regular Canons introduced by the deceased Pontiff. On the 28th July a deputation from the people of Rome appeared in front of the Minerva, where the Cardinals had assembled, demanding, amongst other things, that, for the future, benefices in Rome should be conferred on none but Romans, and that the income destined for the Roman University should no longer be diverted to other objects. The Cardinals answered in a conciliatory manner, whereupon an order was issued that all should lay down their weapons, and that the outlaws should leave Rome. This did much to soothe the popular feeling. Other concessions were also made to the Romans. On the morning of the 29th, forty prisoners, confined in the Capitol for minor offences, were set at liberty. The Cardinals released two citizens of Ascoli and a Baron suspected of heresy, who were imprisoned in the dungeons of St. Angelo, on condition that they should not depart from Rome before the Coronation of the new Pontiff.‡

---

* Buser, Beziehungen, 155.

† *Letter of J. P. Arrivabene, dated Rome, 1471, Aug. 6. (Gonzaga Archives, Mantua.) See N. della Tuccia, 100.

‡ **Letter of Joh. Blanchus de Cremona to the Duke of Milan, dated Rome, 1471, July 29. (State Archives, Milan.) The imprisoned Baron

The City continued tolerably quiet during the ensuing days.*

Sixteen Cardinals were in Rome when Paul II. died. Of those who were absent, none but Roverella and Gonzaga were able to reach the City in time for the Election. Roverella, Legate of Perugia, arrived on the 1st, and Gonzaga on the 4th August.† Many persons expected that the latter would be Pope, others thought the election of Cardinal Forteguerri more probable.‡ A Milanese Ambassador insists on the importance of the Turkish question in regard to the Election; he mentions the persons apparently best fitted to bring about its solution, in connection with the two parties, the Piischi and Pauleschi, already existing in the Sacred College. Of the former, he names in the first place, Forteguerri, then Eroli, Ammanati, and Roverella. Among the Pauleschi he looks upon Amicus Agnifilus and Francesco della Rovere as the most likely candidates.§

The preponderance of the Italian element on this occasion was very remarkable. Of the eighteen electors, all but three (Bessarion, d'Estouteville, and Borgia) were Italians. The thirteen years which had elapsed since the Conclave of

---

was probably the nobleman from Poli mentioned *supra*, p. 113. For a further account of the Canons of the Lateran, see CANENSIUS, 45 ; ROHAULT, 253 ; MAZZUCHELLI, I., 2, 882.

  * *Letter of the same Ambassador, dated Rome, 1471, Aug. 1. (State Archives, Milan.) See *ibid.*, a *Letter from Nicodemus of the 2nd Aug., 1471.

  † *Acta Consist., f. 42b, Secret Archives of the Vatican.

  ‡ REUMONT, Lorenzo, I., 243, 2nd ed. In regard to Forteguerri, J. Blanchus, in a *Despatch of the 1st Aug., 1471, wrote : " *La opinione grandissima del s. pontificato persevera molto sopra Thiano." State Archives, Milan.

  § Second *Letter of J. Blanchus to the Duke of Milan, dated Rome, 1471, July 29. (State Archives, Milan.) See *supra*, p. 124, note *.

Pius II. had brought great changes, and the ascendancy of the foreign Cardinals was at an end.*

Foremost among the aspirants to the Tiara were Cardinals d'Estouteville and Orsini. The former eagerly endeavoured to secure the support of the powerful Duke of Milan. A confidential person was employed to inform him that his brother, Ascanio Sforza, would receive the red hat, and that he himself might be the wearer of a royal crown in the event of d'Estouteville's success.† The wealthy Cardinal Orsini, a man of great capacity for business, was equally energetic in his efforts to obtain the supreme dignity. His brothers and relations had assembled in the neighbourhood of Rome, and it was reported that the former had determined to procure his elevation to the Papal Throne, whether by fair means or foul, and that the King of Naples favoured their design. The Ambassador of Mantua confirms this statement, and adds that Orsini, if his own cause seemed hopeless, would espouse that of Forteguerri and Eroli.‡ Even before the beginning of the Conclave, serious differences occurred between Cardinals Orsini and Bessarion;

---

* The Conclave of 1458 was composed of eight Italian and ten foreign Cardinals ; see our Vol. III., p. 6. The distribution of creations during the last four pontificates was as follows : four Italians, six Frenchmen, one Spaniard, and one German were raised to the purple by Nicholas V. ; four Italians, three Spaniards, one Portuguese, and one Frenchman by Calixtus III. (see our Vol. II., p. 457 *seq.*, and PANVINIUS, 302 *seq.*) ; eight Italians, two Frenchmen, one Spaniard, and one German by Pius II. ; and seven Italians, one Englishman, one Hungarian, and one Frenchman by Paul II. See our Vol. III., p. 293, and *supra*, p. 119.

† **Letter of Paulus Gazurrus de Novaria cap^{nus} d. rev^{mi} Rhotomag. to Duke Galeazzo Maria, dated Rome, 1471, July 29. State Archives, Milan.

‡ Besides the **Letter of P. Gazurrus, cited above, see that of J. P. Arrivabene of the 6th Aug., 1471. Gonzaga Archives, Mantua.

the latter declared that he would not, under any circumstances, suffer the Election to be carried out in the same
way as the last had been. Controversies also arose regarding the admission of Cardinals Savelli and Foscari, who had
not yet been published. Orsini desired their exclusion,
and his opinion prevailed.*

On the morning of the 6th August, after the solemn
obsequies of Paul II. had been concluded, the Mass of the
Holy Ghost was sung, and the College of Cardinals went in
procession into the Conclave in the Vatican. There were
seventeen present, and on the following day Cardinal
Ammanati, who had been delayed by indisposition, was
added to the number.†

On the morning of the 9th August, Francesco della
Rovere, Cardinal of S. Pietro in Vincoli, was elected
Pope.‡ As the Conclave had commenced on the feast
of Pope Sixtus II., the new Pontiff assumed the name
of Sixtus IV.

A number of fresh documents regarding the proceedings
of the Conclave are now before us ; they do much to
complete the scanty details hitherto known, but leave
some important matters still obscure. By far the most
valuable of these are in the State Archives at Milan. They
consist of two lists of the Electors, with an exact account,
on the one hand, of which candidate each Cardinal voted

* See *Despatch of Pietro de Modegnano, dated Rome, 1471, Aug. 1.
(State Archives, Milan.) See PETRUCELLI DELLA GATTINA, 293.

† *Acta Consist., *loc. cit.*, Secret Archives of the Vatican.
REUMONT, III., 1, 163 ; CHRISTOPHE, 209 ; and ROHRBACHER-
KNÖPFLER, 238, are mistaken in asserting that there were nineteen
Cardinals. VAST, Bessarion, 398, makes the Conclave begin on the
20th July !

‡ See the *Despatch of J. P. Arrivabene, dated Rome, 1471, Aug. 9.
(Gonzaga Archives.) Also Appendix, N. 44.

for, and on the other of the number of votes received by each, with the names of the voters.*

The faithful and capable Nicodemus de Pontremoli managed to procure these lists for the Duke, his master, who had expressed a great desire for trustworthy Reports of the Conclave. The Ambassador himself was far from over-estimating their value, and, in order at the present day to appreciate them fairly, it is necessary to bear his observations in mind. After dwelling on the difficulty of obtaining these lists, he draws attention to the fact that most of the Cardinals in the Conclave voted for those whose votes they hoped by this means to win, and not for those whose Election they really desired ; some few, he adds, reserved their votes to conceal secret engagements.† According to these lists, which, unfortunately, do not enable us clearly to distinguish the several scrutinies, Roverella and Calandrini were at first seriously thought of in the Conclave, each of them receiving seven votes ; Bessarion ‡ and Forteguerri followed next, each with six ; d'Estouteville had only four in all, and Orsini but two. The same authority informs us that Cardinals Giovanni Michele, Teodoro of Montferrat, Battista Zeno, Roverella, Forteguerri, Agnifilus, Bessarion, Calandrini, and Orsini gave their votes for Francesco della Rovere ; Borgia, d'Estouteville, and Barbo afterwards adding theirs.

* See Appendix, N. 43. These two lists agree, with only two exceptions ; they are on separate sheets, and have hitherto escaped notice.

† **Despatch of Nicodemus de Pontremoli, dated Rome, 1471, Aug. 20. (State Archives, Milan.) When transmitting the lists on the 28th August to the Duke, the Ambassador again refers to these explanations ; see Appendix, N. 46.

‡ The Venetians had begged their friends in the Sacred College to give him their support ; see G. Colli's Despatch of the 2nd Aug., 1471, in Arch. d. Soc. Rom., XI., 254.

The omission of the name of Cardinal Gonzaga from among the supporters of Rovere in the report of Nicodemus is very strange, for all the other accounts are unanimous in asserting that his Election was chiefly due to Orsini, Borgia, and Gonzaga, and that they were liberally rewarded for their share in securing it.* Ample testimony exists in proof of the part taken by Cardinal Gonzaga. A Despatch from the Ambassador of Mantua to his mother details the reasons which had induced him to espouse the cause of Rovere. In the first place, there was the hope of winning the favour of the future Pope ; secondly, Rovere was a person acceptable to the Duke of Milan ; and thirdly, d'Estouteville had no prospect of success. Accordingly, says the Ambassador, our most gracious Lord Cardinal has taken the greatest trouble on behalf of Cardinal della Rovere, so that it may be said that he, more than any one, has made him Pope. His Holiness has shewn his gratitude by confirming him in his appointment as Legate, and authorising him, if he chooses, to perform his duties by proxy. Moreover, the Abbey of S. Gregorio in Rome has been conferred on the Cardinal, and I believe that he will also have the Bishopric of Albano. The Ambassador then expressly says that the tenth vote for Rovere was given by Cardinal Gonzaga, the eleventh by Barbo, and the twelfth by d'Estouteville.† The Duke of Milan's share in securing the election of Sixtus IV. is confirmed by so many other authorities that we may look upon it as clearly established.‡

* Regarding Borgia's share in the matter, see AMMANATI, Epist. (Frankfort edition), N. 534.

† **Letter of J. P. Arrivabene, dated Rome, 1471, Aug. 11. Gonzaga Archives, Mantua.

‡ In a second *Letter of the 28th Aug., 1471, Nicodemus informs his master that the Pope was grateful to the Duke : " vide

No mention, however, is made in the Ambassadorial Despatches of the part which, according to two chroniclers, the Franciscan Pietro Riario had in the election. Cardinal della Rovere brought him into the Conclave, where he was very useful to his patron in winning for him many undecided votes.* The Election Capitulation, to observe which Sixtus IV. was obliged solemnly to bind himself, is also only alluded to in these Despatches.†

The election of Cardinal Francesco della Rovere caused great joy throughout Rome, especially, Nicodemus informs us, because the well-known piety and holiness of his life led all to hope that he would be an excellent Pastor for the Church and for the Christian Faith everywhere.‡ Francesco, like Nicholas V., owed his elevation to the purple to his reputation as a learned theologian and a man of blameless life. He belonged to an ancient, but impoverished, Ligurian family, and was related to the

et intese quel fo operato pro lui in nome vestro." State Archives, Milan.

* COBELLI, 258, and INFESSURA, 1143.

† On the 13th Aug., 1471, J. A. Ferrofinus relates that on the aforesaid day the Pope had shewn to the Cardinals at St. Angelo Paul II.'s jewels : "de le quali secondo m' ha detto Rhoano hanno *capitulato* in conclavi che non possa disponere ma le conservi a li bisogni de la fede." (State Archives, Milan.) No doubt, then, an Election Capitulation was drawn up in 1471. See also *infra*, p. 211, and the *Despatch of B. Bonattus of 13th Dec., 1471, given in Chapter II., p. 235, and the statement in MAI, Spic., I., 198, that Roverella would not promise anything in the Conclave which might refer to the Election Capitulation.

‡ *Despatch of the 9th Aug., 1471. (State Archives, Milan.) See Appendix, N. 44. The election caused great satisfaction also in the States of the Church ; see Cr. di Bologna, 788, and *Ghirardacci ; also *infra*, p. 206, note †. N. DELLA TUCCIA, 100, speaks of Sixtus IV. as "omo umile e di buona complessione." See SIGISMONDO DE' CONTI, I., 5.

Piedmontese Rovere, Lords of Vinovo.* His father, Lionardo, lived in modest circumstances in the little village
of Abezzola, not far from Savona. To escape from an infectious disease which broke out there, he and his wife,
Luchina Monleone, migrated to Celle on the sea-coast,
and here Francesco was born.†

In consequence of his repeated sicknesses, Francesco's
pious mother consecrated him by vow to St. Francis ;
and, in spite of the opposition of some worldly-minded
relations, entrusted him, when nine years of age, to the
care of the Minorite, Giovanni Pinarolo. Under the
guidance of this excellent religious, the gifted boy learned
to know and esteem the monastic life to which he was
destined to devote himself. Later, he went to the High
School of Chieri, and finally to the Universities of Pavia
and Bologna, where he studied philosophy and theology.
" His talent for dialectics was displayed for the first time
in the General Chapter of his Order held at Genoa when
he was only twenty. On that occasion he acquitted
himself so well in the Latin disputation, that the General,
Guglielmo Casale, embraced him."‡ After he had completed his philosophical and theological studies at Padua,
he undertook the duties of Professor, and taught with

---

* Francesco's letter of 1468 in VILLENEUVE, 31, contradicts the
assertion in REUMONT, Lorenzo, I., 243, 2nd ed., that nothing was
heard of this relationship until he became Pope.

† PLATINA, Vita, Sixti IV., 1053 seq., is the principal authority for
all the following particulars. His detailed narrative gives us what
those most nearly concerned then believed to be true ; see SCHMAR-
SOW, 3, N. 1. We have also a poem, composed in 1477, and entitled
*Lucubraciunculae Tiburtinae cuiusdam protonotarii, which I generally
cite from the MS. in the Court Library, Vienna (Cod. 2403), where
I found it, and an *Oratio ad Sixtum IV., by Naldo Naldi in Cod. 45,
C. 18, f. 113b–117, in the Corsini Library, Rome.

‡ FRANTZ, Sixtus IV., 132 ; MAGENTA, I., 355.

great success at Padua,* Bologna,† Pavia, Siena, Florence, and Perugia.‡ The attendance at his lectures was so great that Johannes Argyropulos and Bonfrancesco Arlati subsequently declared that every learned man in Italy had been a disciple of Rovere's. Cardinal Bessarion is expressly mentioned as having been among his hearers, and ever after having held him in the greatest esteem. So much was this the case, that from that time he would not publish any of his works until the great Franciscan philosopher and theologian had revised and corrected them.§

Francesco was also a distinguished preacher, and was, on many important occasions, a support to the General of his Order. He was afterwards called to fill the post of Procurator in Rome. When the General, Jacopo de Sarzuela, felt the burden of office too heavy for his advanced age, he chose Francesco " as his Vicar for the whole of Italy, and made him Provincial of the Ligurian Province of

* In Naldo Naldi's Oration, cited in preceding page, note †, he speaks in the following terms of Francesco's labours in the City of Padua : *" In ea enim cum homines min. ordinis domi theologiam edoceres, tantus populariter ad te concursus audientium factus est, quod publicis etiam illius civitatis institutis munus tibi philosophie precepta tradendi demandatum esset, ut multi praestantes viri, quidam etiam ex ipsa usque Grecia interessent." According to Naldo, Francesco also professed philosophy in Rome. Cod. 45, C. 18, f. 114, Corsini Library, Rome.

† See *Ghirardacci, St. di Bologna, Cod. 768, University Library, Bologna. The affection of the Bolognese, many of whom were personally acquainted with the new Pope, was, Ghirardacci informs us, manifested in the splendid Embassy sent in 1471 to congratulate him.

‡ See GRAZIANI, 644, and BINI, Mem. Ist. della Perug. Univ., I., 1, 515 seq. (Perugia, 1816).

§ See the testimony of L. Carbo from Cod. Vat., 1195, in SCHMARSOW, 335–6, and CREIGHTON, III., 57.

the Order, where he was very successful in carrying out measures of monastic reform." *

He won yet greater renown by the part which he took in the disputation regarding the Precious Blood, held in December, 1462, in the Vatican before Pius II.† The learning and controversial ability which he then manifested doubtless had a share in bringing about his Election to the Generalate, at the great Chapter of the Franciscans held at Perugia in May, 1464.‡ He at once determined vigorously to undertake the reform of his Order. A violent fever laid him low for a time, but did not hinder the accomplishment of his purpose. The skill and care of Ambrosius Grifus § brought him safely through, and he hardly gave himself time to recover before beginning the work of visitation and reformation in the Franciscan Convents and the educational establishments connected with them.

Francesco so ably defended the privileges of the Institute over which he presided that Pope Paul II. abstained from the measures he had intended to take against the whole Order. A General Chapter was consequently held at Florence in 1467.‖ In the summer, the General went to his home to recruit his health, which had been impaired by his sojourn in Rome ; he then visited Pavia, and meant to proceed thence to Venice, and there to give theological lectures during the winter. He was ready to start on

* FRANTZ, Sixtus IV., 133.
† See our Vol. III., p. 286.
‡ WADDING, XIII., 344–5.
§ See the **Letter of " Franciscus de Saona " to the Duke of Milan, dated Bologna, 1465, Jan. 2, and also a *Brief of Sixtus IV. of the 15th Nov., 1471, to the same. Both documents are in the State Archives, Milan.
‖ WADDING, XIII., 397. I saw in the State Archives at Milan an Autograph *Letter of Franciscus de Saona to Duke Galeazzo Maria Sforza, dated Florence, 1467, Febr. 27.

the journey, when, at the end of September, a letter from Cardinal Gonzaga, accompanied by another from Bessarion, informed him that he had been created Cardinal on the 18th September, 1467, by Paul II.*

On the 15th November, 1467, the new member of the Sacred College reached Rome, where he received the red hat, and had S. Pietro in Vincoli † assigned to him as his titular Church. The condition of the Cardinal's Palace adjoining this venerable Basilica was so dilapidated that Francesco was at once obliged to restore it, a work which his poverty would have rendered impossible, had it not been for the assistance of his colleagues. In the purple, the Cardinal of S. Pietro in Vincoli, as he was styled, continued to be a simple Franciscan ; " in his house, which overlooked a great part of the ancient and of the modern City, questions of scholarship and ecclesiastical affairs were discussed, but no politics." ‡ Whatever leisure his new dignity allowed him was devoted to learned pursuits, and, during the four years of his Cardinalate, he published a number of works which brought him more and more into notice.

In the first place the Cardinal again took up the disputed question regarding the Precious Blood ; his work on the subject, dedicated to Paul II., was printed in Rome in 1470, together with a treatise " On the power of God." A

---

* See *Acta Consist., Secret Archives of the Vatican, and *supra*, p. 122. On the 24th Sept., 1467, Francesco still wrote as General to the Duke of Milan, and, on the 9th and 12th October, as Cardinal. I found these three Autograph *Letters, which are dated from Pavia, in the State Archives at Milan. According to AMMANATI, Ep., 529, and Vespas. da Bisticci (MAI, I., 194), Bessarion induced the Pope to raise Francesco to the purple ; regarding the affection entertained by Paul II. for him, see COBELLI, 258.

† *Acta Consist., Secret Archives of the Vatican : the 20th November is here named as the day of the *aperitio oris.*

‡ REUMONT, Lorenzo, I., 243, 2nd ed. ; VILLENEUVE, 8 and 31.

philosophical and theological dispute in the University of Louvain was the occasion of a writing entitled " De futuris contingentibus." A work on the Immaculate Conception bears witness to that devotion to the Blessed Virgin which continued unabated after his elevation to the Papal throne. With a view of composing the frequent disputes between the Dominicans and the brethren of his own Order, in which the one party appealed to Duns Scotus and the other to St. Thomas Aquinas, he endeavoured to shew that the two authorities, although differing in words, were really of one mind. In the midst of these labours the voice of his colleagues summoned him, at the age of fifty-seven, to fill the Chair of St. Peter.*

A portrait from the hand of his Court-painter, Melozzo da Forli, which is still preserved, represents the new Pope as a man of middle stature and strong, compact frame. The features are regular, the nose and forehead forming an

---

* SCHMARSOW, 6, where Duns Scotus is strangely confounded with Scotus Erigena. Regarding the learned writings of Sixtus IV., see CORTESIUS, XXXIX., Bibl. pontif., 203 *seq.* ; FABRICIUS, VI., 491 *seq.* ; CAVE, II., App., 187 ; QUIRINI, 283 *seq.* ; MÜNTZ, Renaiss., 354. In the eulogistic poem, *Lucubraciunculae Tiburtinae cuiusdam proto-notarii, written in 1477, which has been mentioned at p. 205, occur the following lines :—

> " Tris autem scripsit libros (ut opuscula nondum
>   Edita praeteream), quibus in tribus eminet eius
>   Ingenium excellens ingensque scientia rerum.
>   Ex iis unius titulis (si rite recordor)
>   Est de posse Dei, de contingentibus alter,
>   Tertius inscriptus liber est de sanguine Christi."

Cod. 2403, f. 5–5b, Court Library, Vienna. It is hard to understand how GEIGER, Renaissance, 152, can assert that Sixtus IV. was no scholar or respecter of mediæval theology, and that he had no right to the place which Benozzo Gozzoli assigns to him in his picture as an admirer and expounder of St. Thomas Aquinas.

oblique line, with a gentle curve between them. The powerful head impresses us with an idea of uncommon energy and force, which difficulties could not daunt ; while the lines on the brow bear witness to a life of hard and unremitting toil.

Sixtus IV. commenced his reign by conferring favours on the Cardinals, and in this proceeding formed such a contrast to his predecessor, that, as an Ambassador wrote, every one felt as if they were in a new world.* In the first place, those who had brought about his Election were rewarded. Cardinal Borgia received the Abbey of Subiaco *in commendam*, and Gonzaga that of S. Gregorio, while Orsini was made Camerlengo, and as such took the oath as early as the 12th August. The position of Legate to the Marches was promised to Cardinal Forteguerri, but report said that he declined it, preferring to remain at the Court ; it was accordingly conferred on Roverella, and Ammanati was sent to Perugia.†

On the 13th August the Pope gave a banquet to the Cardinals at St. Angelo. After its conclusion, the money and valuables collected by Paul II. were inspected. Great

---

* "*Ad ugniuno pare vedere principio d'un novo mundo." Letter of J. P. Arrivabene, dated Rome, 1471, Aug. 13. Gonzaga Archives.

† *Report of Nicodemus of Pontremoli, dated Rome, 1471, Aug. 12. (State Archives, Milan.) Borgia completed a wing of the Castle at Subiaco, and added the tower, still standing, where his coat of arms and an inscription may be seen ; see GREGOROVIUS, Wanderjahre, II., 17 ; GORI'S Arch. St., IV., 126 ; and JANNUCELLI, Subiaco, 230. According to the *Acta Consist., f. 43 (Secret Archives of the Vatican), Bessarion's translation from the See of Albano to that of Porto took place on the 30th Aug., 1471 ; Cardinal Borgia, who must then have been a priest, at the same time being appointed Bishop of Albano. GAMS, XXIII., and BRESSLAU, Urkundenlehre, I., 211, are mistaken in giving 1468 as the date of Borgia's elevation to the episcopal See of Albano, as is CLEMENT, 133, in stating that it occurred in 1476.

interest was at this time felt regarding these treasures, which had hitherto been so carefully preserved, and, in conformity with the Election Capitulation, were to be expended on the cause of the Faith.* The Pope and the Cardinals were occupied for the whole day in examining these precious stores. One of the Cardinals told the Duke of Milan's Ambassador that they had found, in the first place, fifty-four silver shells, filled with pearls, valued at 300,000 ducats. These were sealed up by all the Cardinals, and were to be sold to defray the expenses of the war with the Turks. Next were seen the jewels and the gold belonging to the two tiaras which Paul II. meant to have had rearranged, worth about 300,000 ducats. A magnificent diamond, estimated at 7000 ducats, was pledged to Cardinal d'Estouteville for monies which he had advanced to the deceased Pontiff. The amount of gold, silver, jewels, precious objects, and other ornaments filled them with astonishment, and their value was deemed to be a million ducats. " But," the Ambassador adds, " the worth of these things depends on the opinion of those who will buy them." The money found amounted only to 7000 ducats, and was chiefly in the form of carlini. Deposits of 100,000, 60,000, 80,000, and 30,000 ducats were entered in a note laid up in a chest. The place where these sums were concealed could not at first be discovered ; but their actual existence was certified by the fact that Paul II., in a Consistory held not long before his death, had spoken of half a million of ducats which he would expend on the war if the Christian Princes would undertake an expedition against the enemies of the Faith. All these treasures, which the new Pope had

* Besides the passage from Ferrofinus' Despatch of the 13th August, quoted *supra*, p. 204, note †, see two *Letters of J. P. Arrivabene, dated Rome, 1471, Aug. 11 and 13. (Gonzaga Archives, Mantua.) In regard to L. Orsini, see SANSOVINO, Casa Orsina, 5 *seq.*

sworn not to touch, were sealed up by the Cardinals, and placed in the custody of the Castellan of St. Angelo.*

After Sixtus IV. had been consecrated Bishop, his solemn Coronation took place on Sunday, the 25th of August.† The tribune where the Pope received the tiara of St. Gregory the Great from the hands of Cardinal Borgia was so lofty that all the people could witness the ceremony.‡ According to ancient custom, he then proceeded to take possession of the Lateran. In the splendid procession were to be seen the Despot of the Morea and Scanderbeg's nephew. A tumult occurred in front of the Lateran; the Pope himself was in danger, and Cardinal Orsini had much difficulty in appeasing the excited populace. The impression made on Sixtus IV. by this untoward event was such that he returned to the Vatican at the first hour of the night.§

* The above account is drawn from the hitherto unknown *Report which Petrus de Modegnano, apost. protonot., furnished to Duke Galeazzo Maria, dated Rome, 1471, Aug. 14. See also a *Letter of Nicodemus de Pontremoli, dated Rome, 1471, Aug. 20; both these documents are in the State Archives, Milan. As Dr. Gottlob has kindly informed me, the account-books shew that Sixtus IV. sold many of Paul II.'s jewels as early as 1471. On the 31st May, 1472, the Medici paid 23,170 florins, "pro valore plurium jocalium de diversis sortibus emptorum ab ipsis depositariis usque in diem 19 Sept. proxe preteriti;" a further sum of 12,000 florins was realised by the sale of jewels. The King of Naples lent 16,000 florins, and received jewels as security for their repayment.

† See Bull. Vatic., 195. Here and elsewhere the 26th of August is wrongly named as the day of the Coronation, in contradiction to all the best authorities; see following note. FRANTZ, 134, is also mistaken in giving the 22nd August; and the Lib. confrat. b. M. de Anima, 13, the 8th September.

‡ See the *Reports of Nicodemus de Pontremoli, dated Rome, 1471, Aug. 25, and that of Blanchus de Cremona, dated Rome, 1471 Aug. 26th (State Archives, Milan), as well as the *Acta Consist. of Secret Archives, f. 43.

§ The *Letters of the Milanese Ambassadors which we have just

The letters by which the Pope made his elevation known to the temporal powers are dated on the day of his Coronation; in these he begs for the support of fervent prayers that he may rule the Church to the praise and glory of God, and the salvation of the people committed to his care.*

"When the tiara first rested on the brow of Sixtus IV. the figure of Nicholas V., amongst his immediate predecessors, must have presented itself most vividly to his mind, for he also was a native of Liguria, and like Sixtus himself, but unlike Pius II. and Paul II., had risen from a modest position. Again, he was by nature a scholar, and only after his elevation had developed the princely magnificence whose traces were visible wherever ruined Rome bore the aspect of a new city. That the new Pontiff should resolve to follow in his steps, and with the good fortune of the Rovere, to carry out the work begun

quoted, give more details than Infessura and Platina regarding Sixtus IV.'s *Possesso*. The Jews who stationed themselves on the Bridge of St. Angelo are here mentioned. Schmarsow, misled by Platina (see on the other side CANCELLIERI, Possessi, 45), makes the Coronation take place after the *Possesso* and after the tumult. PLATINA, Vita Sixti IV., 1057, estimates the expenses of the Coronation of Sixtus IV. and the obsequies of Paul II. (see *supra*, p. 191, note *) at 28,000 golden florins (see also MÜNTZ, III., 1, 268 *seq.*, and ROHAULT, 253 and 503). The sum is not so extravagant as SCHMARSOW, 8, imagines, for the Coronation alone of Paul II. cost 23,000 florins.

* RAYNALDUS, ad an. 1471, N. 70. I found letters of this description, with some textual variations, in the Gonzaga Archives, Mantua (original), in the Florentine State Archives (Copy, X.-II.-25, f. 35b–36b), and in the Archives of Perugia. VOIGT, Gesch. Preussens, IX., 41, mentions one addressed to the Grand Master of the Teutonic Order in the Archives of Königsberg. The letters of the Sacred College regarding the election are also dated on the 25th August ; see CHMEL, Urkunden und Briefe, II., 267 ; a similar letter to the Duke of Saxony is in the State Archives, Dresden.

by his energetic countryman, was but natural. But he had not the clear start from the first that Nicholas had. Nicholas V. had been freely elected, his actions were untrammelled. Sixtus, in order to be elected, had permitted himself to be bound, and the conditions of the Papal power also had undergone a complete change in the interval."*

In Italy itself the Apostolic See had no trustworthy friends. Sigismondo de' Conti tells us that the excessive obstinacy of Paul II. had almost everywhere provoked distrust and hatred.† The jealous fears of Italian politicians in presence of the increasing power of the States of the Church may have exercised a yet more potent influence. Sixtus IV. at once sought to establish friendly relations on all sides. Under Paul II. the disputes with Naples and Venice seemed to be interminable. Sixtus IV. at once came to an understanding with these two powers,‡ although at the cost of considerable sacrifice on his own part. Without any great trouble Ferrante obtained the satisfaction of seeing the rich Abbey of Monte Casino conferred upon his youthful son, while the Protonotary Rocha was made Archbishop of Salerno.§

"This Pope evidently intends to be on good terms with every one," wrote the Marquess of Mantua's Ambassador,‖ briefly describing the beginning of Sixtus IV.'s pontificate.

---

* SCHMARSOW, 7.

† SIGISMONDO DE' CONTI, I., 5.

‡ Loc. cit., I., 6–7.

§ *Letters of Nicodemus de Pontremoli, dated Rome, 1471, Aug. 31 (State Archives, Milan), and of the Ambassador of Mantua, B. Bonattus, dated Rome, 1471, Sept. 2. (Gonzaga Archives, Mantua.) See also GATTULA, II., 568, and TOSTI, Monte Cassino, III., 181.

‖ "*Questo papa monstra voler star bene cum ogniuno." B. Bonattus on the 2nd Sept., 1471. Gonzaga Archives.

Before he had an idea of being Pope, or even Cardinal, Sixtus IV. had had amicable relations with the Duke of Milan, and this in a measure explains the warm interest taken by Galeazzo Maria Sforza in promoting the election. After it had been carried, he was one of the first to congratulate the new Pope.* Sixtus IV. replied at once on the 16th of August by an autograph letter of the most flattering character. He began by recalling their former relations, praised the Duke's piety and devotion to the Holy See, of which he had given proof in the Romagna during the vacancy of the Chair of St. Peter, and finally assured him that his pontificate should bring the Duke nothing but happiness and blessing.†

The bond between the new Pope and the Florentines was even closer. "He looked upon the Medici, the patrons and friends of the modest Thomas of Sarzano, as his natural allies."‡ This was made very apparent when the Florentine Embassy, headed by Lorenzo de' Medici, arrived in Rome to pay homage on behalf of the Republic. Its reception was most cordial and honourable. Two antique marble busts were presented to Lorenzo, and he was allowed to acquire gems and cameos from the collection of Paul II.

* In the State Archives, Milan, "Roma," I found the draft of this Letter of congratulation, dated 1471, Aug. 11.

† See Appendix, N. 45. (State Archives, Milan.) Nicodemus de Pontremoli, writing to the Duke on the 20th Aug., 1471, says : "As I have already stated, His Holiness has repeatedly declared that he places his chief hopes on your Excellency ; he expresses himself in this manner, not only to me and to Cardinal Gonzaga, but also in the Consistory, and on every occasion when your Highness is mentioned." (State Archives, Milan.) The Cronica di Bologna, 789, gives an account of the great Milanese Embassy, in which Ascanio Maria Sforza took part. See N. DELLA TUCCIA, 101 ; and RATTI, I., 78, 89.

‡ SCHMARSOW, 7.

at a very moderate price. The Pope's confidence and good-will were also manifested in other very substantial ways. The financial affairs of the Papacy were confided to the Roman Bank of the Medici, by which arrangement a rich source of wealth was opened to Lorenzo and to his uncle Giovanni Tornabuoni. Further concessions in regard to the alum works were granted to him. Emboldened by so many favours, "the practical-minded Medici at last took courage to remark that he had but one desire unfulfilled, and that was to see a member of his family admitted into the Sacred College. To this request Sixtus IV. also lent a favourable ear, for he was unwilling to refuse Lorenzo anything. The latter soon left the Eternal City, laden with all possible tokens of the Pope's good-will, which was soon to be repaid with ingratitude."*

For a time indeed Filippo de' Medici, Archbishop of Pisa, endeavoured to maintain good feeling between Florence and Rome. "The Pope has shewn me such honour," he wrote on the 15th November, 1471, from Rome to Lorenzo de' Medici, "that a hundred tongues would fail me to express it. He told me to rest assured that I might dispose of Sixtus IV. as I would. Had you not yourself been here I would write yet more particularly regarding His Holiness' affection for our house, but as you know it, I think it unnecessary."†

On the 28th November the Venetian Envoys appeared

---

* Opinion of SCHMARSOW, 8. See REUMONT, Lorenzo, I., 243 *seq.*, 251 *seq.*, 2nd ed.; MÜNTZ, Précurseurs, 182.; FRANTZ, Sixtus IV., 135 *seq.*; and PERRENS, 358. The *Oration on behalf of the Florentine Embassy was deliver d on the 3rd Oct., 1471, by Donato Acciaiuoli (see MAI, Spic., I., 440; MAZZUCHELLI, I., 1, 41), and is preserved in Cod. 541 of the Chapter Library, Lucca, and in a Manuscript in the Riccardian Library, Florence, from which LAMIUS, 4–5, gives a passage.

† BUSER, Lorenzo, 19; see 23 and 27.

in Rome. One of them, Bernardo Giustiniani, made an
elaborate speech in the Pope's presence, the principal
subject of which was the unspeakably deplorable condition
of the East.* It was not indeed necessary to remind
Sixtus IV. of this, for he had already turned his attention
to the terrible danger with which the steady advance of
Islam threatened Christian civilisation. He aimed at the
formation of a league of the European powers, to be directed
exclusively against the Turks. A great Congress was to
carry the idea into effect. During the days which immediately followed his Election, it was rumoured that, in
accordance with the Capitulation, the Pope intended as
soon as possible to convene such an Assembly. Cardinal
Gonzaga† at the same time endeavoured to have his

---

* CIACONIUS, III., 120–26 ; LÜNIG, Orat., I., 26–46 ; Orat. clar. vir.,
105 *seq*. (Cologne, 1559). A *Letter from the Ambassador of Mantua,
dated Rome, 1471, Nov. 29, speaks of the arrival of the Venetian
Embassy. (Gonzaga Archives.) The 16th November was the day
appointed for the Florentines to pay their homage ; see Filippo de'
Medici's *Letter to Lorenzo, dated Rome, 1471, Nov. 15. (State
Archives, Florence, F. 27, f. 522.) The Embassy of Frederick, Count
Palatine, which was admitted to audience on the 21st April, 1472, also
dealt with the Turkish question ; see JACOB. VOLATERR., 87. In
November of the same year Envoys from Sigismund of the Tyrol were
in Rome. I found in Cod. Q., 41, of the Franciscan Library at Schwaz
the Discourse pronounced on this occasion, *Pro Sigismundo Austrie
duce illustr. ad Sixtum IV. P. M. Ludovici de Fryburgk utriusque juris
doctoris oratio anno sal. septuagesimo secundo die veneris sexta
Novemb. Romae in consistorio publico habita. Ravenna sent a special
Embassy to Rome, payments for which I find entered on the 21st
October and 13th November in *Sixt. IV., Lib. Bullet., 1471–73 (State
Archives, Rome), where appear also payments on the 11th November,
1471, "pro oratoribus regis Ungarie," and on the 18th November,
1471, "pro nuntio regis Portugallie."

† See his *Letter of the 17th Aug., 1471, from which it appears
that the Pope and the Milanese Ambassador had considered this

paternal city chosen as the place of meeting, and his proposal was favourably received, although Cardinal Orsini exerted himself on behalf of Florence.* Piacenza and Pavia were also spoken of.† On the 30th of August the matter was discussed in Consistory. Bessarion and others among the older Cardinals sought to deter the Pope from leaving Rome, and to induce him to hold the Congress in the Lateran ; others again preferred Mantua or Pisa. No definite decision was yet arrived at.‡ A letter was now received from the Emperor, who asked that Udine might be selected, but the Duke of Milan and other Italian Princes declared against this city. Sixtus IV. accordingly proposed, first Mantua and then Ancona—but all in vain ; the Princes neither understood nor sympathised with the aims of the Holy See, and all proposals were wrecked on the rocks of their indifference and private interests.§

Sixtus IV. was not as much distressed by this failure as he otherwise might have been, because at this moment a dangerous enemy was threatening Turkey in the rear. The Turcoman Prince, Usunhassan, "with the hope of completely supplanting the Sultan, seemed disposed to make common cause with European Christendom. At the

---

plan. (Gonzaga Archives.) GROTEFEND, I., 217, speaks of the processions ordered by the Pope to avert the danger of Turkish attack.

* *Despatch of Nicodemus de Pontremoli, dated Rome, 1471, Aug. 20. State Archives, Milan.

† *Letter of Nicodemus de Pontremoli, dated Rome, 1471, Aug. 29. State Archives, Milan.

‡ *Report of Nicodemus of Aug. 31, 1471, and that of the Mantuan Ambassador of Sept. 2, 1471. (Gonzaga Archives.) Regarding the reasons in favour of Rome, see PLATINA, Sixt. IV., 1056 seq.

§ PLATINA, loc. cit. ; FRANTZ, Sixtus IV., 142. On the 21st Dec., 1471, the *Mantuan Ambassador, B. Bonattus, wrote word that a Congress (dieta) was no longer talked of, but rather the despatch of Legates.

time of Sixtus IV.'s accession the conflict between Mahomet and Usunhassan in Caramania appeared to be tending to a great catastrophe, while the relations between Mocenigo, the Doge of Venice, and Usunhassan were such that they seemed only to need to be drawn a little closer to make the position of the Turks absolutely hopeless." The Turkish question might thus be said to have become a matter of world-wide importance, and accordingly the Pope " inaugurated his action in it with a certain magnificence."*

On the 23rd December a Secret Consistory was held, and five Cardinals were appointed Legates de latere, with the object, as the Consistorial Acts declare, of calling upon the whole Christian world to defend the Catholic Faith against the Turk, the enemy of the name of Jesus. Bessarion was sent to France, Burgundy, and England ; Borgia to Spain, Angelo Capranica to Italy, and Marco Barbo to Germany, Hungary, and Poland, while Oliviero Carafa was to command the naval forces which were to be assembled with the assistance of the King of Naples.†

---

* CARO, V., 1, 361-2 ; N. DELLA TUCCIA, 102, mentions the sending of Ambassadors from Great Caramania to Rome.

† "*Die lunae xxii[i] decembris, 1471, idem S.D.N. in dicto consistorio secreto creavit quinque legatos de latere cardinales per universas provincias et regna mundi ad requirendum reges, principes et alios christianos ad defensionem fidei Catholicae contra nefandissimum Turcum qui nomini Jesu infensus, etc. :—

Rev. dom. Nicenum apud regem Franciae, ducem Burgundiae et regem Angliae.

  „   „   Vicecancellarium apud regem Yspaniae et alios.

  „   „   S^tae Crucis apud principes et dominos Italiae.

  „   „   S^ti Marci apud imperatorem et regem Ungariae et alios.

  „   „   Neapolitanum apud regem Ferdinandum et per mare."

Acta Consist., f. 44. (Secret Archives of the Vatican.) See also **Bessarion's letter of the 23rd Dec., 1471, which I shall cite. PALACKY, V., 1, 74, and CARO, V., 1, 362, mention only four Legates, in this

A few days later the Pope issued a solemn Bull, in which he described the Turkish preparations for the conquest of Christendom, and called on the powers to take common measures of defence.*

The aged Bessarion was certainly the most worthy of all the Legates. Although he feared that the burden would be beyond his strength, yet in the hope of being able, at least, to effect something, he had resolved to accept it.† On the 20th April, 1472, he left Rome, but instead of directly proceeding to France, he remained some time longer in Italy.‡ According to Ammanati, he lingered from dread of undertaking the arduous task ; other accounts attribute his delay to the fact that Louis XI. kept him waiting a long time for a letter of safe conduct.§ When once he had

following PLATINA, 1057. The Venetian authorities (SANUDO, 1196 ; MALIPIERO, 70) correctly give five as the number.

* RAYNALDUS, ad an. 1471, N. 72.

† See his **Letter of 23rd Dec., 1471, in the State Archives of Florence.

‡ BANDINIUS, LV. (MIGNE, CLXI.), says that Bessarion left Rome at the beginning of the year. The *Acta Consist. of the Secret Archives of the Vatican record his departure from Rome for France on the 20th April, 1472 ; and so does a *Despatch from the Milanese Ambassador of the 20th April, 1472. In Sixti IV., Lib. Bullet., 1471–73, a sum is entered as paid for "cursori eunti ad regem Galliae et archiepisc, Lugdunen.," who were to announce Bessarion's appointment as Legate. (State Archives, Rome.) On the 21st March, 1472, Sixtus IV. had written to Charles of Burgundy regarding Bessarion's mission. BALUZE, IV., 527–31. On the 27th April the Cardinal was at Gubbio (Chronic. Eugub., 1021); on the 10th May at Bologna (PIERLING, Le mariage d'un Tsar, 368); and on the 16th May at Piacenza (Annal. Placent., 942). The date of the letter in REUMONT, Lorenzo, I., 420, 2nd ed., must accordingly be wrong.

§ VAST, 409. Ammanati's assertions regarding Bessarion's attitude on this occasion (see, especially, Epist., 437 and 534, and also 425 of the Frankfort edition) cannot now be individually verified ;

received it, he travelled as rapidly as his infirm health
permitted. On the 15th August he wrote from Saumur to
the French King, exhorting him to peace, and, on the same
day, he also sent letters to the Dukes of Brittany and
Burgundy.*

Shortly before this time an understanding had been
arrived at, by direct negotiations with Rome, in regard to
the abnormal condition of ecclesiastical affairs in France,
but this agreement met with violent opposition in some
quarters. There can be no doubt that the Greek Cardinal
touched on these matters in his interviews with the King.
He also tried to obtain the release of La Balue, but his
efforts proved unsuccessful, as did also those which he made
to reconcile the French Monarch with Charles the Bold of
Burgundy, and to win him for the Crusade. Sick and
disheartened, he started on his homeward journey. When
he reached Ravenna, his illness assumed a dangerous
character, fever came on and soon consumed the little
strength which yet remained to him, and on the 18th
November, 1472, he died.† His mortal remains were

SCHMARSOW, 9, looks upon his authority as open to suspicion. Vespasiano da Bisticci's account (MAI, I., 195) is doubtful; his statement
that Bessarion did not give his vote for Francesco della Rovere is in
direct contradiction to the documents which we give in Appendix, N. 43.

* D'ACHERY, III., 842, new edit.; MIGNE, CLXI., 699; VAST, 413
seq., 459 *seq.*

† BANDINIUS, LVI.; MALVASIA, 254; VAST, 430. By several
writers, as, for example, REUMONT, Lorenzo, I., 420, 2nd ed.;
ROHRBACHER-KNÖPFLER, 240; CIPOLLA, 565; CHEVALIER, 301, the
19th November is wrongly given as the day of the Cardinal's death;
SCHMARSOW, 13, names the 6th November; ZINKEISEN, II., 400, even
places it in the December of 1473. The *Acta Consist. of the Secret
Archives of the Vatican, amongst other authorities hitherto unknown,
adhere to the date we have adopted in the text. So does *GHIRARDACCI,
St. di Bologna; see our Vol. III., p. 243, note †.

borne to Rome, where they arrived on the 3rd December, and were deposited in the Church of the Holy Apostles.* Sixtus IV. was present at the obsequies.

Cardinal Borgia, who had been appointed Legate for the whole of Spain and the neighbouring islands, was not more successful in advancing the cause of the Crusade. On the 15th May, 1472, he went to Ostia, there to embark for his native land.† His task was no easy one, for the Peninsula was at this time in a state of great agitation and disorder. Ammanati speaks most unfavourably of Borgia's proceedings in Spain. He says that he shewed himself everywhere vain, luxurious, ambitious, and greedy. Yet, in a letter which is still extant, this same Ammanati writes to Borgia in the most flattering terms, and praises the way in which he had carried out his Spanish mission.‡ Such a writer has no claim to our credit. It is, however, extremely probable that Borgia considered a Cardinal Legate as a very important person, and acted accordingly; in fact, treated his countrymen to a considerable amount of Spanish

---

* Acta Consist., *loc. cit.* Regarding the monument, which was afterwards transferred to another position, and is still preserved, see VAST, 432 and 461–62. REUMONT, III., 1, 532, also gives the Epitaph; he is mistaken in asserting (III., 1, 316) that the Cardinal died in Rome. L. MAZIO speaks of Bessarion's palace and of his tomb, Studi Storici, 275–77 (Roma, 1872); and p. 280 of the probable dwelling-place of Platina. See also, in regard to Bessarion's mission to France and d'Estouteville's nomination as Legate for that country, S. LJUBIČ, Dispacci di Luca de Tollentis vescovo di Sebenico e di Lionello Cheregato vescovo di Traù nunzi apostolici in Borgogna e nelle Fiandre, 1472–88 ; ZAGABRIA, 1876, 24 *seq.*, 27 *seq.*, 32.

† *Acta Consist. (Secret Archives of the Vatican), by which CLEMENT, 118, is to be corrected. In *Sixti IV., Lib. Bullet., 1471–1473, on the 12th Febr., 1472, occurs the entry : "Roderico vicecan. legato ad regna Hispaniar. flor. duo millia octuaginta." State Archives, Rome.

‡ Ep., 513, Frankfort edition.

pride. A recent historian, by no means prejudiced in Borgia's favour, speaks of the discharge of his diplomatic duties in terms which form a complete contrast to Ammanati's account. " The Legate," he says, " had, as far as lay in his power, fulfilled his mission to Spain. It was time for him to return to Rome, and render an account to the Pope of the state of things which he had found on his arrival, of that which prevailed during his sojourn in the country, and of the result of his efforts. Matters had certainly improved in Aragon ; in Castille the situation depended on factors which were entirely beyond the sphere of a Legate's authority, and which were working themselves out independently of him. His task was fulfilled when he had done what he could in helping to direct affairs along the only path which could lead to peace and quiet."*

On the 11th September, 1473, Cardinal Borgia made his will, and began his return journey. Off the coast of Pisa he encountered a fearful storm ; one of his galleys sank before his eyes, and the ship in which he himself sailed almost met the same fate. More than 200 of his suite were drowned, and amongst them three Bishops ; the loss of property was estimated at 30,000 florins, and was aggravated by the depredations of wreckers on the coast.†

There can be no doubt that the task entrusted to Cardinal Barbo was undoubtedly the most difficult of all, while at the same time the most important, for, with regard to the Turkish war, " nothing was more indispensable than the aid of Hungary, Poland, and Bohemia,—and these were

* HÖFLER, R. Borgia, 37. See also HERGENRÖTHER, VIII., 199-200.

† See AMMANATI, Ep., 534 ; PLATINA, 1060 ; PALMERIUS, 256-7 ; ZURITA, XVIII., c. 59. I found in the State Archives at Florence a **Letter of Cardinal Borgia's of the 12th Oct., 1473, in which he gives an account of his misfortune. Regarding his Will, see THUASNE, III., App., p. I.-II.

involved in almost hopeless discord."* Barbo's zeal is
evidenced by the fact that he left Rome on the 21st
February, 1472, his instructions directing him to proceed
in the first place to the Emperor.† Until the autumn of
1474, the Cardinal Legate's labours in Germany, Poland,
and Bohemia were unremitting.‡ Even those who judge
him most severely, highly praise his persevering efforts for
the restoration of peace ; success, however, was not granted
him.§ The internal dissensions of the European nations
had reached such a pitch that it was beyond the power of
any individual to allay them. Frederick III., who, from
the point of view of that day, was the natural leader, was
extremely slow in his decisions, especially in cases where a
pecuniary sacrifice was in question.|| Unbounded egotism
prevailed among laity and clergy ; their attitude towards
the great danger in the East was one of almost absolute
indifference.¶

* CARO, V., 1, 362.

† *Acta Consist. (Secret Archives of the Vatican.) The date
commonly given, 22nd February (PALACKY, V., 1, 74 ; SCHMARSOW,
11), is to be corrected by reference to this document. On the 6th
Febr., 1472, Cardinal Barbo received 2083 florins for his journey.
*Sixti IV., Lib. Bullet., 1471–1473. (State Archives, Rome.) The
Cardinal's Instructions are to be found in Cod. epist., 259 ; in TELEKI,
XI., 459 *seq.* ; and THEINER, Mon. Hung., 436 *seq.*

‡ According to the *Acta Consist. (Secret Archives of the Vatican),
Card. Barbo returned to Rome from Germany on the 26th Oct., 1474,
and not in November, as SCHMARSOW, 94, states.

§ PALACKY, V., 1, 74 *seq.* ; FABISZA, 98 *seq.* ; CARO, V., 1, 365 ;
ZEISSBERG, 245 *seq.*

|| "*Dominus Imperator tardus est admodum in [de]liberationibus
suis et in eis presertim in quibus pecuniam effundere oportet." These
words are taken from a Roman *Instruction of this period, but
unfortunately undated, in Cod. S. 1, 1, f. 21–24. Angelica Library,
Rome.

¶ Regarding the return of the Cardinal, whose amiability had won

Sixtus IV., however, did not permit the indifference of the great European powers to damp his zeal in regard to the war. During the earlier months of 1472 he was engaged in negotiations for the restoration of peace in Italy,* and particularly in the equipment of galleys. Repeated letters were addressed to all the Faithful, urging them to contribute towards these warlike preparations ; and at the same time the Pope made repeated efforts to awaken the interest of individual Princes in the cause.†

Sixtus IV. was all the more dependent on extraneous contributions for the naval preparations on account of the deplorable state in which he found the Papal finances at his accession. The general belief that Paul II. had left large sums of money had soon proved to be a delusion. Treasure and jewels were not wanting, but of actual coin there was not more than 7000, or, according to other accounts, 5000 florins. The Cardinal-Camerlengo put the officials of the Treasury in prison, but nothing could be extracted from them. Creditors of previous Popes took the opportunity of coming forward and demanding payment. Sixtus IV. had to sell many of the gems and works of art, handed down by his predecessors, to satisfy them. Some

the affection of the Germans (SCHMARSOW, 25), see AMMANATI, Epist., 595, Frankfort edition.

* See the Letter of B. Bonattus, dated Rome, 1472, Jan. 4 (Gonzaga Archives), and the **Brief of 5th Jan., 1472, to the Duke of Milan. State Archives, Milan.

† See RAYNALDUS, ad an. 1472, N. 2 and 16. A *Brief to Cologne, dated Rome, 1471, Sept. 24 (8 Cal. Oct. is to be rendered by this date, and not, as ENNEN, III., 307, has it, by 8th October), mentions the despatch of a special Ambassador to Frederick III., to inform him of the equipment of a fleet for the Crusade by the Pope. Or. Pgm., with seal appended, is in the City Archives, Cologne.

few of the Cardinals, amongst them d'Estouteville, now presented old claims.*

Notwithstanding these difficulties, the arming of the fleet proceeded. The account-books show that in 1471–72 144,000 golden ducats in all were devoted by Sixtus IV. to this object.† A treaty was entered into with Venice and Naples, in accordance with which both these States equipped a fleet for the war. The Pope himself furnished twenty-four galleys and 4700 soldiers, who embarked at once on the Adriatic. Four ships came up the Tiber for Cardinal Carafa.‡ On the Feast of Corpus Christi, the 28th May, 1472, he sang a solemn High Mass at St. Peter's, in presence of the Pope and the whole Court. Sixtus IV. then blessed the banners for the fleet, which were presented to him on his throne by the Ambassadors. In the afternoon, a new and unwonted spectacle was witnessed ; the Pope on horseback, accompanied by all the Cardinals, went in procession from the Vatican to the ships, which lay at anchor in the Tiber below S. Paolo. Sixtus " went on board the Legate's galley, and, from a platform at the stern, blessed the ships, the commanders with their followers, and the crews.

---

* PLATINA, 1057 ; SCHMARSOW, 8. See the *Letter in the State Archives, Milan, cited *supra*, p. 212, note*. On the 19th Sept., 1471, Bessarion received "ex precio jocalium, S. R. E.," the amount of his expenses in the time of Paul II., and the cost of his journeys as Legate for Germany and Venice under Pius II. *Sixti IV., lib. Bullet., 1471–73. State Archives, Rome.

† GOTTLOB, Cam. Apost. Individual cities in the States of the Church, as, *e.g.*, Jesi, contributed to the cost of the fleet ; see BALDASSINI, Jesi, 175.

‡ GUGLIELMOTTI, 360–65. See CIPOLLA, 566. LANDO FERRETTI, *Storia d'Ancona, says, in agreement with Bernabei : " Delle galee del papa ne furono armate sei in Ancona." Cod. H. III.. 70, f. 307. Chigi Library, Rome.

He then bestowed a farewell embrace upon his lieutenant, and left him in the ship, himself returning to the Vatican as the sun was declining."*

The Cardinal-Admiral Carafa is described as a man " of resolute character and full of good-will." He went by way of Naples, where he was most honourably received, to Rhodes. Having appeased some internal dissensions among the Knights of St. John, he joined the Neapolitan and Venetian ships.† The whole fleet now numbered eighty-seven galleys, to which were added two from Rhodes.‡ In a Council of War, it was determined that an attack should, in the first instance, be made on the port of Satalia on the coast of Caramania. The southern coast of Asia Minor was selected, on account of the alliance which existed between the Caramanian Princes and Usunhassan, who was also on very friendly terms with the Venetians, and with the Pope. Another reason for commencing operations here was the opportunity it afforded for shewing the strength of the Crusaders' fleet to their Asiatic allies.§ The chains which defended

* SCHMARSOW, 11. To the authorities from which we have drawn our account may be added the *Acta Consist. of the Secret Archives of the Vatican, and a *Letter of Arcimboldi's, dated Rome, 1472, May 30. (State Archives, Milan.) According to this last Report, the Pope again blessed the galleys on the 30th May, and the next day Carafa sailed for Ostia. In *Sixti IV. lib. Bullet., 1471–73, the following entries occur on the 23rd May, 1472 : " Oliv. Card. Neapolit. pro stipendio classis flor. auri de camera viginti quatuor millia unum." On the 9th June : "archiepiscopo Pisar. pro expedit. galear. flor triamillia ducentos octo ;" and on the 10th July, 1472, a sum " pro vexillis S^{ce} † rev^{mo} card. Neapolit." State Archives, Rome.

† BOSIO, II., 334.

‡ GUGLIELMOTTI, 371–2. See FINCATI, L'armata Venez., 38, and CHIOCCARELLUS, 289.

§ HEYD, II., 326. From Malipiero, 79, it appears that Ambas-

the harbour of Satalia were burst, and serious injury was inflicted on the Turks by the destruction of its rich warehouses and suburbs, but the city proper, with its strong fortifications, successfully resisted the attack. Jealousies between Naples and Venice soon reached such a point that the Neapolitan fleet returned home, yet it was resolved that the war should be carried on. The wealthy city of Smyrna was taken by surprise. Carafa wished to preserve it as an important basis of operations, but the Venetians were of a different opinion, and it was given up to plunder, and then set on fire. This dispute broke up the friendly relations which had existed between the Papal forces and their Venetian allies, and, when winter began, the fleet of the Republic retired to the harbours of Modone and Napoli di Romania, while Carafa returned to Italy. On the 23rd January, 1473, he made his entrance into Rome, bringing with him a number of Turkish prisoners on camels. The Cardinal hung up portions of the broken harbour-chain of Satalia on the door of St. Peter's; these trophies are now placed over the entrance which leads to the Archives of the Basilica.*

Carafa's successor as Legate, Lorenzo Zane, Archbishop of Spalatro, and a Venetian by birth, sailed with ten galleys for the East at the end of April, 1473;† he was

sadors from Usunhassan came to Rome. I found in *Sixti IV. lib. Bullet., 1471–72, in the State Archives, Rome, an entry made on the 16th Aug., 1471, of payments for "tribus oratoribus Somcassani principis, etc., in alma urbe commorantib."

* GUGLIELMOTTI, 372 *seq.*; F. JULIEN, Papes et Sultans, 110 *seq.* (Paris, 1879).

† I take the above dates, in regard to which GUGLIELMOTTI (396), the most accurate student of these matters, gives no information, from a *Letter of the Milanese Ambassador, Sacramorus, dated Rome, 1473, April 25: "S. Sta questa matina ha benedite et date le bandere al arcivescovo de Spalatro che va legato in Levante cum

not able to do anything, and Usunhassan's defeat at Terdschan (26th July, 1473) gave a decided advantage to the Turks. Moreover, the Venetian Commander, Mocenigo, held aloof from the Papal Legate, fearing that the latter would frustrate his designs on Cyprus.*

Hopes had been entertained that the marriage of Princess Zoë, niece of the last Byzantine Emperor, with the Russian Grand Duke, Ivan III., would enlist a new champion for the Crusade, and bring about the reunion of the Russian with the Roman Church. These hopes were doomed to disappointment. On the 25th May, 1472, Sixtus IV. had received the Russian Ambassadors in Secret Consistory, and, on the 1st June, Zoë, who was acknowledged by her contemporaries to be the legitimate heiress to the Byzantine throne, was married by proxy to the Grand Duke. What took place on this occasion, in regard to the question of religion, is not clear, but Rome was probably deceived by fair promises. The Pope gave the Princess rich presents and the sum of 6000 ducats, provided for her a suitable escort, and sent letters of recommendation to the different States through which she was to pass on her journey to the North.†

The Greek Princess left Rome on the 24th June, 1472;

le X. gallee che se armano in Anchona, cosa che a jaschuno etiam a li piu cardinali pare mala spesa et denaro gettato, ma per piu rispetti dio perdoni a chi l'ha persuaso." If victorious, Zane was to receive the red hat. State Archives, Milan.

* GUGLIELMOTTI, 396 *seq.*, and SISMONDI, X., 420. See also FINCATI, L'armata Venez., 57, and WEIL, Gesch. der Chalifen, V., 340.

† PIERLING, Le mariage d'un Tsar, 375, says that he has discovered only one of these letters, that addressed to the Duke of Modena. I am able to point out two others : (*a*) to Bologna, dated Rome, 1472, June 22 : "Cum dil. in Christo filia nob. mulier Zoe." State Archives, Bologna ; (*b*) to Nuremberg, dated Rome, 1472, June 30. Kreis-archiv, Nuremberg.

everywhere, both in Italy and in Germany, the Pope's letters procured for her a brilliant reception. His kindness was but ill repaid, for, from the moment she set foot on Russian soil, she shewed herself a schismatic.* On her entry into Moscow (12th November), the Papal Legate who accompanied her was only admitted into the city in *incognito*, for it was feared that his public appearance with his cross would imply an acknowledgment of the Pope's Supremacy. The new Grand Duchess completely conformed to the Orthodox Church.†

Four years later, we again hear of negotiations between Sixtus IV. and the Russian Grand Duke, who was then seeking to obtain the Crown. Poland at the time dreaded the consequences of their success, and worked against the Union which it had supported at Kiew.‡ Michael Drucki, the Metropolitan of that place, had, with the consent of his clergy, sent an Embassy with a letter to the Pope, expressly acknowledging his Primacy ; and his successor, Simeon, is said to have been in favour of Union.§

* PIERLING, *loc. cit.*, 376 *seq.*, 379 *seq.*

† STRAHL, Beiträge zur Russischen Kirchengeschichte, 89, 190 (Halle 1827, 2nd ed.), and Gesch. Russlands, II., 335 *seq.* ; KARAMSIN, Geschichte des Russ. Reiches, VI., 51 *seq.* (Riga, 1824).

‡ See THEINER, Mon. Pol., II., 230 ; PICHLER, II., 54–5 ; HERGENRÖTHER, VIII., 265, N. 7.

§ PELESZ, I., 476–7 ; HERGENRÖTHER, VIII., 266. The letter of the Kiew Clergy to Sixtus IV. was first published in 1605, and was for a long time considered apocryphal ; recent and thorough investigation on the part of Malychewski has established the genuine character of this important document ; see Rev. d. Quest. Hist., XVII., 274 (1875).

CHAPTER II.

THE admirable energy with which, in the earlier years of his pontificate, Sixtus IV. devoted himself to the defence of Christendom, is, in great measure, clouded by the extravagance with which, from the moment of his accession, he heaped favours upon his numerous, and, in many instances, unworthy relations.

Foremost among his kindred appear the sons of his brother Raffaello, Giuliano, Bartolomeo, and Giovanni della Rovere, of whom the first two embraced the ecclesiastical state, while Giovanni remained in the world, and, under Federigo of Montefeltre, studied the art of war.* Lionardo, who afterwards became City Prefect,† was the son of Bartolomeo della Rovere, another brother of the Pope's.

* Further details regarding him will be found, *infra*, p. 270. Bartolomeo della Rovere entered the Franciscan Order at an early age, was made Bishop of Massa Marittima in 1473, and of Ferrara in 1474 or 1475 ; see UGHELLI, II., 553, and GAMS, 695 ; also ADINOLFI, Portica, 116. His praises are sung by the author of the *Lucubrac. Tiburtinae, mentioned *supra*, p. 205, note,† in Cod. 2403, f. 19, of the Court Library, Vienna. In the British Museum is a drawing by Melozzo da Forli, representing an old man without a beard, in complete profile, turned towards the right (Photogr. Braun, N. 61). SCHMARSOW, 391, supposes this to be the likeness of Raffaello della Rovere, the father of Julius II.

† VILLENEUVE, 38-9.

Three sisters of the Pope had respectively married into the families of Riario, Basso, and Giuppo; and from these marriages sprang a number of descendants, "over all of whom the oak spread its branches,* so that the golden fruit fell into their laps."† Bianca della Rovere, the wife of Paolo Riario, had two sons, Pietro and Girolamo, and one daughter, Violante; Violante married Antonio Sansoni and was mother of Cardinal Raffaello Riario Sansoni, well-known in connection with the Pazzi conspiracy. Luchina, the Pope's next sister, had, by her marriage with Giovanni Guglielmo Basso, five sons, Girolamo, Antonio, Francesco, Guglielmo, and Bartolomeo, and a daughter, Mariola. Antonio was a man of pure and blameless life; and in 1479 he espoused a relation of the King of Naples.‡ The christian name of the Pope's third sister, who married Pietro Giuppo, is not known; a fourth, Franchetta, is mentioned as married to Bartolomeo Armoino, and dying in 1485.§

A new epoch for his kindred began with the elevation of Francesco della Rovere to the Throne of St. Peter. As early as the autumn of 1471, we find three of his nephews in the Papal service.‖ In the following spring, two of his

---

* The arms of Sixtus IV.

† SCHMARSOW, 30.

‡ VILLENEUVE, 36, 49–50 ; SCHMARSOW, 178. As to Antonio Basso, see Civ. Catt., I., 679, 1868, where are given two hitherto unpublished Briefs relating to him.

§ VILLENEUVE, 51–3, partly from Acts in the Vatican Archives.

‖ On the 31st Oct., 1471, among the payments made by the Thesaurarius, is entered : *"magcis dominis Leonardo, Antonio et Jeronimo S. D. Nri pape nepotibus duc. auri 3250 pro eorum presentis anni provisione." Exitus, 487, f. 150. (Secret Archives of the Vatican.) See *Sixti IV. lib. Bullet., 1471–73, where, f. 20b, on the 30th Sept., 1471, is a payment "pro Leonardo nepoti ad stipendia S. R. E. nuper conducto," and on the 16th Oct., 1471, others " pro Leonardo, Antonio et Hieronymo nepotibus." State Archives, Rome.

sisters, probably Bianca and Luchina, migrated to Rome, where Sixtus IV. had prepared for them a suitable dwelling.* The arrival of the other relations was not long delayed.

All the members of the Ligurian colony which assembled around the Pope well understood how to take advantage of the fact that "Sixtus did not know the value of money, and, having grown up from his youth in a mendicant Order, gave with full hands as long as he had anything to give."† These relations, who had mostly been in very needy circumstances and humble positions, in the course of a few years found themselves in the enjoyment of wealth, and of ecclesiastical and temporal dignities such as hitherto they had never dreamed of.

Sixtus IV. had not occupied the Papal throne for many months before two of his youthful nephews, Giuliano della Rovere and Pietro Riario, were admitted into the Sacred College. The Pope was deeply indebted to Paolo Riario of Savona, the father of the last-named young man. Leone Cobelli, in his Chronicle of Forli, has recorded some interesting particulars regarding their earlier relations.‡ A certain Franceschino of Savona, he tells us, of the Order of the Minorites, was studying in that town, and was on very friendly terms with Paolo Riario. Paolo, a worthy and benevolent man, observing the young monk's love of learning, resolved to receive him into his house, and to

---

* See the entries of the 23rd of March and 8th April, 1472, in *Sixti IV. lib. Bullet., 1471-73. (State Archives, Rome.) The sisters of Sixtus IV. arrived on the 2nd April, 1472 ; see the Milanese Ambassador's *Letter of that day in the State Archives at Milan, in which the nephew, Antonio, is spoken of as "homo de bona conditione," and his care of the Pope, who was suffering from the gout, is mentioned.

† SCHMARSOW, 30.

‡ L. COBELLI, 257-8.

support him. Franceschino accordingly instructed the sons of his patron, and was enabled by the latter to complete his own education. This generous assistance could not have been better bestowed, for the needy student became one of the best professors in his Order. In the fulness of his gratitude to Paolo Riario, Franceschino said to him : " I well know that to you, after God, I owe it that I have become what I am ; I will shew myself grateful ; let me have your son Pietro for my son : I will give him the best possible education, and make a notable man of him." Paolo gladly consented ; Francesco clothed his *protégé* with the Franciscan habit, and shewed him the greatest kindness.* When a Cardinal, he took Fra Pietro with him to Rome, where he is said to have played an important part in the Conclave.† Almost immediately after his accession, Sixtus IV. bestowed on Pietro an Abbey on the Franco-German frontier, with a yearly income of 1000 ducats, and the Bishopric of Treviso.‡ But he was destined ere long to mount yet higher.

* According to the *Funeral Oration for Cardinal Riario in Cod. 45, C. 18, of the Corsini Library, Rome, which we shall hereafter cite, his father died when he was twelve years of age ; Francesco della Rovere was then lecturing on Holy Scripture in Siena, and made the orphan come to him. From the same source, we also learn that Fra Pietro studied at Pavia, Padua, Venice, and Bologna, and subsequently at Siena and Ferrara. CIACONIUS, III., 43, says that the Oratio in funere Petri card. S. Sixti habita a Nicolao episc. Modrusien. has been printed. A complete refutation of the fable, invented by political enemies of Sixtus IV., to the effect that the Riario were his sons, is to be found in the Civ. Catt., III., 417 *seq.*, 1868. REUMONT, in the Allgem. Zeitung, p. 3836, 1877, expresses his astonishment that a man like Villari (MACHIAVELLI, I., 61) should repeat charges so utterly unfounded.

† See *supra*, p. 204.

‡ *Letter of Nicodemus de Pontremoli, dated Rome, 1471, Aug. 31. State Archives, Milan.

In the second week of December, 1471, it was reported that the Pope was about to create new Cardinals ; that he purposed to make an alteration in the Election Capitulation, and meant to elevate his two young nephews to the purple.* Sooner than had been expected, these anticipations were realised.

On the 16th December, 1471, a Consistory was held, and Pietro Riario, aged twenty-five, and Giuliano della Rovere, aged twenty-eight, were created Cardinals, though not immediately published.† To the former was assigned, as his title, on the 22nd December, the Church of S. Sisto, while Giuliano received that of S. Pietro in Vincoli, previously held by Sixtus IV. himself.‡ On the following day, although not yet published, both of the young Cardinals appeared with the Red Hat, a thing which the Marquess of Mantua's Ambassador mentions as hitherto unheard-of.§

The promotion of these two nephews afforded to those

* " * De far cardinali se fa gran praticha et per quello sento al papa se consentirà de farne dui che siano aut de carne sua aut de natione cum far una aditione al capitulo del conclave de questa reformatione per non stringer el resto, et questi serano il vescovo de Carpentrasse suo ninodo [=nipote] ex fratre et il vescovo di Treviso suo alevo [=allievo]." *Letter of B. Bonattus, dated Rome, 1471, Dec. 13.   Gonzaga Archives, Mantua.

† *Letter of B. Bonattus, dated Rome, 1471, Dec. 21.   (Gonzaga Archives.)   The day of the creation, which is not here given, is learned from the *Acta Consist., Secret Archives of the Vatican.   The common statement that the nomination was made on the 15th December is erroneous.   SCHMARSOW (10) is also wrong in saying that this creation of Cardinals took place in "the same sitting" as that in which the Legates for the Turkish war were nominated, and REUMONT, III., 1, 164, in speaking of this Consistory as the first.

‡ *Acta Consist., Secret Archives of the Vatican.

§ " *Res inaudita che prima siano comparsi cum il capello che publicati."   B. Bonattus from Rome, 1471, Dec. 23.   Gonzaga Archives.

who had not approved of the first acts of Sixtus IV., and had deemed themselves overlooked, a welcome occasion for angry and injurious comments. Cardinal Ammanati speaks of the elevation of two youths, now for the first time brought out of obscurity, and altogether inexperienced, as an act of imbecility. "He declaimed against the nepotism of La Rovere, quite forgetting that his own patron, Pius II., had been far from blameless in this particular."*

This first creation of Cardinals by Sixtus IV. was certainly an infringement of the Election Capitulation, "but the uncertain position of the new Pope, surrounded as he was on all sides by experienced, influential, and skilful prelates, who desired to use him as a tool for their own selfish designs, justifies this step, to which Bessarion lent his approval and aid. Sixtus IV., to ensure his independence, required the support of trustworthy coadjutors, whose energies should be absolutely at his disposal."†

Giuliano della Rovere was certainly the most remarkable of the two nephews. "Even at an early age he gave evidence of those qualities which rendered his long and brilliant career so distinguished alike in the political history of Italy and in the annals of intellectual culture. If, like others, he profited by the abuse which had now become a system, and allowed numerous Bishoprics and Abbeys to be conferred upon a single individual, with the

---

* SCHMARSOW, 9.

† With this opinion of SCHMARSOW, 10, may be compared the justification of Sixtus IV. in his Brief to Charles of Burgundy (BALUZE, IV., 528), and the declaration of GREGOROVIUS, VII., 230, 3rd ed., that nepotism " formed for the Pope a governing party, and a bulwark against the opposition of the Cardinalate." As early as the summer of 1472, Sixtus IV. was completely " master of the situation," " potestate, abundat," says AMMANATI, Epist., 454.

sole object of enriching him ; if his uncle made him
Archbishop of Avignon and of Bologna, Bishop of Lausanne, Coutances, Viviers, Mende, and finally of Ostia and
Velletri, and Abbot of Nonantola and Grottaferrata,
heaping benefice after benefice upon him, Giuliano manifested in the expenditure of his income, and in his whole
manner of living, a prudence and seriousness which
contrasted favourably with the conduct of many other
prelates. If his moral character was not unblemished, his
outward demeanour was always becoming, and, immediately after his elevation to the purple, he began to devote
that attention to the fine arts, and especially to architecture,
which won for him lasting renown. The serious character
of his other studies, although they were mostly directed to
secular subjects, contributed to develop those exceptional
abilities of which his labours in later life gave such signal
proof, and which had begun to manifest themselves even
during the pontificate of Sixtus IV."*

Giuliano della Rovere was born on the 5th December,
1443, at Albizzola, near Savona, where his parents were
living in very poor circumstances. Having entered the
Franciscan Order, he pursued his studies at Perugia.
Sixtus IV., even while a Cardinal, treated him with exceptional favour. "The grave and resolute character of this
nephew justly inspired him with confidence. Like himself,
he had been trained in the strict discipline and privations
of the monastic life, and there had been an almost constant
interchange of thought between them." Giuliano's appearance was striking. Melozzo da Forli's fresco of" Sixtus IV.,

---

* REUMONT, III., 1, 165. See SCHMARSOW, 177 seq., 369 seq.
Regarding Giuliano's connection with Grottaferrata, see ROCCHI, 102
seq. About the year 1475 the Abbey of Gorze was bestowed on him ;
see LAGER, Gorze, 85 ; MARTÈNE, II., 1503-4. In reference to the
Bishopric of Lausanne, see Jahrbuch für Schweiz. Gesch., IX., 22 seq.

surrounded by his Court, appointing Platina Librarian of the Vatican" represents his tall figure, his face in profile, looking down upon his uncle with great dark eyes full of seriousness and dignity. He wears the purple cape, lined with ermine. His black hair is surmounted by a bright coloured skull-cap. The "round head, with its angular cheek-bones, and the firmly closed mouth betoken the man of deeds, who wastes no words, but acts."*

Pietro Riario was a very different character. He was intelligent and cultivated, courteous, witty, cheerful, and generous, but his good qualities were counterbalanced by a lust of power, a boundless ambition and pride, and a love of luxury, which rendered him utterly unworthy of the purple. Unfortunately, Sixtus IV. fostered these faults by lavishing rich benefices on him, even more abundantly than on the Cardinal of S. Pietro in Vincoli. The Archbishopric of Florence, which had so lately been held by a Saint, the Patriarchate of Constantinople, the Abbey of S. Ambrogio, and a number of Bishoprics were soon concentrated in the hands of this young man.† His yearly revenues before long exceeded 60,000 golden florins‡ (=about 96,000 pounds); but even this sum was far from satisfying his requirements, for Riario, "transformed in one night from a mendicant friar into a Crœsus, plunged into the maddest excesses." § The Cardinal, says Platina, set himself to collect together unheard-of quantities of gold and silver plate, costly raiment, hangings and carpets, splendid horses, and a multitude of servants in scarlet and silk. He patronised young poets and painters, and delighted in

---

* SCHMARSOW, 44.

† See CIACONIUS, III., 43.

‡ So says CORTESIUS, De cardinalatu, XLIV. SCHIVENOGLIA, 176, estimates the income at 50,000 ducats.

§ GREGOROVIUS, VII., 231, 3rd ed.

contriving and carrying out pageants and tournaments on the most magnificent scale. He gave extravagant banquets to some of the Ambassadors, and to Leonora, daughter of the King of Naples. He was very generous to scholars, and to the poor. Moreover, he began a palace in the vicinity of the Church of the Holy Apostles, the extensive foundations of which bespoke a colossal superstructure. He seemed to vie with the ancients in pomp and grandeur*—and, it may be added, in vices. All morality was openly defied by this upstart. Instead of the habit of St. Francis, he went about in garments laden with gold, and adorned his mistress from head to foot with costly pearls.†

The ostentation of Cardinal Riario, says Ammanati, surpassed anything that our children will be able to credit, or that our fathers can remember.‡

The Reports of Ambassadors then in Rome shew that Ammanati's expressions were not exaggerated ; the Ambassadors of the Duke of Milan seem unable to say enough of the brilliant tournaments and the rich banquets given by the Cardinal, especially during the Carnival.§

* PLATINA, Sixtus IV., 1058. See FULGOSUS, VI., c. 10. The *Funeral Discourse in Cod. 45, C. 18, of the Corsini Library gives, f. 119, the number of his household as about 500.

† FULGOSUS, X., c. 1 : "Amicam Tiresiam non palam solum, sed tanto etiam sumptu alebat quantus ex eo intelligi potest quod calceis margaritarum tegmento insignibus utebatur temporis meliore parte inter scorta atque exoletos adolescentes consumpta." See Cr. di Viterbo di Giov. di Juzzo, 104 ; Annal. Placent., 944 ; KNEBEL, II., 54 ; and the passage from the *Work of Sigismondo Tizio (Chigi Library) in Arch. d. Soc. Rom., I., 478.

‡ AMMANATI, Epist., 548 (Frankfort edition).

§ *Joh. Ferrofinus, in a *Report, dated Rome, 1473, March 4, describes the "giostre ha facto fare in questi di de carnevale il cardinale S. Sisto." (State Archives, Milan.) See also INFESSURA, 1144, and Una cena carnevalesca del Card. P. Riario. Lettera

Great astonishment was excited by a feast to which Riario invited four Cardinals, all the Ambassadors, and several prelates on the 1st February, 1473.* The sons of the Despot of the Morea, the City Prefect, and the Pope's nephews, Girolamo and Antonio, also took part in it. The walls of the dining-hall were adorned with precious tapestry; in the middle, on an elevated platform, was a table where the so-called King of Macedonia sat, in splendid robes, and attended by four Counsellors and an interpreter. At the left of this platform was the Cardinal's table, to which those of the guests were joined; there were two sideboards laden with silver, and a multitude of torches made a blaze of light. The feast lasted fully three hours. Before every course the seneschal appeared on horse-back to the sound of music, and each time in a fresh costume. The banquet was followed by a Moorish dance and other pastimes. At its conclusion, came a Turkish Ambassador, bearing credentials, and accompanied by an interpreter; who complained that Cardinal Riario had bestowed on the King of Macedon a kingdom which belonged to the Turks, and threatened that unless he gave up his usurped insignia, war should be declared. The Cardinal and the King replied that they would let the matter be decided by arms. Accordingly, on the following day, the combat took place in the square before the Church of the Holy Apostles, and the Turk—being taken captive by Usunhassan the King of Macedon's General—was led through the streets of Rome in fetters.†

ined. a di Lud. Genovesi 2 Marzo, 1473. Roma, 1885. (Nozze Vigo—Magenta.)

* I take the description of this feast from a **Report of Johannes Arcimboldus to Galeazzo Maria Sforza, dated Rome, 1473, Febr. 3, which I found in the State Archives, Milan.

† This strange representation seems to have been so much admired

Before the year was over, Riario again gave an entertainment on a yet larger scale, surpassing in mad extravagance
anything that the sumptuous age of the Renaissance had
yet produced.   The occasion for this further display was the
passage through Rome of Leonora, the daughter of the King
of Naples, on her way to her husband, Ercole of Ferrara.*

On the 5th June, 1473, after a short rest at Marino,
Leonora approached the walls of Rome.   Ercole's brothers,
Sigismondo and Alberto, together with many nobles from
Ferrara and Naples, accompanied her.   Cardinals Carafa
and Ausio, and several Prelates, awaited her arrival at
the third milestone from the City, and conducted her to
the Lateran, where she partook of some refreshment, and
venerated the holy relics.†   Meanwhile, the Pope's two
favoured nephews, Pietro Riario and Giuliano della Rovere,
had come to bid her welcome, and, escorted by them,
the Princess proceeded to the residence of the Cardinal
of S. Sisto by the Church of the Holy Apostles, where
preparations for her reception had been made in a style
of unprecedented magnificence.‡   "In the square before the

that it was repeated at the beginning of March, 1473.   *" Heri," writes
Joh. Ferrofinus on the 4th, "se fece uno bellissimo torniamento et
bagordo cum representatione de Ussoncassan da un canto et lo Turco
da l'altro quale tandem fo preso et menato per la briglia per Roma et
poy reducto ad casa de Mᵉᵉ."   State Archives, Milan.

* See the Monograph of OLIVI, who, p. 27, proves, in opposition to
Gregorovius, that Leonora was the legitimate daughter of Ferrante.

† See CORVISIERI, I., 479 seq., and Sacramorus' **Report of the
7th June, 1473, which I found in the State Archives, Milan.

‡ On the 5th June, 1473, Sacramorus writes : *" Questa duchessa
de Ferrara intrera hoggi a le xxi. hore ; smonta in casa de S. Sisto
como V. Ex. è advisata grande apparechio, ymo sumptuosissimo de
tappezarie, ornato e argenti li fa in casa sua."   The Cardinal, the
Ambassador adds, willingly shews his numerous precious possessions.
State Archives, Milan.

Church, Riario had caused to be erected a splendid house constructed of wood, rivalling the Palaces of ancient times. It had three halls, with wreathed pillars, surmounted by a rich frieze, on which the arms of the Pope, the Cardinal, and the Duke of Ferrara were hung. The open sides of these halls looked into the court, which, on its fourth side, was closed by a stage prepared for the theatrical representations which were to be given. In the middle of the court were two fountains, supplied with water from the roof of the Basilica. The whole open space was protected by an awning from the rays of the sun. Five spacious sleeping rooms for the Princess and her ladies opened into the first hall. The gentlemen of her suite were accommodated in fourteen chambers, similarly opening into that of the opposite wing. The middle hall, looking across to the stage, was in front of the Church over against its portico. Externally, the edifice was painted to resemble stone; within, the walls, ceilings, and floors were covered with gold-embroidered carpets and precious tapestries and stuffs, so that the wood-work nowhere appeared."*

The banqueting-hall of this palace was kept cool by means of three bellows, out of sight, and here was to be seen the marvellous tapestry, representing the creation of the world, made by order of Pope Nicholas V., and believed to be unequalled in Christendom. This master-piece of art was afterwards hopelessly lost.† The luxury of the interior was indescribable; silk, damask, and gold brocade were lavished in reckless profusion; even the meanest vessels were made of pure silver and gilt! However highly we may estimate the extravagance of the age,

* SCHMARSOW, 51. To the authorities here cited may be added the Reports in CORVISIERI, X., 645 seq.

† See KINKEL in the Allgem. Zeitung, 1879, p. 3003.

such senseless prodigality must necessarily have given cause for scandal and offence.*

On Whit-sunday, after the Mass at St. Peter's, the Princess, attired with dazzling splendour, was received by the Pope, and in the afternoon the History of Susanna † was represented by a Florentine troupe.

On Whit-monday, Riario gave a banquet in her honour, which, in its sumptuous and unreasonable luxury, recalled the heathen days of Imperial Rome.‡ If the silk-clad servants, and the splendid decoration of the hall, the great sideboard, with its twelve épergnes and masses of silver plate, was enough to astonish the guests, the feast itself was even more marvellous. Before its commencement, sweetmeats, oranges encrusted with sugar, and malvoisie were offered to the company, and then rose-water for the hands. The guests took their places at the table to the sound of trumpets and fifes. Only ten persons sat at the principal table with Leonora, eight belonging to her suite, her host and Girolamo Riario. The banquet lasted six

---

* See INFESSURA, 1144, who indignantly exclaims : "Oh guarda in quale cosa bisogna che si adoperi lo tesauro della chiesa." See also AMMANATI, Epist., 548, and the **Report of T. Calcagnini of 7th June, 1473. University Library, Padua.

† See Leonora's Letter of the 10th June, in CORVISIERI, X., 647 seq., and the **Reports of Sacramorus and T. Calcagnini ; as also a Letter from the Ambassador of the Duke of Modena, dated Rome, 1473, June 7 (State Archives, Modena), now published by OLIVI, 26–7.

‡ Besides the documents published by CORVISIERI, X., 648 seq., and, in particular, the Princess's Letter of the 10th June, we may here refer to the **Reports of Sacramorus (State Archives, Milan) and T. Calcagnini, written on the 7th June, and already cited. The latter of these, which I found in the University Library, Padua, is also interesting, as having furnished the foundation of Corio's account : its length is such that I am obliged to publish it elsewhere. Of more modern writers, see SCHMARSOW, 52 seq., and MÜNTZ, 50 seq.

whole hours ; there were three courses, during which forty-
four dishes were served ; amongst them were stags roasted
whole and in their skins, goats, hares, calves, herons,
peacocks with their feathers, and finally, a bear with a
staff in his jaws. Most of the dishes were for show, the
bread was gilt, the fish and other viands were brought to
table overlaid with silver. The sweets and confectionery
were countless, and all sorts of artistic shapes. Amongst
other devices, the labours of Hercules were represented the
size of life ; and a mountain with a gigantic and apparently
living serpent. Sugar fortresses, with towers and citadels
from which banners waved, were borne in and thrown
amongst the people from the balcony.   "Ten great ships
sailed in, made of confectionery and laden with sugared
almonds, which, in allusion to the arms of the Rovere, were
shaped like acorns. Next came the triumph of Venus,
drawn in a chariot by swans," then a mountain from which
a man emerged and expressed his astonished admiration
of the banquet. Allegorical figures also appeared during
the feast, amongst others, a youth who sang verses in Latin,
and announced: "At the command of the Father of the
Gods I am come, and bring you joyful news: Envy us no
longer the festivals of our Heaven, for Jupiter himself is a
guest at your board." *

Towards the end of the entertainment a ballet was
danced on a stage by ancient heroes with their mistresses ;
while it was going on, ten Centaurs suddenly burst in upon
the scene, with little wooden shields and clubs, and were
driven away by Hercules. Bacchus, and also Andromeda,
were represented, and " other things," says a writer belonging
to the Princess's suite, "which I do not remember or did

* See CORVISIERI, X., 649, where a colon should be inserted after
'jubet.'

not understand, as I was not a proficient in Humanistic studies."*

Leonora received many costly gifts from Sixtus IV. and the Cardinals ; she remained in Rome until the 10th June.† Other spectacles, of a more Christian character, were provided in her honour, forming a striking contrast to the mythological representations we have described.‡

The splendid reception of the Neapolitan Princess had, in part, a political object ; it was intended to make the alliance between the Pope and Ferrante evident to the world. This agreement had cost the Pope considerable sacrifices, but it put an end to a ceaseless series of disputes, and, for a time, delivered the Apostolic See from apprehensions which had caused much distress to Paul II.§ A family connection was to confirm the alliance with Naples. In the spring of 1472, on the death of Antonio Colonna, Lionardo della Rovere had become City Prefect.‖ Soon afterwards, he married a natural daughter of Ferrante, and Sora, Arpino, and other territories were bestowed on the newly-married couple. Both outwardly and inwardly, Lionardo was so poorly gifted that he was the laughing-stock of the Romans. Thus the union was anything but an attractive one. In order to bring it about, Sixtus IV. renounced his right of sovereignty over Sora, and Ferrante agreed to invest Rovere with that fief.¶

* **Report of T. Calcagnini in the University Library, Padua.

† OLIVI, 29, is wrong in naming the 9th.

‡ CORVISIERI, X., 653. For some account of similar feasts in that age of luxury, see MÜNTZ, Renaissance, 225 *seq.* ; and in REUMONT, Lorenzo, II., 310 *seq.*, 2nd ed., the description of B. Salutati's banquet on the 16th February, 1476.

§ Sixtus IV. alludes to this fact in a **Brief of the 30th May, 1472. State Archives, Milan.

‖ **Brief of the 17th Febr., 1472.   State Archives, Florence.

¶ SCHMARSOW, 12.

Not satisfied with what he had already obtained, the Neapolitan Monarch now brought forward the question of the feudatory tribute, and, in this matter also, Sixtus IV. shewed himself exceedingly complaisant, remitting the whole tribute, together with all other debts. The King, in return, bound himself to send a white horse yearly to Rome, in recognition of the tenure of his fief, to take part in the war against the Turks, to defend the coasts of the States of the Church against pirates, and, if necessary, to support the Pope, at his own expense, with an armed force.* Platina admits that this agreement was disapproved of by many.† Sixtus IV., in writing to the Duke of Milan, quotes the advice of the Cardinals and the intention of Pius II. in justification of his renunciation of territory, adding that the fief had brought the Church more trouble than gain, and that the Duke himself had advised the measure.‡

"After this beginning, a crafty diplomatist like Ferrante too clearly perceived the advantages promised by the alliance with the Pope to refrain from making use of it for his own ends. In the spring it was evident that nothing would come of the Italian League. The King soon succeeded in rendering the negotiations with the agents of the different States, who had come to Rome, ineffectual, and lost no time in writing to inform the

---

* See the *Letters of Sixtus IV. to Ferrante, dated Rome, 1472, Febr. 28 and March 11, in Cod. B. 19, f. 122b and 125 of the Vallicellana Library, Rome. Also RAYNALDUS, ad an. 1471, N. 82, and 1472, N. 57-8 ; GOTTLOB, Cam. Apost. and Mél. d'Archéol., 185, 1888.

† PLATINA, Sixtus IV., 1059 ; SCHMARSOW, *loc. cit.* In a *Letter, dated Rome, 1472, April 2, Cardinal Gonzaga mentions the remission of the Neapolitan tribute. Gonzaga Archives.

‡ **Brief of 30th May, 1472. State Archives, Milan.

Milanese of the dissolution of the compact between him and them." *

This disturbance of the relations between Milan and Naples was extremely disagreeable to the Pope, who earnestly endeavoured to prevent a breach between the two powers.† He had reason to hope for success, from the fact that his relations with Milan, which had always been good, had of late been drawn yet closer. Platina informs us that, either from jealousy at Rovere's elevation to the post of City Prefect and to the Dukedom of Sora, or else in obedience to the wishes of the Lord of Milan, the Cardinal of S. Sisto had exerted himself to promote the betrothal of his brother Girolamo with Sforza's grand-niece, the daughter of Conrad of Cotignola. Girolamo had hitherto been a grocer, or, some say, a public scrivener in Savona. The little town of Bosco was now purchased for him at the price of 14,000 golden florins. Riario even went so far as to have Cardinal Giuliano's youthful brother secretly conveyed from Pavia to Rome, because Galeazzo Maria Sforza had cast his eyes upon him, and expressed a wish that this nephew of the Pope's should be connected with his family by marriage. When Giovanni della Rovere so suddenly disappeared from Pavia, Galeazzo changed his plans. The Countess of Cotignola made difficulties about the dowry, with the result that this alliance was relinquished, and Girolamo Riario married instead Caterina Sforza, a natural daughter of the Duke, and was made Count of Bosco.‡

---

* SCHMARSOW, 12.

† **Brief of the 30th May, 1472, *loc. cit.*

‡ PLATINA, 1059; SCHMARSOW, 12–13. Cardinal P. Riario, in a *Letter, dated Rome, 1472, June 20, thanked the Duke of Milan for having invested his brother with Bosco. (State Archives, Milan.) *B. Bonattus, writing from Rome on June 3, 1472, mentions 16,000 ducats

Meanwhile, all danger of war between Milan and Naples had ceased. On the 22nd June, the Pope had urged the Duke to keep on good terms with the King of Naples, assuring him that in no way could he give him greater pleasure.* On the 17th July, he was able to express his satisfaction to Galeazzo in learning that he meant, for the future, to preserve amicable relations with Naples.†

Cardinal Riario was now in the fullest enjoyment of the favour of the Pope. He seemed, says a contemporary, able to do whatever he wished. A chronicler speaks of him as being the first among the Cardinals, having the complete control of the Papal treasure, and the Pope himself entirely in his hands.‡ " Not the reserved, brusque Giuliano, but the versatile and agreeable Pietro was the one to conduct all negotiations, and, with undeniable skill, to assist Sixtus IV., who had little experience in diplomacy, in all the more important business of the State." § The influence of the Cardinal of S. Sisto had in a very short time become so great that he was feared, not only by the Cardinals, but even by Sixtus IV. himself, to whom nothing but the

as the sum paid for Bosco, and says that the whole business was carried out " molto secreta." (Gonzaga Archives.) Girolamo went in person to Milan ; see in Appendix, N. 47, the *Brief of the 22nd June, from the State Archives, Milan. Regarding the splendid presents given by Girolamo to his bride, see MAGENTA, II., 351 seq.

* *Brief of the 22nd June, 1472. (State Archives, Milan.) See Appendix, N. 48.

† *Brief of the 17th July, 1472. State Archives, Milan.

‡ "*Card. de S. Sisto dicto fratre Pietro da Savona ord. min. primo cardinale di Roma lo quale havea ne le mane tutto el thesauro de papa Sisto et che gubernava la Sua Sta come voleva et ad minus cavalchava cum trecento cavali et era de estode de anni circa 23 in 24." U. CALEFFINI, Cronica Ferrariae, f. 38. Cod. I.-I.-4, Chigi Library, Rome.

§ SCHMARSOW, 10–11.

Papal dignity seemed left, while all real power was in the hands of the favourite.*

The year 1473 was one of trouble for Sixtus IV.   In February he was attacked by an illness,† in consequence of which he spent the hot season on the airy heights of Tivoli.‡   All through the summer he was harassed by political anxieties.   In May, tidings came that the Duke of Milan had sold Imola to the Florentines for 100,000 florins, and, at the same time, he heard that the Hungarians had entered into an agreement with the Turks, and meant to attack the Venetians in Dalmatia.§   The last of these reports was false, but the first proved correct.

The Pope was greatly, and very reasonably, disturbed by the sale of Imola.   Neither he nor Ferrante could " calmly witness" the extension of Florentine domination " into the Romagna, which would introduce relations of a very different order from those maintained with the small existing dynasties.   Moreover, the measure was also unwelcome, because it would obviously tend to stimulate the desire of Venice for further annexations."|| On the 16th of May, a Brief of admonition and complaint was addressed to the Duke of Milan, informing him that the Pope would not, on

* NOTAR GIACOMO, 123 ; Cr. di Viterbo di Giov. di Juzzo, 104.   See CORIO, 264.

† See in Appendix, N. 49, the *Brief of the 24th February, 1473. State Archives, Milan.

‡ According to the *Acta Consist. in the Secret Archives of the Vatican, the Pope was absent from Rome from the 19th July to the 13th November.   AMMANATI, Epist., 478, 514, 518, condemns this sojourn of Sixtus IV. at Tivoli.   " He forgot," remarks SCHMARSOW, 17, "when he said this, that Pius II. had loved to stay there." Regarding the care of Sixtus IV. for Tivoli, see VIOLA, III., 108.

§ *Letter of Ol. de Bonafrugis of 26th May, 1473.   Gonzaga Archives.

|| REUMONT, Lorenzo, I., 256, 2nd ed.

any account, permit the sale of Imola.* This declaration was repeated in Papal Missives to Florence itself, to the King of Naples, and to the Bolognese.† A week later, Sixtus IV. again begged the Duke to revoke the sale of this city, which belonged to the Church. "O my son!" he writes, in concluding his letter, "listen to your father's counsel; depart not from the Church, for it is written: 'Whoever separates himself from thee, must perish.'"‡ Shortly afterwards, on the 6th June, another Brief was written to the Duke, who had meanwhile expressed his willingness to comply with the Pope's desire. The importance attached by Sixtus IV. to the matter is manifested by the fact that he again wrote with his own hand.§

On this occasion the Pope obtained all that he wished. Galeazzo Maria Sforza restored Imola to the Holy See for the sum of 40,000 ducats, and, with the consent of the Cardinals, Sixtus IV. conferred it as a fief upon Girolamo Riario.||

There can be no doubt that these circumstances were connected with the tour through Italy which Cardinal Riario undertook, in the middle of the summer of 1473, as Legate for the whole of that country.¶ The commencement of this journey was far from propitious. The Cardinal's efforts to compose the party strife in Umbria

---

* See the **Brief of the 16th May, 1473. State Archives, Milan.

† See the **Brief of 17th May, 1473, in the State Archives, Bologna.

‡ I also found this interesting **Brief, which is in Sixtus IV.'s own handwriting, dated Rome [1473], May 23, in the State Archives, Milan.

§ **Original in the State Archives, Milan.

|| RATTI, II., 35 seq.; BURRIEL, III., XXIX. seq.; TONDUZZI, Faenza, 506; RIGHI, II., 229.

¶ Not late in summer, as SCHMARSOW, 16, says, for, on the 6th August, 1473, *Cardinal Riario writes "ex Tuderto." (State Archives, Florence.) Arch. Med. Filza, 46, f. 263.

were unsuccessful. Spoleto and Perugia refused to obey his commands. "The Legate indignantly turned to Gubbio, whither he had summoned the petty princes of the Flaminian and Pisan territory to meet him; but Niccolo Vitelli, who was practically tyrant of Città di Castello, answered his invitation by saying that he was a private individual, and a simple burgess of his native city; an assembly of Princes in no way concerned him, as he had never coveted so high a title. Thus the Legate was mocked, and the competency of his tribunal denied."* The immediate punishment of the refractory Vitelli being impossible, Riario proceeded to Florence,† to take possession of his Archiepiscopal See, amid great festivities.‡ On the 12th September he entered Milan. The Duke received him with royal honours, conducted him in triumph to the Cathedral, and then to the Castle, where, as if he had been the Pope himself, apartments were given him, and the keys of the Citadel delivered to him each night. In the

* PLATINA, Sixt. IV., 1060; SCHMARSOW, 16. In regard to the dispute concerning the marriage ring of the Blessed Virgin, which at this time occupied the Perugians and then the Pope, see GRAZIANI, 644; PELLINI, 712 *seq.*, 726 *seq.*, 731 *seq.*; BONAZZI, 686 *seq.*; FANTONI, Del pronubo anello della Vergine, Perugia, 1673; CAVALLUCCI, Istoria del s. anello, Perugia, 1783.

† He announced his arrival to Lorenzo in the following words: *"Prest^me vir ut frater car^me. Proximo [die] lune ad vos venturi summemus iter, quod scientes Tue Prest^tie gratum fore scribere voluimus. Vale. Augusti xx., 1473, P[etrus] S. Sixti presb. card., patriarcha Constant. Perusiae etc. legatus." Original in the Arch. Med. Filza, 46, f. 268, State Archives, Florence, where are also a number of *Letters of Riario's, from which the further course of his journey may be learned. He dates ult. Aug. Florentiole, IV. Sept. Bononiae, 18 Octob. ex sancto Cassano.

‡ REUMONT, Lorenzo, I., 255, 2nd ed., where the "eulogistic verses" of Angelo Poliziano, "with their evil bombast and profane idolatry," are mentioned.

negotiations which ensued, the Cardinal succeeded in securing the favour of the Duke for himself. Report, moreover,
spoke of a compact then entered into, by virtue of which
the Pope was to make the Duke of Milan "King of
Lombardy, and give him possession of all the cities and
provinces appertaining to this dignity." The Duke, in
return, it was said, promised to help Cardinal Riario to
obtain the Tiara. It was even asserted that, on his return
to Rome, the Pope would resign the Chair of St. Peter in
favour of his nephew!*

From Milan, Riario proceeded by way of Mantua† and
Padua to Venice, where further festivities awaited him.
By the end of October‡ he was again in Rome. Soon
afterwards Sixtus IV. thanked the Duke of Milan for
his splendid reception of Riario, and confirmed the arrangements entered into by the latter.§

Two months more brought the scandalous life and

* SCHMARSOW, 16 *seq.*, and BURCKHARDT, I., 101, 2nd ed., are
inclined to give credit to Corio's Report. See also Arch. St. Lomb.,
III., 449, and VI., 721 *seq.* I have found nothing concerning this
matter in the Ambassadors' Despatches.

† SCHIVENOGLIA, 175-6.

‡ This appears from a *Brief of Sixtus IV. to Bologna, dated Rome,
1473, Oct. 28, in which he says, "as soon as ever Cardinal Riario
returned, he told me of his splendid reception at Bologna;" the
Pope then expresses his thanks. (State Archives, Bologna, Q. 3.)
With this accords the following notice in the *Cronica Ferrariae of
the Notary Caleffini : *"1473 a di 13 de Octobre arivò in Ferrara il
card. S. Sisto cum circa 300 cavali nominato frate Pietro da Savona ;
he had been in Lombardy and Venice ; the Duke went to meet him,
and shewed him great honour. On the 15th, the Cardinal started
for Rome per la via de la Marcha." Cod. I.-I.-4, Chigi Library,
Rome.

§ See in Appendix, N. 50, the *Brief of 2nd Nov., 1473, from the
State Archives, Milan. See CORIO, 276, whose manner of expressing
himself lacks exactness and clearness.

ambitious projects of the Pope's nephew to an end. In
the third week of December, 1473, Riario was attacked
by a violent fever; * on the 5th January, 1474, he was
a corpse.† Venetian poison was spoken of by some, but
the statement of other contemporaries, who say that the
Cardinal, though only eight and twenty years of age, fell
a victim to his own excesses, is more probable.‡ The

* See the *Report of J. P. Arrivabene, dated Rome, 1473,
Dec. 20, who speaks of "febre continua" and "gran indisposition
del stomacho"; only the physicians were admitted to see him.
(Gonzaga Archives, Mantua.) Riario must soon have recovered;
see the Despatch of the 30th Dec. 1473, in Arch. d. Soc. Rom., XI.,
264, when a relapse ensued.

† *Acta Consist., Secret Archives of the Vatican, and *Letter of the
Mantuan Ambassador, dated Rome, 1474, Jan. 5.

‡ A highly-coloured apologetic article, " Il card. fra Pietro Riario,"
in the Civ. Catt., III., 705, 1868, questions the testimony of Raph.
Volaterranus, because he wrote his "Commentarii" thirty years after
the death of the Cardinal; this objection cannot be raised against that
of PALMERIUS, who expressly says, p. 257 : "morbo ex intemperantia
contracto moritur." See also Arrivabene's *Report of the 20th Dec.,
1473, cited above. Riario was buried in the Church of the Holy
Apostles, where the well-known beautiful monument was erected in
his memory (see SCHMARSOW, 166 seq.). The obsequies took place
on the 18th Jan., according to the *Acta Consist. of the Secret
Archives of the Vatican. In Cod. 45, C. 18, of the Corsini Library,
Rome, f. 117–23, is the *Oratio in funere rev^di d. Petri card. S. Sixti
habita Romae a rev^do patre d. Nicolao episc. Modrusien, a tissue
of flatteries which must be received with the greatest circumspection.
The orator may be more easily credited when he praises Riario's
great "liberalitas"; he then continues : "Extinctus jacet optimarum
artium dedicatissimus amator. Interiit omnium studiosorum prae-
cipuus fautor, cultor bonorum (!) curiae splendor, ornamentum civitatis
et huius urbis diligentissimus restaurator." The notice, f. 119,
"Nullas a ministris impensarum exigebat rationes : nulla computa
exigere volebat," is interesting, as a proof of his neglect of money
matters. CIACONIUS, III., 43, says that the "Oratio in funere Petri
card. S. Sixti habita a Nicolao episc. Modrusien" has been published.

Report of a Milanese Ambassador also informs us that
Riario was converted before his end, received the holy
Sacraments, and died truly penitent.*

All Rome wept with Sixtus IV. over the untimely death
of the pomp-loving Cardinal.   The feeling of the people
is expressed by the Senatorial Secretary, Infessura, who
says : " Our delightful feasts all came to an end, and
every one lamented the death of Riario." †   In the short
period of his cardinalate he had squandered 200,000, or,
according to some accounts, 300,000 golden florins, and
the debts which he left amounted to 60,000 florins.‡
Justice, however, requires us to add that Riario had also
spent some of his wealth on noble objects.   " In his love
of splendour we trace the taste of the period for that
artistic embellishment of existence, without which the
temporal rulers of the day, even the wildest and most
warlike of them, deemed it impossible to live.   During
his sojourn at his Palace of the Holy Apostles," continues Melozzo da Forli's biographer, " his love of the
fine arts was evidenced by the way in which he attracted
to himself, and gathered into his service, all the talent
that Rome afforded." §   This account is confirmed by the
statement of a Roman scholar, who, after a thorough
investigation of the subject, asserts that every poet at

* Letter of Sacramorus, written on the 5th Jan., 1474, in Arch. d.
Soc. Rom., XI., 262-4.

† INFESSURA, 1144. Many cutting satirical verses were also composed on the occasion ; see CORIO, 276, and SCHMARSOW, 338 ;
of this class is the Epitaphium rev. d. Petri card^lis Sixti IV. in the
rare little volume entitled " Epitaphia claror. viror.," Strasburg, 1510.

‡ Cr. di Viterbo di Giov. di Juzzo, 104, and RAPH. VOLATERRANUS,
XXII., f. 234.

§ SCHMARSOW, 50 ; see 54, 163, where it is shewn that, after critical
investigation, the connection of Melozzo da Forli with Cardinal Riario,
although very probable, is not absolutely proved.

that time living in Rome has commemorated the Cardinal as a patron of talent.* The funeral discourse pronounced at his obsequies makes mention of the valuable library which he was preparing to establish in his Palace, and also his restorations and embellishments of churches at Treviso, Milan, Pavia, and Rome.†

* CORVISIERI, in Arch. d. Soc. Rom., I., 478 *seq.* See also COR-SIGNANI, II., 468, and Civ. Catt., III., 696 *seq.*, 1868.

† In particular, S. Gregorio in Rome ; with regard to the Church of the Holy Apostles, the funeral discourse only declares that Riario intended to beautify it. Cod. 45, C. 18, f. 121b-122 of the Corsini Library, Rome.

CHAPTER III.

Christian, King of Denmark and Norway, and Federigo of Urbino in Rome.— Disturbances in the States of the Church.— Cardinal Giuliano della Rovere's Expedition into Umbria.— Federigo becomes Duke of Urbino, and gives his Daughter in Marriage to Giovanni della Rovere.—The League of the 2nd November, 1474.

Sixtus IV. consoled himself more quickly than had been expected for the death of his beloved nephew.* For a few days he gave himself up to his sorrow, no one, not even the Cardinals, being admitted to his presence ; † but on the 10th January, 1474, the Mantuan Ambassador was able to inform the Marchioness that the Pope was beginning to get over

---

* Even the *Brief of the 6th Jan., 1474, to Ercole of Este has a calm and collected tone :   *"Sed quoniam ita fuit Dei voluntas, in cuius potestate omnia posita sunt, ferendum est equo animo iuxta illud : Dominus dedit, dominus abstulit, ut domino placuit, sic factum est, sit nomen domini benedictum." The Original is in the State Archives, Modena.   The same quotation occurs in the *Briefs of like import dated Rome, 1474, Jan. 6, which informed the Florentines and the Duke of Milan of P. Riario's death, and commended Girolamo Riario to them.   (State Archives, Florence, X.–II.–25, f. 59, and State Archives, Milan, Autogr.)   It may indeed be a question how far the official letters of the time represented the feelings of the Pope.

† "His Holiness," Marquess Giov. Francesco Gonzaga writes from Rome on the 9th Jan., 1471, to Marchioness Barbara, *"sta molto strata et cum dolore et ad niuno se lasse vedere fin qui ne ad cardinali ne ad altri." Gonzaga Archives, Mantua.

Riario's loss.* The question as to who would now exercise the influence wielded by the late Cardinal, whose jealousy had kept all others in the background, and on whom would his wealth devolve, was eagerly and generally discussed. Some predicted the elevation of Girolamo Riario, while others thought it would be Cardinal Orsini, who had now no opponent.†

Riario's possessions, regarding which fabulous stories were circulated, passed to his brother, Girolamo, who inherited with them much of his influence.‡ Cardinal Giuliano della Rovere also became a prominent figure. The conduct of this nephew of the Pope formed a happy contrast to that of Pietro Riario. Giuliano "was not distinguished by brilliant intellect or fine literary culture, but he was a man of serious disposition and great prudence, though frequently rough in his manner and proceedings. He did not surround himself with an extravagant number of attendants, and indulged in no needless expense in apparel or in living, yet his taste was good in his house and furniture, and he loved excellent workmanship. On suitable occasions, he knew how to give free play to the

---

* "*Benche N.S. doppo la morte de frate Petro ne in lo giorno de la epiphania uscisse fuori a la messa ne habia fatto consistorio ne voluto udire cardinale che sia andato a palatio, nondimeno se intende che de questo caso se ne porta piu constantemente che la brigata pensava e dice che vol attendere a vivere. Le conte Hieronymo sento gli fa persuasione assai a questo effecto." *Letter of J. P. Arrivabene, dated Rome, 1474, Jan. 10. Gonzaga Archives, Mantua.

† See J. P. Arrivabene's *Letter of the 10th Jan., 1474, cited in preceding note.

‡ See N. Benededei's Report in CAPELLI, 252. *"De qua," to use the words of J. P. Arrivabene in a *Despatch, dated Rome, 1474, March 5, "lo conte Jeronimo continua in grande favore e reputatione e fa piu che tuti li altri." Gonzaga Archives, Mantua.

largeness of his nature."* Such occasions presented themselves when princely persons visited his uncle in the Eternal City, and in 1474 and 1475 they were of frequent occurrence.

Early in March, 1474, it was rumoured that King Christian of Denmark and Norway was coming to Rome. Sixtus IV. at once declared his intention of shewing all possible honour to the Northern Prince, and lodging him in the palace formerly occupied by Frederick III. ;† he also wrote him a very cordial letter of welcome.‡ If, as would seem probable from recent investigations, the motive of the King's journey was principally religious, the joy of the Pope and the attentions paid to his guest can easily be understood.§ Moreover, Sixtus IV. hoped for

---

* SCHMARSOW, 18, where is also a good remark regarding the authority of Jacobus Volaterranus. He also justly observes (see p. 10) that the description of Giuliano's first years as a Cardinal given by BROSCH (5 seq.) needs many corrections.

† *Letter of Card. Gonzaga, dated Rome, 1474, March 3. Gonzaga Archives.

‡ RAYNALDUS, ad an. 1474, N. 1. The date is not given by Raynaldus, and is also wanting in the MS. B.-19, f. 220, of the Vallicellana Library, Rome. Regarding the pilgrimage of Christian I. to Rome (which MANNI, 79, wrongly assigns to the year 1475), see, besides CANCELLIERI, Notizie della venuta in Roma di Canuto II., e di Christiano I., re di Danimarca negli anni 1027, e 1474, etc. (Roma, 1820), LÖHER in the Hist. Taschenbuch, 1869, p. 266 seq., and HOFMANN, Barbara, 23 ; especially the Danish Monograph of F. KROGH, published in Copenhagen in 1872. In this work the documents in the State Archives, Milan, are used but partially, and without accurate references. Krogh is not acquainted with the *Letters from the Gonzaga Archives, Mantua, which we shall cite.

§ KROGH, 7. In Germany, certainly, every one spoke only of the political objects of this journey, and cities and Bishops heard of it with anxiety. LÖHER, loc. cit., 267. There is no doubt that various diplomatic negotiations were connected with Christian's pilgrimage.

the assistance of Christian I. in the war against the Turks ;
he was aware that the King believed in a prophecy which
had declared that a Northern Ruler was destined to
conquer and expel the Infidel.

The King, a grave man, with a long gray beard, came
with 150 followers ; all were soberly clad, and pilgrims'
staves were embroidered on the housings of their horses.*
On the 6th of April the travellers entered Rome. Christian I. was overwhelmed with tokens of honour ; the whole
Court went to meet him and conducted him to St. Peter's.
Here Sixtus IV. would have embraced him at once, but
the King knelt down with all his followers, and begged
for the Papal blessing. When he rose from his knees,
the Pope embraced him and conducted him to his Palace.
Cardinals Gonzaga and Giuliano della Rovere provided
for the hospitable entertainment of the visitors.†

During the whole time of his sojourn in Rome, Christian I. paid such honour and attention to the Pope and
the clergy, that he was often cited as an example to the
Italians of the manner in which they ought to bear themselves towards the Church and her servants.‡ The Pope
gave the royal pilgrim a portion of the true Cross and
other relics, a portable altar,§ a splendid mule with a
bridle studded with gold, a valuable ring, and other

* See SCHIVENOGLIA, 177-8. The Italians wondered at the fair
hair and complexions of the Northerns ; see N. DELLA TUCCIA, 111 ;
*Ghirardacci, Hist. di Bologna, writes : "Era questo re tutto vestito
di negro con una beretta rossa e portava nel petto un segno come
portono li pelegrini che vanno a S. Jacomo di Galezia." Cod. 768,
University Library, Bologna.

† KROGH, 46 ; SCHMARSOW, 18.

‡ S. AMMANATI, Epist., 556, of the Frankfort edition. The date,
April 4, also given in the Milan edition, f. 276b, must be wrong ;
perhaps it ought to be IV. Idus April = 10th April.

§ Now in the Museum at Copenhagen.

precious things.   On Maundy Thursday, after Holy Mass,
Sixtus IV. bestowed his blessing on the King, and granted
him an Indulgence.   On Easter Sunday Christian received
Holy Communion from the hands of the Pope, and the
Golden Rose.   He also received costly gifts from the
Cardinals, and, in return, presented them with beautiful
furs, and other choice products of his kingdom.*

King Christian remained in Rome for three weeks,
Sixtus IV. shewing him honour in every possible way.†
The conversations between the Pope and the King dealt
with the question of the Crusade, the affairs of the
Northern Kingdom, and perhaps other political projects,
such as the possibility of changing the Ducal Crown of
Sforza into a Royal one.‡   As the Papal Bull for the
foundation of the University of Copenhagen is dated 12th
June, 1475, the erection of such an institution in the North
must also, at this time, have come under discussion.§   The
Pope shewed great readiness in meeting the wishes of
his royal guest with regard to several other Bulls, and
Christian was so much delighted with his sojourn in
Rome that he had a medal struck to commemorate it.‖

* KROGH, 52–3.   See Lübeckische Chroniken, published by
GRAUTOFF, II., 358, where, in some cases, dates different from those
of Krogh are given ; the latter, however, being supported by the Letters
of the Milanese Ambassadors, deserves the preference.

† See the *Report of J. P. Arrivabene, dated Rome, 1474, April 19.
Gonzaga Archives.

‡ LÖHER, *loc. cit.*, 267 *seq.* ; KROGH, 47.

§ The University at Copenhagen was opened on the 1st June,
1479, the High School at Upsala having been inaugurated on the
22nd Sept., 1477 ; see KROGH, 54, and C. ANNERSTEDT, Upsala
universitets historia. Första. delen. (Upsala, 1877).

‖ The only example of this Medal, possessed by the Royal
Collection in Copenhagen, was lost in 1805 ; KROGH, 55.   How far
Sixtus IV. consented to the extension of Royal rights over the Danish
Clergy, which, by the advice of Albrecht of Brandenburg, Christian

After again devoutly visiting the seven principal Churches,* Christian I. started on the 27th April on his homeward journey.† The Milanese Ambassador informs us that all the Cardinals conducted him, with every token of respect, to the gate of the City. Two members of the Sacred College accompanied him on his way, as far as the frontier of the Papal territory. According to the same Ambassador, Christian was the bearer of important letters from the Pope to the Emperor, Frederick III., a fact which proves that the opportunity afforded by this pilgrimage for discussing political affairs had not been neglected.‡

Soon after the departure of Christian, Count Federigo of Urbino, a former friend of the Pope, arrived in Rome.§ On this occasion also, Cardinal Giuliano was splendid in his hospitality ; " he had given up his residence in S. Pietro in Vincoli to the City Prefect, and had moved to Bessarion's Palace, near the Church of the Holy Apostles."‖ On the 28th May, the Count was solemnly received by the Pope ; Sixtus IV. had "assigned him a place in the Chapel on the benches of the Sacred College, so that he sat immediately below the last Cardinal, an honour hitherto reserved for the eldest sons of Kings." Although d'Estouteville and Gonzaga were extremely annoyed at this arrangement, the Pope adhered to it.¶ His motive

sought to obtain, I am unable to say. (See Archiv für Œsterr. Gesch., VII., 98-9.)

* This is expressly stated by J. P. Arrivabene in a *Letter, dated Rome, 1474, April 24. Gonzaga Archives, Mantua.

† *Report of Sacramorus, dated Rome, 1474, April 28. State Archives, Milan, "Roma."

‡ See KROGH, 55.

§ BALDI, III., 208 ; REPOSATI, I., 42.

‖ SCHMARSOW, 18-19.

¶ JACOBUS VOLATERRANUS, Diarium, 95. See two *Reports of J. P. Arrivabene, dated Rome, 1474, May 28. Gonzaga Archives, Mantua.

was soon evident. A marriage was in contemplation between a daughter of Federigo and Giuliano's younger brother, Giovanni della Rovere, who was to be given Sinigaglia and Mondavio. Even before it had been discussed in Consistory the Pope had impressed upon the Count the impossibility of obtaining the consent of the Cardinals to the project.* Jacobus Volaterranus informs us that it was looked upon in the Sacred College as a dangerous example of nepotism. Federigo was obliged to depart without effecting his purpose.†

During the Count's sojourn in Rome, and at the very time when the Pope was occupied in taking precautions against an impending dearth, tidings reached him of the murder of Gabriello Catalani, the Guelph Lord of Todi, and of the outbreak in that city of an insurrection which seemed likely to spread.‡ All the discontented from Umbria, and especially from Spoleto, with their partisans, flocked into Todi, and were headed by Giordano Orsini and the Counts of Pitigliano.§ Soon the whole of the province was in commotion. Rioting, murder, and incendiarism were the order of the day. If the whole place was not to be given over to absolute anarchy, " it was necessary to act at once with a strong hand."‖

At the beginning of June, Sixtus IV. sent Cardinal Giuliano to restore peace in Todi by force of arms.¶ The

* *Letter of Cardinal Gonzaga to his father, dated Rome, 1474, May 27. Gonzaga Archives, Mantua.

† See *Cardinal Gonzaga's Letters, dated Rome, 1474, June 2 and 4, *loc. cit.*

‡ PLATINA, Sixtus IV., 1061.

§ The people of Spoleto had already, at the beginning of the year, given trouble to those of Ceretano. See the *Brief of 3rd Febr., 1474. State Archives, Florence.

‖ Opinion of SCHMARSOW, 20.

¶ See the **Letter of Cardinal Giuliano della Rovere to Lorenzo

task was one of great difficulty, but in selecting Giuliano
the Pope had chosen a man well fitted to carry it out.*
" Accustomed to privations, and to the stern discipline of
the cloister, the Cardinal did not shrink from the hardships
of a soldier's life.   With the assistance of the valiant
Giulio of Camerino, he forced his way into Todi.   Giordano
Orsini and the Count of Pitigliano withdrew, some of the
insurgents were cast into prison and others banished, and
all communication between the country people and the city
was cut off." †

Cardinal Giuliano then turned his arms against Spoleto,
which, at the time, was in the hands of the party of the
Orsini.   At 3000 paces from the city he halted, and, through
Lorenzo Zane, Patriarch of Antioch, called upon the
inhabitants to lay down their arms.   Thereupon many of
the citizens fled, carrying their most valuable possessions
to the mountain fortresses in the neighbourhood ; the rest
accepted the Ambassador's offers of peace, went to meet

de' Medici, dated Rome, 1474, June 1 (State Archives, Florence), and
Sixtus IV.'s Brief to Perugia of the same day.   Arch. St. Ital., XVI.,
588.   The day of Giuliano's departure from Rome is not mentioned in
the *Acta Consist. of the Secret Archives of the Vatican, which, for
this period, are very fragmentary and incomplete.   The Pope, at the
same time, appealed to the friendly powers for their support ; see the
*Brief of the 1st June, 1474, in Appendix, N. 51.   (State Archives, Milan.)
The Cardinal's Mission to Todi was announced to the people of
Spoleto by a Brief of the 3rd June, 1474 ; see SANSI, Saggio di Doc.,
43–5.

* Even in 1472 Sixtus IV. had endeavoured to appease disturbances
which had broken out in Todi.   Two *Briefs to Perugia, one dated
1472, April 16, and the other s. die, are excerpted in Cod. C. IV. 1,
University Library, Genoa.

† PLATINA, 1061 ; FRANTZ, 153 ; SCHMARSOW, 20.   See also Sixtus
IV.'s *Brief to Florence of the 20th June (State Archives, Florence,
X.–II.–25, f. 62b–63), and that to Ercole d'Este of the 14th July, 1474.
State Archives, Modena.

the Legate, and begged for pardon. Giuliano garrisoned the gates of the city, and had already begun to endeavour to reconcile the contending parties, when, in defiance of his express command, the greedy mercenaries began to plunder. Most of these men were from Camerino and Ceretano, and were bent on retaliating on the people of Spoleto the depredations which they had suffered at their hands. The Legate's voice was powerless to restrain the lawless troops ; indeed, his own life was at one moment in danger. He could only be thankful that he was able to save the Episcopal Palace and the Convents, and to preserve the women and maidens from outrage. "Such," observes Platina, "was the fate of the Spoletans, who had despised the Pope's commands, and had filled their city with the spoils of their neighbours."*

At the end of June, the Cardinal proceeded to the upper valley of the Tiber, where Niccolo Vitelli, the tyrant of Città di Castello, replied to all remonstrances from Rome with words of open scorn. He was charged with having lent assistance to the insurgents in Todi and Spoleto : the time had come when he must be compelled to submit. His contumacy seemed all the more dangerous, because it found favour with his neighbours. "Whenever any political dispute should break out with Rome, the forcible alienation of the important district on the borders of Tuscany was to be apprehended. The adjacent stronghold of Borgo San Sepolcro was still in the hands of the Florentines, to whom it had been mortgaged by Eugenius IV. The Pope was bound to put an end to this state of

* PLATINA, 1061-2. See SCHMARSOW, 20 ; FRANTZ, 154 seq.; CAMPELLO, lib. XXXVII. ; PELLINI, 740 ; SANSI, Saggio di Doc., 43-4, and Storia, 68 seq. In the *Briefs of June 20 and July 14, 1474, already mentioned, Sixtus IV. speaks of Giuliano's resistance to the plunder of Spoleto.

things." Not till all peaceable means had been exhausted
did he proceed to force.* And even to the last he
declared that, if Vitelli would submit, he would again
receive him into favour, for he only sought obedience,
not vengance.†

Vitelli, meanwhile, had no idea of submission ; he rejected
the easy conditions offered by Cardinal Giuliano, who was
accordingly compelled to lay siege to Città di Castello.
Sorties were made every day, and the Papal troops
repeatedly suffered serious losses. But a far greater danger
threatened them in the consequences of an alliance which
Vitelli had succeeded in negotiating with Milan and
Florence. The Florentines, forgetful of benefits received
from the Pope, even as recently as during the war of
Volterra, had furnished the tyrant with money, and then,
in spite of the absolute promise of Sixtus IV.‡ that their
territory should remain inviolate, had sent 6000 men to
Borgo San Sepolcro near Città di Castello, ostensibly for
the protection of their frontier, but in reality with the
object of assisting Vitelli whenever the situation should
become critical.§ Sixtus IV. justly complained of the
shameful manner in which help was thus given to "a

---

* SCHMARSOW, 21, where details are given in regard to Vitelli's
defiant bearing towards Paul II. and Ammanati ; the latter pleaded in
favour of Vitelli, and thereby incurred the displeasure of Sixtus IV.
See also REUMONT, Lorenzo, I., 257, 2nd ed.

† See in Appendix, N. 52, the *Brief of the 25th June, 1474. State
Archives, Milan.

‡ "*Promittimus enim vobis in verbo pontificis neque nos neque
legatum nostrum neque ullas copias que illuc profecte sunt aut pro-
ficiscentur minimam offensiunculam terris aut agris vestris illaturas,"
are the words of the *Brief to Florence of the 28th June, 1474. State
Archives, Florence, X.-II.–25, f. 63b-64.

§ FRANTZ, 155; SCHMARSOW, 22. See the opinion of REUMONT,
Lorenzo, I., 257, 2nd ed.

rebellious subject, whom no kindness had been able to win to obedience."*

During the siege of Città di Castello the attitude of Galeazzo Maria Sforza was very unsatisfactory. On the 5th June the Pope felt constrained to express his astonishment at the manner in which the Duke had written to him on this occasion, and to defend the justice of his action. The Pope said, "We ask nothing from Vitelli but obedience; if he will submit, and live as a private individual, We will be gracious to him, but no Prince can tolerate open rebellion. The excuse of the Florentines that they feared an attack on Borgo San Sepolcro, was hypocritical, for, on the 28th June, We had already pledged our word on this matter." †

In the middle of July, Milan and Florence began diplomatic action in favour of Vitelli; meanwhile, the Pope refused to accede to the request that he would withdraw his troops from Città di Castello, giving a full account of the motives which influenced his decision.‡ It is worthy of note that the King of Naples, who had received many benefits from Sixtus IV., also interfered on behalf of the rebels. Anarchy in the States of the Church was more in accordance with his wishes than peace and

* See *Brief to Ercole d'Este, dated Rome, 1474, July 14. State Archives, Modena.

† See the *Brief of 5th July, 1474, in Appendix, N. 53. (State Archives, Milan.) On the same day Sixtus IV. again wrote to Florence: *"Monemus et hortamur vos pro mutua benevolentia, pro iustitia ipsa et honestate, desinite ab inceptis favoribus quos Nicolao prestatis ne indignationem Dei contra vos provocetis." State Archives, Florence, X.–II.–25, f. 64b–65b.

‡ This appears from the *Brief to Naples, Milan, and Florence, dated Rome, 1474, July 18 (Copy in the State Archives, Milan and Bologna, Q. 22), in which the Pope refuses the above-mentioned request.

order. The ingratitude of the Duke of Milan seems to have been particularly distressing to the Pope, who, on the 28th July, 1474, sent him an autograph letter, reproaching him in touching language.*

In this serious state of affairs Sixtus IV. turned to the warlike Count Federigo of Urbino. In order to make yet more sure of his fidelity, he bestowed on him, on the 21st August, the Ducal dignity with the same pomp and ceremonies observed in the case of Borso of Este three years before.† Two days after this, Federigo arrived at the Papal camp before Città di Castello. ‡ On the appearance of this General, "who was reputed to be invincible," Vitelli expressed a willingness to negotiate. His bearing, however, was still anything but submissive. He knew that he had powerful friends to fall back upon, and he was also aware that Federigo had no intention of strengthening the Papal authority on his own borders. The daring rebel was able so to manage the negotiations, that the capitulation was not a submission, but an honourable treaty.§ It was decided that the Cardinal, with 200 soldiers, should be admitted into the city. The personal safety of the tyrant was guaranteed; Lorenzo Zane, Patriarch of Antioch, was to remain with a garrison in

* In Appendix, N. 54, I give this *Letter, which I found in the State Archives, Milan.

† Particulars are given in the Letter of J. P. Arrivabene of the 21st August, 1474, amongst AMMANATI, Epist., N. 568, of the Frankfort edition. See PLATINA, Sixtus IV., 1062, and a *Letter of Card. Gonzaga, dated Rome, 1474, Aug. 21. (Gonzaga Archives, Mantua.) REPOSATI, I., 250, wrongly gives the 23rd March, and REUMONT, Lorenzo, I., 259, 2nd ed., the 23rd August as the day when the Ducal dignity was conferred.

‡ This we learn from a *Letter written by J. P. Arrivabene, and dated Rome, 1474, Aug. 26. Gonzaga Archives.

§ L'ÉPINOIS, 441 ; SCHMARSOW, 23.

the castle until the return of the exiles and the completion of a fort, for the erection of which, Giuliano had given orders. The army then withdrew, and the Cardinal, accompanied by Duke Federigo who brought Vitelli with him, started for Rome.*

The tidings of the fall of Città di Castello were received with great rejoicings in Rome; trumpets announced the event from S. Angelo, and more noise could not have been made about the taking of a Spartacus or a Sertorius; yet, adds Cardinal Gonzaga's Secretary, "I do not believe in a real submission, for there are crafty people who know how to mingle fire and water without disturbing any one."†

The capitulation was, indeed, calculated rather to encourage than to subdue Vitelli. It was in harmony with the whole course of this affair, which clearly shewed the character of the confederates with whom Sixtus IV. had to deal. "Surrounded by treachery, with such an ally as the crafty Ferrante of Naples at his side, and with neighbours like Lorenzo de' Medici, can the Pope be blamed for establishing his nephews firmly in the States of the Church, where a Cesare Borgia and a Pope like Julius II. were needed to purge it from its oppressors great and small?"‡

---

* SCHMARSOW, 23, who (p. 21, note 3) draws attention to the fact that Roberto Orsi's (De obsidione Tifernatum, Citta di Castello, 1538; and in TARTINIUS, II., 671 seq.—an Italian translation by E. Manucci appeared in 1866 at Perugia) account is that of a partisan of Vitelli's. See also UGOLINI, I., 507. In a Brief, dated Rome, 1474, Sept. 2, Sixtus IV. informs the Duke of Milan "deditionem civitatis nostre Castelli." The original is in the State Archives, Milan, and it was printed by MARTÈNE, II., 1468.

† Letter of J. P. Arrivabene of the 3rd Sept., 1474, in AMMANATI, Epist., 574, Frankfort edition. See ibid., N. 575, and a *Letter of Cardinal Gonzaga to his father, dated Rome, 1474, Sept. 5. Gonzaga Archives.

‡ FRANTZ, 156-7.

Platina informs us that the Legate, on his journey back to Rome, was met by Envoys from many cities, who congratulated him and brought him valuable presents. These the Cardinal either declined, not from pride, but as unbefitting a servant of the Church, or else devoted to pious objects, like the restoration of Churches and Convents.[*] " On the 9th of September, early in the morning, Giuliano with the Duke reached the Porta Flaminia.   All the Cardinals had been commanded by the Pope to go and meet him, but the hardy Ligurian was too early for them. Before the sun had risen he was in the Church of Sta Maria del Popolo.   Thence he was conducted to his Palace with great pomp.   The Duke, the City Prefect, and Count Girolamo rode in front, preceded by Vitelli amid some nobles."   A Consistory was then held, and the vanquished rebel did homage.[†]   The Pope was prevented by indisposition from taking part in these proceedings.[‡]

During the Duke of Urbino's sojourn in Rome on this occasion he received honours even greater than those bestowed upon him in the spring.   The rooms provided for him were immediately above those of the Pope.[§]   This time the negotiations regarding the marriage were brought

---

[*] PLATINA, Sixtus IV., 1063.   See SIGISMONDO DE' CONTI, I., 9.

[†] Letter of J. P. Arrivabene of the 9th Sept., 1474, in AMMANATI, Epist., 578, Frankfort ed. ; SCHMARSOW, 23.

[‡] On the 9th September, Arrivabene was full of conjectures as to the Pope's malady, but on the 10th he was able to write : *" Lo mal del papa per quanto se habia è piccol cosa ; ha havuto doi legieretti parosismi de terzanetta, de la qual se munda e non ne fanno caso se non per essere papa, e lo secundo de heri doppo'l disnare non fu piu che tre hore."   On the 16th of September, the same Ambassador says : *" La cosa è tardata per questa puocha febre del papa che fu solamente doi parosismi, hora sta bene."   Gonzaga Archives, Mantua.

[§] *Letter of Card. Gonzaga, dated Rome, 1474, Nov. 2.   Gonzaga Archives.

to a satisfactory conclusion.   On the 10th of October Sixtus
IV. informed the Duke of Milan that " to-day the betrothal
of our nephew, Giovanni della Rovere, with the Duke of
Urbino's daughter, has been announced." *   Two days
later, the Vicariates of Sinigaglia and Mondavio, which,
after the death of Pius II., had revolted against Antonio
Piccolomini, Duke of Amalfi, were conferred upon Giovanni.†   The document appointing him Vicar was signed
by all the Cardinals, including those who before had voted
against the measure, with the exception of Cardinal Piccolomini.   The yearly salary was fixed at 600 ducats.‡

In attaching to himself, by benefits and by bonds of
relationship, the warlike Federigo of Urbino, who might
have been a dangerous enemy, Sixtus IV. had achieved an
important political success.   Indeed, the Pope had much
reason to congratulate himself on all that he had gained
during the summer of 1474.   The attempt " to keep his
hands full at home, by making troubles in the States of
the Church, had not succeeded for any time, and its authors
had been exposed.   The intrigues of Lorenzo de' Medici
were laid bare.   He had most unwarrantably interfered in
a private affair of the Pope's.   Even Cardinal Ammanati,
who certainly was no partisan of the Rovere family,
thought it necessary to remonstrate with him.   Not content
with supporting the insurgents, he had, under cover of the
confederation, sent letters and messengers about to excite

* See Appendix, N. 55.   State Archives, Milan.

† SIENA, L., St. di Sinigaglia, 154.

‡ *Report of J. P. Arrivabene, dated Rome, 1474, Oct. 12. (Gonzaga Archives.) SCHMARSOW, 343–4, gives extracts from Cod. Urb.,
1023, concerning the architectural works undertaken by Giovanni
della Rovere in Sinigaglia : *La vita e gesti della buona mem. sig. Johan
Prefetto auct. Fra Garzia de Francia.   A good description is also here
given of Giovanni's person.

disturbances throughout the whole of Italy, with the view
of compelling the Pope to desist from the chastisement of
the rebels."*   His efforts had failed, and Lorenzo de' Medici
saw that his hopes of assistance from Milan and Naples
were vain.†   He at once looked about him for new allies,
and turned to Venice.   The rulers of the Republic, however,
felt that the league against the Turks bound them to
Naples, and yet more to the Pope, who had sent money
and provisions when Scutari was besieged.‡   The Signoria,
Navagiero informs us, answered Lorenzo's overtures by
declaring that they had already concluded a league with
Naples, and with the Pope, and that he was free to join
it.   The matter was to be dealt with in Rome, where
Ambassadors from all parts would soon meet.   The hopes
of the Pope, that his wish for a general alliance among the
Italian powers might yet be fulfilled, began to revive.
The failure of this scheme, so necessary in view of the
warlike preparations of the Turks, was in no way his
fault.§

The progress of the negotiations seemed at first to
justify the brightest expectations.   An agreement, which
satisfied all parties, was framed.   But at the last moment,
when the treaty was about to be signed, Ferrante, according to the testimony of a Venetian chronicler, instructed

* SCHMARSOW, 24.   SIGISMONDO DE' CONTI, I., 9, writes of Lorenzo :
"Nam praeterquam quod Nicolao pecunias et vires subministrabat,
omnem Italiam literis nunciisque sub specie foederis sollicitavit ad
opem illi ferendam, ut pontifex ab incepto turpiter desistere cogeretur."

† PLATINA, Sixtus IV., 1063.

‡ SCHMARSOW, loc. cit.

§ An anonymous *Letter, ex Constant., III. Julii, 1474, says :
*"Imprimis in Constantinopoli publice divulgabatur che in el anno
futoro il Turcho intende de uscire cum una potente armata in el golfo
de Vinexia." (State Archives, Milan.   Milit. Guerre, Turchia.)   See
also Mon. Hung., II., 263.

his Ambassadors to break off the negotiations.* On the 2nd November, 1474, Florence, Venice, and Milan concluded a defensive alliance for twenty-five years.† The Duke of Ferrara, the Pope, and the King of Naples were invited to join this league. The Duke alone consented to do so.‡ Sixtus IV. gave a decided refusal, accompanying it with a full explanation of the reasons which induced it. He looked upon the league "as a coalition against the Holy See, an attempt to isolate him and to reduce him to the position of a mere tool for carrying out the egotistical policy of the Tyrants." § Such was the condition of Italy immediately preceding the Holy Year proclaimed by Paul II.

* Navagiero (in MURATORI, XXIII.), 1144.

† *Renovatio et instauratio pacis et ligae inter Venetos, ducem Mediolani et Florentinos cum infrascriptis capitulis. In nomine s. et ind. trinitatis, etc. A° 1474 die II. mensis Novemb. Compertum est pacem ut rerum optimam mortalibus a nostro redemptore imperatam, ita maxime necessariam non posse in Italia esse diuturnam sola cessatione bellorum, etc. Cod. B. 19, f. 156, Vallicell. Library, Rome. RAYNALDUS, ad an. 1474, N. 15, used this copy; I saw another in the State Archives, Bologna, lib. Q. 22. See also concerning the proclamation of the League, SISMONDI, XI., 33 ; ROMANIN, IV., 373 ; REUMONT, Lorenzo, I., 261, 2nd ed. ; TRINCHERA, I., p. LX. ; VIGNA, II., 2, 473.

‡ According to Califfini, *Cronica Ferrariae, Ercole joined the League on the 14th February, 1475. Cod. I.–I.–4, f. 51, Chigi Library, Rome.

§ FRANTZ, 150. See CHMEL, Mon. Habsb., III., 471, and RAUSCH, 147.

CHAPTER IV.

As early as the 26th March, 1472, Sixtus IV. had confirmed his predecessor's decision that every twenty-fifth year should be a year of Jubilee; a further Bull of the 29th August, 1473, abrogated all other Indulgences and Faculties during the Jubilee Year.* In Rome itself the Pope at once began various works of embellishment in preparation for the approaching solemnity. "From the autumn of 1474," writes Platina, "Sixtus IV. devoted himself to the beautifying of Rome. The bridge, which, from its ruinous state, had long been called by the Romans the Ponte Rotto, was rebuilt from its foundations, at great cost, of square blocks of Travertine. This restoration was an immense boon, both to the Romans and to the strangers who came for the Jubilee, and Sixtus IV., with a justifiable pride, desired that it should bear the name of Ponte Sisto. It was a truly princely gift, and we appreciate it all the more, when we see that no Pope before him had ever attempted it. In my opinion," continues Platina, "this was done principally to guard against the recurrence of the disaster which occurred on the Bridge of St. Angelo, in the time of Nicholas V., and which I have already related, when,

* Raynaldus, ad an. 1472, N. 60; Manni, 76.

owing to a panic, numbers of pilgrims were crushed to death."*

Infessura tells us that this bridge was begun in the spring of 1473. On the 29th of April the foundation stone was laid. The Pope, with the Cardinals and several prelates, proceeded to the bank of the Tiber, and, descending into the bed of the river, inserted, in the foundations, a square stone, with the inscription : " Built by Pope Sixtus IV. in the year of Salvation, 1473."† Two years later the work was completed, so that this " most durable and solid," though not beautiful, bridge was ready for the use of the pilgrims in the Jubilee Year.‡ Two inscriptions on marble tablets also for many centuries bore witness to the care of Sixtus IV. for these pilgrims.§

Another work of great public utility, commenced in 1472, was finished in the Jubilee Year. The Aqueduct, conducting the Aqua Virgo to Rome, which had been almost stopped up, was cleared out and prolonged from the Quirinal to the Fontana Treve.‖ " The architectural decorations at its mouth were entrusted to Antonio Lori

---

* PLATINA, Sixtus IV., 1064. The passage is important, as it shews that Platina's Vita Nicolai V. was at this time completed, and furnishes a further argument in support of the belief that the Vita Sixti IV. in Muratori is really from the pen of Platina. See, on this subject, also *infra*, Chap. XII. The beginning of the works in Rome coincides, according to Platina, with Barbo's return from Germany, which was in the end of October, 1474 ; see *supra*, p. 224, note †, the extract from the *Acta Consist., Secret Archives of the Vatican.

† INFESSURA, 1143.

‡ VASARI, IV., 136, is wrong in naming Baccio Pontelli as the architect ; see MÜNTZ, III., 201 ; SCHMARSOW, 32.

§ In the present day nothing is spared, and these memorials have been removed. For the text of the inscriptions, see REUMONT, III., 1, 533, and FORCELLA, XIII., 54.

‖ PLATINA, 1064 ; MÜNTZ, III., 174 *seq.*

of Florence and Giacomo of Ferrara.   Here, as in many
other undertakings, Sixtus IV. continued what Nicholas
V. had begun.   Opposite to the simple inscription left
by his predecessor, he placed one of his own, and surmounted it with a cornice which, with pillars, formed
the façade."*

The chief solicitude of Sixtus IV. was for the restoration
of those Churches and Sanctuaries which were the special
objects of the pilgrims.   He had St. Peter's thoroughly
cleaned, and inserted several windows to admit more
light.   He caused a portion of the wall on the left side,
which was in a dangerous condition, to be strengthened.
The Basilica of Constantine was cleansed, and the side
aisles were refloored and embellished.†   The Vatican Palace
was restored ; the bronze equestrian statue of Marcus
Aurelius Antoninus, which was falling from age, was
repaired, and placed in front of the Lateran on a larger
marble pedestal decorated with trophies.‡   The Church
of the Holy Apostles was beautified, and many of the
smaller Churches, which, even in those days, were very
numerous in Rome, were renovated.   " There was hardly a
chapel in the whole City," says Sigismondo de' Conti, " to
which the Pope did not contribute something in the Jubilee
Year."   Many inscriptions still remain which bear witness
to his energy in this respect.§

---

* SCHMARSOW, 33.   FEA, Storia delle Acque, p. 16 (Roma, 1832),
and the *Poem in the Court Library, Vienna, 2403, f. 10, cited p. 209.

† PLATINA, Sixtus IV., 1064 ; SCHMARSOW, 34 ; ROHAULT, 254.

‡ Albertini Opusculum de mirabilibus Romae, 1509, ed. Schmarsow,
Heilbronn, 1886.

§ MÜNTZ, III., 154 *seq.* ; SCHMARSOW, 35.   The passage in SIGIS-
MONDO DE' CONTI is I., p. 205.   See also FORCELLA, VIII., 301 ; IX.,
263, 345, 531 ; X., 35, 219, 221, 319, 322, 323 ; ARMELLINI, 112, 133,
199, 245, 260, 577, 593.

The Cardinals vied with the Pope in their care for the Sanctuaries of the Eternal City. "The ancient saying, that the people copy their Princes, was verified," wrote Platina, in the year 1474, "for so much building is going on throughout Rome, that, if Sixtus lives, the whole City will soon be transformed. Inspired by these examples, Guillaume d'Estouteville, the Cardinal Archbishop of Ostia, had vaulted the side aisles of the Basilica of the Holy Crib, now called Santa Maria Maggiore, and so embellished it, that nothing finer can be found in Rome."*

In the early part of this pontificate the restoration of the ruined Hospital of Santo Spirito was begun. Here, also, care for the expected pilgrims was the chief inducement for taking the work in hand.† Amongst many other instances of his solicitude for their welfare, we find exhortations addressed to the Italian Powers, calling on them to take care that the roads should be good and secure, to provide a sufficient number of inns for their accommodation, and not to burden them with tolls.‡

Similar considerations led Sixtus IV. "to revert to the plans for the improvement of the streets, already contemplated by the patron of Leon Battista Alberti."§ In a Brief, addressed to the Papal Commissary, Girolamo de Giganti, on the 14th December, 1473, we find the following passage: "Amongst countless other cares we must also

---

* PLATINA, Sixtus IV., 1064; SCHMARSOW, 36; PAULUS DE ANGELIS, Bas. Mar. Mag, Descriptio, 44 and 52 (Roma, 1621).

† Further details are given *infra*, Chap. XII. In 1475 the foundation stone of the new Church at the Hospice of the Campo Santo al Vaticano was also laid; see DE WAAL, National-Stiftungen d. Deutsch. Volkes in Rom., 11 (Frankfurt, 1880).

‡ **Brief to Florence, dated Rome, 1474, Nov. 25. (State Archives, Florence, X.–II.–25, f. 78–78b.) See also MARTÈNE, II., 1476, and PEZZANA, III., 367.

§ SCHMARSOW, 33.

attend to the purifying and beautification of our City;
for, if any city should be clean and fair, certainly this one
should be so, since, by reason of the Chair of St. Peter, it
is the head of the whole world. Considering, then, that
through the negligence of those whose duty it is to keep
the streets in good order, they are in many places foul and
unsightly, we command you for the future to pay special
attention to this matter."*   Already in the year 1474 the
paving of the streets between the Bridge of S. Angelo
and the Vatican was put in hand.   The other principal
thoroughfares were then paved with blocks of stone, the
road from Monte Mario to the Borgo repaired, and the
walls and gates of the City restored.†

   In the beginning of the Jubilee Year appeared the celebrated Bull, "which had, for its chief provision, the renovation of Rome."   It opens with the following sentences : " If
it is a part of our common duty to see to the welfare of
all the cities in the States of the Church, then, certainly,
our best-beloved daughter, the chief City of the Church,
hallowed by the blood of the Princes of the Apostles, has a
special claim on our care and attention.   Unhappily, many
calamities have befallen her, through which her buildings
have fallen into decay, and the number of her citizens has
been diminished.   We therefore earnestly desire to see her
population increased, her houses and palaces rebuilt, and
all her other necessities duly provided for."   Many valuable proprietary rights and privileges are promised to all
who will contribute to the accomplishment of these objects.‡

   It may easily be understood that the Pope met with
"great difficulties in carrying out his improvements, when

* MÜNTZ, III., 179–80.

† SCHMARSOW, *loc. cit.*

‡ THEINER, Cod. Dipl., III., 480–81 ; MÜNTZ, III., 180–81 ;
SCHMARSOW, 34.

they involved clearances to be effected in the narrow streets beyond the Leonine City, belonging to the Roman burghers. Haughty barons could not easily be induced to sacrifice their private property, or the unkempt comfort of their dwellings, to the higher end of the common good. Thus progress was necessarily slow, but the Romans dated the obnoxious measures from the visit of the King of Naples, who certainly encouraged the Pope in his plans, although he was not their originator."*

In December, 1474, an approaching visit from the Neapolitan monarch began to be talked of, the motives of which were rather political than religious.† Ferrante and Sixtus IV. had been drawn closer together by the League of November 2, 1474, which was a cause of grave apprehension to them both. A personal interview was now to afford the opportunity of deciding on the attitude to be adopted towards this new combination.

The reception of the King of Naples was honourable in the extreme. Rodrigo Borgia and Giuliano della Rovere,‡ two of the most distinguished among the Cardinals, welcomed him in Terracina, on the borders of the States

---

* SCHMARSOW, 170, is no doubt correct in thus understanding Infessura's well-known anecdote, according to which the King told the Pope that he was not lord of the City as long as the streets remained so narrow and so obstructed with porticoes, balconies, and erections of all kinds.

† *Despatch of Cardinal Gonzaga, dated Rome, 1474, Dec. 18. (Gonzaga Archives, Mantua.) A *Letter from the Cardinal, preserved in the same Archives, and dated Rome, 1474, Dec. 24, says that Ferrante's visit was to be expected on the 20th January, 1475. *On the 2nd January, 1475, he writes that the King would leave Naples on the 7th or 8th of the month.

‡ They left Rome on the 14th January ; see *Letter of J. P. Arriva-bene, dated Rome, 1475, January 17. (Gonzaga Archives.) See also NOTAR GIACOMO, 128.

of the Church. When he entered Rome on the 28th January, 1475, all the Cardinals met him before the Porta S. Giovanni.* Splendid festivities followed. The King and his brilliant suite, however, remained but three days in Rome. Infessura says that the numbers of falcons which the Neapolitans brought with them completely cleared the City and all the neighbourhood of owls.

The King and the Pope interchanged rich presents, nor did Ferrante forget the Roman officials and the Churches.† When he left Rome, on the 1st February, all the Cardinals accompanied him to the Porta S. Paola, and four of their number as far as S. Paola itself, where he heard Mass before starting for Marino, Rodrigo Borgia and Giuliano della Rovere being with him on this occasion, and Federigo of Urbino having also arrived.‡ At Grottaferrata he received the Order of the Garter, sent to him by the King of England.

On the 8th February, 1475, the Mantuan Ambassador wrote word that Ferrante was to return to Rome secretly by night. On the 5th a report was current that the King

---

* Not on the 6th January, 1475, as REUMONT, III., 1, 169, following the inaccurate INFESSURA, 1144, says ; see Cron. Rom., 35 (where certainly 1475 should be read for 1476) ; SUMMONTE, III., 490, and the *Despatch of J. P. Arrivabene, dated Rome, 1475, January 29 : *" Heri introe in Roma la M^ta del Re al qual tuti li cardinali andorono contro un puocho fuora de la porta de S. Janni." (Gonzaga Archives.) The description of Ferrante's entry, given by Giovanni Santi in his *Reimchronik von Urbino (Cod. Ottob., 1305, f. 211b), is, MÜNTZ informs us (III., 279), inaccurate.

† INFESSURA, *loc. cit.* NOTAR GIACOMO, 128-9, where Ferrante's entrance is assigned to the 25th February ; a mistake repeated by REUMONT, Lorenzo, I., 262, 2nd ed. See SUMMONTE, III., 490, and SCHMARSOW, 34.

‡ So we learn from a *Letter written by J. P. Arrivabene, dated Rome, 1475, Febr. 1. Gonzaga Archives, Mantua.

had come privately to the Pope.* According to Paolo della Mastro's Chronicle, he was in Rome on the 13th and 14th February.†

The subject of these interviews between the Pope and Ferrante was at first unknown to the majority even of the Cardinals. On the 17th February, Cardinal Gonzaga thought he had some inkling of it. On that day Sixtus IV. summoned a Consistory, in which he announced that the danger from Turkey called for a general League of all the Italian Powers, and the levy of a tithe from the clergy. This decision was then imparted to the Ambassadors appointed to attend the Consistory, but the Neapolitan Envoy was the only one who displayed any alacrity in responding to the wishes of the Pope.‡ There can be no doubt that negotiations had also been carried on between Sixtus IV. and Ferrante regarding the attitude to be adopted by them towards the League of the 2nd November, 1474.§

The concourse of Jubilee pilgrims, which commenced on Christmas Day of that year, did not at first equal the great expectations entertained. The wars in France, Burgundy, Germany, Hungary, Poland, Spain, and other countries were, according to the Chronicle of Viterbo, the reason why so few people came ; also, respect for the clergy had been much shaken by former experiences.‖ An encouraging token of a return to a better state of feeling was, however, manifested by the much-decried

---

* *Despatches of J. P. Arrivabene, dated Rome, 1475, Febr. 5 and 8. Gonzaga Archives, Mantua.

† Cron. Rom., 35.

‡ **Letter of Card. Gonzaga, dated Rome, 1475, February 17. Gonzaga Archives.

§ See PALMERIUS, 258.

‖ Cron. di Viterbo di GIOV. DI JUZZO, 411.

courtiers, who eagerly availed themselves at Easter of the graces of the Jubilee.* The pilgrims now became more and more numerous. One of the Ambassadors gives 200,000 as the number present when the Pope solemnly blessed the people on Ascension Day.† This is, no doubt, an exaggerated estimate, but the report of this eye-witness fully establishes the fact that the concourse was immense.

Entries in the Confraternity-Book of the Church of the Anima shew that a great many pilgrims, both clerical and lay, came from Germany during the "golden year." ‡

Among the princely personages at Rome on this occasion we may mention Queen Dorothea of Denmark,§ Nicholas of Ujlak,‖ whom Matthias Corvinus had made King of

---

* " "*Questi di sancti benche la Ex. V. soglia havere male opinione de cortesani se attesto tanto al spirituale et a visitar questi luochi sacri per guadagnar lo iobileo che le cose del mundo erano in tuto mese da canto." *Letter of J. P. Arrivabene, dated Rome, 1475, April 1. (Gonzaga Archives, Mantua.) LANDUCCI also went as a pilgrim to Rome in 1475, see Diario, 14.

† *Letter of J. P. Arrivabene, dated Rome, 1475, May 5. He further says : *" Qua concorre gente asai a questo iobileo et piu che mai non se haveria veduto." Gonzaga Archives.

‡ Lib. confrat. b. Mariae de Anima, 25 *seq.*, 78, 105, 260. For an account of the pilgrimage of the Bishop of Ratisbon, see JANNER, III., 574 ; of that of the Abbot of Melk, KEIBLINGER, I., 644 *seq.* Regarding the editio princeps of the tract entitled "Indulgentiae et reliquiae urbis Romae" of 1475, see ROSSI, I., 163.

§ DAAE, Kong Christian, 92, cites only the account of the Chronicle published by Gherens (Norsk. Hist. Tidsskr., IV., 105). The Queen's journey is mentioned also by SCHIVENOGLIA, 180 ; GIOV. DI JUZZO, 411 ; and SIGISMONDO DE' CONTI, I., 204. See also KROGH, 25 ; and HOFMANN, Barbara von Hohenzollern, 23.

‖ See ENGEL, Welthist., XLIX., 3, 431 ; *Califfini, Cronica Ferrariae (Cod. I.-I.-4, f. 51-2, Chigi Library, Rome), says that the Re di Bossina arrived at Ferrara on the 21st February, 1475, with 110 horses (andava a Roma al perdono del jubileo), and was again there on the

Bosnia ; Anthony of Burgundy, the "Great Bastard ";* and finally, Charlotte of Lusignan. Charlotte had left Rhodes on the 4th July, 1474, and was never again to see that island or Cyprus. She had gone first to her husband at Montcalier, and now journeyed to Rome, where her rights were recognised.† In the latter part of May she reached Civita Vecchia,‡ and on the 3rd June entered Rome. The Cardinals went to meet the deposed Princess, and during her stay in Rome she was entertained at the Pope's expense.§

Sixtus IV. caused the reception of Charlotte of Lusignan to be portrayed among the frescoes in the Hospital of S. Spirito. "Beneath the picture, still visible, which represents the Queen, adorned with the insignia of her rank and surrounded by her attendants, kneeling before Sixtus IV., is a somewhat fulsome inscription, which

---

5th April on his return journey. J. P. Arrivabene also says, in a *Letter, dated Rome, 1475, March 24, that the King of Bosnia came only on account of the Jubilee. Who the "ill. madama ducessa d'Alemagna," mentioned in a *Letter of Arrivabene's, dated Rome, 1475, March 6, as then arriving in Rome, may be, I am unable to say. Gonzaga Archives.

* Jahrbuch der Preuss. Kunstsammlungen, II., 253. Anthony's visit to Naples in the month of April is mentioned by the Giornali Napol., 1135, and his arrival at Ferrara on the 15th June, by Califfini, *loc. cit.*, f. 52. (Chigi Library, Rome.) Arrivabene, in a *Despatch, dated Rome, 1475, May 22, also says, "to-morrow the bastardo de Bergogna will depart." Gonzaga Archives, Mantua.

† HERQUET, Königsgestalten, 89–90, and Charlotta, 186 *seq.*, who, however, like MAS–LATRIE, III., 114, is ignorant of the exact time of her arrival in Rome. See also Bibl. de l'École des Chartes, p. 268 (1877).

‡ See *Letters of J. P. Arrivabene, dated Rome, 1475, May 18 and 22. Gonzaga Archives, Mantua.

§ *Letter of Arrivabene, dated Rome, 1475, June 8 (El papa li fa le spese). *Loc. cit.*

declares that the Pope received the unhappy lady with
such kindness, that, in her overflowing gratitude, she was
incapable of words and could only weep." *   Charlotte
spent the next year in Rome, supported by a pension from
the Pope; a house in the Leonine City, now the Palazzo
de Convertende, was assigned to her as a residence.†

The Jubilee year closed sadly for the Pope. The City
Prefect fell ill at the end of October, and died on the 11th
November.‡ Sixtus IV. conferred the vacant post on his
nephew, Giovani della Rovere.§ During the same month,
the Tiber rose and overflowed a great part of the City.
The mud, which it deposits more abundantly than almost
any other river, and the continued dampness of the flooded
quarter, produced malaria and pestilence.‖ Under these

* HERQUET, Königsgestalten, 90, and Charlotta, 194.

† See ADINOLFI, Portica, 96 *seq.*   Regarding the maintenance given
by the Pope, see MAS-LATRIE, III., 148 *seq.*; and GOTTLOB, Cam. Ap.

‡ J. P. Arrivabene wrote from Rome on the 3rd Nov., 1475:
*"Heri sera lo prefetto laborabat in extremis destitutus omni spe
medicorum.   Nra Sre [= Card. Gonzaga] fu a visitarlo . . . Sua Bne
fa mostra de haverne extrema passione." (Gonzaga Archives.) Regarding his death, see INFESSURA, 1145.

§ On the 17th December, 1475, see Cod. XXXIII.-129, f. 115.
(Barberini Library, Rome.)   A * "Panegyricus cum Joannes Rovere
praefectus urbis creatus est," composed by D. Calderino, is preserved
in Cod. 157 of the Chapter Library, Verona.   Giovanni, by his
marriage with the Duke of Urbino's daughter, solemnised in 1478,
"with Persian pomp" (Palmerius), Lord of Sinigaglia, was, as
SCHMARSOW, 43, remarks, the most permanently prosperous of the
Pope's nephews, and his son, Francesco Maria della Rovere, became
heir to the Duchy of Urbino.   In regard to Giovanni's popularity in
Sinigaglia, see SIENA, Sinigaglia, III., 160.

‖ INFESSURA, 1145, and NOTAR GIACOMO, 130. See A. DE WAAL,
Das Böhmische Pilgerhaus in Rom., p. 70 (Prague, 1873). The Plague
soon spread through a great part of the Italian Peninsula ; see
HÖRSCHELMANN in the Allg. Ztg., 1884, N. 177 ; BONAZZI, 728 ; and
MASSARI, 46 *seq.*

circumstances, many were prevented from coming to Rome to gain the Jubilee Indulgence. The roads had also become more insecure, and accordingly, to avoid exposing pilgrims from a distance to these risks, the Pope commanded that the Jubilee should be held at Bologna during the Eastertide of 1476, and granted the Plenary Indulgence to all who, besides fulfilling the usual conditions, should visit the Churches of S. Pietro, S. Petronio, S. Antonio, and S. Francesco in that city.* Countless pilgrims, therefore, flocked to Bologna, which had never before seen so many strangers within her walls.† Participation in the graces of the Jubilee Year, without leaving home, was also granted to several other foreign Princes and countries ; in most cases with the condition that the Jubilee alms should be devoted to the defence of Christendom from the Turks.‡

Besides his consultations with the King of Naples in the beginning of the Jubilee Year, the Pope was repeatedly occupied with the affairs of the Turkish war. "Owing to the hostile complications in which Central Europe was involved through the Burgundian war, it had become powerless to resist the advance of the Turks." Sixtus IV., accordingly, on the 15th February, 1475, appointed Bishop Alexander of Forli Papal Legate for the restoration of

---

* NOETHEN, Gesch. der Jubeljahre, p. 67, is mistaken in stating that this change was made in the year 1475. Cardinal Gonzaga, in a *Letter of the 6th May, 1476, speaks of the concession in favour of Bologna as recently granted. Gonzaga Archives.

† See FALEONI, 510.

‡ NOETHEN, 68 ; MANNI, 85 ; Freib. Kirchenlexikon, II. 317, 2nd ed. ; VITTORELLI, 317. See THEINER, Mon. Hung., II., 449 seq. ; Mon. Slav., 503 seq. ; Mon. Hibern. 474-6. FINKE in the Zeitschr. für Gesch. Westfalens, 45, p. 113 seq., mentions a volume preserved among the Libri decime of the State Archives at Rome, with the Notaries' Deeds regarding the Jubilee alms in Burgundy and the adjacent countries.

peace.* In the ensuing months the Pope made repeated
appeals to the Italian Powers for help.†   The state of
affairs in the East was indeed calculated to cause the
greatest anxiety.   Usunhassan had never been able to
recover from his defeat, and thus the hand of the Sultan
pressed more and more heavily on the Christians in Albania,
the coasts of the Adriatic, and the Danubian Provinces.‡
At the end of 1474 a powerful Turkish army attacked
the brave Woiwode of Moldavia, Stephen the Great, who
refused any longer to pay tribute.   Stephen, with great
skill, decoyed the superior forces of the enemy on through
the forest to the Lake of Rakowitz (north-west of Galatz),
and there inflicted on them a severe defeat (10th January,
1475).§

Meanwhile, a fleet of 300 sail, with 40,000 men on board,
had been made ready at Constantinople.   Candia was, at
first, supposed to be its destination, but it took an easterly

* CHMEL, Mon. Habsb., III., 435 ; RAUSCH, 135, see 146, in regard
to the Legate's success.

† On the 16th April, 1475, Sixtus IV. commended Usunhassan's
Ambassadors to the Florentines. MÜLLER, Doc., 220. On the 1st
July, 1475, he wrote to the Italian Powers, describing the increasing
danger from Turkey, and claiming from them assistance. * " Quare
eandem devotionem vestram per viscera, etc., hortamur in Domino ac
deprecamur, ut iuxta vires vestras aliquam subventionem facere
velitis." *Brief to the Florentines in the State Archives, Florence,
and on the same day, 1st July, to the Marquess of Mantua. Gonzaga
Archives, Mantua.

‡ HERTZBERG, Osmanen, 630.

§ See the Letter of the 24th January, written from Torda, to King
Matthias, and the Report of Woiwode Stephen of the 25th January in
Mon. Hung., II., 299–302. See MAKUSCEV, II., 13 *seq.* ; also HAMMER,
II., 137, and Arch. St. Lomb., I., 315 *seq.*, besides the documents
published by C. ESARCU in the year 1874 at Bucharest. Stephen sent
some of the banners he had taken from the Turks to Sixtus IV. ; see
RAYNALDUS, ad an. 1474, N. 10–11.

course, ran into the Black Sea, and, on the 31st of May, appeared before Caffa in the Crimea, a rich and important Genoese colony. On the 6th of June the place was in the hands of the Turks, and its fate was soon shared by the whole southern coast of the Crimea.*

Strenuous efforts for the preservation of this city had in former days been made by Popes Calixtus III., Pius II., and Paul II.† The tidings of its fall reached Rome in September, 1475. Further details were soon received from the Knights of St. John,‡ and the accounts of the cruelties exercised by the Turks on its unfortunate inhabitants caused general horror and dismay, which were intensified by the impossibility, under the melancholy circumstances of the West, of that united defensive action which alone could have promised success. Discouraging as the result of his former attempts had been, the Pope again fulfilled his duty. He sent special Briefs to all the Princes of Christendom, informing them of the disaster, and calling on them to resist the indefatigable foe.§ Sixtus IV., at the same time, exhorted them to send Ambassadors

---

* VIGNA, II., 2, 163 *seq.*, 177, 474 *seq.*, 480 *seq.* ; SERRA, 248 *seq.* ; ZINKEISEN, II., 386 *seq.*; HERTZBERG, Osmanen, 633 ; HEYD, II., 400 *seq.* ; CARO, V., 1, 445, N. 2.

† See our Vol. II., p. 435 *seq.* ; VIGNA, II., 1, 164 *seq.*, 559-60, 645 *seq.*, 665 *seq.* ; and THEINER, Mon. Slav., I., 464 *seq.*

‡ AMMANATI, Epist., 641, Frankfort edition. See RAYNALDUS, ad an. 1475, N. 23-6, and VIGNA, II., 2, 176.

§ Cardinal Gonzaga wrote from Rome on the 18th Sept., 1475 : * "La Sta de N. S. havuto mo la certeza de la perdita de Caffa ne da aviso a tuti li principi e potentie de Italia." Gonzaga Archives, Mantua, where is also the *Brief to Mantua, dated Rome, 1475, Sept. 12. I saw in the State Archives of Modena, and in those of Florence, X.-II.-25, f. 89b-90b, similar Briefs of the same date. It appears from Mon. Habsb., III., 437 *seq.*, that Briefs were also addressed to other Princes besides those of Italy.

to Rome. It would seem that he still hoped to bring about a League of all the Powers against the Osmanli; but he met with little response! * In November negotiations began, and they lasted for months. "Their result may be learned from the fact that the flames of the places the Turks had set on fire were soon visible from the belfry of St. Mark's." † In March, 1477, Cardinal Ammanati wrote: "Our Pope is doing everything in his power. He did not dismiss the Italian Ambassadors, as he wishes to obtain more than the tithe. The tithe from the clergy, and a twentieth part from the Jews, has been granted to him, but how little is that compared to such a war. What are a few hundred thousands for the defence of a needy king ‡ against the ruler of all Asia and a good part of Europe? The assistance of the laity, so anxiously desired by His Holiness, has not yet been afforded. We strive as far as in us lies, to copy the indefatigable zeal and courage of our Father. May God enlighten our minds and hearts, that we may not walk in darkness and the shadow of death, and, when we have lost this valiant champion, too late lament that we have not sooner known the way of our salvation." §

* Sixtus IV. was obliged frequently to urge the sending of Ambassadors ; see his *Briefs of the 17th and 30th Sept., 1475, in the Gonzaga Archives, Mantua, and the State Archives, Florence, X.-II.-25, f. 91 and 91b-92 ; *ibid.*, 94b-95b, a long *Brief, dated Rome, 1475, Dec. 21, in which he earnestly prays that assistance may be sent against the Turks.

† REUMONT, Lorenzo, I., 263, 2nd ed. Regarding the persons of the Ambassadors, see PEZZANA, III., 378. PERUZZI, Ancona, 383, and SERRA, III., 252, shew that Sixtus IV. cannot be accused of negligence as to the Turkish war.

‡ Matthias Corvinus of Hungary.

§ AMMANATI, Epist., 644, Frankfort edition.

CHAPTER V.

Beginning of the Rupture of Sixtus IV. with Lorenzo de' Medici.

THE pestilence, which had already visited Rome in the Jubilee Year, returned early in the summer of 1476, with such violence that residence in the City became almost intolerable.* At the beginning of June the Pope determined to seek the heights of Viterbo;† on the 3rd he commended his States to the Protection of King Ferrante;‡ on the 10th he left Rome, accompanied by Cardinals d'Estouteville, Borgia, Carafa, Nardini, Gonzaga, and Michiel.§ Cardinal Cybò remained behind as Legate. Later on, the City was visited by terrible thunderstorms and tempests. The Palace of the Senate was closed, and justice

---

* This epidemic, which broke forth with great virulence in March, was consequent on the inundations in January. See the Roman Letter of the 21st March, 1476, in KNEBEL, II., 408-9 ; Cron. di Viterbo di GIOV. DI JUZZO, 412 ; and a *Notice in Cod. Vatic., 7239, f. 157. (Vatican Library.) In the course of the month of April, Duke Albrecht of Saxony came to Rome (RÖHRICHT, Pilgerreisen, 160), where Girolamo Riario held a splendid tournament on the 25th (INFESSURA, 1145). On the 1st May, *Cardinal Gonzaga mentions the return of the Plague, which rapidly increased. See J. P. Arrivabene's *Letter, dated Rome, 1476, May 24. All these Papers are in the Gonzaga Archives.

† *Letter of J. P. Arrivabene, dated Rome, 1476, June 5, *loc. cit.*

‡ MARTÈNE, II., 1452-3.

§ See Acta Consist. of the Secret Archives of the Vatican in MARINI, II., 17, and INFESSURA, 1145.

was administered at the foot of the steps. Penitential processions thronged the streets. Infessura mentions one in July, in which the venerated image of our Lady from S. Maria Maggiore was carried with much devotion.*

The Pope was obliged, immediately on starting, to alter his route, for the terrible malady had appeared at Viterbo; he went, therefore, first to Campagnano, then to Vetralla, then for a time to Amelia and Narni, and finally settled at Foligno.† Thence he visited Assisi, where, in the month of August, he celebrated the Feast of St. Francis, the founder of his Order, and venerated his relics with great devotion.‡

* INFESSURA, 1145. A Brief of 5th Aug., 1476, commending Cardinal Cybò, is given in MARTÈNE, II., 1548.

† See MARINI, II., 217 *seq.*, and Cron. di Viterbo di Giov. di Juzzo, 413. See also the incomplete *Reports of the Bishop of Parma, S. Sacramorus, which are in the State Archives at Milan. One of these *Letters, written in July (the date is effaced), speaks of the terrible ravages of the Plague in Rome, whence every one had fled : it appears "non ci sia rimasto quasi niuno"; the pestilence had also reached Todi. A *Report by Sacramorus, written ex Amelia on the 8th July, 1476, shews that the Plague continued in Rome ; isolated cases had occurred in Viterbo, Spoleto, and Todi ; the Pope was suffering from the gout. A Letter, dated Foligno, 1476, Sept. 26, shews that the Pope was then in that town. See also, in reference to Sixtus IV.'s sojourn at Foligno, the Cronica di Suor Caterina Guarneri in Arch. St. p. le Marche, I., 300 (Foligno, 1884). Ammanati's Letter of the 13th July, 1476, in Anecd. Litt., III., 372, speaks of the ravages of the Plague in the Sienese district. In Perugia it was so violent that Sixtus IV., by a *Brief of the 7th July, 1476, authorised the magistrate to pass important resolutions when only two-thirds of the members of the Council were present. Regest. in Cod. C.-IV.-I., University Library, Genoa.

‡ SCHMARSOW, 110, after WADDING, ad an. 1476, XIV., 145 *seq.* See Cronich. di S. Francesco, III., 182. In a *Letter, dated Foligno, 1476, Aug. 29, Bonfrancesco Arlotti also mentions that Sixtus IV. went to visit the bodies of St. Francis and St. Clare. (State Archives Modena.) GRAZIANI, 647, says that Sixtus IV. left Assisi on the 25th August on account of the Plague.

As the pestilence abated very slowly, Sixtus IV. remained at Foligno until the autumn. When Cardinal Giuliano della Rovere returned, on the 4th October, from his mission to France, he found the Pope still in this charming little town,* which he only left on the 7th of the month. He spent the first night at Spoleto, and then, probably because the Plague was still claiming many victims,† travelled so slowly that he did not reach his capital until the 23rd of October.‡

Just as this calamitous year was closing, all Italy was struck with horror at the assassination of the Duke of Milan (26th December, 1476). This crime was a tyrant-murder of the ancient type, and was directly attributable to the influence of ideas zealously propagated by the false Humanist, Cola Montano. The Annals of Siena expressly state that the conspirators had studied Sallust, and Sigismondo de' Conti also informs us that Lampugnani had, from early youth, chosen Catiline as his model.§

"The peace of Italy is at an end!" exclaimed the Pope, on hearing of the death of Galeazzo Maria Sforza; and,

* *Acta Consist., Secret Archives of the Vatican.

† See a *Letter of Card. Gonzaga of the 24th Oct., 1476. Gonzaga Archives, Mantua.

‡ *Acta Consist., Secret Archives of the Vatican. SCHMARSOW, 110, N. 5, has already pointed out the error of Infessura in giving the 27th December as the date of the Pope's return to Rome. Many condemned his long absence, as we learn from the justification offered in the *Lucubrac. Tiburtin., Cod. 2403, Court Library, Vienna. To this subject also refers *Oratio habita ad pontif. Xistum qua cohortatur ut remota sevitie pestis ab urbe dignetur repetere urbem Romam et ipsam presentia sua consolari. Cod. Ottob., 2290, f. 172b–173, of the Vatican Library.

§ SIGISMONDO DE' CONTI, I., 17. See REUMONT, Lorenzo, I., 266, 2nd ed.; BURCKHARDT, I., 58, 134, 3rd ed.; and, besides the literature alluded to in our Vol. II., p. 216 seq., Atti d. deput. p. l. prov. di Romagna, 1869, VIII., 121 seq., and Arch. St. Lomb., II., 284 seq., XIII., 140 seq., 414 seq.

indeed, the existing political system seemed entirely upset. The Duke of Milan was the only Prince sufficiently rich and powerful permanently to counterbalance the ambitious King of Naples, his heir was still a child ; the Regency was in the hands of the Duchess Bona, a weak woman, entangled in the meshes of her intriguing brothers-in-law.*

Fully alive to the dangers which threatened Italy, Sixtus IV., on the first day of the new year (1477), addressed a Brief to all the Italian Princes and Rulers, earnestly exhorting them to the maintenance of peace.† Cardinal Giovanni Mellini was also sent as special Legate to Milan and Lombardy, and instructed to use every effort for the same object.‡ The newly-appointed Legate was a man venerable alike for his age, his learning, and his goodness ; he started on the 27th January, and returned on the 7th May.§

The course of affairs in Milan was watched, not only by the Pope, but also by Lorenzo de' Medici, with the keenest interest. Peace was for the present preserved, and the Duchess remained in power,‖ but her authority rested on

* SCHMARSOW, 109, 111. See REUMONT, Lorenzo, I., 267 *seq.*, 2nd ed. Duchess Bona's letter, informing the Pope of the murder, is given by MURATORI, Chron. Est., XV., 546.

† All these *Briefs are dated Rome, 1477, Jan. 1, and their words are identical. I have seen the Originals in the Gonzaga Archives, Mantua, and the State Archives, Modena and Bologna (Lib. Q. 3), and a contemporary copy in the State Archives, Florence, X.–II.–25, f. 103b–104.

‡ See *Acta Consist., Secret Archives of the Vatican, and a *Brief from Sixtus IV. to Florence, dated Rome, 1477, January 3. State Archives, Florence, *loc. cit.*, f. 104b.

§ *Acta Consist., Secret Archives of the Vatican. See SIGISMONDO DE' CONTI, I., 17.

‖ See the **Letter of Ascanio Maria Sforza to Albrecht of Bonstetten of the 20th March, 1477, in Cod. 719, N. 51, of the Chapter-Library at St. Gall.

no solid foundation. Lorenzo sought in every way to confirm it. "But," as a friend of the Medici writes, "it is perfectly incomprehensible how, at so critical a moment, when
the support of Milan was most uncertain, he could think
of giving just cause of complaint to neighbours whom he
knew to be already dissatisfied with him. Yet this is
what he did." *

At the beginning of his reign, Sixtus IV. had been very
favourably inclined towards the Medici; the reception
which Lorenzo met with in Rome, the fact that the
financial affairs of the Holy See were, much to their advantage, entrusted to their care, and that the Alum works
at Tolfa were farmed out to them, were plain proofs of
this good-will.† If these friendly relations were of brief
duration, it was only because Lorenzo openly manifested
his ungrateful purpose of making troubles for the Pope.‡

The Florentine Expedition against Volterra, in the year
1472, was the first occasion on which these differences
appeared. The Pope had sent auxiliary troops to aid the
Florentines in suppressing the revolt of that city; this act
of friendship towards Lorenzo led to disastrous results.
After twenty-five days of bombardment, the city capitulated,
on condition that the lives, honour, and property of the
burgesses should be spared. No sooner, however, had
the undisciplined troops entered the place, than a general
plunder began. "In vain did Federigo of Montefeltre
remonstrate; Volterra was sacrificed in the most shameful
manner. This seemed to have delighted the Florentines.
When the victor came, with a heavy heart, to their city,
they overwhelmed him with marks of gratitude to console

---

* REUMONT, Lorenzo, I., 270, 2nd ed.

† See *supra*, p. 215. From GOTTLOB, Cam. Apost., we learn that,
previously to 1478, the Medici farmed the customs in Rome.

‡ SCHMARSOW, 111. See *supra*, p. 265 *seq.* and 268 *seq.*

him for the wound that his honour had sustained; but the Pope saw his credit abused, and general compassion excited on behalf of the ruined city. His magisterial hand, which had been laid upon the balance in favour of the Medici, was stained with blood."*

Then followed the purchase of Imola. The acquisition of this territory from the Duke of Milan interfered with the designs of the Republic, which had eagerly sought an extension of its domain in that direction.† Lorenzo had made the greatest efforts to make it impossible to obtain the money required. Henceforth "the Court of Rome could no longer employ him in a financial capacity. That which had once been so generously offered to him was now withdrawn. The management of the Apostolical Exchequer was transferred to the Bank of the Pazzi, who, in spite of the Medici, had advanced the sum; that was all, but it was enough."‡

* Such is the judgment of SCHMARSOW, 13. See REUMONT, Lorenzo, I., 249, 2nd ed., and II., 455, where the special literature on the subject is indicated. FRANTZ, 141, believes the first alteration in the relations between Sixtus IV. and Lorenzo was due to the Pope's decided refusal to elevate Giuliano de' Medici to the purple. An ecclesiastical difference (taxation of the clergy) is mentioned in the *Brief of 14th Sept., 1471. State Archives, Florence, X.–II.–25, f. 37b–38.

† FRANTZ, 141.

‡ SCHMARSOW, 24. See FRANTZ, 177, and BUSER, Lorenzo, 31. SIGISMONDO DE' CONTI, I., 16, speaks of the withdrawal of the financial business in Rome from the Medici in 1476. "Fisci tamen administrationem apud eum amplius esse non passus est, credo ne posset sanctam Romanam ecclesiam viribus propriis oppugnare." But a Letter of Lorenzo, of the 14th Dec., 1474 (in BUSER, Lorenzo, 132), implies that this had already been done. According to information kindly communicated by Dr Gottlob, from July, 1474, the Medici no longer appear as depositarii generales S.R.E. in the Libri introitus et exitus of the Secret Archives of the Vatican. DAUNON, I., 279, is

The tension between Sixtus IV. and Lorenzo was also greatly increased by the faithless conduct of the latter at the time of the siege of Città di Castello. He repaid the assistance rendered to him by the Pope, during the war with Volterra, by vigorously supporting rebellion in the States of the Church.* The persistent aid accorded by Florence to Vitelli rendered his complete subjugation impossible. Thus the capitulation, which was at last brought about, is characterised by Cardinal Ammanati, favourably disposed as he was towards the Medici, as an insult to the victors, for the terms were dictated by the vanquished.†

The next dispute had to do with a more ecclesiastical question. On the death of Cardinal Riario, Francesco Salviati had aspired to the Archbishopric of Florence, but had been compelled to give way to Lorenzo's brother-in-law, Rinaldo Orsini ‡ In 1474, Filippo de' Medici, Archbishop of Pisa, a man much devoted to the interests of his relations, died. Without consulting the Florentines, the Pope now raised Francesco Salviati to the vacant throne.§ It is not to be supposed that the Pope made this appointment with the intention of wounding the Medici and the Republic, but "from a letter of Cardinal Giuliano to Lorenzo, it is evident that he knew it would not be welcome. The Cardinal commends the Archbishop-

---

altogether incorrect in saying : "Un des premiers soins de Sixte IV. fut d'ôter à la famille de Medicis l'emploi de trésorier."

* FRANTZ, 160. See *supra*, p. 265.

† REUMONT, Lorenzo, I., 258, 2nd ed.

‡ GAMS, 748, does not give the day of his appointment. A *Brief of Sixtus IV., dated Rome, 1474, quinto Cal. Mart., acquainted the Florentines with Orsini's nomination. State Archives, Florence, X.-II.-25, f. 59b-60.

§ On the 14th Oct., 1474, Sixtus IV. communicated the elevation to the Florentines ; see the *Brief of that date in the State Archives, Florence, X.-II.-25, f. 69b-70.

elect to Lorenzo, and emphatically declares that there had been no intention of offending his Magnificence by the nomination."* Girolamo Riario earnestly entreated Lorenzo to overrule the opposition that would be made to the acceptance of Salviati. As this letter was not answered, Girolamo Riario wrote again on the 26th October, 1474, and this time with his own hand. "If," he says, "you would have me see that I am loved by you, and that my friendship is agreeable to you, and would also have our Master perceive that you are towards His Holiness all that I have ever declared you to be, then deal with me in this matter as you wish me to deal with you and your affairs."†

Two days before this letter was written, the Pope had exhorted the Florentines to be reasonable, and to acknowledge the newly-appointed Archbishop; but neither the Republic nor Lorenzo had any idea of yielding.‡ Lorenzo, writing to the Duke of Milan, declared that to consent to recognise the Archbishop would be to betray the honour of the city.§ Early in 1475 Girolamo sent his Chancellor to Florence to enter into negotiations for an agreement; but a long time passed without any settlement.‖ All the

* REUMONT, Lorenzo, I., 270–71, 2nd ed.

† BUSER, Lorenzo, 30.

‡ *Brief, dated Grottaferrata, 1474, Oct. 24. *"Nos quidem," it says, "eo animo sumus, ut digne a nobis factam provisionem substineamus; vos quidem cum prudentes sitis nobiscum convenietis in sententiam et electo ipsi statim possessionem tradi facietis." State Archives, Florence, X.–II.–25, f. 70–70b.

§ BUSER, Lorenzo, 31 and 132.

‖ Regarding the result of the negotiations, see the Report of the Milanese Ambassador; BUSER, Lorenzo, 32–3. J. P. Arrivabene writes on the 13th April, 1475: *"Le cose de Lorenzo de Medici dico de le rasone suoe de la depositeria qui presso al papa sono in speranza d'acordo, el qual seguendo stimase che lui habia a venir qui in brevi personalmente." Gonzaga Archives, Mantua.

Pope's exhortations failed to obtain Salviati's reception.* For three whole years the Florentines held out. Salviati remained in Rome, and the resentment which he cherished was soon shared by others. "Lorenzo," says an historian by no means prejudiced against him, "could not fail to perceive that this affair was seriously disturbing his relations with the Pope and his adherents. It is easy to understand that the feeling of animosity was directed against Lorenzo personally ; men had come to look upon him as the head of the Republic, and everything, whether good or evil, was ascribed to his influence."†

A fresh manifestation of the hostile disposition of the Florentines towards Sixtus IV. occurred in the autumn of 1475. Niccolo Vitelli was then endeavouring to regain his former position in Città di Castello. The enterprise failed, but the Pope's request, that the faithless rebel should no longer be permitted to dwell in the territory of the Republic, was refused.‡

After all this, it is not surprising that Sixtus IV. did not grant the petition that a Florentine should be admitted into the Sacred College, but put off the Republic with hopes for the future.§

In the spring of 1477 Lorenzo placed further difficulties

* On the 6th October, 1475, Sixtus IV. wrote to Florence : *"Per integrum fere annum exspectamus, ut dil. filio electo Pisano posses-sionem ecclesie traderetis" ; they must at last do this. State Archives, X.-II.-25, f. 92-92b.

† REUMONT, Lorenzo, I., 278, 2nd ed.

‡ SIGISMONDO DE' CONTI, I., 19. See in Appendix, N. 56, the *Brief of 21st October, 1475. State Archives, Florence.

§ In a *Brief on the subject, dated Rome, 1476, Jan. 12, Sixtus IV. says : *"Non tulerunt tempora quemadmodum nobis supplicastis ut ante hac ornare vestram rempublicam cardinali Ro. ecclesiae potu-erimus" ; he then holds out hopes of the ultimate accomplishment of their desires. State Archives, Florence, X.-II.-25, f. 95b.

in the Pope's way, by encouraging the mercenary captain, Carlo Fortebraccio, to abandon the Turkish war and return to the Umbrian frontier.   Carlo desired to win for himself the quasi free city of Perugia, where his father and brother had formerly ruled.* Without the consent of the Florentines this was impossible, as free passage through their States and maintenance for his troops were indispensable ; but they also had designs upon the city. They wished to draw it into their league, to alienate it from the Pope and to bring it under their own influence.   They therefore incited Carlo to attack the Sienese ; he nothing loth began, on the most frivolous pretexts, to plunder and to levy contributions in the valleys of the Chiana and the Arbia. The Medici viewed with satisfaction these troubles of their neighbours, hoping that they would tend to incline them to submit to their domination.   Moreover, it was desirable that the Pope's attention should be diverted from Perugia, until the conspiracy for the betrayal of the city should be mature.†

The Sienese, thus attacked in time of peace, complained to the Pope and the King of Naples, and from both received promises of assistance.   Sixtus IV. remembered that Carlo's father had threatened to make Pope Martin say twenty Masses for a *bolognino*.‡   A division of the army, under Antonio of Montefeltre, advanced to chastise the mercenary chief, who had thus wantonly disturbed the peace of the

---

* In *Letters of the 3rd and 11th Jan., 1477, Sixtus IV. had already forbidden the Perugians to admit Fortebraccio into their city. On the 22nd March he thanked them for having given a good reception to the Bishop of Rieti, whom he had sent as Governor. Regest. in Cod. C.-IV.-1, University Library, Genoa.

† SCHMARSOW, 135 ; REUMONT, Lorenzo, I., 273, 2nd ed. ; LEO, IV., 388.

‡ See Cronica di Viterbo di Giov. di Juzzo, 414.

district.* Carlo Fortebraccio made a feint of going to
meet the enemy, but on a day agreed upon with some of
the nobles who were in league with him, suddenly appeared
before Perugia.   Happily the plot was discovered, and the
seizure of the place prevented.   Carlo thus saw the scheme,
for whose accomplishment he had come to Tuscany, frustrated, and, as the hostile army had meanwhile increased
in strength, he retired first to Montone and afterwards to
Florence.   Duke Federigo of Montefeltre had, by this time,
led a large force into the Perugian territory.   Montone
was surrounded.   The stronghold of the Bracci stood on
a steep height, and was defended by lofty walls and various
outworks, erected by the old Condottiere.   All the plunder
amassed by Fortebraccio was collected in this mountain
fortress, and his wife, who was in charge, appeared with
dishevelled hair, urging the garrison to offer a brave resistance.   Carlo himself also sent messengers and letters from
Florence to encourage them, promising that a powerful
army should soon arrive to raise the siege, for he was
assured of the assistance of the Medici and their allies ;
but no castle had yet been able to hold out against
Federigo, "a stormer of cities like Demetrius, the son of
Antigonus."   The troops sent from Florence were repulsed,
and Montone compelled to capitulate.   "As pardon had
been promised to them," says Sigismondo de' Conti, "they
remained unharmed from first to last, and were, moreover,
through the Pope's goodness, indemnified for their losses,

---

* See L'ÉPINOIS, 441 ; REUMONT, Lorenzo, I., 273, 2nd ed. The
*Brief in the State Archives of Florence, here cited, was already
known by means of a Regest. in Arch. St. Ital., XVI., 2, p. 588.
*Briefs regarding the sending of troops to Perugia were addressed
to that city by Sixtus IV. on the 25th and 28th of June and
the 6th July, 1477. Regest. in Cod. C.-IV.-1, University Library,
Genoa.

but the walls were destroyed, and a nest of rebellion was thus rooted out."[*]

The Sienese from this time forth were greatly alarmed: they concluded a close alliance with Sixtus IV. and Ferrante of Naples (8th February, 1478). Lorenzo himself could cherish no illusions as to the untoward position in which his own fault had placed him. He looked round about him for allies. He thought he might depend upon Milan, and then turned to Venice to ask if he might, in case of necessity, reckon on the troops of the Republic; the answer was in the affirmative. Interests and parties became more and more sharply separated. Sixtus IV., Count Girolamo, Ferrante, and Siena being on one side, and Florence, Venice, and Milan on the other.[†]

Lorenzo's attitude towards the Pope remained unchanged. "It is hard to discover in these proceedings his customary circumspection and political penetration. Even his biographer, Niccolo Valori, is not able to reconcile his conduct towards Sixtus IV. with the claims of either statesmanship or gratitude."[‡]

[*] SIGISMONDO DE' CONTI, I., 20; SCHMARSOW, 136, where the date of the 2nd September, as that of the fall of Montone, is wrong. ALLEGRETTI, 783, mentions the 27th September, and in accordance with this is a *Brief of the 30th Sept., 1477, to the Marquess of Mantua, informing him of the surrender of the place. Gonzaga Archives, Mantua, where is a long *Brief of the 2nd Sept., 1477, in which the Pope speaks of the shameful conduct of Fortebraccio.

[†] BUSER, Lorenzo, 34.

[‡] REUMONT, Lorenzo, I., 274, 2nd ed.

CHAPTER VI.

THE CONSPIRACY OF THE PAZZI, 1478.

AT the beginning of the year 1478 the tension between Rome and Florence was such as to render a catastrophe almost inevitable. Wherever the opportunity had occurred, Lorenzo de' Medici had thwarted the Pope; he had done everything in his power to prevent the consolidation of the temporal principality of the Pope and to foster the elements of weakness which existed in the States of the Church.* His ambition and masterfulness had increased beyond all bounds: he would have been prepared to sacrifice even the precious blessing of ecclesiastical unity to carry out his own schemes. His confidential letter of the 1st February, 1477, to Baccio Ugolini shews that he would have contemplated a schism without shrinking. In this letter he says, in so many words: "For any one in my position, the division of power is advantageous, and, if it were possible without scandal, three or four Popes would be better than a single one."†

The downfall of the Medici, who had become the very soul of the anti-Papal agitation in Italy, appeared the only

---

* SUGENHEIM, 350–52.

† The passage to which BUSER, Lorenzo, 32, first called attention is as follows: *"Per mia pari fa che la auctorita si distribuischa et se potessi esser sanza scandalo sarebbono meglo tre o quattro Papa che uno." Arch. Medic. innanzi il princ. F., 89, f. 351. State Archives, Florence.

hope of security for the future. No one maintained this view with more warmth and eloquence than the Pope's nephew, Girolamo Riario, who felt that, as long as that family governed Florence, his hold upon Imola must remain precarious. The weakness of Sixtus IV. allowed to Girolamo an overweening influence in public affairs, and his ambition had become absolutely unbounded since his marriage with Caterina Sforza (May, 1472), a woman of a spirit kindred to his own.* " I am not," she said, " Duke Galeazzo's daughter for nothing : I have his brains in my head."†

Lorenzo, more or less by his own fault, had made many enemies in Florence as well as in Rome. Eaten up with pride, "he cared for no one and tolerated no rival. Even in games he would always be first. He interfered in everything, even in the private lives of the citizens, and in their marriages ; nothing could be done without his consent. In the work of casting down the mighty and raising up those of low degree, he refused to act with that considera- tion and discretion which Cosmo had always been careful to observe."‡ Among the old nobility, in particular, there was great dissatisfaction. It was an essential part of the policy of the Medici to prevent any family, even if allied

* See **Report of Sacramorus ex urbe, 1477, May 25 (State Archives, Milan), and Juzzo's Chronicle in the edition of N. DELLA TUCCIA, 414 ; F. OLIVA, Vita di C. Sforza, 2 *seq.* (Forli, 1821) ; and BONOLI, 248.

† SCHMARSOW, 137, conjectures that it was Caterina Sforza's account of her father's assassination which suggested to Girolamo that the haughty Prince who stood in the way of his further advancement might be removed in a similar manner. FRANTZ, 178, is convinced that the Milanese conspiracy encouraged the Pazzi to follow in the same track.

‡ Thus VILLARI, I., 40, judges Lorenzo de' Medici. The documents subsequently brought to light by Buser are not calculated to modify his opinion.

or related to their own, from becoming too powerful or too rich. Lorenzo de' Medici carried out this principle to the utmost. The Pazzi soon perceived that he was planning their ruin. They saw themselves excluded from all honourable offices and influential positions in the Republic, and at last found their property also attacked. Grievances such as these drove them into the party of Lorenzo's opponents, "whose motto was, the Liberty of the Republic."*

The enemies of the Medici soon formed themselves into two groups, one of which gathered round the Pazzi, and the other round Girolamo Riario. The hostility of the Pazzi towards the Medici was purely political, or, perhaps, social and political, in its character. With Sixtus IV. and his right hand, Riario, its motives were chiefly ecclesiastical.

The indignation of the Florentine nobility against the purse-proud tyranny of the Medici was so deep and so wide-spread that, independently of Roman influence or co-operation, it must sooner or later have led to a catastrophe such as it had often already produced. The outbreak was hastened on by the alliance of the Pazzi with Girolamo, which had become closer since the purchase of Imola.

It is uncertain whether the idea of effecting a change in the form of government in Florence by violent means originated with the Pazzi or with Girolamo. However this may be, Francesco de' Pazzi, the Roman banker, was quite as active and as eager in the matter as Riario.† Together

---

* See REUMONT, Lorenzo, I., 278, 2nd ed., who thinks that the Pazzi were not the principal offenders. See SCHMARSOW, 137, and FRANTZ, 175 seq.

† See FRANTZ, 204. According to a passing observation of JAC. VOLATERRANUS, 128, the Roman Palace of the Pazzi was near the Bridge of S. Angelo, therefore in the Street Canale del Ponte, now Via del Banco di S. Spirito, where the Sienese and Genoese bankers also lived.

they induced the Archbishop of Pisa, Francesco Salviati, who was living at the Roman Court, and very bitter against the Medici, to join them.

The first most important point was to discover what line the Pope would take in regard to their plan. " There was no doubt that, in his present state of irritation, he would favour any attempt to bring about a change of government in Florence. But Girolamo Riario was also well aware that his uncle would not lend himself to any undertaking which could imperil the honour of the Papacy. They must aim at securing a free hand to carry out the revolution, without letting the Pope know how it was to be accomplished."* He must be led to believe that the ill-will in Florence against the Medici was already so great that they could be easily overthrown in the usual manner, that is to say, by an insurrection without assassination. Giovan Batista da Montesecco, a vassal of Riario's, was selected, after the blow had been struck, to march into Florence with an armed force, and follow up the advantage gained. He consented, but warned the conspirators that the business might not be so readily accomplished as they thought.†

* REUMONT, Lorenzo, I., 280–81, 2nd ed. When VILLARI, I., 40, writes of the Pazzi conspiracy : "It was planned in the Vatican by Sixtus IV., and many members of the most powerful Florentine families took part in it," he, by an unworthy perversion of facts, falsely attributes the origination of the crime to one who was only drawn into connection with it afterwards. For there is no doubt but that "Salviati and Fr. de' Pazzi, with Count Girolamo," were, as CIPOLLA, 582, says, "primi autori di tutta quella intricata matassa" ; see Montesecco's confession in CAPPONI. Reumont, in his day, also protested, in the Allg. Ztg., against Villari's violent condemnation of Sixtus IV. See *supra*, p. 234.

† See Montesecco's depositions in CAPPONI, II., 548-58. This edition is henceforth cited, as being the only one taken from the

Montesecco had also another misgiving as to what the Pope would say to the plan. The answer given by Girolamo and Salviati is most significant. "Our Lord, the Pope," they said, "will always do what we persuade him, and he is angry with Lorenzo, and earnestly desires this." "Have you spoken to him of it?" "Certainly," was the reply, "and we will arrange that he shall also speak of it to you."*

This interview, at which Salviati and Girolamo alone were present, soon took place. According to the later and thoroughly credible statement of Montesecco, the Pope from the first declared that he wished for a change of government in Florence, but without the death of any man. "Holy Father," replied Montesecco, "these things can hardly be done without the death of Lorenzo and Giuliano, and, perhaps, of others also." The Pope answered: "On no condition will I have the death of any man : it is not our

original MS. Montesecco merely details the preliminaries of the conspiracy ; as to the crime itself, see (*a*) Politianus, De conjurat. Pactiana commentarius, 1478 (published again in OPERA POLITIANI, Basil., p. 636–43, 1553, and in an old Italian translation, in P.'s Prose volgari, ed. G. Adimari, Napoli, 1769), a contemporary work, substantially true, but written with great bitterness (see ROSCOE, Lorenzo, 155, and REUMONT, II., 456, 2nd ed.) ; (*b*) LANDUCCI, Diario, 17–19 ; (*c*) Strozzi's Report, first published by Bini e Bigazzi, Vita di Fil. Strozzi il vecchio, 55–9 (Firenze, 1851), and afterwards by FRANTZ, 207 *seq.* ; (*d*) *Parenti (see *infra*), used by REUMONT, I., 287, 2nd ed., in his excellent description. As to further authorities, see CAPPONI, II., 379 ; REUMONT, II., 456, 2nd ed. ; and PERRENS, 384 *seq.* Diplomatic Reports regarding the crime were hitherto unknown ; I was fortunate enough to find the *Reports of the Milanese and Mantuan Ambassadors, written two days after the event ; the text of these two important pieces is given in Appendix, N. 57 and 58. As the Milanese Ambassadors were invited by Lorenzo, we have here a fresh account from eye-witnesses.

* CAPPONI, II., 550 ; REUMONT, Lorenzo, I., 283, 2nd ed.

office to consent to the death of any, and, even if Lorenzo is a villain (villano), and has wronged us, I in no way desire his death; what I do desire is a change of government."* Girolamo then said, "What is possible shall be done to avoid such a casualty, but if it should occur, will your Holiness forgive its authors?" "You are a brute," rejoined Sixtus, "I tell you I do not desire the death of any man, but only a change in the government; and to you also, Giovan Battista, I say that I greatly wish that the government of Florence should be taken out of Lorenzo's hands, for he is a villain and an evil man, and has no consideration for us, and if he were out of the way we should be able to arrange matters with the Republic according to our mind, and this would be a great advantage." "What your Holiness says is true," said Riario and the Archbishop. "If, after a change of government in Florence, the State is at your disposal, your Holiness will be able to lay down the law for half of Italy, and every one will have an interest in securing your friendship. Therefore, be content to let us do all that we can for the attainment of this end." Hereupon Sixtus IV. again spoke very decidedly, without any reserve or ambiguity. "I tell you," he said, "I will not. Go and do as seems good to you, but no one's life is to be taken."† At the close of the audience, he gave his consent

---

* "Io non voglio la morte de niun per niente, perchè non è offitio nostro aconsentire alla morte de persona; e bene che Lorenzo sia un villano e con noi se porte male, pure io non vorria la morte sua per niente, ma la mutatione dello Stato sì." CAPPONI, II., 552; FRANTZ, 199.

† "Io te dico che non voglio: Andate e fate chome pare a voi, purchè non cie intervengha morte." CAPPONI, II., 552; FRANTZ, 200; REUMONT, Lorenzo, I., 284, 2nd ed. All these strong words of prohibition, although spoken in a private audience and to confidants, must, according to GREGOROVIUS, VII., 242, 3rd ed., have been a mere farce. "If," writes this historian, "he" (Sixtus) "did not

to the employment of armed men. Salviati said, as he withdrew : " Holy Father, be content to let us steer this bark, we will guide her safely." The Pope said, " I am content." " Sixtus IV. could only understand that those present fell in with his views, and he gave his consent."

The Pope, who had grown up in the cloister, and was little acquainted with the world, evidently believed that the advance of the troops assembled on the frontiers of the Republic, to join the discontented Florentines, would make it possible to overpower and capture the Medici.* The conspirators had other views. After repeated consultations, Girolamo and Salviati determined to act in opposition to the clearly expressed desire of the Pope. Preparations were at once commenced.

It is important to observe that Sixtus IV. again sent a message through a Bishop to urge the confederates to consider the honour of the Holy See and of Girolamo himself.† Had he known anything of the purpose of assassination, such an exhortation would have been absolutely unmeaning. " For, even if it succeeded, if both the Medici fell at once, and the Republic declared itself free, the

expressly desire their " (the Medici's) " death, he cared little whether blood was shed or not." Dr. Joseph Schmid has very kindly communicated to me the following extract from the work of Dr. Kempter, a gifted writer, too early taken from us : " How," he says, " can such an assertion, which is not merely prejudiced, but utterly unfounded, be reconciled with history and justice ? According to the literal sense of the documents, we should be condemned by any tribunal as guilty of libel and calumny, if we were to say that Sixtus IV. intended the death of the two Medici in the year 1478."

* FRANTZ, 203.

† See Montesecco in CAPPONI, II., 555. It is hard to understand how Reumont's critic can maintain, in the Rev. Hist., XXVI., 164, that the words in question are not to be found in Montesecco's confession in Capponi.

honour of the Holy See would be compromised. Sixtus IV. accordingly remained, as is perfectly clear from the whole of Montesecco's deposition, under the impression that the plan was to take both the Medici prisoners : Lorenzo on his journey to or from Rome, Giuliano perhaps on his way from Piombino, and then to issue a Proclamation from the Republic. An unprejudiced critic cannot arrive at any other conclusion from the documents before us." *

Circumstances had hitherto been unfavourable to the execution of the scheme. As, however, many had been initiated, it became necessary to act promptly, to avoid the risk of discovery. Francesco de' Pazzi had at last won over his brother Jacopo, the head of the family : among the other conspirators may be named, Bernardo di Bandini Baroncelli and Napoleone Franzesi Jacopo, son of the well-known Humanist, Poggio Bracciolini, two of the Salviati, and two clerics, Stefano of Bagnone, a dependent of Jacopo de' Pazzi, and Antonio Maffei of Volterra, "who had been led to take part in the plot by grief at the misfortunes of his native city, whose ruin he attributed to Lorenzo." Francesco de' Pazzi and Bandini were to murder Giuliano, while Lorenzo was to be killed by Montesecco ; Salviati was to seize the Signorial Palace, and Jacopo de' Pazzi to arouse the Florentines.†

Just at this time, in the spring of 1478, the young Cardinal Rafaello Sansoni-Riario came to Florence, in consequence of an outbreak of the Plague at Pisa, and took up his abode at the Villa of the Pazzi. According to the original plan, the Medici were to be assassinated at a banquet; but, as Giuliano was prevented by indisposition from attending it, the murder was postponed. Cardinal Rafaello, who was but eighteen, had no suspicion of all

* FRANTZ, 206-7.
† REUMONT, Lorenzo, I., 286 *seq*., 2nd ed. ; FRANTZ, 197.

that was going on, and held free and friendly intercourse
with Lorenzo de' Medici.   Lorenzo repeatedly urged him
to visit his Palace and the Cathedral, and Rafaello Sansoni
promised to do so on Sunday, the 26th April, 1478.   The
conspirators determined to take advantage of this favourable opportunity for carrying out their purpose.

Lorenzo had invited a brilliant company to dinner in
honour of the Cardinal.   Many Ambassadors and Knights,
among them Jacopo de' Pazzi and Francesco Salviati, were
invited.   On the morning of the eventful day, the Cardinal,
with a few companions, among whom were the Archbishop
and Montesecco, went into the city.   Giuliano de' Medici
excused himself from the feast on the plea of ill-health,
but promised to be present in the Cathedral.   " This caused
a change of purpose, and the church, instead of the
banqueting-hall, was selected as the scene of the murder."*
Montesecco, however, at the last moment refused to per-
petrate the crime in the Cathedral, either because he
shrank from shedding blood in a church, or, on maturer
consideration, from the affair altogether.†   In his stead,

---

* REUMONT, Lorenzo, I., 287, 2nd ed.   Regarding the frequency of
paid assassinations at this period, see, besides the work of Lamansky,
GOTHEIN, 22 ; and BURCKHARDT, II., 222 seq., 2nd ed., who, in
I., 56 seq., 2nd ed., also speaks of murders in churches ; see VILLARI,
I., 27 ; and GEIGER, Renaissance, 192.

† So says SIGISMONDO DE' CONTI, I., 23 (o fosse mosso da religione
o piu attentamente considerando a che impresa si sarebbe sobarcato—
in the very carelessly-given Latin text the Preface is omitted).   POLI-
TIANUS (Op., 638) only says : " Destinatus ad Laurentii caedem Joannes
Baptista negotium detractarat."   *PARENTI, f. 9b, only remarks at first,
" ricussolo poi dicendo nolle fare in chiesa secondo che molti dichono."
Later on he speaks of Montesecco's refusal in the following words :
" o che non li bastasse alhora la vista o che l'amicitia teneva con
Lorenzo lo rattenesi o che religione l'impedisce o che altra occulta
causa lo movessi in effetto lo recuso."   National Library, Florence.

the two clerics, Stefano and Maffei, undertook the deed.

The beginning of the second part of the High Mass was the signal of action for the conspirators.* With the cry "Ah! traitor!" Bernardo di Bandini Baroncelli made a rush at Giuliano, and plunged his dagger in his side. Severely wounded as he was, he strove to defend himself, and, in doing so, pushed against Francesco de' Pazzi, from whom he received a thrust in the breast. After this he staggered about fifty paces further, and then fell to the ground, where Francesco de' Pazzi stabbed him repeatedly till life was extinct.† Stefano and Maffei had meanwhile

---

* On no point do accounts vary so much as with regard to the exact time appointed for the deed ; see the comparison of passages in FRANTZ, 208, N. I. The Milanese Ambassador, in his *Report, says the *Agnus Dei;* the Mantuan and LANDUCCI, 17, mention the *Elevation;* these two moments are so near that it was very easy to confound them. Vespasiano da Bisticci (MAI, I., 448), writes : "levato il corpo di Cristo circa la communione"; the Synodus Florentina expressly declares : "Evenit autem ut in ecclesia ab elevatione ad communionem res differretur." F. Strozzi, on the other hand, observes, "in sul dire missa est"; whereupon PERRENS, 385, adds : "A ce moment, quoiqu'il y ait encore quelques prières à dire, chacun se leve, sort de sa place, s'achemine vers les portes. Il y a dans l'église un va-et-vient, un brouhaha très favorable aux violences. En outre les cloches sonnent alors : elles devaient avertir l'archévêque Salviati," &c. But the bells were also rung at the *Elevation* and the *Communion.* In opposition to Strozzi's statement is the fact, expressly mentioned by himself and several other writers, that Giuliano and Lorenzo, according to their custom, were then walking about in the church (see Appendix, N. 57), which, at the end of the Mass, would be natural and not worthy of notice, but during its continuance was unusual, and a bad habit of a corrupt age. The conspirators cannot then have chosen the *Ite missa est* as their signal, for their victim in that case might easily have escaped.

† " *Venuto el tempo a hora circa xiv. Bernardo Bandini secondo che ciaschuno afferma perche fu chosa quasi invisibile si cacciò adosso a

attacked Lorenzo, but only wounded him slightly. While his servants and some youths warded off further blows with their cloaks, he fled into the old sacristy, and its bronze door was fastened at once by Angelo Poliziano.*

All this was the work of a moment. Very few persons could see exactly what took place. This, and the horror which paralysed the senses of the immediate witnesses, accounts for the many variations in the details which have reached us. Those who were at a little distance did not know what was going on, and many thought that the dome of the Cathedral was about to fall in.†

Salviati's attempt to take possession of the Signorial Palace was equally a failure. Jacopo de' Pazzi's cry of liberty met with no response, while the people rose on all

---

Giuliano et con una coltella li menò nel fianco dicendo : hai traditore. Giuliano ispaurito si mosse per volersi aiutare et retornarne et rintoppò in Francesco che medisimamente li menò un altro colpo nel petto. Il perche discostatosi Giuliano qualche cinquanta passi dal primo luogho dove fu ferito cascò in terra et Francesco addossoli tante ferite li dette che lo lasciò morto.   Similmente trasseno fuori l'armi alcuni famigli di Francesco intorno a Giuliano ; in nella baruffa ferirono Francesco in una gamba et gravemente." PARENTI, f. 11.   (National Library, Florence.)   Machiavelli's assertion, repeated by REUMONT, I., 288, 2nd ed., that Francesco wounded himself, is therefore erroneous ; see also PERRENS, 386, N. 2.

* See, besides the authorities cited above and in PERRENS, 387, the detailed account of the attack on Lorenzo in the *Reports of Don Albertinus (Gonzaga Archives), and of the Milanese Ambassadors. (State Archives, Milan.)   Appendix, N. 57 and 58.

† POLITIANUS, Op., 639.   See also STROZZI'S description (*loc. cit.*, 56), and PARENTI, who writes * " Fatto questo la confusione fu grande tra cittadini che si trovavano nella chiesa.   Chi si fuggi di chiesa e corse a casa sua, chi per paura si noscosse nella calonica di S. Reparata, chi nelle case vicine, chi ando per l'arme et tornò in chiesa in difesa di Lorenzo, chi pure vi si rimase senza suspetto per veder le cose dove restavano et chi prese un partito e chi un altro."

sides to that of " Palle" (the balls in the armorial bearings
of the Medici). The slaughter of the guilty at once began.
Archbishop Salviati, his brother, and his nephew Jacopo
Bracciolini, with Francesco de' Pazzi, were all hung up
together from the window-bars of the Signorial Palace.
Then the ropes were cut, so that the bodies fell amidst the
crowd,* where they were torn in pieces, and the severed
heads and limbs borne in triumph through the streets.
All who were supposed to be enemies of the Medici,
whether guilty or innocent, were butchered.† The two
assassins who had fallen upon Lorenzo had their noses and
ears cut off before they were killed.

Montesecco was seized on the 1st, and beheaded on the
4th, May. Neither his withdrawal at the last moment, nor
the disclosures which he made in regard to the ramifications
of the conspiracy, availed to mitigate his sentence.‡ His
statements are of the greatest importance in their bearing
on the question of the participation of Sixtus IV. in the
events of the 26th April. "It is certain that he desired
that the Medici should be overthrown by force. It is
equally certain that he can have known nothing beforehand
of the details of the attempted assassination, for these were
only arranged in haste on the very morning of the deed,
when it had been found necessary to abandon the plan of
murdering the brothers at a banquet." §

The further question, whether Sixtus IV. approved of the
murderous intention of the conspirators, must be answered

* See the Milanese Ambassadors' *Report of the 28th April, 1478, in
Appendix, N. 57. State Archives, Milan.

† LANDUCCI, 19; POLITIANUS, Op., 640; REUMONT, Lorenzo, I.,
291 seq., 2nd ed. ; PERRENS, 391 seq.

‡ PERRENS, 393.

§ H. HÜFFER in the Allg. Ztg., 1875, p. 1010, indirectly against
RANKE, Päpste, I., 31, 6th ed.

in the negative.   Had this been the case, "Montesecco, whose interest it was to make the least of his own share in the crime, would scarcely have concealed the fact.   His depositions bear upon them the stamp of truth; they have sometimes been taken in their obvious sense, and sometimes arbitrarily interpreted.   In face of such evidence, to continue to make the Pope an abettor in the murder is worse now than it was 400 years ago."*

It is, however, deeply to be regretted that a Pope should play any part in the history of a conspiracy.   Lorenzo had given Sixtus IV. good ground for a declaration of war; the principle of self-preservation demanded active measures for future security, and amongst them, the overthrow of this malignant enemy; but open warfare would certainly have been more worthy of a Pontiff than participation in a political plot, even had it involved no bloodshed.

---

* Opinion of REUMONT, Lorenzo, I., 292, 2nd ed., see II., 456, 2nd ed.; and CREIGHTON, III., 75, in regard to the credibility of Montesecco's statements, which have been well described as an honourable, soldierly avowal.   See also HEFELE-HERGENRÖTHER, VIII., 214, N. 2, against BROSCH, Julius II., p. 10.

CHAPTER VII.

The Tuscan War.—French Intervention in Favour of the Florentines.—Relations of Louis XI. with the Holy See.—The Pope's Reconciliation with Florence.

An unsuccessful conspiracy always strengthens the power against which it has been directed. Lorenzo, who shewed admirable skill and tact in making the most of his advantage, now rose to absolute power in Florence. " Even those who had hitherto been heartily opposed to him, from Republican convictions, came over to his side. The baseness of this attack on his life, to which was added the abuse of the sacred place and the most solemn act of worship, and the presence of a Cardinal, had called forth the greatest indignation." * Immediately after the failure of the plot, this anger found vent in the indiscriminate slaughter of all the enemies of the Medici ; and, as time went on, far too much license was permitted to the mob. Twenty-three days after the event, boys were allowed to drag the half-clad corpse of Jacopo de' Pazzi through the streets, and fling it, with ghastly jibes, into the Arno.† Cruel reprisals continued even into the year 1480: a well-informed contemporary doubts the guilt of those then sentenced. Renato de' Pazzi, a peaceful man, devoted to study, who had refused to take any part in the conspiracy,

* Frantz, 213.

† Landucci's description of this scene (Diario, 21-2) makes one shudder.

was certainly innocent. Nevertheless, he was executed.* Bandini was pursued to Constantinople, where the Sultan gave him up to Lorenzo. This circumstance, and, in a yet greater degree, the letters of condolence which he received from all sides, from Princes and Republics, Statesmen and Cardinals, helped to make him haughtier than ever.†

Many ecclesiastics who had nothing to do with the conspiracy were also executed.‡ The Archbishop of Pisa was brutally scourged, without trial of any sort, and Cardinal Rafaello Sansoni-Riario, although perfectly innocent, was imprisoned. These things greatly angered Sixtus IV. Sigismondo de' Conti thus describes his feelings when the tidings first arrived from Florence. "The Pope expressed his horror at the crime, in which the conspirators had added sacrilege to murder. He was also deeply grieved at the danger of Cardinal Sansoni, the disgraceful slaughter of innocent priests, and the ignominious death of the Archbishop. He saw that a serious indignity had been inflicted on the Church. This latter point was specially distressing to him, because it made peace impossible, for it would

---

* REUMONT, Lorenzo, I., 292, 2nd ed. PERRENS, 396, agrees with Reumont in saying that the vengeance exceeded all bounds, and was quite unparalleled ; see also p. 391, where Perrens speaks of an *orgie de vengeance*, and VILLARI, Machiavelli, I., 41.

† In the State Archives, Florence, X.-II.-25, we find *Letters of condolence from Lucca, Perugia, and Venice, and also from Cardinal d'Estouteville. The last of these *Letters is dated Rome, 1478, April 28, and contains the following words : *" Per l'antiqua affectione et singulare amore che havemo portato et portiamo a quella E.S. non sanza grande dolore et despiacere de animo havemo intesa questa matina la novita che li e stata et dallo altro canto inteso el buon fine per la V. tranquillita et pace che e seguito secundo el dolendo caso ; habiamo ringraziato dio," &c. Spoleto also condoled with the Florentines ; see SANSI, Storia, 80, and Doc. 46.

‡ SIGISMONDO DE' CONTI, I., 24.

be a dangerous example for the future, if those who had so gravely infringed her rights were to be left unpunished." *
Accordingly, Sixtus IV. claimed satisfaction from the Florentines for their violations of ecclesiastical immunities, and also demanded the liberation of Cardinal Sansoni, and the banishment of Lorenzo.

The first two demands were undoubtedly just. Donato Acciaiuoli, the Florentine Ambassador in Rome, though he had been deeply affronted by Riario,† strongly advised his Government to fulfil the promise which they had made in writing to release the unoffending Cardinal. Florence, he observed, gained nothing by his detention, and the refusal to comply with the righteous request of the Pope must lead to serious danger. But "the reasonable representations of their trusty servant," and Ferrante's warning not to add fuel to the fire,‡ were alike unheeded.

It was decided that the Cardinal should for the time be retained in captivity, as a hostage for the safety of the Florentines in Rome.§ On the 24th May, Sixtus IV. sent the Bishop of Perugia to the city with a letter from the Cardinal-Camerlengo to Lorenzo, informing him that a commission was already appointed to commence proceedings against the Republic, unless the Cardinal was

* SIGISMONDO DE' CONTI, I., 25 ; see ibid., 39, Sixtus IV.'s circular letter. In 1476 the Pope had remonstrated against the practice, which prevailed in England and Wales, of summoning clerics to appear before secular judges, as a breach of ecclesiastical law. HARDOUIN, Conc., IX., 1496 seq. ; ROSCOVÁNY, Monum., I., 115-17 ; WILKINS, III., 609-10 ; Mon. Acad. Oxon., I., 348 seq.

† Sixtus IV. maintained that this had occurred without his knowledge, and regretted the incident ; see Vespasiano da Bisticci in MAI, I., 451.

‡ BUSER, Lorenzo, 37 ; FRANTZ, 218.

§ See *Letter from the Milanese Ambassadors, dated Florence, 1478, May 20. Ambrosian Library.

at once set free. Venice also advised the Florentines not
to give their enemies just cause of complaint by keeping
Sansoni in prison.*   All, however, was in vain ; although
there had been ample time to establish the innocence of
the young Prelate, they would not hurry themselves, and
matters daily grew worse.†

Sixtus IV. was at last weary of waiting. He " would,
no doubt, have preferred a reconciliation with Florence,
but that had been rendered impossible." ‡   Accordingly,
on the 1st June, fully four weeks after the tragedy,
and, therefore, when the excitement of the first moment
had subsided, he issued a Bull excommunicating Lorenzo
and his adherents. The Bull began by enumerating the
whole series of Florentine offences : the protection afforded
to the Pope's enemies, the attack on the Papal territory,
the hindrances placed in the way of those who were going
to Rome, and the detention of convoys carrying provisions
to the Court there, finally their treatment of Francesco
Salviati. Passing on to the events which had succeeded
the conspiracy, Sixtus IV. declared that the vengeance
taken in the form of executions and banishments had been
cruel and excessive. Lorenzo, the Gonfaloniere, and the
Prior in their mad fury, and by the instigation of the devil,
had even laid hands on ecclesiastics. They had hanged
the Archbishop at the window of the Palace in the sight
of the crowd, and, cutting the rope, allowed the corpse to
fall down into the street. Other innocent clerics, of whom
some belonged to the suite of Cardinal Sansoni, had also
suffered death. Finally, although the Bishop of Perugia
had been sent as Legate to apply, in the name of the
Pope, for the release of the Cardinal, he had not been

---

* ROMANIN, IV., 390 ; FRANTZ, 219.

† REUMONT, Lorenzo, I., 299, 2nd ed.

‡ REUMONT, loc. cit., 300.

released.   On account of these crimes, the sentence of the greater Excommunication was pronounced against Lorenzo and the other functionaries, and, in the event of these guilty persons not being delivered up, the city would be laid under an Interdict and its Archiepiscopal dignity cancelled.*

In spite of the severity of this Bull the Cardinal was still kept in prison, though the rigour of his captivity was somewhat mitigated.   Its character may be gathered from the description a Sienese chronicler gives of his appearance when he was at length set free.   " On the 13th June," says Allegro Allegretti, " Cardinal Sansoni-Riario came to Siena, more dead than alive from the terror he had endured, and still feeling as if the rope were about his neck."†

On the 20th June the Cardinal arrived in Rome.   The deadly pallor of his face bore witness to the torments he had undergone, and this he retained to the end of his life.‡ Francesco Gonzaga had left the City two days previously for Bologna, where the friendship of the Bentivogli with the Medici awakened some anxiety.   The instructions given to Gonzaga betray the Pope's " uneasiness, and his consciousness of the bad impression produced by Florentine events."   They also shew that there had been a possibility

---

* Bull, " Iniquitatis filius et perditionis alumnus Laurentius de Medicis," in RAYNALDUS, ad an. 1478, N. 4 *seq.*, and FABRONIUS, II., 121 *seq.*   See FRANTZ, 221 *seq.* ; HEFELE-HERGENRÖTHER, VIII., 216 ; and L'ÉPINOIS, 444.

† ALLEGRETTI, 784, who also says that the Cardinal had been repeatedly threatened with hanging.   In regard to Sansoni's Letter to the Pope, " which was apparently dictated" (REUMONT, I., 299), see the excellent observation of CIPOLLA, 586.

‡ *Acta Consist., f. 55, Secret Archives of the Vatican.   According-ing to the same authority, the ceremony of opening the Cardinal's mouth was performed on the 22nd June, and on the 26th he went as Legate to Perugia.

of reconciliation ; for, after exhorting the Bolognese to be faithful, Sixtus IV. observes, " We have not taken it ill, nor do we blame our people for their friendliness towards the Florentines when the tidings of these disturbances first reached them. On the contrary, we approved of this manifestation of sympathy with their neighbours, as the Republic had as yet done nothing against the Church, and we ourselves wrote to Florence to express our regret at the occurrence. But, now that they have committed such shameful outrages on the ecclesiastical state, and have incurred the censures of the Church for their persistent violations of her rights, the Bolognese can no longer in honour continue to stand by them. Such a course would constitute an attack upon us, and would not assist them."*

The long-deferred, but practically inevitable, release of the Cardinal, whose innocence could not be denied, was the only concession made by Florence to the Pope. The Excommunication was despised ; the Interdict,† pronounced on the 20th June, was disregarded ; and the alliance of other Powers, especially that of France, was sought. Memorandums, couched in violent language, and evading any real answer to the very definite charges made by the Pope,‡ threats of a Schism, and preparations for war were the only reply vouchsafed by the once pious and fastidiously refined Florentines to the exhortations of

---

* REUMONT, I., 303, 2nd ed. The copy here used of the *Instructio pro R. Card. Mantuano in the Cod. Capponi, XXII. (now in the National Library at Florence), is without date ; the date may, however, be gathered from the statement in the *Acta Consist., Secret Archives of the Vatican, that Gonzaga started on the 18th June on his Mission to Bologna.

† See RAYNALDUS, ad an. 1478, N. 12–13.

‡ See FRANTZ, 228 *seq.*, and REUMONT, I., 318, 2nd ed.

Sixtus IV., who was convinced of the justice of his cause.*

Although the Florentine Government set the Excommunication and Interdict at naught and constrained the clergy to perform their sacred functions, they still complained of the distress which these censures had occasioned. The document known by the name of the "Synodus Florentina" bears eloquent testimony to the fanatically anti-Roman temper of the party of the Medici. In it Sixtus IV. is called "the adulterer's minion" and the "Vicar of the Devil." He is loaded with accusations, and the hope is expressed that God may deliver His people from false shepherds who come in sheep's clothing, but inwardly are ravening wolves.†

---

* See, in particular, the autograph Letter to the Duke of Urbino, of 25th July, 1478, in FABRONIUS, II., 130–31.

† See HEFELE-HERGENRÖTHER, VIII., 218, and FRANTZ, 242 *seq.* There is no room for doubt as to the authenticity of the document known as the Synodus Florentina, and published in FABRONIUS, II., 136 *seq.*, for the original, probably in the handwriting of Gentile Becchi, Bishop of Arezzo, is preserved in the State Archives, Florence (C. STROZZ., 387). The further question, whether the Synodus Flor. was the work of an actual and formal Conciabulum, or was a more or less individual production of Gentile Becchi, has been treated at length by FRANTZ, 237 *seq.* This conscientious writer believes that, "to the shame of the clergy who had grown up under the Medici," we must admit "that the Council was really summoned, and asserted the principles of the Synodus Flor." Striking as are Frantz's observations in detail, and thoroughly as he analyses the document, his reasons do not seem to me, nor to the latest biographer of Lorenzo (REUMONT, I., 318, 2nd ed.), sufficient to establish his conclusion. FABRONIUS, Döllinger, 354 ; CAPPONI, II., 385 ; and CREIGHTON, III., 287, are of opinion that there was no Synod ; HEFELE-HERGENRÖTHER, VIII., 218 *seq.*, and REUSCH, II., 969, believe that there was. The lamented C. Guasti was kind enough, at my request, to make minute investigations regarding this matter ; but neither in the State Archives, nor

War began in July.   Ferrante, hoping by this means to gain Siena, espoused the Pope's cause.   Lorenzo looked for support to Venice and Milan, and especially to Louis XI., King of France.

The relations between this monarch and Sixtus IV. had, from the first, been precarious.   In 1472 he had, indeed, sent an Embassy to Rome* to do homage, but it soon became evident that the King adhered to his former policy of holding the Pragmatic Sanction and the Council over the Pope's head, to be used as a bait or a rod according to circumstances.†   The agreement arrived at by direct negotiation with Rome, in the summer of 1472, lasted but a short time.   The University resisted it as contrary to the Basle Decrees.   Although Louis XI. ratified the Concordat on the 31st October, 1472,‡ the Pragmatic Sanction continued practically in force.§   The Mission of the Bishop of Viterbo to France made no change in the state of affairs.‖   In the following year the tension between France and Rome increased.   At the French Court it was asserted that the

those of the Duomo at Florence, is there any notice of this supposed Synod : in the latter, however, the expenses incurred on such an occasion would necessarily appear, yet no trace of them is to be found.

* Regarding the reception given to the French Ambassadors in Rome, see LJUBIČ, *loc. cit.*, 22.   Cardinal Gonzaga gave them a splendid banquet.   See MOTTA in Bollet. st. d. Suizz., VI., 21.

† REUMONT, I., 305, 2nd ed.   See PHILLIPS, III., 328 ; Kirchen-lexikon, II., 754, 2nd ed. ; GUETTÉE, VIII., 36 ; FIERVILLE, 146-7 ; and LEGEAY, II., 90.

‡ CHARAVAY, Sur les lettres de Louis XI., 9 (Paris, 1881) ; PICOT, I., 425 ; and FIERVILLE, 147.

§ FIERVILLE, 147 ; BULAEUS, V., 701 *seq.*

‖ The *Acta Consist.*, Secret Archives of the Vatican, mention d'Estouteville's nomination as legatus in Gallias on the 12th October, 1472 ; but he declined the appointment, and the Bishop of Viterbo went in his stead.   See GINGINS LA SARRA, I., 3 *seq.*

creation of Cardinals by Sixtus IV. on the 7th May, 1473,
was simoniacal. The Pope justified himself in a letter
addressed to the King on the 22nd August, 1473.* Louis'
reply is a combination of reclamations and insults. He
angrily complained that the Pope had passed over the
names of those whom he had proposed for the purple,
while the wishes of other Princes were taken into consideration. He thought that he deserved better treatment than
this, after having abolished the Pragmatic Sanction in his
kingdom. He concludes with an appeal to Almighty God
and to St. Peter and St. Paul!

At the end of 1474 Sixtus IV. had remonstrated with
the King about his breach of the treaty of 1472.† Louis
answered by issuing an Ordinance on the 8th January,
1475, "for the protection of Gallican liberties," making the
Royal Placet necessary for the publication of all Papal
Decrees.‡ Measures of a more hostile character soon
followed. The King began to agitate for the holding of a
General Council, in which the "Church might be reformed,"
and "a lawful Pope elected in the place of Sixtus IV., who
had obtained his elevation by simony." Secret Despatches,
taken from a Hungarian Envoy, shew that Louis was
seeking to win over the Emperor Frederick to this scheme.
The King of Hungary, upon this, represented to the Duke
of Burgundy that he and the King of Naples thought
that the only way of counteracting these manœuvres was
for the Pope himself at once to summon a Council. He

* I found in the State Archives of Milan a contemporary copy of
this hitherto unknown *Document, and will publish it elsewhere,
together with the *Answer of the French King. GUETTÉE, VIII., 38,
may be corrected by reference to these documents.

† D'ACHERY, Spicil., III., 844 *seq.* (Paris, 1723).

‡ See Archiv für Kirchenrecht, XVIII., 170; and DAUNON,
II., 263.

had obtained the consent of Sixtus IV., and urged the Duke
to join them.*

In January, 1476, Louis XI. issued a decree convening
an Assembly of the French Church at Lyons.† Thus, the
Council so much dreaded in Rome threatened to assume
a tangible form. There can be no doubt that the Mission
of the Legate, Giuliano della Rovere, to France was connected with this movement.‡ His presence there was also
rendered desirable by the state of affairs in Avignon,§ of
which city Giuliano was Archbishop; to this dignity was
now added that of Papal Legate.‖ Louis XI., who was by
no means favourably disposed towards the Cardinal,¶ did
everything in his power to have the former Legate, Charles
of Bourbon, reappointed. A violent dispute ensued, in
which it seemed probable that Avignon would have been
lost to the Holy See. At last the difficulty was settled

* DROYSEN, II., 1, 301; SEGESSER, Beziehungen der Schweizer
zu Matth. Corvinus, 72 *seq.* (Luzern, 1860); RAUSCH, 148 *seq.*;
MENZEL-SCHLIEPHAKE, Geschichte von Nassau, V., 424 (Wiesbaden,
1879), doubts, but without sufficient reason, whether this agitation for
a Council was serious.

† GINGINS LA SARRA, I., 285, see 321.

‡ Although this Mission of Giuliano's (see next page, note *) is
mentioned in universally accessible publications, BROSCH, in his Monograph, 7–9, knows nothing of it! SCHMARSOW, 110, has already observed that, in consequence of this gross ignorance, Brosch "takes
upon himself to suggest that the Cardinal Legate may at this time
have fallen under the Pope's displeasure." We have here a characteristic example of this writer's want of circumspection, and of his
mania for hazarding injurious conjectures on every occasion.

§ Giuliano left Rome on the 19th February, 1476, as Cardinal
Gonzaga and J. P. Arrivabene concur in stating in their *Letters,
dated Rome, 1476, February 20. (Gonzaga Archives, Mantua.) See
also the Brief of the 24th February in MARTÈNE, II., 1528.

‖ FANTONI, I., 343.

¶ See LAGER, Gorze, 85; MARTÈNE, II., 1503–4.

by the elevation of Charles of Bourbon to the purple.* Giuliano founded a College in Avignon for poor students, and was received with great honour in Rome when he returned in the autumn. In the difficult negotiations with the French monarch, he received much assistance from his skilful judicial adviser, Giovanni Cerretani.†

In March, 1476, while Giuliano was still in France, a letter from Louis XI. was affixed to the door of St. Peter's, commanding all Cardinals, Prelates, and Bishops of his kingdom to appear at Lyons on the 1st May, to deliberate upon the assembling of a General Council.‡ In the latter part of April a French Embassy presented to the Pope the strange request that he would consent that a Council should be held at Lyons, and would be present there in person! Naturally, this request was not granted.§ For a considerable time it was reported that the Pope, in order to be beforehand with the opposition, would himself summon a General Council to meet in Rome.‖ In the end, neither Assembly came to anything.

* Besides FANTONI, *loc. cit.*, see, regarding Giuliano's Mission to France, GINGINS LA SARRA, II., 33 *seq.*, 97, 131, 185; N. DELLA TUCCIA, 413; KNEBEL, II., 429; AMMANATI, Epist. (Frankfort edition), ep. 877 and 886; MARTÈNE, II., 1529, 1547; SCHMARSOW, 109-10; REUMONT, Lorenzo, I., 305, 2nd ed.; FRIEDBERG, II., 477; CHARPENNE, Hist. des réunions temp. d'Avignon, I., 10 (Paris, 1886).

† PALMERIUS, 259. According to the *Acta Consist. of the Secret Archives of the Vatican, Giuliano reached Foligno on his homeward journey on the 4th Oct., 1476, "ubi papa cum curia sua tunc residebat." This date was hitherto unknown.

‡ KNEBEL'S Tagebuch, II., 391-2; RAUSCH, 150. See also MARTÈNE, II., 1535, and the **Despatch of J. P. Arrivabene, dated Rome, 1476, May 14. Gonzaga Archives, Mantua.

§ Sixtus IV. explained his reasons in a **Brief to the Duke of Milan, dated Rome, 1476, April 21. (State Archives at Milan.) A similar *Brief to Ercole d'Este is in the State Archives, Modena.

‖ See KNEBEL'S Tagebuch, II., 408; also 405 and 406.

Trusting in the schismatical tendencies of Louis XI., Lorenzo had, on the 2nd May, 1478, begged him to interfere in the contest between Florence and Rome, and a little later had recommended that the usual means of intimidation, the proposal to hold a Council, should be employed.* Louis XI. did not need much persuasion. " The King," writes a contemporary Ambassador, " has long cherished the plan of bringing about a schism in the Church. That which has taken place in Florence has furnished him with an excellent pretext. He is, therefore, sending Philippe de Commines to Turin, Milan, and Florence. Commines will not go to Venice, the King being persuaded that, in consideration of the close alliance existing between him and the Signoria, the intimation of his wishes by a simple letter will suffice."†

Sixtus IV. did not allow himself to be cast down by the threats of the French King. On the 11th July an outbreak of the Plague obliged him to betake himself to Bracciano,‡ where he was joined by the representatives of Venice, Milan, Florence, and Ferrara, together with two new French Envoys. On the 1st August all the Envoys met together

* BUSER, Beziehungen, 193–4. See DESJARDINS, Polit. de Louis XI., 29, and Négociat., 171 *seq.*

† Despatch of the Milanese Ambassador of the 16th June, 1478, in KERVYN DE LETTENHOVE, I., 173 *seq.* See FRANTZ, 261, and HEFELE-HERGENRÖTHER, VIII., 220. Nothing, unfortunately, is known of the negotiations with the Pope carried on by Commines ; even the time of his visit to Rome has not been exactly ascertained ; see REUMONT, I., 310, 2nd ed.

‡ *Acta Consist., f. 55, Secret Archives of the Vatican. We learn from this authority that Sixtus IV. did not return to Rome until the 17th September. HEFELE-HERGENRÖTHER, VIII., 223, is, accordingly, mistaken. The Plague, as J. P. Arrivabene in a *Despatch, dated Rome, 1478, May 24, declares, had broken out in May. Gonzaga Archives, Mantua.

in the Castle of the Orsini, and declared that the conduct of Sixtus IV. towards Florence and towards Lorenzo was a scandal to Christendom, because it hindered the Turkish war. Repeated requests for the removal of the censures had been made to him without any effect. For this reason, and also because all countries, chiefly through the faults of their rulers, needed thorough reform, they demanded the assembly of a Council in France.* On the 16th August Louis XI. strictly forbade the transmission of any money to Rome. In September the temporal and spiritual magnates of France met at Orleans. They left it to the King's choice, " either in the following year to summon a National Council at Lyons, or to prevail on the Pope to hold an Œcumenical Council. Louis XI. deemed it best to attempt the latter alternative."†

At the beginning of December, 1478, Sixtus IV., with the object of counteracting French intervention in the contest with Florence, as well as the schismatic tendencies of Louis XI. and his Italian allies, sent two Nuncios to the Emperor Frederick III., requesting his mediation and assistance.‡

---

* The *Document drawn up on this occasion, which GREGOROVIUS, VII., 246, 3rd ed., was the first to point out, is in the State Archives, Florence, Atti publ., CLXI. It begins with the words : " In nomine, &c., 1 Aug., 1478. Cum Sixtus IV. injuste," &c., and concludes as follows : "Acta facta et gesta fuerunt predicta omnia et singula supra-scripta Brachiani Sutrin. dioc. terrar. (*not* territ., as Gregorovius reads) dom. Neapoleonis de Ursinis et in palatio sive fortitio dicti oppidi Brachiani." The French Envoys were Tristanus comes Claramontis and Gabriel Vives. Regarding the unjust accusations made by the King, see FRANTZ, 261 *seq.* On the 5th Aug., 1478, entrance into France was denied "à ung nommé Herosme Riaire, homme de bas lieu," &c. ; see BASIN-QUICHERAT, III., 67.

† REUMONT, Lorenzo, I., 327, 2nd ed. ; GUETTÉE, VIII., 40 *seq.* ; LEGEAY, II., 318 ; BUSER, Beziehungen, 478 ; PERRENS, 413.

‡ Sixtus IV. had already written to the Emperor about Lorenzo on

The Ambassadors of the King of France reached Rome
in January, 1479, and at once presented a memorial desiring
the assembling of a General Council. Sixtus IV. replied
that, if it were possible, such a measure would be very
agreeable to him. At the same time, he made it plain that
the Pope presides in an Œcumenical Council, and that to
him belongs the right to summon it. He pointed out that
the Prelates, who are all bound to maintain the liberty of
the Church, would sit in it. No one of them would say
that Lorenzo had the right to cause the Archbishop of
Pisa to be ignominiously executed. All would rather be
of opinion that he ought first to have been sentenced by an
ecclesiastical tribunal. No Council could be called without
the consent of the Emperor and the other Princes. The
summoning of such an Assembly belongs to the Pope, and
he would take council with the Cardinals on the subject.
Sixtus IV. went on to speak in detail of the ecclesiastical
policy of Louis XI. As to the Pragmatic Sanction, he
said, either it was a just measure, in which case the King
ought not to have revoked it, or an unjust one, in which
case he ought not to think of reviving it. In recalling the
Prelates from Rome, he had done wrong : their Superior is
the Pope. The King would do better to lead Lorenzo to
acknowledge his errors, and to persuade him to make fitting
atonement ; if he did this, he would obtain pardon, and all
else would be easily settled. A Papal Ambassador had,
moreover, been sent to France, and would be able to
give the King further explanations. Numerous letters
received from members of the clergy bear witness to the
indignation that would be felt if the Pope did not appear

the 23rd May, and again on the 6th Aug., 1478 ; on the 1st December,
he informed him of the arrival of L. de Agnellis ; see Mon. Habsb.,
451, 454. The *Instruction for L. de Agnellis and A. de Grassis are
in Appendix, N. 59. Secret Archives of the Vatican.

as the avenger of the insults offered to the Church in Florence.*

On the 15th February another Consistory was held, and the Emperor's Ambassadors, who had meanwhile arrived, took part in it. They expressed themselves with decision regarding the rights of the Holy See, and did not think a Council necessary, but were of opinion that the Pope should deal mercifully with the Florentines, and conclude a peace, considering the present danger from the Turks.†

Most of the Cardinals also desired the restoration of peace, but Count Girolamo and Ferrante laboured with all their might against it, and were at first successful.‡

The uncertain attitude of Bologna at this time caused the greatest anxiety to Sixtus IV., and Cardinal Gonzaga was sent there.§

---

* RAYNALDUS, ad an. 1478, N. 18 *seq.* ; FRANTZ, 283 *seq.* ; HEFELE-HERGENRÖTHER, VIII., 224 *seq.*

† HEFELE-HERGENRÖTHER, VIII., 227 *seq.* ; GUETTÉE, VIII., 41–2, where are details regarding the negotiations which followed. DESJARDINS, Polit. de Louis XI., 31, sees the matter completely from the French King's point of view, and believes in his honourable feeling for Christendom !

‡ See N. DELLA TUCCIA, 421, and in Appendix, N. 60 and 61, Pandolfini's *Letters of the 20th and 25th March, 1479. State Archives, Florence.

§ See *Ghirardacci, St. di Bologna, *loc. cit.* (see our Vol. III., p. 243), and an autograph **Letter of Sixtus IV. to Cardinal Gonzaga, dated ex urbe 20 Martii, 1479 (Orig. in the Episcopal Archives, Mantua), from which it appears that Gonzaga was also to go to Germany. This Mission, however, came to nothing ; for on the 21st April, A. tit. S. Sabine card. Montisregalis [=Auxias de Podio] was appointed legatus de latere in partibus Alamanie ; he set off on the 17th May. (*Acta Consist., f. 57, Secret Archives of the Vatican.) On the last day of March Sixtus IV. commanded Card. Gonzaga, should the Bolognese continue obstinate in their disobedience, at once to leave the city. *Brief of this day in the State Archives, Milan. By the end of the

In the struggle with Florence, things at last seemed taking a more favourable turn, for, on the 4th April, 1479, the ecclesiastical censures were suspended, and a temporary cessation of hostilities proclaimed by the Pope.* Emboldened by this partial success, the Florentines, on the 28th April, rejected the terms of peace then proposed by him. In order to bring pressure to bear upon Sixtus IV., on the 27th May the League, through the Venetian Ambassador, declared that, unless within a period of eight days he should agree to a peace, their representatives should be instructed to leave Rome. Sixtus IV. was justly astounded at this communication, which "was tantamount to a refusal to make any concession to his demands. The limit of eight days, also, was an insult, since it was obviously impossible for him to conclude a peace without the consent of his allies, Naples and Siena."† On the 31st May the Ambassadors again assembled in the Pope's presence for further negotiations. Sixtus IV. caused a long statement to be read, shewing that he had tried every possible means for the restoration of peace. "The Venetian Ambassador replied in a speech in which he greatly incensed the Pope, by dwelling largely on the obnoxious topic of the Council." When the French Ambassador, in the name of his master, and in accord with the League, endeavoured to enter a protest against the

year, partly through the conciliatory action of the Pope (see *Letter of Joh. Angelus de Talentis, dated Rome, 1479, May 27, State Archives, Milan), matters were so far settled that in a *Brief, dated Rome, 1479, November 20, Sixtus was able to praise the Bolognese for their obedience. State Archives, Bologna.

* Sixtus IV. and Giuliano della Rovere lost no time in informing the French Ambassadors of the fact. See in Appendix, N. 62 and 63, *Letters of the 6th and 7th April, 1479, from the Milanese State Archives.

† HEFELE-HERGENRÖTHER, VIII., 231.

failure of the negotiations, Sixtus IV. brought the meeting to a close. Soon after this the Envoys of the League left Rome, unaccompanied, however, by those of the French King.*

The position of the Florentines grew much worse in the autumn.† Discontent was more and more openly expressed ; Lorenzo was told to his face that the city was weary of war and needed peace. It became evident that there was no hope of assistance from Louis XI., and this conviction had a great effect on public feeling.‡

In his necessity Lorenzo boldly resolved to go himself as a suppliant to Naples (6th December, 1479). The utter faithlessness of Ferrante now became evident. Regardless alike of the alliance concluded with the Pope, and of the loyalty which he owed to his suzerain, he did not hesitate to betray him. The treaty of peace, which was the result of his negotiations with Lorenzo and Lodovico il Moro, regarded nothing but his own interests, although he had but recently sworn that he would lose ten kingdoms and his crown rather than let Lorenzo go without securing the conditions desired by Sixtus.§ The Pope bitterly complained that the victory which had been in his hands was filched away, as it were, behind his back ; but, that no one might accuse him of being an obstacle in the way of peace, he ratified the treaty, stipulating, however, that

* BUSER, Beziehungen, 208–12, and Lorenzo, 141 *seq.* ; DESJARDINS, Négociations, I., 185–6 ; PERRENS, 426–7.

† The Pope was at this time more than ever resolved on the expulsion of Lorenzo from Florence ; see the *Briefs of the 20th and 22nd Sept., 1479, to Alfonso of Calabria and Federigo of Urbino. State Archives, Milan.

‡ FRANTZ, 332 *seq.*

§ FRANTZ, 351. Regarding Ferrante's artfulness and faithlessness, see GOTHEIN, 32, and SYBEL'S Hist. Zeitschrift, N. F., XXI., 365.

Lorenzo should come in person to Rome; from this time "the Tuscan war languished."*

Meanwhile Otranto had been taken by the Turks, and this loss did more than anything else to turn attention from these internal disputes to the dangers in the East, and to remove the last obstacles in the way of a complete reconciliation. "The advantage which the Florentines derived from the altered condition of affairs was so manifest that many voices were heard which accused Lorenzo of having encouraged the Sultan to attack Apulia."† Florence decided to send a solemn Embassy to Rome, praying for the removal of the Interdict. It arrived on the 25th November, 1480, and the negotiations for peace were promptly brought to a happy conclusion. On the 3rd December the Florentines were released from all ecclesiastical censures.‡

* HEFELE-HERGENRÖTHER, VIII., 236; GREGOROVIUS, VII., 247, 3rd ed.

† REUMONT, Lorenzo, I., 368, 2nd ed. ; FRANTZ, 352.

‡ Particulars of the ceremonies and of the conditions of peace are given by JACOB. VOLATERRANUS, 113 *seq.*

CHAPTER VIII.

TURKISH EXPEDITIONS AGAINST RHODES AND OTRANTO.—RESIST-
ANCE OFFERED BY SIXTUS IV.—DEATH OF SULTAN MAHOMET.
—THE POPE'S REPEATED ATTEMPTS AT A CRUSADE.

IT has always been a part of the policy of the Eastern
conquerors to profit by the quarrels of the Western Powers.
From this point of view the last thirty years of the 15th
Century had been an exceptionally favourable period for
the Sultan. Half Europe was convulsed with wars, and,
from 1478, Rome, hitherto always the foremost in the
defence of Christendom, had been involved in an unholy
struggle, with the result that for a time Sixtus IV. did
nothing in this direction.

From 1477 the outlook in the East had grown more
and more gloomy. "In May of that year, while a Turkish
army blockaded Lepanto and Leucadia, Achmed Bey
attacked Kroja, the capital of Albania, and, on the 15th
June, 1478, this stronghold was compelled to capitulate.
Schabljak, Alessio, and Drivasto also fell into the hands
of the Turks; only Antivari and Scodra continued to hold
out though besieged." *

Even more distressing than these losses were the barbarous incursions of the Turks into the Austrian Alpine
Provinces,† Friuli, and Upper Italy. The Tuscan war

---

* HERTZBERG, Osmanen, 630. See FALLMERAYER, Albanes. Element, 103 *seq.*, and MAKUSCEV, Slaven, 115.

† See HUBER, III., 234 *seq.*, where are also details regarding the

deprived the Venetians of all hope of assistance from their
fellow-countrymen ; and an alarming outbreak of the Plague
added yet more to their discouragement. The Signoria
took the momentous resolution of abandoning the contest.
On the 25th January, 1479, a treaty of peace was signed at
Stamboul by Giovanni Dario, the Venetian Commissioner.
The conditions were hard. Not only Kroja and Scodra,
the Albanian chieftains, and the house of Tocco, but also
even Eubœa and Lemnos were abandoned to the enemy ;
however, the trade of the Republic with the Levant was
preserved.* From this moment a period begins during
which the whole policy of Venice is devoted to the one
object of maintaining this advantage.†

In the very nature of things, for a conquering state there
is no standing still. This was evident after the great
successes gained by the Turks over the first naval power
of the West. In the summer of 1479, Leonardo Tocco the
Third was driven from Leucadia. The unfortunate man
sought refuge in Rome, where the number of fugitives from
the East was constantly increasing. Sixtus IV. generously
gave him 1000 ducats at once, and allowed him twice that
sum as a yearly pension, promising to do more when better
times should come.‡

The next year an attempt was made to put an end to
the rule of the Knights of St. John in Rhodes. They had

conflicts in Moldavia and Wallachia. Huber seems to have been
unacquainted with Haselbach's work, Die Türkennoth im 15 Jahr-
hundert mit besonderer Berücksichtigung der Zustände Oesterreichs,
Wien, 1864.

* See ZINKEISEN, II., 432–7 ; HERTZBERG, 632 ; HEYD, II., 327
seq. ; HOPF, Griechenland, LXXXVI., 161 ; Cal. of State Papers,
Venet., I., 139 seq.

† ZINKEISEN, II., 441.

‡ JACOB. VOLATERRANUS, 102.

long been the terror of the Turks, and the object of their
bitterest hatred. As there was no Christian naval power
now to be feared, the task seemed an easy one; but the
heroic valour of Pierre d'Aubusson and his Knights
wrought marvels, and this last bulwark of Eastern
Christendom was saved for a time (Summer of 1480).[*]
Tidings of the approach of succour from the West hastened
the departure of the Turks.[†] Sixtus IV. had granted a
special Indulgence to all who should do anything to aid
the Knights; had called upon the Italian Powers to assist
them, and besides himself sending two ships with provisions
and war materials, was preparing for further exertions.[‡]

Western Christendom had not yet recovered from the
agitation caused by the struggle in Rhodes, when a fresh
disaster filled all hearts with terror and dismay.

Mahomet had long been gazing with covetous eyes on
the wealth of Italy, the seat of his great enemy, the Papacy.[§]
There can be no doubt that the insane jealousy of Venice
at the increase of the power of Naples, hurried on the impending attack. If the Signoria did not actually invite the
Turks into Italy, they certainly allowed them to believe
that their arrival would be far from unwelcome to them.[||]

The result appeared in the despatch of a Turkish fleet,
with a number of troops on board, to Apulia. On the 11th

---

* ZINKEISEN, II., 464 *seq.*; BERG, Die Insel Rhodus, 60, 133 *seq.*
(Braunschweig, 1862). The Knights were praised by all for the courage
displayed in this war; see RÖHRICHT-MEISNER, Pilgerfahrten, 22
(Berlin, 1880).

† SIGISMONDO DE' CONTI, I., 102.

‡ RAYNALDUS, ad an. 1480, N. 2 *seq.*, 24; JACOB. VOLATERRANUS,
106; Diario Parm., 334, 345, 348; FOUCARD, Dispacci, 104 *seq.*, 106 *seq.*,
118 *seq.*, 131, 139; THEINER, Mon. Pol., II., 214; GUGLIELMOTTI, 423.

§ See MAKUSCEV, Slaven, 90.

|| BROSCH, Julius II., p. 18. See CIPOLLA, 605, and FOUCARD,
Dispacci, 132.

August, 1480, Otranto was in the hands of the Infidel.*
Of its 22,000 inhabitants, 12,000 were put to death with
terrible tortures, and the rest carried away into slavery.
The aged Archbishop, who, with heroic courage, had remained to the last before the altar imploring the help of
God, was sawn in two, as was also the Governor. Indescribable horrors were perpetrated. Many captives, who
refused to become Mahometans, were slaughtered on a hill
before the city, and their bodies thrown to the dogs.†

The tidings that the victorious banner of the Crescent
had been planted on Italian soil "produced unutterable
consternation." ‡ " In Rome," says Sigismondo de' Conti,
" the alarm was as great as if the enemy had been already
encamped before her very walls. . . . Terror had taken such
hold of all minds that even the Pope meditated flight. I
was at that time in the Low Countries, in the suite of the
Cardinal Legate Giuliano, and I remember that he was commissioned to prepare what was necessary at Avignon, for
Sixtus IV. had decided upon taking refuge with the French,
if the state of affairs in Italy should become worse." §

---

* See *Copia della presa d'Otranto da Turchi nel anno 1480 in Cod.
X.–IV., 52, N. 17.   (Casanatense Library, Rome.) See JAC. VOLATER-
RANUS, 110; FOUCARD, Dispacci, 85, 88, 92, 111, 153, 165 *seq.*; M.
SANUDO, 1213 ; Diar. Parm., 352 ; CIPOLLA, 604.

† The height on which these victims died for their Faith has ever
since borne the name of the Martyrs' Hill. They were at once venerated as saints by the people, and ultimately canonised by Clement
XIV. Acta Sanctorum, 18th Aug., p. 179 *seq.*; ROHRBACHER-
KNÖPFLER, 248 ; SUMMONTE, III., 501 *seq.*

‡ See BASIN-QUICHERAT, III., 68 ; SERRA, Liguria, 267 ; CIAVARINI,
I., 195 ; BLASI, Sicilia, II., 665, see also his Storia dei vicerè, &c., di
Sicilia, 118 (Palermo, 1842).

§ SIGISMONDO DE' CONTI, I., 107–9 ; SCHMARSOW, 142 ; GUGLIEL-
MOTTI, 429. Ferrante had sent a special messenger to inform the
Pope of the fall of Otranto ; see FOUCARD, Dispacci, 86.

Ferrante's dismay was even greater than that of the Pope. His son, Alfonso, was immediately recalled from Tuscany,[*] and the assistance of Sixtus IV., and all the other Princes of Italy, vehemently invoked with the threat that, unless active support were speedily given, he would throw in his lot with the Sultan for the destruction of all the others. We see, from the report of a contemporary historian on the Papal side, how unfriendly were the relations between the Pope and the King of Naples at this time. "Sixtus IV.," he writes, "would have witnessed with great indifference the misfortunes and losses of his faithless ally, had Ferrante's enemy been any one but the Sultan; but it was a very different matter when the common foe of Christendom had actually got a footing on Italian soil, and speedily the Papacy and Rome itself were threatened with utter ruin, unless he were promptly expelled. He at once sent all the money that he could get together, permitted tithes to be levied from all the clergy in the kingdom, and promised a Plenary Indulgence to all Christians enlisting under the banner of the Cross."[†]

Immediately on the landing of the Turks in Apulia, Sixtus IV. had appealed to the Italian Powers, and his cry for help was soon repeated in yet more pressing terms.[‡] "If the faithful," he said, "especially the Italians, wish to preserve their lands, their houses, their wives, their children, their liberty, and their lives, if they wish to maintain that Faith into which we have been baptised,

* NOTAR GIACOMO, 146; G. A. PECCI, Mem. di Siena, I., 14 *seq.* (Siena, 1755); FOUCARD, Dispacci, 82, 121, 153; REUMONT, Lorenzo, II., 368 *seq.*, 2nd ed.

† SIGISMONDO DE' CONTI, *loc. cit.* See FOUCARD, Dispacci, 110 *seq.*, 142, 609 *seq.*

‡ Florence also received similar *Briefs, dated Rome, 1480, July 27 and August 5. (State Archives, Florence, X.–II.–25, f. 154b–156b.) The Pope had already, in July, the intention to fit out a fleet in Genoa, and so to meet the Turkish danger. CHMEL, Briefe, 278 *seq.*, 299 *seq.*, 302, 325 *seq.*

and through which we are regenerated, let them at last trust in our word, let them take up their arms and fight."*

In a Consistory, held on the 14th August, it was determined that every possible effort should be made to expel the Turks from Otranto.†

On the 18th August Gabriele Rangoni was appointed Cardinal Legate to Naples, and, on the 23rd, he started for his post.‡ On the 22nd September fresh Briefs were addressed to all the Italian States, desiring them to send representatives to a Congress to be held in Rome at the beginning of November.§ The example set by Sixtus IV., in his reconciliation with Florence, could not fail to have a good effect on his efforts for the restoration of peace in Italy. One of the conditions of the treaty with the Republic was that it should furnish fifteen galleys for the war with the Turks.‖ On the 4th December Cardinal Savelli was sent to Genoa, to endeavour to reconcile the contending parties there, and to superintend the equipment of the Papal fleet in the harbour.¶

---

* See RAYNALDUS, ad an. 1480, N. 20-28, and Diar. Parmen., 352.

† FOUCARD, Dispacci, 98, 112.

‡ *Acta Consist., Secret Archives of the Vatican. See FOUCARD, Dispacci, 114, 142, and 154-5, Brief of Sixtus IV., of the 16th August, regarding the purposed Mission of the Bishop of Terracina to Naples. An undated *Brief of Sixtus IV., referring to Rangoni's Mission, is in the Library at Bamberg (bound up with Incunabel, Q. II., 24).

§ *Brief to Florence, dated Rome, 1480, Sept. 22. State Archives, Florence, X.-II.-25, f. 158b ; a copy is in the State Archives, Milan, Autogr.

‖ REUMONT, Lorenzo, I., 370, 2nd ed.

¶ *Acta Consist., Secret Archives of the Vatican. The 20th December is here mentioned as the day of Savelli's departure, while JACOB. VOLATERRANUS, 116, has the 19th. From the *Acta Consist. we learn that the Cardinal had only returned from Perugia on the 2nd of the month.

The Divine assistance was invoked by an ordinance of the Pope, desiring that the Octave of the Festival of All Saints should henceforth be solemnly celebrated throughout Christendom.* The preparations for the Crusading fleet were at once commenced ; twenty-five galleys were to be built, partly in Ancona, and partly in Genoa.† As the Papal Treasury was empty, Sixtus IV. was compelled to have recourse to extraordinary taxation. A tax of a gold ducat was, in the first instance, laid upon every hearth‡ in the States of the Church, and then a tithe imposed for two years on all churches and convents in the Papal territory.§

A Brief of Sixtus IV. to Bologna, dated 3rd January 1481, furnishes detailed information regarding the deliberations of the Envoys assembled in Rome. The Pope explains that, as a tax for the expenses of the Turkish war has to be imposed on all Princes, he and the Cardinals, in order to set a good example, have undertaken to contribute the sum of 150,000 ducats, although so large an amount is almost beyond his powers. 100,000 ducats of this is to be expended on the equipment of twenty-five triremes, and the remaining 50,000 to be sent to the King of Hungary. He, moreover, engages to collect 3000 soldiers for the recovery of Otranto, to which place he has already sent troops. With regard to the building of the fleet, the Ambassadors

* RAYNALDUS, ad an. 1480, N. 29.

† JACOB. VOLATERRANUS, 115 ; GUGLIELMOTTI, 432.

‡ See the **Brief to Card. Gonzaga of the 29th Nov., 1480. (State Archives, Bologna.) A Sienese Ambassador, whose *Report is, unfortunately, half-destroyed, writes, under date Rome, 1480, Nov. 20, that the Pope said : * " Nos una cum istis venerab. fratribus nostris sumus parati pro posse et ultra posse facere debitum nostrum et exponere introitus nostros et omnia bona nostra et calices, &c." State Archives, Siena.

§ See RAYNALDUS, ad an. 1480, N. 28, and a *Brief to Bologna, dated 1480, December 17. State Archives, Bologna, Lib. Q. 3.

are of opinion that 100 triremes must be prepared, and
200,000 ducats be sent annually to the King of Hungary.
The money required for these purposes is to be raised
among the several Powers; he and the Cardinals having
already contributed their share, the preparation should be
completed by March. The Bolognese must not delay, for
the danger was imminent.[*]

The action of the Pope was not confined to Italy. He
was unremitting in his endeavours to unite all the Princes
of Europe against the common foe. The results varied in
different places. King Edward IV. of England declared
that it was unfortunately impossible for him to take part
in the war.[†] No help was to be expected from distracted
Germany. Even now, the States assembled to take counsel
together were unable to come to terms.[‡]

Tidings of a more favourable nature arrived from France,
where Giuliano della Rovere was at this time acting as
Papal Legate.[§] He had been charged to bring about a
peace between Louis XI., Maximilian of Austria, and the
Flemings, to obtain the release of Cardinal de La Balue, and
procure French assistance for the Crusade.[||] Giuliano had

---

[*] MAKUSCEV, I., 311–12. See also the Milanese Report of 13th
Dec., 1480, in CHMEL, Briefe, 347 seq.

[†] Cal. of State Papers, Venet., I., 142–3.

[‡] ENNEN, III., 308.

[§] BROSCH, Julius II., pp. 15 and 304, following Jac. Volaterranus,
only mentions the 9th June as the date of Giuliano's departure. From
the Acta Consist., Secret Archives of the Vatican, f. 59, we learn that the
Cardinal was appointed legatus de latere for France on the 28th April;
the 9th June is also given here as the day when he left Rome.
Giuliano was at Parma on the 3rd July. See Diar. Parm., 343.

[||] This appears from a *Letter, written by Giuliano della Rovere to
Sixtus IV., dated Vendôme, 1480, Aug. 24, in which he speaks of his
favourable reception by Louis XI. I found a copy of this document
in the State Archives, Milan.

been obliged to renounce the exercise of his full powers as
Legate, but he was in great measure successful in regard
to the Crusade.* On the 28th August he was able to
forward to the Pope a royal letter, containing the most
satisfactory assurances as to the share France would take
in the war.† Envoys were to be sent to Rome to settle
the details. In the instruction for this Mission, Louis XI.
says : " No sufficient resistance can be offered to the Turks
at less cost than at least 100,000 golden scudi a month.
He proposed himself to furnish 100,000 annually, and
twice that sum if the Pope would allow him to impose a
tribute on all ecclesiastics in his kingdom, and would send
him a Legate provided with all the faculties desired by the
King, and especially with full powers to absolve in cases
reserved to the Pope. Other Christian Princes, however,
must also contribute their share. The King counted on
40,000 scudi annually from Italy and the States of the
Church ; on 200,000 from Germany, which had so many
rich Archbishops, Bishops and Beneficiaries, Princes and
cities ; and on the same amount from Spain. The King of
England might contribute 100,000 scudi. Venice, he had
heard, would not be unwilling to declare war against the
Turks if help from Italy were certain. The plenipo-
tentiaries were accordingly authorised to unite with the
other Italian Powers in promising an annual subsidy of
300,000 scudi to the Republic. In the event, however, of
the other Kings and nations not giving any definite promise,
the French Envoys were only to undertake that their
Government would contribute its just share of the burden.

* Authenticated by BROSCH, Julius II., 16. See also FRIEDBERG,
II., 477.

† This *Letter of Louis XI. to Sixtus IV., dated Vendôme, 1480,
Aug. 28, was hitherto unknown ; I found a copy in the State Archives,
Milan.

The Pope must also, above all, secure France against England."*

Soon after the arrival of the French Mission (8th March)† Sixtus IV. wrote a circular letter to the Italian Powers, laying before them the proposals of Louis,‡ as expressed in a Memorandum, in which the Envoys had embodied the result of their negotiations. It proclaimed a general peace throughout Italy, and decreed that speedy assistance against the Turks should be rendered with the least possible delay. France promised troops, and was to be included in the alliance. The Emperor was also invited to join it, and a subsidy of 50,000 ducats was allotted to the King of Hungary. The Pope undertook to furnish twenty-five, and King Ferrante forty triremes. Genoa promised five galleys, Ferrara four, Siena three, and Bologna two, Lucca, Mantua, and Montferrat one each; while Milan engaged to give 30,000 and Florence 40,000 ducats. §

According to the testimony of a contemporary historian, the Milanese and Florentines were not remiss in contributing money; the Venetians only held aloof, because they had concluded peace with the Sultan. ‖

On Passion Sunday, the 8th April, 1481, Sixtus IV. published an Encyclical, calling on all the Princes of Europe

---

* GOTTLOB in the Hist. Jahrb., VI., 447.

† JACOB. VOLATERRANUS, 123. See BASIN, III., 70.

‡ *Brief to Milan, dated Rome, 1481, March 23 (the Original is in the State Archives, Milan); one of the same day to the Duke of Ferrara (Original in the State Archives, Modena), and to Florence (Copy in the Florentine State Archives).

§ RAYNALDUS, ad an. 1481, N. 4 *seq*. See GRASSO, 323.

‖ SIGISMONDO DE' CONTI, I., 110. In a *Brief of the 3rd Jan., 1481, Sixtus IV. exhorted the Milanese Government to pay the tax; on the 10th April he again called upon them for aid against the Turks. Both these *Bulls are in the State Archives, Milan.

to take part in the Turkish war.* Indulgences were proclaimed throughout Italy, and the tithe for the war was
levied. On the 9th April the tithe was announced in
France and Dauphiné, and Giuliano della Rovere appointed
Collector-General.† Notwithstanding the daily increasing
danger, there was still in many places but little zeal. The
wealthy city of Bologna, for instance, declared that the
tribute of hearth-money and the equipment of two triremes
were too much for her ; the Pope accordingly, on the 1st
February, 1481, forgave the tribute, but urged that the two
vessels should be prepared at once.‡ A Papal Brief of the
3rd May to the Vice-Legate at Bologna shews that the
city then professed itself willing to contribute 2000 ducats
towards the expenses of the war. The Pope considered the
sum very small, but had all the more hope that it would be
sent without delay. In June we hear of difficulties. On
the 7th of August it was still unpaid. At last, on the 11th
of September, it arrived ! § Several other cities behaved in
the same manner.

Personally, Sixtus IV. gave the best possible example.
He parted with his own silver plate, and sent a large
quantity of sacred vessels to the Mint to meet the expenses
of the Crusade.||

* See RAYNALDUS, ad an. 1481, N. 19, 20 seq.; FABRICIUS, VI., 492 ;
and GRASSO, 351. A complete copy of the Bull of the 8th April,
beginning with the words, " Cogimur jubente altissimo," is in the State
Archives, Milan.

† GOTTLOB in the Hist. Jahrb., VI., 448.

‡ *Brief of Sixtus IV. to Bologna, dated Rome, 1481, Febr. 1.
State Archives, Bologna, Lib. Q. 3.

§ *Briefs of Sixtus IV. to the Legate's representative at Bologna,
dated Rome, 1481, May 3, June 16, Aug. 7, and Sept. 11, *loc. cit.* See
also on next page, note †.

|| Diar. Parm., 364-5. See CORTESIUS, De cardinalatu, f. CXXIV.,
and Anecdot. Litt., III., 258.

In the midst of these anxious and hurried preparations came tidings of the death of the mighty conqueror, whose name, during one whole generation, had filled Europe and Asia with terror. By the end of May rumours of this event began to circulate in Rome, and, on the 2nd June, the report was confirmed by letters from the Venetian Government to its Envoys.* Cannons were fired, and all the Church bells rang to announce the good news. The Pope himself went at once in thanksgiving to the Vespers at Sta Maria del Popolo, which the Sacred College and all the Ambassadors also attended. As darkness came on, bonfires were lighted in all directions. On the 3rd of June, processions of thanksgiving were ordered during three successive days, and Sixtus IV. personally took part in them.† Briefs, dated the 4th June, pointed out to all Christian Powers that this was the moment for dealing a decisive blow. Sixtus IV. was able to announce that he had already equipped a fleet of thirty-four ships at Genoa, which would soon be in the Tiber, and that men-of-war were being built at Ancona and would be added to the Neapolitan fleet.‡

* **Despatch of B. Bendedeus of the 2nd June, 1481. (State Archives, Modena.) See JACOB. VOLATERRANUS, 134.

† *Letter of B. Bendedeus, dated Rome, 1481, June 3rd. (State Archives, Modena.) See NOTAJO DI NANTIPORTO, 1071, and INFESSURA, 1147. Throughout all Italy similar rejoicings took place ; see Diar. Parm., 374. In many instances the newly-kindled zeal for the Crusade grew cold. The Bolognese, seeking to withdraw from their promise of a subsidy, said "mortuo nunc Turcorum tyranno necessitatem amplius non imminere." Sixtus IV. expressed his astonishment at such language in a *Brief to the Vice-Legate, dated Rome, 1481, June 16, and urged them to take advantage of this opportunity of crushing the enemy. He was himself determined, he added, to do everything in his power to accomplish this end. State Archives, Bologna, Lib. Q. 3.

‡ MÜLLER, Docum., 233.

On the 30th June the Pope, with all the Cardinals, went to S. Paolo for the blessing of this fleet, which brought the Cardinal Legate Savelli back to Rome, and also its recently appointed Admiral, Cardinal Fregoso. After Vespers, the Pope held a Consistory. Savelli gave an account of his mission, and the ceremony of opening the mouth of Cardinal Fregoso then took place.* Sixtus IV. made him an address on the task which he was called upon to undertake, "gave him his Legate's ring and the banner which he had consecrated for the fleet. The captains of the ships then came in, kissed the foot of the Pope, and were signed with the cross on their breasts. At the close of the Consistory, the Pope, with the Cardinals and a great number of Prelates, proceeded to the river, where the galleys were lying at anchor, went on board each of the vessels, and gave the Apostolic blessing. The crew stood fully armed on the decks and saluted when he appeared. Weapons were brandished, swords drawn and struck upon the shields, and military evolutions executed as in actual battle. Hundreds of hoarse voices shouted the Pope's name amid the thunder of artillery ; it was a feast for both eye and ear," writes the chronicler, Jacobus Volaterranus.†

On the ‡ 4th July the Cardinal Legate sailed by way of Naples for Otranto, and, together with Ferrante and his ships, took part in the siege of that place. The resistance of the Turks was most obstinate, and they did not lay down their arms until the 10th September. Ferrante at once informed the Pope of the happy event, and he, in his turn, transmitted the news to all the Powers.§

* *Acta Consist., f. 62, Secret Archives of the Vatican.

† SCHMARSOW, 181, according to JACOB. VOLATERRANUS, 139. See also Diar. Parm., 377 ; and NOTAJO DI NANTIPORTO, 1071.

‡ *Acta Consist., f. 62, Secret Archives of the Vatican.

§ Ferrante's letter in JACOB. VOLATERRANUS, 146 *seq.* ; in regard to

Sixtus IV. had, from the first, intended that, after Otranto had been retaken, his fleet, joined by the ships of the other Powers, should proceed to Vallona, and, with the help of the Albanians, wrest this important fortress from the Turks. As early as the 30th of August he had written to Genoa to this effect.* The Portuguese fleet of twenty-five vessels, which had appeared before Ostia, was to form part of this expedition. Its Commander, the Bishop of Elbora, begged permission to go to Rome and receive the Pope's blessing, a favour which Sixtus IV. could not refuse. But his annoyance may be imagined, when, on his return from a short absence, he found that the Portuguese officers had preferred sight-seeing in Rome to going to the war, while the sailors occupied themselves in robbing the Roman vineyards. It required stringent orders from the Pope to induce them at last to weigh anchor and proceed to Naples, but only to linger there in a similar manner, under pretext of completing their equipment.† Sixtus IV.

the Papal Brief of the 18th Sept., 1481 (National Library, Florence), see Appendix, N. 64. Also GRASSO, 481 and 484-5. PRUTZ, Mittel-alter, II., 553, gives a medal struck by Sixtus IV. to commemorate the expulsion of the Turks from Otranto. Luca Pasi, in a *Letter, dated Rome, 1481, Sept. 20, speaks of the feasts and processions by which this victory was celebrated. State Archives, Modena.

* "*Januensibus," dated Rome, 1481, Aug. 30. This Brief is one of the first in the extremely important collection of Sixtus IV.'s Briefs in Cod. Magliab., II.-III.-256, of the National Library, Florence (in future, where this Library is cited, this MS. is to be understood). RAYNALDUS, ad an. 1481, N. 19, laments the loss of the Register for the year 1481 ; we have here almost a complete collection of the Briefs of Sixtus IV. from the end of August, 1481, till the end of August, 1482. The Florentine MS. is from the Rinuccini Library, and no doubt originally came from the Secret Archives of the Vatican ; in the University Library, Genoa, I found a fine copy of this valuable collection ; Cod. B. VIII., 17.

† JACOB. VOLATERRANUS, 154 ; SCHMARSOW, 185. In a *Brief to

repeatedly complained of the conduct of these Crusaders, and especially of that of their unprincipled chief.* But it was all in vain.

Meanwhile, still more deplorable events had occurred at Otranto. Disputes had arisen among the victors about the partition of the spoil. On the 1st September the Cardinal Legate wrote word that the captains of the triremes were bent on leaving, because the Plague had broken out on board four ships, and, moreover, their pay had not arrived. Sixtus IV. wrote to the Legate on the 10th September, maintaining that he was in no way to blame, he had fulfilled all his promises ; he also exhorted Fregoso to use every effort to retain these captains.† On the 18th September, after hearing that Otranto had been recaptured, Sixtus IV. again urged his Legate to follow up the victory to the best of his power.‡ Great, therefore, was his surprise when he learned from the King of Naples that the Legate had given out that the Pope had desired him to return with his fleet after the capture of Otranto! Sixtus IV. at once, on the 21st September, wrote to the King that he had, on the contrary, always intended and desired that the fleet, after delivering Otranto, should sail to Vallona.§ At the same time, he sent strict orders to the Legate to proceed

the Bishop of Elbora, dated Bracciano, 1481, Sept. 15, the Pope says : * " Intelleximus frat. tuam audita Hydronti recuperatione nolle ulterius progredi, sed statuisse istic morari. Miramur vehementer, &c." National Library, Florence.

* See **Briefs of the 17th September to the Cardinal of Lisbon and to the King himself. National Library, Florence.

† " *Tibi mandamus expresse et quemadmodum per alias litteras scripsimus omni studio, cura et ingenio enitaris ad continendos et refrenandos animos eorum. Legato classis, 1481, Sept. 10." National Library, Florence.

‡ See Appendix, N. 65.

§ *Regi Ferdinando, 1481, Sept. 21. National Library, Florence.

thither at once, recapture the place, and destroy the
Turkish ships.* On the 23rd September Sixtus IV. sent
one of his naval captains to prevent the return of the
Papal fleet, and to urge the Legate to start for Vallona.†

All the Pope's efforts were, however, fruitless. By the beginning of October the Legate and his ships appeared before
Civita Vecchia. Sixtus IV. hastened there to endeavour to
prevail upon him to turn back. Protracted consultations ensued, in which the Pope presided, and the Legate, the Neapolitan Ambassador, and the captains of the ships took part.

* " *Volumus et ita expresse tibi precipiendo mandamus ut . . .
redeas omnino et unacum classe regia Vallonam proficiscaris ad eam
expugnandam et classem Turcorum comburendam, ita enim est firme
et immutabilis nostre voluntatis. Cardli Januensi, dat. Bracciani, 1481,
Sept. 22." (National Library, Florence.) There is also a similar
*Brief from Sixtus IV. to Fregoso, dated 23rd Sept., 1481, in Cod.
Vatic. 4103, P. II., f. 105, Vatican Library.

† *Cardli Januensi and *Melchiori Zocho triremium nostrar.
capitaneo, dat. Bracciani, 1481, Sept. 23, loc. cit. GREGOROVIUS
completely misrepresents the facts of the case when, after dwelling
on the favourable opportunity for carrying on the war with the Turks
afforded by the deliverance of Otranto, he says (VII., 249, 3rd ed.) :
"Andreas, the last of the Palæologi, had at this time found an asylum
in Rome after appearing as a suppliant at the gates of every European
court. Sixtus generously granted him a yearly pension of 8000 ducats ;
but he would hear nothing of the East (in the 2nd edition, here follow
the words, 'and continued completely engrossed by his territorial
policy'). His fleet, with the Cardinal Legate, P. Fregoso, returned to
Civita Vecchia, and in vain did the Neapolitan Ambassador, Anello,
urge the prosecution of the war." Regarding Andreas Palæologus, see,
in contradiction to Gregorovius, a *Brief of Sixtus IV. to the Bishop
of Elbora, dated Bracciano, 1481, Sept. 15, in which he is directed to
assist Andreas to pass over to the Peloponnesus, so that he might be
able to reconquer his country. (National Library, Florence.) An
admirer of Gregorovius has lately observed that "he looks at the
deeds of the past with the eye of a poet" ; this is evidently a doubtful
course.

These last complained much of the conduct of the Duke of Calabria, while Fregoso represented, with all due deference, the impossibility of carrying out the undertaking. " The outbreak of the Plague on board the ships, the impracticability of the men, whom no amount of pay could persuade to serve any longer, the advanced season of the year, the essential difficulty of the enterprise, its immense cost—for the repair of the fleet alone, 40,000 ducats would at once be required —all these things were brought forward to prove the enterprise hopeless ; but Sixtus IV. declared himself ready for every sacrifice. He would, like Eugenius IV., pawn his mitre, he would sell the rest of his silver plate : all was in vain." *
He was obliged to return to Rome without effecting his purpose, only leaving orders that the harbours of Civita Vecchia and Corneto should be thoroughly repaired.†

* ZINKEISEN, II., 461, from JACOB. VOLATERRANUS, 147–52. See CIPOLLA, 608, N. 2, and BALAN, 221, both of whom express their disagreement with Gregorovius. See also GUGLIELMOTTI, 459, 461 ; SERRA, Liguria, 268 seq., and GRASSO, 339 seq. I have failed to find, either in Rome or in Florence, the ten letters of Sixtus IV. belonging to this period, mentioned by Guglielmotti as published by de Romanis (Notizie istoriche della terra di Canino con alcune lettere di Sisto IV., Roma, 1843) ; the pamphlet is reviewed in Arch. St. Ital., App. VI., 412 seq. ; but I have sought for it in vain in the editorial library of this Review.

† JACOB. VOLATERRANUS, 152–3. The Pope returned to Rome on the 17th Oct., 1481. For an account of the Embassy of the Prete Gianni, which arrived in Rome in November, 1481, see the Report of the Milanese Ambassadors in Arch. St. Lomb., 1889, p. 151 seq. which also treats of Turkish affairs.

CHAPTER IX.

Sixtus IV. and Venice at War with Ferrara and Naples.—
Andreas of Krain's attempt at a Council.—The Battle
at Campo Morto, and the dissolution of the Alliance
between the Pope and Venice.

While Sixtus IV. was zealously devoting himself to the
Turkish war, Count Girolamo was occupied with matters
of a very different nature. His ambition soon involved the
too indulgent Pontiff in a new war in the immediate neighbourhood of Rome, and even in the City itself. Giuliano
della Rovere was at this time Legate in the Low Countries,
where he had been sent to make peace between Louis XI.
of France and Maximilian of Austria. His prolonged
absence rendered it easy for Count Girolamo to carry out
his plans and abuse the affection of the Pope.[*]

It was intolerable to Girolamo that Lorenzo had not only
escaped the attempted assassination on the 26th April, 1478,
but that it had actually served to render his position more
secure. All his thoughts and desires were directed to the
one aim and object of obtaining some compensation for
this failure. His uncle's advanced age urged him to
prompt action. "Wholly incapable of making himself a

---

[*] Schmarsow, 177; Reumont, III., 1, 174, and Lorenzo, II., 182,
2nd ed. Regarding Giuliano's Mission, see the Report of his private
secretary, Sigismondo de' Conti, I., 108-9; also Legeay, II., 400
seq., and Commines-Lenglet, III., 574 seq., 595 seq., 598 seq., 600 seq.,
616 seq., 623 seq., 630 seq.

name by valorous deeds, Girolamo, who cared for nothing but his own aggrandisement, was perpetually, by his schemes, running counter to all statesmanlike plans of policy.   He thus entangled a generous nature like that of Sixtus IV. in deplorable inconsistencies, and took advantage of his uncle's affection to urge him further and further down the steep incline which ends in ruin."*

Ferrante of Naples had, during the Tuscan war, faithlessly abandoned the Pope and constrained him to make peace on very unfavourable terms.   From this time forth, the chronicler says, the Pope's confidence, withdrawn from Naples, was bestowed on the Venetians.   At the beginning of February, 1480, negotiations were set on foot which led to the conclusion of an alliance with Venice. Here Count Girolamo stepped in.   Even during the war of Otranto he had formed close relations with Venice. Not content with Imola, he had taken advantage of the dispute which broke out after the death of Pino of Ordelassi, regarding the succession, and seized on the Countship of Forli.†   After this success he cast his insatiable eyes on Faenza.   In January, 1481, Venice had made known her willingness to gratify him in this point also.   The Council of Ten, however, warned him that another project of his, which aimed at nothing less than the expulsion of Ferrante from Naples, must be kept a profound secret.‡   According to Sigismondo de' Conti, it was Virginio Orsini, the heir of Napoleone, who urged the Count on to this enterprise.   "Virginio claimed from Ferrante the Countships of Alba Fucense and Tagliacozzo, which formed part of his patrimony, and which the King

* Such is the opinion of SCHMARSOW, 178.

† See the detailed account of SCHMARSOW, 179 ; REUMONT, Lorenzo, II., 365, 2nd ed. ; BONOLI, 247 ; and BURRIEL, III., p. xliii.

‡ BROSCH, Julius II., 21.

had sold for 12,000 ducats to Lorenzo Oddone Colonna and his brother." Orsini was deeply wounded by this transaction, because his family had always been true to the King. He now hoped, by Ferrante's humiliation or downfall, to recover his rights. He promised Girolamo that his family would assist to the utmost in the war against the King of Naples. Sixtus IV., in his irritation against Ferrante, gave his consent to the scheme, but he and Girolamo were well aware that the co-operation of Venice was indispensable. This could only be obtained by offering some tangible advantage to the Republic. Ferrara was accordingly held out as a bait. Sixtus IV. was incensed with the Duke, because, in the Florentine war, he had been at the head of his enemies, and because he persistently strove to evade his yearly tribute. Moreover, Ercole of Ferrara had so far forgotten himself as to prohibit the publication of several Apostolic Rescripts in his State, which he governed in the name of the Holy See.[*]

In September, 1481, Girolamo Riario went to Venice. He was received like an Emperor, the Doge meeting him at the foot of the Palace steps.[†] In a Secret Council the Count unfolded his plan for overthrowing Ferrante, and promised the Venetians Ferrara if they succeeded in conquering it. They were only asked to furnish a fleet, to keep the King in check, and a few troops. Girolamo claimed nothing for himself, except Lugo and Bagnacavallo, two

---

[*] SIGISMONDO DE' CONTI, I., 114 *seq.*; SCHMARSOW, 182; BALAN, 223. An admonitory Brief to the Duke regarding the tribute to be paid, written as early as the year 1475, is given in MARTÈNE, II., 1480. BROSCH'S statement, Kirchenstaat, I., 12, that Ferrara had paid 5000 ducats as tribute, is, according to GOTTLOB, Cam. Ap., mistaken; the *Introitus-Register of the Secret Archives of the Vatican mention 4000 florins.

[†] FRANTZ, 370; BONOLI, 249.

cities in the Flaminia, on the border of his Countship of Imola.*

After the Pope's nephew had left the Council, deliberations began. Opinions were divided. The elder men, whose judgment was the clearest, objected to involving the Republic in a fresh war. They represented the difficulty of taking Ferrara, a strong and populous city, surrounded by swamps and a wide river; they averred that Ercole d'Este was a skilful soldier; that his neighbours were bound to him by ties of kindred and friendship, and that he had at his disposal treasures amassed by a long line of ancestors. Doubts were also expressed as to the trustworthiness of Riario, who was not considered scrupulously truthful; it was further urged that Sixtus IV. was but mortal and had reached an age when death could not probably be distant, that he was a Ligurian and inconstant in his resolutions, that even if he adhered to his purpose the Sacred College would not stand by him, as they had never desisted from claiming the restoration of Cervia and Ravenna from the Venetians. The votes of the younger members of the Council, however, prevailed against these considerations, and war was decided upon. Girolamo returned to Sixtus IV., after having received the freedom of the city and been admitted amongst her nobles.†

The beginning of the year 1482 seemed to offer some hope that peace might still be maintained. Giuliano della Rovere returned at this time from his Mission to France, and Ercole d'Este and Lorenzo de' Medici sought, by

---

* SIGISMONDO DE' CONTI, I., 119; SCHMARSOW, 184.

† SIGISMONDO DE' CONTI, I., 120. While Girolamo was occupied with these far-reaching projects, the ground under his feet began to give way. Three conspiracies occurred in succession, and were with difficulty suppressed. Florence persistently stirred up discontent against Girolamo. See SCHMARSOW, 274.

means of his powerful influence, to avert the war.   They
were well acquainted with the Cardinal's opinion of the
ambitious and restless Riario,* who just then had scarcely
recovered from a violent fever,† and this fact also made it
more probable that the Pope might be induced to withdraw
his consent.

In the middle of April the King commenced hostilities
by the advance of his troops into the States of the Church.‡
In Rome, preparations for war were but half completed,
and Venice would not be ready till the end of April.   Two
fleets had been equipped by the Republic: one of them,
under Vettor Soranzo, was to commence operations on the
coast of Naples, while the other, under Damiano Moro,
was to penetrate to the States of Ferrara.   The land forces
were also divided into two armies, under the command of
Roberto Malatesta and Roberto da Sanseverino.   At the
beginning of May Venice declared war against Ferrara.§
The Marquess of Montferrat, Genoa, and Pietro Maria
de Rossi, Count of San Secondo in the Parmesan territory, joined the Papal and Venetian league.   Ferrara
and Naples found powerful allies not only in Milan
and Florence, but also in the Marquess Federigo of

* SCHMARSOW, 188.

† See *Letters of Alexander Arrivabene, dated Rome, 1482, January
23 and 26. Gonzaga Archives, Mantua.

‡ BALAN, 228. On the 2nd April, 1482, Sixtus IV. had issued the
following *Order : "Gubernatori Reatis et Interamnis . . . volumus
ac tibi presentium tenore expresse mandamus ut omnia loca et passus
istius gubernii ex quibus transire solent aut possunt qui in regnum
proficiscuntur diligenter custodiri facias" ; no troops were to be allowed
to pass without a written permission from him or Count Girolamo.
"Simile gubernat. Campanie, praefecto urbis, Virginio de Ursinis."
National Library, Florence.

§ See SANUTO, Commentarii della guerra di Ferrara nel 1482, 11–12,
and SIGISMONDO DE' CONTI, I., 121. See CIPOLLA, 612.

Mantua, Giovanni Bentivoglio of Bologna and Federigo of Urbino.*

Unhappily for the Papal cause, the ancient feud between the Colonna and the Orsini at this time broke out again.

The immediate occasion of this outbreak was the hostility between the rich and noble families of della Valle and Santa Croce. In the autumn of 1480 the whole City had been involved in this contest, the della Valle being supported by the Colonna, and the Santa Croce by the Orsini. Not till April, 1481, did the Pope, after much trouble, succeed in restoring peace. A Commission of three Cardinals was appointed to watch over its maintenance, and to arrange all differences that might arise.†

As most of the great Roman Barons, with the Pope's consent, had entered the service of Ferrante, and were fully occupied by the war at Otranto, tranquillity for a time continued; but after the recovery of that city, quarrels recommenced, and, fomented by the King of Naples, became more and more violent.

In consequence of the tension which existed between Rome and Naples in the spring of 1482, the Pope recalled the Barons who, since the war with the Turks, had remained in Ferrante's pay. The Orsini, headed by Virginio, the intimate friend of Girolamo Riario, obeyed, and the Conti also, as well as Stefano Colonna of Palestrina, with his sons Giordano and Giovanni, re-entered the Papal service. The Savelli, on the other hand, and the Colonna of Paliano-Genazzano cast in their lot with the King of Naples. Their alienation was partly due to the enmity between them and the Orsini, which Ferrante took pains to foster, but partly

---

* SISMONDI, XI., 227.

† JACOB. VOLATERRANUS, 126. SIGISMONDO DE' CONTI, I., 134 *seq.*, gives a full account of the origin of the animosity between Valle and Sᵗᵃ Croce.

also to the domineering ways of Girolamo Riario. The Pope endeavoured, by gentleness and consideration, to repair the harm which his nephew had done, and several Cardinals, amongst whom were Giuliano della Rovere and Stefano Nardini, did their best to pacify the offended Colonna, even at the last moment, but all these efforts were fruitless.*

At the beginning of April a fresh incident occurred, which made matters worse. During the night of the 3rd of that month the Santa Croce, aided by the Palace guards, whom Girolamo had given them, attacked the house of the della Valle. Most unfortunately, in the struggle which ensued, Girolamo Colonna, an illegitimate brother of the Cardinal of S. Maria in Aquiro and of Prospero of Paliano, was killed.† The Pope, in consequence, outlawed the Santa Croce, and caused their palaces to be destroyed. The exasperation of the Colonna from this time forth knew no bounds.

At this critical moment, several weeks before the Venetian declaration of war, the King of Naples commenced hostilities against Rome. In the middle of April his troops appeared in sight of the Papal residence at Marino, ostensibly for the purpose of defending the Colonna against the Orsini. Ferrante informed the Conservators that he was not taking up arms against Rome, but for the deliverance of the City and of Italy from the slavery to which the bad government of Girolamo Riario had reduced them.‡

---

* SIGISMONDO DE' CONTI, I., 132 *seq.*; SCHMARSOW, 191, who very justly observes: "BROSCH, Julius II., 23, completely misapprehends the position of affairs when he considers Giuliano della Rovere to have been guilty of a breach of confidence in regard to the Pope." Brosch is very unfortunate in his most prejudiced conjectures; see *supra*, p. 322.

† BALAN, 227, note 4.

‡ *Ibid.*, 228.

On the 18th April the Pope admonished King Ferrante to withdraw his troops from Rome; * on the 23rd he complained in Consistory of the presence of the Neapolitans at Marino, and declared that he could not grant the request of the King's son, Alfonso of Calabria, for a free passage through the States of the Church to support Ferrara.†

The Ambassadors of Naples and Ferrara left Rome on the 14th May. They went, in the first instance, with great pomp to Lorenzo Colonna at Marino. Strengthened by the Savelli, and by constant reinforcements from Naples, Lorenzo now ventured to lead his men up to the very gates of Rome. On the 30th May his troops entered the City, but were driven back by the Orsini and Girolamo Riario. Prospero Colonna had previously gone over to the side of the Pope's enemies, and had received in Paliano (on the 22nd May) a garrison from the Duke of Calabria, who had meanwhile appeared before Rome as Commander of the Neapolitan troops.

Sixtus IV. was naturally much incensed by this treachery, and all the more so because Prospero had recently drawn a portion of his pay. The Pope also fully realised how injurious to him was the loss of these villages. Therefore, Sigismondo de' Conti informs us, he resolved on a hazardous step, which, however, the sequel proved to have been a judicious one.‡

A Consistory took place at mid-day on the 2nd June. Count Girolamo and Virginio Orsini attended it, and accused Cardinals Colonna and Savelli of treason. The

---

* *Sixtus IV. regi Ferdinando, dated Romae die XVIII. Aprilis, 1482. National Library, Florence.

† BALAN, 228, from Despatches in the State Archives, Modena. Here also are the particulars of a last attempt made by the Pope to win the Colonna.

‡ SIGISMONDO DE' CONTI, I., 137.

two Cardinals warmly defended themselves, openly condemning the conduct of their kinsmen and casting all the blame upon them. The meeting was stormy, and lasted until the evening. At last the Pope, to avoid worse evils, gave orders that the accused Cardinals should be kept as hostages for their disaffected families. Cardinal Savelli's brother, Mariano, who had a command in the Papal army, was also arrested. As disturbances were apprehended from the partisans of the Colonna, the Vatican was guarded by horse and foot soldiers. The captured Cardinals were honourably treated during the first day and the following night : Savelli in the house of Giuliano della Rovere, and Colonna with Girolamo Basso, who at that time lived in the Vatican. At the close of the second day an order arrived to transfer them to St. Angelo.*

Several hundreds of light Turkish horsemen from the garrison of Otranto had gone over to Alfonso of Calabria, and now formed part of his army, which was encamped within sight of Rome. These wild troops ravaged the Campagna, and spread terror in every direction. On the 6th of June the Papal force was ready. Count Girolamo was Commander-in-chief, and under him were Count Niccolo of Pitigliano, Virginio and Giordano Orsini, Giovanni Colonna, Giacomo and Andrea de' Conti, the Count of Mirandola, and many others.†

Sigismondo de' Conti has left us a graphic picture of the state of things in Rome at this crisis. " In the Pope's antechambers," he says,‡ "instead of cassocked priests, armed

---

* FRANTZ, 375-6. In contradiction to the Venetian Documents (see SCHMARSOW, 192), SIGISMONDO DE' CONTI, I., 137, maintains the innocence of the Cardinals.

† REUMONT, III., 1, 175.

‡ SIGISMONDO DE' CONTI, I., 137-8. For "qui impar" *read* "quia i.," and for "quornm" *read* "quorum." The Roman edition of

guards kept watch. Soldiers, equipped for battle, were drawn up before the gates of the Palace. All the Court officials were filled with terror and anguish ; the fury of the populace was only restrained by the fear of the soldiers."

Thus, with the assistance of the Colonna, Alfonso of Calabria had succeeded in effecting his purpose, and transferring the war to Roman soil. He was perpetually making raids in the vicinity of the City walls, and carrying off men and cattle. The Papal army, encamped near the Lateran, did not venture out, either from a sense of its own weakness or from a fear that the angry townspeople, in whose vineyards it lay, might shut the gates and prevent its return. To add to all, the Plague again broke out in the City. Alfonso took Albano, Castel Gandolfo and Civita Lavinia, without encountering any resistance. His father, Ferrante, meanwhile was active. With a fleet of twenty triremes he harassed the shores of the Roman territory. He further succeeded in making himself master of Terracina and Benevento by treachery. The Florentine army, under the command of Costanzo Sforza, took Città di Castello. The Pope was greatly alarmed, and commanded his chamberlains and domestics to take turns in keeping nightly watch. His anxiety increased from day to day, more particularly as the Venetian fleet, on which all his hopes rested, had not yet sailed.*

this author, published in 1883, is far from perfect in this respect. See also *supra*, p. 308, and GOTTLOB in the Hist. Jahrb., VII., 303 *seq*.

 * SIGISMONDO DE' CONTI, *loc. cit.* The Romans had much to suffer from Girolamo, whose soldiers even desecrated the Lateran Church. On the 20th June Città di Castello fell into the enemy's hands, whereupon Sixtus IV. sent troops against this city. (*Brief of the 5th July to the City Prefect. National Library, Florence.) The citadel of Terracina was lost four weeks later, and Benevento in the middle of July ; see the Despatches to Modena in BALAN, 229. Sixtus IV. then drew as many troops as he could into Rome ; see his

Rome was insufficiently defended, and was shut in on every side by enemies.* The perplexity and anxiety of the Pope were increased by accounts which reached him from the North of attempts which the Dominican, Andrea Zuccalmaglio, Archbishop of Carniola,† was making to revive the Council of Basle. He had come to Rome in 1478, as Envoy from the Emperor,‡ and received many presents and marks of distinction from the Pope.§ His ambition led him to aspire to greater dignities, and even to the purple, and, in October 1480, he induced the Emperor to address to the Pope and the Sacred College letters

*Briefs of the 11th, 12th, and 24th of July to the City Prefect. (National Library, Florence.) At the beginning of August the Pope even recalled his troops to Rome from Bologna, which was unsafe ; see *Brief to Perugia, dated 1482, Aug. 3. Cod. G.–IV.–1, University Library, Genoa.

* In his necessity, Sixtus IV. even applied to France ; see REUMONT, Lorenzo, II., 183, 2nd ed.

† Recent students, such as BURCKHARDT, Andreas von Krain, and FRANTZ, 435, are certainly incorrect in adopting Hottinger's idea that Andreas lived at Laibach (Aemona), for, until 1788, Laibach was not an Archbishopric (GAMS, 283). From 1452–1525, seven, or possibly eight, Archiepiscopi Crainenses are known. Andreas succeeded his predecessor on the 18th January, 1476 (loc. cit., 405). Several Slav provinces bear the name of Krains ; according to FARLATTI, III. Sacr., IV., 189 seq., the coast about Macarsca is here meant (see Kirchenlex., I., 837, 2nd ed.) ; GAMS, loc. cit., thinks that a somewhat more southerly district is to be understood.

‡ BURCKHARDT, 25 ; FRANTZ, 434 ; and GEBHARDT, 47, say that Andreas first came to Rome between 1480 and 1482 ; the Briefs in Mon. Habsb., III., 453, and II., 330, which certainly Burckhardt had not the means of consulting, shew this statement to be mistaken. In his table of contents, p. xlii., CHMEL wrongly designates Andreas as Archbishop of Gran.

§ SIGISMONDO DE' CONTI, I., 157 ; Lib. confrat. B. M. de Anima, 27 ; and the Briefs of 10th Sept., 1481, and 4th May, 1482, to which we shall presently refer.

recommending him in pressing terms.* In consequence of these letters, Sixtus IV., who readily made promises, seems to have given him some encouragement; but, as the red hat did not arrive, Andrea soon began to pour forth torrents of insolent abuse against the Pope, his nephews, and the Roman clergy. Sixtus IV. admonished and warned him, but in vain. There was nothing for it but to call him to account for his calumnies. The Emperor's mediation soon procured his liberation from confinement in St. Angelo, where, out of consideration for Frederick III., he had been treated leniently. The same motive induced the Pope, in opposition to the desire of the Cardinals, to abandon the suit which had been commenced against him, and then to set him at liberty.† Sixtus IV. soon had cause bitterly to regret his indulgence. Andrea Zuccalmaglio went by way of Florence to Basle, where he falsely announced himself as the Emperor's representative, and even went so far as to assume the title of Cardinal of S. Sisto. On the 25th March, 1482, he entered the Cathedral of Basle during the celebration of Mass, and, with violent invectives against the Pope, proclaimed a General Council, to be held in that city. Even at this time, his secretary, Numagen, clearly perceived that he was not quite right in his head. He could not control himself, was incapable of deliberation, and would listen to no one's advice.‡

In April, Andrea went to Berne, and was at first cordially received by the authorities, but at the end of eight days

* Mon. Habsb., III., 48.

† See the important Brief of the 10th Sept., 1481, published in the Appendix to SIGISMONDO DE' CONTI, I., 410. This at last throws some light on a matter hitherto involved in obscurity, and decides the date of the conflict. BURCKHARDT, 25, has placed it at too late a period.

‡ HOTTINGER, 356; BURCKHARDT, A. von Krain, 28–89.

the Bernese had discovered his real character. On the 4th May the alarmed Council sent a letter to Basle to warn that friendly city against the danger of espousing his cause. Berne apologised to Rome for having unwittingly shewn honour to one who placed himself in opposition to the Church and the Pope.*

In Basle, also, Andrea's abuse of the Pope had awakened some doubts, and a suspicion that he was influenced by personal hatred. Nevertheless, he was left quite free when he formally announced the assembling of a Council at the beginning of May. The Emperor was duly informed, but did nothing, and waited to see what would come.

Sixtus IV. was greatly disquieted, and, on the 4th May, wrote to Frederick III., and sent a special Envoy to ask him to take measures to secure the arrest of the Archbishop.† The Emperor's attitude now became so strange as to excite suspicions in Rome that Andrea was acting on secret instructions from him. On the 21st July he called the Archbishop "trusty and well-beloved," and asked for information about his project, and, on the 23rd July, he merely recommended the Councillors at Basle to act with caution.‡

Andrea chose this very time to cut off all means of retreat. On the 20th and 21st July he issued two violent and ill-written appeals, the last of which "was no better than a pasquinade." In the opening words of this detestable production, Sixtus IV., whom he had but a few days before invited to attend his Council, is addressed, no longer as Pope, but as "Francesco of Savona, Son of the Devil, thor who hast climbed to thy high dignity through the window

---

* Jahrb. für Schweiz. Gesch., IX., 13–14.

† I found this **Brief, which, as far as I know, was up to this time undiscovered, in the National Library, Florence.

‡ BURCKHARDT, A. von Krain, 34.

of simony instead of entering by the door, thou art of thy father, the Devil, and seekest to do his will."[*]

If we remember that the Archbishop had not a single adherent among the German or French Prelates, these outrageous railings against the Head of the Church seem almost like the ravings of a maniac; but when we find that Andrea had allied himself with the enemies of the Pope in Italy, it is easier to account for his violence. This evidently took place when he went from Rome to Basle by way of Florence. He must then have received from the Florentines and other conspirators assurances without which he could scarcely have ventured on his hazardous enterprise. "A bitterly exasperated Prelate, who promised to raise the whole of the North against the Pope, was, under the circumstances, an important ally, however dubious might be his motives, and however great the peril to which he exposed the Church."[†] The last consideration did not certainly weigh with Lorenzo de' Medici, who already was of opinion that it would be for his advantage to have three or four Popes instead of one.[‡]

The experiences of Lorenzo during his first conflict with Sixtus IV., however, deterred him from again exposing himself to the risk of Excommunication. Andrea was, there-

---

[*] HOTTINGER, 360 *seq.*, 368 *seq.*; BURCKHARDT, 36.

[†] BURCKHARDT, 49. BUSER, Lorenzo, 158, has referred to the summons to Basle addressed by Andreas to Lorenzo de' Medici. It begins in the following words: * "Spiritus sanctus qui per totum terrarum orbem dispersos in unitatem fidei congregat dignetur fovere ignem suum accensum in te, fidei et ecclesie Christi zelatore fidelissimo. Agimus nempe in gaudio magno gratias ei qui te nobiscum sollicitare hoc opus sanctum et necessarium accendit; ille eciam labores tuos si perseveraveris legitime eternis gaudiis compensabit. Age igitur pro Christo, pro fide et ecclesia illius et pro tota christianitate constanter et veni." State Archives, Florence.

[‡] See *supra*, p. 300.

fore, for the time, "only to be supported in secret, and very cautiously. When he had been in a measure successful, and the Pope had been thoroughly intimidated, the allies would proceed to advocate a Council."* Not till the 14th September did Lorenzo's confidant, Baccio Ugolini, accompanied by a Milanese Envoy, arrive in Basle.

Ugolini's Reports to his master enable us to estimate the hostility of Lorenzo to the Papacy, and to appreciate the reasons which induced Sixtus IV. to make the efforts he did for his removal from Florence. " I offered him " (Andrea of Carniola), writes Ugolini on the 20th September, 1482, " in your (Lorenzo's) name all that I could and knew to favour this undertaking (the Schism), praising him and flattering him as is customary. . . . It is a great thing that he is a Friar; that is the crown of all his qualities, and he has a fearless countenance, which awakens confidence and knows how to keep a man in his place, and let no one approach him. . . . The citizens (of Basle), too, could not be better disposed . . . they would not by any means allow their priests to observe the Interdict, and they openly favour the Archbishop as much as they can. . . . This man is quite fitted to serve out the Pope and the Count (Riario), and that is enough." Ten days later this Florentine again wrote confidentially to Lorenzo, saying, amongst other things : " I afterwards made a long speech (to the Magistracy of Basle) in favour of the Council, praising the lords for this honourable enterprise, and extolling the person of Carniola, while I drew a contemptible picture of the government of Sixtus IV., and insisted on the necessity for a Council.† They listened thankfully to everything. . . . As regards the matter of the Council, they declare that they are well-

---

* BURCKHARDT, *loc. cit.* See also BUSER, Beziehungen, 228.

† The Venetian-Papal troops were just at this time victorious.

disposed towards the Holy See, and so far as they can
have their way they will take care (they, the Councillors
of Basle!) that the Church, which they see to be in great
danger, or rather in ruins, shall be reformed to the faith
of Christ. . . . Moreover, I (Ugolini) have gained such an
ascendancy over the Carniolan (the Pope and 'Reformer'
of the future), that it rejoices him more than anything. . . .
Every hour he raises his hands to heaven and thanks God
who has sent me to him. I need not say how eagerly
the Doctors of the University read the letters which I
have communicated to the Council here. What more can
we desire? The Pope is more hated here than there." *

* FABRONIUS, II., 227 *seq.* In consequence, however, of the
energetic action of the Pope, who sent a great number of Nuncios
in succession to the Emperor and to Basle (see BURCKHARDT, A. von
Krain, 29 *seq.* ; in another place I will give supplementary extracts on
the subject from Sixtus IV.'s *Briefs, which are before me. Secret
Archives of the Vatican and National Library, Florence), and especially
because the condition of the League had completely changed, it was
in the end deemed well to leave their tool (RANKE, III., 5, 6th ed.)
to his fate. Basle had at first refused either to give up or to imprison
the Archbishop, and had thus fallen under an Interdict, which, however,
was not regarded. No change took place until October, when the
Emperor openly declared against Andrea. On the 18th December,
1482, the authorities of Basle at last arrested Andrea, but still refused
to give him up. The Bishop of Suessa accordingly published a Bull
of Crusade against Basle, which occasioned great distress. The
matter was not settled when Sixtus IV. died, and was succeeded by
Innocent VIII. ; it was finally concluded by the suicide of Andrea,
who was found hanged in his dungeon on the 13th November, 1484.
For details I refer to BURCKHARDT, 65 *seq.*, 93 *seq.* GLASSBERGER
in Anal. Francisc., II., 483, gives a full description of the danger
involved by Andrea's proceedings. In Chap. XI. we shall mention
that Ferdinand and Isabella of Spain also threatened to hold a
Council. Regarding the open and secret opposition to Rome in
Germany in the time of Sixtus IV., see GEBHARDT, 48 *seq.*, and
DROYSEN, II., 1, 328, 341.

Under these circumstances, it is not surprising that Girolamo Riario, the cause of all this trouble, became very unpopular in Rome, and a powerful party, headed by Cardinal Giuliano della Rovere, strongly urged the Pope to conclude a peace. But when the Venetian General, Roberto Malatesta, who had hitherto been fighting against Ferrara, appeared in Rome on the 23rd July, the war-party again got the upper hand.*

His arrival caused great rejoicing. "This is he who will redeem Israel!" shouted the people in the streets. On the 24th July Roberto was received in secret audience by the Pope, after which he at once began to make his preparations. The Proveditore, Pietro Diedo, brought money by command of the Republic to help in raising fresh troops for the Papal army ; 1000 young Romans, ready armed, were enlisted in a week. On the 15th August the Venetian auxiliaries came in, and were blessed by the Pope from a window of the Vatican. Rome was full of warlike enthusiasm. "The banners of the Republic, together with those of the Pope, were borne through the whole City, and harmony reigned in the common camp." †

On the same 15th August the army advanced as far as Bovillae on the ancient Appian Way.‡ Castel Gandolfo, Castel Savello, and Albano surrendered.§ Alfonso retired before the superior forces of the enemy behind Velletri to the neighbourhood of Nettuno and Astura, where he expected succour by sea from Naples.

---

* REUMONT, III., 1, 176.

† FRANTZ, 381–2 ; SCHMARSOW, 194.

‡ SIGISMONDO DE' CONTI, I., 139.

§ On the 19th August, 1482, Sixtus IV. wrote to Count Girolamo: * "Gratissimum nobis fuit quod scribit nob. tua de castello Gandolfo et de castello Sabello ;" the Pope hopes that all will go on well. National Library, Florence.

Along this sea-shore stretches a woody morass, a desolate wilderness, the home of the buffalo and the wild boar. " In the whole of the Roman territory there is not another district so pestilential as this desert of Maremma." Its air is full of deadly fever, which has given the place the name of the Campo Morto (field of death) ; even down to the time of Pius IX. it has been a safe refuge for murderers. In the midst of these marshy thickets, at about an equal distance from Velletri and Nettuno, was a " fortified enclosure for the breeding of buffaloes and cattle ; this castrum took from its Church the name of San Pietro, and from its moats the surname in Formis."* Alfonso of Calabria had here assembled his troops to await the attack. His position was a strong one, for his army occupied a sort of island, covered to the south by a small swamp, and protected on the north and east by trees and brushwood. To the west, where the Papal forces made the attack, there was a meadow about 500 paces in width, which was crossed by a ditch about two feet deep to carry off the water. Behind this, Alfonso's artillery was placed ; some 300 paces further back he caused a considerably deeper trench to be made for the defence of his troops.†

---

* GREGOROVIUS, VII., 256, 3rd ed.　See Mél. d'Archéol., V., 84 seq.　NOTAR GIACOMO, 148, calls the place Campo Morto, as do also Infessura and P. Cyrnäus (see GREGOROVIUS, loc. cit.).　The mistaken statement, that the name was due to the battle, occurs in PAPEN-CORDT, 490, and REUMONT, III., 1, 177.

† SIGISMONDO DE' CONTI, I., 142 seq., who also gives a very good description of the battle, largely used by Sansovini in his History of the Orsini.　See also SANUDO, Comment., 39-40 ; a Sienese Despatch in Arch. d. Soc. Rom., XI., 606 seq. ; the Este Reports in CAPELLI, 31-3 ; Roberto's Letter in TONINI, 390 seq. ; and a second Letter from him, which Valentini published, with other Reports, in Arch. Veneto, 1887, fasc. 65, p. 72 seq. ; to these we may add the **Report of Pasius, dated 24th Aug. 1482, from the State Archives, Modena.

Roberto Malatesta, to whom Riario had resigned the
command, having set his troops in order of battle and
exhorted them to bravery, ordered the foot soldiers to
make the attack.   These were mostly recruits, and were
so alarmed by the appearance of the Turks, whom Alfonso
opposed to them, that they fled almost immediately.   The
whole of the Papal army would have been cast into confusion had not Roberto, at the right moment, rushed forward
with a chosen band of tried soldiers, by which means he
not only repelled the onslaught of the enemy but drove
him back behind the trench.   Sword in hand, Roberto
here held his ground for a whole hour, acting at once as
soldier and as leader.*

While the battle was raging at this point, Giacomo de'
Conti, with six companies, attacked the camp on the right.
This movement was hidden from Alfonso by the thicket.
Roberto, at the same time, renewed his assault on the
front.   Alfonso's forces were not able to resist the two-fold
onslaught of an enemy superior in numbers; they began to
waver and then to fly.

Up to this moment Alfonso had "fought like a lion";†
several horses had been killed under him ; now, fearing he
would be surrounded and made prisoner, he also took to flight.
He had some difficulty in making his way through the
wood to Nettuno, where, with a few followers, he took boat
for Terracina.   Here, under the protection of his father's
galleys, he gathered together the remnant of his army.

The battle of "Campo Morto in the Pontine Marshes"
thus ended in a complete victory for the Papal troops.
Both sides had fought desperately.   The field was strewn
with wounded, and the number of dead who lay there was

---

* SIGISMONDO DE' CONTI, *loc. cit.*

† See the **Report of Pasius, quoted on preceding page, note †.
State Archives, Modena.

proportionately large; almost all the Janissaries were among them. Many flags and cannons fell into the hands of the conquerors, who also took a number of prisoners, including almost all the Chiefs and Barons.*

Roberto proceeded at once to Velletri, to attend to the wounded and rest his wearied troops. On the following day he sent his light cavalry forward to collect the baggage of the enemy.

When the news of the victory reached Rome, bonfires were lighted, the bells of the Capitol rang out, and all the Churches answered. Sixtus IV., with a numerous suite, attended a Mass of Thanksgiving at Santa Maria del Popolo.†

The very day after the battle, Marino surrendered to the Pope the keys of the Citadel and the captive Fabrizio Colonna; the idea of pressing on into the kingdom of Naples with the victorious army was spoken of in Rome.‡ Sixtus IV. informed the Emperor and all friendly States of the great success obtained by his General,§ and thanked the latter in a highly eulogistic Brief.‖

Girolamo Riario made a splendid pageant of his entry into Rome with his prisoners. The Romans were treated with the spectacle of the enemies who had but recently

---

* SIGISMONDO DE' CONTI, *loc. cit.* In reference to the number of dead here given, the small strength of the army is to be borne in mind, and the fact that the warriors were clad entirely in mail.

† NOTAJO DI NANTIPORTO, 1077; SCHMARSOW, 195; FRANTZ, 385.

‡ See the *Despatch of the 24th August from Pasius in the State Archives, Modena, cited *supra*, p. 365, note †.

§ See RAYNALDUS, ad an. 1482, N. 9, and the **Briefs to Genoa and Perugia of the 22nd and 24th August, 1482. National Library, Florence, and University Library, Genoa (G.–IV.–1).

‖ **Rob. Malatestae, dated Rome, 1482, Aug. 24. National Library. Florence.

threatened their very walls, now led through their streets as captives, with heads bowed low, in the triumphal procession. Antonio Piccolomini, Duke of Amalfi, and Vicino Orsini, son of the Grand Constable of the kingdom of Naples, attracted the greatest attention. The Pope received the captives with kindness, and honourably entertained the Duke of Amalfi, Pius II.'s nephew, in his Palace, before sending him back to his family.*

" It is a true saying," writes Sigismondo de' Conti, " that human happiness is never long unalloyed." The sounds of rejoicing were soon silenced and exchanged for lamentations over the premature death of the victor.

Roberto Malatesta was engaged in dispersing the hostile troops scattered about the neighbourhood of Rome, when " the effects of his tremendous exertions in the great heat of the unhealthy swamps overtook him. The fatal breath of Campo Morto proved stronger than youth and courage." †

On hearing of the sickness of his General, the Pope at

* SIGISMONDO DE' CONTI, I., 144; SCHMARSOW, 195; FRANTZ, 385. Regarding the Triumphal Procession, see also NOTAR GIACOMO, 149, and the Sienese Despatches in Arch. Stor. Rom., XI., 608.

† SCHMARSOW, 195, rejects the idea that Roberto was poisoned, and CREIGHTON, III., 91, agrees with him, as also GREGOROVIUS, VII., 257, 3rd ed., who inclines to the same opinion. Even SIGISMONDO DE' CONTI, I., 144, mentions the report of poison. Count Girolamo Riario has been suspected of the murder ; see, in his defence, TONINI, 393, and App., 289. Any idea that Roberto's death was due to foul play is set aside by a Despatch given by BALAN, 230, and also by a *Letter of Cardinal Gonzaga, dated Rome, 1482, Sept. 11, which I found in the Gonzaga Archives, Mantua, and a passage in the *Cronica Ferrariae of Caleffini. Cod. I.–I.–4, f. 156, Chigi Library, Rome (see Appendix, N. 66). These authorities, who are by no means prejudiced in Girolamo's favour, may be considered as conclusive on this question. The *Diario del Corona also says : " Mori Roberto Malatesta di febre." Barberini Library, Rome, LIV., 10, f. 410.

once sent his own physician to Val Montone, where Roberto lay, and caused him to be transported in a litter to Rome. He was most carefully tended in the house of the Cardinal of Milan, but he did not rally. When his condition left no room for hope, the Pope, with his own hands, administered Extreme Unction. On the 10th September the brave warrior breathed his last.*

Sixtus IV. paid every possible honour to the deliverer of his capital. He personally took part in the obsequies, and afterwards caused a marble monument to be erected in St. Peter's. After many vicissitudes, this monument, on which the figure of the leader, mounted on his war-horse, is carved in relief, found its way to the Louvre, where it now adorns the hall devoted to Sculpture of the Renaissance period.†

On the 11th September the Pope legitimatised the sons of Roberto and invested them with the paternal inheritance, thus refuting the imputation that he was influenced by designs upon the fief of the Malatesta; though some such hankerings, perhaps, had been cherished by Girolamo Riario.‡

The immediate consequence of Roberto's death was to nullify the good effects of the victory of Campo Morto. The Venetian troops, regardless of the promises and entreaties of the Pope, withdrew. The siege of Cavi by the

---

* MARINI, I., 209; BALAN, 229; FRANTZ, 387. The different dates given for Roberto's death (see CIPOLLA, 617) are set at rest by Cardinal Gonzaga's Letter, which we publish in the Appendix, N. 66. Caleffini, *Cronica Ferrariae, Cod. I.-I.-4, f. 156, Chigi Library, Rome, also names the 10th September as the day. Roberto's epitaph is to be found in DE ROSSI, Inscript., II., 421.

† See COURAJOD in the Gaz. des Beaux-Arts, 1883, p. 233, and YRIARTE, 354 *seq*.

‡ TONINI, 394-5.

Papal forces was unsuccessful, either because of the strength of its fortifications or because the Orsini, who disliked any further extension of the power of the Pope, neglected to render assistance.*

Meanwhile, Alfonso had again rallied his soldiers, and the war continued, generally to the disadvantage of the Papal troops and the detriment of the Romans, whose fields were laid waste and whose flocks were carried off. The Orsini, incensed by Girolamo's selfish proceedings, at last declared that, if no other auxiliaries arrived, they would withdraw. Without them—as Sigismondo de' Conti justly insists—it was impossible to carry on the war against the King of Naples, and especially against the Colonna. The Venetians, on their side, made it plain that the only thing they wanted was Ferrara, and that which might befall the Pope was nothing to them.†

Meanwhile, the revived opposition in the North added to all these troubles the threat of a Council and a Schism, and Andrea of Carniola was still unchecked in his career.‡

Sixtus IV. now began to perceive " that, by his own action, he was strengthening the hands of a Power which, by its persistent efforts to acquire dominion over the cities of the Adriatic littoral, was likely soon to prove a source of serious danger to him. Giuliano della Rovere seems to have been the person who induced the Pope to separate himself from

* SIGISMONDO DE' CONTI, I., 156.

† SIGISMONDO DE' CONTI, I., 156 ; SCHMARSOW, 196-7. Sixtus IV. writes, on the 20th October, 1482, to Jordano Orsini regarding the proceedings of the enemy in the immediate neighbourhood of Rome: *" Dilecte, etc., Quottidie hostes per Latium discurrunt nemine prohibente et versus S. Sebastianum et alia loca urbi vicina irrumpunt et predas abigunt." Lib. brev., 15, f. 96b, Secret Archives of the Vatican.

‡ See *supra*, p. 363.

the Republic, while Girolamo Riario, the soul of the war party, was probably won over by a hope of eventually obtaining the Malatesta fiefs."* On the 28th November a truce was concluded with the Duke of Calabria. On the 12th December a treaty of Peace between Rome on the one side and Naples, Milan, and Florence on the other was signed. By this treaty the possession of his States was guaranteed to the Duke of Ferrara, territories conquered during the war were mutually restored, an alliance for twenty years, which the Venetians also were free to join, was concluded, and finally, a pension was secured to Girolamo Riario.†

On the following day, the 13th December, Sixtus IV. went in procession to the newly-built Church of Sta Maria della Virtù and bestowed on it the name of Sta Maria della Pace (Our Lady of Peace). At Christmas Peace was publicly proclaimed.‡ The important point now was to obtain the adhesion of the Venetians to this alliance, which had been concluded without their knowledge. Failing this, the peace would be little more than a name.

* REUMONT, Lorenzo, II., 187, 2nd ed.

† SISMONDI, XI., 242.

‡ NOTAJO DI NANTIPORTO, 1080 ; *Diario del Corona. (Barberini Library, LIV., 10, f. 411.) See FEA, La chiesa di S. M. d. p. (1809), and ARMELLINI, 433.

CHAPTER X.

THE POPE'S STRUGGLE WITH VENICE AND THE COLONNA.—THE PEACE OF BAGNOLO AND THE DEATH OF SIXTUS IV.

THIS one-sided treaty which, under the stress of circumstances, had been concluded by Sixtus IV., had a most prejudicial influence on his relations with Venice. Sigismondo de' Conti, known as an historian, was sent in December, 1482, to pacify the Venetians, and to obtain the cessation of hostilities against Ferrara. The reception which awaited him was far from encouraging ; no one ventured to speak to him. The Envoy, however, was not to be deterred from the accomplishment of his Mission ; he delivered the letters which the Pope and the Sacred College had entrusted to him, and endeavoured, with honied words, to persuade the Doge and the Council to a truce ; all his efforts, however, were ineffectual. The Signoria, after the great sacrifices which had been made, would not draw back. They believed victory to be in their hands, and were determined in any case to carry on the war. Sigismondo's Mission was a complete failure.*

The irritation of the Venetians against Sixtus IV. was at this time so great that they proceeded to violent menaces. They declared that, if the Pope should be led to employ his spiritual weapons, he would find himself involved in a

---

* See his own Report, in which (I., p. 158 *seq.*) the Briefs to Venice are inserted ; also MALIPIERO, 269 *seq.*, and Hist. Jahrbuch, VII., 308 *seq.*

disastrous war in Italy, the end of which he would not live
to see. They said they were in league with all the
Christian Powers, and were resolved, if necessary, even to
call in the Turks!*

Sixtus IV. did not allow himself to be intimidated.
A State Paper repelling the accusations of the Venetians
was drawn up,† and it was then determined that, besides
Girolamo Riario, Cardinal Gonzaga should be sent as
Legate to Ferrara.‡ On the 5th February, 1483, Cesare de
Varano was commanded immediately to proceed thither
with all the troops he could collect.§

---

* SIGISMONDO DE' CONTI, I., 165 *seq.* That these were no empty
threats is evident from the Report of Sanudo (Comment., 58), who
informs his Government that Melchiore Trevisan had been sent to
Constantinople. See CIPOLLA, 619.

† I found in the Secret Archives of the Vatican this document,
which, as far as I know, has not yet been printed, with the Title :
Responsio dom. nostri Sixti papae IV. ad objecta sivi per venetos in
causa belli Ferrariensis ; Politic. varia, VII., f. 309-30. The charges
against Sixtus IV., which the Venetians, through their Ambassadors,
had disseminated at the different Courts, are here refuted, and the
ambition of Venice is sharply rebuked. The special ground of her
animosity is declared to be "quod non ad eorum libitum pontificatum
administramus." The importance of Ferrara as the "antimurale
totius Romandiole" is asserted ; were Ferrara Venetian, Forli would
be imperilled. In conclusion, His Holiness still expresses the hope
that Venice would perceive her error, &c. There is no date, but the
document must certainly belong to the spring of 1483. See also the
justificatory piece in RAYNALDUS, ad an. 1483, N. 3.

‡ *On the 13th Dec., 1482, Sixtus IV. announced to Ercole of
Ferrara the Mission of Gonzaga, in order that "presentia sua consolari ac spiritualibus et temporalibus favoribus sicut necessitas exegerit
promptius iuvare et reintegrationi status tui intendere possit." Copy in
the State Archives, Modena. On the same 13th December the Legate's
Representative at Bologna was also informed of Gonzaga's Mission.
The *Brief on the subject is in the State Archives, Bologna, Q. 3.

§ **Brief of 5th Febr., 1483, in the State Archives, Florence (Urbino).

At the end of February the Venetian Ambassador left Rome; fearing that Sixtus IV. would proclaim a Crusade against Venice, he let fly a parting threat, that in that case there should be no more peace for the Pope. If it came to the worst they would make a league with the Devil!*

At the same time, the Congress at Cremona, which, besides the Papal Legate, the Duke of Calabria, and Lorenzo de' Medici, comprised Lodovico and Ascanio Sforza, Ercole d'Este, Federigo Gonzaga, Marquess of Mantua, and Giovanni Bentivoglio, determined to put down the Venetians by force of arms.†

Preparations for war were hastily begun in every direction. There was no time to be lost, for Ferrara could not hold out much longer. The Pope was unwearied in his exhortations.‡ He especially insisted on the necessity of attacking Venice by sea.§ No less than 50,000 ducats were allotted for the equipment of the fleet, the sum being raised by the creation of new offices.||

Early in April, Branda Castiglione, Bishop of Como, was appointed Legate of the fleet.¶ On the 30th of the month the Pope proclaimed his alliance with Naples, Milan, Ferrara,

---

* CAPELLI, 37.

† REUMONT, Lorenzo, II., 189, 2nd ed. ; FRANTZ, 421 *seq.*, 458; CIPOLLA, 620. Girolamo Riario was not present, as SCHMARSOW, 200, shews, in opposition to Reumont.

‡ See in Appendix, N. 67, 69, 70, 71, 72, the *Briefs of 4th March, 16th and 21st April, and 1st May, 1483, as well as Girolamo Riario's Letter of the 7th May, 1483, from the State Archives, Milan.

§ See *Brief of 3rd April, 1483, in Appendix, N. 68.

|| CAPELLI, 37.

¶ Bonfrancesco Arlotti, Bishop of Reggio, writes from Rome on the 9th April, 1483 : *" El vescovo de Como per concistorio et da N. Sʳᵉ è publicato legato suxo l'armata." (State Archives, Modena.) Regarding the operations of the fleet, see SIGISMONDO DE' CONTI, I., 181 *seq.*

and Florence, and reiterated his promises of assistance to the Ferrarese through Cardinal Gonzaga, who died soon afterwards, a victim to the fatigues of the war.*   The Venetians on their side entered into negotiations with the Duke of Lorraine, " in order again to harass King Ferrante by a popular Angevine rising, while their fleet harried the coast of Apulia and took possession of the important stronghold of Gallipoli."†

By the end of May the spiritual weapons of the Pope were also launched against Venice.   From the month of February the Ambassadors of Ferrara had been urging him to proclaim an Interdict.‡   Girolamo Riario exerted his influence in the same direction, and succeeded in determining Sixtus IV. to take this important step.

The Bull of Interdict was laid before the Consistory on the 24th May.   All the Sacred College, with the exception of the Venetian Cardinals, declared their concurrence.   Their opposition, which greatly incensed the Pope, was not calculated to alter his purpose.   On the same day the Bull was affixed to the Gates of St. Peter's.   In the Archives of Modena the jubilant Report is still preserved in which the Ferrarese Envoy tells the Duke that he had at once hastened to St. Peter's to convince himself of the fact.§

The Pope at once communicated the Bull to the Emperor, the King of France, and the other Kings

---

* RAYNALDUS, ad an. 1483, N. 4, 5 ; CIPOLLA, 621.

† REUMONT, Lorenzo, II., 189.

‡ See *Letter of B. Arlotti, dated Rome, 1483, Febr. 21. State Archives, Modena.

§ *Letter of B. Arlotti, dated Rome, 1483, May 24, *loc. cit*. The Bull (dated X. Cal. Junii=23rd May, *not* June, as CIPOLLA, 621, has it) is in RAYNALDUS, ad an. 1483, N. 8–16 ; it was sent to Milan on the 25th May. See Appendix, N. 73, *Brief from the State Archives, Milan.

and Princes of Christendom for publication in their dominions.*

As the Venetian agents in Rome refused to transmit the Bull to their native city, the Pope sent a herald to deliver it to the Patriarch of Venice, whom he charged, under pain of Excommunication and suspension, to impart it to the Doge and the Signoria. "The Patriarch pleaded illness, and apprised the Doge and the Council of Ten, who enjoined strict silence, and commanded him to continue the celebration of public worship as if nothing had happened."† "The indignation of the Venetians against the Pope is extreme," wrote the Ferrarese Ambassador. "They threaten to recall all their Cardinals and Prelates from Rome, and Sixtus IV. has prepared, in anticipation of this, a new Bull against Venice."‡ The Signoria, in the first place, appealed to a future Council,§ and at once began to agitate at the Imperial Court,‖ as well as at those of France and of England,¶ for its convocation, but these efforts were fruitless. Louis XI., on the contrary, at once complied with the wishes of the Pope,** and had

---

* RAYNALDUS, ad an. 1483, N. 17 ; FRANTZ, 429. See Appendix, N. 73 and 74, Cathedral Archives of St. Gall.

† FRANTZ, 426 ; ROMANIN, IV., 413 seq.

‡ *Report of Bonfrancesco Arlotti, dated Rome, 1483, June 16. State Archives, Modena.

§ This appeal was affixed to the Church doors of S. Celso in Rome, in the night between the 2nd and 3rd July ; see MALIPIERO, 283. The Informatione circa l'interdetto di Sisto IV. contro Venetia in Cod. LIX.–120 of the Barberini Library, Rome, is merely an extract from Malipiero. The Pope already, on the 24th June, knew of the "vain and unlawful" Appeal, for the Venetians had sent a copy to their Cardinals ; see *Letter of Bonfr. Arlotti, dated Rome, 1483, June 24. State Archives, Modena.

‖ See in Appendix, N. 75, the *Letter of the 15th June to the Emperor. Secret Archives of the Vatican.

¶ See Cal. of State Papers, Venetian, I., 146.

** See *Brief to Louis XI., dated Rome, 1483, June 15, in which

the sentence against Venice published in his dominions. The Venetian Ambassadors were dismissed. This happy result was chiefly due to the exertions of the Archbishop of Tours and of St. Francis of Paula. The latter had come to Rome in the beginning of 1483. " All the Cardinals went to see him. He had three audiences from the Pope, who placed him on a seat of honour by his side, and conversed with him for three or four hours. He was so struck with admiration at the wisdom of his discourse that he granted him permission to found a new Order."* From Rome St. Francis went to the French Court, and was there when Louis XI. died (29th August).†

Sixtus IV. had never allowed himself to be alarmed by

the necessity of resorting to spiritual weapons is asserted. " De con-silio igitur fratrum nostrorum sententias et censuras ecc^cas adversus prefatos Venetos pro tulimus sequuti fe. re. Clementum predecessorem nostrum. . . . Bullam autem censurarum huiusmodi ad Maj. tuam in praesentiarum mittimus, ut eam per totum regnum tuum si ita tibi videbitur publicari facias." Lib. brev., 15, f. 620–21, Secret Archives of the Vatican.

* REUMONT, III., 1, 180; SIGISMONDO DE' CONTI, 176–7; RAY-NALDUS, ad an. 1483, N. 22. See also VICTON (Vita Francisci a Paula, p. 121, R. 1625); FANTONI, 345; LEGEAY, II., 503; and the Mono-graphs on S. Francis of Paula by SYLVAIN (P. 1874), DABERT (P. 1875), and ROLLAND (P. 1876, 2nd ed.); as also F. ROLLE, Documents relatifs au passage de S. François à Lyon (1483), Lyon, 1864.

† Under the new monarch, Charles VIII., to whom Sixtus IV. expressed his condolences on the 11th Sept., 1483 (in the *Brief Lib. brev., 16 B., f. 27, Secret Archives of the Vatican, the Mission of a Legate is also announced), the anti-Papal tendency revived again in France. The restoration of the Pragmatic Sanction was demanded, and Cardinal de La Balue, who had been sent as Legate to the French Court, could do little or nothing. See HEFELE-HERGENRÖTHER, VIII., 260; GUETTÉE., VIII., 53 seq., 59 seq.; FIERVILLE, 147; PICOT, I., 426 seq.; HÖFLER, Rom. Welt, 186; and, especially in regard to La Balue's Lega-tion, BULAEUS, V., 763; FRIEDBERG, II., 503 note; BUSER, Beziehungen. 240 seq.; and Mèm. de la Soc. de l'Hist. de Paris, 1884, XI., 35 seq,

the threat of a Council. He declared in Consistory that he was quite willing that one should be held, only it must be at Rome in the Lateran, for the right of summoning it belonged to him ; moreover, added the Pope, the Council will necessarily afford an opportunity for the reformation of the ecclesiastical and temporal Princes, and also for calling the Venetians to account for their appropriation of portions of the States of the Church, which must be restored.*

No decisive advantage had meanwhile been gained at any one of the various seats of war. Not one of the enterprises begun by the allies had been brought to a conclusion. Contending interests threatened the League with dissolution. But Venice also was in a deplorable condition ; " her treasury was exhausted, her arsenals empty."†

There seemed, indeed, to be a hope of peace in March, 1484, when, at the desire of the allies, Ascanio Sforza, a brother of Lodovico Moro's, was raised to the purple. The Portuguese Cardinal, Giorgio Costa, who possessed the full confidence of the Signoria, had already made considerable progress in this direction, when Girolamo intervened. The selfishness of this insatiable man completely destroyed the prospect of peace, " which, at this moment, would have been more honourable to the Pope and more favourable to himself than it ever again could be."‡

While the Ferrarese war engrossed general attention, internal dissensions again broke out with great violence in Rome. The year 1483 had been a year of peace for the

---

* See the **Report of B. Arlotti or the 7th July, 1483. (State Archives, Modena.) Sixtus IV.'s Protest against the Appeal of the 15th July is given by RAYNALDUS, ad an. 1483, N. 18–21.

† FRANTZ, 459–61.

‡ SCHMARSOW, 202, from SIGISMONDO DE' CONTI, I., 185-6.

Eternal City ; towards its close, Cardinals Colonna and Savelli were liberated.* They were joyfully welcomed by their dependents when released on the morning of the 15th November, and at once took part in the Consistory in which Sixtus created five new Cardinals.†

If the year 1483 had been one of tranquillity, the next year was stormy. In January the Orsini, confident in the friendship of Girolamo Riario, began the conflict by expelling Antonio Savelli from Albano. The " factions flew to arms. On the 21st February the della Valle stabbed their enemy, Francesco Santa Croce," and fortified their Palace. The Colonna now espoused the cause of the della Valle, and the Orsini that of the Santa Croce, and also barricaded their Palaces.‡ The disturbances came to such a pitch that, as we learn from an Ambassador, soon no one in the City felt his life or property secure.§ "Never," wrote another

---

* " Instances of brutal outrage were not wanting, the after effects of the calamity of war and of inconsiderate tyranny." SCHMARSOW, 199. Regarding the horrible scenes at d'Estouteville's funeral, see NOTAJO DI NANTIPORTO, 1081–2.

† " *Questa matina son liberati li rev^mi cardinali Savello et Columpna de castel S. Angelo, ondo erano carcerati, cum omnium consensu et plausu incredibili. In questa medema hora et eodem consistorio son creati cardinali cinque." Bonfrancesco Arlotti, dated Roma, 1483, Nov. 15. According to a *Report of this Ambassador, of the 1st June, the release of the Cardinals was, even at that time, expected. (State Archives, Modena.) See also a *Letter of Stefano Guidotto, dated Rome, 1483, Nov. 18 : * " Io gionsi qua a Roma sabbato mattina a 15 del presente e ritrovai tutta la terra in festa per esser alhora cavati di castel S. Angelo quelli dui rev^mi cardinali Colonna e Savello." They were present at the election the same morning. (Gonzaga Archives, Mantua.) GRAZIANI, 653, is mistaken in stating that the Cardinals were liberated on the 17th November.

‡ GREGOROVIUS, VII., 261, 3rd ed.

§ See a *Letter from B. Arlotti, dated Rome, 29th May, 1484. State Archives, Modena.

contemporary, "did I see such confusion. It was the 29th
of May; the whole of Rome was in arms. It was said that
they wished to seize the Protonotary by night; he kept
watch and secured himself as well as he could. I had two
hand-barrows full of stones set inside my doors, which I
barricaded, and I had heavy stones brought up to the
windows and into the loggia. All through the night
the cry of Bear! Bear! was heard in the Rio Ponte, and
on Monte Giordano watch-fires burned, shots were fired,
and trumpets blown."*

On the following day, May 30, the Pope made an effort
to settle the dispute in an amicable manner. He sent
messengers to the Palace of Cardinal Colonna, on what is
now called the Piazza della Pilotta, where Lorenzo Oddone,
the Protonotary, had entrenched himself, inviting him in the
most friendly terms to his presence, and promising him all
that his justice and generosity could grant. Lorenzo's
intimate friend, Cardinal Sansoni, endeavoured to persuade
him to accept the Pope's invitation. Finally, Giuliano della
Rovere himself came and offered to remain as a hostage
in the house of the Colonna until such time as Oddone
should return from the Pope, an offer, as Sigismondo de'
Conti observes, suggested rather by affection than prudence.†

Lorenzo was fully inclined to go, but his friends, fearing
for his safety, prevented him. When Sixtus IV. sent the

---

* See REUMONT, III., 1, 181, who is mistaken in assigning these
disturbances to the 29th March. This error is due to the omission
of the name of the month in Notajo di Nantiporto. INFESSURA, 1158,
and JACOB. VOLATERRANUS, 196, are correct in mentioning the end
of May. SCHMARSOW, 250, misled by Sigismondo de' Conti, speaks of
the 28th and 29th April. See, on the other hand, B. Arlotti's *Letter of
the 29th May, already cited, and a **Report of Stefano Guidotto,
dated Rome, 1484, June 1. Gonzaga Archives, Mantua.

† SIGISMONDO DE' CONTI, I., 189.

Conservators for the second time, and promised to forgive everything, he mounted his horse and rode away alone.   But some armed followers of his met him on the Piazza Trevi and obliged him to return.

Girolamo and the Orsini had meanwhile ascertained, through Leone Montesecco, the Prefect of the Body Guard, that Oddone had only a crowd of untrained and unwarlike retainers in his house.

All fear vanished.   After a proclamation had been made to the effect that all who should take part with the Colonna incurred the guilt of high treason, an order for the forcible arrest of the Protonotary was issued.   The attack at once began.   A panic seized the Colonna ; a great many of them left the Palace, which was soon surrounded on all sides. During the fight, which lasted but two hours, forty of the Colonna and only thirteen of their adversaries were killed. The barricades were then scaled, the Palace was relentlessly plundered, and Lorenzo Oddone taken prisoner.   On the way to the Vatican, Virginio Orsini had to defend the unarmed captive from Count Girolamo, who, in his rage, twice drew his sword against him.   Sixtus IV. reproached him in violent language, and accused him of having twice sought to drive him from Rome.   "The Protonotary tried to excuse himself on the ground that his people had prevented him when he tried to go to the Vatican, but after all the terror he had undergone he could hardly utter a sound.   He was given over to Virginio Orsini and confined in St. Angelo." *

"It was fortunate," says Sigismondo de' Conti, "that the conflict was not protracted into the night, under cover of which shame and fear are put aside, and many more would

* Sigismondo de' Conti, I., 190 *seq.* ; Schmarsow, 251.   See Arch. d. Soc. Rom., XI., 612, and Stefano Guidotto's **Reports of the 1st and 4th June, 1484.   Gonzaga Archives.

have taken part with the Colonna, so that the Pope and the Orsini might have been in great danger." *

The houses of the della Valle were, like the Palace of the Colonna, razed to the ground.† The undisciplined soldiers billeted themselves in the houses of the Colonna quarter and wrought cruel havoc there.‡

A portion of the Roman burghers determined to beg the Pope to make peace with the Colonna. Cardinal Giuliano also earnestly advocated a reconciliation, but again the Orsini and Count Girolamo prevented it. The conduct of the latter became more and more insupportable. "He extorted money from the Roman churches, and even from the College of Papal Secretaries and that of the Stradioti."§ If we may believe Infessura, whose sympathies are with the Colonna party, high words passed between Girolamo Riario and Cardinal Giuliano, even in presence of the Pope. Cardinal Giuliano had granted asylum in his Palace to some fugitives from Cardinal Colonna's dwelling, and had expressed his displeasure at Riario's violence. Girolamo accused the Cardinal of protecting rebels and enemies of the Church. Giuliano replied that the men whom he protected were no rebels against the Church, but some of her most faithful servants; that Girolamo was hunting them out of Rome,

* SIGISMONDO DE' CONTI, I., 191. Bonfr. Arlotti writes on the 2nd June, 1484: * "El non si poteria dir quanto stano di bona voglia el papa et conte per questa victoria et sbatimento di Colonesi." State Archives, Modena.

† See S. Guidotto's **Report of the 1st June, 1484, and the *Diario volgare del Corona in Cod. LIV.-10, f. 413. Barberini Library, Rome.

‡ Particulars, especially with regard to the ill-treatment of P. Laetus, in SCHMARSOW, 251.

§ GREGOROVIUS, VII., 262-3, 3rd ed. See also SCHMARSOW, 252-3, who gives a graphic picture of Girolamo's doings in Rome, of his exactions, his usurious speculations in corn, and his insolence towards the Rota.

setting the Church of God on fire and destroying her.   He was
the cause of all the evil deeds which were bringing ruin on
the Pope and on the Cardinals.   The Count, on this, flew into
a rage and declared that he would drive him out of the
country, burn his house over his head, and give it up to
plunder, as he had done to that of the Colonna.*

The attack on the Colonna still went on in the neighbourhood of Rome.   The whole of Latium was soon a prey to
fire and rapine.   On the 27th June Marino fell, and the
Colonna retired to Rocca di Papa.†

Three days later Lorenzo Oddone was beheaded in St.
Angelo, after retracting the confessions torn from him on
the rack.   The unhappy man met death with calmness and
dignity.   The corpse was taken, in the first instance, to the
neighbouring church of Sᵗᵃ Maria Traspontina, whence, in
the evening, it was conveyed to that of the SS. Apostoli.
Here it was received by his mother and many other women,
wailing and lamenting, and was buried that same night by
Infessura and a vassal of the Colonna.‡

* INFESSURA, 1168 ; SCHMARSOW, 253.

† "*Marino hogi s'è dedito et accordato cum el papa," writes B.
Arlotti on the 27th June, 1484. (State Archives, Modena.) SCHMARSOW,
254, is, accordingly, mistaken in giving the 25th as the date.

‡ NOTAJO DI NANTIPORTO, 1087, and INFESSURA, 1174-5. The
former merely says of Colonna's mother, "fece gran lamento" ; the
latter, although a partisan of the Colonna, and very hostile to Sixtus
IV., is (like the Cron. Rom., 37, and the above-mentioned *Diario del
Corona) silent as to the words of accusation which ALLEGRETTI, 817,
says she uttered at the sight of her dead son : " Questa è la testa
del mio figlio e la fede di Papa Sisto che ci promesse, come lassassimo
Marino, ci lassarebbe el mio figliulo." GREGOROVIUS, VII., 264, 3rd
ed., and RANKE (Päpste, I., 31, 6th ed.) both incorporate the words
in their text, but the former is fair enough in a note to call attention
to the fact that they rest solely on Allegretti's authority. REUMONT,
III., 1, 183, does not mention them. SCHMARSOW, 254, repeats them,
but, as CREIGHTON, III., 99, admits, "there is no evidence that the

On the 2nd July Girolamo and Virginio Orsini, with their troops, took the field against the Colonna.* Events soon proved that they had been very ill-advised in thwarting the efforts made to re-establish peace. Prospero and Fabrizio Colonna defended themselves bravely. "The Savelli allowed themselves to be corrupted, and thus many strongholds were indeed lost, but Paliano held out," and Girolamo found it necessary to apply to the Pope for reinforcements. He was soon compelled to own that he had little hope of subduing the Colonna.

Sixtus IV. was greatly disturbed by these tidings; he had never anticipated such determined resistance.† In the month of March his health,‡ which, till then, had been very

Pope made any promise to release Lorenzo." It is worthy of notice that the Mantuan Ambassador, S. Guidotto, does not even allude to the mother's words. Writing on the 2nd July, 1484, he says : * " La Sta del N. S. el fece portare in una cassa ad una certa chiesa propinqua al castello e fu monstrato ad alcuni e poi etiam a la madre e fu sepelito la sera assai honorevolmente a S^{to} Apostolo." *On the 8th July he reports that Colonna's mother had died of grief; but says nothing of these words. I found these two *Letters in the Gonzaga Archives, Mantua. The Sienese Report in Arch. Rom., XI., 614, contains nothing in regard to the supposed exclamation. All rules of criticism require us to reject the statement of an absent writer, when all the witnesses who were on the spot are ignorant of the circumstance mentioned.

* " *Hogi a l'alba lo ill. s. conte è andato in campo, cussi el s^{re} Virgineo." S. Guidotto on the 2nd July, 1484. (Gonzaga Archives.) See B. Arlotti's *Letter of the same day. (State Archives, Modena.) Payments for Girolamo's troops are entered in July, 1484, in *Div. Sixti IV., 1484. State Archives, Rome.

† REUMONT, III., I, 184 ; SCHMARSOW, 255.

‡ On the 7th January, 1483, Stef. Guidotto wrote : * "La Sta de N. S. za tri o quatro di è stato per uno puoco di catharo col collo tuto incordato, non ge stato tempo ne honesto di chieder audientia perche etiam il feci dir a li cardinali che non ge andassimo. S. Sta me fece

good, had begun to give way.* Constant agitation and anxiety naturally told upon him at last. In the middle of June he fell ill of a fever.† Early in August his old malady, the gout, attacked him with such violence that he received the Sacraments of Penance and the Holy Eucharist.‡

Meanwhile, the rumour that peace had been concluded with the Venetians continued to gain more and more credence in Rome. This was actually the case.

The warlike zeal of Milan had been gradually cooling ever since the July of 1483. The urgent demands of Sixtus IV. had failed to produce any effect.§ A year later, " Lodovico Moro had succeeded in severing himself from the League, of which he had been but a half-hearted member." " When the Venetians were getting the worst of it, and their finances were nearly exhausted," says Commines, " Duke Lodovico came to the aid of their honour and credit, and every one again got his own, excepting the poor Duke of Ferrara, who had been drawn into the war by himself and his father-in-law, and was now obliged to abandon the Polesina to the Venetians. It is said that the affair brought Duke Lodovico in 60,000 ducats. I know not," adds Commines, " if that is true, but I found the Duke of Ferrara, who, however, had not at that time yet given him his daughter in marriage, under this belief."‖

dire una matina che ge andassi e ritrovai che la notte gera venuto quello disturbo, non è percho gran male, anci l'è gaiardo e bello continuo comel fussi de 40 anni." Gonzaga Archives, Mantua.

* Sienese Despatch of the 17th March, 1484, in Arch. Rom., XI., 610.

† BURCHARD-THUASNE, I., 493.

‡ *Report of B. Arlotti, dated Rome, 1484, August 3. State Archives, Modena.

§ See in Appendix, N. 76, 77, 78, 79, 80, and 81, the *Briefs of July 15th, August 20th and 25th, Sept. 20th, and Oct. 2nd and 13th, 1483. State Archives, Milan, and Secret Archives of the Vatican.

‖ REUMONT, Lorenzo, II., 190, 194, 2nd ed.

Gallipoli and other places on the coast, which had been taken from him, were restored to the King of Naples. Roberto da San Severino, the Captain-General of the Venetians, became commander of the troops of the League, with a yearly salary of 20,000 florins. Riario went away empty. The Peace of Bagnolo (7th August, 1484) became, as Sigismondo de' Conti justly observes, a victory for Venice, for Ercole of Ferrara was obliged to come there in person as a suppliant, and Lodovico sent his son ostensibly to take part in the festivities, but really as a hostage for the fulfilment of the conditions of the treaty.*

The Pope would not at first believe in this disgraceful Peace. When, however, he could no longer doubt that his authority had been thus set at naught, his grief was extreme. "Faithless Lodovico!" he was heard to exclaim, in a voice shaken with sighs.†

His illness was no doubt aggravated by excitement. A Consistory had been summoned to meet on Wednesday, the 11th August, but as the Pope had become worse in the

---

* SIGISMONDO DE' CONTI, I., 194; SCHMARSOW, 256, who draws attention to the fact that Gianfrancesco Tolentino, as Procurator and Mandatory of Sixtus IV., had the first place among those who conducted the Peace negotiations, and that, accordingly, it cannot be said that the treaty was concluded behind the Pope's back (as BROSCH, Julius II., p. 27, represents it to have been), and without his knowledge or consent; but the conditions, to which the majority agreed, broke his heart.

† SIGISMONDO DE' CONTI, I., 204. "Hardly five months had passed," says REUMONT, Lorenzo, II., 195, 2nd ed., "since he had conferred the Red Hat on Ascanio Maria Sforza, brother of the man who was now thwarting all his plans. Ascanio began a troubled cardinalate under warlike auspices." See also SCHMARSOW, 256. The assertion that Sixtus IV. took delight in wars and troubles, and, accordingly, was greatly vexed that any kind of Peace should be concluded, is a malicious invention, irreconcilable with his last authentic utterances. LÄMMER in Histor. Jahrbuch, I., 179.

night, the assembled Cardinals were dismissed. Nevertheless, after Vespers, the Ambassadors of the League were
admitted into his presence. " When he had heard them,"
says Jacobus Volaterranus, "he complained, not, as evil-
minded and malicious persons have asserted, that Peace had
been concluded, but that its conditions were so unfavourable.
' Up to this time,' he said, ' we have carried on a dangerous
and difficult war, in order, by our victorious arms, to obtain
an honourable Peace for the security of the Apostolic See,
our own honour, and that of the League. Now, when as
you know, by the will of God, success was at hand, you
bring back conditions of Peace suited to the vanquished,
not to the victor. The Venetians had already offered our
Apostolic Legate terms much fairer and more profitable to
your Princes, terms which were honourable to the Apostolic
See, whereas these are disgraceful. The cities taken in the
war were to be entrusted to our protection, the nobles were
to send us hostages and await our judgment, Ferrara was
not mentioned. You propose none of these things, but, on
the contrary, shameful conditions, fraught with the seeds of
confusion and future evil rather than good. This Peace, my
beloved sons in Christ, I can neither approve nor sanction.'"*

During the night and the following day the weakness of
the Pope hourly increased ; the fever consumed his strength.
On the Feast of S. Clara, 12th August, in the fourth hour of
the night, he passed peacefully away. " Four days previously," Jacobus Volaterranus informs us, " he had received
Holy Communion. After his death the Penitentiaries of
the Friars-minor washed him, vested him, and laid him out
on his bier. In the evening the corpse was brought to the

---

* JACOBUS VOLATERRANUS, 199 ; FRANTZ, 476 *seq.* See also
Bonfrancesco Arlotti's **Letter of the 12th August, 1484. State
Archives, Modena.

Basilica of St. Peter, and, with all fitting honour, deposited in the chapel which he had himself built in his lifetime, until his monument should be ready. The obsequies commenced on the fourth day, and continued for nine days without intermission." *

* JACOBUS VOLATERRANUS, 200; FRANTZ, 477. Regarding the Pope's last hours, see the Despatch of Guidantonio Vespucci in BURCHARD-THUASNE, I., 496, where the actual account of his death is, however, wanting. * " In questo punto che siamo a hore V. è passato di questa vita la santa mem. di papa Sisto." *Despatch of Vespucci of the 12th August, Arch. Medic. filza 39, f. 320. (State Archives, Florence.) With this, accord Bonfrancesco Arlotti's *Despatches of 14th and 15th August, which say that death took place between the fifth and sixth hours. (State Archives, Modena.) Stef. Guidotto's Letters of the 12th and 13th August from the Gonzaga Archives, printed in Appendix, N. 82, mention an earlier hour. The imposing bronze monument, which Cardinal Giuliano erected to his uncle's memory, was executed by Antonio Pollajuolo, a Florentine, in 1493, and is now in the Chapel of the Blessed Sacrament in St. Peter's; it represents the departed Pope in his Pontifical robes : " a thick-set, almost small figure, a bony hand with dry sinews, covered with loose leathery skin, but with veins which seem almost throbbing with warm blood, and a long history written in the deep furrows and angular lines of the weather-beaten face" (SCHMARSOW, 259); round about are ill-chosen and, in some instances, objectionable, allegorical figures of the Sciences. See BURCKHARDT, Cicerone, 358 ; GREGOROVIUS, Grabmäler, 101 seq. See also CROWE-CAVALCASELLE, III., 127 ; BURCKHARDT, Gesch. der Renaissance, 292 ; PIPER, Mythologie, I., 89 ; The Ecclesiologist, XXIX., 161 ; SEMPER, Donatello, 120 (Innsbruck, 1887); Plate in LITTA, fasc. 147.

CHAPTER XI.

IN following the course of Sixtus IV. through the mazes of
Italian politics, it is often difficult to believe that he was
once the General of a Mendicant Order ; but in the ecclesiastical sphere the case is quite different, and his action fully
corresponds to what we should naturally expect.* As early
as the year 1472 the decision of Gregory IX. regarding the
powers of the Cardinal-Protector of the Franciscans was
confirmed.† A Bull of the 3rd October of that year made
the Feast of St. Francis henceforth a holiday of obligation.‡
This was followed, on the 31st August, 1474, by the Bull
known as "Mare magnum" (the Great Sea), by which the
privileges of the Franciscan-Conventuals were so greatly
augmented. In it those granted by Clement IV. and
Eugenius IV., which were already very extensive, were not

---

* Regarding the abolition of the exemptions of the Mendicant
Orders from common law jurisdiction, which was contemplated by
Calixtus III., and then by Paul II., and the protest of Francesco della
Rovere against the measure, see PHILLIPS, VII., 997.

† Bull., 205-7.

‡ Bull., 209. A copy of the Bull is in the State Archives, Dresden,
D P O, No. 64.

only confirmed but considerably increased. Most ample
powers were conferred upon the Conventuals in regard to
Divine Worship during an Interdict, jurisdiction in cases
reserved to the Pope, exemption from tithes and from
episcopal jurisdiction, the administration of the Sacraments,
and the burial of the faithful in the habit and in the ceme-
teries of the Order. All who opposed them were threatened
with severe punishments.* A similar Bull was also issued
in favour of the Dominicans.†

Even this was not enough, for in 1479 Sixtus IV.
granted yet further favours by the "Golden Bull." ‡ To
enumerate the good things bestowed on the Mendicant
Friars, and more particularly on the Franciscans, during this
long pontificate would be an almost endless task.§ Highly
as we may estimate the manifold and important labours of
these Orders, there can be no doubt that the indulgence
shewn to them was excessive. Sixtus IV. also assisted the
Brothers of the Common Life, and approved the order of
the Minims and that of the discalced Augustinians.‖

* Bull., 217 seq. See WADDING, 1474, N. 17 ; Anal. Francisc., II.,
457. PANZER, Annal., III., 488, gives information regarding a very
ancient printed copy of the 'Mare magnum.' A copy of it is in the
City Library, Frankfort, Rit. Cath., 151.

† Bull., 224 seq. ; Bull. praedic., 516 seq.

‡ Bull., 278 seq. ; Bull. praedic., III., 578 seq.

§ See, besides Wadding, the Croniche di S. Francesco, III., 319
seq., and EUBEL, II., 223.

‖ JANSSEN, I., 66, 15th ed. ; HEFELE-HERGENRÖTHER, VIII., 199.
Sixtus IV. repeatedly came forward as the Protector of Monastic
Institutes (see his *Decree for the Dominicans at Ghent, dated
Rome, 1483, Febr. 18 ; Minute brevium Sixti IV., &c., f. 18, N. 79,
Secret Archives of the Vatican ; and a *Bull, dated 1484, iv. Cal. Julii,
in reference to the Monast. Trinit. Milet. in the Archives of the
Greek Seminary, Rome, L. II.), and, especially, of ecclesiastical liberty ;
see supra, p. 314 seq., and the *Brief to the Doge of Venice of the 7th

The many disputes of the Religious Orders among themselves were deplorable. Accordingly, in the " Golden Bull " Sixtus IV. expressly forbade the office of Inquisitor to be exercised by a Franciscan against a Dominican or *viceversa ;* and, to prevent the perpetual conflicts between the Secular and Regular clergy, he also issued a decree that Parish Priests were not to accuse Mendicants of heresy, and, on the other hand, prohibited the latter from telling the people that they were not bound to hear Masses of obligation in their Parish Church. Seculars and Regulars were alike forbidden to influence the faithful in regard to their place of sepulture. Sixtus IV. confirmed the rule that the Easter Confession was to be made to the Parish Priest.*

There seems to be no doubt that Sixtus IV. also desired to effect a reunion between the Franciscan Conventuals and the Observantines. As he had himself been a Conventual, this would have meant the abolition of the Observantines. They were greatly disturbed about this scheme. Glassberger writes in his chronicle : " During the whole course of his pontificate, Sixtus IV. did nothing that could justly be blamed, except that he wished to subject the Observantines to the Conventuals; for this reason God raised up an adversary against him in Andrea of Carniola. From all sides, even from temporal Princes like the Duke of Milan, petitions were showered upon Rome, so that the Pope exclaimed : ' The whole world is for the Observantines ! ' " St. Jacopo della Marca is said to have predicted to Sixtus IV.

Nov., 1480, in Lib. brev., 13, f. 160. (Secret Archives of the Vatican.) For evidence of the care of Sixtus IV. for the Greek Christians, see Bibl. de l'École des Chartes, 1877, p. 269.

* HERGENRÖTHER, VIII., 253. See REMLING, Speier, II., 172-3 ; LEA, I., 293, 302. KOLDE, 205, relates the unavailing attempt of four Electors from the Rhine Provinces to induce Sixtus IV. to suppress the Mendicant Orders.

that he would die suddenly if he carried out this plan.   As a fact, the Bull, which had been drafted, never appeared.*

The partiality of Sixtus IV. for his own Order doubtless contributed to bring about the canonisation of St. Bonaventura, which was proclaimed with much solemnity in Rome on the 14th April, 1482.† In the previous year he had raised to the altars the Minorites martyred in Morocco in the time of Honorius III.‡

The exertions of Sixtus IV. on behalf of the due celebration of Divine worship and chanting of the Liturgy are also especially worthy of record. It was by him the famous Sistine Choir was instituted and attached to this Chapel for the daily chanting of the Divine Office. The reign of this Pontiff was the beginning of a new artistic life in the Papal Chapel ; " the most highly-gifted singers from all countries flocked to Rome, allured by the opportunity afforded to them of exercising their art, making their talents known, and reaping rich rewards." §

Sixtus IV. laboured assiduously to preserve the integrity

---

* GLASSBERGER in Anal. Francisc., II., 455, 463 ; EUBEL, II., 278.

† INFESSURA, 1148 ; JACOB. VOLATERRANUS, 169 *seq.* ; RAYNALDUS, ad an. 1482, N. 47 *seq.* ; Bull., 284 *seq.* ; WADDING, XIV., 285 *seq.* ; Anal. Franc., II., 284 ; BALUZE-MANSI, Miscell., IV., 471 *seq.* ; MARTÈNE, II., 1672–3 ; OROLOGIO, Canonici di Padova, 157 ; SCHULTE, Quellen, II., 332 ; VALENTINELLI, Regesten, 522 (München, 1865); SUMMONTE, III., 503 *seq.* ; STÄLIN, III., 594.

‡ RAYNALDUS, ad an. 1481, N. 52–3.

§ HABERL, Bausteine, I., 72, and III. : Die Römische Schola Cantorum und die päpstlichen Kapellsänger bis zur mitte des 16 Jahrhunderts, Leipzig, 1887.   Extract from the Vierteljahrsschrift für Musikwissenschaft, Jahrg., 3.   Part II. of the " Bausteine " contains the musical catalogue of the Archives of the Papal Chapel (1888). The well-known editor of Palestrina has in this work far surpassed his predecessor (SCHELLE, Die päpstl. Sängerschule, Wien, 1872), and has rendered valuable service by his researches in the musical treasures of the Roman Archives.

of the Faith, and, in particular, took measures against the Waldensees in Piedmont and France.*

The Pope was, as the preceding history bears witness, most solicitous for the maintenance of the monarchical constitution of the Church.   In 1478 he formally annulled the Decrees of the Council of Constance.   Martin V. had already refused to recognise them, with the exception of those concerning the Faith.   In 1483 he revived the Bull of Pius II. prohibiting appeals to a Council.†

His ardent devotion to the Blessed Virgin was an admirable trait in the character of this Pope.   Sigismondo de' Conti says that he used to pray before her statue with such

* LEA, II., 159, 187, 266, 416 ; BERNINO, 208 *seq.* ; Bull. praedic., III., 487, 501, 577 ; MARTÈNE, II., 1507, 1510; Bull., 263 *seq.* See PELAYO, I., 548, 788 ; REUSCH, I., 42. Regarding Sixtus IV.'s ordinances against Slavery, see RAYNALDUS, ad an. 1476, N. 21–2.

† RAYNALDUS, ad an. 1478, N. 46, 1483, N. 18 *seq.* ; GEBHARDT, 45, and *supra*, pp. 326 and 377 *seq*. That Sixtus IV. was an energetic champion of Papal authority, in opposition to the false Conciliar theories, is evident from his autograph *Observations on the official Acts of the Council of Constance, which Dr. Finke has most kindly made known to me.   After the words : " Nos votis—conspiciebamus" in the Convocation Bull "Ad pacem" of 1413, December 8 (MANSI, XXVII., 537 *seq.*), is the remark : "Sixtus papa IIII. manu propria addidit et glosavit in originali existenti in bibliotheca : Deceptus fuit papa Johannes." After "deinde securit. civ. Const.," Sixtus IV. wrote : " Papa habet determinare locum concilii et tempus et solus habet congregare concilium, ideo petitur ab eo, &c." At the 5th November Sixtus IV. has added to the marginal note, "Inchoatio concilii" (see MANSI, 532) "Parvi roboris." On the Bull of Publication he wrote : "Nota quod papa statuit et concilium approbat, ideo papa est super concilium, quemadmodum rex, qui statuit, est super concilium suum, quod facta per regem approbat." (Barberini Library, XVI., 63.) With reference to Sixtus IV.'s observations on the Acts of the Council of Constance, see H. FINKE, Forschungen und Quellen zur Gesch. des Konstanzer Concils., 54 (Paderborn, 1889).

fervour and recollection, that for a whole hour his eyes
never wandered from it.*   The Italian shrines of our Lady,
especially those of Loreto and Genazzano, were the objects
of his particular care.†   In the year 1475 he instituted the
Feast of the Visitation and published an Encyclical on the
occasion.‡   He also, in many ways, promoted the devotion
of the Rosary.§   In Rome the Pope's veneration for the
Mother of God found expression in the erection of the celebrated churches of Sᵗᵃ Maria del Popolo and Sᵗᵃ Maria della
Pace, and of the Sistine Chapel, which was dedicated to her
Immaculate Conception.|| In 1475 he approved of a special
Office of the Immaculate Conception for the 8th December.¶
Here also his Franciscan sympathies appear.   His Order,
in opposition to that of the Dominicans, were ardent
champions of this doctrine, which was already widely diffused
in the Church.   The contention between the two Orders on
this subject now broke forth anew.   A Dominican, named
Vincenzo Bandelli, had asserted in public disputations and
in writing that those who declared the Conception of the
Blessed Virgin to have been Immaculate were guilty of
heresy and, accordingly, of mortal sin.   The dispute became
so violent that Sixtus IV. had to interfere.   Although he
did not pronounce any definite decision, the Constitution,
which he published in 1483, clearly shews to which side he
personally inclined.   "We," he says, "reject and condemn

---

* SIGISMONDO DE' CONTI, I., 204.

† TURSELLINUS, 140 *seq.*; DILLON, Unsere liebe Frau vom guten
Rathe, Einsiedeln, 1887.

‡ RAYNALDUS, ad an. 1475, N. 34.   See FABRICIUS-MANSI, VI.,
491.

§ Bull. praedic., III., 567, 576 *seq.*; Bull., 268 ; GIESELER, Kirchengesch., II., 4, 337.

|| Bull., 269 *seq.* ; Bull. Vatic., 205 *seq.*   FRANTZ, 514, has misunder-
stood this Bull.

¶ FRANTZ, 513.

the assertions of those preachers, who allow themselves to be
so far carried away as to represent such as believe or maintain that the Mother of God was preserved from the stain of
original sin, to be thereby tainted with heresy or guilty of
mortal sin, and those who solemnly celebrate the Office of
the Conception of Mary, or listen to sermons in which that
doctrine is declared, as thereby committing sin—we reject
and condemn, by Apostolical authority, all such statements
as false, erroneous, and completely devoid of truth, together
with the books which contain them. We also determine
and appoint that preachers of the Word of God and others,
of whatever station, rank, calling, and character they may
be, who shall henceforth rashly venture to maintain that the
statements we have thus disapproved and condemned are
true, or who shall read books containing them, holding or
considering them to be true, after the preceding constitution
has been made known to them—*ipso facto*, incur the sentence
of Excommunication."

In order, however, to guard against the impression that
any special dogmatic decision of the doctrine in question
was here involved, the Pope adds to this decree the express
declaration that no such decision has yet been given by the
Apostolic See, and that, accordingly, the opponents of the
view of Scotus and of the Doctors of Paris cannot at
present be accused of heresy.*

In the sphere of ecclesiastical policy, Sixtus IV. made
considerable concessions to governments with whom he was
on good terms, or from whom he expected assistance of a
political nature. The influence of the secular power on

---

* Extrav. commun., lib. III., tit. XII., c. 2. See the beautiful
work, Zum Lobe der unbefleckten Empfängniss der allers. Jungfrau,
58–9 (Freiburg, 1879); DENZINGER, Die Lehre von der unbefl. Empfängniss, 30 *seq.* (Würzburg, 1855, 2nd ed.); FRANTZ, 513 *seq.*;
HERGENRÖTHER, VIII., 213 ; Kirchenlexikon, IV., 473, 2nd ed.

ecclesiastical affairs was thus unduly strengthened.* Besides confirming the Bulls granted to the Emperor Frederick III. by Eugenius IV. and Nicholas V., regarding the exercise of patronage for the episcopal Sees of Trent, Brixen, Gurk, Trieste, Chur, Piben, Vienna, and Wiener-Neustadt, on the 8th April, 1473, he also granted him the right of presentation to 300 benefices.† A Bull of 1478 also accorded to Frederick the temporary patronage of other Bishoprics.‡

Dukes Ernest and Albrecht of Saxony received from Sixtus IV., in 1476, the right of presentation to several high dignities belonging to the Chapter of Meissen, and, nine years later, that right was extended to all such posts in that city.§

A Bull of the 8th July, 1479, allowed the Government of Zurich to fill up all benefices belonging to the Great Cathedral and that of our Lady and the Monastery of Embrach, even such as should fall vacant in the Papal months.‖ In consideration of the number of clerical state criminals and falsifiers of the coinage in the Republic of Venice, Sixtus

---

* An example of "the truly pertinacious energy" with which even minor States sought to impose upon the Holy See prelates devoted to their interests, may be found in the Jahrb. für Schweiz. Gesch., IX., 21 seq. See also, in STÄLIN, III., 539, the utterances of the Duke of Wurtemberg regarding his right to confer ecclesiastical fiefs. For an account of the dispute concerning the appointment to the Bishopric of Fréjus, in which Sixtus IV. carried out his purpose, see LECOY DE LA MARCHE, I., 543.

† Mon. Habsb., I., 316, 318.

‡ Mon. Habsb., II., 386 seq. See Archiv für Œsterr. Gesch., LV., 175.

§ Cod. Dipl. Sax. Urkundenbuch des Hochstiftes Meissen, III., 240, 263, 272, 278; GESS, Klostervisitationen des Herzogs Georg von Sachsen, 2 (Leipzig, 1888).

‖ Geschichtsfreund, XXXIII., 46 seq.; Jahrbuch für Schweiz. Gesch., IV., 9.

IV. consented that such should be tried by the secular judges in presence of the Vicar of the Patriarch.*

The control of the State over the Church in Spain had at this time assumed an immense development. Efforts to strengthen and extend this power led to important contests concerning presentations to Bishoprics. In the autumn of 1478 Cardinal Peter Ferrici, Bishop of Tarragona, died.† Sixtus IV. then conferred the Bishopric on Andreas Martinez; but King Ferdinand, who desired this preferment for Cardinal Pedro Gonzalez de Mendoza, commanded Martinez to resign at once, threatening him with exile and other severe penalties to be inflicted on himself and his relations.‡ The See of Cuença (1482) was the occasion of an even more serious dispute. Sixtus IV. had appointed his nephew, Raffaello Sansoni, to this Bishopric, while Isabella wished it to be given to her Confessor, Alfonso de Burgos. The remonstrances of the Royal pair being disregarded, they broke off communication with Rome and threatened to hold a Council. The friendship of the Spanish monarchs was of great importance to the Pope in his Italian difficulties. In consequence, he had granted them extensive concurrent rights in episcopal nominations, and Alfonso de Burgos eventually became Bishop of Cuença. Isabella, however, it must be said, used her privilege in favour of really excellent men.§

---

* FRIEDBERG, 692 ; see 690. As to the treatment of obnoxious Bishops by Venice, see the information given by MAS-LATRIE in the Rev. des Quest. Hist., 1878, April, p. 571 *seq.*

† PANVINIUS, 325.

‡ PRESCOTT, I., 255 ; Archiv für Kirchenrecht, N. F., IV., 11 ; FRIEDBERG, 539 *seq.*

§ MAURENBRECHER, Studien, 13 (Leipzig, 1874), and Kath-Reformation, 378 (Nördlingen, 1880) ; FRIEDBERG, 540 ; PRESCOTT, I., 256 *seq.*, II., 586 ; SENTIS, Monarchia Sicula, 102. See also HERGENRÖTHER in Archiv f. Kirchenrecht, N. F., IV., 15 ; PHILLIPS-VERING, Kirchenrecht, VIII., 1, 199 *seq.*

Sixtus IV. shewed greater firmness in regard to the question of the Spanish Inquisition. This tribunal, whose office it was to punish obstinate heretics or notorious sinners who were nominally members of the Church,* was created, in the first instance, to deal with the special circumstances of the Jewish community in Spain. No other European State had suffered, to the extent that Spain was then suffering, from the unrelenting system of usury and organised extortion practised by these dangerous aliens. Persecutions were the natural consequence, and often the only alternative before the Jews was baptism or death. Thus the number of merely nominal converts to the Christian Faith soon became very great. The secret Jews were incomparably more dangerous than those who openly professed their religion. "If the latter monopolised the greater part of the wealth and commerce of the country, the former threatened alike the Spanish nationality and the Christian faith. On the one hand they contrived to insinuate themselves into a number of ecclesiastical charges, and even to become Bishops, and on the other to attain high municipal honours and to marry into all the noble families. These advantages, and their great wealth, were all covertly devoted to the gradual subjugation of the Spaniards and the undermining of their Faith in favour of the Jews and Judaism."† Things had latterly come to such a pass that the very existence of Christian Spain was at stake.‡

The Inquisition was created as a remedy for these evils.

---

* Only such as having, through baptism, become members of the Church were viewed as rebels against her authority, and the unbaptised were not subject to the Inquisition. See GRISAR, 551, N. 1.

† HEFELE, Ximenes, 277-8.

‡ Such is the opinion of A. HUBER, Ueber die Spanische Nationalität und Kunst, Berlin, 1852.

The necessary authorisation of the Holy See was given in a Brief of the 1st November, 1478.* Ferdinand and Isabella were hereby empowered, after due examination, to nominate two or three Archbishops and Bishops, or other dignitaries of the Church, who should be secular or regular priests, commendable for their prudence and virtue, at least forty years of age, and of blameless morals, Masters or Bachelors of Theology, Doctors or Licentiates of Canon Law. These Inquisitors were to proceed against relapsed Jews who had been baptised and other apostates. The Pope granted them the necessary jurisdiction for proceeding, according to law and custom, against the guilty, and permitted the Spanish monarchs to dismiss them and appoint others, with the reservation that the Bull itself could not be annulled without express mention of its contents.†

By the desire of Queen Isabella another effort was made to bring back those who had been led away by preaching and other peaceable means. These attempts being obstinately and scornfully rejected, the Spanish monarchs, in virtue of the Papal Bull, nominated, on the 17th September, 1489, two Dominicans, Michael Morillo and Juan Martin, as Inquisitors for the city and Diocese of Seville. Two secular priests were associated with them. They began their work without delay. Jews who obstinately persisted in their errors were handed over to the secular power and burned.‡

Very soon vehement complaints of the harsh and irregular proceedings of the Inquisitors began to arrive in Rome. Sixtus IV.'s Brief of the 29th January, 1482, shews that grave abuses had arisen. The Pope, in the first place, expresses

---

* Not on the 1st September, as GRISAR says, 560.

† LLORENTE, I., 167–8 ; see IV., 410.

‡ LLORENTE, I., 171 seq. See HEFELE, Ximenes, **282** seq. ; RODRIGO, II., 71 seq. ; GRISAR, 561.

his displeasure at the omission, without his knowledge, of certain clauses in the former Brief, which, as it appears, would have guarded more securely against abuses, brought the methods of procedure into greater harmony with the course of common law, and facilitated the concerted action which had been usual between the Inquisitors and the Bishops. The result had been that these former, under pretext of the Papal Brief, had unjustly imprisoned many persons without trial, subjected them to cruel tortures, pronounced them heretics, and confiscated the possessions of those who were executed, so that numbers had fled the country in dread of a similar fate.   Moved by the complaints of persons who had turned to the Holy See as "the defender of all the oppressed," after consultation with the Cardinals, he issued his commands that the Inquisitors should henceforth proceed in conformity with law and justice, and in concert with the Bishops.   Sixtus IV. further declared that nothing but consideration for the King, whose Ambassadors in Rome interceded for the Inquisitors, could have induced him to continue them in their office.   Should they persist in these evil practices, and act without consulting the Bishop of the Diocese, or considering what the salvation of souls demanded, he would put others in their place.   The Pope refused to grant the request of the Spanish monarchs for the appointment of Inquisitors in the other portions of their kingdom, as the Dominican Inquisition was already in force there.*

Sixtus IV., though approving of the new Inquisition in itself,† had soon fresh cause for dissatisfaction with the con-

---

* LLORENTE, IV., 394-7 ; GRISAR, 561, where, naturally, 1482 is to be read for 1492.

† This is evident from the Brief of the 23rd February, 1483, in LLORENTE, IV., 402-6.   No Pope has condemned the Spanish Inquisition in itself, but many for these abuses, as, especially, Sixtus V. in the Bull of the 22nd January, 1588, where he speaks of the

duct of the Inquisitors.   His displeasure was directed not against the institution, but against the manner in which it was carried out.   There can be little doubt that the Spanish monarchs desired to give it too worldly a character, and at times made the real danger which existed from the feigned Christians, a pretext for bringing the tribunal to bear upon their other enemies, and that the new Inquisitors were but too ready to play into their hands.   Against these abuses Sixtus IV. insisted on the strict observance of the provisions of the common law.   We learn something of the domineering character of Michael Morillo from a Bull of Sixtus IV., dated 21st January, 1479.   From this document it appears that Morillo had removed the former Inquisitor of Valença who had been appointed by the General of the Dominicans, and had given his post to another.   The Pope cancelled this act, and desired the original appointment to be maintained.*

The abuses in the Spanish Inquisition, however, did not cease ; consequently, when the jurisdiction of the tribunal was extended to Castille and Leon, Sixtus IV. pronounced the severest penalties against Inquisitors who should fail to exercise their office in a conscientious manner, and in accordance with the canonical prescriptions.†

It is important to note, as a significant fact bearing on the character of this institution, that " not only the ecclesiastical authorisation of the first Inquisitors, but also the first regula-

Spanish Inquisition as established by the authority of the Holy See (see RODRIGO, II., 153).   An Edict of their Spanish Majesties in 1487 affirms that the introduction of the Inquisition into Spain was due to the Holy See ; see REUSS, Instructionen, 134.   On the other hand, it is certain that Rome did everything to mitigate the severity of the Inquisition, and to guard against its employment for political objects ; see HEFELE, Ximenes, 315 *seq.*

* Bull. praedic., III., 572.

† LLORENTE, IV., 410.

tions as to the mode of procedure, emanated directly from the Pope." In order to avoid constant appeals to Rome, often made as mere subterfuges and with a view of impeding the course of the law, he, in 1483, appointed the Archbishop of Seville, Papal Judge of Appeals for the Inquisition.*

Notwithstanding all these precautionary measures on the part of the Holy See, accused persons were still treated in Spain with arbitrary cruelty and injustice. To remedy this evil, Sixtus IV., on the 2nd August, 1483, decreed :—(1) That decisions on appeals given in Rome were to be held valid in Spain ; (2) that shamefaced penitents were to be absolved in secret ; (3) that those once absolved were not again to be molested by the Inquisitors. In conclusion, Sixtus expressly admonished the Royal pair to leave those who had retracted, in peaceful possession of their property. "As it is mercy alone that makes us like God, we beg and exhort the King and the Queen, for the love of Jesus Christ, to imitate Him, whose property it is always to have mercy and to spare. Let them have compassion on their subjects in the city and Diocese of Seville, who are sensible of their errors and ask for pardon."†

The appointment of a Grand Inquisitor, which took place in this year, was another important step in the organisation of the new tribunal. The idea appears to have originated with the Spanish monarchs. In the autumn of 1483 Sixtus IV. entrusted the spiritual powers of this office to Thomas Torquemada, the Dominican Prior of S. Cruz.‡ "He was

* LLORENTE, IV., 411–12 ; GRISAR, 562.

† LLORENTE, IV., 408–21. See HEFELE, Ximenes, 287 ; BAUMSTARK, Isabella von Castilien, 98 (Freiburg, 1874) ; ROHRBACHER-KNÖPFLER, 69.

‡ See, for further information, BARTHÉLEMY, Erreurs Hist., IV., 170 seq. (Paris, 1875). Torquemada's Instruction of 1484 is in REUSS,

to direct all the business of the Inquisition, was empowered
to delegate his Apostolic Mission to others, and, especially,
as the Pope's representative, to hear appeals made to the
Holy See, superseding the former occupant of this office."*
The Grand Inquisitor's sphere of jurisdiction was, by a
special Papal Brief of the 17th October, 1483, extended to
the kingdom of Aragon.† A Council of Inquisition was
now established, mainly with the object of assisting in the
hearing of Appeals. Torquemada instituted this Council
"by virtue of the plenary powers which he had received
when his authority was conferred upon him by the Pope."
Sixtus IV. gave his sanction to this measure.‡ The
members of the Council have often been spoken of as mere
State officials; this, however, is a mistake. They were
State officials, and, as such, derived their temporal jurisdiction from the King, but, in their primary ecclesiastical
capacity, they had no authority until it was imparted to
them by the Papal Delegate. The Grand Inquisitor,
nominated by the King, always received his ecclesiastical
jurisdiction from an Apostolic Brief.§ He proposed, and
the King nominated, the Councillors, who derived their
spiritual jurisdiction from his approbation, by which he
imparted to them a share in his Apostolic authority.‖

The Spanish Inquisition, accordingly, appears as a mixed,
but primarily ecclesiastical, institution.¶ The fact that the

Instructionen, 1 *seq.*; the ecclesiastical character of the Inquisition is
clearly manifested in the documents here printed (p. 67, form of Ab-
juration, and p. 70, Oath of Absolution).

* GRISAR, 563 ; HEFELE, Ximenes, 288.

† Bull. ord. praed., III., 622.   See RODRIGO, II., 101 *seq.*

‡ RODRIGO, II., 163.

§ In addition to the testimonies adduced by Rodrigo, see the passages
from L. a Paramo and Carena in GRISAR, 564, note 2.

‖ RODRIGO, *loc. cit.* ; GRISAR, 564.

¶ Rodrigo's work, which is somewhat prolix and inaccurate, has the

condemned were handed over to the secular arm testifies to the correctness of this view. Had the Spanish Inquisition

merit of shewing that the Spanish Inquisition cannot justly be looked upon as a purely State institution. The Spanish scholar sums up his opinion in the following terms : " The tribunals of the Holy Office had no essentially secular character. They were ecclesiastical in regard to the matters of which they took cognizance, and to the authority by which they were created. But, in consideration of the Royal delegation conferred upon the judges, they may be said to have had a mixed character" (I., 276) ; " in fact the Spanish Inquisition was a spiritual court, armed with Royal weapons." The view which regarded it as a purely State institution was popularised in France by DE MAISTRE (Lettre à un gentilhomme Russe sur l'Inquisition Espagnole, 11–12, Lyon, 1837), and in Germany by RANKE (Fürsten und Völker, I., 241 seq., Hamburg, 1827 ; and, with slight alterations, also in the 4th edition of 1877, p. 195 seq.). It has been recently put forward, on the Catholic side, by three other historians : GAMS (Zur Gesch. der Span. Staatsinquisition, Regensburg, 1878); HERGENRÖTHER (Kirchengesch., II., 765, 3rd ed., and Staat u. Kirche, p. 607 seq.) ; and KNÖPFLER (Rohrbacher's Kirchengesch., 68 f., and Hist.-polit. Bl., XC., 325 seq., and XCI., 165 seq.). In favour of the opinion we have adopted above, may be cited the old theologians of the Inquisition, such as Paramo and Carena, who must have been accurately acquainted with the matter ; and, among modern writers, BALMES (Protest. und Kath., II., 177, Regensburg, 1845); PRAT (Histoire du P. Ribadeneira, 347 seq., Paris, 1862); ORTI Y LARA (La Inquisicion, Madrid, 1877); RODRIGO, GRISAR (see Innsbr. Zeitschr. für Kath. Theologie, 1879, p. 548 seq.) ; BAUER (loc. cit., 1881, p. 742 seq.); F. X. KRAUS (Alzogs Kirchengesch., II., 106, N. 3, 10th ed.); FUNK (Lit. Rundschau, 1880, p. 77 seq., and Kirchengesch., 360) ; BRÜCK (Kirchengesch., p. 533, 4th ed., and Kirchenlexikon, VI., 765 seq., 2nd ed.); and JULIO MELGARES MARIN (Procedimientos de la Inquisicion, 2 vols., Madrid, 1886, I., 82 seq.). This last, who is keeper of the Archives at Alcala, speaks with full knowledge of their contents. On the Protestant side, see HERZOG, VI., 740 seq., 2nd ed. (Benrath), and Allg. Ztg., 1878, p. 1122. Excessive regard for the authority of Ranke has prevented the general acceptance of the correct view of this question, and, in the case of Catholic publicists, it is hard to decide how far apologetic con-

been a State institution, a royal court of justice, there would have been no necessity for this. " A court which invariably hands over those whom it finds guilty to the secular arm for punishment cannot itself be a secular tribunal." It was precisely the ecclesiastical character ot the new Inquisition which made its judges decline to execute capital sentences, and follow the custom always observed by the ecclesiastical Inquisition of requesting that the prisoner " might be leniently dealt with," a formality prescribed by the Canon Law.*

The action of Sixtus IV., as General of his Order, would have led to the expectation that he would prove a reforming Pope. Admonitions and exhortations on this point were not wanting. Apart from those voices which clamoured for reform as a means for compassing other ends, many memorials reached Rome from abroad, animated by the purest motives, and urging the need of it on the Pope. The abuses in the Cistercian Order, particularly that regarding *commendams,* were thus brought under his notice.† In Rome itself zealous Friars went preaching penance and

---

siderations may have weighed in their adoption of the theory of a State institution. Apologetic ends must not, however, be allowed to influence the historian, whose sole aim should be truth.

* GRISAR, 572.

† I found this remarkable *Document in a collection in the University Library at Würzburg, M. ch. q. 15 (formerly belonging to the Convent of Ebrach), f. 239-43 : * "Ad beatissimum in Christo patrem et dominum nostrum dom. Sixtum divina providentia papam quartum . . . exhortatio de et super quibusdam gravaminibus ac injuriis per quosdam cardinales Romanae curiae . . . Cisterciensis sacri ordinis quibusdam abbatiis ac coenobiis violenter illatis per rev. dom. Johannem Cistercien. s. theol. profess. producta." Here, at f. 240b, we read : "Commenda est vipera matris ecclesie rumpens viscera, exterminans spirtualia et devorans temporalia secundum ethimologiam nominis . . ."; f. 241b : "Testis est fere tota Italia, testis est ipsa Lumpardia ubi vix ordinis sunt vestigia . . . Testis est Sabaudia (where a Convent had been

amendment. Many secular priests were equally earnest, warning their hearers that God would let the Turks come to Rome as a judgment for their sins. The Pope placed no obstacle in the way of such men, but, on the contrary, gave them every encouragement, remembering how valuable the preachers of penance had been in stemming the tide of depravity during the period of the Renaissance.* A secular priest, who had come to Rome in 1473 and spoken in this strain, was not only permitted by the Pope to preach everywhere, but also received material support.† Sixtus IV. sent the celebrated St. Jacopo della Marca in October, 1471, to pacify Ascoli, which was torn with hatred and factions.‡

A further proof that the Pope was favourably disposed towards ecclesiastical reform is furnished by a Bull, drawn up at his command, and containing minute provisions for the amendment of the Court. Abuses which had crept in among the Cardinals were relentlessly exposed in it, and rules laid down which, had they been carried into effect, would have completely changed the aspect of the Sacred

granted *in commendam* to a boy three years of age !). Testis est ipsa Burgundia ubi monasteria nobilia sunt ad devorandum exposita." The author is deeply attached to his Order, whose ruin he desires to arrest, by the help of the Pope.

* See, on this subject, the particulars we have given in our Vol. I., p. 36 *seq.*

† *Letter of J. Arcimboldus, dated Rome, 1473, Febr. 26, in the Arch. Veneto, 1888, fasc. 71, pp. 241–2. From VOLATERRANUS, 173, we learn that Sixtus IV. did not interfere when Father Paolo Toscanella preached in the strongest manner at the Papal Court against the Pope, his family, and the Cardinals.

‡ Jacobo de Marchia, ord. min. prof., dated Romae, 1471, Octob. 17 : *"Hortamur te charitate paterna, ut ad civitatem ipsam te conferre et in eadem gratia tibi assistente divina quidquid boni poteris operari velis." Lib. brev., 14, f. 1, Secret Archives of the Vatican.

College and of the whole Court.* Unhappily, this Bull was
never published. The cause of this must be sought not in
the remissness of the Pope, but in the opposition of those
who surrounded him.† His nephews well knew what the
consequences of reform would be to them. The Sacred
College also put obstacles in the way. A letter of Petrus
Barrocius, written in the year 1481, expressly states this,

* *Bull "Quoniam regnantium cura," s. d. in Cod. Vat., 3884,
f. 118–132b (Vat. Library. Thence in Arch. d. Soc. Rom., I., 479 *seq.*;
also in Cod. Vat., 3883; see HABERL in the Vierteljahrsschrift für
Musikwissenschaft, III., 242), and in Cod. 422, f. 239 *seq.*, of the State
Library, Munich. Extracts from this Reformatio Sixti IV. are also
to be found in Cod. Capponi, LXXXII., N. 26, National Library,
Florence.

† It cannot, however, be denied that Sixtus IV. ought to have done
far more than he did for the cause of reform. Even if the stormy
character of his reign be taken into account, that which was actually
accomplished in the way of remedying the sad state of things was far
too little. It related principally to the Religious Orders; see
GROTEFEND, I., 22 ; MOHR, Regesten, I., 98 ; Jahrb. f. Schweiz. Gesch.,
IX., 75; MAZZUCHELLI, II., 3, 1863; WADDING, *passim*; Bull.
praed., III., 526, 585, 588 ; Chroniche di S. Francesco, III., 204 ; and
*Brief to episc. Acien., dated Rome, 1480, Oct. 1 ; Lib. brev., 13, f. 87,
Secret Archives of the Vatican ; *ibid.*, f. 190 : Abbati monasterii S.
Pauli de urbe, dated Rome, 1480, Nov. 22 (Reform of the Convent
at Todi); *ibid.*, f. 221, a Brief for Hermann. elect. et confirmat.
Colonien., &c., dated Rome, 1480, Dec. 6, urging the removal of abuses.
Lib. brev., 14, f.15b and 32 (Monastic Reform in Ireland and Sicily).
See also RAYNALDUS, ad an. 1483, N. 36 (Reform of the Clergy in
France). Of even more importance than these isolated Decrees is the
Constitution of the 22nd May, 1472, against simony ; see Bull., 208–9
Regarding a measure of reform attempted by Sixtus IV., in opposition
to the Election Capitulation in the Bishopric of Bamberg, see Quellen-
sammlung f. Fränk. Gesch., IV., LXXXXI. *seq.* The above-mentioned
Orders, confirmed by Sixtus IV., were also appointed to labour for
reform. His appointment of good Bishops is recorded by MAS-
LATRIE in the Rev. des Quest. Hist., 1878, Avril, p. 570 *seq.*

while giving a detailed account of the corruption of the Court. "Sixtus IV.," he writes, "wished to set his face against these practices, and appointed a Commission of reform, but the majority of the Cardinals negatived the suggestions of the better disposed."* This could not have happened but for the unfortunate changes which had taken place in the members composing the Sacred College.

Torquemada and Carvajal, two unflinching champions of ecclesiastical purity, had died during the pontificate of Paul II.† In the time of Sixtus IV., many of the elder Cardinals had gone to their reward. Bessarion, amongst others, in 1472, and, on the 21st December in the following year, at Verona, the brave Forteguerri.‡ Three other admirable members of the Sacred College died in 1476: Roverella (3rd May), Calandrini (24th July §), and Agnifilus (9th November). On the 11th August, 1477, Latino Orsino, and ‖ in 1478, the austere Capranica passed away ; Eroli and Amma-

---

* Letter of P. Barrocius to Card. Petrus Fuscarenus, dated Belluno, 1481, Aug. 13, in Anecdota Veneta, ed. Contarini, p. 202. With the description given by Barrocius, compare those of Card. AMMANATI, Epist., 272 (820 *seq.*, Frankfort ed.); of B. FULGOSUS, II., c. 1 ; and Savonarola (see VILLARI, I., 15 *seq.*, 19 *seq.*). I shall revert to this last in the Introduction to my next Volume.

† See *supra*, p. 145. Torquemada died on the 26th Sept., 1468.

‡ These dates are taken from the *Acta Consist. of the Secret Archives of the Vatican. Regarding Forteguerri's death, see also N. DELLA TUCCIA, 105.

§ See FALEONI, 511, and SFORZA, Nicolaus V., translated by Horak, 134 (Innsbruck, 1887).

‖ The important post of Camerlengo was then conferred on d'Estouteville (in a Letter of the 12th August, 1477, he announces to the Florentines his nomination, which had taken place on that day ; see State Archives, Florence, X.-II.-25, f. 124b), and, after his death, on Raffaello Sansoni Riario ; see MARINI, II., 245 ; and *Div. Sixti IV., 1482-4, f. 135. State Archives, Rome.

nati in 1479 (2nd April and 10th September).* The loss
of these representatives of better days was not adequately
repaired ; during the thirteen years of Sixtus IV.'s pontificate, eight creations of Cardinals took place, and thirty-four
prelates, twenty-two of whom were Italians, were raised to the
purple ; † but, in the majority of cases, these appointments
were not made from purely ecclesiastical motives, and the
worldly-minded Cardinals, such as Jouffroy (†1473), Alain
(†1474, May 3), d'Estouteville (†1483, January 22 ‡), and
Gonzaga (†1483, October 21), who died in the time of this
Pope, were but too soon succeeded by others of like character.

The first creation of Cardinals by Sixtus IV. was much
to be deplored. On this occasion his two young nephews,
one of whom was utterly unworthy of this dignity, were
raised to the purple. In the second creation, on the 7th
May, 1473,§ the wishes of temporal Princes had predominant
weight. The Archbishop of Arles, Philippe de Lévis, had
been recommended for the dignity by King René, and
Giovanni Arcimboldo, Bishop of Novara, by the Duke of
Milan. The selection of Philibert Hugonet, Bishop of Macon,
seems to have been due to the Duke of Burgundy's influ-

---

* For an account of Ammanati's last years, his death, and his tomb,
see PAULI'S rare monograph, 91–8.

† Of the twenty-two Italians, six were Romans. According to the
common account, Sixtus IV. nominated thirty-five Cardinals ; but the
elevation of Theobald of Luxemburg (see Lettres de Louis XI., III.,
107) is very uncertain ; according to FRIZON, 523–4, Theobald was
designatus, but not *publicatus*. The *Acta Consist. and other authorities say nothing about him, and I have therefore thought it right
to exclude him from the number.

‡ This date is given by the *Acta Consist., Secret Archives of the
Vatican, while BORGIA, Velletri, 382, maintains the 22nd Febr.

§ See *Acta Consist. of the Secret Archives of the Vatican, and
*Letter of Oldroandus de Bonafrugiis, dated Rome, 1473, May 10.
Gonzaga Archives.

ence.* As to Stefano Nardini, Sixtus IV. himself said of him that he had made him a Cardinal, in order to encourage the members of the Court to emulate his zeal and industry.†

If Nardini, the founder of a College for poor students,‡ was worthy of a place in the Senate of the Church, the same cannot be said of the two other Italians who received the purple on the 7th May, 1473. Giov. Batista Cybò had passed a frivolous youth, and the wealthy Antonio Giacomo Venier was living in a style of princely luxury The two Spaniards, Auxias de Podio and Pedro Gonzalez de Mendoza, Archbishop of Toledo,§ created at this time, were, however, excellent men.

More than three years elapsed before Sixtus IV. again added to the numbers of the Sacred College. An Ambassador, then living in Rome, speaks of violent disputes between the Cardinals and the Pope, who, notwithstanding all his efforts, only succeeded in accomplishing the creation of five new Cardinals.‖ This took place on the 18th December, 1476.¶ Among those promoted, but one, G. B. Mellini,

---

* That the nomination of Ph. Hugonet was due to the Duke of Burgundy's influence is evident from LJUBIČ, Dispacci, &c., 33.

† Letter to Louis XI. of the 22nd Aug., 1473. (State Archives, Milan.) See *supra*, p. 321.

‡ ARMELLINI, 645 ; FORCELLA, XIII., 171.

§ Details regarding the eight Cardinals created in 1473 may be found in CIACONIUS, III., 47 *seq.* ; CARDELLA, III., 182 *seq.* ; CONTELORIUS, 69 ; FRIZON, 519 *seq.* See also DOMINICUS, De dignit. Episcop., 33. The titles were, according to the *Acta Consist., conferred on the 17th May.

‖ *Letters of J. P. Arrivabene, dated Rome, 1476, Dec. 10, 18, and 22. Gonzaga Archives, Mantua.

¶ INFESSURA, 1145, is mistaken in saying the 17th December ; the Cron. Rom., 34, rightly gives the 18th as the date ; see also *Acta Consist., Secret Archives of the Vatican. The Cardinals were published on the 20th ; see CONTELORIUS, 71.

Bishop of Urbino, was an Italian ; two, Charles de Bourbon and Pierre de Foix, were French ; one, Pedro Ferrici, was a Spaniard ; and one, Giorgio da Costa, Archbishop of Lisbon, a Portuguese. This last died in 1503, at the age of 100, one of the wealthiest Princes of the Church of his time.*

In the following March we hear of negotiations for the nomination of new Cardinals. On the 24th of that month, Sixtus IV. proposed in Consistory, John of Aragon (a son of Ferrante),† Ascanio Maria Sforza, Pietro Foscari, and his own two nephews, Cristoforo della Rovere and Girolamo Basso della Rovere.‡ The preliminary discussions lasted all through the summer,§ ending on the 10th December, 1477, in a complete victory for Sixtus IV. On that day all those whom he had proposed were, with the exception of Ascanio Sforza, raised to the purple, and to their number were added the Minorite, Gabriel Rangone,|| George Hesler, who had rendered important service to the house of Habsburg,¶ and, finally, a third nephew of the Pope's, Raffaello

* REUMONT, III., 1, 262 ; CIACONIUS, III., 55 *seq.* ; CARDELLA, III., 192 *seq.* ; FRIZON, 524 *seq.* Concerning P. de Foix, see MARTÈNE, II., 1517, 1530, and MIGNE, 921.

† Giorn. Nap., 1138 ; MAZZUCHELLI, I., 2, 927.

‡ I find this fact, which has hitherto been unknown, in a *Letter of Card. Gonzaga, dated Rome, 1477, March 24. Regarding the Pope's nephews, he says : " El castellano de S. Agnolo qui el qual è arcivescovo de Tarantaso gientilhomo piamontese dicto de la Rovere buon dottore e prelato assai commendato e lo vescovo di Recanati nepote d. S. Sᵗᵃ ex sorore." Gonzaga Archives, Mantua.

§ *Letter of Card. Gonzaga, dated Rome, 1477, June 18, *loc. cit.*

|| He had been recommended for elevation by the King of Hungary as early as the year 1475 ; see Mon. Hung., II., 295.

¶ Frederick III. had for some years actively sought to procure Hesler's elevation (regarding this prelate's life, see WÜRDTWEIN, Nov. subsid., XIII., 63 *seq.*), and was expecting it in March, 1474 ; see Mon. Habsb., I., 329 *seq.* Also the Brief of 1475 in MARTÈNE, II., 1497-8, and a Despatch of 1476 in GINGINS LA SARRA, I., 288. In

Sansoni Riario.* These numerous additions to the Sacred College gave occasion for the creation of a new Title, the first which had for several centuries taken place. Sixtus IV. gave Pietro Foscari, St. Nicholas at the Colosseum (S. Nicolaus inter imagines)† as his titular Church.

If the simultaneous elevation of three Papal nephews was in itself an extraordinary proceeding, Raffaello Sansoni's age—he was only seventeen—did not tend to diminish its exceptional character! The spiritual element was no better represented by him than by Cristoforo and Giuliano della Rovere. "Though presenting many radical differences in personal character, they were all great lords with essentially worldly interests. The fourth of the Pope's nephews on the sisters' side, Girolamo Basso della Rovere, was a prelate of blameless life, who never abused the favour of his uncle or of his cousin, Pope Julius II."‡ Cristoforo della Rovere dying on the 1st February, 1478,§ Sixtus IV., on the 10th of

February, 1477, the dignity had been promised to Hesler (see ENNEN, III., 530), Sixtus IV. then making the provision that, in the event of his own death before Hesler's publication, the latter should be reckoned among the Cardinals ; see RAYNALDUS, ad an. 1477, N. 11. Hesler was not published until December ; see *Acta Consist., f. 53, Secret Archives of the Vatican. On the 13th January, 1478, Sixtus IV. sent him the Red Hat ; Mon. Habsb., III., 447. Hesler came, for the first time, to Rome on the 21st January, 1480 ; on the 28th January took place the ceremony of the opening of the Mouth ; on the 1st of May he started on his homeward journey ; see *Acta Consist., f. 59, *loc. cit.*

* See CIACONIUS, III., 63 *seq.* ; CARDELLA, III., 202 *seq.* ; CONTE-LORIUS, 72, who repeatedly corrects Ciaconius.

† See ARMELLINI, Chiese, 23 ; PHILLIPS, VI., 224 ; and PAN-VINIUS, De episc. titulis, &c., 20 ; *ibid.*, 28 and 42, concerning other innovations made by Sixtus IV. connected with this subject. For an account of P. Foscari, see also OROLOGIO, Canonici di Padova, 82 *seq.*

‡ REUMONT, III., 1, 261.

§ *Acta Consist., Secret Archives of the Vatican. TOSI, Plate 126, gives an engraving of Domenico's beautiful grave in S. Maria del Popolo.

that month, received his brother, Domenico, into the Senate
of the Church.   He "built for himself the much-admired
Palace on the Piazza Scossacavalli, and a villa in the neighbourhood of Ponte Molle, without the City, which was often
visited by Sixtus IV.   He also built the Chapel in Sta Maria
del Popolo, which, like his Palace, was adorned with paintings from the hand of Pinturicchio.   The little town of
Montefiascone owes to him its principal church, and his
native city, Turin, its Cathedral, which, being the work of
Meo dal Caprino, bears a striking resemblance to the churches
built by the same architect in Rome.   This member of the
Rovere family had no merit in the way of talent to recom-
mend him.   He had but little literary culture, and was not
either learned or naturally quick-witted.   It was the grace
of God, his good reputation, and his true and loyal disposition which brought him to the front." *

These last nominations, together with the increasing influence of the Pope's nephews, who came in greater numbers
to Rome at this time, gave to the Court a more and more
worldly character.   The crafty Girolamo Riario, who was
made Burgher of the City and a member of the Roman
nobility in the year 1477, and, in 1480, Commander-in-Chief
of the Church, surpassed all the Cardinals in influence.†
The whole demeanour of this upstart was in keeping
with his extravagant expenditure on all festal occasions.
He took pride in eclipsing all the Cardinals, even those who

---

* SCHMARSOW, 145 ; MÜNTZ, III., 37–8 ; ADINOLFI, Portica, 144
seq., 251 *seq.*

† INFESSURA, 1147.   Regarding Riario's influence, see, besides the
passages from different authorities collected by SCHMARSOW, 367,
the Florentine Ambassadorial Despatches in Appendix, N. 60 and
61 ; GRASSO, 332 ; and the treatise of DE LA NICOLLIÈRE-TEIJEIRO,
Institution du comte palatin de Latran en faveur de Jérôme Riario,
&c., Nantes, 1886.

were of princely birth.* The purely worldly tendencies
displayed, especially by Rodrigo Borgia, Francesco Gonzaga
and d'Estouteville, among the older Cardinals, the frequent
admission of others of similar disposition into the Sacred
College, and the removal by death of so many of those who
were truly devoted to the interests of the Church, led pious
and earnest men like F. Piccolomini and Marco Barbo to
absent themselves as much as possible from Rome. Giovanni Michiel and Pietro Foscari, the kinsmen and countrymen of the latter, were essentially Venetian patricians, and
found the new order of things by no means uncongenial.†

The next creation still further promoted the worldliness
and pomp of the Sacred College. It took place on the 15th
May, 1480,‡ and was, in many respects, an important one.
With hardly an exception those raised to the purple were
of high birth : they were, Paolo Fregoso, Ferry de Clugny,§
Cosimo Orsini de' Migliorati, the "excellent Giovan Battista
Savelli, whose elevation had, up to this time, been hindered
by the Orsini party. He had given proof of his abilities in
several Legations, was endowed with an enterprising spirit
and a talent for organisation ; he had been designated for the
cardinalate by Paul II., but the sudden death of that Pope,
and the influence of Latino Orsini with Sixtus IV. had so
far kept him from that dignity. In conjunction with him,
Giovanni Colonna was also created, and the seeds of party

---

* See Jac. Volaterranus, 104. For a description of Girolamo's
Palace, see Schmarsow, 116, and Adinolfi, La torre de' Sanguigni,
49 seq. (Roma, 1863).

† See Schmarsow, 144 seq., and also Knebel, II., 392.

‡ Not the 5th May, as Ciaconius, III., 77 ; Cardella, III., 215 ;
and Contelorius have stated, but die lunae XV. Maii, according to
the *Acta Consist., f. 59, Secret Archives of the Vatican.

§ Frizon, 527 seq., speaks of him as a distinguished man. See also
Bibl. de l'École des Chartes, 1881, p. 444 seq., and Migne, 688 seq.

strife introduced into the Sacred College; for Giuliano della
Rovere was a friend of the Colonna and the Savelli, while
Girolamo Riario's interests, as a temporal lord, drew him to
associate himself more and more closely with the Orsini." *

The next creation, on the 15th November, 1483, did yet
more to increase the influence of the great Roman families
in the Sacred College, Giovanni Conti of Valmontone and
Battista Orsini being then raised to the purple. The same
dignity was conferred on Juan Moles, a Spaniard, on the
Archbishop of Tours, Elie de Bourdeilles, and on Giovanni
Giacomo Sclafenati, Bishop of Parma, who was but twenty-
three years of age.† The choice of this youthful Prelate
gave occasion to much unfavourable comment, and completely nullified the good impression which the simultaneous
elevation of the saintly Bourdeilles might have produced.‡
A yet greater error was committed in the promotion of
Ascanio Maria Sforza (March, 1484) dictated as it was
by worldly and political motives.§

* SCHMARSOW, 147.

† *Acta Consist., f. 67, Secret Archives of the Vatican. CIACONIUS,
III., 81 seq. CARDELLA, III., 221, is uncertain as to the date which
the diligent CONTELORIUS, 76, gives correctly. See also, in relation
to Sixtus IV. and the Orsini Cardinals, Lett. eccles. di P. Sarnelli,
332 (Naples, 1686).

‡ Stefano Guidotto, in the Postscript to a *Letter, dated Rome, 1483,
Nov. 18, speaks of Bourdeilles as "sanctissimus et observandissimus
s. religionis." (Gonzaga Archives, Mantua.) See also the statements
of FRIZON, 529 seq., and MIGNE, 588.

§ According to CONTELORIUS, 76, Ascanio's nomination took place
on the 6th March "in secreto consistorio et die 17 fuit publicatus."
The *Acta Consist. of the Secret Archives of the Vatican mention only
the latter event. Stefano Guidotto says, in a *Letter, dated Rome,
1483, March 16, that it was believed that Ascanio would be published
as a Cardinal on the following day. (Gonzaga Archives.) In the Lib.
brev., 16 A, of the Secret Archives of the Vatican, I found, f. 60, a
*Brief to Ascanio, dated 1484, March 17, informing him of his nomina-

When we consider that it was this man, in conjunction with Cardinals Riario, Orsini, Colonna, Sclafenati, and Savelli (all of them admitted by Sixtus IV. into the Senate of the Church), who in 1492 carried the election of Rodrigo Borgia, we are naturally inclined to form an unfavourable opinion of this Pope, from whom so much had been hoped.*

Nevertheless, an impartial study of history must lead us to protest against the picture drawn by Infessura of Sixtus IV. Infessura was a violent partisan of his deadly enemies, the Colonna. He blesses the day when God delivered his people out of the hand of this "most profligate and unjust of Kings." Neither fear of God nor love for his people, no spark of kindness or good-will, according to this author, were to be found in him ; nothing but sensuality, avarice, love of show and vain-glory. After this tremendous general accusation he proceeds to enter into details. He cannot say a good word anywhere of Sixtus IV. It is plain from this, and from the violence of his language, that we have here a collection of everything that was reported to the Pope's disadvantage in Rome, at a time when a strong opposition to his person and to his Court prevailed there.†

tion as Cardinal, which had taken place on that day, "de unanimi consilio et consensu" of the Cardinals. From a *Letter of Cardinal Arcimboldus to the Duke of Milan, dated Rome, 1476, Dec. 22, it appears that great efforts had at that time been made to procure Ascanio's elevation. (State Archives, Milan.) See also *supra*, p. 409. Regarding A. Sforza, see also BÜCHI'S work, Albrecht von Bonstetten (Frauenfeld, 1889), which has just come under my notice, especially pp. 35 and 38. A request addressed by Richard III. to Sixtus IV., with regard to the appointment of a Cardinal, is mentioned in RYMER, XII., 216.

* Regarding these hopes, see JORDAN, Podiebrad, 358-9. Of the twenty-three Cardinals who composed the Conclave of 1492, fourteen had been created by Sixtus IV.

† This is the opinion of SCHRÖCKH, Kirchengesch., XXXII., 364

As regards Infessura's most serious accusation, that of gross immorality, in that corrupt age such a charge was but too frequently flung at any enemy.   Later on, the austere Adrian VI. was himself a victim to the slanderous tongues of the Renaissance age.   Things had come to such a pass that "no one could escape calumny, and the most exemplary virtue provoked the worst detraction."* Atrocious crimes of this kind are not proved by the malignant gossip collected by a writer so open to suspicion as Infessura.† No trustworthy contemporary, not one of the

As opposed to BROSCH, who (Julius II., p. 29) inclines to Infessura's view, and speaks of Sixtus IV. as "a man without truth and faith, without shame and conscience," we may mention not only HEFELE-HERGENRÖTHER, VIII., 268, but also SCHMARSOW, 262, who express themselves in very different terms, and maintain that Sixtus was deeply penetrated with a sense of the sacredness of his priestly office. CREIGHTON, III., 115, also writes : "Infessura . . . has blackened his memory with accusations of the foulest crimes. These charges, made by a partisan who writes with undisguised animosity, must be dismissed as unproved."

* BURCKHARDT, Cultur, I., 187 *seq.*, 3rd ed. Even in the lifetime of Pius II. an Invective appeared from the pen of an offended Humanist (probably Filelfo), making the most infamous accusations against him, many of which were quite absurd ; see VOIGT, Pius II., III., 636. Here a charge similar to that made by Infessura against Sixtus IV. is not wanting, yet the moral life of Pius II. as Pope was blameless.

† The passage in question, with "ut fertur vulgo, ut dicunt quidam, ut dicitur," is only in Eccard's edition, 1939. Muratori omits it, deeming it too disgraceful to place before the eyes of respectable men ; referring any one who finds pleasure in such filth to Eccard (MURATORI, III., 2, 1110). Even opponents of the Papacy have protested against these accusations. GREGOROVIUS, VII., 268, 2nd ed., writes : "The text of Infessura, as given in Eccard, brings terrible charges against the moral character of Sixtus ; these are certainly exaggerated." SYBEL'S Zeitschr., N. F., XXI., 358, admits that Gregorovius is not prepossessed in favour of Sixtus IV. In his third edition Gregorovius

numerous Ambassadors, who reported everything that took place in Rome with scrupulous accuracy, has a word to say on the subject ; one indeed of these Envoys, immediately after the election of Sixtus IV., extols his blameless and pious manner of life.* Whatever faults Sixtus IV. may have committed as Pope, there was no change for the worse in regard to morals or religion. The fact that he chose as his confessor the blessed Amadeus of Portugal, a man of extraordinary sanctity and mortification, is in itself a proof of this.† We have ample evidence to prove that Sixtus IV. discharged his religious duties zealously and seriously, and venerated his holy patrons, St. Francis and the Blessed Virgin, with the same devotion which he had manifested before his elevation. Though suffering acutely from gout, he never allowed this to prevent him from assisting at the solemn Easter Mass. " With touching perseverance the feeble old man made his pilgrimages of devotion to the Churches of Sta Maria del Popolo and della Pace, which he had built in honour of the Blessed Virgin."‡ Sixtus IV. must indeed have been a consummate hypocrite if his private life was infamous while he appeared so fervent a client of the most Pure Mother of God.§

has struck out the last four words of our quotation, but he produces no evidence in support of Infessura's statements.

* *Despatch of Nicodemus of the 9th Aug., 1471. Appendix, N. 44.

† Regarding Amadeus, see AA. SS. Aug. II., 572 *seq.* ; Freib. Kirchen-lexikon, I., 669, 2nd ed.

‡ JACOBUS VOLATERRANUS, 131 ; SCHMARSOW, 263.

§ See my observations in the Hist. Jahrbuch, VIII., 729, against SCHMARSOW, 4, 261, 327. These last passages seemed, not only to me, but to other students, to prove that the worthy biographer of Melozzo looked upon Infessura's charges as well-founded. I am glad now to be able to say that Professor Schmarsow, in writing to me (1887, Oct. 26), protested against the idea that he adopted Infessura's shocking view of the life of Sixtus IV. In the further course of our

Infessura's other charges against Sixtus IV. must equally be either dismissed or modified. An impartial student admits that "the historian who represents this Pope as avaricious and greedy of gain, double-faced in his policy, insatiable in his lust of conquest, passionate and tyrannical in character, without taking into account how much in his conduct is entirely, or in great measure, due to Girolamo Riario, is guilty of a serious error. History belies herself when she paints her subject in a glare of light, oblivious of the deep contrasting shadows."*

Among the darkest of these shadows is that unfortunate attachment to his nephews, in spite of his many estimable qualities, which entangled him in a labyrinth of political complications, from which at last no honourable exit was possible.† The difficulties into which this deplorable weakness for his relatives led Sixtus IV. also had other most injurious effects. "In order to procure the required resources, it was necessary to resort to all sorts of financial expedients, which resulted in a terrible amount of venality and corruption."‡ Even before the time of this Pope there

correspondence the Professor wrote (1887, Nov. 11): "I am willing to accept what you say against my words, only you must not make me appear to be a blind follower of Infessura ;" and "with the kind of documents that are before us, it would hardly be possible to prove the charge of immorality." If LEA, III., 639, still maintains the truth of Infessura's accusations, we may understand it, considering the standpoint of the author of "An Historical Sketch of Sacerdotal Celibacy."

* SCHMARSOW, 260. See CIPOLLA, 626. An example of the manner in which Sixtus IV. is made responsible for the sins of his nephews is given in WOLF, Lect., I., 952.

† "Le népotisme," writes RIO, II., 66, "fut la grande plaie, la plaie honteuse du règne de Sixte IV."

‡ ROHRBACHER-KNÖPFLER, 255. See BURCKHARDT, I., 150, 3rd ed. Both refer to the melancholy picture drawn by BAPT. MANTUANUS, De calamitatibus temp. l. III., Op. ed. Paris., 1507, f. 302b.

existed offices which could be purchased, and to which were
attached certain sources of income.   The revenues of these
offices are said to have amounted in 1471 to something like
100,000 scudi.*   When the danger from Turkey made the
want of money more and more pressing, Sixtus IV. further
added to this crowd of officials.   Four Colleges, those of the
"Stipulatori, Giannizzeri, Stradiatori, and Mamelucchi," were
revived by him.†   While the expense of every Bull or Brief
went on constantly growing, as the host of officials connected
with it increased, the Annates were again raised,‡ and a
new tax (Compositio), to be paid to the Dataria in Rome §
on collation to a benefice, imposed.   Besides this there was
the so-called "Quindennien," a tax to be paid every fifteen

---

* See RANKE, Päpste, I., 262, 6th ed.   I found also in the Ambrosian
Library, Milan, Cod. A., 13 Inf., the account of *Gli ufficii piu antichi,
cited above by Ranke from Cod. N., II., 50, of the Chigi Library.
REUMONT, III., 1, 283, again repeats the erroneous statement that
the creation of ecclesiastical posts in the Roman Court began with
Sixtus IV.

† MORONI, VII., 186, LXVII., 172 ; BANGEN, 447.   The "Mamelucchi" were abolished by Innocent VIII.

‡ See KIRSCH, Die Annaten und ihre Verwaltung in der zweiten
Hälfte des 15 Jahrhunderts in the Hist. Jahrbuch, IX., 307.   The
Manuscript of the National Library, Rome (F. XLVI.–1471, MS.
Sessorian, 46), here mentioned, is not so little known as Kirsch
imagines it to be, for the Anz. f. Schweiz. Gesch., N. F., 1887,
18, Nos. 2 and 3, gives extracts from it.   Regarding a list of
Annates in the Library of S. Pietro in Vincoli, see DUDIK, I.,
66 seq.

§ The extreme party of Reform looked on the Compositio as a
pretium collationis, and pronounced it simoniacal ; a more moderate
party, on the other hand, considered it as a stipendium attached to the
benefice itself ; see Sixti IV. S. P. ad Paulum III., compositionum
defensio, ed. Dittrich, Braunsberg, 1883.   DITTRICH, Regesten Contarini's, 279 seq. (Braunsb., 1881).   See also DÖLLINGER, Beiträge,
III., 218, and DITTRICH, Contarini, 381 seq. (B., 1885).

years by all benefices subject to Annates, which dated from the reign of Paul II.*

The venality of many of the Court officials, and the excessive exercise of the Pope's rights in the matter of taxation, occasioned, especially in Germany, a feeling of deep dissatisfaction with the Holy See, which did more than has generally been supposed to pave the way for the subsequent apostacy. When the great assembly of the clergy of the Metropolitan Churches of Mayence, Trèves, and Cologne was held at Coblence, in the year 1479, numerous complaints were formulated for transmission to the Pope. Their principal subjects were the non-observance of the Concordat, unfair taxation, the great privileges of the Mendicant Orders, and the number of exemptions.†

If, notwithstanding the many imposts levied, the Papal Treasury was almost always in difficulties, this was due, not only to extravagant expenses, but also to defective financial administration. Serious and growing negligence is to be observed in the manner in which the accounts of the Apostolic Treasury were kept. The monthly audit had become little more than a formality. The salaries of the officials were often five or eight months, or even a year or two, in arrear. The deficit, which increased month by month, necessitated constant loans.‡ Under such circumstances we cannot be surprised to learn that Sixtus IV.

* See *supra*, p. 106.

† Further particulars will be found in GEBHARDT, 53 *seq*. The gravamen of 1479 has been often printed ; as, for example, by LEIBNIZ, Cod. I., 439 *seq*., and GEORGI, Grav. coll., 254.

‡ Everything was mortgaged, even, on one occasion, the Registrum Bullarum, upon which Petrus Mellinus lent 1000 flor. auri. It was redeemed on the 20th Aug., 1482. This fact has been kindly communicated to me by Dr. Gottlob, whose book on the Cam. Ap. will throw much light on these matters from authentic sources. Regarding mortgages, see also REUMONT, III., 1, 283.

at his death left behind him debts to the amount of 150,000 ducats.*

This financial pressure led to a considerable augmentation of indirect taxation in the States of the Church, and also to the diversion of the revenues of the Roman University to other objects, and the imposition of taxes on the salaries of the Professors. As Infessura, who was a member of the teaching staff of this University, speaks with peculiar bitterness of the injury inflicted on it by Sixtus IV.,† there is ground for supposing him to have been among the sufferers.‡ In this circumstance, and in Infessura's alliance

---

* MÜNTZ, III., 64-5.

† Infessura in ECCARD, 1941.

‡ See TOMMASINI, Il diario di Stef. Infessura, in Arch. d. Soc. Rom., XI., 494-5. In this study, the prelude to a much needed critical edition of Infessura's Diarium, the various MSS. are indicated and described, and valuable information regarding the family and the life of Infessura is furnished. Tommasini's work as critic is, however, incomplete, and coloured by partiality. Even the enumeration of critical judgments of the chronicler is, with all its apparent minuteness, very imperfect. Tommasini ignores the opinions of SCHRÖCKH ; HERGENRÖTHER (see *supra*, p. 416) ; CHRISTOPHE, II., 295 *seq.* ; BRÜCK, 450 ; Civ. Catt., 1868, I., 147 ; HAGEN, Die Papstwahlen von 1484 und 1492, p. 2, &c. He even thinks it well completely to omit the important observations of SCHMARSOW (416, note †, to which may be added Schmarsow's words, p. 196, where, in speaking of the death of R. Malatesta, he says : " Infessura alone directs suspicion to the Pope, on whom, without examination, he casts the chief responsibility of Girolamo's crime"), as well as the opinion expressed in REUMONT'S Lorenzo, II., 456, 2nd ed. (" Infessura exaggerates the faults of the Pope with regard to truth "). It is even more extraordinary that the passage from REUMONT, III., 1, 367, is not given completely in this special study. Here Reumont, in the first place, points out that Infessura's special value as an authority begins with the time of Martin V. and Eugenius IV., and continues during the last three pontificates of the Century down to the year 1494, and then proceeds to observe : " This genuine representative of undying Roman slander has provided those who delight

with the Colonna and his Republican sentiments, may be found the motive of the unmeasured reproaches heaped

in scandalous gossip with materials as rich as, if not richer than, those furnished by the well-known J. Burchard of Strasburg, Bishop of Orte and Master of Ceremonies of the Papal Chapel from the days of Innocent VIII. to those of Julius II. ; but a little experience of the manner in which, even up to the present day, truth and falsehood are mingled in the history of Rome, and cartloads of fabrication accredited by a few ounces of fact, will guard us against taking such narrators absolutely at their word, however evil the age may be. The Roman Liutprand of the 15th Century demands the same severely critical examination as that of the 10th." Tommasini is also silent regarding the manifest falsehoods of Infessura, of which Gregorovius has given proof (L. BORGIA, 11–12, Stuttgart, 1874), and the misrepresentation exposed by FRANTZ, 481 *seq.*, 483 *seq.* In the face of such proceedings, Tommasini's reiterated professions of impartiality can deceive no one ; his purpose is clear : Infessura must, at any cost, be raised to the position of a thoroughly trustworthy authority. As yet he has been unsuccessful in this attempt ; it remains to be seen whether in his edition he can adduce anything further in support of his thesis. It is unjust to say that I represent Infessura as a "violento avversario della dominazione papale" (TOMMASINI, p. 488) ; Infessura himself does far more to represent himself in that light by the praises which he bestows on a murderer like Porcaro (see our Vol. II., p. 233, note †), and therefore even Gregorovius describes him as "an enemy of the Papal power." At p. 482, Tommasini himself admits "l'amore dell' Infessura alla liberta communale di Roma," as well as his sympathies with the Colonna and the Republican party (see pp. 526, 547, 554), but he fails to draw the evident conclusion from these admissions. Infessura's position as a partisan necessarily incapacitates him from forming an impartial judgment in regard to Sixtus IV. It is really time that the name of a chronicler who admits lampoons as serious evidence in his work, should be struck out of the list of impartial narrators of history (see TOMMASINI, 550). The writings of such an author are only to be employed with the greatest prudence, and after the most critical investigation. Tommasini, however, has not thought an examination, such as we have made, of Infessura's individual charges against Sixtus IV. necessary. He has saved himself much

upon Sixtus IV., the friend of the Orsini, and the advocate of strongly monarchical ideas. Violent personal feeling, arising from the position of the author, and perhaps from his unpleasant experiences, is here openly expressed.* We have a repetition of the relations which existed between Platina and Paul II. Platina is not an impartial and truthful authority in regard to the builder of the Palace of S. Marco, neither is Infessura to be trusted when he tells the history of the head of the Rovere family.

trouble by not entering into the most serious accusations, or those which some critics have proved to be absurd. On the other hand, he brings evidence to shew that, in matters of secondary importance, Infessura's charges are true ; see p. 559. Here, however, he is not very fortunate, for the evidence in regard to the purchase of corn (560) by no means proves any usurious dealing on the part of Sixtus IV. The justice of Reumont's remarks on the mixture of truth and falsehood in Roman slander is here exemplified. The Sienese Despatches, published by TOMMASINI, p. 606 *seq.*, in a general way confirm Infessura's picture of the state of things from 1482, but they do not contain a syllable in support of his shocking accusations against the Pope. It would certainly be an error totally to reject Infessura's testimony (as SANESI, St. Porcaro, p. 108, Pistoja, 1887, seems to suppose me to do. I will here observe, as a curious fact, that Sanesi himself says he has "esaminato soltanto poche pagine" of Infessura), but it is a still greater error to accept it unconditionally, especially when, as in regard to Sixtus IV., it is dictated by passion, and its exaggeration is patent. That Infessura is here as unfair as P. DELLA MASTRO, whose point of view is most narrowly Roman (Cron. Rom., 37), has already been declared by an authority like MÜNTZ, III., 8. As TOMMASINI, p. 577, cites an article written by Burckhardt thirty-seven years ago, he will be interested to hear that Burckhardt's opinion is now different. The worthy author of the Cultur der Renaissance, writing to me on the 12th May, 1889, said : "I am now aware that I have set far too much value on Eccard's Infessura, and other muddy sources, and been too much guided by them."

* This observation applies to the Florentine historian ; see *infra*, p. 433.

Many abuses no doubt existed in the Rome of those days, and Girolamo Riario was certainly guilty of many unbecoming actions, but Infessura is not justified in accusing Sixtus IV. of usurious speculation in corn for his own covetous purposes.   The Pope's great care for Rome of itself contradicts this statement, and witnesses above suspicion testify to the relatively favourable condition of the inhabitants of the States of the Church under Sixtus IV., excepting, of course, in times of war.   Philippe de Commines, who went to Rome with no favourable prejudices, after he had become personally acquainted with the state of things there, expressed his opinion that the Popes were wise and well advised, and that, but for the strife between the Colonna and the Orsini, the dwellers in the States of the Church would be the happiest people on earth, inasmuch as they paid no poll-tax and practically hardly any other taxes.*   If this last statement is to be taken with some reservation, it is still certain that " hardly anywhere, on an average, was the taxation so low as in the States of the Church."†

* Mém. (ed. Lenglet), II., 367 ; KERVYN DE LETTENHOVE, I., 184.

† REUMONT, III., 1, 279.   "In his civil administration," says SCHMARSOW, 262, "Sixtus IV. manifests extraordinary talents.   No one so well understands how to ensure the accomplishment of his orders ; he foresees everything, directs everything, takes account of everything beforehand : for he is well aware that quite as much prudence and determination are necessary in dealing with the insubordination of the starving Roman populace as in the task of bridling the Barons.   Everything is thought out thoroughly and in detail.   If we find liberal measures restricted by conditions which almost nullify their effect, we must recognise in this the hand of a revising financial adviser.   Parsimony had no place in the nature of Sixtus IV." Such is the judgment of an impartial investigator.   In his article on Infessura, where Tommasini, in addition to all this author's other charges, also maintains those of avarice and misgovern-

The history of the speculations in corn of Sixtus IV., about
which Infessura has so much to say, is actually that the
magistrate of the Annona or Abondanza bought corn by
his orders, laid it up in granaries and distributed it to
the bakers at a settled price, according to which the value
of bread was regulated.   Abuses on the part of the subordinate officials no doubt occurred ; while men are men,
such things will arise in similar cases.   But the new system
was devised by the Pope in order to facilitate and secure the
provisioning of Rome, and affords no ground for charging
him with usurious dealing in corn.   Practically, under the
successor of Sixtus IV., the Annona protected the Roman
people from want, when, in the year 1485, the Duke of
Calabria was encamped in the Campagna and cut off
supplies.*   The energetic measures adopted by Sixtus IV.,
in order to ensure public safety in Rome and other cities of
the States of the Church, as, for example, Perugia, were
appreciated by his contemporaries.†

ment, it is easy to see that he is bent on branding Sixtus IV., on any
terms, as the corrupter of Rome.   Such partiality is all the more shocking in one who always seeks to call in question the fairness of other
writers.   See *e.g.*, Arch. Rom., XI., 482, 488, &c.

* REUMONT, III., 1, 285 *seq.*   See, regarding the Annona in general,
MORONI, II., 145 *seq.*; RANKE, Studien, 100 (Leipzig, 1877) ; also
Römische Briefe, II., 170 *seq.*, where evidence is given of the sacrifices
made by later Popes, in order to provide the Roman people with good
bread at the lowest possible price.   Further proof of the care taken
by Sixtus IV. for the provisioning of Rome, especially in years of
scarcity, is furnished by numerous *Briefs : *e.g.*, to Bologna, dated
Rome, 1473, Sept. 14 (State Archives, Bologna) ; to Perugia, dated
1474, Febr. 24 (University Library, Genoa, C. IV., 1) ; also Lib. brev.,
15, f. 12, 122, 297, 696 ; 16 A, f. 6, 30, 45 ; 16 B, f. 2, 21, 75b, 111, 139,
171b (Secret Archives of the Vatican) ; see MARTÈNE, II., 1540,
1541, 1542, 1548.

† THEINER, Codex, III., 484, and *Brief to Perugia, dated 1479,
May 23. (University Library, Genoa, C. IV., 1.) A *Speech made by

The solicitude of Sixtus IV. for the welfare of his subjects is further evinced by his efforts to check the devastation of the Campagna, and to promote tillage there,* his re-
introduction of the Constitution of Albornoz,† his solicitude
about the coinage,‡ and his exertions for the regulation of
the rivers,§ and the drainage of unhealthy places in the
States of the Church.   Works of this description were promoted by him in the neighbourhood of Foligno,‖ and in the
Maritima.   At the latter spot there was an idea of making
an attempt to dry up the well-known Pontine Marshes.   In
1476 the Pope requested the Duke of Ferrara to send him

the Milanese Ambassador praises Sixtus IV. for the restoration of
security in Rome and its neighbourhood.   Cod. Vatic., 6898, Vatican
Library.

* THEINER, Codex, 491 *seq.*, *ibid.*, 482 *seq.*; and Römische Briefe,
II., 166 *seq.*, as well as REUMONT, III., 1, 284 *seq.*   In regard to the
promotion of agriculture by the Popes, and their relation to the
Roman Campagna, see, in general, SOMBART, Die Römische Campagna
(Schmoller's Forschungen, Vol. 8), and, to complete his account,
RATTINGER, Kirchenstaat, 42 *seq.*; Hist.-polit. Bl., 1884, I., 24 (against
LÖHER, Das neue Italien, 1883).   MILELLA, I papi e l'agricoltura
nei dom. temp., Roma, 1881, was not accessible to me.

† In the year 1478; see THEINER, Cod., 494 *seq.*; LA MANTIA, I.,
462.

‡ L'ÉPINOIS, 450.   See MÜNTZ, III., 244; THEINER, Cod., 488.
Sixtus IV. was, according to Friedländer, the first who had his likeness
stamped on the coins; see MÜNTZ, L'atelier monét. de Rome, 2 (Paris,
1884).   The regard of Sixtus IV. for uniformity of coinage appears
in his *Brief to Perugia of the 21st March, 1477.   University Library,
Genoa, C. IV., 1.

§ See the *Briefs to Perugia of the 4th Febr. and 20th April, 1482
(University Library, Genoa, *loc. cit.*), and THEINER, Cod., 497.

‖ See **Briefs to Cardinal Savelli, Legate in Perugia, dated Rome,
1482, May 18 (National Library, Florence), and to Barthol. archipresbyt. plebis Scandiani, dated Rome, 1482, Aug. 30, Lib. brev., 15,
f. 17. (Secret Archives of the Vatican.)   Even in time of war, Sixtus
IV. found leisure for such occupations.

an hydraulic architect, competent to direct these difficult works.*

The accusations of greed and cruelty, which Infessura has brought against the Pope, must also be absolutely dismissed. " The most trustworthy authorities," on the contrary, bear witness to the inherent kindliness which was expressed in his countenance and speech. " He was won by the least token of attachment ; the more disposed he himself was to kindness, the less worthy of further benefits did he esteem those whom he saw to have abused former ones."†

Equally unanimous is the testimony which assures us of his generosity. He could refuse nothing, " so that the pleasure he felt in satisfying people often made him grant the same appointment to several troublesome petitioners. Accordingly, for the sake of avoiding misunderstandings, he found it necessary to entrust to an experienced and firm man, like John of Montmirabile, the revision of requests, grants, and presents. Even in the Vatican, the Mendicant Friar so little understood the value of money that, if he saw any coin on the table, he could hardly refrain from at once distributing it, through his chamberlains, to friends or to the poor. His saying, ' A stroke of the pen suffices to pro-cure for a Pope any sum that he desires,' is an evidence of his simplicity in matters of this kind. No Pontiff was fonder of giving, or of kinder disposition, and he was always willing to advance men and to bestow honours upon them. This amiable and benevolent temper of mind led him to adopt, in his intercourse with those around him, both high and low, a tone of affability and goodness, and even of expansive

* This appears from a **Brief of the 10th Febr., 1476, which I found in the State Archives, Modena.

† SCHMARSOW, 260 ; see SIGISMONDO DE' CONTI, I., 204. Also TIRABOSCHI, VI., 1, 64 ; Tommasini has never seen the critical observations of these eminent students.

confidence, which, in diplomatic negotiations, often gave cold
politicians an advantage over him.   His unpleasant experiences with the Cardinals, who had carried his election, and
with Ferrante of Naples, who was solely influenced by selfish
considerations, furnished the reasons which induced him
later on to confide practical affairs to the crafty brothers
Pietro and Girolamo Riario."*   The foregoing pages have
shewn the disastrous influence exercised especially by the
latter.   Girolamo was like the evil genius of Sixtus IV. ;
bred in the cloister, and without experience of the world, the
better judgment of Francesco della Rovere succumbed but
too often to his headstrong policy.   It may truly be said,
that nothing so much tended to obscure the good, and even
brilliant, qualities, of this Pope, as his inability to shake himself free from influences which stained his honour.   It may

* SCHMARSOW, 260–61. See ARTAUD, Gesch. der Päpste, IV., 164
(Augsburg, 1854). *Sixti IV. lib. Bullet., 1471–73, records, as early as the
5th Nov., 1471, alms to the amount of tria millia octingentos quinqua-
ginta duc.   From the same Register it appears that gifts were regularly
bestowed upon the poor at Christmas and Easter. (State Archives,
Rome.) Dr. Gottlob will treat, in a special work, of the support accorded
to the fugitives from the East. Regarding Charlotte of Cyprus, who
again lived in Rome from the year 1482, see BELLI, 35 seq.;
HERQUET, Charlotta, 205 ; and ADINOLFI, Portica, 99 seq., 102 seq.
Generous assistance was also given to the cities of the States of the
Church.   Perugia, which had suffered from the Plague and from a
year of scarcity, received in 1477 a thousand ducats as a free gift;
see *Brief to Perugia of the 18th January, 1477. (University Library,
Genoa, C. IV., 1.) On the 17th October, 1471, money was sent to
assist in the restoration of the walls and bridges at Folignano near
Ascoli. *Lib. brev., 14, f. 1 (Secret Archives of the Vatican) ; the same
volume affords many proofs of the liberality of Sixtus IV. on behalf of
needy convents. See f. 95b : *Abbati S. Placidi ord. S. Benedicti et
Henrico de Avellino canonico et decano eccl. Messanen. (1472,
January 2) ; f. 116 : *Archipresbyt. et Jacobo de la Fossa canonico
eccl. Reginae ; f. 146b : *Assistance pro fabrica infirmarie conventus
ord. min. Bononien. (1472, Febr. 29).

be asked how such weakness can be reconciled with the great energy often manifested in the conduct of Sixtus IV. ; the best answer is, in the words of Melozzo's biographer, that his was one of those peculiar characters "which are capable at times of strong efforts of will, during which they display really commanding ability, but which are followed by intervals of weakness and indifference which seem necessary to enable them to collect their forces again." * The crafty Girolamo relentlessly turned these weaker moments to account.

Side by side with many excellent and praiseworthy qualities, we see in Sixtus IV. great defects and failings ; there are many bright points, but there are also dark shadows.

If our unbiassed researches lead us, for the most part, to dismiss the intemperate accusations brought against Sixtus IV. by a partisan of the Colonna like Infessura, on the other hand, they forbid us to look upon him as an ideal Pope. Francesco della Rovere was admirable as General of his Order ; the contemplation of his pontificate awakens mingled feelings in our minds.   It is but too true that the father of Christendom often disappears behind the figure of the Italian prince ; that, in the exaltation of his own kindred, he exceeded all due bounds, and allowed himself to be led into worldly ways, and that great relaxation in ecclesiastical discipline and manifold abuses prevailed in his reign, although they were not unaccompanied by measures of reform.   Ægidius of Viterbo may be guilty of exaggeration in dating the period of decadence from his pontificate,† yet there can be no doubt that he steered the Barque of St. Peter into dangerous and rock-strewn waters.

* Schmarsow, 260.

† The passage is to be found in Gregorovius, VII., 266, 3rd ed. See Christophe, 214

In his relations to learning and art Sixtus IV. appears to far greater advantage than in the sphere of ecclesiastical policy. "When we remember that this man was a poor Friar, suddenly transformed into the mightiest Pontiff of his age, we are struck with astonishment at finding nowhere in him the least trace of the straitened surroundings of his youth and early training. Instead of the narrowness and pettiness we should expect, we find him entering into the spirit of the past, and making the magnificent taste of the day his own to a degree that no other Pope had done. We see him vying with the most renowned Italian Princes in raising his capital from the dust and degradation of centuries of ruin to be a seat of splendour, a worthy and beautiful abode ; endeavouring not merely to place her on an equality with the greatest cities of Italy, but to make her once more the intellectual literary and artistic centre of the world. Noting all this, we are filled with respect for a man so capable and so powerful, in spite of some violence in his temper and inequalities in his character. Notwithstanding all his faults, there is something imposing in the first of the Rovere Popes ; we are constrained to admire him, and, without hesitation, place him on a level with his predecessor, Nicholas V., and his nephew and successor, Julius II."*

* SCHMARSOW, 263.

CHAPTER XII.

SIXTUS IV. AS THE PATRON OF ART AND LEARNING.—(*a.*) RE-
FOUNDING AND OPENING OF THE VATICAN LIBRARY.—THE
SECRET ARCHIVES OF THE VATICAN.—INTELLECTUAL LIFE IN
ROME.—ENCOURAGEMENT OF THE HUMANISTS.—PLATINA AND
HIS "HISTORY OF THE POPES."—(*b*) RENOVATION AND EMBEL-
LISHMENT OF ROME.—THE POPE AND THE CARDINALS AS
CHURCH-BUILDERS.—THE CAPITOLINE MUSEUM.—THE HOS-
PITAL OF S. SPIRITO.—ARTISTIC VERSATILITY OF SIXTUS IV.—
MELOZZO DA FORLI.—THE FRESCOES OF THE SISTINE CHAPEL.

ONE title to renown, possessed by Sixtus IV., is uncontested;
he was unwearied in his zeal for the promotion of art and
learning. Fresh from the poverty of the Franciscan Convent in which his earlier days had been spent, and from the
arduous philosophical and theological studies which had
occupied his mind, Francesco della Rovere, on his elevation to
the Chair of St. Peter, at once set to work to adorn Rome with
the most precious and varied works of art and learning, and
to raise her to the position of the chief city of the Christian
world, and the artistic and literary centre of the Renaissance.
The prosecution of the great work of Nicholas V. was the
ideal which filled his mind, and, amid all the political and
ecclesiastical perplexities which troubled the thirteen years
of his reign, the realisation of this ideal was pursued with
a steadfast earnestness which even his opponents were constrained to admire. In the history of Intellectual Culture
the name of Sixtus IV. must ever find an honourable place,
together with those of Nicholas V., Julius II., and Leo X.

It may safely be said that, in regard to the development of the Renaissance in Rome, Sixtus IV. occupies a position similar to that of Lorenzo de' Medici in Florence. "If the Golden Age which he introduced was often the subject of exaggerated praise from the admirers of his brilliant literary Court, it is nevertheless true that he has a right to be numbered among the most popular National Popes."*

I.

Of all the works undertaken by Sixtus IV. none has a greater claim on the sympathy and interest of the historian than the re-establishment of the Vatican Library, and its opening for general use. This "most admirable of all his foundations"† occupied the Pope even in the earliest months of his pontificate. On the 17th December, 1471, he took the first step towards rescuing the forgotten Library of Nicholas V., and providing the necessary accommodation for its preservation.‡ As time went on, "he adopted the idea of Nicholas V. in its fullest extent, and made further additions to the treasures which had been saved. He endeavoured to procure valuable manuscripts, ancient codices, and modern copies from all parts, so that a book-dealer like Vespasiano da Bisticci speaks of the Pope's love of collecting as marking a new epoch, from which he occasionally dates, although, as a Florentine, he is not otherwise favourably disposed towards this Pope."§

* CROWE-CAVALCASELLE, III., 326, referring to an Eulogium in Cod., 1092, University Library, Leipzig.

† CROWE-CAVALCASELLE, III., 327. See RENAZZI, I., 179–80. The Poem mentioned *supra*, p. 209, note *, in Cod., 2403, f. 11b *seq.* of the Court Library, Vienna, is enthusiastic in the praise of the Library of Sixtus IV.

‡ MARINI, Archivi, 18 ; Arch. St. Ital., 3 Serie, III., 215 ; MÜNTZ, III., 118 *seq.* ; and Regestum Clementis V., I., p. xlv.

§ SCHMARSOW, 37.

The zeal with which Sixtus IV., assisted by Platina, Jacobo di Volterra, Lionardi Dati, Domizio Calderino, Mattia Palmieri, and Sigismondo de' Conti, laboured to increase the Vatican Library is evidenced by the fact that in 1475 it contained no less than 2527 volumes, 770 of which were Greek and 1757 Latin. Between 1475 and 1484, 1000 more were added, bringing the number up to more than 3500 volumes, something like three times as many as appear in Nicholas V.'s Inventory drawn up twenty years before.* In order to appreciate the importance of the collection, let us remember that ten years later the library of the wealthy Medici contained about a thousand Manuscripts.†

In the collection of Pope Sixtus IV. we observe a decided preponderance of ecclesiastical works. Theology, Philosophy, and Patristic Literature form its chief contents. The Inventory of 1475 mentions 26 volumes of St. Chrysostom's writings, 28 of St. Ambrose, 31 of St. Gregory, 41 of Canon Law, 51 of Records of Councils, 51 of the works of St. Thomas, 57 of St. Jerome, and 81 of St. Augustine. The Old and New Testaments occupy 59 volumes, and Glosses on the Scripture 98. Celebrated Greek authors are represented by 109 volumes, and there are 116 on religious subjects by less-known writers of the same nation. Compared with the collection of Nicholas V., the total absence of any writings in the vernacular is a defect. The classics occupy the second place; there are 14 volumes of the works of Seneca, 53 of the Latin Poets, 70 of Greek Poetry and Grammar, 125 of Roman, and 59 of Grecian History. The Latin writers on Astrology and Geometry contribute 19, and Greek Astrologers 49 volumes; Latin Philosophers 103, and

* MÜNTZ, Bibliothèque, 135, 141.

† See our Vol. II., p. 212. The particulars there given in regard to Nicholas's Library are supplemented by MÜNTZ, Bibl., 315 *seq.*, and Rev. critique, 1886, p. 282.

Greek 94. There were 55 Latin and 14 Greek works on Medicine.*

The first Librarian of the Vatican under Sixtus IV. was Giandrea Bussi, Bishop of Aleria, a man of classical culture. The appointment of this ardent promoter of the art of typography in Rome renders it probable that the productions of the printing-press were not excluded from the Papal collection. An Inventory of the year 1483 distinguishes between printed books and Manuscripts.†

Bussi, who died in the Jubilee Year, was succeeded by Bartolomeo Platina. New and regular revenues were, at the same time, assigned by the Pope to the Library,‡ and energetic measures were taken for the recovery of books which had been borrowed and not restored.§ Platina received a yearly salary of 120 ducats (= £240 sterling) and

---

* MÜNTZ, Renaissance, 121, and Biblioth., 142 and 159 *seq.* In regard to the Inventories, see also the articles of MÜNTZ and DE ROSSI (355) in the Serapeum, I., 334 *seq.*, VI., 301 *seq.*, XII., 130 *seq.*

† MÜNTZ, Bibl., 141. In 1472 Bussi drew up a petition to Sixtus IV. in the name of the printers, Schweynheim and Pannartz, who had fallen into great distress ; to this petition is appended a most valuable list of the works which, up to that time, had issued from their press, with the number of copies of each ; see LINDE, I., 167 *seq.* ; LORCK, Gesch. der Buchdr., 57 *seq.* (Leipzig, 1882). The two printers had then printed 12,475 volumes ; Bussi's letter was probably of little use to them. Competition was increasing, and at length they abandoned the struggle. Pannartz died after 1476 ; Schweynheim entirely gave up printing. According to JANSSEN, I., 15 (14th ed.), Rome had, in 1475, as many as twenty printing-offices, and by the close of the Century 925 works had been produced ; most of these were mainly supported by the clergy ; see also FROMANN, 9 ; FALK, 18 ; LINDE, I., 172, III., 715.

‡ **Bull of Sixtus IV., dated Romae, 1475, XVII. Cal. Jul., Armar. XXXI., N. 62, f. 113. Secret Archives of the Vatican.

§ The Bull on the subject is printed in the Regestum Clementis V., I., p. xlvi. See also MARINI, Archivi, 18.

apartments. Three officials, called Scriptores or Custodes, were placed under him, and also a bookbinder. They were paid 12 ducats a year each, and were generously supported by Sixtus IV. in every way that he could. One of them, Demetrius of Lucca, was a man of considerable learning.* Platina soon died, and his place was filled by Bartolomeo Manfredi, surnamed Aristophilo, Secretary to Cardinal Roverella. In July, 1484, the new Librarian went, by the Pope's desire, to Urbino and Rimini to copy Manuscripts.†

The appointment of Platina, the employment of subordinate officials, and the assignment of a regular income were the first steps towards the reorganisation of this noble Institution, which soon acquired a world-wide reputation. On the 1st July, 1477, Sixtus IV. published another Bull regarding the revenues of the Library and the stipend of its custodians. In the introduction to this Bull, he says that the objects of this Institution are the exaltation of the Church militant, the spread of the Catholic Faith, and the advancement of learning.‡

Another important work of the Pope was the separation of the Manuscript books from the Documents and Archives. A special place, called the Bibliotheca Secreta, was prepared, in which the Documents arranged by Platina were to be preserved in walnut-wood chests. "The whole room was wainscoted, and the free space on the walls above adorned with frescoes in chiaroscuro. This costly undertaking must have been completed in the latter part of the Summer of 1480." §

* Müntz, Bibliothèque, 137. See also Vogel in the Serapeum, VII., 296 seq.

† See Sixtus IV.'s Briefs of the 18th Oct., 1481, and 14th July, 1484, in Müntz, Bibl., 300-303. Also Regestum Clementis V., I., p. xlvii.

‡ Müntz, Bibl., 300.

§ Schmarsow, 206.

Documents of special importance had, from the beginning of the 15th Century, been kept at St. Angelo. Having regard to the troubled state of the times, Sixtus IV. caused the Charters containing the chief privileges of the Roman Church to be transferred to this place ot safety, after authentic copies of them had been made by Urbino Fieschi and Platina.*

The Library proper consisted, until 1480, of two halls opening into each other, one for the Latin and the other for the Greek Manuscripts. From the registers of payments it appears that, in the summer of 1480, Sixtus IV. added a third hall, which was distinguished by the name of the Great Library, and was in all probability situated on the other side of the Cortile del Papagallo, beneath the Sistine Chapel. Its walls and ceiling were painted by Melozzo, with the assistance of Antoniasso. Twenty-five years later, Albertini wrote a description of the Library, which is shorter than we could wish. He places the three portions of the Public Institution in juxtaposition, so as to separate the Library from the Secret Archives. "In the Apostolic Palace at the Vatican," he writes, "is that glorious Library, built by Sixtus IV., with his portrait exquisitely painted and the epigram beneath.† There are also paintings of the Doctors, with other verses, which I give in my collection of epigrams. Beside this Library is another, called the Greek one, also built by Sixtus, together with the chamber of the Custodians. There is, moreover, a third very beautiful Library, also erected by Sixtus IV., in which are the Codices

---

* BRESSLAU, Urkundenlehre, I., 129 ; Löwenfeld in RAUMER'S Hist. Taschenbuch, 6th Series, V., 318 ; DUDIK, II., 14 *seq.*; Regestum Clementis V., I., p. xlix. ; MARINI, Archivi, 18 ; GACHARD, Arch. du Vatican, 7–8 (Brussels, 1874) ; Mél. d'Archéologie, 1888, p. 150 ; and Studi e Doc., VIII., 11.

† See *infra*, p. 453.

adorned with gold, silver, and silk bindings. I saw Virgil's works in this hall, written in capital letters, besides geometrical, astronomical, and other instruments connected with the liberal arts, which are also decorated with gold, silver, and paintings." Albertini then proceeds to speak of the Secret Library (Bibliotheca Secreta), which had been re-arranged by Julius II.*

The Great Library, which contained the collection of ancient Manuscripts, had the advantage of the two other halls in being well-lighted by "a large glass window containing the arms of the Rovere family. The German glass-maker Hermann had been obliged to bring this himself from Venice." † Here stood the long tables to which the Manuscripts were secured by little chains—just as they now are in the splendid Laurenziana at Florence ; but in the 15th Century the comfort of scholars was more considered than it is in the 19th. In the cold and damp winter days the grand Library was warmed.‡ Although the Manuscripts were chained, they were most liberally lent out. Platina's list of books lent is preserved,§ and shews

---

* SCHMARSOW, 40 *seq*. His researches concerning the Vatican Library have essentially rectified and completed the earlier descriptions of GREGOROVIUS, ZANELLI (Bibl. Vat. [R. 1857], p. 13), and REUMONT (Arch. St. Ital., N. S., VIII., 1, 132 *seq*.). Schmarsow's Monograph has unfortunately escaped the notice of the worthy M. Müntz in his valuable work on the Vatican Library.

† SCHMARSOW, 42 ; MÜNTZ, III., 119 *seq*.

‡ MÜNTZ, Bibliothèque, 140.

§ Cod. Vat., 3964, published by MÜNTZ, Bibl., 269-99. In order justly to appreciate the liberality of Sixtus IV., the extreme difficulty of procuring Manuscripts in those days must be remembered ; Lorenzo de' Medici, in the period of his greatest magnificence, had to write an autograph letter to Ercole d'Este, a Prince who was under great obligations to him, for the loan of ' Dio Cassius,' and, notwithstanding the confidential relations which existed between them, Ercole did not send the original ; see REUMONT, Lorenzo, II., 106, 2nd ed.

that several volumes were entrusted at once to the same person. Among those who availed themselves of the literary treasures of this Library, were the Pope himself, Cardinal Giuliano, numerous Bishops and Prelates, Johannes Argyropulos, Sigismondo de' Conti, Pomponius Laetus, Johannes Philippus de Lignamine, Hieronymus Balbanus, Augustinus Patritius, Jacobus Volaterranus, Francesco de Toledo, and others. The negligence of some borrowers compelled the administrators from the year 1480 to require pledges to be deposited for books lent.

The reorganisation of the Vaticana, and its opening to the public, would suffice to secure for Sixtus IV. an abiding record in the history of scholars. But his other efforts for the promotion of learning were by no means inconsiderable.

In the early days of his pontificate, the Humanists seem to have felt much anxiety as to the attitude the former Franciscan friar might adopt in regard to their pursuits. This feeling is evidenced by a work which Sigismondo de' Conti dedicated to the Pope, reminding him that Nicholas V., the most famous Pontiff of the age, had gained great renown by his patronage of scholars. Sigismondo warned Sixtus IV. not to attach too little importance to the opinion of the learned, and to what might be written of him by celebrated men. He reminded him of the words of Francesco Sforza, who said that the wound of a dagger was less to be dreaded than that of a satirical poem. In conclusion, the anxious Humanist again begged the Pope to shew honour to men who were in a position to preserve his name from oblivion and to immortalise his actions.*

* "*Habeantur in pretio viri qui tuum nomen ab interitu vendicare, qui tuas res gestas immortalitati mandare possunt." Fol 603 of Sigismondo de' Conti's *Work, Ad Sixtum IV. pro secretariis, which I found in Cod. Vat., 2934, P. II., Vatican Library. Sixtus IV. restored the College of Abbreviators, and fixed their number at seventy·

Exhortations of this kind were not needed. Sixtus IV.
perfectly understood the importance of the Renaissance ; he
was well aware that the Humanists were indispensable, and
that it was impossible, on account of some isolated excesses,
to adopt a position of antagonism towards the intellectual
life so ardently cultivated on all sides.   " Full of intellect
and of taste for high culture," the ex-general of the Mendicant Order from the first resolved " to surround the Papal
Throne and his own relations with all that could give him
prestige in the eyes of the world." *   Although the attraction
which the Eternal City exercises on lovers of antiquity had
already drawn a numerous colony of learned men to Rome,
the Pope constantly sought to add to their number.   One
of his greatest acquisitions was Johannes Argyropulos of
Constantinople, the most highly gifted among the Greeks
who had migrated to Italy.   In winning him to Rome,
Sixtus IV. gained a victory over the Medici, in whose
service he had been for some time.   Argyropulos was very
successful there.   He had the satisfaction of numbering
amongst his hearers men of the greatest distinction, Bishops
and Cardinals, and even notable foreigners such as Johann
Reuchlin.†   Angelo Poliziano was also his disciple.‡   The
worthy Bartholomäus Fontius was appointed to a Professorial
Chair in the Roman University under Sixtus IV.   In 1473
Martino Filetico became Professor of Rhetoric in that Insti-

two ; see CIAMPINI, 33 *seq.*; PHILLIPS, VI., 394. In regard to the
sale of these places, see GOTTLOB, Cam. Apost.

* PAPENCORDT, 517.

† Reuchlin was among the audience of Argyropulos in the Spring
of 1482 when staying in Rome with Count Eberhard of Württemberg.
See MÜNTZ, Renaissance, 83 ; STÄLIN, III., 592 *seq.*; GEIGER,
Reuchlin, 25.

‡ MÜNTZ, Renaissance, 83. Concerning Argyropulos, see VOIGT,
Wiederbelebung, I., 372, 2nd ed., and LEGRAND, Bibliographie
Hellénique, Paris, 1885, 2 vols., *s. v.*

tution.* Even non-Italian scholars were summoned by the Pope to Rome. Among these, was, in 1475, the famous Regiomontanus (Johann Müller of Königsberg in Franconia). Unfortunately, this great discoverer, who, by the Pope's desire, would have assisted in the work of reforming the Calendar, died in July, 1476.†

But the ambition of Sixtus IV. was not yet satisfied. He desired to win for his beloved Rome the prince of the neo-platonic philosophy, the scholar whose writings cast a halo of glory over Florence. Several of the Cardinals supported him in this project. Marsilio Ficino, however, was bound to the Medici by bonds which could not be severed. He requited the Pope's gracious summons by a letter couched in the most flattering terms.‡

* Filetico had previously taught Greek there ; see MARINI, II., 208 ; SCHMARSOW, 55, 75 note, and 345 ; and CORVISIERI in the Review, Buonarotti, Ser. II., Vol. IV., 1869.

† FULGOSUS, VIII., c. 13 ; ASCHBACH, Wiener Universität, I., 556 ; KALTENBRUNNER, Kalenderreform, in the Sitzungsberichten der Wiener Akad. Hist. Cl., LXXXII., 374 ; JANSSEN, I., 124 (14th edit.) ; TIRABOSCHI, VI., I, 356. The statement that Regiomontanus was poisoned (BECHSTEIN, Deutsches Museum, I., 253) is a pure invention ; Aschbach supposes him to have succumbed to the summer fever raging in Rome, which was of a pestilential character ; this hypothesis, which Jovius gives as a fact, is all the more probable, inasmuch as the Plague actually prevailed in Rome at the time ; see our account, *supra*, p. 288. There is an interesting statement in the Koelhoff'schen Chronik to the effect that, after hearing Johann Cantor dispute in Rome, Sixtus IV. wrote an extremely friendly Brief to his Father. Städtechroniken, XIV., 877. In regard to the Pope's relations with Joh. Wessel, see ULLMANN, II., 353 *seq.*, and to his encouragement of Universities, PRANTL, I., 68 ; Tüb. Theol. Quartalschr., p. 206, 1865. See F. STÄLIN, Gesch. Württembergs, I., 2, 671 *seq.* (Gotha, 1887) ; PELLINI, 813 ; and *supra*, p. 260, regarding Copenhagen.

‡ MÜNTZ, Renaissance, 83. See the Revue des deux Mondes, 1881, Nov., p. 163. Regarding the jurists whom Sixtus IV. invited to Rome, see RENAZZI, I., 185 *seq.*

The Roman Humanists in the time of Sixtus IV. formed
a very brilliant circle. While Pomponius Laetus lived
almost entirely by his labours as a Professor,* "Platina
wrote his History of the Popes, Campanus composed his
elegies and epigrams, Aurelio Brandolini charmed even the
unpoetical Pope with his verses, while a bevy of youthful
writers produced Latin poems of more or less merit." † The
favour shewn by Sixtus IV. to Gasparo and Francesco, the
sons of Flavio Biondi, shewed his willingness to reward the
services rendered by departed scholars.‡ Johannes Philippus
de Lignamine, the editor of many ancient authors, was in
his service. His kinsman, Philippus de Lignamine, a Dominican, continued Ricobaldo's Chronicle of the Popes down to
the year 1469, and dedicated his work to Sixtus IV.§

His pontificate was very fruitful in historical works. The
example of Pius II. in writing the history of his own time
produced many imitators. Sigismondo de' Conti holds the
first place amongst these. His "Contemporary History," in
seventeen books, comprising the period from 1475 to 1510,
"ensures him an honourable mention among the Cinquecento
writers." Sigismondo, who is spoken of with the greatest
respect by contemporaneous authors, was a Christian
Humanist. These men, "the sympathetic outcome of the
age of the Renaissance, had themselves experienced the
antagonism between the ancient classical world and the

---

* Petrus Martyr was, from the year 1477, a disciple of P. Laetus;
see HEIDENHEIMER, P. M., 4 (Berlin, 1881).

† GEBHARDT, Adrian von Corneto, 4. See RENAZZI, I., 187 *seq.*;
MÜNTZ, Renaissance, 408–9; and VILLENEUVE, 14, for an account
of Brandolini. For the relations of D. Calderino to Sixtus IV., see
GIULIARI, 76 *seq.* See also MANSI-FABRICIUS, I., 297.

‡ This information is furnished by Wilmanns from the Registers
of the Secret Archives of the Vatican in the Gött. Gel. Anz., 1879,
pp. 1502–3.

§ FABRICIUS-MANSI, V., 279–80.

mediæval point of view, but able justly to distinguish between the means and the end, were not blinded by the
splendour of the past, and held fast to the principles of Christianity." Sigismondo requited the favours of Sixtus IV. and
the Rovere by a frequent and far too partial mention of them
in his work, which otherwise is both trustworthy and candid.*
" Jacopo Gherardi of Volterra (Volaterranus), attracted by
Pope Sixtus IV. to the Court of Rome, followed the
example of his first patron, Cardinal Ammanati, by writing
Memoirs of his time. Mattia Palmieri of Pisa, Papal Scrip-
tor, who died in 1482, continued the chronicle of his famous
Florentine namesake, Matteo Palmieri." †

Notwithstanding the love of literature which distinguished
Sixtus IV., the unfortunate circumstances of the time robbed
the Roman University of much of her splendour. " The
revenues destined for the maintenance of the Institution
were often employed in the war, and taxes were imposed on
the salaries of the Professors. Different posts connected
with the University came by purchase into unworthy
hands."‡

Sixtus IV. also encouraged literary men by appointments
to diplomatic Missions. In 1476 Georgios Hermonymos
went to England as Orator to the English§ Embassy, and in
1482 Sigismondo de' Conti, who had previously accompanied
Cardinal Giuliano to the Netherlands, was sent to Florence.||

---

* GOTTLOB in the Hist. Jahrb., VII., 304–23. See also SYBEL'S
Hist. Zeitschr., N. F., XXI., 359. The Life of Sigismondo by Bartol.
Alpeus, preserved in the Archivio Communale of Ancona, has been
published by Faloci Pulignani, S. de C. Il Topino, I., N. 26.

† REUMONT, III., 1, 350.

‡ RENAZZI, I., 195 ; PAPENCORDT, 521 ; CHRISTOPHE, II., 295 seq.
See supra, p. 422.

§ OMONT, G. Hermonyme in the Mém. de la Soc. d'Hist. de Paris,
XII., 65 seq., and GEIGER, Vierteljahrsschrift für Renaissance, II., 197.

|| See supra, pp. 334 and 372.

Johannes Philippus de Lignamine had, in 1475, the honour of welcoming the King of Naples at Velletri, and was subsequently entrusted with Missions to Mantua and Sicily.*

The excessive self-esteem of these favoured Humanists often took a very offensive form. Theodoros Gaza, considering the payment given him by the Pope for his translation of Aristotle's Animals insufficient, is said to have scornfully cast it into the Tiber.† The anecdote may be an invention, but it exemplifies the insolence and greed of many Humanists, one of whom, George of Trebizond, even went so far as to beg money from the Sultan, to whom he wrote two fulsome letters.‡ Francesco Filelfo, who made presents and money

* MARINI, I., 193 *seq.*

† So says Jovius, while PIERIUS VALERIANUS, De infelicitate literat., II., 159, makes Trapezuntios die of it. Hodius doubts the whole story ; BÄHR, in Ersch-Gruber, I., Section 55, p. 135, refuses to reject it altogether. See LEGRAND, I., xxxviii.

‡ Perotti (how far he received directions from Sixtus IV. remains still uncertain ; see REUMONT'S Vermuthungen, III., 1, 350, and *cf.* Vespasiano da Bisticci [in MAI, I., 279], who, however, being a Florentine, is not an impartial witness ; Civ. Catt., I., 148, 1868) accordingly made a furious attack on Trapezuntios. VOIGT, Wiederbelebung, II., 144, 2nd ed., cites : N. Perotti, Refutatio deliramentorum Georgii Trapezuntii in Morelli ; Codices ms. lat. bibl. Nanianaep., 51. The last-named book was not within my reach. On the other hand, there is in *Cod. Vat., 2934, I., f. 219 *seq.*, an " Invectiva Nic. Perotti in Georg. Trapezunt. quia Turcum omnibus quicumque fuerunt imperatoribus natura praestantiorem esse voluit," which is, perhaps, identical with the " Refutatio." Perotti here takes both the letters of Trapezuntios to the Sultan to pieces, sentence by sentence, heaps reproaches upon him, and calls on the Pope, the Emperor, and all Christian Princes to punish him : " Hancine luem, hancine pestem . . . sustinere amplius poteritis ? . . . Exurgite igitur, exurgite . . . et hunc sceleratissimum hominem, hanc trunculentam feram, hoc immanissimum monstrum non ex urbe abigite, non ex Italia exterminate . . . sed cadendum flagris et usque ad ossa dilaniandum discerpendum dilacerandum tradite."

the chief subject of his verses, was even more covetous.* If the insolent petitions of this insatiable man were not favourably received he revenged himself by the coarsest invectives. Each new Pope was addressed immediately upon his elevation by the "King of importunate poets," and if, like Pius II., he failed to satisfy the immense expectations of the petitioner, was loaded with abuse. The attacks which this most repulsive of Humanists made on the memory of the departed Pius II. were so horrible, that the College of Cardinals caused him to be imprisoned at the very time when he was striving to obtain a place at the Court.† On the accession of Sixtus IV., Filelfo renewed his efforts in this direction. The Pope at first gave him no encouragement, and Filelfo's flatteries soon changed to complaints, and finally to threats. When he was summoned to Rome in 1474, he owed his appointment mainly to the dread of his pen.‡ Filelfo was employed for three years as Professor at the Roman University ; dissensions were not wanting during this period ; the most important was his quarrel with Miliaduca Cicada, Master of the Papal Treasury. For the first time, however, "he was delighted with the City, its climate, the exuberance and elegance of its life, and, above all, with the incredible liberty which there prevailed."§

The "incredible liberty" was most strikingly displayed in

* VOIGT, Wiederbelebung, I., 531, 2nd ed., gives a detailed description of Filelfo's system of begging.

† VOIGT, Pius II., III., 637 seq. ; GASPARY, 116.

‡ This fear is manifest in the friendly manner in which Sixtus IV. caused him to be treated on his arrival in Rome ; see MÜNTZ, Renaissance, 89. BUSER, Lorenzo, 26, informs us that Filelfo begged assistance from Lorenzo de' Medici for his journey to Rome.

§ "Et quod maximi omnium faciendum videtur mihi, incredibilis quaedam hic libertas est." Ep. LX. in ROSMINI ; see GREGOROVIUS, VII., 531, 3rd ed., and MÜNTZ in the Rev. des Deux Mondes, 1881, Novemb., p. 168.

the permission given by the Pope to the Roman Academy to resume their meetings, which had been suppressed. Sixtus IV. looked upon Humanism as a purely literary movement in no way dangerous to religion. The apprehensions which the extravagances and the heathen tendencies of many literary men had awakened in the mind of his predecessor were not shared by him. " He may also have thought that the Humanists had had their lesson and taken it to heart." Pomponius Laetus was again perfectly free to lecture, and the Academy held its sittings without the slightest hindrance. The spectacle was a strange one. " While a Minorite occupied the Papal Throne the worship of antiquity, with its excesses as well as its good side, flourished unrebuked, and no offence seems to have been taken at the pontificate of Pomponius Laetus.   The assemblies at his house on the Quirinal near the Gardens of Constantine were more brilliant than ever.   The Academy was openly recognised, and this, in fact, was the simplest way of rendering it harmless."*   High dignitaries of the Church were on friendly terms with it.   On the 20th April, 1483, when the Academicians celebrated the birthday of Rome, a solemn High Mass, followed by a discourse from Paulus Marsus, preceded the banquet, at which six Bishops were present.   At this Academic Feast the " Privilegium," by which the Emperor Frederick granted to the body the right of conferring the title of Doctor and crowning Poets, was publicly read.†

In his treatment of Platina, one of the most violent members of the Academy, Sixtus IV. shewed great tact and knowledge of human nature.   " He managed to win this ringleader of the opposition by treating him as an old friend, and assigned to him successively two tasks, which removed all danger of anti-Papal dispositions, by enlisting all his

* REUMONT, III., 1, 351. See also SCHMARSOW, 28.
† JACOB. VOLATERRANUS, 185.

energies and talents in the service of the very power against which he had rebelled.   He first encouraged him to write a History of the Popes, and then requested him to make a collection of all the Documents regarding the rights of the Holy See."*   By the end of the year 1474, or the beginning of 1475,† Platina was able to offer his "History of the Popes" to his august patron.‡   It is, in many respects, a remarkable

* SCHMARSOW, 28.

† This appears from the fact that Platina's work comes down to November, 1474.   DÖLLINGER, Papstfabeln, 22, is, therefore, in error when he says that Platina's History of the Popes was written in 1460. VAIRANI, I., 6, gives 1473 as the year in which the work was begun.

‡ I found in Cod. Vat. 2044, of the Vatican Library the copy presented to Sixtus IV.   It is a splendid Renaissance Codex, of 236 folio pages, written on parchment.   It begins, f. 1 : "Prohemium Platynae in vitas pontificum ad Sixtum IIII. P. M. Multa quidem, &c." The 'M' is illuminated with an exquisite miniature of the arms of the Rovere, supported by two naked genii.   Each word is written in many colours : blue, red, green, lilac, and gold, and the effect on the fine parchment is splendid.   There is a still finer miniature at f. 2b, a portrait of the Pope, surrounded by the inscription : "Sixtus Pont. Max," and framed in a wreath with golden acorns.   The many-coloured letters often recur, as in f. 3, where the naked genii again appear, but this time without the coat-of-arms.   Here the actual history begins . "Platynae historici liber de vita Christi ac omnium pontificum qui hactenus ducenti fuere et XX. Nobilitatis maximam partem, &c." This original copy of the History, which has become so celebrated, has a threefold importance.   (a.) It contains, f. 229–236b, the Life of Sixtus IV., as found by MURATORI, III., 2, 1045-65, in a Cod. Urb. ; that is to say, without the addition regarding the Hospital of S. Spirito.   This tends to confirm Schmarsow's view that Platina was the author of this Vita ; see also *supra*, p. 272.   (b.) It contains all the passages calculated to give offence, as, *e.g.*, that against John XXII., fol. 177b, as well as the violent language, of which we shall speak presently, condemning the state of ecclesiastical affairs at that period.   (c) There are many interesting notes, probably in Platina's own handwriting, some of which are mere corrections, and others, especially in the Biography of Paul II., alterations of the text ; expressions are in some instances,

work for the period in which it was written.   Instead of the confused and often fabulous Chronicles of the Middle Ages, we find here for the first time a clear and serviceable hand-book of real history.   The graphic descriptions, the elegant, perspicuous, and yet concise, style of the work have won for Platina's " Lives of the Popes" many readers even down to the present day.*

In his Preface, which is addressed to Sixtus IV., Platina begins by emphasising, in the Humanistic style,† the dignity and importance of history.   His declaration that he will, on principle, avoid applying expressions belonging to classical heathenism to Christian subjects, is remarkable.   He begins his work with Christ, " so that, springing from the Emperor of Christians as from a living fountain, it may flow on through the Roman Bishops down to the days of Sixtus." In the lives of the earliest Popes, Platina repeatedly mentions the ancient monuments with admiration.   " In the Church of Sant' Andrea near Santa Maria Maggiore," he writes, in his life of Simplicius, " as I looked at the relics of antiquity which it contains, tears often filled my eyes at the neglect of those whose duty it is to preserve it from decay."‡

toned down, and in others intensified.   Further particulars will be given in another place.

* See TIRABOSCHI, VI., 1, 279 ; VILLARI, I., 130 ; BISSOLATI, 73 seq. ; MÜNTZ in the Rev. des Deux Mondes, 1881, Nov., p. 174.   An English translation of Platina's Lives of the Popes appeared in 1888. The book was first printed by two Germans in Venice, in 1479 ; in 1481 another edition came out at Nuremberg (Hain, 13,047) ; this was followed by numerous others, some of which were mutilated ; see VAIRANI, I., 11–12 (here p. 119, also the " Prohoemium Platinae ad Sixtum IV. in libellum Plutarchi de ira "), and POTTHAST, Bibl., I., 495. What BISSOLATI, 165 seq., adduces is unsatisfactory.

† See, in general, VOIGT, Wiederbelebung, II., 495, 2nd ed., and SIGISMONDO DE' CONTI, I., 4.

‡ His interest in antiquity is often betrayed.   In opposition to the

The critical acumen repeatedly manifested by Platina is worthy of note, "though he keeps this faculty under restraint, not wishing to interrupt the flow of his narrative."* The freedom with which, in a work dedicated to Sixtus IV., he treats of the faults of both the older and the more recent Popes, is to be commended, and does equal honour to the author and to his patron. It is all the more painful to find that, in dealing with the life of his former adversary, Paul II., Platina has been unable to rise to the height of an impartial historian. Death is a great peacemaker, and it might have been expected that, when Paul II. was no longer on earth, Platina would have done justice to his memory. This, however, is by no means the case. The labours of Paul II. are described in a very one-sided manner, and indeed often wilfully travestied and ridiculed.† Even in passages in which there is no occasion for mentioning this Pope, Platina seeks one, in order to give vent to his hatred.‡ This is all the more to be deplored, inasmuch as the biographies of the Popes of the Renaissance period constitute the only original portion of his work.

Platina's language, also, in speaking of the ecclesiastical affairs of his own time, is often very intemperate. Strangely enough, these outbreaks do not occur in the lives of the 15th Century Popes, but are interpolated in those of an earlier period. They are, in fact, masked attacks. When writing of Dionysius I., Platina drags in complaints of the

ignorant chroniclers of the 14th Century, he clears St. Gregory the Great from the slanderous accusation of having ruthlessly destroyed the relics of the past.

* GREGOROVIUS, VII., 589, 3rd ed. Platina looked with suspicion on the fable of Pope Joan, but would not omit it, as almost every one maintained it; see DÖLLINGER, Papstfabeln, p. 22.

† See SCHMARSOW, 29. See also *supra*, p. 64 *seq.*

‡ See the passages in the Life of Hadrian I. and Stephen VI.

pomp and pride of the higher clergy. In the histories of
Julius I., Socinus I., and Boniface III. he introduces censures, obviously aimed at the clergy of the 15th Century.
The immorality of Sixtus IV.'s Cardinals is severely casti-
gated in the biography of Stephen III. A still more violent
passage is inserted in his account of Gregory IV.* There
was doubtless good cause for his animadversions, but they
come somewhat strangely from a man whose own life was
so dissolute.† Platina, however, is guilty of a worse fault,
when, in dealing with the reign of John XXII., he repeats
the assertion of the party of the opposition, who maintained
that the Pope contradicted Scripture, in saying that Christ
possessed no property. The truthfulness of this historian
may be gauged by the frivolous inscriptions discovered to
have been written by some of the Roman Academicians in
the Catacombs of S. Callisto, on the occasion on which he
describes himself as having visited it out of devotion‡ with
a few friends.§

We cannot but be surprised that Sixtus IV. accepted the
dedication of a work like Platina's. Probably he was only
acquainted with its contents in so far as they concerned the
history of his own pontificate. This portion, which comes
down to November, 1474, contained nothing but what would
have given him perfect satisfaction. This feeling found
expression in Platina's appointment as Librarian of the
Vatican in the following year. While he occupied this post,
the Pope commissioned him to arrange the collection of

---

* Reflections on the danger threatened by Turkey in the 15th
Century are placed in the history of Boniface V., and coupled with
charges against the clergy of Platina's own time.

† See the evidence from *Cod. Vat., 9020, *supra*, p. 64, note ‖.

‡ "Invisi ego haec loca cum amicis quibusdam religionis causa."
Vita Calisti I., p. 56.

§ See *supra*, p. 63.

Documents containing the Privileges of the Roman Church, which are now preserved in three volumes in the Vatican Archives. This useful work, which is invaluable to the annalists of the Church,* was brought to a conclusion during the war with Florence.† Here, also, Platina proved his critical discernment in excluding the "Donation of Constantine" from his collection of Documents. The Preface to the work is interesting, inasmuch as Platina not only avoids everything of an anti-Papal tendency, but also speaks with approval of the proceedings of the Popes against heretics and schismatics.‡ There appears to be no doubt that Sixtus IV. succeeded in completely winning him over to the cause of the Church. The same may also be said in regard to the proud Pomponius Laetus, who now composed poems in honour of Sixtus IV.§

Platina died in 1481. His friends, among whom were some Bishops, celebrated the anniversary of his death in the Church of Sta Maria Maggiore, where he was buried.‖ Mass was said by the Bishop of Ventimiglia, an Augustinian, and the tomb was sprinkled with holy water and incensed.

---

* RAYNALDUS, ad an. 1478, N. 48. Kaltenbrunner is going to publish an exact description of the Coll. Platinae, together with a partial Catalogue of its rich contents; see Mittheil. des Œsterr. Instituts, VI., 208.

† This appears from the Preface, of which MARINI, Archivi, 21, and Regestum Clementis V., I., p. xlix., give short passages; through the kindness of Professor Kaltenbrunner, I was able to make use of a complete copy.

‡ *" De auctoritate anathemizandi eos qui contra sedem apost. moliti aliquid fuerint quique heresim et seditionem in ecclesia Dei severint tam latus in his bullis apparet campus ut fulmina quedam in prevaricatores ipsos et scismaticos e celo missa videantur." Preface to the first volume of the Coll. Platinae. Secret Archives of the Vatican.

§ GREGOROVIUS, VII., 574-5, 3rd ed.

‖ See BISSOLATI, 82, and Archivio Veneto, 1887, fasc. 67, p. 161.

Pomponius Laetus, the President of the Academy, then mounted the pulpit to pronounce an oration in memory of his departed friend. Jacobus Volaterranus informs us that it was of a thoroughly religious and serious character. A poet from Perugia, named Astreus, then, from the same pulpit, recited an elegy in verse, lamenting his loss! That such a thing could have been done is indeed an evidence of that "incredible liberty" so triumphantly praised by Filelfo. We cannot, however, suppose that serious men could fail to disapprove, when, in the very sanctuary of the Queen of Heaven, just after the Mass for the Dead, a layman, without the least token of any spiritual office, pronounced, from the pulpit, verses which, although very elegant, yet—as Volaterranus remarks—were quite alien to our religion, and out of keeping with the sacred function which had just taken place.*

The Rome of that day was indeed full of strange contrasts, against which no one protested. Christian and heathen Humanism are to be seen walking side by side in daily life, and apparently incommoding each other as little as did the reforms and abuses which prevailed together in the Church.†

II.

During his long pontificate, Sixtus IV. did incomparably more for the promotion of Art than for that of Literature. It has been justly observed, that the artistic activity of

---

* JACOBUS VOLATERRANUS, 171 ; SCHMARSOW, 189 ; BURCKHARDT, Cultur, I., 278, 3rd ed.

† See *supra*, p. 406 *seq.* This may also be a fitting place to mention that Cod. 14 of the Archives of the Papal Chapel contains most unseemly mythological figures, and a naked Cupid with violet stockings ; see HABERL, Bausteine, I., 72. Things of this kind cannot have come to the knowledge of the Pope, who, although an enthusiastic lover of Art, punished an obscene painter. INFESSURA, 1178.

the 15th Century reached its climax in Rome in his days.[*]
Francesco della Rovere started with the firm determination
of carrying on the work of Nicholas V., in adorning the
capital of the Christian world with all that sheds lustre on
a secular power.   But as his individual character differed
widely from that of the first patron of Art among the Popes,
the manner in which he proceeded naturally differed also.
Sixtus had, in common with Nicholas V., that love of the
ideal which was so strong in the earlier Pope, but he " confined himself to what was practical and possible, and did not
let his imagination run wild " in gigantic projects.   Accordingly, Sixtus IV. had the happiness of reigning long enough
to accomplish the greater part of what he had undertaken.[†]

The verses from the pen of Platina, on the opening of the
Vatican Library, which adorn the portrait of Melozzo da
Forli, tell, in a few words, what Sixtus did for Rome :—

> Templa domum expositus ; vicos, fora, mœnia, pontes :
> Virgineam Trivii quod repararis aquam.
> Prisca licet nautis statuas dare commoda portus :
> Et Vaticanum cingere Sixte ingum :
> Plus tamen Urbs debet : nam quæ squalore latebat :
> Cermitur (*sic*) in celebri bibliotheca loco.[‡]

The approach of the Jubilee Year was, as we have shewn,
the primary occasion of the external renovation of the Eternal
City, and her transformation from the mediæval type to one
in keeping with the advancing needs of the age.   At the
present day there are but few parts of Rome that give any

[*] GREGOROVIUS, VII., 639, 3rd ed.   See MÜNTZ, III., 11, and
REUMONT, III., 1, 402.

[†] See REUMONT in the Lit. Rundschau, 1878, p. 334, and MÜNTZ,
III., 17.

[‡] See SCHMARSOW, 37.   Milanesi has shewn that Baccio Pontelli
was never Sixtus IV.'s chief Architect ; Meo del Caprino, Giovanni de'
Dolci, Giacomo da Pietrasanta, and others were employed in that
capacity.

idea of the City as it was four hundred years ago.   There was an irregular collection of narrow, crooked, and dirty streets, in which the common requirements of a great town were utterly neglected.   In many cases, projecting porticoes, stalls, and balconies seriously obstructed the ordinary traffic, not to speak of that which might be expected in the Jubilee Year.   In some places, two horsemen could not pass each other.   Pavements, with the exception of some which had been begun in the time of Nicholas V., were almost unknown, either in the middle of the streets or alongside of the houses.*

Into this gloomy and unhealthy chaos Sixtus IV., following the schemes of Nicholas V., first brought air and light.   The most important streets were paved, and it then became possible to think of cleansing them.†   We have already spoken of the difficulties encountered in the work of widening the streets, which was undertaken in preparation for the Jubilee Year.‡   The Pope, however, was not to be deterred from it.   In January, 1480, he began by the removal of the armourers' shops on the Bridge of S. Angelo. "The Romans at first opposed this innovation, but soon became reconciled to what was a real benefit."§   In June of

* See REUMONT, III., 1, 403 seq.

† CORIO, 264, expressly states that the measures of Sixtus IV. rendered Rome more healthy.   It is hard to realise the state of the streets in former times.   Many of the principal thoroughfares in London were not paved until the 15th or 16th Century.   Berlin was not completely paved even in the earlier half of the past Century; and its streets were not swept before the year 1600.   The highly-civilised Italian cities were the first to have their streets paved; see the dates in BURCKHARDT, Gesch. der Renaissance, 212–13.

‡ See supra, p. 276 seq.

§ GREGOROVIUS, VII., 631, 3rd ed.   "Every one nowadays," says SCHMARSOW, 149, "takes the part of the energetic Pope who proceeded relentlessly against these abuses, although Roman chroniclers of his own time complain of his tyranny."

the same year an order was promulgated, requiring that "in all the most frequented streets projections should be cleared away, pavements laid down, at least at the sides, houses jutting out into the street wholly or partially removed, the ruined ones rebuilt, new squares laid out and those already existing widened and made more symmetrical. Cardinal d'Estouteville was to superintend these improvements." * The Pope himself came from time to time to ascertain personally how his directions were being carried out.

In the Leonine City he laid out a handsome street, originally known by his own name, extending from the moat of the Castle to the great gate of the Papal Palace (now Borgo S. Angelo) ;† a third street here met the old Via de' Cavalli, which took much the same direction as the present Borgo S^{to} Spirito, and the old Via Santa, now Borgo Vecchio. The erection of the Ponte Sisto effected a complete transformation in that part of the City which lay on the right bank of the Tiber. Sigismondo de' Conti says that, in consequence of the accommodation afforded by the Bridge, this dirty and uninhabited district became thickly populated.‡ Distinguished persons built houses there, and, even to the present day, the Vicolo Riario, near the Corsini Palace, remains as a memento of the villa belonging to that family which was situated there.§

Besides all that he did for the Library, Sixtus IV. carried

---

* REUMONT, III., 1, 404 ; MÜNTZ, III., 182 ; MARCELLINO DA CIVEZZA, III., 92 ; P. BELLONI, La costituzione " Quae publice utilia . . ." intorno al decoro publ. e la città di Roma, 11 (Roma, 1870).

† ADINOLFI, Portica, 51 and 218 seq. ; FORCELLA, XIII., 68, 78, 85. The *Eulogy of Sixtus IV., mentioned supra, p. 209, note *, expressly lays stress on the formation of the Via Sistina. Cod. 2403, f. 11, Court Library, Vienna.

‡ SIGISMONDO DE' CONTI, I., 204.

§ See BURRIEL, Caterina Sforza, I., 31.

on other works of restoration in the Vatican, and built the Chapel which bears his name. The interior of the Palace was fitted up anew, and a barrack erected for the guard. The roof of St. Peter's, its Sacristy, and the Chapel of S. Petronilla were restored, and the Tabernacle of the Confession and the Chapel of the Immaculate Conception were constructed.[*]

We have already spoken of the restoration of the churches before and during the Jubilee Year.[†] These works were very rapidly carried on, and Sixtus IV. also found time for building new churches. Foremost among these we must mention Sta Maria del Popolo, begun in 1472, and St Maria della Pace, both of which are worthy memorials of the Pope's devotion to the Queen of Heaven. Sta Maria del Popolo is a Basilica, with three naves surrounded by chapels, and with an octagonal dome supported on a drum, the first of the kind erected in Rome ; unlike the other buildings of the period, which were, for the most part, very hurriedly built, the façade of the year 1477 is a good specimen of pure Renaissance.[‡]

Sta Maria del Popolo was the favourite church of the Pope and of the Rovere family. Sixtus IV. visited it almost every week, and the chief events of his reign were mostly celebrated there.

The Cardinals, especially his nephews, followed the Pope's

---

[*] MÜNTZ, III., 111, 139, 147 ; SCHMARSOW, 229. Regarding the Tabernacle of the Confession, probably erected in 1475, see Jahrb. der Preuss. Kunstsammlungen, VIII., 12 seq.

[†] Supra, p. 275.

[‡] SCHMARSOW, 113–14, see pp. 35, 115, 117 ; REUMONT, III., 1, 408 ; FORCELLA, I., 319 seq. ; FRANTZ, 167 ; PAPENCORDT, 521. "In the edifices of the time of Sixtus IV.," says SPRINGER, Rafael, 103, "we observe that massive forms and grand proportions are avoided ; they have, however, the advantage of presenting in their interior ample space for sculpture and painting." See infra, p. 465 seq.

example. "Two Churches and palatial Convents, S. Pietro in Vincoli and SS. Apostoli, are, in their entirety, memorials of the Rovere."* In the first-named Basilica, Cardinal Giuliano continued the work of his uncle, and in the latter, that of the nephew, Pietro Riario. This Cardinal also restored the portico of S. Agnese.†

The Castles of Grottaferrata and Ostia, in the neighbourhood of Rome, are also abiding monuments of the powerful Cardinal. After the death of Bessarion, Grottaferrata was granted *in commendam* to Giuliano, who at once began to build there. On account of the strategical importance of its position, the Convent was surrounded by a fortification. Those who have visited the Alban hills will remember this "incomparably picturesque group of buildings at the foot of the green hills of Tusculum, on a smooth space overshadowed by old elms and plane-trees."‡ The Castle of Ostia is of kindred character—even now, "in its decay, the most beautiful ruin of the later mediæval period in the vicinity of Rome"; but the surrounding landscape is very different. Grottaferrata lies amidst rich fields and fruitful hills ; about Ostia is a "melancholy, silent tract of barren, low-lying ground, formed of rubbish and sand-hills," through which the yellow, sluggish stream makes its way to the sea. A long inscription on the principal tower of the Castle records that "Giuliano of Savona erected this stronghold as a refuge from

---

* GREGOROVIUS, VII., 635, 3rd ed. See MÜNTZ, Anciennes Basiliques, 21 *seq.* Vasari has assigned to Pontelli a share in the building of SS. Apostoli ; this cannot however be admitted. Müntz supposes Giovanni de' Dolci to have been the Architect of this church. JANITSCHEK in the Repertorium, IV., 214, concludes from its style, that it is the work of Giacomo da Pietrasanta.

† FORCELLA, II., 228, X., 350.

‡ REUMONT, III., 1, 409, and SCHMARSOW, 10 and 118. See also ROCCHI, 103 *seq.*

the perils of the sea, a protection to the Roman Campagna, a defence to Ostia, and to the mouth of the Tiber." He began it in the reign of Pope Sixtus IV., his uncle, and concluded the work by digging out, at his own expense, the moat which had been silted up by the river in the time of Pope Innocent VIII., in the year of Salvation 1486, the 2115th after the building of Ostia, the 2129th after Ancus, the founder of the city. The architect of the Castle at Ostia and probably also of the fortifications at Grottaferrata, was the celebrated Giuliano Giamberti, surnamed da San Gallo.*

Before Cardinal Giuliano built the Castle of Ostia, the wealthy d'Estouteville, its Bishop, had provided the ruined city with walls, streets, and houses.† In 1479, d'Estouteville, who had, two years previously, succeeded Orsini as Camerlengo, began to rebuild the Church of S. Agostino in Rome : this work was completed in four years.‡ He was also a great benefactor to other Roman Churches, especially to Sᵗᵃ Maria Maggiore and S. Luigi de' Francesi.§

Mention has already been made of the buildings erected by Cardinal Domenico della Rovere. Girolamo Basso della Rovere completed the Pilgrimage Church at Loreto, and

---

* GUGLIELMOTTI'S work, Della rocca d'Ostia, &c., Roma, 1862, is admirable. See also REUMONT, III., 1, 410 seq., 519. For an account of Giuliano's magnificent constructions in Bologna, see Atti dell' Emilia, II., 194 seq., and SPRINGER, Rafael, 104.

† See Anecdota Veneta, ed. CONTARINI, 267 ; ARMELLINI, 145.

‡ SCHMARSOW, 145. See MÜNTZ, III., 41 ; JANITSCHEK'S Repert., IV., 76 ; ARMELLINI, 107 ; FORCELLA, V., 18. Regarding the removal of the market from the Capitol to Piazza Navona by order of d'Estouteville, see CANCELLIERI, Il Mercato, 16 (1811).

§ DE ANGELIS, Basilicae S. Mariae Majoris descriptio, 137 seq. ; BARBIER DE MONTAULT, Le Card. d'Estouteville bienfaiteur des Églises de Rome (Angers, 1859), and Inventaires des établ. nationaux de S. Louis des Français et de S. Sauveur in Thermis à Rome (Paris, 1861) ; also MÜNTZ, III., 285 seq.

caused the Cappella del Tesoro to be painted by Melozzo
da Forli ; the paintings, which are in excellent preservation,
are very original and striking.*   Another important edifice
of this time was the Palace of Cardinal Stefano Nardini
(Palazzo del Governo Vecchio), built in 1475.   "It is the
last Roman Palace which still retains something of the
character of the mediæval fortress."†   .

It would take too long to go further into details.   The
relations of Sixtus IV. were undoubtedly admirable patrons
of Arts ; the armorial bearings of Riario Rovere and Basso on
many ancient piles bear witness to their splendid achieve-
ments in this line.

Sixtus also did much in the way of restoring the bridges,
walls, gates, towers, and other buildings of the City.‡   At
the Capitol these works were connected with the opening of
a museum of antiquities, the first public collection of the
kind in Italy, and indeed in Europe.§   The practical Sixtus
IV., by admitting the public to visit the collection, rendered
it more popular than it had been in the time of its founder,
Paul II.   Museums now began to appear everywhere
in connection with and as supplementing the Libraries.
The characters of distinguished men frequently present
great contradictions, and we find Sixtus IV., almost simul-
taneously with the opening of the Capitoline Museum, dispersing many of the costly treasures of the Palace of S.
Marco.   With similar inconsistency, he restored the equestrian statue of Marcus Aurelius and destroyed many ancient

---

* A detailed description is given by SCHMARSOW, 124 *seq.*

† GREGOROVIUS, VII., 638, 3rd ed.   See FORCELLA, XIII., 171.
An inscription on a restoration undertaken by Cardinal Gonzaga in
Bologna is given in Atti dell' Emilia, II., 188.

‡ MÜNTZ, III., 188 *seq.* ; FORCELLA, XIII., 13.

§ MÜNTZ, III., 168 *seq.*, and Le musée du Capitole, Paris, 1882.
See also MARCELLINO DA CIVEZZA, III., 91.

temples and triumphal arches.* But, however great the injury he may have inflicted on the ancient monuments, it was more than outweighed by his artistic embellishment of Rome, to which he imparted a completely new aspect. In order to encourage building in his capital, and to increase the number of its inhabitants, he had, in 1475, conferred the right of ownership on all who should build houses within the City district.†

One of the most beneficial works accomplished by Sixtus IV. was the restoration of the Hospital of S^{to} Spirito, a foundation of Innocent III., which had fallen into decay.‡ Pity for children deserted by unnatural mothers induced this Pope, whom his enemies depict as another Nero, to adopt Eugenius IV.'s undertaking. When Sixtus IV., in his frequent visits to the dilapidated house, saw these poor, forsaken children at play, his heart was touched, and he decided to have the Hospital thoroughly rebuilt and richly endowed. "He engaged the best Architects, hired a number of labourers, and commenced operations at once. Sixtus IV. considerably extended the original plan; he provided portions for the girls as they grew up, so that they might not be exposed, without resources, to the temptations of the world." § Although the building was certainly hurried on

* See MÜNTZ, III., 15. By a special Bull of 1474, Sixtus IV. protected the old Basilicas; MÜNTZ, Anc. Basil., 8.

† THEINER, Cod., III., 480–81. See MARCELLINO DA CIVEZZA, II. 725.

‡ ". . . Verum hoc quum longa vetustas
   Demolita foret, vix relliquiae ut remanerent,
   Sixtus id instaurat novaque omnia sumptibus illic
   Efficit immensis."

These lines are from the *Poem, cited p. 209, note * ; which is in Cod. 2403, f. 12, Court Library, Vienna.

§ PLATINA, Sixtus IV., 1064 ; SIGISMONDO DE' CONTI, I., 205 ; Bull., 226 ; FRANTZ, 165. S. Spirito was situated on the Tiber, and most

for the Jubilee Year, it was not until 1482 that the works were completed. The Architect of the whole is unknown; he could not have been Baccio Pontelli, who, until 1482, lived at Pisa and Urbino, not in Rome. Sixtus IV. also shewed his predilection for the Order of the Holy Ghost and for the Hospital "by a grant of various privileges and an increase of its fixed revenues."* Following the example of Eugenius IV., he re-established the confraternity in the spring of 1478, and himself became a member.† All the Cardinals and the whole Court followed him. From that time forward, it became more and more the custom to enter this pious society. The Confraternity-book of S^{to} Spirito has accordingly become, in its way, a unique collection of autographs.‡

of the German Hospitals of the Holy Ghost were also by the water, partly for sanitary reasons; see Zeitschr. des Vereins für Erforschung Rheinisch. Gesch., II., Part 4 (Mainz, 1864). A ground-plan of the whole institution is given by LETAROUILLY, Édifices de Rome, III., Pl. 256.

* BROCKHAUS, S. Spirito, 284–5, 289, 290. See also, in regard to Pontelli, REDTENBACHER, 147.

† Not 1477, as GREGOROVIUS, VII., 633, 3rd ed., and BROCKHAUS, 285, N. 10, state; in Bull., 245 seq., for A° VI. should be read A° VII., as RAYNALDUS, ad an. 1477, N. 12, has it, and, which is conclusive, the *Confraternity-book in the Archives of S^{to} Spirito, f. 65. The Bull was printed at the time (HAIN, pp. 14809–12). Only these Latin editions were hitherto known, but a German one also exists. In 1885 a copy of this most rare early-printed book (s. l. e. a., fol. 6 sheets) was offered by the antiquary, Alb. Cohn, in Berlin (Mohrenstrasse, No. 53, Catalogue 164, No. 429), for forty marks.

‡ See DUDIK, I., 86; GREGOROVIUS, loc. cit.; and Mon. Vat. Hist. Hung. illust., Ser. I., Tom. V., Budapest, 1889. The following entry, written in a firm hand, at f. 69 of the *Confraternity-book, is interesting: "Ego Rodericus de Boria episcopus Portuen. card^{lis} et ep. Valent. S. R. E. vicecancellarius intravi predict. sanct. confraternitatem die XXI. Martii, 1478, ea mente ut indulgentiam prefatam a S. D. N. concessam consequar ideo propria manu me suscripsi." Archives of S^{to} Spirito.

The magnificent scale on which the reconstruction of this
Hospital was carried out, so that even Alberti was satisfied
with it, is an abiding memorial of the benevolence of Sixtus
IV. Much pains were bestowed on the decoration of the
interior ; the spacious and airy hall for the sick was ornamented with frescoes as far as the tops of the windows, and
above them with a broad frieze of pictures arranged in
panels. Attention has recently been directed to these half-
faded paintings, which are of the ancient Umbrian type.
They portray the foundation of the Hospital by Innocent
III., and, in a very attractive form, the life of Sixtus IV.
from his birth. The inscriptions under them are from the
pen of Bartolomeo Platina.*

The architectural works of Sixtus IV. extended to almost
all the cities of the States of the Church, and even as far as
Savona and Avignon. Assisi, Bertinoro, Bieda, Bologna,
Caprarola, Cascia, Cesena, Citerna, Città di Castello, Civita
Vecchia, Corneto, Fano, Foligno, Forli, Monticelli, Nepi,
Orvieto, Ronciglione, Santa Marinella, Soriano, Spoleto,
Sutri, Terracina, Tivoli, Todi, Tolfa, Veroli, and Viterbo,
were all, in this respect, indebted to this Pontiff.†

---

* To BROCKHAUS belongs the merit of having first appreciated these
frescoes, which are not even mentioned by Crowe-Cavalcaselle ; he
gives a minute description of them, 429 *seq.* See also SCHMARSOW,
202 *seq.*, who establishes Platina's authorship of the inscriptions. A
copy of the legend under each picture is given in Cod. Barb., XXX.,
113, *f.* 80, of the Barberini Library. VILLENEUVE, 8, is mistaken in
his observations regarding this MS.

† See the accounts from the Archives given by MÜNTZ, 207–39. To
supplement these, see also *supra*, p. 427, and, with regard to what was
done in Assisi, CRISTOFANI, 332 *seq.* ; LASPEYRES, 7, 10, 13, 14, 32
seq. ; and REDTENBACHER, 164 ; for those at Bologna, a **Brief of
the 10th Nov., 1471, in the State Archives of that city. A *Brief to
Savona (*s. d.* preceding one of the 17th April, 1483) begins with these
words : * " Magno tenemur desiderio, ut capella quam in ecclesia

It is worthy of remark that Sixtus IV.'s patronage of
the Arts was universal in its character.   Sculpture was encouraged in the persons of Verocchio and Pollajuolo, and
he also did much for the promotion of the minor arts ;
medallists, engravers, glass-makers, cabinet-makers, gold-
smiths, weavers, and embroiderers were all employed by
him, and he also took an interest in pottery.*

In his orders for Works of Art, the Pope did not spare
expense, as is evident from the fact that the Tiara made
for him cost over 100,000 ducats.   In this, as in all other
things, he fully realised that the duties of a Pope are very
different from those of the General of a Mendicant Order.†

The artistic chronicle of this pontificate is not yet exhausted.   Sixtus IV. seems to have been even more active
as a promoter of painting than as a builder.   His practical
spirit was shewn in his command, that the painters settled
in Rome should form themselves into a Guild and draw up
statutes ; and this was the beginning of the famous Academy
of St. Luke.‡

B. Francisci istius civitatis construi facimus absolvatur et perficiatur."
They were to take care that this should be speedily done. (Lib. brev.,
15, f. 489, Secret Archives of the Vatican.) In Viterbo a palatium ad
habitationem presidis provincie patrimonii was built (see the *Decree of
Card. Sansoni, dated Viterbo, 1484, Mai 18, Lib. brev., 17, f. 37, Secret
Archives of the Vatican) : this building, now the Palazzo Pubblico,
still bears the Pope's arms with the inscription : Sixtus IIII., Pont. Max.

* UGOLINI, II., 530, and REUMONT, III., 1, 520.

† MÜNTZ, III., 30 ; REUMONT, III., 1, 426. Here is an account of
the medals and coins of Sixtus IV. See also MÜNTZ, Atelier monét.,
p. 2 ; Jahrb. der Preuss. Kunstsammlungen, II., 105, 232–3, III., 143.
The influence of the Renaissance on the leaden seals attached to
the Bulls of Sixtus IV., is noticed by MAS-LATRIE in the Rev. des
Quest. Hist., 1887, Avril, p. 433 seq.

‡ MISSIRINI, Mem. p. serv. alla storia della Romana Accademia di
S. Luca, Roma, 1823 ; PIAZZA, Opere pie, 621 ; SCHMARSOW, 149 seq. ;
MÜNTZ, III., 99–111.

Sixtus IV. was, in fact, for Painters what Nicholas V. had been for Architects. We find, employed in his service, men whose names are held in honour by the whole civilised world: Ghirlandajo, Botticelli, Signorelli, Perugino, Pinturicchio, and finally, the great Melozzo da Forli.*

This last-named artist was specially in touch with the stately characteristics of the Rovere family. Every one who has visited the Vatican galleries must remember Melozzo's picture of Sixtus IV., surrounded by his kindred, appointing Platina Prefect of the Vaticana. This was originally a fresco, and was afterwards transferred to canvas. If no other work of Melozzo's had been preserved, this one, " which captivates the eye at once by its simple and reposeful presentation of clearly defined personalities," would suffice to give us a very high idea of the painter's power.†

This magnificent picture was painted in 1476 and 1477. In the following year the master was working at Loreto, in 1479 he decorated the Chapel of the Choir in St. Peter's, and during 1480 and 1481 he was fully occupied in painting the Vatican Library.‡ Vasari does not mention any of these works, or, indeed, any one of Melozzo's, with the exception of his picture of the Ascension in the Church of SS. Apostoli. This, the most splendid masterpiece produced in Rome during the pontificate of Sixtus IV., was unfortunately

---

* See MÜNTZ, III., 89 *seq.* Pinturicchio worked, in the first instance, in the Sistine Chapel as assistant to Perugino, who was eight years his senior, and afterwards independently in the Capella Bufalini of Sta Maria in Araceli ; see SCHMARSOW, B. Pinturicchio in Rom (Stuttgart, 1882), and Gött. Gel. Anz., 1884, p. 796 *seq.* Regarding Signorelli's sojourn in Rome (1482–83), see VISCHER, L. Signorelli und die Ital. Renaissance, 88 (Leipzig, 1879).

† SCHMARSOW, 1 *seq.*, 42–8, 162 *seq.*, 204, 311. The Arundel Society has brought out a very good chromo-lithograph of this picture. The wood-cut in LÜTZOW, 425, is unsatisfactory.

‡ SCHMARSOW, 167.

destroyed, all but a few fragments, when the church was rebuilt in 1711. Vasari, who saw it, speaks of it with enthusiasm. "The figure of Christ," he says, "is so skilfully fore-shortened, that it appears to pierce the vaulting, and the surrounding angels equally seem to be soaring or floating in air. The Apostles, in their various attitudes, are also drawn with such admirable adaptation to the eye of the spectator, who views them from below, as to have won for Melozzo the highest praise from the artists both of his own day and of ours. The buildings in the picture display a perfect mastery of the laws of perspective."* The few remains of this painting still extant in the Chapter-house of St. Peter's and in the Quirinal, are just sufficient to enable us to guess what the beauty of the whole must have been.† A recent writer justly observes: "In boldness of conception, in largeness and freedom of execution, the fresco in the tribune of SS. Apostoli is a real masterpiece, and is an unanswerable proof of the excellence which it was given to this artist to attain."‡

The Chapel in the Vatican which bears the name of Sixtus IV. contains many splendid memorials of his artistic tastes. This simple and noble edifice was begun in 1473 §

* VASARI, Opere, III., 52, and SCHMARSOW, 167 *seq.*, and p. 71 regarding Melozzo as the special inventor of the " sotto in su."

† Authentic original photographs of the figures of the four Apostles, five Angels, and Christ, have been for the first time, published by SCHMARSOW, Plates, 13–22. The Arundel Society has a chromo-lithograph of two Angels.

‡ SCHMARSOW, 175, who is disposed to adopt 1481 as the year in which this painting was completed. Against the earlier view, that this great work was accomplished under the auspices of Cardinal P. Riario, see also Gött. Gel. Anz., 1882, p. 1616 *seq.*

§ PLATTNER-BUNSEN, Beschreibung von Rom, II., 1, 245. In the Vierteljahrsschrift für Musikwissenschaft, III., 234, Haberl seems to think that the Chapel was finished as early as 1473. In the *Eulogy

and finished in 1481. Vasari attributes the Cappella Sistina to Baccio Pontelli, but this is a mistake. It is the work of the Florentine, Giovannino de' Dolci, who must be looked upon as Sixtus IV.'s head Architect. The Sistina, henceforth the special Papal Chapel for ecclesiastical ceremonies of a semi-public character, is in form a parallelogram, and measures 132 feet by 45. "For two-thirds of its height the wall on the longer sides is unbroken, then there is a cornice, and above this six round-headed windows ; formerly there were two similar ones on the altar side, but these are now blocked up. Their position, however, is shewn by two false ones, painted with a fac-simile of the glass that filled them, on the opposite wall adjoining the Sala Regia. Each of these latter windows has a bull's eye in the centre. In the interior, all architectural divisions are purposely avoided, with the exception of the cornice, about 3 feet in width and provided with an iron balustrade, which runs round beneath the windows. The ceiling forms a shallow circular vault resting upon brackets, and is pierced by a skylight over each of the windows. The whole was, from the first, evidently intended to be covered with paintings."*

written in 1477, which has been mentioned *supra*, p. 209, note *, the following passage occurs :—

> *" Quumque intra divi sacra ipsa palatia Petri
> Nonnullas pater ille domos ornat reparatque
> Tum illic aedificat pulchrum praestansque sacellum.
> Quod quum perfectum fuerit pleneque politum
> Taleque iam factum, quale ipsum destinat auctor
> Amplo et celso animo, tum demum fas erit illud
> Praesulis absque pari monumentum dicere Sixti."

Cod. 2403, f. 11b, Court Library, Vienna.

* SCHMARSOW, 208. See BURCKHARDT, Cicerone, 99. Regarding the Architect of the Sistina, who had settled in Rome in the time of Nicholas V., and was much employed by Pius II., and appointed

A richly-sculptured balustrade of white marble, with the arms of Sixtus IV., divides the space in front intended for the Pope and the Cardinals from that of the laity. The tribune for the singers, which projects but slightly to the left, is similarly enclosed. The floor is beautifully inlaid in stone.

For the decoration of this modest and unpretending building, Sixtus IV. summoned to his Court all the most distinguished painters of Umbria and Tuscany. Domenico Ghirlandajo, Sandro Botticelli, Luca Signorelli, Cosimo Roselli, Pietro Perugino, and Pinturicchio vied with each other in a noble rivalry in its embellishment.* The time taken to complete the paintings on the walls of the Sistina, which were begun in the year 1480, "greatly tried the patience of the Pope. Like Julius II. at a later period, when Michael Angelo was painting the roof, Sixtus IV. could scarcely bear to wait for the termination of the work. On the anniversary of his election, the vigil of S. Lawrence," Jacobus Volaterranus tells us, "he came unannounced, and quite against his usual custom (*extra ordinem*), to Vespers in the Chapel to see how the frescoes were getting on. At last, on the 15th August, 1483, came the long-desired day of their completion."† On the Feast of the Assumption of our Lady, which that year fell on a Saturday, the Pope, we learn from a contemporary, came to the new Chapel and

praesidens fabricae under Paul II., see MÜNTZ, Giovannino de' Dolci con docum. inediti., Roma, 1880.

* LERMOLIEFF (Die Werke Italienischer Meister, 304 *seq.*, Leipzig, 1880) infers, from the landscape, the composition, and many peculiarities, that Pinturicchio probably executed the pictures of the Baptism of Christ and the journey of Moses, which Perugino had been commissioned to paint. This is not the place for a more detailed treatment of the subject, on which see SCHMARSOW, B. Pinturicchio in Rom (Stuttgart, 1882), and Preuss. Jahrb., XLVII., 50 *seq.*, XLVIII., 129.

† JACOBUS VOLATERRANUS, 188; SCHMARSOW, 209–10. Volaterranus is as trustworthy in his dates as Infessura is the reverse.

there heard Mass. There was no further ceremony. All the Prelates and some others assisted at the function. The only Cardinal present was Raffaelo Sansoni. This was the first Mass said after the completion of the Chapel, and only the ecclesiastics belonging to it attended. In commemoration of the event, the Pope published an Indulgence for all who should visit the sanctuary, including women. Sixtus IV. also attended Vespers there that same day. The Prelates were placed below Cardinal Sansoni on the benches assigned to the Sacred College. The Pope blessed the people, both at Mass and at Vespers. When it became known that an Indulgence had been granted to those who should visit the Chapel, the whole City was astir in a moment. The crowd in the Sistina was so great that it was extremely difficult either to enter or to leave the Church, and the throng continued to pass through until after midnight. On the Pope's coronation day, the first solemn High Mass was celebrated in the new Chapel; Giuliano della Rovere being celebrant and all the Cardinals assisting.*

The whole series in the Sistina consisted originally of fifteen frescoes, twelve of which still remain on its longer sides, the other three having given place to Michael Angelo's colossal picture of the Last Judgment.† On the left wall, looking to the right from the altar, are represented events from the history of Moses. According to the custom and taste of the period, several scenes are grouped in the same picture around the principal subject. Moses slaying the Egyptian, driving away the shepherds who hindered Jethro's daughter from drawing water, going into Egypt, and, with his sandals put away, worshipping God in the burning

---

* JACOBUS VOLATERRANUS, *loc. cit.*

† The series of the life of Moses and of Christ has thus been deprived of its beginning.

bush, are thus combined, due to the pencil of Botticelli. The whole forms "a masterpiece of vivid feeling and expression and technical facility."*

Signorelli's farewell and death of Moses is another glorious creation, full of dramatic power. In contemplating it, "we perceive at once that the artist was thoroughly aware that the strength of his rivals lay in composition and in the management of light and shade. In his grouping, largeness of conception and combination are united with great clearness of detail. The drawing is bold and strongly marked, and the entire execution bears the impress of great care and taste, as also the employment of gold on the draperies."†

On the right wall are paintings by Pinturicchio, Botticelli, Ghirlandajo, Roselli, and Perugino, representing scenes from the life of our Lord. Two of these frescoes, the Vocation of SS. Peter and Andrew, by Ghirlandajo, and St. Peter receiving the Keys, by Perugino, "stand out from among the other mural paintings in so marked a manner, indicating the approaching triumph of the noble ideal style in art, that nothing but the overpowering proximity of Michael Angelo's work could prevent the immediate recognition of this important fact."‡ All artists agree in considering Perugino's Institution of the Primacy "one of his most perfect productions." The solemn grandeur of this marvel-

---

* RUMOHR, II., 272. See The Ecclesiologist, XXIX., 195. The date of Botticelli's arrival in Rome is uncertain ; according to LIPPMANN in the Jahrb. der Preuss. Kunstsammlungen, IV., 71, perhaps it may have been in October, 1482.

† CROWE-CAVALCASELLE, IV., 8-9, who also remarks : "Signorelli unquestionably deserves a place of honour among the painters of the Sistina" ; see also BURCKHARDT, Cicerone, 552. Roselli's pictures are the least successful ; Sixtus IV.'s expression of opinion regarding them is, however, a mere legend ; see RIO, II., 65 and 83.

‡ SCHMARSOW, 227.

lous creation fully corresponds with the dignity of its subject, and this latter is enhanced to the imagination by
the situation of the picture.

Ghirlandajo, however, surpassed all his companions. His
masterly genius enabled him to grasp the vocation of SS.
Peter and Andrew in its most impressive and solemn
aspect. "His picture is, so to speak, a foreshadowing of
Raphael's Miraculous draught of Fishes and Feed my
Sheep."*

The wall behind the altar was adorned by a painting of
the Assumption of our Lady, with Sixtus IV. praying
beneath it. Vasari believes this to be the work of Perugino,
but Sigismondo de' Conti remarks, in regard to this fresco,
that the Blessed Virgin seems actually to rise from the
earth towards Heaven ;† Perugino never possessed the art
of fore-shortening in its perfection. "So marvellous is the
view from beneath, so real the ascent towards Heaven, that
no man then living, save Melozzo da Forli, could have
created the like," and the most recent investigations are
perhaps right in assigning the work to the great Master,
who has been called the forerunner of Raphael and
Michael Angelo. ‡

As we survey this sanctuary of Italian Renaissance, we
cannot fail to acknowledge that the choice of subjects for
the frescoes in the Papal Chapel could not have been improved. § To the chief scenes from the life of Moses on the

* BURCKHARDT, Cicerone, 552. See PLATTNER-BUNSEN, Beschreibung der Stadt Rom, II., 1, 252, and The Ecclesiologist, XXIX., 195
seq.

† SIGISMONDO DE' CONTI, I., 205.

‡ SCHMARSOW, 214 ; see 317 seq. In the Repert., XI., 199, are to
be found Janitschek's remarks in support of a contrary opinion.

§ See PRUDENTIUS ROMANUS, Römisches Leben, in the Wiener
"Vaterland," 1888, May 20, and REUMONT'S Römische Briefe, I., 75
seq.

one side, correspond on the other those from the life of our Lord, as the fulfilment of their typical signification. What Moses, the leader of the chosen people, foreshadowed, has been perfected by Christ for all time.   Peter, who lives in his successors here, reigns as the Vicar of Christ.   Through him the human race is brought to the Saviour, as the Jewish nation, the type of Christendom, was led by Moses to the feet of the Christ.   The development of the whole plan of Salvation is concentrated in the three names : Moses, Christ, Peter.   Thus, the magnificent drama of the Story of the Church is presented to the spectator as the Life and the Truth in the frescoes of this Chapel, which, in its historical aspect, is the most remarkable in the world, and thus worthily was the building fitly inaugurated, which afterwards, under another Pope of the house of Rovere, was to be enriched with the marvellous productions of the giant genius of Michael Angelo.

APPENDIX

OF

UNPUBLISHED DOCUMENTS

AND

EXTRACTS FROM ARCHIVES.

APPENDIX.

1. Cardinal Ammanati to Francesco Sforza, Duke of Milan.*

1464, Sept. 1, Rome.

La Ex. V. havera inteso la nova creatione del pontefice et forse in se medesma pensera quanto sia da stimarla. Signore, primum et ante omnia, questi r^{mi} cardinali antichi, creati da altri papi che Pio deliberorno unanimiter fra loro de non eleggere se non de loro medesmi parendoli che N. S. defuncto per esser stato pocho nel cardinalato non li havesse charezati ne stimati tanto quanto haveriano voluto, che imputavano allo haver poco provato ch' è esser cardinale. Ne da questo proposito se potiano revocare. Alchuni de novi, non essendo dacordo, ne vedendo haverli a riescire il fatto loro proprio per gratificarsi se ne andorono con li prefati antichi. Onde che ancora io vedendo la necessita della cosa per non esser scluso dalla gratia sua et perche sempre me haveva mostrata optima voluna verso de V. Ex. ne andai con li altri. A Dio se vole referire tutto che in tal loco et tempo mirabiliter opera. Io sono de opinione ch' ogni giorno piu V. Ex. sara satisfacta et che le demonstrationi et opere de questo pontefice ve saranno accepte et grate et il parlare suo quotidiano assai efficacemente lo demonstra . . . .

[Original in Ambrosian Library, Milan. Cod. Z.-219, Supp.]

* The above letter is entirely in his own handwriting ; see *supra*, p. 13.

2. JOHANNES PETRUS ARRIVABENUS TO MARCHIONESS BARBARA
OF MANTUA.*

1464, Sept. 2, Rome.

The Archbishop of Spalatro (L. Zane), che foe nepote del
vicecancelliere vechio è facto thesaurere.† El. rev. monsignor
vicecancelliere secondo el iudicio havera gran conditione et
merito chè s'è fatigato a la real.‡

[Original in Gonzaga Archives, Mantua.]

3. CARDINAL GONZAGA TO HIS FATHER, LODOVICO DE
GONZAGA.§

1464, Sept. 4, Rome.

. . . Costui comincia a far del altiero e molto stima suoa
dignitate; puoria accadere chel concilio che è statuito de far in
termino de tre anni lo faria puoi humiliare.

[Original in Gonzaga Archives, Mantua.]

4. JOHANNES PETRUS ARRIVABENUS TO MARCHIONESS BARBARA
OF MANTUA.

1464, Oct. 3, Rome.

The Plague is raging in Rome.‖ Questo papa ha mutato la
stampa del piombo de le bolle; da un canto fa S. Paulo e S. Petro
che sedeno; da l' altro lui è in cattedra e doi cardinali presso cum
alcune persone denanti in ginochione.¶

Discontent on the part of the Secretaries, because most of them
had not yet had audience.** The influence of the Bishop of
Vicenza with Paul II.††

[Original in the Gonzaga Archives, Mantua.]

---

* See *supra*, p. 124.   † See GOTTLOB, Cam. Apost.

‡ This account of Card. Borgia is repeated by J. P. Arrivabenus in a
*Despatch of 4th Sept., 1464 : * " El rev. mons. vicecancelliere ha gran credito
et certo l'ha meritato cum costui." (Gonzaga Archives.) Regarding Borgia's
part in the Conclave, which is here alluded to, see also *supra*, p. 12.

§ See *supra*, p. 25.   ‖ See *supra*, p. 29, note §.

¶ See *supra*, p. 108.   All Paul II.'s leaden Bulls are distinguished by their
tasteful and delicate execution ; see Arch. St. Ital. (3rd series), IX., 2, 195 ; and
Mél. d'Archéologie, 1888, p. 454.   The Medals of this Pope are equally fine ;
see Jahrbuch der Preuss. Kunstsammlungen, II., 92 f.

** See *supra*, p. 26.   †† See *supra*, p. 111 *seq.*

5. Jacopo de Aretio to Marchioness Barbara of Mantua.*

1464, Oct. 9, Rome.

. . . Lo r^{mo} mons. vicecancelliere ne ha hauta una pesta de questa sua malattia insino al presente, pur heri comenzo ad usir fora, non è perho ancor salda la cicatrice de la peste; molto gla giovato l'alegreza che ha hauta de la restitution sua al pristino officio, che papa Pio glavia interdetto; † cum detrimento perho è facta questa restitutione de molti poveretti che haviano compero l'officio et io so uno di quelli; è perho dato ordine che sieno restituiti li denari che difficil cosa sira perche non è picciola somma onde forse per questa casone qualche sancto ce aiutera . .

[Original in Gonzaga Archives, Mantua.]

6. Tristano Sforza to Francesco Sforza, Duke of Milan.‡

1464, Oct. 21, Rome.

. . . Disse§ poy come con Veneciani non credeva poter mantener amicitia perche erano molti in quel regimento li quali gli erano inimici; item di sua natura erano tanto insolenti che non li potria comportare et diceva che se rendeva certo venendo qua la loro ambasciata, non li stariano XV. di, che seriano in discordia con S. Sta . . .

[Original in the Ambrosian Library, Milan.   Cod. Z.–219, Supp.]

7. Cardinal Gonzaga to his Mother, Marchioness Barbara of Mantua.‖

1464, Dec. 28, Rome.

Hoggi havendo terminato la Sta di N. S. che li cardinali portino di continuo berette rosse parendo essere colore conveniente a la dignitate, ne donoe una per ciascuno et ha inhibito che in corte niuno altro le posse portare rosse su la fogia da preti et la S. Sta portara la beretta e capuzino de cremesino. El di de natale celebroe esso nostro S^{re} et io cantai l'evangelio nel quale me feci grande honore . . .

[Original in the Gonzaga Archives, Mantua.]

---

* See *supra*, p. 38.   † See Voigt, III., 553, N. 1.
‡ See *supra*, p. 95.   § Paul II.   ‖ See *supra*, p. 25.

8. Pope Paul II. to the Doge Cristoforo Moro, and the Senate of Venice.*

s. d. [1464/5].†

Paulus II. . . . . Christoforo Moro duci universoque senatui Veneto salutem. "Vas electionis, etc." The Pope draws the attention of the Venetians to the many misfortunes which they endured, to the calamities in the East, Plague, &c. These are judgments from God for their cupido dominandi. Intermissa fidei causa Tergestum ‡ imperialem urbem oppugnare aggressi quantum eris et temporis perdideritis et quod iacturis affecti fueritis, ipsa rebus infectis soluta obsidio patefecit. Serious charges are then made against the Venetians :—(1) You despise the priests and Bishops; (2) you have occupied lands belonging to the Church; (3) you have, without permission, imposed tithes on benefices, but prohibited the Papal tithes; (4) you exclude the clergy from public offices "ut iam quicunque apost. sedis gratiam promeruerit in propinquo ab omnibus publicis rebus se cognoscat extorrem." Warning and admonition to turn from this course.

[Cop. s. d. Cod. Ottob., 1938, f. 9–16. Vatican Library.]

9. Metrical Inscription on the Church and Palace of S. Marco.§

Patritius Veneta Paulus de gente secundus
Barbo genus magni princeps vicerector Olympi
Hec patribus monumenta dedit decora alta . . . ||
Marmoribus templum Marci reparavit et arte
Et posuit latis miranda palatia muris
Cesareae quales fuerant sub collibus aedes
Hinc hortos dryadumque domos et amena vireta
Porticibus circum et niveis lustrata columnis.

[Secret Archives of the Vatican, Armar., XXXIX., T. X., f. 83b.¶]

---

* See *supra*, p. 96.

† As the contest about tithes lasted until 1468, this very ample letter (rather a treatise than a letter) may be assigned to a later date. I have selected an earlier one on account of the mention of the war with Trieste.

‡ Manuscript: *Trigrestum*.

§ See *supra*, p. 78.

|| An illegible word, perhaps meaning "reformans."

¶ These verses are preceded by others, which also occur "in frontispicio

10. Jacopo de Aretio to Marchioness Barbara of Mantua.*

1465, Jan. 31, Rome.

. . . La Sta de N. S. sta anchor bene et attende a far una mirabil mitra la qual chiamano el regno, perche se fa al exemplo de quella de S. Silvestro cum li tri corone, chiamata el regno ; vole anchora come per altra ho scripto che questi r^{mi} s. cardinali usino insegni cioe ornamenti differenti da li altri prelati † et perche similmente è honesto che Sua B^{ne} sia differentiata da li cardinali comenza a usare lo scapuccino de cremesi, non so quello usaranno li cardinali, ditto messer Johanni porra referire. Questo so che S. Sta è molto tenace et strecta a concedere gratie exorbitanti da rasgione come sono dispense et altre gratie difficili et per tanto tutti li officiali se lamentono perho che simili gratie son quelle che mettono dinari in corte per rispecto de le taxe et nel dare audientia S. B. fa a modo usato cioè che pena usa a darla, ma ristora in una cosa che quando la da ascolta volontieri et non fa caso che nel dire l' homo. sia longo . . . .

[Original in the Gonzaga Archives, Mantua.]

11. Augustinus de Rubeis ‡ to Francesco Sforza, Duke of Milan.§

1465, April 21, Rome.

. . . De le altre cerimonie facte per la Sta del N. S^{re} a questa pasqua et de una mitria in tre corone papale de precio forsi de piu de LX^m ducati, quale ha facta fare il papa nova, portatola il di de pasqua et con essa celebrata la messa informarà a piena la V. S^{ia} praedict. Francesco de Varese che ha veduto ogni cosa.‖

[Original in the Ambrosian Library, Milan.]

---

hortorum divi Marci " ; MARINI, II., 199, has published them without more exactly mentioning their source. Some verses on Paul II.'s palace, composed by Porcello de' Pandoni, are in MÜNTZ, II., 54. Verses "in laquearibus templi S. Marci" in DE ROSSI, Inscript., II., 439 ; see also Mél. d'Archéol., 1888, p. 455, N. 3.

* See *supra*, p. 26.　　　　　　　† See *supra*, p. 477, No. 7.

‡ Regarding this Ambassador, see also PORTIOLI, 23.

§ See *supra*, p. 107.

‖ I have sought in vain for this Report. In the Gonzaga Archives, Mantua, I found a *Letter of Bald. Suardo to Marchioness Barbara, which speaks of

12. Instruction for the Milanese Ambassador, Emanuel de Jacopo * to Louis XI.†

1466, March 3, Milan.

Cose che sono da dire per Emanuele a la M^{ta} del re de Franza. The Venetians are always spreading injurious reports regarding France.

Item diray a la M^{ta} sua chel ne pare per bene de la M^{ta} Sua che sopraseda ad dare l' obedientia al papa perche, soprasedendo, el papa se sforzarà sempre ad compiacergli et fargli cosa grata per indurlo ad questa obedientia et questo finche la M^{ta} Sua havera assetato ad suo modo le cose de suo regno, perche dapoy sempre pora fare quello sera de suo piacere . . . .

[Copy in National Library, Paris. Fonds Ital., Cod. 1611.]

13. Pope Paul II. to Bologna.‡

1466, April 29, Rome.

Intelleximus quod Rhenus fluvius qui iam pridem proprium alveum egressus fuit magnam partem agri nostri Bononiensis inundat maximumque damnum ex huiusmodi inundatione resultat tam civibus civitatis nostre Bononie quam incolis comitatus territorii eiusdem . . . .

Yet greater damage is to be feared for the future. Therefore they are to take measures to have the river led back to its bed. Dat. Romae apud S. Marcum sub annulo piscatoris die XXIX. Aprilis 1466 pont. nostri a° 2°.

[Original in the State Archives, Bologna, lib. Q.–3.]

14. Timoteo Maffei to Piero de' Medici.§

1466, June 15, Rome.

The Pope will again take measures to promote peace in Italy, although he found the Venetians disinclined for it. Tuum dolorem

---

the new mitre made by order of Paul II. The cost is here estimated at 30,000 ducats; much higher sums are named by Canensius, 43-4, and Ammanati, Comment., p. 371 (Frankfort ed. of 1614).

* See Reumont, Diplomazia, 367, and Lettres de Louis XI., III., 10, 55, 145, 327.

† See *supra*, p. 100. ‡ See *supra*, p. 34.

§ See *supra*, pp. 86 and 154.

tuasque lachrymas, quas pro irruptione Turcorum in Albaniam emisisti, gratas habuit : sed gratiorem oblationem quam illi tuo nomine tuoque iussu feci . . . .

[State Archives, Florence. Av. il princ., f. 17, N. 506.]

15. CARDINAL GONZAGA TO MARQUESS LODOVICO OF MANTUA.*

1466, July 5, Rome.

Illmo S^r mio patre. Veneri proximo † in consistorio la Sta de N. S. molto turbato et alteramente propose che de novo la S. de Vinesia ha fatto publicare ne le terre suoe de vuolere riscuotere da preti sei decime, per la qual graveza pare chel clero se ne sia dogliuto et ha havuto ricorso a la sede apost^{ca}. Parse che la S. B^{ne} ne fosse grandemente sdignata e che chi li havesse consentito de facto haveria mandato de la excommunicatione et interdicti cominciando a rumpere cum lor con larme spirituali. Pur essendo iudicata la cosa de grande importantia e digna de molto contrapeso foe determinato che se gli facesse pensiere sopra e puoi nel primo consistorio se pigliasse el partito de quanto se havesse a fare pro honore sedis apostolice. Qui è opinione dalcuni che essendo Venetiani secretamente in acordio col Turcho vogliano cum questo riscuotere fare doe cose : restaurarsi de le spese fatte per el passato et occultare tanto piu la intelligentia de la pace col Turcho credendo che quando la brigata veda fare queste aspere exactioni debba stare in opinione che pur siano in guerra dal canto de là . . . Romae v. Julii, 1466.

Ill. D. V. filius observ^{mus}.

F. CARD^{LIS} DE GONZAGA.

[Original in the Gonzaga Archives, Mantua.]

16. CARDINAL GONZAGA TO MARQUESS LODOVICO OF MANTUA.‡

1466, July 19, Marino.

. . . Circa quelle decime da Vinesia foe pur concluso doppo molti ragionamenti de mandarli un messo ea de causa ut desisterent da metterle e casu che nol facessero mettere man a l' arme spirituali e mandare excommunicatione et interdicti. Tamen el messo fu

---

* See *supra*, p. 96. † July 4. ‡ See *supra*, p. 97.

fatto soprastare de qua per alcuni dì che penso sia o per vedere se interim cum littere et altre trame se puotesse assettare o che el *papa** voglia prima vedere de havere qualche intelligentia o cum *el re Ferando** o cum *qualche potencia* per non rimanere solo a la pugna . . . . Marini, xix. Julii, 1466.

[Original in the Gonzaga Archives, Mantua.]

17. BARTHOLOMAEUS DE MARASCHIS TO MARCHIONESS BARBARA OF MANTUA.†

1466, Sept. 1, Rome.

A questi di scrissi como in Alemagna era scoperta una setta de heretici quasi simili a questi fratizelli de la opinione.‡ Qua a la corte erano mandate littere sopra cio dal vescovo Laventino al quale daria pocha fede cum sit chel ne habia puocha se non se havesse per altre vie questo esser vero; pur ho cercato havere copia de una littera mandata da esso Laventino al vescovo de Ratisbona § che in vero è una brutta cossa et questa copia mando a la Ex. V. El papa pur ha habuti tri termini de febre terzana, non grande, credese presto guarirà . . .

[Original in the Gonzaga Archives, Mantua.]

18. CARDINAL GONZAGA TO HIS FATHER, MARQUESS LODOVICO OF MANTUA.||

1467, Jan. 7, Rome.

. . . Questa matina in consistorio secreto fossemo sopra la materia del soccorso che dimanda el Scandarbec et in summa el papa disse che li daria cinque milia duc^{ti} ne piu voleva dargene allegando che anche lui bisognava provedere a li fatti suoi,

---

* These words are in cipher with the key annexed.

† See *supra*, pp. 116 and 189.

‡ Regarding these heretics, see *supra*, p. 113 *seq.*

§ I found this letter, dated Breslau, 1466, June 11 (which JANNER, III., 565, cites from Cod. 716 of the Königl. Kreissbibl., Ratisbon), also in Cod. 4764, N. 14, of the Court Library, Vienna; it is printed in the Anal. Francisc., 422, now also by DÖLLINGER, Beitr. z. Sectengesch. d. M.-A., II., 625-6 (München, 1890), from Cod. Paris Library, 5178, with the wrong date, ii. Jan., 1466, and other variations.

|| See *supra*, pp. 89 and 155.

monstrando pur de temere de qualche novitate. Qui el card^le de li Ursini comincioe a dire che la S. Sta non haveva a temere da niuno lucco, allegando le ragione perche non; el papa se ne scaldoe e corruciato usci a campo dicendo che sapeva del certo chel re haveva consultato cum cinque soli, di quali uno ge ne haveva dato adviso, se doveva assaltare el stato de la chiesia o non, e che questi cinque gli havevano persuaso che lo facesse e cussi anche lo re se li monstrava molto animato. . . .

[Original in the Gonzaga Archives, Mantua.]

19. Joh. Blanchus* to Galeazzo Maria Sforza, Duke of Milan.†

1468, Febr. 28, Rome.

. . . Haveano bene essi ambasciatori‡ tutti insieme pensato de andare hozi tutti al papa ad visitarlo et dolersi de questi tractati che gli sono stati facti contra et ad offerirli voy sig. principali de la liga molto largamente per consolarlo alquanto, etc., ma havendo loro mandato da S. Sta ad richiederlo de audientia per potere exequire dicto loro pensiero senza farli assapere alcuna cosa de quello gli volessero dire et essendoli facta lambassata venne de fuori el suo cubiculario et dixe al misso che l' haveva per doe volte facta lambassata, ma che S. Sta non havea resposto ne si ne non, el che se iudica sii per grande affanno che ha S. Sta de questi tractati come e da credere debba havere. Credo starano mo ad expectare che S. Sta mandi per loro.

Questi tractati hano molto diminuita la reputatione del papa appresso quelli che intendeno qualche cosa. S. Sta se partite da le habitatione de S. Petro et venne ad habitare ad S. Marco § per levarse de le mano de Orsini et stare fra Colonesi. Ma ad quello se vede l' è ‖ periculo per tutto. Credo che S. Sta sii in grande affanno et como el tractato se andara scoprendo maiore tanto maioremente gli crescera l' affanno et cosi e converso sel tractato ser de poca stima.

[Original in the State Archives, Milan, Cart. gen. ad an.]

---

* See, regarding this Ambassador, Gingins, Dép. Mil., I., xvi., II., 37, 308, 368.

† See *supra*, pp. 46 *seq.* and 58.   ‡ Of the League.

§ In MS.: *Maro.*   ‖ In MS.: *le.*

20. Augustinus de Rubeis to Galeazzo Maria Sforza, Duke of Milan.*

1468, Febr. 29, Rome.

Illustr., etc. El me occorre de presente de scrivervi una nova hystoria accaduta qua acio V. Ex. sapia la cossa como passa, perche so bene se ne dira variamente. Nam in questa corte erano alcuni docti, gioveni, poeti e philosofi tra li quali se domandaveno li principali uno Calimacho Venetiano, secretario del rev^mo cardinale de Ravenna,† uno Glaucho Coldelmero pur de Venesia, Petreo secretario del rev^mo cardinale de Pavia,‡ non so di che payse fusse; uno altro Platano Mantovano, secretario del rev^mo cardinale de Mantua§ et uno familiaro del rev^mo vescovo de Feltro,‖ thexaurero apostolico con molti altri scriptori et cortesani de diversi lochi, sed del dominio vostro non ce ne era veruno. Quali havevano facti una certa secta za piu di de persone asay et tuta volta multiplicava de gente de ogni condicione, la piu parte famiglii de cardinali et de prelati. Et costoro tenevano opinione chel non fusse altro mondo che questo et morto il corpo morisse la anima et demum che ogni cossa fusse nulla se non attendere a tuti piaceri e volupta, sectatori del Epicuro et de Aristippo dummodo potesseno far senza scandalo, non za per tema de Dio, sed de la iusticia del mondo, havendo in omnibus respecto al corpo, perche l' anima tenevano per niente. Et ita non facevano altro che goldere manzando carne la quadragesima, non andar may a la messa, non se curar de vigilie ne de santi et al tutto contempnendo papa, cardinali et la giesia catholica universale. Dicevano che santo Francesco era stato uno ypocrita et demum se facevano beffe de dio e de li santi, vivando al suo modo usaveno maschii e femene promiscue et indifferenter cum singulis similibus, etc. Se vergognaveno esser domandati per nome christiani. Propterea se li havevano facti mutare et se chiamaveno li soprascripti nomi stranei et de simile. Dicevano che Moyses era stato un grande inganator de homini con sue leze et Christo un seductore de popoli e Machometo homo de grande ingegno, che se tirava dreto tuta gente per industria e malitia sua, siche era grande manchamento ali moderni docti sequir tal leze e norme se non viver al

---

** See *supra*, p. 50 *seq.*
§ F. Gonzaga.*

*† B. Roverella.
‖ A. Faseolus; see *supra*, p. 112.*

‡ Ammanati.

suo modo, etc. Gli era ancora uno de li principalissimi chiamato Julio Pomponio doctissimo homo, Romano, qual circha uno anno ando a Venesia et li par legesse et modo sia destenuto pur per tal cason. Tandem devenerant isti ad tantam insolentiam ultra laltre pacie che tutoldi andaveno vociferando et digando che certamente il papa morirà presto inante passasse il mese de marzo proximo mo luno mo laltro et in diversi lochi et modi siche se ne faria un altro et che le cosse andariano per altra via. Intanto ch' essendone piu fiate avisata S. Sta se ne faceva beffe credando fusse per vaticinii o per astrologia, etc. Et tra laltri lo nostro rev^mo cardinale de Thyano * sentendone pur qualche cossa ghe ne dedi notitia per scaricho suo et anche non lo extimo Sua B^ne ni may monstrò farni caso fin ch' un Juliano de l' Aquila, altre fiate factor de monsig^re de Pavia † la in quele parte et nunc fora de casa sua cum pocha gratia et qual era molto mal contento, fu temptato da alcuni de questi ita superficialiter de la morte del papa maxime dal dicto Petreo per esser stati piu domestici in una casa medesima, al qual dando parole generale subito pensò retornare in gratia del patrono col scoprir questa cossa. Et ita fecit et immediate esso monsignore feci chiamare dicto Petreo interrogandolo de questa materia ac etiam examinandolo suptilmente. Qui confessus fuit et non negavit qualiter erano una brigata che havevano determinato amazar lo papa et mettere sotto e sopra tuta la corte e nominò Calimacho dicto de sopra per lo capo de la brigata et che questo facto havevano ordinato far il di primo de quaresma ala messa papale in dacione cinerum. Dil che replicandoli lo cardinale como haveva potuto consentir saltem a la pernicie sua chel sapeva pur li voleva ben, gli rispose haveva pensato dirli quello giorno et confortarlo che non andasse a la messa per bene de la persona sua et camparlo a quelo modo. His autem intellectis immaginò S. R^ma S. scrutari hanc rem medulitus per poterne meglio chiarire la Sta del papa et dixit isti chel dovesse andar a veder da quelo Calimacho et informarse bene de la cossa, postea ritornar con intentione sel se ne trovava fondamento de poterne certificare lo papa et darli ne le mane luno et laltro. Sed fo tristo et fece notitia ad esso Calimacho, a Glaucho, et luy insemo, quali erano capita istius factionis, et se ne fugireno senza altro indusio ni retornar dal cardinale. Tamen incontinenti fece sapere il tuto al papa, sed non

* N. Forteguerri. † Ammanati.

se potereno havere costoro; ma alchuni altri seguaci foreno pigliati, che non sano lo trattato formaliter. Nientedemeno son stati examinati e cosi se recitava questa hystoria multifariam et multis modis. Alchuni dicevano che havevano tractato de amazare lo papa et mettere a carne e sacho tuti li preti et altri quando gli fosse stato possibile menando le mano a tuti, etc. E per fornir meglio tal pensere havevano trama etiamdio con uno d. Lucha de Tocio,* citadino Romano, bandito za piu anni passati; ma perche è doctore e valente homo stava presso la M^{ta} del sig^{re} re Ferando con bona reputatione e nome de regio consiglero, il qual haveva luy anchora intelligentia de molto altro numero de banditi e sfidati da Roma bene piu de quatro o cinque cento persone, le qual tute dovevano entrar in questa terra secretamente cum ordine dato al primo di de quaresima nel hora de la messa papalle quando zetasse la cenere in capo lo papa, retrovarsse insemo nascosti per le ruine sono a canto al palazo de le case zetate a terra per ampliarlo e farlo mazor, qual e grandissimo spatio dascondere nedum tanti homini, ma uno exercito, etc. Da laltra parte dovevano venir circha L. o LX. persone cum quili altri cortesani soprascripti su la piaza de dicto palazo et incomenzare questione con li famigli di cardinali e prelati, che stano expectando li patroni li, per occupare alcuni pochi fanti che stano a la guarda del papa, perche a dire lo vero viveva molto liberamente e cum pocha custodia. E cossi quisti altri nascosti, atachato lo rumore dal canto di qua, subito dovivano entrar la giesia, amazar lo papa et quanti ne havessero voluto de nuy altri. Postea sachezar, rubar e far al suo modo con intentione esso d. Lucha de Tocio de introdur uno novo stato di populo e farsi luy patrono de li altri se la fantasia li sequeva. Alcuni altri dicono questo facto se doveva far hogi, che è la dominica de carneval et tuto lo populo va a festo in Testazo e li fanti de la guarda e li altri officiali, ita che restano poche persone per Roma e ne le case e nel hora de la festa far lo insulto al palazo, zetar a terra le porte et amazar lo papa; il che seria stato fornito in ante se fusse sentuto la cossa e potuto gionger lo succorso, deinde andare de casa in casa a li cardinali et altri e far lo medesimo. Et alcuni

---

* Compare our Vol. III., p. 107 *seq.* and *supra*, pp. 49, 52, 58. In a *Brief of Sixtus IV. (without address), dat. Rome, 1483, Sept. 23, "Lucas Tozolus eques Romanus car^{mi} in Christo filii nostri Ferdinandi Sicilie regis ill. orator," is mentioned. Secret Archives of the Vatican.

dicevano se doveva far lo di de le palme per lo soprascripto modo, etc. Il perchè non se potendo sapere ben el vero, deliberassemo nuy oratori de la liga andar al papa per sapere avisar li nostri principali de la verita intesa de Sua B^ne e per offerirse li in tal caso, etc. Fu contenta haverci auditi et ce ringratiò. Postmodum ce narrò tuto il facto de le heresie ut supradictum est nominando li sopradicti principali tuti et su questa parte monstrò far un gran caso de voler extirpar tal heresia dolendose non haver havuta prima notitia, etc. De questa altra conspiracione in la persona sua ce disse haver inteso tuto quanto e scripto de sopra, sed che anche non trovava lo fundamento, perchè non se erano potuti haver li principali, quali cerchava tuta via de trovare e credeva li haveria. Et lo piu havesse potuto intervenir fin a mo era la confessione de uno di presi chi diceva del certo lo predicto d. Lucha de Tocio esser dentro de Roma per questa cason et che li haveva parlato luy ben che non se ne sia potuto trovare indicio ne certeza alcuna ; imo a mandato il papa fin a Napoli a sapere sel se absentato niuno di de là et anche non è venuto la risposta ; adjungendo costuy ultra de cio che esso d. Lucha haveva etiamdio tractato in castello S. Angelo et haveva mandato mille ducati a certi fanti de la guardia per dover pigliar lo castello a sua richesta, etc. A facto fare inquisitione grande il papa per cavarne la verita et non ha trovato altro fundamento. Se crede che quisto tal confesso simile cosse lo habia * facto per intrichar et alongar la iusticia de la persona sua. E questo è usque nunc cio che se trova. Non se cessa de fare ogne diligentia per haver li principali, et ha lo papa facto bandir che li da uno de li tri caporali in le mane videlicet Calimacho, Glaucho e Petreo o che li acusa in modo che li se possano haver li sera donato CCC. ducati per chiaschuno e de d. Lucha de Tocio V^e ducati. Cum questo poteria forte essere se sentirea piu ultra et non dubita il papa de haverne qualche uno o tuti, confidandosi non se debiano reducere in diminio alcuno che li siano mandati fin qua, e dice del tuto ne avisarà nuy altri et io a V. Ex. scrivaro quanto succederà, a la qual me recommando.

Romae die xxviii. Februarii, 1468

Eiusdem i. et ex. D. servulus Augustinus de Rubeis.

[Original in the State Archives, Milan, Cart. gen. *Placed by mistake in the fasciculus*, "Florence, 1478."]

* In MS.: *habiano.*

21. Joh. Blanchus to Galeazzo Maria Sforza, Duke
        of Milan.*

1468, Feb. 29, Rome.

Ill^me, etc.   Per la alligata de XXVII. del presente ho scripto a
V. Ex. quello se diceva per Roma et per alcuni di principali de
questa corte circa questa coniuratione et tractati.   Dapoy heri sera
la Sta de N. S^re mando ad dire ad questi rev^di et mag^ci ambaxatori
de la liga che potevano andare da Sua B^ne et cosi gli anday ancora
io con loro et doppo condolutose essi ambaxatori in nome de voy
signori principali de la liga de questa coniuratione et offerto le
persone e stati et gente vostre ad soe deffese e favori et demum
domandato come passavano queste cose, S. Sta respose et dixe che
uno signore del mundo l' haveria avisato che la se guardesse perche
lera certificato che per alcuni in Roma se tractava de stranie cose
etiam contra la persona soa et che deinde vennero alcuni cardinali
da se et nomino solamente el cardinale de Mantoa † ad dirli de
certa mala vita et heresia che seguivano alcuni scellerati scolari
nominandone quatro per principali, cioe Calimaco, Petreo, Glaucho
et un altro extraneo nome dicendo che costoro se havevano electo
una vita achademica et epicurea perche ultra che haveano manzato
la quaresima passata et tutta via manzavano li venerdì et sabbati
carne et non servavano vigilia alcuna et seguivano li appetiti
carnali con maribus et feminis et facevano mille altre scelleragine
quod abhominabilius est negavano la divinità cioè non esser Dio
et negavano che fosse l' anima dicendo che morto el corpo era
morta l' anima et subjungevano che Moyses fo seductore del
popolo et che Christo fo falso propheta et ultra questo non se
volevano per niente chiamare ne lassare chiamare per li proprii
nomi, ma se havevano posti li nomi predicti che forono nomi de
achademici et epicuri dicendo S. Sta che non gli bastava esser loro
cativi ma che andavano seducendo questo et quello altro et che
ne havevano seducto alcuni et maxime uno Lucido che stava
con suo parente che è qua suo depositario, subjungendo S. Sta che
non solamente se andavano gloriando de questa loro scellerata
vita et heresia, ma andavano detrahendo al honore de Dio et de
la chiesa dicendo male de S. Sta et delo clero del mondo et
dicendo : guarda se questi preti sono inimici de layci che hano
facta la quaresma et voleno che nuy la jeiuniamo et piu ce hano

* See *supra*, p. 59, *seq.*   † F. Gonzaga.

ligati che non possiamo pigliare piu che una mogliere et multa huiusmodi, dicendo ancora S. Sᵗᵃ che non gli bastava questo ma che piu ultra dicevano che presto se vederia de nove cose et maxime verso uno certo prete dixero date de bona voglia che fra pochi di non te bisognera fare piu tante supplicatione perche havemo uno iudicio chel papa ha ad morire presto et sapemo che ad ogni modo el morirà presto et seguirano de le altre cose relevate et similia et dice S. Sᵗᵃ che per questo loro avantarse de simile cose li dicti cardinali hano voluto intendere la facenda et poy gli lo sono venuti ad dire ut s.

Ma dice S. Sᵗᵃ che per alhora non pote haver gratia de fare prendere dicti quattro scellerati perche fugirono, ma spera haverli perche vano latitando qui dintorno et che è su la via de haver almanco Calimaco ch' è el principale et dice S. S. non potendo havere loro ha facto prendere le loro cose et hagli trovati soy epygrammata et versi et soneti intitulati ad pueros in genere turpe dove demonstravano molte loro ribaldarie et dice che havendo facto pigliare alcuni che practicavano con loro per questo et per la fuga de loro se comenzò ad credere che la conjuratione fosse de grande importantia et questo . . . * mercordi proxime passato et che quello di medesmo che se corse el palio de le gioveni † venire uno Roma [no] ad dire ad S. Sᵗᵃ che se guardasse intorno perche l' haveva veduto alcuni banditi che erano venuti in Ro[ma] et che non gli degono esser venuti se non per fare male, etc., et gli ne mostrò uno addito che era . . . * alla festa del palio. Et dice S. Sᵗᵃ che alhora fece demandare el vicecamerlengo et reprehendolo che [non §] havesse mandato bando che li banditi non potessero venire in Roma ad queste feste de carnevale . . .* commise che dovesse andare ad fare prendere dicto bandito et cosi fu preso luy et uno suo [compagno ‡] et dice che interrogandolo el vicecamerlengo et reprehendolo chel fosse venuto in Roma essendo bandito per la vita come era, el repose et confessoe che l' era venuto ad videre le feste, ma dice S. Sᵗᵃ che como cativo che le fece una inventione dicendo che l' era venuto in Roma con uno factore de d. Luca Tozolo § Romano bandito che sta ad Napoli con la Mᵗᵃ del re et che esso d. Luca doveva

---

* What follows is destroyed by damp.   † See *supra*, p. 31 *seq.*
‡ Destroyed in original.
§ Regarding this matter see CANENSIUS, 80, and PLATINA, 779.

anche luy essere gionto in Roma perche el l' haviva lassato in la silva de Velitri et piu ultra accusò dicto d. Luca dicendo che esso d. Luca haveva mandato in Roma mille ducati in mano de li suoi parenti per dispensarli in certi suoy pensieri che l' haveva facto. Et dice S. Sta che intendendo questo gli crescette el suspetto e che ha mandato ad cercare per tuta Roma esso d. Luca et postoli la taglia adosso como per l' altra littera io scrivo et che interim che lo faceva cercare è venuto S. S. un cittadino Romano cognato desso d. Luca ad pregare S. Sta che non se fatichi piu in cercarlo perche el non era venuto et che sel fosse venuto l' haveria facto capo ad casa soa et che luy voleva obligare la vita chel non era partito da Napoli et diceloli S. Sta come nuy intendiamo che l' ha mandato qua mille ducati da farne certi suoy designi, etc. : el gli respose che l' e vero che per littera di cambio l' ha mandato mille ducati per la dote de una soa figliola la quale S. Sta sa che l' hano voluta maritare al suo medico et che non li [ha] mandati per altra casone. Et dice S. Sta che l' e vero chel suo medico li di passati gli richiese licenza de prendere dicta soa figliola per mogliere, ma che el gli dissuase questa cosa con dirgli che may ad sua instantia ne de homo del mondo el non faria gratia al dicto d. Luca de retornare ad Roma perche l' era bandito che havendo facta pace con un altro Romano et havendoli data sicurta de non lo offendere, lo fece poy amazare et che la seria cosa de troppo male exempio et che facendo quella gratia bisognaria poy farne molte altre simile et che non voleva tiarse questo carico ad le spalle et per questo pare quasi che S. Sta sii fuori d' ogni suspecto de d. Luca et dice che l' expecta per tutto hozi la certeza da Napoli. Nientedimeno S. Sta non abandona la impresa de investigare meglio la cosa et dice S. Sta che per questo ha cognosciuto che dicto bandito che ha accusato d. Luca ut supra lo ha facto per dare favore et dilatione alla pena che l' ha ad patire luy et piu ultra dice che gli ha accusato uno signore ben grande et grande et che crede chel dica le boxie dechiarando S. Sta che pro certo el non gli ha accusato el re Ferrando. Dice S. Sta che da principio che gli fo dicto che questi conjuratori havevano intelligentia con uno gran signore gli andò l' animo sopra el re de Boemia dicendo chel credeva che l' uno heretico se intendesse con l' altro. Item dice che questi ribaldi hano qualche volta dicto de volere andare ad trovare el Turco et ch' unaltro de questi scolari che al presente e a Venetia fin l' anno passato andò ad Venetia per volere deinde andare ad trovare el Turcho et qui comenzò S. Sᵗᵃ ad damnare molto questi studii de humanità dicendo che se Dio gli prestava vita, voleva providere ad due cose : l' una che non fosse licito studiare in queste vane historie et poesie perche sono piene de heresie et maledictione ; l' altra che non fosse licito imparare ne exercire astrologia perche da essa nascono molti errori dicendo li putti non hano ad pena dece anni che senza che vadano ad scola sano mille ribaldarie, pensate come se degono poy impire de mille altri vicii quando legeno Juvenale, Terentio, Plauto, Ovidio et questi altri libri, dicendo Juvenale monstra de reprendere li vicii, ma el ne fa docto et li insigna ad chi lo lege, come fano anche questi nostri predicatori quali qualche volta havemo reprehesi che predicando insignano fare de le cose lascive che l' homo non le intese may piu et questo quando se metteno ad volere dire : in questi modi se po fare uno peccato ; dicendo S. Sᵗᵃ che gli sono tanti altri libri che se possono legere et che legendoli l' homo se farà tanto docto quanto bastarà et che le meglio dire una cosa per li proprii vocabuli cha per queste circuitione che usano poeti. Retornando ad damnare molto li dicti 4 coniuratori che ex toto negano Dio dicendo che li pagani et gentili et li altri antichi servavano qualche religione et costoro negano el tucto. Et qui el magᶜᵒ d. Lorenzo da Pesaro* allegò molte cose et de Romani et de altri antichi in le quale servarono grandissima religione et tante cose allegò ad questi propositi esso d. Lorenzo chel papa ne prese piacere assay et lo stava volunteri ad audire. Fo etiamdio allegato et testamento vechio et testamento nuovo et rasone civile et rasone canonica per esso d. Lorenzo et per li altri ambaxatori de la liga perche tutti sono doctori chi in utroque et chi in jure civili tantum. Fo etiamdio recordato che como è prohibito alli preti de seguire le lege civile per le conditione differente che sono dal temporale al spirituale così se po prohibere el studio de le poesie et astrologie perche da esso se cava mille heresie, etc. Ad un altra cosa dixe S. Sᵗᵃ che la voleva providere cioè alle zanze et bosie che se dicono qua in campa de Fiore et che ordinarà uno decreto opportuno ad questo et che farà fare de li schrizzi ad questi zanzatori che se fano ad Venetia dicendo che quando Pier

* In reference to this Ambassador, see *supra*, p. 60, and Lettres de Louis XI., Vol. III., 278-9, 343.

Brunoro fo mandato in la Morea uno Venetiano gli dixe va pur che tu non ne tornaray may et che essendosene doluto Piero Brunoro cosi la S^{ria} fo statim preso dicto Venetiano et dattoli XXV. squassi de corda et poy bandito et molte altre cose dixe ad questo proposito dicendo maxime che tutto quello fo dicto in campo de Fiore o vero o boxia, o ben o male che sia fu scripto per tutto el mondo et che del vero et bene se po havere l' homo per excusato, ma che de la bosia et male el se voria castigare cioè castigare quelli che lo andasseno fingendo et seminando.

Demum la S. Sta dixe che ad ogni modo l' haveria deliberato communicare questa cosa con li prefati ambaxatori et con li cardinali, ma che l' era stato fin hora ad non dirne altro perche el non sapeva ancora dire alcuna verità de tradimento se non le bestialitate suprascripte et cosi li cardinali sono andati questa matina ad palazo per questa casone le quale tutte cose me è parso significare a V. Ex. alla quale humilmente me recommando. Datum Romae ult. Februarii, 1468.

[Original in the State Archives of Milan. Cart. gen. *Wrongly placed under February*, 1463.]

22. Aug. de Rubeis to Galeazzo Maria Sforza, Duke of Milan.*

1468, March 4, Rome.

Circha li tractati contra la persona del papa de li quali ve scripsi per altre mie, se facta ogni diligencia et inquisicione per sentir piu oltra et tandem non se trovato fin a qui altro che parole paze e vane de coloro che zanzaveno † chel se voria amazare lo papa et chel se poteria bene far per quello modo che io scripsi et ch' essendo questo popolo et tuta la corte mal contenta ‡ et disposta non manchava se non che qualch' uno incomenzasse che tutol mondo poy gli tirarey dreto, &c. L' è § vero che quelli principalli per anchora non se suni potuti havere. Se cercha per ogni modo haverli ne le mano et crede prefata Sta da loro se saperia piu inanti. De d. Luca Tozo s' è ‖ trovato non essere vero se sia ullo tempore partito da Napoli ni sia intervenuto ni

---

* See *supra*, p. 59.   † =cianciavano, dicevano ciance.
‡ See our account, *supra*, p. 27 *seq.*   § Manuscript: *Le.*
‖ Manuscript: *se.*

conspirato a la cosa. Lo papa ha molto piu che prima ordinate le guarde de palazo et sta con pur asay major respecto chel non soleva. Le feste de carnevale, corsi de palii, convito al popolo la domenica pasata et laltre tute se sonno facte al modo usato como laltri anni ho scripto et nulla è inmutato ni manchato.

P.S.—Del resto de quella heresia se ne trova pur molti intricati et tutavolta se va cercando de laltri et lo papa ha intentione de stirpare questa secta.

[Original in the State Archives, Milan, Cart. gen.]

23. POPE PAUL II. TO FLORENCE.
1468, May 16.

The Pope expresses his affection for Florence (see *supra*, p. 14) and praises the Florentines for having accepted the peace. Paul II. then speaks of his constant zeal from the beginning * of his reign for war with the Turks. Hactenus enim ducenta milia florenor. in huiusmodi christianorum subsidia erogavimus † . . .

Datum Romae apud S. Marcum, xvi. Maii, 1468.

[Copy in the State Archives, Florence X.–II.–23, f. 172.]

24. GIACOMO TROTTI ‡ TO BORSO, DUKE OF MODENA.§
1468, July 8, Rome.

The Pope is going to leave Rome because the Plague is raging there.‖ Persona non rimane qui,¶ chi va de qua chi de la, ne mor[ono] 40 e 50 el di. All are fleeing from the Plague-stricken

---

* The Milanese Ambassadors, Laurentius de Pesaro and Joh. Blanchus, writing home from Rome, on the 24th April, 1468, speak in the following words of the Pope's disposition on this subject : " * El papa monstra secundo ha dicto questa sera chel voglia che se attendi omnino ad fare expeditione contra el Turco." State Archives, Milan.

† See *supra*, p. 158. The statement of Paul II. is corroborated by the testimony of Sixtus IV. ; see RAYNALDUS ad an. 1471, N. 71.

‡ This diplomatist was still with Paul II. in the autumn of 1470 ; see WÜRDTWEIN, Nov. Subsid., XIII., 69.

§ See *supra*, p. 190.

‖ The Plague had reached Rome in the beginning of April ; see *Despatch of Augustinus de Rubeis, dated Rome, 1468, April 2. (State Archives, Milan.) By the end of the month it was making great ravages ; see *Letter of A. Patritius, dated Rome, 1468, April 27, Angelica Library, S. 1, 1, f. 117.

¶ Laurentius de Pesaro writes from Rome on the 3rd June, 1468 : " *omne persona fugge." State Archives, Milan.

city where are only to be seen sick people being carried. Three
Cardinals have remained in Rome, but with closed doors, so that
no one of their household may go out.

[Original in the State Archives, Modena.]

25. Tommaso Soderini* to Florence.†

1468, Nov. 29, Venice.

News reached Venice that the Emperor had arrived in Porde
none.‡ Questa S. per honorare la M^{ta} Sua ha electi sedici
imbasciadori. Quattro gli sono iti incontro insino a Frigoli et
domattina si partono gli altri dodici per riceverlo a Padova.
Haveano apparechiato qui splendissimamente la casa del marchese
di Ferrara per la stanza sua; ma dicono ha mandato a dire non
vuole passare per Vinegia, ma che fa la via di Padova a Ferrara.
Manda questo dominio due oratori che anno a compagnare la
persona sua insino a Roma e quali sono M. Piero Mozanigho et
M. Triadono Gritti. . . .

[State Archives, Florence, X.–II.–24, f. 81b–82.]

26. Joh. Petrus Arrivabenus to Marchioness Barbara
of Mantua.§

1468, Dec. 26, Rome.

Illma madonna mia. L' ordine dato de mandare incontra a
limperatore prima quatro prelati e insieme doi auditori de rota e
doi advocati consistoriali come scrissi a V. Ex. vene servato e
cussi subsequenter li doi card^{li} || e Suoa M^{te} ad una terra chiamata
Otriculi lontana de qua quaranta miglia entroe in barcha nel
Tevere e vennesene fin presso a Roma a sette miglia ad un luoco
che se dice la Valcha dove smontoe in terra, e qui da quelli doi
card^{li} etprelati mandati, li qualilhavevano per terra seguitato era
aspettato e da molte altre persone che li erano andate in contra.

---

* Florentine Ambassador in Venice.

† See *supra*, p. 161.

‡ See Toderini, 13 and 113. The Oration pronounced at Pordenone in
presence of the Emperor, by Petrus Molinus, one of the Venetian Ambassadors,
is in the British Museum (MS. 15906, f. 14b).

§ See *supra*, p. 162 *seq.*

|| d'Estouteville and F. Piccolomini.

Quello di che foe la vigilia de natale stimandose che havesse ad giongere de di, el collegio di card[li] se congregoe a la porta de S. Maria del populo, e cussi tuta la corte e la citade col baldachino fatto cum larme del papa e suoe de damaschino biancho brochato doro, ma retardoe infina a le tre hore de notte ad intrare, che dicono alcuni foe per la giornata longa, alcuni per esserli data quella hora da astrologi.* Sentendo la suoa venuta li card[li] se li fecerono incontro un puocho fuora de la porta, et a la porta Suoa M[te] entroe sottol baldachino vestita dun vestitello de panno negro e col suo capuzino et capello, de nanti li andavano el S. de Camarino . . . et questi altri signori e baroni ecclesiastici cum le torze in man; la terra era apparata de panni et altri ornamenti dove haveva a passare et feceronoli fare un longo circuito et passarono'da S. Marco, passate le cinque hore gionse a S. Petro dove la S[te] de N. S. laspettava in la capella magiore e qui se inginochioe a basarli el pede e puoi la mane di puoi levandose a basare el volto el papa se levoe un puocho da la sede suoa. Era presso la cathedra del papa per spacio de doi homini al lato dextro apparichiata una sede per limperatore ma piu bassa dun brazo e piu eminente che el luoco di card[li] un grado; qui fatte alcune oratione e cerimonie ascesero in palatio tuti doi al pare e N. S. teneva limperatore per mane allato mancho e cussi se andarono fin a la camera del papa e di puoi el collegio compagnoe limperatore a la camera suoa, che è piu bassa in palatio dove allogioe anche altra fiata; puoi la messa de la nocte che foe perho cantata presso al giorno, N. S. li dede la beretta e la spatha et al ma† . . . tore levangelio exiit edictum a cesare augusto et mons. mio ‡ disse la omelia, heri a † . . . . andoe giuso col papa sottol baldachino pur a mane in S. Petro et communicosse in la messa† . . . N. S. ascese nel tribunal alto avanti le scale de S. Petro dove deda la benedictione e † . . . sotol baldachino e vedevase lo imperatore che certo monstro una gran reverentia col capo scoperto, e S[te] Suoa lo faceva coprire; nel tornare suso N. S. compagnoe limperatore insina a la camara suoa e li voleva lasciarlo, ma Suoa M[te] fece resistentia et volse venire cum N. S. bene doe sale fin a piede de una scala per la qual puoi se ascende a le sale de sopra e qui

---

* Frederick III. was greatly given to Astrology; see FRIEDRICH, Astrologie und Ref., 29 *seq.*

† What follows is completely destroyed ‡ Card. Gonzaga.

se lasciarono che erano passate le xxiii. hore; portoe indosso limperatore una turcha de veluto negro senza altro ornamento; questa matina credo uscira anche fuori a la messa. In palatio è dato logiamento a S. M^te e parichii di suoi; li altri che se dice ha di cavalli 600 sono divisi per le hostarie* e sento che N. S. a li hosti ha fatto gia el pagamento per octo di, che tanto se ragiona habbia a stare qui, et ha ordinato li sia facto honore. Sono fatti venire in la terra giente darme assai et di fanti e balestrieri quatro milia. Finqui cussi è stato el progresso suo; cum S. M^te è uno abbate de Casanova Savoino el qual è tanto inimico al duca de Milano, e sento ha buona condicione seco in modo che essendo mal dispuosto el papa e lo collegio a la promotione del vescovo de Bressa è opinione dalcuni che forsi questo abbate se habia a fare card^le a petitione de limperatore el qual non pare voglia domandare todescho alcuno. Doi ambasciatori Venetiani sono venuti col imperatore, messer Paulo Moresini e messer Antonio Preoli . . . Rome xxvi. Decem^is, 1468.

Ser^or Jo. PETRUS ARRIVABENUS.

[Original in the Gonzaga Archives, Mantua.]

27. POPE PAUL II. TO BOLOGNA.†

1469, March 6, Rome.

Concerning the overflow of the Reno.‡ The Pope expresses his astonishment that nothing had yet been done to prevent it, and desires that measures should at once be taken against this calamity. He gives this command because he (the Pope) is bound to watch over the general welfare. Dat. Romae vi Martii, 1469, Pont. nostri A° 5°.

[Original in the State Archives, Bologna. Lib. Q., 3.]

28. POPE PAUL II. TO CARDINAL STEPHAN DE VARDA.§

1471, Jan. 14, Rome.

Stephano tit. sanctor. Nerei et Achillei presbyt. card^ii et archiep. Colocensi. Dudum siquidem, etc. . . . The King has often

---

* See GOTTLOB, Cam. Apost.
‡ See *supra*, p. 34.

† See *supra*, p. 34.
§ See *supra*, p. 123.

requested him to send him the Cardinal's Hat as he has long since raised him to the purple. He had expected him to come in person to Rome ; now, however, he sends him the hat by Gabriel de Verona, ordin. minor. nuntium nostrum.

[Lib. brev., 12, f. 77b. Secret Archives of the Vatican.]*

29. CARDINAL FR. GONZAGA TO HIS FATHER.†

1471, Jan. 17, Rome.

He gives an account of the deliberations of the Commission of Cardinals appointed to consider the Turkish business. This Commission held its sittings in the house of Cardinal Bessarion and resolved : che per quest' anno non se havesse ad fare provisione de offendere, ma solum che bastasse a defendre et per mare tantummodo, ad che pareva bastariano cento quaranta galee e xx. nave grosse, ma che ben se disponesse come per li anni seguenti se havesse e per terra e per mare tendere a la ruina del Turco; ma tre cose concorrevano qui chel se intendesse la celeritate de le provisione, la perseverantia desse che pareva se dovesse promettere per xxv. anni aut ad minus per x. e la rata che ciascuno volesse contribuire a questa impresa. Non li fue de ambasciatori chi facesse offerta alcuna speciale ; quelli del re e de Venetiani assai dissero in persuadere le provisione opportune se facessero, Fioren-tini temporezano cum parole generale, quelli del duca disserono non havere commissione a questo, ma chel suo signore è cussi ben dispuosto a fare tutto quello che li metta bene et honore che volendo N. S^{te} da lui cosa alcuna ge lo puo scrivere et trovarallo per la observantia chel ge ha obedientissimo a fare ciò che sia dovere suo, e tuti insieme conclusero che essendo el papa capo e pastore dugniuno li parera che S. Sta havesse prima a specificare la rata suoa per dare exemplo a li altri et che anche quella che sa e conosce la potentia de ciascuno puoria taxare quanto li paresse che ugniuno havesse a conferire. Questa fue la relatione de le cose agitate apud deputatos. The Cardinals were summoned to treat further on the subject dominica proxima in furia. The deliberations lasted from the 22nd hour fin presso le sei hore de nocte : ne la qual consultatione furono varie sententie e parole assai che non accade de extendere ; demum fatta la conclusione

* Kindly communicated by Dr. Gottlob.　　　† See *supra*, p. 193.

secundo lo comune parere furono chiamati dentro li ambasciatori
a li quali N. S. se duolse che in omnibus li facessero cussi puocha
demonstratione de reverentia che havendoli fatto richiedere non
hanno voluto fare dechiaratione alcuna de suoa voluntate. . . .
The Pope then informs the Ambassadors: che communicata re
cum cardinalibus et examinate le facultate suoe li offereva de darli
lo quarto de le intrate suoe che pigliava L^m duc^{ti} l' anno, perche
dice l' intrate suoe tanto del temporal quanto del spiritual senza
lalumiera, la qual gia è dedicata a la crociata,* non essere piu che
cc^m ducati † e per suoa iustificatione offerse de fare monstrare li
libri daltri pontifichi e suoi, e de ciò ne fue data commissione al
card^{le} de Theano ‡ chi fue thesauriere a tempo di Pio et al
card^{le} de S. Marco, § el qua ha fatto un gran tempo lofficio del
camarlengo, che insieme havessero ad examinare li conti et intrate
suoe. . . . Non parse che la offerta satisfacesse a la brigata et
maxime a Venetiani ‖ li quali hanno havuto a dire che N. S.
deveria vendere le suoe zoie, darli el tuto de le intrate suoe reser-
vato solamente quanto bisogna per lo vivere etiam extenuato et
che nui cardinali li doveressimo mettere la metade de le intrate
nostre et in summa metteno la taglia come se ce havessorno in
presone. Replicorono che la S. B^{ne} specificasse quante galee
voleva mantenere alimpresa dicendo che non volevano questa
offerta de denari ne del quarto ; perche lhora era tarda la cosa fu
remessa ad un altro consistorio. . . .

[Original in the Gonzaga Archives, Mantua.]

30. Pope Paul II. to the Inhabitants of Rhodes.¶

1471, Jan. 20, Rome.

In view of the common danger all must render assistance.**
The Pope exhorts them to courage : Aderit et Deus ipse nosque
quoad poterimus nihil in tanta re pretermittemus. In conclusion,
he urges them speedily to repair the ruinous walls of Rhodes.

[Lib. brev., 12, f. 86b. Secret Archives of the Vatican.]

---

* See *supra*, p. 80.   † See Gottlob, Cam. Apost.
‡ N. Forteguerri.   § M. Barbo.
‖ See Romanin, IV., 353, note 1.   ¶ See *supra*, p. 183.
** Regarding the sufferings of the people at Rhodes, see also Bosio, 253 *seq.*,
257 *seq.*

31. POPE PAUL II. TO THE GRAND MASTER OF RHODES, GIAMBATISTA ORSINI.*

1471, Jan. 20, Rome.

He had received their letters, from which he perceived their fear of the Turks. Timendum quippe est, sed non ita ut ab auxiliis ac remediis desistatur, quinimo est eo melius et celerius providendum. Itaque nolite vobis ipsis deesse, sed bono animo sitis. He promises help, and urges them to lose no time in improving the fortifications and moats of the island.

[Lib. brev., 12, f. 87b, *loc. cit.* Secret Archives of the Vatican.]

32. POPE PAUL II. TO DUKE BORSO OF MODENA.†

1471, March 3, Rome.

The Pope in a few words informs the Duke, who intended to visit Rome, that he was sending the Archbishop of Spalatro [Lor. Zane], who is "thesaurarius ac provinciae nostrae marchiae Anconitanae gubernator," to greet him. He will inform the Duke that his arrival is very agreeable to him (the Pope).

[Original in the State Archives, Modena.]

33. POPE PAUL II. TO THE GRAND MASTER OF RHODES, GIAMBATISTA ORSINI.‡

1471, March 12, Rome.

An exhortation to courageous constancy against the attacks of the Turks, *as above*, No. 31.

[Lib. brev., 12, f. 112. Secret Archives of the Vatican.]

34. POPE PAUL II. TO THE GOVERNOR OF SPOLETO.§

1471, April 5, Rome.

Habes bullam de non recipiendis muneribus alias per nos editam.‖ This is to be observed exactly (ad unguem). Prohibe-

---

* See *supra*, p. 183. G. Orsini had been appointed Grand Master of Rhodes by Paul II., in 1467, on the death of Zacosta (see Cron. Rom., 32), and died in 1476; see REUMONT, III., 1, 521.

† See *supra*, p. 184.   ‡ See *supra*, p. 183.

§ See *supra*, p. 35.   ‖ Printed in Bull., V., 184 *seq.*

mus ne aliquo pacto in causis vertentibus in prima instancia
sportule alique recipiantur preterea ne gratis paleas nec ligna
deferri tibi facias.

Simile rectori Patrimonii.

    ,,   ,,   Campanie.

,, gubernatori Fulginei, Fani, Cesene, Asculi, Reatis et
Interamni, Urbis veteris, Vetralle.

[Lib. brev., 12, f. 142. Secret Archives of the Vatican.]

35. CARDINAL FR. GONZAGA TO HIS FATHER.*

1471, April 10, Rome.

. . . Che parlamenti siano stati fati fra lor † non posso altramente de certo sapere, bene uso ugni industria possibile per
cavarlo per indirecto e quando el S^r fue qui a visitarme sabbato
passato ‡ cussi inter loquendo me li acostai e dissi che queste suoe
visitatione davano molto da dire a la brigata la qual pensava che
fusserono per condure el papa a Ferrara, il che a me piaceria
grandemente perche essendo io cupido del bene de N. S. e de la
sede apostolica lo comprobaria parendomi che seria molto expe-
diente e proficuo considerato come sta tuta la Germania verso di
nui et che la Franza pui volte ha domandato el concilio e questo
io lhaveria piu caro ad Ferrara perche seressemo in una terra libera
et buona e ne la qual per la mia particularitate essendo non manco
fiolo a Suoa S^{ria} che al marchese de Mantuoa seria bene visto.
Rispuoseme che parlava prudentemente e Dio volesse che tuti li
altri fussero de questo parere le qual parole me fecerono credere
che qualche cosa ne fusse. Io mandai puo per Jacomo Trotto §
cum monstrare de voler per lo mezo suo fare intendere al S. el
fatto de quella bolla,|| a la qual non era stato presente lui e puoi
entrai a dirli de questa andata a Ferrara commendandola et infer-
endo che lo fusse quodamodo necessaria et chel S. faria una

---

* See *supra*, p. 188.

† Paul II. and Borso d' Este.

‡ 6th April.

§ The Ambassador of Modena to Rome, of whom in the *Report from the
Chigi Library, cited *supra* p. 186, Fr. Ariostus speaks in most favourable
terms.

|| Concerning a "fraternitate o compagnia che se chiamasse de la pace."

sancta opera a usarli ugni industria. Rispuoseme tacete monsignor
che ad ugni modo la conduremo. Lo rev^{mo} monsignor cardinale
de S. Maria in Portico * el qual è nepote del papa me disse questi
dì, el seria pur bene fatto de celebrare una dieta in qualche buon
luoco in Italia et anticipare avanti che per necessitate fussemo
costretti da altri a farla e forsi puoi dove nui non voressimo. Tute
queste parole e coniecture me fanno presumere che qualche cosa
ne sia ; andaro investigando piu che puotrò per darne aviso a V. S.
et maxime passati che siano questi di sancti ne li quali se attende
a lanima. . . .†

[Original in the Gonzaga Archives, Mantua.]

36. Pope Paul II. to John II., Margrave of Baden and Archbishop of Trèves. ‡

1471, April 19 ——

The Pope returns thanks for the iocale addamantibus ac rubinis
ornatum sent to him through Hermann Frank, and praises the
Archbishop : sed ne te lateat nos munera recipere non consuevimus.
He accepts the present, however, in order that the Archbishop may
have no doubt of the favour he bears him, and sends him in return
crucem etiam addamantibus atque rubinis et unionibus redimitam
que multas sacras reliquias . . . tetigit.§

[State Archives, Venice.] ‖

37. Pope Paul II. to Cardinal Fr. Piccolomini.¶

1471, June 26, Rome.

Card^{ll} Senensi legato. Accepimus plures litteras tue circ^{nis} ex

---

* Bat. Zeno.

† Further particulars of the negotiations, which undoubtedly took place in
1471, concerning a fresh Congress or Council, are wanting. The sudden death
of the Pope afterwards turned the thoughts of all in another direction ; but this
question soon came again to the front ; see *supra*, p. 217.

‡ See *supra*, p. 110.

§ See also the Brief to the King of Portugal (Marini, II., 201), and that to the
King of Hungary in Teleki, XI., 122-3.

‖ I am indebted to the kindness of Canon Fraknói, Vice-President of the
Hungarian Academy, for a copy of this Brief.

¶ See *supra*, p. 181.

Ratispona, ex quibus intelleximus, quid usque in eam diem a te factum sit circa ea quae tibi a nobis sunt demandata in causa expeditionis in Turchos, et quomodo ad illos principes qui Ratispone aderant concionem habueris mentemque nostram spem et rei necessitatem aperueris illorumque responsionem. Commendamus plurimum prudentiam et diligentiam tuam. Ita enim est faciendum . . . Quare non cessabis similiter in futurum ab ipso bono opere, sed instabis et perseverabis industria et diligentia, ut nichil boni quod fieri in hanc rem possit postponatur praesertim autem nunc, quum Turchus . . . illam (scl. religionem christianam) extinguere contendit. Super his et aliis etiam lator praesentium, qui ad te revertitur, poterit coram latius referre, quae a nobis audivit ; de occurrentibus successu temporis Nos tuis literis facies certiores.

[Lib. brev., 12, f. 162.   Secret Archives of the Vatican.]

38. Pope Paul II. to Borso, Duke of Ferrara.*

1471, July 10, Rome.

A melancholy report had lately been circulated in Rome regarding a danger which threatened the Duke.† He now hears that this danger has happily been overcome. The Pope exhorts the Duke to strengthen his health, and thanks him for his beautiful present.

[Lib. brev., 12, f. 175b.   Secret Archives of the Vatican.]

39. Pope Paul II. to Cardinal Fr. Piccolomini.‡

1471, July 13, Rome.

Cardinali Senensi legato. Sollicitabat nos antea cura non mediocris, quod car^{mi} in Christo filii nostri Friderici imperatoris tardior ad istam Ratisponensem dietam adventus de die in diem videbatur diferri, cum ad praescriptum diem multi iam convenissent. Vere-

---

* See *supra*, p. 190. Among the Briefs of Paul II. in the State Archives of Modena I saw neither this nor the Brief of 20th July.

† According to the Diario Ferrar., 229, Borso had been suffering since the 27th May from "febri continue flemmatiche che mai non lo abbandonorno insino a ia morte" [20th August]. The Duke had probably contracted this sickness in Rome ; see also Atti e mem. d. deput. di storia patria Moden., V. (1870), 418 *seq.*

‡ See *supra*, p. 181.

bamur namque, ne si ejus optata presentia deesset, dissolveretur quicquid tam necessario tempore principum consiliis et subsidiis iuste desiderabamus fieri in Turchum. Sed tu, dilecte fili, qua soles diligentia progressum omnem et quae ad eam diem sequuta sunt, tuis literis datis Ratispone *duodecima iunii* plene significans nos admodum recreasti . . . Speramus namque et ita optamus, quod et ipsius car^{mi} filii nostri pium studium et sincere principum voluntates te maxime operam dante accendentur ad tam sanctum opus magis ac communi periculo consulent . . . Confidimus enim devotionem tuam cunctos principes in ipsa dieta presentes efficaciter cohortari et inducere ad prosecutionem hujus rei posse.

[Lib. brev., 12, f. 174b. Secret Archives of the Vatican.]

40. POPE PAUL II. TO BORSO, DUKE OF FERRARA.*

1471, July 20, Rome.

Up to this time he had no tidings regarding the Duke's state of health ; he exhorts him to thank God for his recovery. The Pope in conclusion assures Borso of his prayers.

[Lib. brev., 12, f. 176b. Secret Archives of the Vatican.]

41. POPE PAUL II. TO ALBRECHT, MARQUESS OF BRANDENBURG.†

1471, July 20, Rome.

Marchioni Brandeburgensi principi electori. Intelleximus, dil° filio nostro tit. sancti Eustachii diacono card^{li} Senensi isthic in Ratisponen. conventu sedis apost. legato per suas maxime significante, nobilitatem tuam absolutionis beneficium devote suscepisse, quod ipse tibi auctoritate nostra impendit et te sancte matris ecclesie mandatis ac nostris etiam reverenter parere velle accepimus ; placet hoc nobis quam maxime . . . Here follow words of praise . . . . Cuius (scil. Dei) quoque gratiam maiorem ut denique assequaris, nunc potissimum assurgere debes et totus pio operi intendere atque accingi ut scilicet pro fidei puritate

---

* See *supra*, p. 190.

† See *supra*, p. 128. Albrecht had been excommunicated, 1446, Oct. 15, because he persisted in marrying his daughter, Ursula, to the son of the excommunicated G. Podiebrad, in spite of all warnings to the contrary.

servanda atque eius tutela in hac contra Turchos expeditione penitus studeas et alios principes adesse diligentissime horteris, ingenium tibi ut praediximus perspicacissimum est atque ad omnia mature cogitanda et aggredienda prudentissimus haberis et nos scimus te gratia multum valere et auctoritate . . .

[Lib. brev., 12, f. 176b. Secret Archives of the Vatican.]

42. Nicodemus de Pontremoli to Galeazzo Maria Sforza, Duke of Milan.*

1471, Aug. 2, Rome.

. . . Per altre mie havera inteso V. Cels. che la morte del papa fo in un subito in questo modo che essendo lui stato la matina in consistorio cioè el venerdi a vintisei del passato da le dodece hore fino a le deceocto de la megliore voglia del mondo, cenò a le vintidoe hore, mangiò tre poponi† non molto grandi cossi alcune altre cose di trista substantia come si era assuefacto mangiare da alcuni mesi in qua. Poi ad una hora de nocte disse ad un M. Petro Franzoso suo cubiculario chel se sentiva tutto grave. Esso M. Petro gli recordò non desse audientia per quella sera, ma andasse un poco a posare. Giettosse in suso un letuzo dove gli pigliò grande ambascie e tale che essendo uscito esso M. Petro de la camera per licentiare la brigata et lassarlo dormire un poco, senti passate de poco le doe hore bussare lusso‡ de la camera dove el papa se era a pena possuto condure et aprendo lusso trovò el papa presso de morto cum molta bava a la bocca et atacandossegli el papa al colo hebero a cadere ambe doi in modo se abandonò. Essendo li presso una cadrega M. Petro cum molta difficulta ce l' assectò suso et tornò al usso a domandare M. Doymo suo compagno. Quando tornarono dentro el papa havia posate le mane in suso li pomeli de nanti de la cadrega et appozato el capo al muro et vedendolo cum molta bava ala bocca volendolo aiutare el trovarono morto passate de poco le doe hore,§ adeo che dal principio del dolorse

---

* See *supra*, p. 190.

† The death of Frederick III. is also said to have been caused by too liberal an indulgence in melons ; Mailath, I., 319.

‡ = l' uscio.

§ According to our reckoning eleven at night. Our statement is confirmed by the best authorities ; see *Acta Consist. (26 July, 2nd hour of the night,)

et morire non fo una hora. Cardinal Barbo was at once summoned. Disturbances had, up to this time, occurred only in Todi. Qui sono concorsi molti sbanditi et facte alcune picole vendete et robarie, tamen el popolo se deporta fin mo assai bene.

[Original in the State Archives, Milan. P. E. Roma.]

43. VOTING LIST OF THE CONCLAVE OF THE YEAR 1471.*

[I.] *Voce pate ne la creatione del Papa successore ad Papa Paulo.*

Niceno [1] ad Rohano,[2] Bologna,[3] Sanct.†,[4] Pavia,[5] S. Petro. in vinc.[6]

Rohano [2] ad Niceno,[1] Bologna,[3] Sanct. †,[4] Mantoa.[7-8]

Orsino ad Thiano,[9] Ravenna [10] et S. Petro in vinc.[6]

Bologna [3] ad Niceno,[1] Rhoano,[2] Sanct.†,[4] Ravenna [10] et Pavia.[5]

S. Croce [4] ad Niceno,[1] Rhoano [2] et Bologna.[3]

Secret Archives of the Vatican. N. d. TUCCIA, 100; LANDUCCI, 11; GRAZIANI, 643 ; Cron. Rom., 34 ; NOTAR GIACOMO, 108. *Letter from the Archbishop of Milan to Galeazzo Maria Sforza, dated Rome, 1471, July 27 (ii. hore di nocte ad xxvi.) ; State Archives, Milan (P. E. Roma) ; *Letter of Cichus by order of the Duke of Milan, dated Gonzaghe ult. Julii, 1471 (venerdi di prox. passato la nocte sequente fra ii. et tre hore). *Loc. cit.* Infessura is wrong in giving the 25th July as the date ; the Cronica di Bologna, 788, has the 27th. PALACKY, V., 1, 61; and CARO, V., 1, 360 *seq.*, follow the last statement. This is adopted by CHEVALIER, 1740, and KRAUS, 802 ; PLATINA also falls into the same error. REUMONT, Lorenzo, I., 223, 2nd ed., is also in error in asserting that the Pope died in the night between the 25th and 26th of July. TROLLOPE, The Papal Conclaves (London, 1876), even gives the 18th July as the date. Regarding the foolish reports which at once arose concerning the death of Paul, see CIPOLLA, 558.

* See *supra*, p. 202. The above list is certainly the oldest extant. AMMANATI's statements are somewhat different, Epist., f. 209 (Frankfort ed., N. 395) ; but little weight can be attached to them because the letter in question is an apology. *Cichus Simoneta had, on the 31st July, 1471, by desire of the Duke, informed the Roman Ambassadors in writing that the Duke wished one of the following Cardinals to become Pope : Rhotomag. (d'Estouteville), S. Crucis Reatinus (Capranica), Gonzaga, S. Pietro in vinc. (Fr. della Rovere), S. Crisogoni Papien. (Ammanati), Card. Aquilan. (Agnifilus). State Archives, Milan.

[1] Bessarion. [2] d'Estouteville. [3] Calandrini.
[4] A. Capranica. [5] Ammanati. [6] Francesco della Rovere.
[7,8] Fr. Gonzaga. [9] Forteguerri. [10] Roverella.

Spoleti [11] ad Thiano [9] et Ravenna.[10]

Thiano [9] ad Spoleti [11] et S. Petro in vinc.[6]

Ravenna [10] ad Bologna,[3] Thiano,[9] Napoli [12] et S. Petri.[f]

Pavia [5] ad Niceno,[1] Rhoano [2] et Bologna.[3]

Napoli [12] ad Niceno,[1] Spoleto [11] et Ravenna.[10]

Aquila [13] ad Thiano,[9] S. Marco [14] et S. Petri.[6]

S. Marco [14] ad Niceno [1] et Spoleti.[11]

S. Piero [6] ad Orsino, Bologna,[3] S.†,[4] Thexno,[9] Aquila.[18]

Vicecanc.[15-16] ad Ravenna.[10]

Mantoa [7-8] ad Rhoano [2] e Vicecancell.[15-16]

Monferrato [17] ad Rhoano,[2] Bologna,[3] Theano,[9] Pavia,[5] Aquila,[18] S. Petro [6] e Mantova.[7-8]

S. Maria in portico [18] ad Ravenna,[10] Aquilla,[13] S. Petro in vinc.[6]

S. Lutia [19] ad Orsino, Aquilla,[13] S. Petro in vinc.[6]

[II.] *Voce havute.*

Niceno da S. Marco, Napoli, Rohano, Bologna, S.†, Pavia.

Rohano da Mantoa, Monferrato, Niceno, Bologna, S.†, Pavia.

Orsino da S. Lutia S. Piero in vinc.

Bologna da Monferrato, Ravenna, Niceno, Rohano, Pavia, S.†, S. Petro.

S.† da Niceno, Rohano, Bologna, S. Pietro.

Spoleti da Thiano, S. Marco, Napoli.

Thiano da Monferrato, Ravenna, Aquila, Orsino, Spoleti, S. Pietro.

Ravenna da S. Maria in port., Napoli, Vicecanc., Bologna, Orsino, Spoleto et S. Pietro.*

Pavia da Monferrato, Niceno, Bologna.

Napoli da Ravenna.

Aquila da S. Lucia, S. Maria in port., Monferrato, S. Petro.

S. Marco da Aquila.

S. Pietro ad vinc. da S. Lutia, Monferrato, S. Maria in port., Ravenna, Thiano, Aquilla, Niceno, Bologna † et Orsino.

---

[11] Eroli.   [12] Carafa.   [13] A. Agnifilus.
[14] Barbo.   [15-16] R. Borgia.   [17] Theodore of Montferrat.
[18] B. Zeno.   [19] G. Michiel.

* This is a variation from List I. where the name of Roverella does not occur among those who voted for F. della Rovere.

† In List I. it is not stated that Calandrini gave his vote to F. della Rovere.

Vicecancell. da Mantoa.

Mantoa da Monferrato, Rohano.

Monferrato : *niente.*

S. Maria in port. : *niente.*

S. Lucia : *niente.*

Voce agiunte al papa altra le prime nove : Vicecanc., Rohanno, S. Marco.

[Contemporary Copy in the State Archives, Milan, Roma ad an.]

44. NICODEMUS OF PONTREMOLI TO GALEAZZO MARIA SFORZA, DUKE OF MILAN.*

[1471, Aug. 9, Rome.†]

The Cardinal of S. Pietro in Vincoli had that very hour been elected Pope. All Rome rejoices : essendo stato cognosciuto relligioso et sanct^mo homo etiam in minori gradu et perho e anche opinione de ognuno che debia essere optimo pastore per s. chiesa et per tutta la fede christiana.

[Original in the State Archives, Milan.]

45. SIXTUS IV. TO GALEAZZO MARIA SFORZA, DUKE OF MILAN.‡

1471, Aug. 16, Rome.

He returns thanks for the Duke's congratulations on the Papal dignity, quam Dei clementia non meritis nostris adepti sumus. The Duke had loved him when he was yet in minoribus ; he, on his part, had continually loved the Duke. Erit igitur noster hic pontificatus ad omnem honorem et dignitatem tuam facillimus. He knows him to be one of the Princes most devoted to the Apostolic See, quod clarissimis argumentis nuper vacante sede in Romandiola demonstrasti.§ "Dat. Romae apud S. Petrum sub

---

* See *supra*, p. 204.

† The original bears as date vii. Aug., wrongly written instead of ix. Aug., and the superscription : "cito, cito."

‡ See *supra*, p. 215.

§ See the **Brief of Sixtus IV. to the Duke of Milan of 31st August, 1471. State Archives, Milan.

annulo piscatoris xvi. Aug., 1471 ante coronationem." His autograph signature follows.

"F[ranciscus]* vester ex optimo corde manu p.pᵃ."

[Original in the State Archives, Milan. Autograph.]

46. NICODEMUS OF PONTREMOLI TO GALEAZZO MARIA SFORZA, DUKE OF MILAN.†

1471, Aug. 28, Rome.

Cum questa sera la lista ‡ de li voti dati in conclave in la assumptione de questo novo pontefice, qual me è stato difficile havere respecto al juramento, hanno ex consuetudine nedum de darla, ma de non participarla cum persona. Recordomi haver scripto per altra mia a § V. Cels. quello havete ad extimare et persuadervi di questi voti. Rimettomi a quel medesimo et a V. C. me rec. Ex Roma, xxviii. Aug., 1471.

[Original in the State Archives, Milan.]

47. POPE SIXTUS IV. TO GALEAZZO MARIA SFORZA, DUKE OF MILAN.‖

1472, June 22, Rome.

Ad veterem benevolentiam quae tibi nobiscum semper intercessit¶ nova accessit necessitudo by the betrothal of Girolamo Riario to Caterina Sforza; he sends Girolamo to Milan as the Duke wished. Sit super hec sponsalia benedictio nostra, super te et filios tuos et filios eorum . . .

[Original in the State Archives, Milan. Autograph.]

48. POPE SIXTUS IV. TO GALEAZZO MARIA SFORZA, DUKE OF MILAN.**

1472, June 22, Rome.

He earnestly exhorts the Duke, carissimum in Christo filium

---

* The Brief is not signed "Sixtus IV.," because it was written before the Coronation. Only the baptismal name is therefore used.

† See *supra*, p. 202.

‡ See No. 43 of this Appendix.

§ Of the 20th Aug., 1471 ; see *supra*, p. 202.

‖ See *supra*, p. 248.　　¶ See *supra*, p. 215.　　** See *supra*, p. 248.

Ferdinandum, Sicilie regem illustrem, affinem tuum eo amore prosequi qui esse debet inter amantissimos affines. He could do nothing more pleasing to him than this.

[Original in the State Archives, Milan. Autograph.]

49. POPE SIXTUS IV. TO GALEAZZO MARIA SFORZA, DUKE OF MILAN.*

1473, Febr. 24, Rome.

He thanks him for his good reception of Girolamo Riario. His pauculis diebus laboravimus aliquantulum eodem morbo pedum qui et superiore anno nos invasit licet minus doloris et molestie nunc nobis attulerit . . .

[Original in the State Archives, Milan. Autograph.]

50. POPE SIXTUS IV. TO GALEAZZO MARIA SFORZA, DUKE OF MILAN.†

1473, Nov. 2, Rome.

Rediit ad nos dil. filius noster Petrus tit. S. Sixti presbyter cardinalis, patriarcha Constantinopolitanus, noster secundum carnem nepos, qui quanta cum humanitate, quo apparatu, qua liberalitate, qua iocunditate animi eum exceperis abunde nobis explicavit . . . The Pope thanks the Duke for this, and confirms all that the said Cardinal has settled with the Duke.

[Original in the State Archives, Milan. Autograph.]

51. POPE SIXTUS IV. TO GALEAZZO MARIA SFORZA, DUKE OF MILAN.‡

1474, June 1, Rome.

The Pope declares his intention of taking care for the peace of his subjects; he will, in particular, take measures against the rebellion in Todi; he therefore requests the Duke to send troops iuxta requisitionem Hieronymi generis tui Imole in temp. vicarii . . .

[Original in the State Archives, Milan. Autograph.]

---

* See *supra*, p. 249.　　　† See *supra*, p. 252.
‡ See the Brief to Perugia in Arch. St. Ital., XVI., 588, and *supra*, p. 263.

52. Pope Sixtus IV. to Galeazzo Maria Sforza, Duke of Milan.*

1474, June 25, Rome.

The Papal Legate is advancing with an army against Città di Castello : nihil tamen aliud quam obedientiam exacturus et res civitatis illius pro omnium quiete compositurus. Eam si Nic. Vitellius prestare voluerit clementiam et pietatem inveniet, nam et natura ipsius nepotis et legati nostri mitissima est et nos obedientiam quaerimus non vindictam . . . †

[Original in the State Archives, Milan. Autograph.]

53. Pope Sixtus IV. to Galeazzo Maria Sforza, Duke of Milan.‡

1474, July 5, Rome.

The Pope expresses his astonishment at a letter of the Duke's concerning the affair of Città di Castello. Sixtus IV. justifies his action in the matter, A. Nic. Vitello nihil aliud quam obedientiam exegimus ; deponat dominatum, vivat ut privatus et clementiam in nobis inveniet ; exititios introducere non est nobis consilium . . . Quis est regum aut principum qui in dominio suo populum inobedientem aut rebellem aut tyrannum possit tolerare? Quare miramur quod nobis hoc persuadeas cum potius presidium a te speremus. The Florentines say they fear on account of Borgo S. Sepolcro : vana est ista suspicio, for he had assured them on his Papal word that his troops should undertake nothing against Florence.§

[Original in the State Archives, Milan. Autograph.]

---

* See *supra*, p. 265.

† Sixtus IV. expressed himself in similar language in his *Brief to Florence, dated 1474, June 28 (a Copy is in the State Archives, Florence), and in that to Ercole d'Este, dated 1474, July 14 (the Original is in the State Archives, Modena).

‡ See *supra*, p. 266.

§ The principal passage of this Brief of the 28th June, 1474, is printed *supra*, p. 265, note ‡, from the State Archives, Florence. Sixtus IV. also communicated the document on the same 28th June, 1474, to the Duke of Milan ; see *Brief of this date in the State Archives, Milan. Autograph.

54. POPE SIXTUS IV. TO GALEAZZO MARIA SFORZA, DUKE
OF MILAN.*

1474, July 28, Rome.

Yhs

Sixtus papa IIII.

Carissime fili salutem et apost. benedict.

Ve habiamo scripto molti brevi per li quali asai amplamente
avete potuto intendere la iustitia nostra in li fati de cita di Castello.
E per questo si maravigemo asai e non possiam credere quillo ne †
scripto de Fiorense cioche voi non solo incitati Fiorentini contra
di noi, ma anco prometete a loro ogni subsidio contra ‡ di noi.
A fili carissime quid tibi fecimus? Non se ricordiamo averve
offeso mai nec verbo neque opere; anco per lo singulare amore
vi portiamo tuto quello abiamo potuto fare per voi habiamo fato
e faremo sempre. A a numquid redditur pro bono malum?
quare § foderunt foveam anime mee.‖ A fili carissime consciderate
la iustitia de le mie petitione. Considerate contra quem agitur,
quod contra dominum, cui illa civitas subiecta est, contra ecclesiam
suam, contra vicarium suum, contra patrem te cordialiter amantem,
contra affinem, contra illum qui ortum habuit ex civitate tibi
subiecta. Velis ergo fili mi desistere ab inceptis ut ira Dei non
veniat super te, quod absit et velis bene consciderare petitiones
meas iustas et faveas Deo pro debito ac honore tuo, cuius con
servationem semper quesivi. Speramus pro nobilitate animi tui
quod sicut ego sum tibi bonus pater, ita eris nobis bonus filius.
Fomo riquiesti pro parte vostra se volemo v' intromitesti in acordare questa cossa. Dicemmo quello habiam risposto ad ogni altro
chi na ¶ fato simile domanda che non ne pare via honesta dovere
mendicare acordio con nostri subditi, ma quando voi o altro
lo facesse come da si ch' eravamo contento quod non petebamus
a subditis nisi obedientiam veram e de questa mia risposta
non credo vi dovesti scandalisare. Precamur igitur vos ut pro

---

* See *supra*, p. 267. The letter is all written by his own hand. Regarding
the rarity of such Papal autographs, see CAMPORI, Lettere ined. di sommi
pontefici, p. vii. (Modena, 1878).

† = n'è.

§ Manuscript: *qr*.

¶ = n'ha.

‡ Manuscript: *c*.

‖ JEREM., 18, 20.

conscientia vestra ac honore vestro non velitis esse contra * ecclesiam domini prout vos facturos speramus.   Bene valete.

Ex urbe 28 Iulii, 1474.

[A tergo:]

Cariss. in Christo filio Galeaz. Marie duci Mediolani ill.
dentur in propriis manibus.

[Original in the State Archives, Milan.   Autograph.]

55. Pope Sixtus IV. to Galeazzo Maria Sforza, Duke of Milan.†

1474, Oct. 10, Rome.

Hodie conclusum est Deo auctore et publicatum inter dil.
filium Johannem nostrum secundum carnem nepotem et natam
dil. fillii nobilis viri Friderici ducis Urbini matrimonium. . . .‡

[Original in the State Archives, Milan.]

56. Pope Sixtus IV. to Florence.§

1475, Oct. 21, Rome.

He can hardly believe that they shew favour to N. Vitelli, who
is fighting against the Church.   They must not do this: Secus
autem quod absit et quod non credimus iniurie resistere lacessiti
cogeremur.

[Copy in the State Archives, Florence, X–II.–25, f. 9?–92b.]

57. Report of the Milanese Ambassadors in Florence regarding the Conspiracy of the Pazzi.‖

1478, April 28, Florence.

Il cardinale nipote del conte Girolamo per la peste de Pisa

---

* Manuscript : *c.*   † See *supra*, p. 270.

‡ On the 14th October, 1474, Sixtus IV. wrote to Florence : *"Nuperrime
cum dil. fil. nob. viro Federico Urbini duce de nata eius dilecto filio Jo. de
Ruere nostro secundum carnem nepoti in matrimonio locando transegimus,
quod gratum vobis esse non dubitamus." (State Archives, Florence, X.-II.-25,
f. 69b.) See the Brief to the Duke of Ferrara, dated 1474, Oct. 14, in Martène,
II., 1670.

§ See *supra*, p. 296. Lorenzo's letter of apology, dated Florence, 1475,
Dec. 25, is published in Moreni, Lettere di Lorenzo il M. al S. P. Innocenzo
VIII., 1 *seq.* (Florence, 1830), but—as Reumont, Lorenzo, I., 258, 2nd ed.,
observes—assigned in an incomprehensible manner to the successor of Sixtus IV.

‖ See *supra*, p. 304 *seq.* Eine Münze auf die Pazzi-Verschwörung in Richa,
VI., 142.

stavasi ad un palazzo di M. Jacopo de Pazzi non molto discosto da Firenze ed aveva molte volte detto a Lorenzo de Medici trovandosi con lui che voleva un giorno venire a Firenze per vedere il suo palazzo e chiesa maggiore per cui Lorenzo lo aveva invitato a venire ed a disinare in casa sua domenica scorsa che fu ai 26 di Aprile e col cardinale aveva pure invitato l' arcivescovo de Pisa governatore suo e da Firenze M. Jacopo de Pazzi e moltri altri cavalieri e cittadini per onorare il cardinale ed erasi disposto un solennissimo apparato ; el cardinale col arcivescovo venne la domenica mattina e smontato si pose nel duomo alla messa grande che era cantata solennemente e circa il momento che si intonava l'agnus Dei,* etc., quando Giuliano e Lorenzo ambedue se trovarono in duomo che secundo l' usanza passegiavano pero ben separati l' uno dall altro Lorenzo fu assaltato da alcuni, tutti forastieri e per la piu parte Spagnuoli della famiglia del cardinale o forse dell' arcivescovo, ma che se seppe presto reparare, mentre dal famiglio ed alcuni giovani fu ajutato essendosi essi interposti ripararono i colpi coi loro mantelli che ancora si vedono traorati. Lorenzo scappò il pericolo e fu soltanto leggermente ferito alla gola e tosto ritirato in sacrestia ; certo Francesco Neri suo compagno nel ripararlo fu ammazzato. Mentre che Lorenzo fu cosi assaltato ed in un punto medesimo da un altra parte del duomo a Giuliano fu facto simile assalto da costoro insieme con uno Franceschino de Pazzi e Bernardo Barunzelli che ambedue proditoriamente quella matina si erano accompagnati con Giuliano e loro due furoni i primi a dargli delle ferite e così il povero Giuliano rimase morto con innumerevoli ferite che doveva essere pietà a vederlo. Dio non volle la morte de Lorenzo per evitare maggiore male. . . . Non si potrebbe esprimere quanta dimonstrazione abbia fatto questo popolo a Lorenzo e casa de Medici. The people shout : Palle, palle ! Execution of the guilty : L' arcivescovo dopo gli vene concesso di potersi confessarse e comunicare fu appicato per la gola lui ed il fratello con Jacopo Salviati suo nipote, Jacopo de M. Poggio con tutti quelli che erano presi in palazzo ed erano gettati fuori dalle finestre del palazzo de S^{ri} col capestro appicato al colonello delle finestre e di la un pezzo tagliavasi i capestri e cadevano in piazza ; in piazza che erano caduti straziavansi dal

* NOTAR GIACOMO, 133, gives the same acccunt.

popolo e dalla moltitudine in pezzi. . . . El numero delle persone impiccate, tagliate a pezzi e morte in questo facto forse ascende ad un centinajo di persone. . . .

[State Archives, Milan, Cart. gen.]

58. ALBERTINUS, PRIOR OF S. MARTINO, TO MARCHIONESS BARBARA OF MANTUA.*

1478, April 28, Florence.

He arrived in Florence on the 27th. Nui habiamo trovato Firenza in grande travaio cum credo sapia la prefata V. S. Lordine de la cosa sicondo posso intendere è questo : zoè essendo venuto il card[le] nepote del conte Jeronimo a Fiorenza non si dice perche se non che mal per lui et per altri, ditto card[le] non volse intrar in Fiorenza, ma si redusse di fora a uno zardino de quelli de Pazi e de li a certi di questi Pazi fezeno uno convido a Fesole dove fu invitado Lorenzo de Cosimo e Zuliano de Cosimo, ma Zuliano no possette andarli che haveva due anguinalie, sichel disegno de Pazi non potete haver effetto, ma non pentiti fezeno che Lorenzo convidoe il card[le] a casa sua a pasto per haver ditto Lorenzo e Zuliano a suo a piacere, siche aparichiatto il convido amplo e magnifico venuta lora de la messa andono in S. Liberata e tardono la messa piu che fu possibile per far fastidio al popolo azio se havesse a partire, ma pur seguendo la messa quando il prete fui a la levatione[†] se levò Franceschino de Pazi e amaza de fatto cum certe sui compagni Zuliano de Medici ; da po volse e menò per dar a Lorenzo e uno suo compagno li volse piliar il colpo e piliò la morte de fatto per modo che ditto Franceschino taliò la testa cum una spala a ditto compagno de Lorenzo e cum quello medesmo colpo ferì Lorenzo in de la gola, ma non ha grande male. Il card[le] fuzi e larcivescovo de Pisa corse al palazo[‡] cum certi fanti . . . e funo a li mane ; il popolo corse e non potendo intrare andono a una altra porta e brusola e introno dentro e preseno larcivescovo e de fatto lo inpicono lui e il fratello ; possa preseno il card[le] cum tuti quelli de li sui che poteno havere e furono inpicati e similiter il prete che havea cantato la messa e dui garzoneti che erano ragazi del card[le] per modo che quello di

---

* See *supra*, p. 304 *seq.*   † See *supra*, p. 309, note *.
‡ For what follows, see REUMONT, Lorenzo, I., 289 *seq.*, 2nd ed.

fui la domenica ne forono inpichati 36 ; il luni seguente* ne fono
inpichati 16 ; ozi che martidi ancho non e fatto altro ; ma questa
notte è sta menato Ser Jacomo de Pazi cum circha 18 altri e tuta
via ne sono menati e tuti secondo se dice siranno impichati ; il
card^{le} e pur vivo, ma in presone in del palazo de li S^{ri} cum grande
guarda ; se tene perho che non morirà ; altro non ho presentuto
fin a questa hora presente e che hore nove et di 28 del presente. . . . Dopo questa hora siamo a messa a l' Anunciata et
havemo fatto oratione speciale per V. S. e tornati a lozamenti ne
stato ditto alcuni soldati del conte Jeronimo sono stati taliati a
pezi venendo lor a Fiorenza. Non ho potuto intendere altro mi
ric^{do} a V. M. S. Florentie die 28 Aprilis, 1478.

E. D. V. ser^{or} fid^{mus} don Albertinus prior S. Martini.

[Original in the Gonzaga Archives, Mantua.]

59. INSTRUCTION FROM SIXTUS IV. FOR LUDOVICO DE AGNELLIS
AND ANTONIO DE GRASSIS, NUNCIOS TO EMPEROR FREDERICK
III.†

1478, Dec. 1.

Instructiones datae r. patrib. dom. Ludovico de Agnellis
protonot. apost. et Antonio de Grassis ‡ s. palatii causar. auditori
ad M^{tem} Imp. S. D. N. oratoribus. Primo salutabunt ser^{mum}
Imperatorem. . . . Complaints against Lorenzo de' Medici. Item
audivimus Venetos misisse ad suam M^{tem} Jacobum de Medio,§
qui diu in curia nostra ista versatus est et cognitus, cuius dicta
bene advertat, est enim magnus fabricator et Cretensis, qui iuxta
apostolum consueverunt esse mendaces ‖ . . . Insuper sciat
Serenitas S., quod Veneti convenerunt cum rege Franciae, ad

* 27th April.   † See *supra*, p. 326.
‡ Some Manuscripts have Frassis, a mistake which RANKE, Päpste, III., 4*,
has not noticed. It is hard to understand how RANKE, *loc. cit.*, can speak of
this Instruction as "the oldest" which came before him among the Manuscripts
which he saw. The Berlin Historian made use of Cod. VII., G. 1, 99, of the
Altieri Library in Rome, which contains the well-known Instruction of 1472
for Card. Barbo, cited *supra*, p. 224, and frequently to be met with among the
Manuscripts in the Roman Libraries. The texts communicated by Ranke are
not correct.
§ See, regarding him, Gött. Gel. Anz., 1879, p. 282.
‖ Tit., 1, 12.

quem cum istis de liga miserunt oratorem, ut fiat scandalum in ecclesia, obliti quot quantasque pecunias exposuerimus contra Turcum in eorum et caeterorum defensione Christianorum. Miramur certe, quod ipsi qui se profitentur Christianos velint maiorem fidem servare erga Laurentium de Medicis quam erga Deum et sedem apost. .... miramur potissimum, quia anno superiori, ut per coniecturas satis per omnes cognitum est, Carolus de Montone instigatione ligae venisset ad damna ecclesiae; nam habebat in Perusia tractatum civitate ecclesiae, qua habita omnes aliae civitates et tota ecclesia fuisset perturbata, cum etiam detecta proditione publice aggressus fuisset Senenses et pax Italiae fluctuaret cum tamen Turcus esset prope Forum Julii et iam abduxisset magnam praedam, ipsi nihil dicebant, Carolum non reprimebant, nec per ligam quidquam dicebatur de Turco, sed potius de iuvando eundem Carolum, contra cuius oppidum misimus exercitum nostrum, ne amplius perturbaret pacem Italicam. Juvabatur iste ab omnibus, prout per nostros suae Ser^ti iam scripsimus, et cum reverteret Florentiam colebatur ab omnibus ac si Deus esset. Scripseramus tum primo ad Venetos, ut vellent eum revocare ... et nunquam nobis responderunt. Nunc autem ecclesia juste contra ipsum Laurentium mota, clamant Veneti, clamat tota ista liga, petunt cum rege Franciae concilium in Gallis in dedecus nostrum ... parum advertentes, ad quos spectat congregare concilium ... eapropter hortamur M^tem suam, ut non praestet eis aures ... sed rogamus M^tem Suam, ut pro debito suae protectionis quod habet ad ecclesiam et pro honore suo ... velit scribere regi Franciae similiter et isti ligae ostendendo, quod non recte faciunt et ... quod debent magis favere ecclesiae iustitiam habenti, quam uno mercatori, qui semper magna causa fuit, quod non potuerunt omnia confici contra Turcum, quae intendebamus parare et fuit semper petra scandali in ecclesia Dei et tota Italia.

His age and infirmities make it impossible for him to leave Rome, but he hopes to see the Emperor in Rome, and there to take counsel with him regarding the affairs of Christendom.

Reddat igitur nos certos et de tempore et de via, per quam venturus erit ... Item dicat suae Ser^ti, quod rex Franciae et alii complures principes querunt se intromittere, ut fiat ista concordia inter nos, Laurentium et alios, quibus respondimus, quod semper parati sumus ad pacem, dummodo fiat cum honore Dei et ecclesiae. Tamen cum ipse sit primus inter principes temporales . . optaremus, ut ipse, qui est ecclesiae protector, haberet istum honorem. He should do this.

[Cop. in the Secret Archives of the Vatican ; Instruct. divers., II., 30, f. 55b–57 et LV., f. 43b *seq.* ; Vatican Library, Cod. Ottob., 2726, f. 40b–43 ; Altieri Library (see *supra*, p. 515, note ‡); Barberini Library, XXVII., 4, f. 81 ; Borghese Library, I.–34b. ; Chigi Library, Q. 7, 6 ; Corsini Library, 33, F. 1, f. 68–70.]

60. PIER FILIPPO PANDOLFINI TO FLORENCE.*

1479, March 20, Rome.

Tutta questa corte generalmente desidera et vorrebbe pace et ne parlono publicamente ; in questa medesima sententia è la maggior parte de cardinali, ma sono in luogo che non ardiscono parlare quello intendono et alcuni che lanno fatto ne sono stato molto represi et con parole non conveniente dal conte Je[ronimo] et da M. Aniello imb^{re} del re in modo che qui ogni cosa si fa secondo la voglia del conte Je[ronimo] il qual in omnibus dipende dal re . . . .

[State Archives, Florence, X.–II.–24.]

61. PIER FILIPPO PANDOLFINI TO FLORENCE.†

1479, March 25, Rome.

The Cardinals wish that the negotiations for peace should not be broken off: ma il conte ‡ puo piu lui solo che tutto il collegio et pero sanza lui nulla e da sperare si possi fare.

[State Archives, Florence, X.–II.–24.]

62. POPE SIXTUS IV. TO LOUIS XI., KING OF FRANCE.§

1479, April 6, Rome.

He announces the suspension of the censures and the cessation of hostilities with the Florentines : Quod significamus tue M^{ti} ut optimum animum nostrum et dispositionem cognoscat ad com-

---

* See *supra*, pp. 327, 413.
‡ Girolamo Riario.

† See *supra*, pp. 327, 413.
§ See *supra*, p. 328.

placendum **tue** M^{tl} et ad pacem ipsam dummodo fiat cum honore apost. sedis.

[Contemporary Copy in the State Archives, Milan.]

63. Cardinal Giuliano della Rovere to Louis XI., King of France.*

1479, April 7, Rome.

He has been silent because there was nothing important to tell, et fere nulla spes pacis erat.   Now, however, the Pope has yielded to his Majesty's request : arma deposuit censurasque et interdicta suspendit. . . .

[Contemporary Copy in the State Archives, Milan.]

64. Pope Sixtus IV. to Duke Philibert I. of Savoy.†

1481, Sept. 18, Bracciano.

Quod toto nostro desiderio expectabamus et iocundissimum nobis fuit, hodie intelleximus a nostris : the reconquest of Otranto. This opportunity must be seized to resist the Turks : it will never return if now allowed to escape.   Ecce tempus salutis, tempus glorie, tempus victorie quod si negligatur nullum tale unquam recuperare poterimus.   Parvo negocio bellum nunc confici potest quod non sine maximo dispendio maximis calamitatibus nostris . . . postea conficietur.   He has done everything, and ought now to be supported.

Simile imperatori.

Regi Francie, Anglie, Scocie, Polonie, Dacie, Hungarie, Hispanie, Portugallie.

Duci Maximiliano, Britanie, Mediolani.

Electoribus imperii.

Duci Ferrarie, Sabaudie.

March. Montisferrati, Mantue.

Florent. Lucens. Senensib.‡

[National Library, Florence.   Cod. Magliab., II.–III.–256, f.52b.]

---

* See *supra*, p. 328.   † See *supra*, p. 344.

‡ Of these Briefs I found that addressed to the Duke of Milan in the State Archives, Milan, and that to the Florentines in the State Archives, Florence (X.-II.-25, f. 168b).   Both are dated Bracciano, 1481, Sept. 18, and agree with each other : the text, however, differs from the one given above.

65. Pope Sixtus IV. to Cardinal Fregoso, Legate of the Crusader Fleet.*

1481, Sept. 18, Bracciano.

He has received the Legate's letter of the 11th of September concerning the conquest of Otranto. Great joy at this success, which will confer everlasting glory on the Legate and the Duke of Calabria.

Reliquum est ut quod prospere inceptum est felicibus incrementis perficiatur hostesque ipsos omni conatu persequamur ut hac cura et periculo Italiam perpetuo liberemus, ad quam rem intrepide capessendam omnes christianos principes exhortati sumus.† Quare quod in te est cum classe nostra reliquias belli prosequere et hostes quam maximis potes damnis contere ne oblate divinitus occasioni desimus. . . . Quod prestare ipsi possumus libenter facimus utinamque soli possemus neminem certe requireremus. The Pope is surprised that the patroni triremium complain without cause.

[National Library at Florence. Cod. Magliab., II.–III.–256, f.38.]

66. Cardinal F. Gonzaga to Federigo I. of Gonzaga.‡

1482, Sept. 11, Rome.

. . . Essendo accaduta questa accelerata et immatura morte de la bo. me. del Sʳ Roberto Malatesta causata da una febre continua terzana dopia cum fluxo vehementissimo per il che tandem heri tra la prima e seconda hora de nocte expiravit.§ The Pope has to-day legitimatised Roberto's sons per la successione.

[Original in the Gonzaga Archives, Mantua.]

67. Pope Sixtus IV. to the Duke of Milan.‖

1483, March 4, Rome.

Dispensatio duci Mediol. pro impositione novae gabellae seu

---

* See supra, p. 345. † See No. 64 of this Appendix.
‡ See supra, p. 369.

§ Caleffini, in his *Cronica Ferrariae, writes, Roberto died yesterday * "de una ferita che l' have adi passati in lo facta d' arme fra lui, conte Hieronymo, duca de Calabria et Romani ;" a "fluxo" having supervened. Nothing is here said of poison. Cod. I.–I.–4 of the Chigi Library, Rome.

‖ See supra, p. 374.

datii ad succurrendum eius gravissimis impensis presertim pro
defensione Ferrariae.*

[Original in the State Archives, Milan.   Autograph.]

68. Pope Sixtus IV. to the Duke of Milan.†

1483, April 3, Rome.

A long letter urging the importance of naval warfare against
Venice.   Verum quia et a principio et semper expedire ac necessarium esse diximus ut valida classis maritima instrueretur sine
qua ullus bonus rerum successus vix sperari posset huiusmodi rem
tanti momenti esse ut in ea certissima victoriae spes collocata sit,
commemoramus. . . .

[Original in the State Archives, Milan.]

69. Pope Sixtus IV. to the Duke of Milan.‡

1483, April 16, Rome.

Instat apud ducem ut contribuere velit quam citius pecunias per
eum solvendas pro armanda classe. . . .

[Original in the State Archives, Milan.]

70. Pope Sixtus IV. to the Duke of Milan.§

1483, April 21, Rome.

Sixtus IV. hortatur ducem ad solvendum stipendia promissa pro
armanda classe contra Venetos.

[Original in the State Archives, Milan.]

71. Pope Sixtus IV. to the Duke of Milan.‖

1483, May 1, Rome.

An exhortation to send aid to Parma for the rescue of Ferrara.

[Original in the State Archives, Milan.   Autograph.]

---

* Thus in a contemporary statement of contents.
† See *supra*, p. 374.
§ See *supra*, p. 374
‡ See *supra*, p. 374.
‖ See *supra*, p. 374.

72. GIROLAMO RIARIO TO THE DUKE OF MILAN.*

1483, May 7, Rome.

As Ferrara is in the greatest danger, the Duke is urged to send help as soon as possible.

[Original in the State Archives, Milan. P. E. Milano.]

73. POPE SIXTUS IV. TO THE DUKE OF MILAN.†

1483, May 25, Rome.

Dilecte fili, etc. Mittimus nobilitati tue bullam censurarum adversus Venetos quam publicari hic fecimus. He is to allow this Bull to be published in his domains.

[Original in the State Archives, Milan. Autograph.]

74. POPE SIXTUS IV. TO ULRICH VIII.,‡ ABBOT OF ST. GALL.§

1483, June 5, Rome.

. . . : Cum superioribus diebus decrevimus bullam censurarum adversus Venetos, qui . . . ab oppugnatione civitatis nostrae Ferrariensis . . . desistere noluerunt, mittimus ad te bullam . . . allegatam, te quoque hortamur . . . ut personaliter ad confoederatos omnes tamquam orator noster accedas et . . . opereris ut bulla ipsa publicari possit. . . .

[Original in Cathedral Chapter Archives, St. Gall. ‖]

75. POPE SIXTUS IV. TO EMPEROR FREDERICK III.¶

1483, June 15, Rome.

He sends him the Bull against Venice, and exhorts him to let it be published in the Empire et cum effectu observari. Describes the ambition and thirst for conquest of the Venetians. The Pope hopes that the Emperor will proceed against these enemies qui

---

* See *supra*, p. 374.   † See *supra*, p. 376.

‡ Rosch aus Wangen, Abbot from 1463-91 ; see MOOYER, Onomasticon Hierarchiae Germ., 138 (Minden, 1854).

§ See *supra*, p. 376.

‖ This Brief is also in Lib. brev., 15, f. 601, Secret Archives of the Vatican, and there is a contemporary Copy in the State Archives, Milan.

¶ See *supra*, p. 376.

scisma in ecclesia Dei querunt. The Emperor must shew himself a Catholic Prince.

[Lib. brev., 15, f. 623.   Secret Archives of the Vatican.]

76. Pope Sixtus IV. to the Duke of Milan.*

1483, July 15, Rome.

The Pope again most urgently begs him to begin the war against Venice in Lombardy.

[Original in the State Archives, Milan.   Autograph.]

77. Pope Sixtus IV. to the Duke of Milan.

1483, Aug. 20, Rome.

Exhorts him to send assistance to Ferrara, for this is the most important point.

[Original in the State Archives, Milan.   Autograph.]

78. Pope Sixtus IV. to the Duke of Milan.

1483, Aug. 25, Rome.

The necessity of still maintaining the fleet is urgently insisted on.

[Original in the State Archives, Milan.   Autograph.]

79. Pope Sixtus IV. to the Duke of Milan.

1483, Sept. 20, Rome.

The fleet must still be kept up for some time.   The Duke ought to lend his aid.

[Original in the State Archives, Milan.   Autograph.]

80. Pope Sixtus IV. to the Duke of Milan.

1483, Oct. 2, Rome.

Urgent exhortations to send support, especially for the fleet, whose maintenance is very necessary.

[Original in the State Archives, Milan.   Autograph.]

* For Nos. 76 to 80, see *supra*, p. 385.

81. Pope Sixtus IV. to the Duke of Milan.*

1483, Oct. 13, Rome.

Non possumus satis mirari quod res Ferrariensis ita negligatur. . . . Nihil factum est eorum quae in dieta et post dietam ordinata sunt. The Duke must send help most speedily. He (the Pope) is not to blame if Ferrara be lost. Similia Regi et Florent.

[Lib. brev., 16 B., f. 98. Secret Archives of the Vatican.]

82. Stefano Guidotti to Mantua.†

1484, Aug. 12, Rome.

A quest' hora che sono quattro de notte ‡ le passato di questa vita el papa. The Cardinals assemble in the Palace during the night. The beginning of disturbances is already to be seen.

[Original in the Gonzaga Archives, Mantua.]

---

* See *supra*, p. 385. † See *supra*, p. 388.

‡ The same *Stefano Guidotti writes still more precisely on the 13th Aug. : "Ale 4 hora e ¼ el passò di questa vita, benissimo disposto e recevuti tuti i sacramenti ecclesiastici resi il spirito a Dio." (Gonzaga Archives.) The Lib. confrat. Sta M. del. Anima also says that the Pope died between the 4th and 5th hour of the night, as does the record from the Library at Munich in Schmarsow, 377. A Sienese Despatch mentions the 3rd hour ; see Arch. d. Soc. Rom., XI., 618.

INDEX OF NAMES IN VOL. IV.